SUCCEEDING IN CIVICS

COMPANION WORK TEXT FOR MASTERING FLORIDA ASSESSMENTS

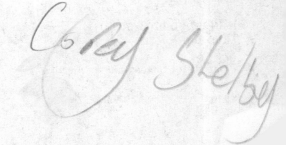

Cover Photo Credit: Getty Images/iStockphoto

mheducation.com/preK-12

Send all inquiries to: McGraw-Hill Education
8787 Orion Place
Columbus, OH 43240

ISBN: 978-0-07-676709-0
MHID: 0-07-676709-4

Printed in the United States of America.

8 9 10 11 QSX 23 22 21 20 19

Table of Contents

CHAPTER 1

The United States: Location and Lands

Chapter Overview

Geographic factors help determine location and boundaries. Describing where a place is in relation to other places or landmarks provides its relative location. Geographers use tools such as lines of latitude and longitude to describe the absolute location of a place. Geographers also divide Earth into hemispheres. The United States is in the Northern and Western Hemispheres and is organized into political units called states. The United States also has other lands such as territories and commonwealths.

The United States is such a large country that it has many types of landforms and bodies of water, as well as variety in its climate. Its landforms include lowlands, plains, wetlands, highlands, and plateaus. Its bodies of water include rivers and lakes, and the Pacific and Atlantic Oceans form part of its border. Most parts of the country have a temperate climate, but some states do have extreme climates. Climate plays an important role in people's daily lives and affects where they live, what they wear, how they earn a living, and even what they do for fun.

CHAPTER BENCHMARKS

SS.7.G.1.1 Locate the fifty states and their capital cities in addition to the nation's capital on a map.

SS.7.G.1.2 Locate on a world map the territories and protectorates of the United States of America.

SS.7.G.1.3 Interpret maps to identify geopolitical divisions and boundaries of places in North America

SS.7.G.2.2 Locate major physical landmarks that are emblematic of the United States.

SS.7.G.2.3 Explain how major physical characteristics, natural resources, climate, and absolute and relative location have influenced settlement, economies, and inter-governmental relations in North America.

LAFS.68.RH.1.2 Determine the central ideas or information of a primary or secondary source; provide an accurate summary of the source distinct from prior knowledge or opinions.

WHAT I NEED TO KNOW

TERMS

- ☐ continent
- ☐ nation
- ☐ border
- ☐ state
- ☐ capital
- ☐ territory
- ☐ protectorate
- ☐ commonwealth
- ☐ landform
- ☐ lowland
- ☐ plain
- ☐ wetland
- ☐ highland
- ☐ plateau
- ☐ climate

PEOPLE, PLACES, EVENTS

- ☐ United States
- ☐ Canada
- ☐ Mexico
- ☐ North America
- ☐ Florida Everglades
- ☐ Great Plains
- ☐ Rocky Mountains
- ☐ Grand Canyon
- ☐ Mississippi River
- ☐ Great Lakes
- ☐ Great Salt Lake
- ☐ Lake Okeechobee

The United States: Location and Lands

CHAPTER BENCHMARKS, *continued*

LAFS.68.RH.2.4 Determine the meaning of words and phrases as they are used in a text, including vocabulary specific to domains related to history/social studies.

LAFS.68.RH.2.6 Identify aspects of a text that reveal an author's point of view or purpose (e.g., loaded language, inclusion or avoidance of particular facts).

LAFS.68.RH.3.7 Integrate visual information (e.g., in charts, graphs, photographs, videos, or maps) with other information in print and digital texts.

LAFS.7.SL.1.2 Analyze the main ideas and supporting details presented in diverse media and formats (e.g., visually, quantitatively, orally) and explain how the ideas clarify a topic, text, or issue under study.

HE.7.P.8.2 Articulate a position on a health-related issue and support it with accurate health information.

The United States: Location and Lands

Create the Foldable® below. Label one tab *Locations and Boundaries* and label the other tab *Landforms, Waterways, and Climates*. Under the left tab, describe the unique geographic location of the United States and identify its boundaries. On the right side, identify and list landforms, important waterways, and climate zones across the country. On the back of the Foldable, describe where you live based upon what you have learned.

Step 1
With the paper arranged horizontally, fold the left side over to the right edge and fold paper in half.

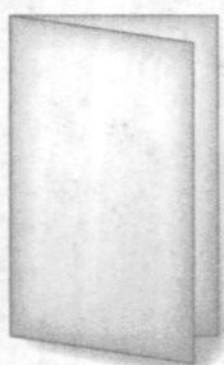

Step 2
While the paper is folded in half, fold the top of the paper down to the bottom to fold in half again.

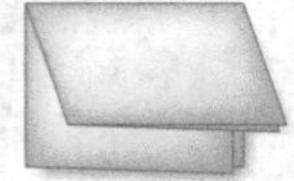

Step 3
Unfold the paper and cut the horizontal fold from the left edge to the center of the paper.

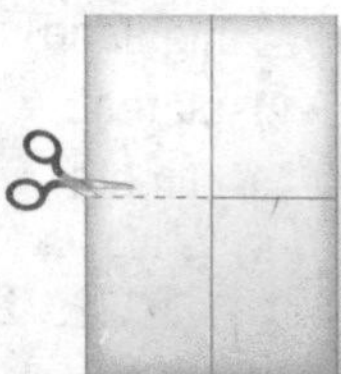

Step 4
Fold shutters down and label as directed.

LESSON 1 SUMMARY

Location

SS.7.G.1.1, SS.7.G.1.2, SS.7.G.1.3, SS.7.G.2.3

Where Is the United States?

You can describe the United States according to its relative location, or where it is in relation to natural or political landmarks. You might say it lies between the Atlantic and Pacific Oceans or between Canada and Mexico.

How Geographers Locate Places

Geographers use various tools to describe the absolute, or exact, location of a place. One way geographers describe absolute location is by naming natural features, such as rivers, mountains, or oceans. Think about Florida's absolute location. You might say that it is bordered by the Atlantic Ocean to the east, the Gulf of Mexico to the west, the Florida Straits and Caribbean Sea to the south, and land to the north. Political boundaries are another tool that geographers use to describe absolute location. For example, Georgia is bordered to the south by Florida. In addition, geographers use imaginary lines of latitude and longitude. Latitude indicates how far a place lies north or south of the Equator, which is at 0° latitude. Longitude indicates how far a place lies east or west of the Prime Meridian, which is at 0° longitude.

Geographers use certain lines of latitude and longitude to divide the planet into hemispheres. Each hemisphere is one-half of the Earth. The Equator divides the Earth into the Northern and Southern Hemispheres. The Prime Meridian divides the Earth into the Eastern and Western Hemispheres.

Locating the United States

Every place on Earth is located in two hemispheres. The United States is north of the Equator and west of the Prime Meridian, so it is located in the Northern and the Western Hemispheres. It lies on the **continent**, or large landmass, of North America. Large bodies of water provide natural barriers for this continent. The Arctic Ocean lies to the north. The Gulf of Mexico lies to its southeast and extends to the Caribbean Sea. The Atlantic Ocean forms its eastern boundary. The Pacific Ocean forms its western boundary.

1. ANALYZING INFORMATION

Underline the details that describe the difference between relative and absolute location. Then, on a separate sheet of paper, explain how you think relative location might affect human settlement, economies, and intergovernmental relations.

Name ____________ Date ____________ Class ____________

LESSON 1 SUMMARY, *continued*

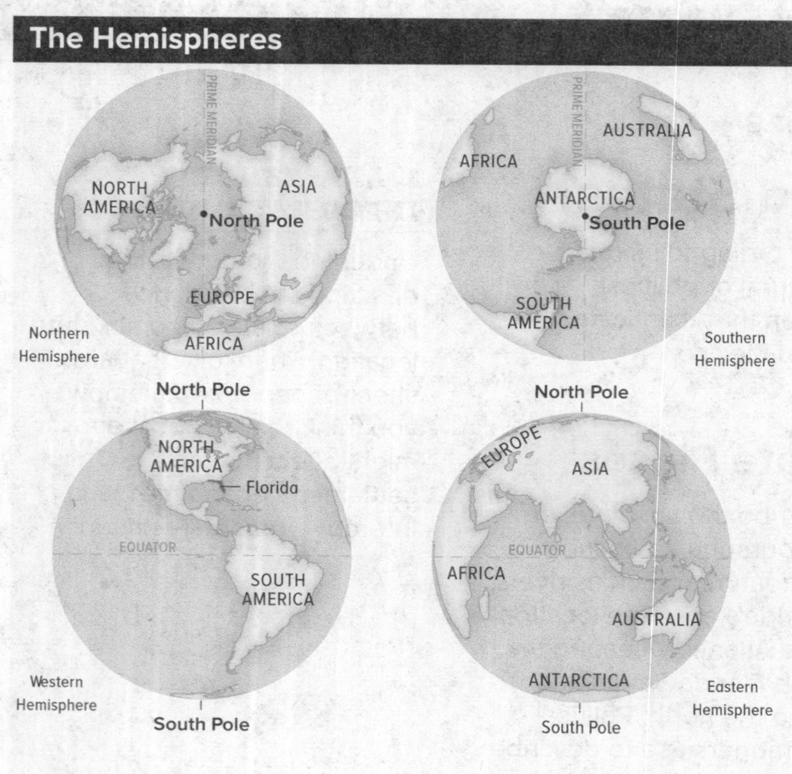

Having water on both sides of the continent has enabled people to settle on both coasts and has allowed goods to be imported and exported. It has also provided people with outdoor activities such as swimming and other water sports.

Many nations may be located within one continent. A **nation** is an area of land defined by political boundaries and under the authority of a specific government. **Borders** are the boundaries that separate nations. Located within North America, the United States also has the Atlantic and Pacific Oceans as its eastern and western borders. The United States shares a political border with Canada to the north and Mexico to the southwest. Being close neighbors makes it important for the three governments to have good relations. The United States has made trade agreements with these close neighbors. Seven smaller North American nations lie south of Mexico on a strip of land called Central America. Greenland is an island northeast of Canada. It is also part of North America.

The United States is made up of 50 states. Most of the nation is located in the middle of North America. All but two of the states are contiguous, or joined together, inside a common boundary. Alaska and Hawaii are separated from the contiguous part of the nation. Alaska is bordered by both land and water. Canada forms its eastern border, the Arctic Ocean forms its northern border, and the Gulf of Alaska forms its southern border. The Bering Sea and the Bering Strait form Alaska's western border. These bodies of water separate Alaska from the nation of Russia in Asia. Hawaii is not located in North America. It is a group of islands in the Pacific Ocean west of the U.S. mainland.

2. IDENTIFYING

Complete this chart to identify the details that support the main idea.

Main idea: Water forms natural barriers for North America.
Detail:
Detail:
Detail:
Detail:

Name ______________________ Date ______________ Class __________

U.S. political borders are partly formed by waterways. For example, the Rio Grande marks more than 1,000 miles (1,600 km) of the U.S.–Mexican border. The five Great Lakes and the St. Lawrence River form part of the U.S.–Canadian border.

ANALYZING MAPS

3. Study the Political Map of North America. What nations make up the continent of North America?

____

____

____

____

____

____

____

____

Political Map of North America

What Are the United States?

The United States has many features, such as special places and groups of people. Natural forces have created some of these features, such as mountains. Other features have been made by humans to serve specific political purposes, such as state boundary lines.

States

The political borders of the United States are useful in several ways. They mark the nation's size and shape. They help organize its land and people. A **state** is a political unit within a nation. Each state has clear borders. A state has its own government but is also subject to the national government.

Name ______________________________ Date ______________ Class __________

ANALYZING MAPS

4. On this political map of the United States, a star shows the location of each state capital. A star within a circle shows the nation's capital. Complete the following list by writing the name of the capital of each place beside it on the list.

California ______________

Florida ______________

Texas ______________

United States ______________

States differ in size, location, and features. Alaska is the largest state in the United States. It is about 400 times larger than Rhode Island, the smallest state. Some states such as Iowa are surrounded only by land. Other states are bordered by oceans, and Hawaii is an island state. Florida is one of the few states that is a peninsula. A peninsula is a piece of land almost entirely surrounded by water but attached to a larger body of land. Florida is bounded by the Gulf of Mexico and the Atlantic Ocean. Northern Florida, including the northwestern part, called the panhandle, is attached to the mainland.

National and State Capitals

Nations and states have capital cities where their governments are located. Each of the 50 states has its own **capital.** The United States has a national capital where government offices are located. The capital of the United States is in a special area called the District of Columbia, also known as Washington, D.C. The District of Columbia is located on the Potomac River between the states of Maryland and Virginia, and it has its own borders.

Political Map of the United States

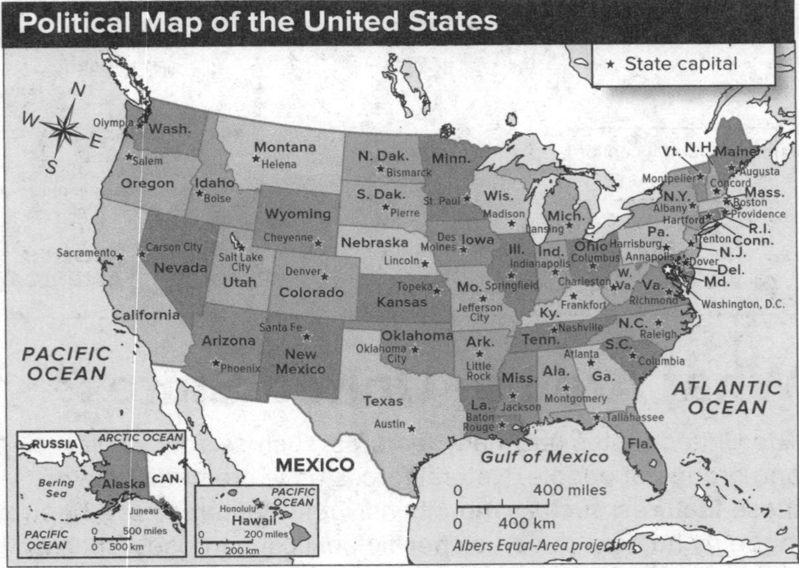

U.S. Territories and Possessions

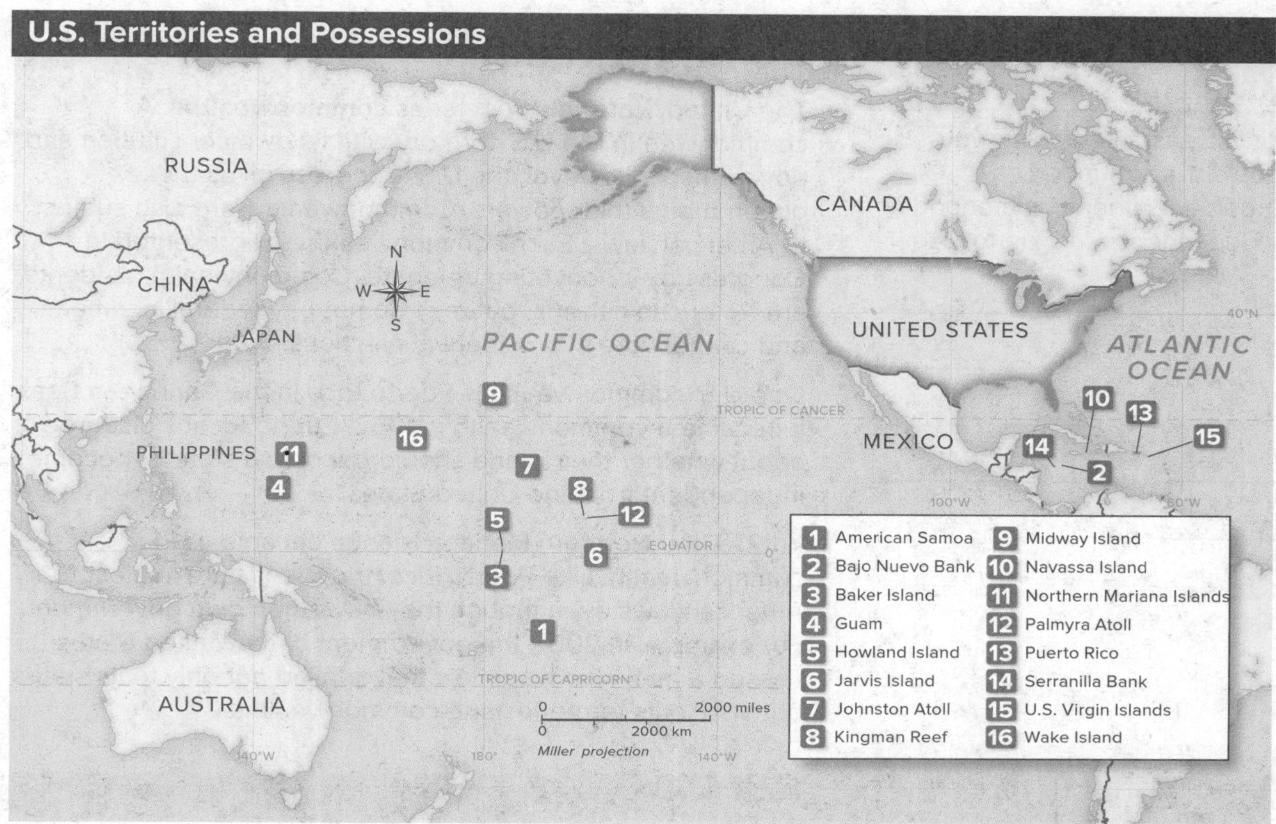

U.S. Territories

The United States holds other lands scattered across the Pacific Ocean and the Caribbean Sea. These political units are U.S. territories. A **territory** is an area of the country that is neither a state nor a part of a state. The U.S. government oversees each territory, but most have their own government, like states do. Each territory also has its own political borders. However, territories are not as closely connected to the United States as states are.

Many U.S. territories came under American control following conflicts in the late 1800s or during the 1900s. These include the U.S. Virgin Islands in the Caribbean Sea, and Guam, American Samoa, Wake Island, and the Midway Islands in the Pacific Ocean.

The United States has also had **protectorates** in the past. Most of these lands were independent. The United States provided them with protection against other nations that were rivals of the United States. Cuba, Panama, Haiti, the Philippines, and Hawaii were U.S. protectorates at one time.

ANALYZING MAPS

5. List at least three facts about U.S. territories, possessions, and former protectorates based on the map.

____

____

____

____

____

____

____

____

____

____

Name ______ Date ______ Class ______

6. CONSTRUCTING AN ARGUMENT

List at least three points you could use to support an argument either for statehood or independence for Puerto Rico.

______

______

______

______

______

______

Commonwealths

The United States also oversees **commonwealths.** A commonwealth is a U.S. territory with its own constitution and government. However, the U.S. Congress gives those governments their powers. Commonwealths are also subject to American laws. Each commonwealth is represented in Congress by a nonvoting delegate. Commonwealth residents are American citizens, but they do not pay federal income tax and cannot vote in presidential elections.

One U.S. commonwealth is Puerto Rico in the Caribbean Sea. It became a commonwealth in 1952. Puerto Ricans disagree about whether their island should become a state or become independent from the United States.

In 1978, the Northern Mariana Islands became a U.S. commonwealth. Like Puerto Rico, the islands are subject to American laws even though they have their own government. For example, in 2007, the government of the United States passed a minimum-wage law that applied not only to its states but also to its territories and commonwealths.

REVIEW LESSON 1

1. Use the chart below to list the political units other than the United States that are located in North America. Then indicate whether they share a border with the United States.

POLITICAL UNITS IN NORTH AMERICA	LOCATION RELATIVE TO UNITED STATES	SHARES A BORDER WITH UNITED STATES
Nations of Central America		

2. **MAKING INFERENCES** Each of the political units in the chart has a different location relative to the United States and has its own physical features. Some physical features help form national borders. How do you think relative location and physical features affect trade and economic relationships among these countries?

LESSON 2 SUMMARY

Landforms, Waterways, and Climates

SS.7.G.2.2, SS.7.G.2.3

Major Landforms

The United States is so large that its landscape varies greatly. It features many different types of landforms. A **landform** is a natural feature on the Earth's surface. Lowlands and highlands are two general types of land on Earth.

Lowlands

Lowlands are areas of flat land at or near sea level. Two large lowland areas are found in the central United States.

CENTRAL U.S. LOWLAND AREAS	
Eastern Central Lowlands	**Western Central Lowlands**
• west from the Appalachian Mountains to the Mississippi River	• west of the Mississippi River extending from the Canadian to the Mexican border
• fertile soil, good for farming	• called the Great Plains; **plains** are large areas of flat land with few trees • prairie, or rolling grassland, with rich soil; farmers raise wheat and cattle

Both the Atlantic and Gulf coasts feature lowlands. The lowland area along the Gulf of Mexico is wide. Atlantic coastal plains stretch eastward, gradually changing from grasslands to woodlands. In the southeastern Atlantic coast, woodlands turn to wetlands. A **wetland** is a large area of moist land, often covered with a shallow layer of water.

Florida's Everglades are the country's largest wetland system and the largest designated wilderness in the southeastern United States. It stretches from Lake Okeechobee in south central Florida to the Gulf of Mexico. Thousands of unique plants and animals live in these marshes, including some endangered species.

The Atlantic and Gulf coasts also feature coastal islands. Small islands are scattered along Florida's Gulf coast. Barrier islands and sandbars lie along its Atlantic coast. South of Florida are a series of islands called the Florida Keys.

ANALYZING VISUALS

1. DETERMINING CAUSE AND EFFECT

The two large lowland areas in the central United States are important farming regions. What physical factors make these areas good for agriculture? How might this affect human settlement and economies?

2. COMPARING AND CONTRASTING

In what ways are the highland areas in the eastern United States similar to the highland areas in the West? How are they different?

____

____

____

____

____

____

____

____

Another important feature of the coastal plains of the United States are busy port cities. They support economic growth from trade and related businesses. New Orleans, Louisiana, and Miami, Florida, are two examples.

Highlands

In addition to lowlands, the United States has **highland** regions, where the land is elevated much above sea level. Most highland areas are located west of the Great Plains, stretching north and south along much of the length of North America. The longest mountain range on the continent is the Rocky Mountains at 3,000 miles (4,800 km) long. It extends from Alaska to Mexico. The Continental Divide runs through these mountains, separating rivers that flow to the east from those that flow to the west.

Smaller mountain ranges lie near the Pacific coast. These include the Sierra Nevada, the Cascade Range, the Coast Ranges, and the Alaska Range. Another type of highland is a **plateau,** a large area of flat highland. The Colorado Plateau and the Columbia Plateau are located between the Pacific ranges and the Rocky Mountains. Among the highlands are dry lowlands—the Great Basin, the Mojave Desert, and Death Valley. Also found here is the Grand Canyon in Arizona, one of North America's most unusual physical features. A canyon is a deep valley with steep rock sides created by a river. The Colorado River carved the Grand Canyon out of the Colorado Plateau. It is so deep that scientists can study the Earth's history in its rock layers. It also has many different ecosystems with a variety of plants and animals.

The eastern United States also features highland areas. The Ozark Plateau rises from the plains in Arkansas and Missouri. The Appalachian Mountains, the oldest mountain range on the continent, is farther east. Its peaks are rounded because erosion has worn them down. The Appalachians stretch from eastern Canada to Alabama for more than 2,000 miles (3,200 km). The Blue Ridge Mountains, the White Mountains, and other smaller ranges make up this chain.

Name ______________________ Date ______________ Class __________

U.S. Landforms and Waterways

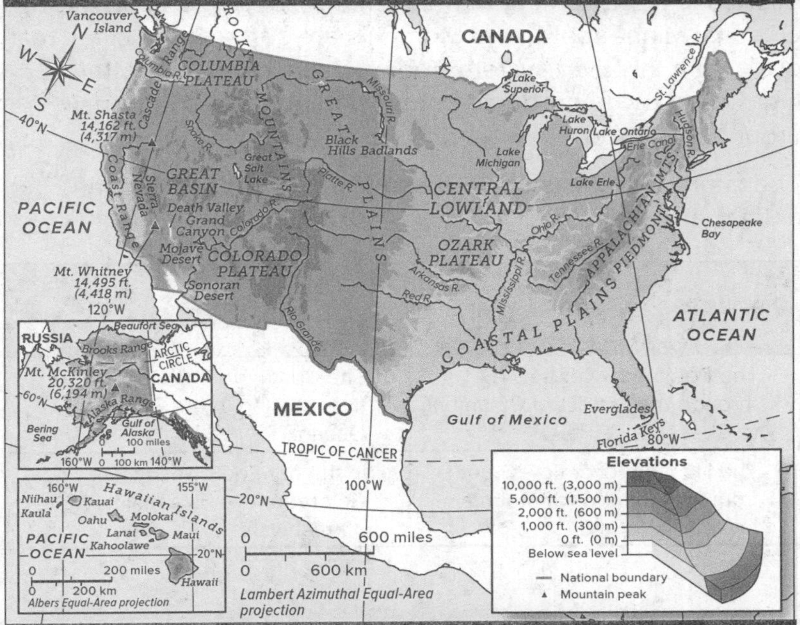

Most of the high elevations in the United States are found west of the Great Plains while most of the lowland areas are in the eastern part of the country.

Major Waterways

A strong connection exists between American history and the nation's bodies of water. The United States is connected to Europe and Asia by the Pacific and Atlantic Oceans. Millions of people migrated to this country by crossing these oceans. They began or joined settlements along the coasts near natural harbors. Many of these settlements grew into great port cities. Similar settlement took place along rivers and lakes within the country. Rivers provided transportation, irrigation, and economic activities, such as fishing and shipping goods.

Rivers

The longest river in the United States is the Mississippi River. It flows south from Lake Itasca in Minnesota 2,350 miles (3,780 km) into the Gulf of Mexico. Along the way it travels through 10 states and collects water from many tributaries. A tributary is a stream or small river that feeds into a larger river. The Ohio River, the Tennessee River, and the Missouri River are the main tributaries of the Mississippi.

3. IDENTIFYING EVIDENCE

The Mississippi River has been important to the physical and economic growth of the United States. Name at least two facts that support this statement.

____

____

____

____

____

____

4. MAKING CONNECTIONS

Think about the bodies of water that are located near you. How did they influence settlement in the region? What contributions do they make to the region's economy?

Together these rivers have made possible the settlement and economic development of much of the nation. St. Louis, New Orleans, Minneapolis, and Memphis are some of the cities that grew from this river system. Today, ships travel this water highway, moving products from inland port cities to ports around the world.

The chart below lists other U.S. rivers that support human, animal, and plant life.

U.S. RIVERS	
Eastern United States	**Western United States**
• The Potomac River flows through the District of Columbia to Chesapeake Bay.	• The Columbia River is the largest river flowing to the Pacific Ocean.
• The Hudson River flows south from the Adirondack Mountains to New York City.	• In the dry Southwest, the Colorado River is a main source of freshwater.

Lakes

The Great Lakes—Superior, Michigan, Huron, Erie, and Ontario—are among the largest freshwater lakes in the world. Their total area is 94,000 square miles. Both Americans and Canadians get their water supply from the Great Lakes. The lakes are connected and form a chain. Their water flows into the St. Lawrence River, which empties into the Atlantic Ocean. The Great Lakes are an important shipping route. Canada and the United States worked together to build the St. Lawrence Seaway, which expanded the shipping route. Through the river and canals of the seaway, ships carry goods from Great Lakes cities, such as Chicago and Detroit, to the world.

Another key American lake is the Great Salt Lake in northern Utah. It has no outlet where water can flow out of it. Three rivers flowing into this lake carry small amounts of dissolved salt. After mixing into the Great Salt Lake, much of the water evaporates. The salt remains in the lake, making it the largest inland body of salt water in the Western Hemisphere.

Many states have lake systems that provide important benefits. Communities get water, and residents can enjoy recreational activities such as fishing. Florida is fortunate to have thousands of lakes. The state's largest lake is Lake Okeechobee in south central Florida. It is the seventh-largest freshwater lake in the country.

Climate

Climate is the pattern of weather that a place experiences over a long period of time. Climate is affected by several factors. Latitude, or distance from the Equator, elevation, and nearby bodies of water can influence climate. Generally, the climate is warmer in places near the Equator. Climate often influences where people settle and what they do. It affects what people wear, the type of shelter they live in, and even their recreational activities.

The United States is so large that the climate varies greatly from place to place. Factors that influence the nation's climate include two oceans, many different landforms and waterways, and varying distances from the Equator.

Temperate Zones

Most regions of the United States have a temperate climate. In this type of climate there are few extremes in temperature and precipitation. Precipitation is water that falls to the ground in the form of rain or snow.

TEMPERATE CLIMATE		
Kind of Temperate Climate	**Where is It?**	**What is it Like?**
humid subtropical climate	southeastern United States	moderate to plentiful rainfall throughout the year; generally warm to hot and humid in summer; mild winters with limited snowfall
humid continental climate	much of the United States from New England to the Great Lakes and the Midwest	cool, wet weather; mild summers; cold winters with snowfall
marine climate	along the West Coast from Washington to central California	affected by moist winds from the Pacific Ocean; moderate temperatures for much of the year; mild, warm winters; much rainfall
Mediterranean climate	southern California	warm, dry summers; mild, rainy winters

5. COMPARING

Compare the climate in the southeastern United States to the climate along the West Coast from Washington to central California.

______

______

______

______

ANALYZING VISUALS

6. DRAWING CONCLUSIONS

Why are places with a Mediterranean climate popular summer tourist destinations?

______

______

______

______

7. EXPLAINING

What is the relationship between latitude and climate?

______

______

______

______

ANALYZING VISUALS

8. ANALYZING INFORMATION

Look at the table on this page. How do average temperatures differ in Fargo, North Dakota, and Miami, Florida? Why do you think this is the case?

______

______

______

______

______

How do you think temperature affected the settlement and the present-day population of each of these cities?

______

______

______

______

______

______

______

Extremes

While most of the United States has a temperate climate, a few states have extreme climates. A subarctic climate exists in much of Alaska. Most of the year, the weather is cold and produces large amounts of snowfall. The summers there are short and cool. Tropical climates are found in Hawaii and southern Florida. Most of the year, the weather is warm or hot with a lot of rain. The rainy season takes place near the end of the year, when tropical storms and hurricanes may occur.

There is a semiarid steppe climate in much of the West and Southwest, but some areas have a midlatitude desert climate. It is very dry in these regions, with little rain or snowfall. During the day, it is usually warm to hot for much of the year. However, it can become quite cold at night in these desert areas.

A highland climate exists in the Rocky Mountains. There are wide ranges in temperature and a great deal of precipitation. Higher elevations above sea level cause colder temperatures. For this reason, the mountains have cooler summers and cold winters with heavy snowfall. The snow results from moisture in the air that cools as it rises over the mountains and falls as snow.

AVERAGE TEMPERATURES IN KEY U.S. CITIES

CITY	AVERAGE JANUARY TEMP.	AVERAGE JUNE TEMP.
Chicago, Illinois	22°	73°
Denver, Colorado	29°	73°
Fargo, North Dakota	7°	71°
Honolulu, Hawaii	73°	81°
Houston, Texas	52°	84°
Juneau, Alaska	26°	57°
Los Angeles, California	57°	69°
Miami, Florida	68°	84°
New York City, New York	32°	77°
Seattle, Washington	41°	65°

Variations in temperature are one element of climate. Average temperatures in different parts of the country vary throughout the year.

REVIEW LESSON 2

1. Use the chart below to locate and describe some important physical landmarks in the United States.

PHYSICAL LANDMARKS	DESCRIPTION
Grand Canyon location:	
Everglades location:	
Great Salt Lake location:	
Mississippi River location:	
Great Plains location:	

2. **REFLECTING** The United States has physical landmarks that have been preserved for generations to appreciate. Based on what you know about the physical landmarks you described in your chart, why are they considered emblems, or symbols, of the United States? How do they help unite Americans?

Benchmark Skill Activities

DIRECTIONS: Write your answers on a separate piece of paper.

LAFS.68.WHST.1.2

1. DETERMINING CAUSE AND EFFECT

Use your FOLDABLES to write an essay.

You have written a description of the place where you live. Think about the geographic factors you mentioned, such as location, waterways, and climate. Explain how these factors have affected the settlement and economy of the place where you live.

LAFS.68.RH.2.4

2. USING DEFINITIONS ACCURATELY

Turn to the "Terms" list on the first page of Chapter 1. Choose at least three words from the list to include in a paragraph that describes the locations of North America and of the United States.

LAFS.68.RH.2.6

3. IDENTIFYING POINT OF VIEW

The following statements are from President Obama's announcement of his Clean Power Plan in August, 2015. As you read, underline any words or phrases that can be considered loaded language. Think about how this language helps you determine the author's point of view. Then identify possible facts that have not been included.

Write a paragraph that explains the effect of loaded language. Name any missing facts that could have been included. Then identify President Obama's purpose.

> *"Climate change is no longer just about the future that we're predicting for our children or our grandchildren; it's about the reality that we're living with every day, right now.*
>
> *The Pentagon says that climate change poses immediate risks to our national security. . . ."*
>
> *—President Barack Obama, August 3, 2015*

LAFS.68.RH.1.2, HE.7.P.8.2

4. CONSTRUCTING AN ARGUMENT

The excerpt below is from the same speech announcing the Clean Power Plan. President Obama stated several reasons to justify this plan. Read one of his reasons below. What evidence does President Obama present to support the Clean Power Plan? Which statement do you think would be most likely to make the public take notice?

> *"Over the past three decades, nationwide asthma rates have more than doubled, and climate change puts those Americans at greater risk of landing in the hospital. As one of America's governors has said, 'We're the first generation to feel the impact of climate change and the last generation that can do something about it.'"*
>
> *—President Barack Obama, August 3, 2015*

Now research on the Internet to find information about the relationship of climate change to asthma. Then write an argument that either supports what President Obama has stated or refutes his claim. Provide support for your argument.

Benchmark Note Cards

DIRECTIONS: Use these note cards to help you prepare for the test.

SS.7.G.1.3 Interpret maps to identify geopolitical divisions and boundaries of places in North America

BOUNDARIES OF NORTH AMERICA	• western boundary: Pacific Ocean • eastern boundary: Atlantic Ocean • northern boundary: Arctic Ocean • southeastern boundary: Gulf of Mexico
POLITICAL DIVISIONS OF NORTH AMERICA	• Canada: north of the United States • Mexico: southwest of the United States • Seven small nations in Central America: south of Mexico • Greenland: island northeast of Canada
BOUNDARIES OF THE UNITED STATES	• Rio Grande marks U.S.–Mexican border • St. Lawrence River and Great Lakes make up U.S.–Canadian border • U.S. shares a political border with Canada to the north • U.S. shares a political border with Mexico to the southwest
POLITICAL DIVISIONS IN THE UNITED STATES AND THEIR BOUNDARIES	• 50 states; each a political unit with clear borders within the nation • 48 contiguous states inside a common boundary • Alaska bordered by Canada to the east, Arctic Ocean to the north, Gulf of Alaska to the south; Bering Sea and Bering Strait to the west • Hawaii in the Pacific Ocean west of U.S. mainland

SS.7.G.1.2 Locate on a world map the territories and protectorates of the United States of America.

TERRITORIES OF THE UNITED STATES	• political units located in Pacific Ocean and Caribbean Sea • each with its own political borders, but subject to U.S. government • in Caribbean Sea: U.S. Virgin Islands • in Pacific Ocean: Guam, American Samoa, Wake Island, and Midway Islands • former protectorates: Cuba, Panama, Haiti, the Philippines, and Hawaii

COMMONWEALTHS OF THE UNITED STATES	• U.S. territories with their own constitution and government • Puerto Rico in the Caribbean Sea • the Northern Mariana Islands in the Pacific Ocean

SS.7.G.1.1 Locate the fifty states and their capital cities in addition to the nation's capital on a map.

U.S. STATES AND THEIR CAPITAL CITIES	• 50 states • each state government in its capital city • separate state governments, but all subject to U.S. national government

NATIONAL CAPITAL OF THE UNITED STATES	• national capital: District of Columbia, or Washington, D.C. • located on Potomac River between the states of Maryland and Virginia • location of national government

SS.7.G.2.2 Locate major physical landmarks that are emblematic of the United States.

THE GREAT PLAINS	• located in Western Central Lowlands, west of the Mississippi River • extends from the Canadian border to the Mexican border • flat land with few trees • rolling grassland, or prairie, with rich soil
THE EVERGLADES	• wetland, or a large area of moist land often covered with a shallow layer of water • the country's largest wetland system and the largest designated wilderness in southeastern United States • Stretches from Lake Okeechobee in south central Florida to the Gulf of Mexico • home to thousands of unique plants and animals, including some endangered species
THE GRAND CANYON	• located in a highland region, where the land is elevated much above sea level • located west of the Great Plains, carved out of the Colorado Plateau • one of North America's most unusual physical features • so deep that it reveals the Earth's history in its rock layers • contains many ecosystems and a variety of plants and animals

THE MISSISSIPPI RIVER	• longest river in the United States • begins at Lake Itasca in Minnesota and flows south 2,350 miles (3,780 km) into the Gulf of Mexico • runs through ten states • with its tributaries, made possible settlement and economic development • helped develop cities such as St. Louis, New Orleans, Minneapolis, and Memphis • route for ships to move products from inland port cities to foreign ports

THE GREAT SALT LAKE	• located in northern Utah • salty because it does not have an outlet • the largest inland body of salt water in the Western Hemisphere

SS.7.G.2.3 Explain how major physical characteristics, natural resources, climate, and absolute and relative location have influenced settlement, economies, and inter-governmental relations in North America.

LOCATION AFFECTS HUMAN SETTLEMENT, ECONOMIES, AND INTER-GOVERNMENTAL RELATIONS	• U.S. location between Atlantic and Pacific Oceans enabled people to settle on both coasts • allowed goods to be imported and exported and made travel easier for people • provided people with outdoor activities such as swimming and water sports • U.S. location between Canada and Mexico emphasizes importance of good relations among the three governments • opportunities for trade among the three nations

PHYSICAL CHARACTERISTICS/ NATURAL RESOURCES AFFECT HUMAN SETTLEMENT AND ECONOMIES IN LOWLANDS	• lowland areas: rich in resources • eastern central lowlands: fertile soil for farming • western central lowlands, or the Great Plains: rolling grassland with rich soil for wheat and cattle • Atlantic and Gulf Coast lowlands: port cities build local economies

PHYSICAL CHARACTERISTICS/ NATURAL RESOURCES AFFECT HUMAN SETTLEMENT AND ECONOMIES NEAR WATERWAYS	• Pacific and Atlantic Oceans made U.S. settlement possible • settlement along coasts near natural harbors, spurring growth of port cities • rivers and lakes used for transportation, irrigation, and varied economic activities • Mississippi River a major shipping route • Great Lakes—Superior, Michigan, Huron, Erie, and Ontario—used to supply water to Americans and Canadians • St. Lawrence Seaway expanded the Great Lakes shipping route to connect Great Lakes cities to the world

CLIMATE AFFECTS HUMAN SETTLEMENT AND ECONOMIES	• often determines where people settle • affects what people wear and the type of shelter they live in • affects what people do for a living and their entertainment activities • may be extreme in some places; affects economies when there are tropical storms, hurricanes, blizzards, or other natural events • sparse population in places with extreme temperatures

Chapter 1

VISUAL SUMMARY

DIRECTIONS: Complete the graphic organizer below.

The United States: Location and Lands

LOCATION AND BOUNDARIES

1. The United States is between ____________________ ____________________.
2. Having water on both sides made it possible for people to settle on both coasts and to trade.
3. The United States shares a political border with Canada to the north and Mexico to the southwest.
4. The Pacific Ocean forms North America's western boundary.
5. ____________ forms its eastern boundary.
6. ____________ is to the north.
7. The Gulf of Mexico lies to its southeast and extends to the Caribbean Sea.

U.S. TERRITORIES AND COMMONWEALTHS

1. Territories are areas of the U.S. that are neither a state nor part of a state.
2. Territories are political units scattered across the Pacific Ocean and the Caribbean Sea.
3. Some territories are the U.S. Virgin Islands in the Caribbean Sea, and American Samoa and the Midway Islands in the Pacific Ocean.
4. Puerto Rico is a commonwealth. It is a U.S. territory with its own constitution and government.

STATES AND CAPITALS

1. The United States has 50 political units called ______.
2. Each state has its own border and ______.
3. The U.S. capital is in ____________.

PHYSICAL LANDMARKS THAT ARE U.S. EMBLEMS

1. ____________________
2. ____________________
3. ____________________
4. ____________________
5. ____________________

USING PRIMARY SOURCES

INTERPRETING Below are two parts of a report entitled "Climate Change in the American Mind, March 2015." The report was part of a project on climate change communication. It tells the results of a survey, a process where interviewers ask questions to find out what people think about something. Read each part and then answer the questions on a separate sheet of paper.

Part A
Beliefs & Attitudes

- *About two in three (63%) Americans think global warming is happening. By contrast, only about one in five Americans (18%) thinks global warming is not happening.*
- *One in three Americans is either "extremely" or "very" sure global warming is happening (37%). One in ten Americans is "extremely" or "very sure" global warming is not happening (9%).*
- *About half of Americans (52%) think that global warming, if it is happening, is mostly human caused. Three in ten (32%) say they believe it is due mostly to natural changes in the environment.*
- *Only about one in ten Americans understands that over 90% percent of climate scientists think human-caused global warming is happening.*
- *About half of Americans (52%) say they are at least "somewhat worried" about global warming, but only 11% say they are "very worried" about it.*
- *Only about one in three Americans (32%) thinks people in the U.S. are being harmed "right now" by global warming.*

— "Climate Change in the American Mind," March 2015; Yale Project on Climate Change Communication

Leiserowitz, A., Maibach, E., Roser-Renouf, C., Feinberg, G., & Rosenthal, S. (2015). *Climate change in the American mind: March, 2015.* Yale University and George Mason University. New Haven, CT: Yale Project on Climate Change Communication.

Part B
Communication

- *Most Americans (74%) say they only "rarely" or "never" discuss global warming with family and friends, a number that has grown substantially since 2008 (60%).*
- *Only four in ten Americans (40%) say they hear about global warming in the media at least once a month (21%) or once a week (19%). Only 16% say they hear people they know talk about global warming at least once a month. One in four (25%) say they never hear people they know talk about global warming.*
- *Two-thirds of Americans are at least "a little interested" in hearing about global warming, whether in the media, in conversation, or somewhere else.*

—"Climate Change in the American Mind," March 2015;
Yale Project on Climate Change Communication

1. Why do you think this report was published?
2. Which two statistics could you use to encourage scientists and the news media to increase communication to the public about global warming?
3. How does each part of the source support or challenge your understanding of global warming?
4. What questions does each part of the document raise about global warming?

Leiserowitz, A., Maibach, E., Roser-Renouf, C., Feinberg, G., & Rosenthal, S. (2015). *Climate change in the American mind: March, 2015.* Yale University and George Mason University. New Haven, CT: Yale Project on Climate Change Communication.

Chapter Practice Test

DIRECTIONS: Circle the best answer for each question.

SS.7.G.1.3 (Moderate)

What is the purpose of this map?

A to show natural resources in the United States

B to show elevations within North America

C to show relative locations of nations in the Southern Hemisphere

D to show the boundaries of nations in North America

2 **SS.7.G.2.3 (High)**

Why did the location of Miami, Florida, most likely affect its early development?

A It was located near major highways, which meant people could travel more easily.

B It was near the coast, so many people likely settled there for economic opportunities.

C Its northern location created a mild climate, so people had more success growing crops.

D Its location along the border of Mexico offered opportunities for trade.

---

3 **LAFS.68.RH.2.4 (Moderate)**

How would geographers describe the relative location of the United States?

A by describing its location with lines of latitude and longitude

B by describing its physical features

C by describing its location between other countries

D by describing its political borders

---

4 **SS.7.G.2.2 (Moderate)**

How has the Mississippi River served as an important waterway for the United States?

A It gave people who sell goods an outlet to the Gulf of Mexico and foreign countries.

B It separated the original colonies from New England.

C It provided a connection between the Great Lakes and the Pacific Ocean.

D It served as a shipping route to Canada.

5 **SS.7.G.1.1 (Moderate)**

Political Map of the United States

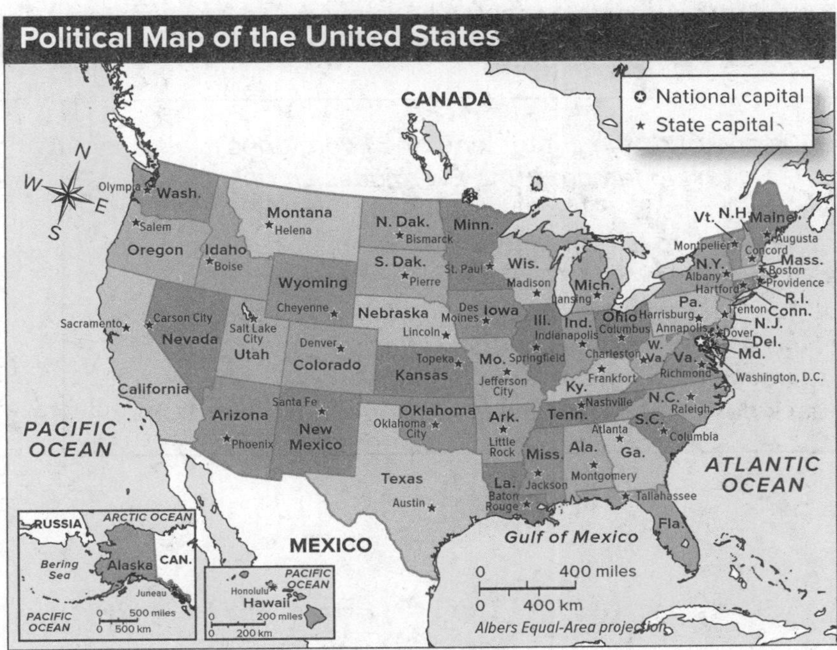

Which of the western states in the contiguous United States has the northernmost capital city?

A Wyoming

B Washington

C Colorado

D Idaho

 **SS.7.G.2.3 (Moderate)**

Which phrase best describes what is represented by the construction of the St. Lawrence Seaway?

A the power of the U.S. Congress related to trade

B the media coverage about economic development

C the cooperation between governments related to a physical feature

D the level of tourism around the Great Lakes

LAFS.68.RH.1.2 (Moderate)

Which section of this primary source best shows what steps could be taken to protect the Everglades?

> **[A]** *Then, in the 1940s and after, the character of the Everglades itself began to change. As South Florida grew, the Everglades shrank, its waters controlled for man's uses.* **[B]** *By the mid-1970s, wading-bird numbers had dropped back to a few hundred thousand, about 10 percent of what it had been a century before.* **[C]** *Biologists actively study these birds, looking for clues that might lead to stopping or even reversing the decline.* **[D]** *As yet the only thing that is certain is that life in the Everglades is more fragile than anyone ever thought."*
>
> —Jack de Golia, *Everglades: The Story Behind the Scenery*

A A

B B

C C

D D

SS.7.G.2.3 (Low)

Which of the following correctly pairs a city with the geographic feature that influenced its settlement and growth?

A New Orleans — Mississippi River

B St. Louis — Great Salt Lake

C Jacksonville — Everglades

D Fargo — Great Plains

9 **SS.7.G.1.2 (Moderate)**

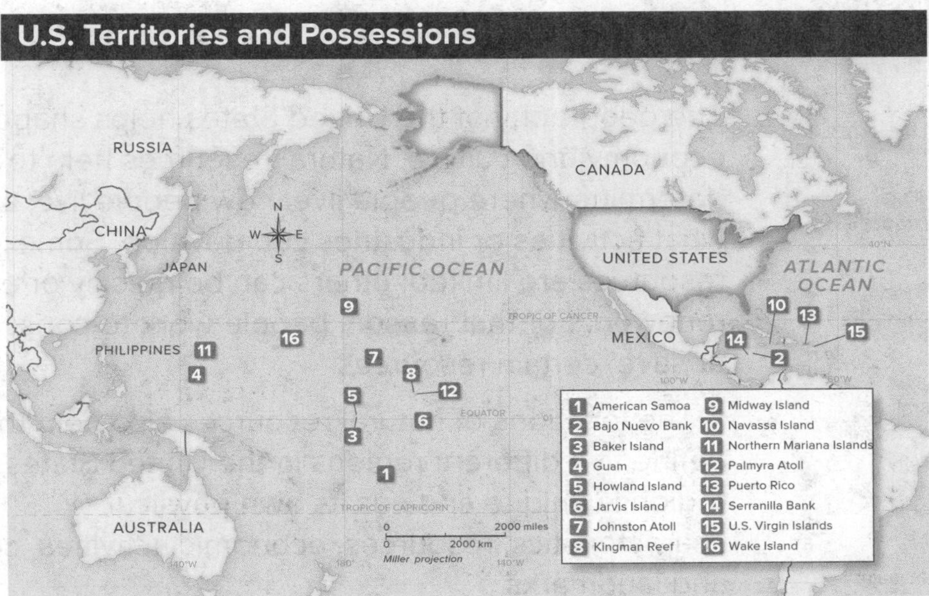

Which of the following statements is supported by the map?

A Most U.S territories are found in the Caribbean Sea.

B Most U.S. territories are located in the Pacific Ocean.

C The United States has more territories than other countries.

D The United States' territories were acquired through conflict.

10 **SS.7.G.1.2 (Moderate)**

What former U.S. protectorate is located in the Pacific Ocean west of the U.S. mainland?

A American Samoa

B Northern Mariana Islands

C Puerto Rico

D Hawaii

The United States: Resources and Regions

CHAPTER BENCHMARKS

SS.7.C.2.3 Experience the responsibilities of citizens at the local, state, or federal levels.

SS.7.G.2.1 Locate major cultural landmarks that are emblematic of the United States

SS.7.G.2.2 Locate major physical landmarks that are emblematic of the United States.

SS.7.G.2.3 Explain how major physical characteristics, natural resources, climate, and absolute and relative location have influenced settlement, economies, and inter-governmental relations in North America.

SS.7.G.2.4 Describe current major cultural regions of North America.

SS.7.G.3.1 Use maps to describe the location, abundance, and variety of natural resources in North America.

SS.7.G.5.1 Use a choropleth or other map to geographically represent current information about issues of conservation or ecology in the local community.

Chapter Overview

The geography of the United States helps shape its economy and culture. Natural resources help to determine where people live, how people live, and what activities or industries can develop. Some resources are limited; others can be quickly or easily renewed. For that reason, people work to conserve, or save, certain resources.

The locations of natural resources also help to define five different regions in the United States. Each region is unique and has its own physical characteristics, resources, economic activities, culture, and landmarks.

WHAT I NEED TO KNOW

TERMS

- ☐ environment
- ☐ natural resources
- ☐ nonrenewable resources
- ☐ renewable resources
- ☐ mineral
- ☐ energy
- ☐ fossil fuel
- ☐ pollution
- ☐ conservation
- ☐ urban
- ☐ Latino
- ☐ trade
- ☐ service sector
- ☐ aerospace
- ☐ textile
- ☐ rural

PEOPLE, PLACES, EVENTS

- ☐ The Northeast
- ☐ The South
- ☐ Everglades
- ☐ The Midwest
- ☐ Great Lakes
- ☐ Great Plains
- ☐ The Interior West
- ☐ The Pacific

CHAPTER BENCHMARKS, *continued*

LAFS.68.RH.2.4 Determine the meaning of words and phrases as they are used in a text, including vocabulary specific to domains related to history/social studies.

LAFS.68.RH.2.5 Describe how a text presents information (e.g., sequentially, comparatively, causally).

LAFS.68.WHST.1.1 Write arguments focused on discipline-specific content.

LAFS.68.WHST.2.6 Use technology, including the Internet, to produce and publish writing and present the relationships between information and ideas clearly and efficiently.

The United States: Resources and Regions

Create this Foldable® like a small booklet. Label the front *Resources and Regions*. Open the Foldable and label the top of the two inside sections *Natural Resources* and *Regions*. On the left side, note and describe renewable and nonrenewable natural resources found in the United States that supply human needs. On the right side, describe the five regions of the country and note how they differ. On the back of the folded booklet, roughly sketch the five regions and label each.

Step 1
Arrange a piece of paper horizontally and fold in half from left to right.

Step 2
Label the inside of your booklet as shown.

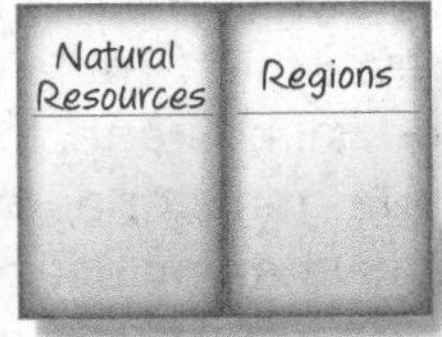

LESSON 1 SUMMARY

Natural Resources

ANALYZE VISUALS

1. EXPRESSING

In which column of the resources chart would you put diamonds? What about fish? How would the discovery of minerals in a region affect its development? Explain your answers.

SS.7.C.2.3, SS.7.G.2.3, SS.7.G.3.1, SS.7.G.5.1

Types of Resources

The **environment** is the air, water, and land that surround you. A vital part of the environment are **natural resources,** materials found in nature that people use for activities such as growing food, fueling cars, and heating homes.

The mix of natural resources in a place affects the things the people there make, the jobs they do, and the way they live. The United States has a rich variety of natural resources, which has helped the country develop a strong industrial, technological economy.

There are two basic types of natural resources. **Nonrenewable resources** cannot be replaced within our lifetime. **Renewable resources** can be replaced in a reasonable amount of time.

NONRENEWABLE RESOURCES	RENEWABLE RESOURCES
iron ore	sun
gold	wind
oil	water
coal	forests

Nonrenewable Resources

One type of nonrenewable resource is minerals. **Minerals** are natural materials that are found in the earth. They do not come from living organisms. The United States has a wealth of mineral resources. They include silver, iron ore, zinc, copper, gold, quartz, limestone, lead, granite, and magnesium. They also include gemstones, which are used in making jewelry. Minerals have many uses. They are needed in the construction industry, and they are used in new technologies, including the creation of computer chips. Iron ore is used to produce steel, which is used in building and manufacturing.

LESSON 1 SUMMARY, *continued*

Another critical nonrenewable resource is energy. **Energy** refers to power, such as heat and electricity. The United States relies on the nonrenewable resources of oil, natural gas, and coal to produce most of its energy. These three natural resources are known as **fossil fuels,** because they result from the breakdown of organic, or once-living, materials. Fossil fuels take thousands or even millions of years to form.

2. DRAWING CONCLUSIONS

Why is it dangerous for the United States to depend on fossil fuels for its energy?

Renewable Resources

The United States has an abundance of renewable resources. One of its most important renewable resources is its land. Fertile soil is critical to farming and other agricultural industries. Fish and other sea animals are a valuable food source. Lumber, which comes from trees, is used for everything from energy production to building homes to making paper. Life cannot exist without water. It is one of the nation's most important natural resources, and it meets a broad range of critical human needs.

Today, many citizens believe the United States needs to develop energy sources that use renewable resources. As a result, scientists are exploring ways to generate power from the tides, the wind, the sun, plant materials, and atomic reactions.

3. MAKING CONNECTIONS

Why might energy industries play an important role in the Texas economy?

Locating Nonrenewable Resources

Different resources can be found in different areas of the United States. The minerals gold, silver, and copper are found mostly in the western states. Most iron ore comes from Minnesota and Michigan, and zinc is located in Tennessee, Alaska, and Missouri. Limestone deposits lie near the Great Lakes and in Florida.

Like minerals, fossil fuels such as oil and natural gas are found in underground deposits. Large oil deposits have been found under the land in Alaska, California, Oklahoma, Texas, and Louisiana. Reserves of oil are also located beneath the Gulf of Mexico. Most of the nation's natural gas fields are found in Oklahoma, Texas, and Kansas. Most of the nation's coal is beneath the Appalachian Mountains and in Wyoming.

ANALYZING MAPS

4. Based on the map, what types of industries would you expect to find in Texas, Louisiana, and Mississippi?

____

____

____

5. CREATING MAPS

Using information that you have learned about the natural resources of the United States, create a map on a separate piece of paper showing the natural resources of the United States. Be sure to include the following on your map and in its key:

- M for minerals
- H for hydroelectric dams
- F for fossil fuels
- L for the most fertile land

Oil Rigs in the Gulf of Mexico

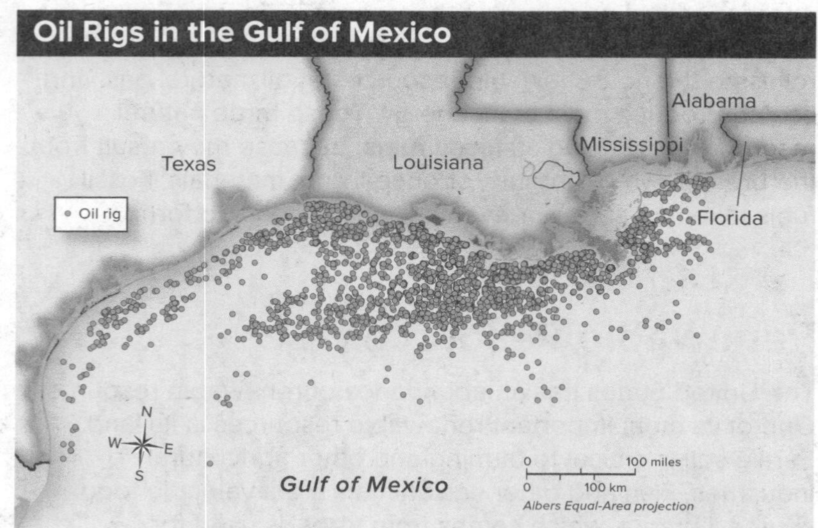

Using Renewable Resources

Governments at all levels are working with businesses and citizens to better manage our natural resources and find ways to use renewable resources to meet the needs of people in the future.

Land and Water

Nearly half of the land in the United States is used for farming or ranching. Most fertile land is found in the central part of the nation, on the coastal plains, and along rivers. Farmers use this land to grow corn, wheat, cotton, tobacco, vegetables, and fruits. They also raise poultry, pigs, and livestock. Rangeland, or open grassland in the western half of the nation, is used to graze cattle and sheep.

The nation's many rivers and lakes provide water for much of the country. Water is used for drinking, washing, farming and gardening, travel, and other purposes. It can also be used as a renewable source of energy. Hydroelectric dams create power for thousands of homes and businesses. For example, hydroelectric dams provide electricity for people living in Tennessee, Kentucky, Mississippi, and Alabama. Niagara Falls, along the border between New York State and Canada, also produces hydroelectric power. Currently, water is the second-largest source of electricity after fossil fuels.

Wind and Solar Resources

The United States also uses wind resources to generate electricity. Wind farms now operate in 36 states. The Great Plains and coastal areas are especially good areas for wind power.

Solar power, or power generated from the light and heat of the sun, is another renewable resource. Solar panels produce electricity for individual homes and businesses. There are also solar energy plants in California, Arizona, and Florida. In 2011, solar panels and a solar water heater were installed on the roof of the White House.

6. MAKING INFERENCES

Why is Florida a good location for solar energy plants? Which other states would be good locations for solar energy?

Lumber Resources

Lumber is used in countless products, and forests cover about one-third of the United States. More than half of the nation's tree resources are in the Pacific Northwest. Large forest areas also blanket the Appalachian Mountains. Timber companies plant new trees to replace the ones they cut.

7. MAKING CONNECTIONS

What responsibilities do citizens have concerning the conservation of resources? What are some ways you or your community participates in conservation?

Fish

Fish are another renewable resource. The term *fisheries* refers to the waters in which fish and other sea creatures are caught, and there are many fisheries in the country's coastal regions. Overfishing in some areas threatens the survival of certain types of fish. Fish farming, where businesses raise fish in tanks or enclosed areas, is one solution to this problem.

Consequences of Human Activity

Natural resources help people survive, but accessing them impacts the environment. Many human activities cause **pollution,** materials that dirty the air, water, and soil. Over time, pollution damages the environment, which in turn can harm people.

Name ______________________ Date ______________ Class __________

ANALYZING MAPS

8. Why are the Everglades important to the economy, resources, and geography of Florida?

____

____

____

____

____

____

____

____

Conservation means planned, careful use of natural resources in order to prevent overuse of natural resources and reduce pollution. State and federal agencies work to manage resource use and protect public lands. Citizens can also participate in conservation programs at the local, state, and national level.

Loss of Wetlands: The Everglades

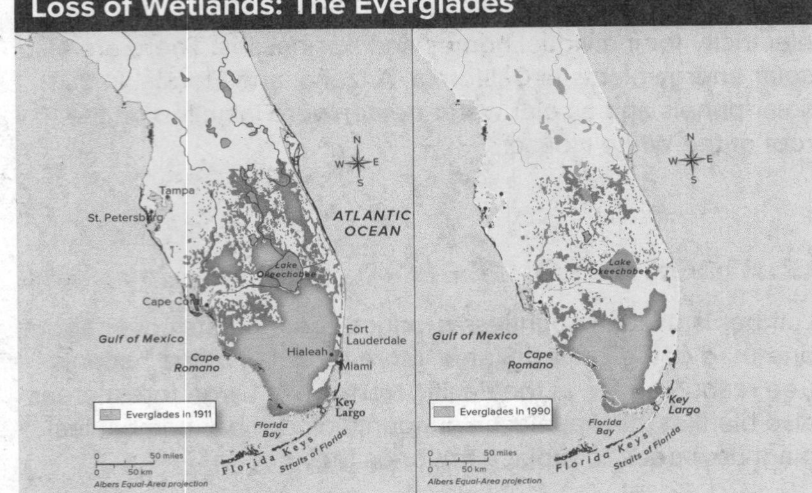

REVIEW LESSON 1

1. Use the Venn diagram below to compare and contrast renewable and nonrenewable resources.

RENEWABLE

- can be easily replaced or cannot be used up
- includes wind, water, and ____________

(Both)

- ____________ ____________
- ____________ ____________ ____________
- ____________ ____________ ____________

NONRENEWABLE

- cannot be replenished in a human lifetime
- includes minerals and ____________

2. **DRAWING CONCLUSIONS** Why does a nation need both renewable and nonrenewable resources? Use the Venn diagram above to write an essay that explains how both types of resources contribute to a nation's survival and success, giving specific examples about the United States from the text.

Regions of the United States

SS.7.G.2.1, SS.7.G.2.2, SS.7.G.2.3, SS.6.G.2.4

The Northeast

The United States can be divided into five major regions. They are the Northeast, the South, the Midwest, the Interior West, and the Pacific.

The Northeast has the smallest land area but is the most densely populated of the regions. Its 11 states are mostly **urban,** or thickly settled. Its population is mostly of European descent, but it also has many African American, Asian, and Latino residents. **Latino** is a term for people of Latin American origin.

Early settlers adapted to the land in the Northeast. The rocky soil, mountainous landscape, and cold winters made farming difficult. The coastline and rivers, however, provided resources for fishing, shipping, and trade. Settlements grew into towns, and towns grew into cities.

Today, the economy of the Northeast remains based on industry and trade. **Trade** is the buying and selling of goods and services. Services are jobs performed by one person for another, such as health care, banking, and tourism. In recent years, the Northeast's **service sector,** or part of the economy that does not produce things to sell but rather performs work that helps others in some way, has expanded. Industries such as technology, communications, research, publishing, and chemical production are part of the region's urban economy.

The region also boasts cranberry bogs in Massachusetts, coal mines and timber in the Appalachian Mountains, farms in Pennsylvania and New York, maple syrup producers in Vermont, jewelry makers in Rhode Island, and naval shipyards in New Hampshire.

Historic sites play an important part in the culture of the Northeast. Philadelphia is the home of Independence Hall and the Liberty Bell, symbols of the nation's birth. Boston is also steeped in early American history that can be viewed on the Freedom Trail. One of the most famous landmarks is the Old North Church. The church bell was rung to let people know that the British were marching on Concord and Lexington. New York City boasts the Statue of Liberty in its harbor and the Empire State Building at its center—both U.S. landmarks.

1. SYNTHESIZING

Which five words best describe the Northeast region of the United States? Briefly explain each choice.

1. ______________________

____

____

2. ______________________

____

____

3. ______________________

____

____

4. ______________________

____

____

5. ______________________

____

____

ANALYZING VISUALS

2. EXPLAINING

Where is the Statue of Liberty located? Why is the Statue of Liberty an important cultural landmark?

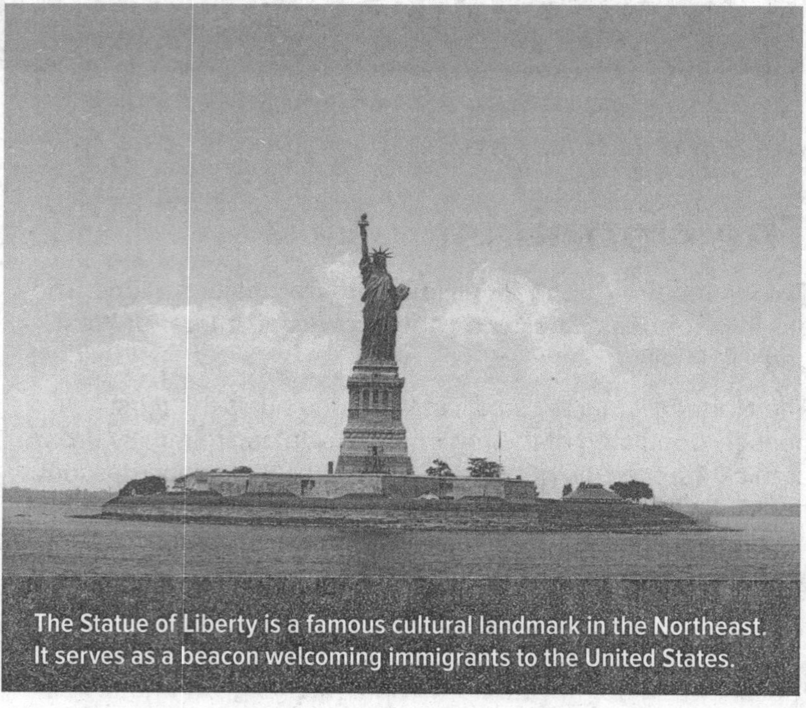

The Statue of Liberty is a famous cultural landmark in the Northeast. It serves as a beacon welcoming immigrants to the United States.

3. COMPARING AND CONTRASTING

How is the South similar to the Northeast? How is it different?

The South

The South has a warm climate, rich soil, and lots of rain. As a result, farming has become a key part of the region's economy. Major crops include citrus fruits, cotton, rice, tobacco, nuts, and soybeans. Cattle ranching also thrives, especially in Texas.

In recent years, the South's economy has grown and new industries have developed. West Virginia, Kentucky, Louisiana, Texas, and Oklahoma are major coal, oil, and natural gas producers. The **aerospace** industry develops aircraft, spacecraft, missiles, and satellites. It is centered in Cape Canaveral, Florida, with other facilities in Alabama and Texas. Southern industries produce **textiles,** or cloth, along with electrical equipment, computers, airplanes, and parts. Like the Northeast, the South also has an expanding service sector.

In recent years, the population in the South has increased. At the same time, the South has become more diverse. In addition, the warm climate has attracted retirees, and thousands, if not millions, have moved to the region. States such as Florida also have many Latino and Haitian immigrants.

Although the population is growing, the South still has large rural areas. A **rural** area is one that is not heavily populated. Forest, farmland, and coastal plains cover much of the region. One notable rural area is the Florida Everglades. About half of this huge, unique wetland area is national parkland reserved for diverse wildlife, including alligators, bobcats, manatees, turtles, and rare panthers.

The growth in population has resulted in large urban areas and bustling cities. Dallas, Houston, Atlanta, New Orleans, and Miami are busy port cities and business centers. Washington, D.C., the nation's capital, lies between Maryland and Virginia.

Like the Northeast, the South is also home to important cultural landmarks. The Capitol and the White House are among the famous sites in Washington, D.C. Texas is the home of the Alamo, the site of an important battle in Texas's fight for independence from Mexico.

4. EXPLAINING

Why is the Midwest so well-suited for farming?

____

____

____

____

The Midwest

The geography of the Midwest is characterized by the Great Lakes and the Great Plains. The Great Plains are composed of millions of acres of flat, fertile land. Winters are colder in the Midwest than in the South, and the climate is drier. However, farmers raise crops such as wheat, corn, oats, soybeans, fruits, and vegetables. In fact, so much grain is grown here that the Midwest is called the "breadbasket of the nation." Farms here also produce pork, beef, and dairy products. Valuable minerals include iron, coal, lead, and zinc.

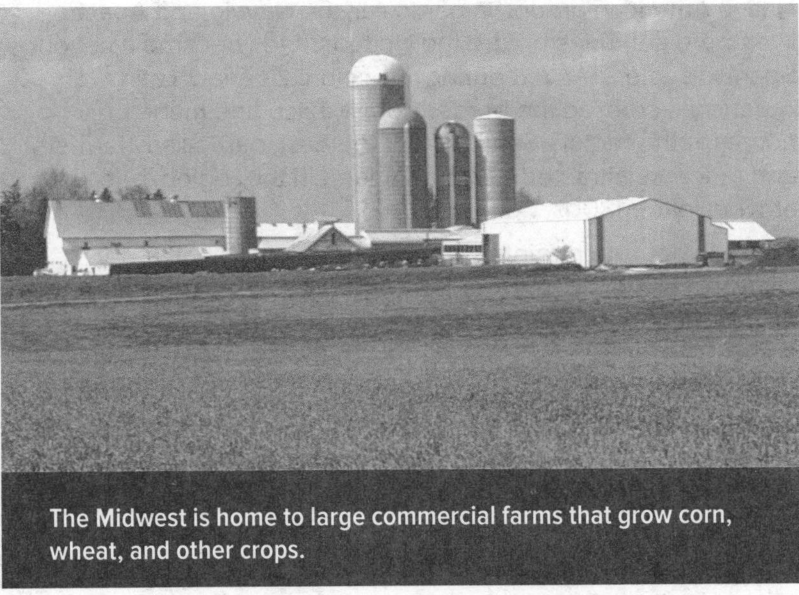

The Midwest is home to large commercial farms that grow corn, wheat, and other crops.

The Midwest formed a crossroads for settlers heading west in the 1800s. The famous Gateway Arch monument in St. Louis, Missouri, marks this historic westward movement. Another major cultural landmark is Mt. Rushmore in the Black Hills of South Dakota. The faces of four presidents—George Washington, Thomas Jefferson, Abraham Lincoln, and Theodore Roosevelt—are carved into the mountainside.

5. THEORIZING

Is it still appropriate to call the Midwest the Rust Belt? Why or why not?

6. ANALYZING INFORMATION

How have the residents of the Interior West adapted the environment to their needs?

Over time, with access to coal and iron and shipping channels on the rivers and the Great Lakes, the Midwest developed manufacturing centers in cities such as Cleveland and Detroit. The automobile industry was particularly important in the region. Midwestern factories struggled during the latter part of the twentieth century. Because of the sharp decline in the economy and the loss of jobs, the region became known as the Rust Belt.

Some parts of the Midwestern manufacturing industry have recovered. The automobile industry is in a recovery period. Despite the problems the industry suffered during the past decade, it still plays a role in the regional economy. Today, in addition to manufacturing and agriculture, the Midwest has developed thriving service industries.

Many African Americans, Asian Americans, and Latinos make their home in the Midwest. In fact, according to some estimates, African Americans make up approximately 80 percent of the population in Detroit, Michigan.

The Interior West

The people who settled the Interior West have diverse roots. Two Native American groups in particular, the Navajo and Apache, lived here centuries before the United States became a nation. Spanish settlers arrived during the colonial period. Latin Americans crossed the border from Mexico and made their homes in the region. Settlers from the East, particularly farmers and ranchers attracted to cheaper land in the region, began arriving in the 1800s.

There is not much rainfall in the region, and it has a dry climate. Farmers use irrigation systems that enable them to grow cotton, alfalfa, and other crops. Ranchers raise livestock, and there are large cattle ranches in the Interior West. Lumbering and the mining of copper, iron, coal, and other minerals occur here. The region's natural resources also include oil and natural gas.

Manufacturing, especially for the aeronautics and electronics industries, has grown in recent years. Research and development, especially for the aerospace, nuclear weapons, and energy industries, is another rapidly developing part of the economy.

This region has fewer people than others. Still, it is home to some major cities. Denver and Salt Lake City are booming and have become important hubs for technology. Tourists flock to Albuquerque and Phoenix, which has created a thriving service industry. The warm, dry climate of Arizona attracts retired Americans as well as visitors.

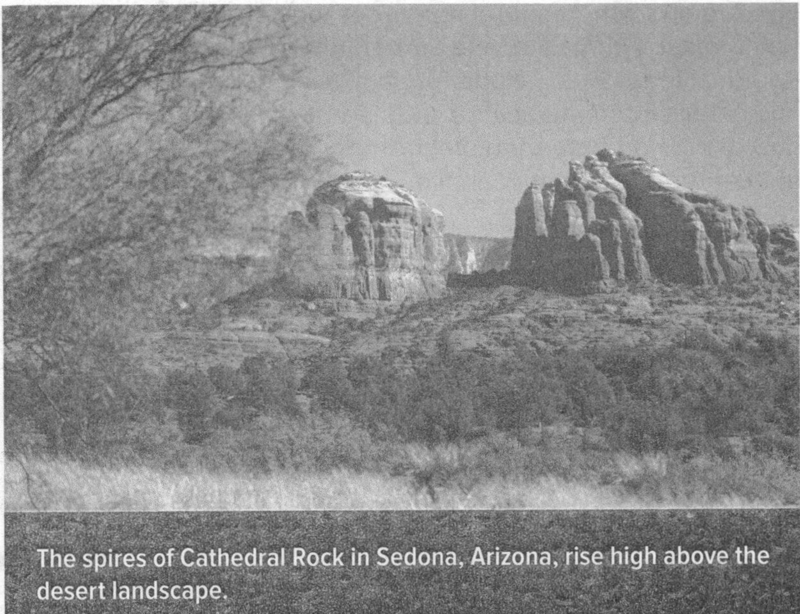

The spires of Cathedral Rock in Sedona, Arizona, rise high above the desert landscape.

ANALYZING VISUALS

7. DRAWING CONCLUSIONS

What makes Cathedral Rock such a dramatic geographic feature?

The Interior West is marked by its rugged geographic features. From the Rocky Mountains to the Arizona desert, the landscape attracts visitors from all around the world. Millions of Americans and foreign visitors travel to Arizona's Grand Canyon each year. Another natural wonder is the Great Salt Lake in Utah. The lake is known for its high salt content. Hoover Dam, an amazing engineering feat on the Arizona-Nevada border, also draws visitors. The dam provides electricity, flood control, farm irrigation, and drinking water to millions of people.

The Pacific

The Pacific region borders the Pacific Ocean. Throughout these states, coastal plains rise to mountain ranges, including California's Sierra Nevada and Washington's and Oregon's Cascade Range. The Alaska Range includes Denali (Mt. McKinley), the highest peak in North America. Volcanoes also dot the region. Hawaii is actually a chain of volcanic islands.

In general, these states have plentiful rain and mild temperatures. This climate helped fertile valleys in California, Washington, and Oregon become centers of agriculture. California, for example, grows more than half of the produce consumed in the United States. Hawaii grows sugarcane, pineapples, bananas, papayas, and coffee in its rich volcanic soil.

8. COMPARING

How is the Pacific region similar to the Northeast?

The region's other natural resources include minerals in California, oil in Alaska, and timber in Washington and Oregon. Regional industries include tourism, fishing, livestock, plastics, and satellite communications. California's Silicon Valley is a hub of the computer and electronics industries. Los Angeles is the center of the American film industry.

Many Native Americans, Latinos, and Asian Americans call the Pacific region home. In California, nearly half the people are Latino or Asian American.

REVIEW LESSON 2

1. Use the chart below to compare and contrast the regions of the United States.

REGION	PHYSICAL AND CULTURAL LANDMARKS	CULTURE AND ECONOMY
Northeast		
South		
Midwest		
Interior West		
Pacific		

2. **RECOGNIZING RELATIONSHIPS** How do the different regions of the United States work together to create a single economy? Use the chart above to write an essay that explains the relationship among the regions.

Benchmark Skill Activities

DIRECTIONS: Write your answers on a separate sheet of paper.

LAFS.68.WHST.1.1

1. COMPARING AND CONTRASTING

Use the notes from your FOLDABLES to write an essay answering the following questions:

How does the abundance or lack of renewable and nonrenewable resources affect the economy of a region? What differences might there be in the economies and growth of regions that have renewable resources versus those that have nonrenewable resources? What kinds of industries flourish in areas that have renewable or nonrenewable resources?

LAFS.68.RH.2.4

2. DETERMINING WORD MEANINGS

Read the excerpt below from a speech given in 1999 by Carol Browner of the Environmental Protection Agency. Then, write a definition for each of the underlined words. Use the words around these words, or context clues, to help you determine their meaning.

> "Not only is tourism, fishing and farming dependent upon adequate flows of clean water, but so too are the six million people who live here. Just as we might invest in traditional infrastructure—roads and schools—so too must we invest in the Everglades if we are to guarantee a sound future for south Florida and to preserve this treasure for future generations."

LAFS.68.RH.2.5

3. COMPARING AND CONTRASTING

Examine the text in each lesson. How did the author organize the ideas in each lesson? How is the presentation similar? How is it different?

LAFS.68.WHST.1.1

4. ARGUMENT

Is conservation more important for renewable or nonrenewable resources? Write an argument with a clearly stated claim, supporting reasons, and relevant evidence drawn from details in the text.

LAFS.68.WHST.2.6

5. INFORMATIVE/EXPLANATORY

Travel blogs and Web sites are important resources for people planning vacations. Create a travel blog aimed at people who want to travel across the United States. Your blog should:

- describe each of the nation's cultural regions
- describe the "must see" cultural and physical landmarks in each region, and include each landmark's significance
- be formatted appropriately
- use appropriate images, headings, and hyperlinks
- be published online

Benchmark Note Cards

DIRECTIONS: Use these note cards to help you prepare for the test.

SS.7.C.2.3 Experience the responsibilities of citizens at the local, state, or federal levels.

CITIZEN RESPONSIBILITIES	Citizens have the responsibility to: • use resources wisely • participate in conservation efforts

SS.7.G.2.1 Locate major cultural landmarks that are emblematic of the United States.

MAJOR CULTURAL LANDMARKS	**Northeast** • Independence Hall and the Liberty Bell (Philadelphia, Pennsylvania) • Statue of Liberty and the Empire State Building (New York, New York) **South** • Cape Canaveral (Florida) • The Capitol and White House (Washington, D.C.) • The Alamo (Texas) **Midwest** • Gateway Arch (St. Louis, Missouri) • Mt. Rushmore (South Dakota) **Interior West** • Hoover Dam (Nevada-Arizona border)

SS.7.G.2.2 Locate major physical landmarks that are emblematic of the United States.

MAJOR PHYSICAL LANDMARKS

Northeast
- Appalachian Mountains

South
- The Everglades (Florida)

Midwest
- The Great Lakes
- The Great Plains

Interior West
- Grand Canyon (Arizona)
- Cathedral Rock (Arizona)
- Great Salt Lake (Utah)

Pacific
- Sierra Nevada (California)
- Cascade Range (Washington and Oregon)
- Denali (Mt. McKinley) and the Alaska Range (Alaska)
- Volcanoes and volcanic islands (Hawaii)

SS.7.G.2.3 Explain how major physical characteristics, natural resources, climate, and absolute and relative location have influenced settlement, economies, and inter-governmental relations in North America.

PHYSICAL CHARACTERISTICS

Economic Influences
- The Northeast's rocky soil, mountainous landscape, and cold winters make farming difficult. The region's coastline and rivers allow fishing, shipping, and trade.
- The South's warm climate, rich soil, and plentiful rain encouraged the development of farming.
- The Great Plains of the Midwest are noted for miles of flat, fertile land that helped the region become the nation's breadbasket.
- The dry nature of the Interior West requires irrigation and hydroelectric dams to provide water for farming, drinking, and energy.
- The fertile valleys of the Pacific helped the region become the nation's top producer of fruits and vegetables.

NATURAL RESOURCES	**Economic Influences** • Minerals contribute to the construction, heating, and manufacturing sectors of the U.S. economy. • Fossil fuels contribute to the petroleum industry in states along the Gulf of Mexico. • The energy industry uses fossil fuels, wind, and the sun to provide electricity in different states. • Plentiful trees in the Pacific Northwest and Appalachia are the basis of the lumber industry. • Fertile land and fisheries provide the nation with food.

SS.7.G.2.4 Describe current major cultural regions of North America.

THE NORTHEAST	• smallest region • densely populated • mostly urban • mostly of European descent • large industrial and service sectors • important historical landmarks

THE SOUTH	• large rural areas • growing cities • increasing diversity • farming and aerospace industries • includes the U.S. capital

THE MIDWEST	• population includes African Americans, Asian Americans, and Latinos • the “breadbasket of the nation” • the Rust Belt • farming and manufacturing, especially automobiles • gateway for pioneers heading west in the 1800s

THE INTERIOR WEST	• dry climate • Navajo, Apache, and Spanish heritage • farming, ranching, mining, and tourism • least populated • dramatic geographic features

THE PACIFIC	• borders Pacific Ocean • coastal plains rise to mountains • diverse population • diverse resources • tourism, computer, electronics, and film industries

SS.7.G.3.1 Use maps to describe the location, abundance, and variety of natural resources in North America.

RESOURCES BY REGION	• **Northeast:** water, trees, coal • **South:** fertile land, fossil fuels, minerals • **Midwest:** fertile land, wind, minerals • **Interior West:** minerals, sun • **Pacific:** fertile valleys, fisheries, trees, sun, wind

SS.7.G.5.1 Use a choropleth or other map to geographically represent current information about issues of conservation or ecology in the local community.

LOCAL CONSERVATION ISSUES	• Between 1911 and 1990, the Everglades lost one-third of its territory. As a result, it has been designated a protected area.

Chapter 2

VISUAL SUMMARY

DIRECTIONS: Complete the graphic organizers below.

NATURAL RESOURCES

NONRENEWABLE

Definition: cannot be replenished in a human lifetime

Examples and Uses:

★ fossil fuels, energy

★ ______

★ ______

CONSERVATION

Definition: ______

Purpose: ______

RENEWABLE

Definition: ______

Examples and Uses:

★ ______

★ ______

★ ______

U.S. REGIONS

NORTHEAST

Population: ______

Economy: little farming, lots of industry, trade, and services

Landmarks: ______

SOUTH

Population: ______

Economy: ______

Landmarks: ______

MIDWEST

Population: ______

Economy: ______

Landmarks: ______

INTERIOR WEST

Population: small; Native American and Spanish heritage

Economy: ______

Landmarks: ______

PACIFIC

Population: ______

Economy: ______

Landmarks: ______

USING PRIMARY SOURCES

DIRECTIONS: Write your answers on a separate sheet of paper.

Both of these photographs were taken in Washington State by Darius Kinsey in the early 1900s. Kinsey was an important photographer who documented logging activities in the Pacific Northwest. Based on what you see in each photograph, answer the following questions.

1. Analyzing Visuals What natural resource is the focus of these photographs? Is it a renewable or nonrenewable resource?

2. Making Inferences What activity or activities caused the situation shown in the second photograph?

3. Interpreting What feelings does each photograph inspire? Explain.

4. Hypothesizing How might these photographs be used to encourage conservation?

Chapter Practice Test

DIRECTIONS: Circle the best answer for each question.

SS.7.G.5.1, SS.7.G.2.4 (Low)

This map shows the extent of the 2010 oil spill in the Gulf of Mexico.

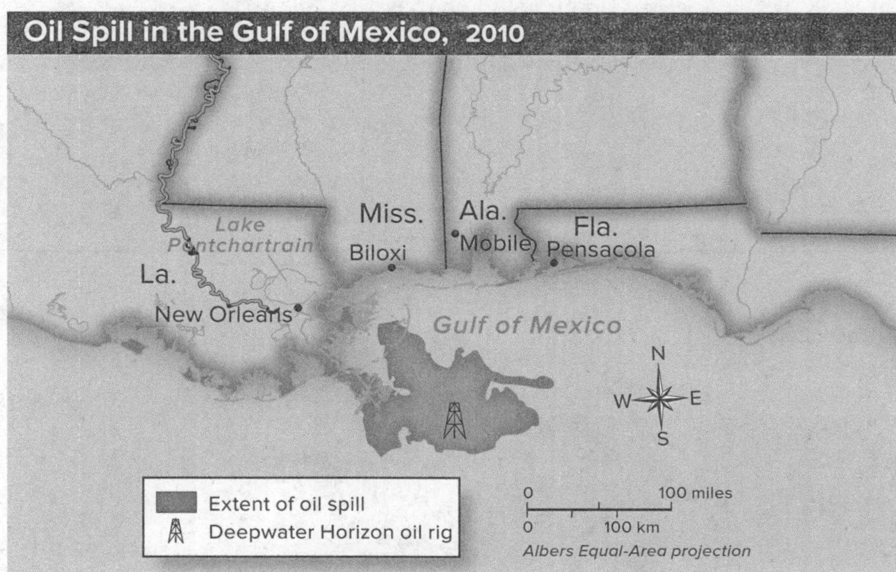

Which U.S. region was most directly affected by the oil spill?

A Northeast

B Midwest

C Pacific

D South

SS.7.G.2.3 (Moderate)

When an oil spill occurs in a coastal region, which renewable resource is most threatened?

A sun

B fish

C petroleum

D fertile land

SS.7.G.2.1, SS.7.G.2.2 (Moderate)

Lake Mead is a human-made lake fed by waters from the Colorado River system that supplies water and electricity. Which region of the United States would be most directly affected by issues confronting Lake Mead?

A Interior West

B Northeast

C Pacific

D South

SS.7.G.2.1, SS.7.G.2.2 (Moderate)

Why might the object in this image be considered both a cultural and a physical landmark?

A The statue welcomes European immigrants to the United States, and it is located on an island.

B The statue is a symbol of freedom and democracy, and it is located in New York City's harbor.

C The statue was a gift to the United States from France and because of its height, it is visible for miles.

D The statue is a popular destination for both Americans and visitors to the United States.

SS.7.G.3.1 (Moderate)

Natural Resources of the United States

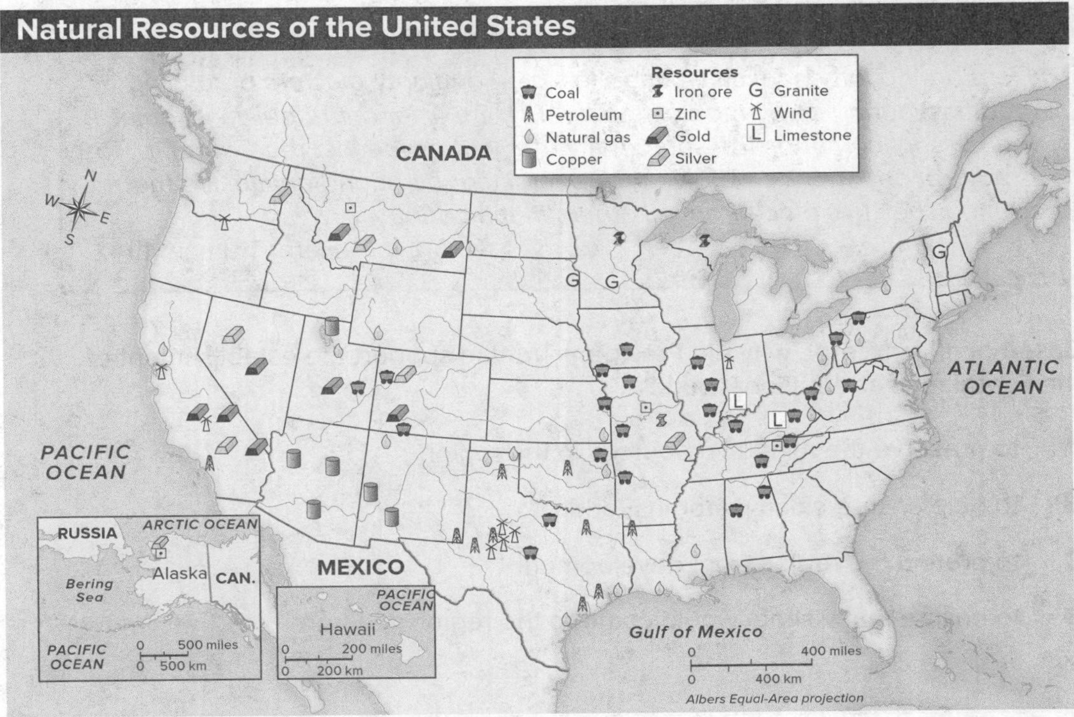

Which region is home to most of the nation's mineral deposits?

A the Midwest

B the South

C the Northeast

D the Pacific region

SS.7.G.2.1 (Moderate)

Someone interested in learning about the founding of the United States should visit landmarks in which region?

A the Pacific

B the Midwest

C the Northeast

D the Interior West

7 **SS.7.G.2.4 (High)**

> *"Here are no lofty peaks seeking the sky—no mighty glaciers or rushing streams wearing away the uplifted land. Here is land, tranquil in its quiet beauty, serving not as the source of water, but as the last receiver of it. To its natural abundance we owe the spectacular plant and animal life that distinguishes this place from all others in the country."*
>
> —Harry Truman, 1947

Based on this excerpt, why did President Truman support the establishment of the Everglades as a national park?

A to preserve the mineral resources in the region

B to help ensure clean water in Florida

C to protect the region from development

D to ensure that visitors would come to the region

---

8 **SS.7.C.2.3 (Moderate)**

What can a citizen do locally to help conserve fossil fuels?

A use natural gas for heating instead of oil

B buy unleaded gasoline instead of diesel

C travel by foot or bicycle as much as possible

D set emissions requirements for motor vehicles

9 **SS.7.G.2.3 (Moderate)**

Why are most U.S. farms found in the Midwest and South?

A That is where most of the nation's fertile soil is located.

B That is the area that gets the most annual sunshine.

C It is the region where there are many transportation options.

D It is the region in the nation that is best suited for wind turbines.

---

10 **SS.7.G.3.1 (High)**

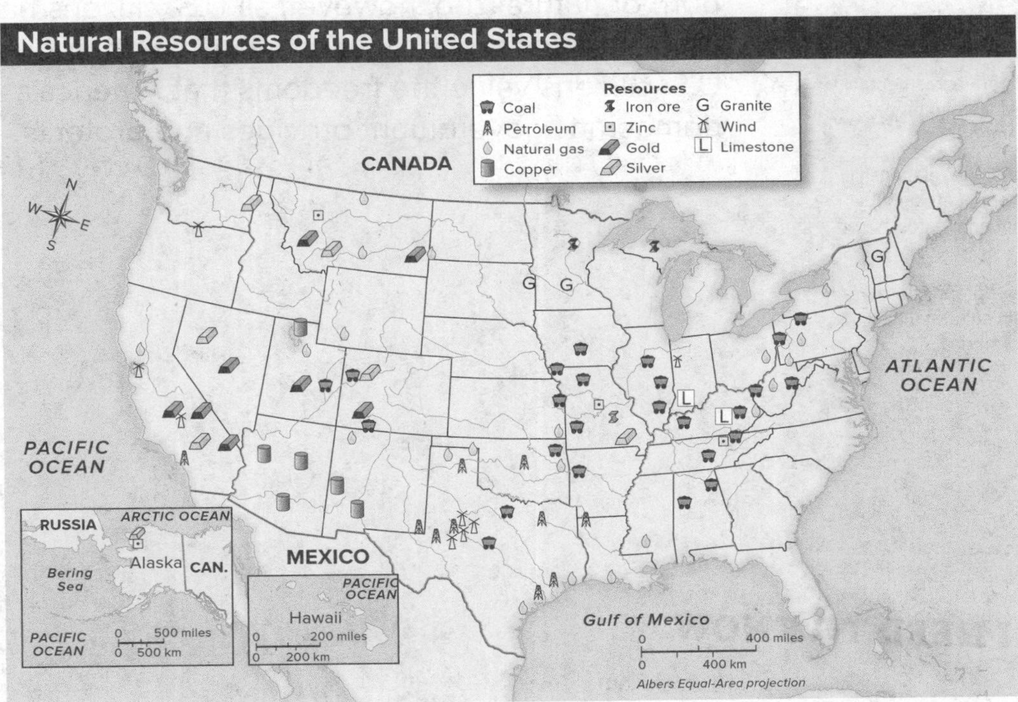

Which region provides the largest variety of energy resources?

A the South

B the Interior West

C the Northeast

D the Pacific

CHAPTER 3

Americans, Citizenship, and Governments

CHAPTER BENCHMARKS

SS.7.C.2.1 Define the term "citizen," and identify legal means of becoming a United States citizen.

SS.7.C.2.2 Evaluate the obligations citizens have to obey laws, pay taxes, defend the nation, and serve on juries.

SS.7.C.2.3 Experience the responsibilities of citizens at the local, state, or federal levels.

SS.7.C.3.1 Compare different forms of government (direct democracy, representative democracy, socialism, communism, monarchy, oligarchy, autocracy).

SS.7.C.3.2 Compare parliamentary, federal, confederal, and unitary systems of government.

SS.7.C.3.4 Identify the relationship and division of powers between the federal government and state governments.

SS.7.G.4.1 Use geographic terms and tools to explain cultural diffusion throughout North America.

Chapter Overview

For hundreds of years, people from all over the world have come to America and worked to become citizens of the United States. American citizens are a diverse group of people. The culture of the United States has been enriched by the wide range of beliefs and backgrounds that immigrants have brought to the country. Like native-born Americans, immigrants can become citizens of the United States. Whether native-born or naturalized, however, all U.S. citizens have certain duties and obligations. Despite their diversity, all U.S. citizens value the freedoms that America's democratic government provides and protects.

WHAT I NEED TO KNOW

TERMS

- ☐ ethnic group
- ☐ citizen
- ☐ citizenship
- ☐ naturalization
- ☐ majority rule
- ☐ direct democracy
- ☐ representative democracy
- ☐ monarchy
- ☐ socialism
- ☐ communism
- ☐ oligarchy
- ☐ autocracy
- ☐ federal
- ☐ parliamentary
- ☐ unitary
- ☐ confederation

Americans, Citizenship, and Governments

CHAPTER BENCHMARKS, *continued*

LAFS.68.RH.1.2 Determine the central ideas or information of a primary or secondary source; provide an accurate summary of the source distinct from prior knowledge or opinions.

LAFS.68.RH.2.4 Determine the meaning of words and phrases as they are used in a text, including vocabulary specific to domains related to history/social studies.

HE.7.P.8.2 Articulate a position on a health-related issue and support it with accurate health information.

Americans, Citizenship, and Governments

Create the Foldable® below and label the tabs with the lesson titles. Under each tab, list two important things you read about that relate directly to your life or to the lives of family, friends, and/or neighbors. Based upon what you learn, give a brief description of each item on your list. On the back of the Foldable, explain two of the rights or responsibilities of an American citizen. How do you think United States citizenship might differ from citizenship in another country?

Step 1
Fold the right side of the paper over, leaving a vertical margin on the left side.

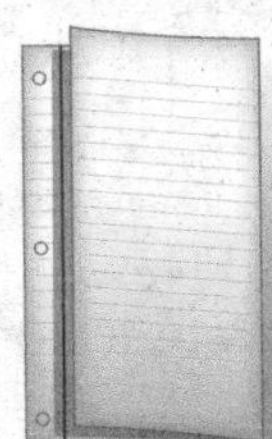

Step 2
Cut a horizontal line across the top flap, dividing it into two equal parts. Make an additional horizontal cut, dividing each of the two sections.

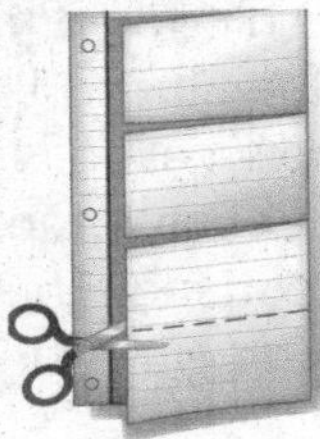

Step 3
Label the tabs as shown.

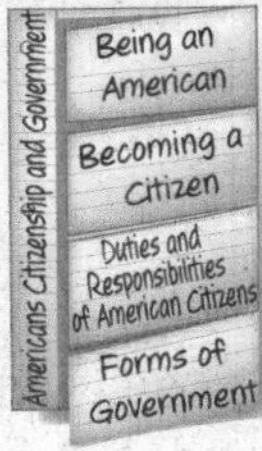

LESSON 1 SUMMARY

Being an American

SS.7.G.4.1

A Diverse Population

In the United States, many people have similar customs and celebrate the same national holidays. However, some people have different customs. Their families may have come from other countries and continued the traditions of their homelands. About 13 percent of all Americans were born in another country. These foreign-born people are immigrants, or people who move permanently to a new country.

Almost everyone now living in the United States has ancestors who lived in another country at one time. People have been coming here ever since colonial times. Despite their different backgrounds, they have worked together to build a nation.

1. DETERMINING CENTRAL IDEAS

People have come from other countries throughout the history of the United States. What effect did they have on the country?

A History of Immigration

According to most scholars, the earliest immigrants came to North America from Asia. The first group arrived about 20,000 years ago. As they continued to travel, they gradually spread throughout North America. They formed separate groups, and their cultures and languages changed. Together as a group they are called Native Americans.

2. IDENTIFYING

Who were the first immigrants to North America?

Much later the Spanish came to what is today the United States. In the 1500s, they arrived in what is now Florida. They built permanent homes to settle there. Later they built settlements in the Southwest, including the present-day states of Texas and California.

Later, immigrants came from other countries. In the 1600s, English immigrants settled along North America's east coast. People from France settled in present-day Canada. Some made their homes near the Great Lakes and the Mississippi River. The Dutch arrived from the Netherlands. They began farming near the Hudson River and established New Amsterdam, now called New York City. By the late 1600s and the 1700s, other immigrants arrived from Germany, Sweden, Ireland, and Scotland. They started the thirteen colonies that eventually became the United States.

Some people from western and central Africa did not want to come to the Americas. They were taken from their homes and forced onto ships. They traveled across the Atlantic Ocean to the Americas. There they were sold into slavery. Almost 500,000 Africans were in the United States by the early 1800s.

From the 1830s to the 1860s, the United States took in more than 5 million people. Most had left Ireland and Germany to escape poverty and disease. Many from other countries were drawn by the discovery of gold in California in 1848. They hoped to get rich. Thousands of immigrants came from China.

Between 1860 and 1890, another 10 million immigrants came from Europe. Many were from northern and western European countries such as Denmark, Norway, and Sweden. Then a shift in immigration occurred. From 1890 to 1924, about 22 million immigrants arrived. Most came from southern and eastern European nations such as Italy, Greece, Poland, and Russia.

By the late 1900s, a larger share of immigrants than ever before came from Asia and Latin America. Today, more than half of all the people in the United States who were born in another country come from Latin America.

United States Immigration

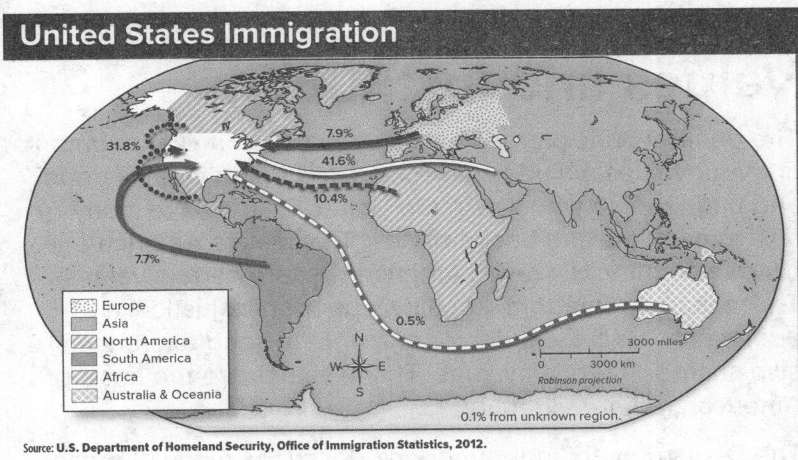

Source: U.S. Department of Homeland Security, Office of Immigration Statistics, 2012.

Ongoing Transformation

The U.S. population grew dramatically between 1830 and 1930. It went from about 12 million people to almost 120 million. Immigrants made up about 40 million of that increase. They helped make the United States a diverse country. Many different foods and cultures became part of the nation.

Other changes came to the American population. In the mid-1800s, people from rural areas began moving to cities. New industries developed, and they needed workers. Workers in a factory could earn more than they could from farm work. Better jobs drew many people from farms to the cities. After the Civil War, freed African Americans left the South for cities in the North. They were looking for jobs and a better life. By 1920, more than half of all Americans lived in towns or cities.

3. SPECULATING

How might the United States be different today if large numbers of Latinos had not immigrated to the country in recent decades?

4. ANALYZING MAPS

From which part of the world do most U.S. immigrants come? The least?

5. ANALYZING INFORMATION

How have changes in work affected the American population since the mid-1800s?

6. IDENTIFYING EVIDENCE

Reread Values and Institutions. Underline the values that are shared by all Americans. Then, explain why those values might be attractive to people who immigrate to the United States.

Changes in the working world have continued in more recent times. More and more women are in the workforce. Many factory jobs have been replaced by service jobs. Service jobs are work that is done for someone else. Examples of service jobs include programming computers, providing health care, and practicing law.

American Diversity

Americans belong to a variety of racial and ethnic groups. People of the same racial group share distinctive physical traits. Members of an **ethnic group** share a common national, cultural, or racial background. About 16 percent of Americans call themselves Latinos. They share a heritage from Latin America. Latinos and other groups, such as African Americans and Asian Americans, are said to be members of minority groups. However, these minority groups will be the majority of the population by the 2040s.

Values and Institutions

The general principles, or beliefs, you use to make judgments are your values. Values are broad ideas about what is good and bad. People who live in the United States have many different beliefs and backgrounds. This makes America a diverse country. However, Americans share certain values. These include freedom, equality, opportunity, justice, and democracy. Unity, respect for one another, and tolerance are also shared American values. These values are the basis of Americans' shared identity.

The Declaration of Independence describes many of these shared values. For example, the Declaration states that all people are equal. This means that the law should treat everyone equally. Freedom is another important value to Americans. The Declaration states that all people have the right to "life, liberty, and the pursuit of happiness." *Liberty* is another word for freedom.

Social Institutions

America's institutions are reflections of our shared values. Institutions are the key practices, relationships, and organizations in a society. Examples include families, schools, places of worship, clubs, and volunteer groups. Members of these groups share similar values. These institutions help their members develop a shared sense of being American.

Government Institutions

The American value of freedom is demonstrated in its government institutions. Freedom is the right to make choices without undue interference from the government. American government is based on the principle of popular sovereignty. This is the idea that the government receives its power from the people.

The Constitution reflects the principle of limited government power. It sets up a three-part government in which no one part can have more power than the other two. In addition, the Bill of Rights makes sure that the government cannot abuse its power over the individual.

7. REFLECTING

Choose one of the social or government institutions. How might you share values with that institution?

____

____

____

____

____

____

REVIEW LESSON 1

1. Use the chart to identify where most U.S. immigrants came from during the time period listed.

TIME PERIOD	LAND/COUNTRY OF ORIGIN OF IMMIGRANTS
Prehistoric era	
1500s	
1600s	
Late 1600s and 1700s	
Early to mid-1800s	
Mid- to late 1800s	
Late 1800s to early 1900s	
Late 1900s and today	

2. **EXPRESSING** In an essay on a separate sheet of paper, answer these questions: How does having a variety of cultures in the United States benefit all Americans? Are there any disadvantages to cultural diversity?

LESSON 2 SUMMARY

Becoming a Citizen

1. PARAPHRASING

What is a *citizen*? Define the term in your own words.

______

______

______

______

______

______

2. MAKING CONNECTIONS

Use the quote from Jefferson to speculate on the connection among education, citizenship, and democracy.

______

______

______

______

______

3. REFLECTING

On a sepate sheet of paper, write an essay that answers this question: Do you believe there are any groups in the United States that are still being denied citizenship? Explain.

______

SS.7.C.2.1

What Is Civics?

Civics is the study of the duties and rights of citizens. **Citizens** are members of a community who owe loyalty to a government and who are protected by that government. Government is the ruling authority for a community. Citizens need to understand their rights and responsibilities. Citizens support their community and government when they carry out their responsibilities.

The Founders of the United States believed in the value of civics. Thomas Jefferson wrote, "Whenever the people are well-informed, they can be trusted with their own government." Informed citizens are able to make wise decisions about public issues. They are also better able to make decisions about candidates for public office.

Roots of Citizenship

The idea of **citizenship,** or the rights and duties of citizens, began in ancient Greece and Rome. Greek and Roman citizens had legal rights and could take part in government. However, only men who owned property could be citizens. In addition to rights, they had duties to their government. They had to pay taxes and serve in the armed forces.

Later, other ideas about citizenship arose. In the 1700s, thinkers in America and France changed the ancient ideas. They said that being a citizen meant belonging to a nation. Another important idea was the "consent of the governed." This means that governments get their power from the people being governed. Citizens consent, or agree, by participating in government.

People had the chance to gain more power with this new idea. However, the power was still not shared by all. In the United States, citizenship at first was limited mostly to white men. Other groups struggled to gain full citizenship. In 1868, the Fourteenth Amendment gave citizenship to African American men. In 1920, women gained suffrage with the Nineteenth Amendment. In 1924, all Native Americans became citizens when Congress passed the Indian Citizenship Act.

Today, there are two ways that a person can become an American citizen. These are either by birth or by going through a special process.

Natural-Born Citizens

A person automatically becomes an American citizen if he or she was born

- in any of the 50 states or in the District of Columbia
- in an American territory
- on a U.S. military base overseas
- on American soil to people who are not U.S. citizens

A person born in another country can claim American citizenship, but there are requirements. If both parents are American citizens, the child can be an American citizen. The same is true if one parent is a citizen who has lived in the United States. A person can also choose to be a citizen of both the United States and another country. This is called dual citizenship.

Naturalized Citizens

Naturalization is the legal process for foreign-born people to obtain citizenship. Immigrants who want to become United States citizens must meet certain requirements:

- They must be age 18 or older.
- They must have been a lawful permanent resident for five years, or three years if married to a U.S. citizen.
- They must be able to read, write, and speak English.
- They must be of good moral character.
- They must show an understanding of American civics.

First, the person must complete an application and send it to the U.S. Citizenship and Immigration Services (USCIS). Next, a USCIS official talks to the applicant to make sure that the person meets all five requirements.

An applicant must then take a citizenship exam covering the history and government of the United States. The exam also tests the applicant's ability to read, write, and speak English. Many people take classes to prepare for this test.

Finally, applicants participate in a special ceremony. They take an oath in which they swear to be loyal to the United States above all other countries. They also make other promises. For example, they swear to obey the Constitution and the country's laws. After taking this oath and signing a document, they are citizens. If they have children under 18, the children automatically become citizens too.

4. CONSTRUCTING AN ARGUMENT

Some people want to amend the U.S. Constitution to remove automatic citizenship for children born in the United States to parents who are not U.S. citizens. Would you support such an amendment? Why or why not?

____
____
____
____
____
____
____

5. POSING QUESTIONS

Write a question you believe should be included on the exam to become a U.S. citizen. Explain why you think a prospective citizen should be required to answer this question.

____
____
____
____
____
____
____
____
____

6. RECOGNIZING RELATIONSHIPS

Individuals found guilty of any of three very serious crimes can lose their citizenship. Circle those three crimes. In what way are these three crimes related?

Complete the flowchart to show the sequence of events that are involved in the naturalization process.

The Naturalization Process

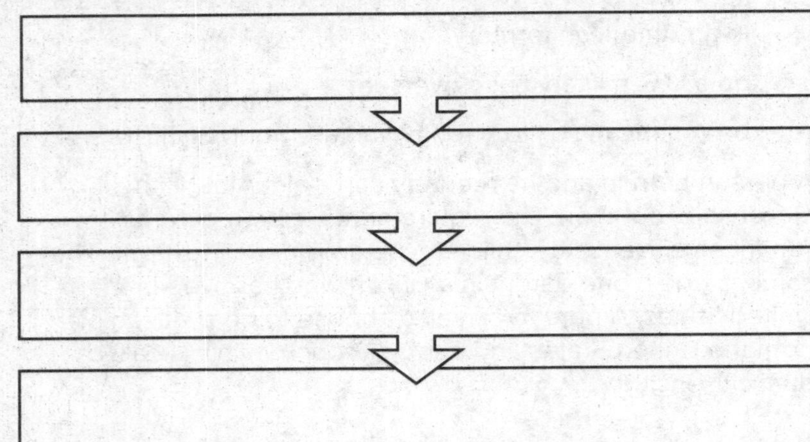

Losing Citizenship

Americans can lose their citizenship in three ways:

- *Expatriation.* Someone who gives his or her loyalty to a foreign country is expatriated. An example is a person who chooses to become a naturalized citizen of another country.
- *Denaturalization.* Naturalized citizens who are discovered to have lied on their citizenship application are denaturalized. They lose their citizenship and may be deported, or sent out of the country.
- *Being convicted of certain crimes.* Anyone convicted of any of three serious crimes can lose citizenship. These crimes are treason, taking part in a rebellion, or using violence to try to overthrow the government.

Only the federal government can grant citizenship or take it away. However, states can deny, or take away, some privileges of citizenship. For example, states can take away the right to vote from some criminals, but states cannot take away that criminal's citizenship.

REVIEW LESSON 2

1. Use the chart below to identify the ways a person can become a natural-born citizen of the United States.

A PERSON AUTOMATICALLY BECOMES AN AMERICAN CITIZEN IF HE OR SHE WAS BORN:	A PERSON BORN IN ANOTHER COUNTRY CAN CLAIM AMERICAN CITIZENSHIP IF:

2. **CONSTRUCTING AN ARGUMENT** The Constitution says that only "natural-born" citizens can become president of the United States. Should the Constitution be amended to allow naturalized citizens to become president as well? Write your essay on a separate sheet of paper.

LESSON 3 SUMMARY

Duties and Responsibilities of American Citizens

1. DRAWING CONCLUSIONS

Why is paying taxes a duty and not merely a responsibility?

2. PRIORITIZING

Reread the section Duties of Citizens. Underline the civic duties of American citizens. Then, rank the duties from most to least important. Explain your ranking.

SS.7.C.2.2, SS.7.C.2.3

Duties of Citizens

Citizens help make our communities safe and agreeable places to live. We do this by living up to our duties and responsibilities. Responsibilities are things we should do. They are actions that we choose to do, even though they are not required. Duties are actions that citizens are required to carry out. National, state, and local governments establish those duties by law. Anyone who fails to perform his or her duties is subject to penalties, such as being fined or sent to prison.

Obey Laws

The most important duty for citizens is to obey the law. People establish laws in order to live together in peace. Laws help people understand what is acceptable behavior and what is unacceptable. Laws enable governments to keep order and protect our safety, health, and property. Communities suffer harm and conflict when people do not obey the law.

Pay Taxes

Citizens must also pay taxes. There are different kinds of taxes: income, property, sales. Tax money keeps the government running. Without taxes, the federal government could not pay its employees, defend the country, or help those in need. Local governments could not hire police officers and firefighters, run schools, or pave roads. People who try to avoid paying taxes face stiff fines and other penalties.

Defend the Nation

Most male citizens aged 18 to 25 must register with the Selective Service System (SSS). They may be needed to defend the nation. In the event of war or extreme national emergency, the government may need to draft, or call for military service, men from this list. The United States has not had a draft since 1973. Since then, volunteers have met the needs of the armed forces.

Serve in Court

Every adult citizen must be prepared to serve on a jury. A person accused of a crime has a right to a trial by jury. That right is guaranteed by the U.S. Constitution. A jury is a group of citizens who listen to the evidence presented in court. They are required to think about it fairly and decide whether the accused is guilty. During the trial, the accused has the right to hear and present witnesses. If citizens are asked to be a witness at a trial, they have a duty to do so.

Attend School

Attending school is also a duty. Most states require children aged 7 to 16 to attend school. Schools teach students how to become good citizens. They also prepare students to become skilled employees who can contribute to the nation's economy.

Responsibilities of Citizens

For society to work, all citizens must do their part. Citizens must help one another. They must also allow one another to voice their ideas and concerns. When everyone participates and works together, they enjoy a society that works well.

Be an Informed and Active Citizen

Your city, state, and federal governments make decisions that affect your life. These decisions might involve changing tax rates or spending government money on services. Citizens have a responsibility to be informed about what is happening. They also must make an effort to understand the issues. Then they can express their opinions or decide how to vote on an issue.

Citizens are also responsible for making sure that the government is working properly. They must communicate their opinions and concerns to government officials. Public officials need to hear what citizens need and want. Then their actions can reflect citizens' interests. There are various ways to make your voice heard. You might support a cause that you care about by contacting elected officials and, above all, by voting. As President Franklin D. Roosevelt said:

> "The ultimate rulers of our democracy are not a President and Senators and Congressmen and Government officials but the voters of this country."
>
> —Franklin D. Roosevelt (1938)

3. CONSTRUCTING AN ARGUMENT

Imagine that an adult friend has been called to jury duty but does not want to attend. Write an argument convincing your friend otherwise.

____

____

____

____

____

____

____

____

____

____

4. DESCRIBING

What are some ways citizens can fulfil their responsibilities for becoming informed?

____

____

____

____

____

____

____

____

Name ______________________ Date ______________ Class ________

5. CONSTRUCTING AN ARGUMENT

In some countries, citizens are legally required to vote. Do you think voting should be a civic duty rather than a responsibility? Explain.

Voting is a responsibility that gives citizens the opportunity to shape the future of their communities, states, and nation. In the United States, all citizens 18 years of age and older have the right to vote. Responsible voters take time to learn about the candidates and the issues before they vote. They also pay attention to the actions of their elected officials. Voters can replace poorly performing officials in the next election. Voting ensures peaceful and orderly changes in leadership.

Respect the Rights of Others

Another responsibility of good citizens is to treat others politely and respectfully. People of many different backgrounds live in the United States. Everyone has the right to his or her opinions, beliefs, and practices. Respecting and accepting others, regardless of differences, is called tolerance. Tolerance allows America's diverse population to live together peacefully.

Contribute to the Common Good

In order for communities and governments to grow, people need to participate. Responsible citizens are willing to give time, effort, and money to improve community life. The members of a community must contribute to the common good, or the things that benefit all members of the community. For example, everyone benefits from having safe streets, good schools, and a clean environment.

6. CREATING VISUALS

Select a volunteer organization in your community or a civic activity that you support. Then, on a separate piece of paper, create a flyer to get the group's message out to the public.

Being Involved

Good citizens care about the welfare—the health, prosperity, and happiness—of all members of their community. One way to help others is by volunteering. Volunteerism is the practice of offering your time and services to others without receiving payment. Millions of Americans do volunteer work. Without their efforts, many important community needs would not be met.

People do many kinds of volunteer work. Neighbors get together on a weekend to clean up a park. Community organizations collect supplies for needy families. Retirees record books for the blind. You might go with friends to visit nursing homes or collect food for a local pantry.

People also support causes by giving money to charities. There are more than 1 million charities in the United States. They are focused on issues such as health, hunger, youth activities, and animal welfare. Americans give more than $300 billion to charity each year. Much of this money comes from small gifts made by ordinary people.

Volunteers by Type of Organization

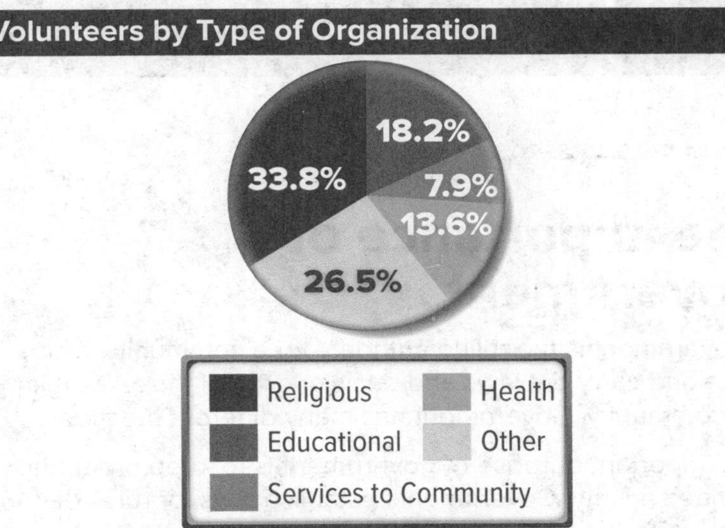

Source: Bureau of Labor Statistics, 2010.

The federal government supports volunteerism through many agencies. The Corporation for National and Community Service provides money, training, and other help for volunteer groups. It also manages other agencies that work in education, public safety, health, and the environment.

ANALYZING VISUALS

7. ANALYZING GRAPHS

Why do you think that so many volunteers represent religious organizations?

REVIEW LESSON 3

1. Use the chart below to name some ways a person can carry out the responsibilities of American citizenship.

WAYS TO BE INFORMED
WAYS TO RESPECT OTHERS' RIGHTS
WAYS TO CONTRIBUTE TO THE COMMON GOOD

2. **GATHERING EVIDENCE** Do you believe most Americans are fulfilling both their duties and their responsibilities as citizens? Why or why not? Cite specific examples as evidence for your views. Write your response on a separate sheet of paper.

LESSON 4 SUMMARY

Forms of Government

SS.7.C.3.1, SS.7.C.3.2, SS.7.C.3.4

1. REASONING

List each purpose of government and explain why each is necessary.

2. ASSESSING

Could your state pass a law setting requirements for becoming a citizen of the United States? Explain.

The Importance of Government

A government is the ruling authority for a community. It can make and carry out laws and decisions for all those living in the community. Government has many different functions.

One important purpose of government is to keep order and provide security. Governments establish laws, or rules of conduct, for people to follow. They set up armed forces to keep people safe from foreign enemies. Governments also provide services that people need, such as schools, roads, police departments, and assistance for the poor or unemployed.

Public policy refers to the decisions and actions a government takes to solve problems. Governments develop public policy plans to reach goals. Since governments have limited amounts of money, they must create realistic plans to wisely spend money.

Governments also need to have good relations with other governments. Sometimes they can cooperate on shared goals. National government officials work with foreign governments to cooperate on projects or resolve conflicts.

Levels of Government

The United States has a federal system of government. In this system, government power is divided between the federal, or national, government and state governments. In each state, local governments run towns, cities, and counties.

The national government has the highest level of authority over U.S. citizens. It sets the basic rules for citizenship, and it makes and enforces laws for the entire country. A state or local government cannot make any laws that would go against the laws of the national government or the U.S. Constitution.

Each state government makes laws and decides matters for the people of that state. States set rules for education, organize elections, oversee public health, and build public facilities such as roads. States also have the power to set up local governments in counties, cities, and towns. Local governments establish schools, provide police and fire departments, and organize local court systems. They also must obey the laws or authority of the national government.

Name ______________________ Date ____________ Class ________

The Types of Government

Nations have different types of government. Not all nations are governed like the United States. Two main types of government are democratic and authoritarian. Under a democratic government, the citizens hold the power to rule. An authoritarian government is one in which one leader or group of people holds absolute power. Other differences include the role of political parties and the way the government makes sure citizens obey laws.

Several specific types of government fall under these two main categories. They include democracy, monarchy, socialism, communism, oligarchy, and autocracy.

Democracy

Democracy works on the principle of **majority rule**. For example, a decision is made by a group when more than half of the people vote for it. Citizens agree to follow what more than half the people want. At the same time, people in the minority still have all their rights as citizens. In a democracy, candidates from two or more political parties compete for the voters' approval. Ruling majorities are determined through free and fair elections.

Democracy began in ancient Greece more than 2,500 years ago. The Greek city of Athens had a **direct democracy**. In a direct democracy, all voters meet to discuss and vote on issues in person.

ANALYZING VISUALS

3. SUMMARIZING

The chart contrasts two types of government. Write a one- or two-sentence summary of the information about each type of government.

____

____

____

____

____

____

____

____

____

COMPARING DEMOCRATIC AND AUTHORITARIAN GOVERNMENTS				
	Selection of Leaders	Extent of Government Power	Means of Ensuring Obedience	Political Parties
Democracy (including republic, constitutional monarchy)	Leaders are chosen in free and fair elections.	The government is limited in power by the constitution and laws; citizens' rights and freedoms are protected.	The government relies on the rule of law.	Multiple parties compete for power.
Authoritarianism (including absolute monarchy, dictatorship, and totalitarianism)	Rulers inherit their positions or take power by force.	Rulers have unlimited power; the government may impose an official ideology and control all aspects of political, economic, and civic life.	The government relies on state control of the media, propaganda, military or police power and terror.	Power lies with a single party.

4. HYPOTHESIZING

Do you think it might be possible to have direct democracy in the United States? Describe what tools could be used to make that work.

5. COMPARING

Of the types of government described, which type of government is most similar to the U.S. government? Explain.

Today, nations are too large for direct democracy to be practical. Instead, many countries, including the United States, have a **representative democracy**. In this kind of democracy, citizens elect leaders to represent them. The representatives make laws and govern on behalf of citizens. The United States is the world's oldest representative democracy.

There are two types of representative democracy. One type is a republic, such as the United States. In a republic, citizens have a role in choosing the person who will be the head of the government. The other type is a constitutional monarchy.

Monarchy

A **monarchy** is a government with a hereditary ruler. A monarch, either a king or queen, inherits this position. In the past, monarchs held complete power over their country and its people, a type of government called an absolute monarchy.

Today, the power of most monarchs is limited by the country's constitution. For that reason, this type of government is called a constitutional monarchy. The monarch has just a small, often ceremonial role. Actual political power is found in a legislature whose members are elected by the voters. The legislature chooses a prime minister to head the government.

Socialism

Socialism is a system in which the government owns the businesses and industries that produce products. The government decides how resources are used and how much workers are paid. It also provides the people with services. These include education, health care, and help for poor or unemployed people. In democratic socialism, citizens have democratic rights such as free speech and free elections. People have private property, but the government owns and makes decisions about certain industries and businesses.

Communism

Communism is a system developed by Karl Marx in the 1800s. In communism, the state owns all natural resources, industries, and businesses. The central government usually is run by a single party. It decides what products are made and how to distribute products and services. It also controls all forms of communication. Today few nations have communist governments.

Oligarchy

An **oligarchy** is a type of government in which a small group of people holds the power. Oligarchs usually gained their power from their wealth, social position, or military power. If the ruling group holds elections, there is only one candidate. If there is a legislature, it can only approve the ruling group's policies. Oligarchies often use force to prevent people from disagreeing with their decisions.

Autocracy

An **autocracy** is a government in which one person has all the power to rule. In the past, kings or emperors who inherited their position often ruled autocracies. Another form of autocracy is a dictatorship. Dictators also have complete control of the government. They often come to power by the use of force. They overthrow an existing government and take power. Many dictators force their people to accept totalitarian rule. In a totalitarian state, the government controls almost all aspects of people's lives. Totalitarian leaders use fear, violence, and propaganda to control the people.

Systems of Government

Nations also differ in their systems, or structure, of government. Governments are organized in various ways. The structure is related to the way power is shared or not shared among the levels of government.

Federal

As you learned earlier, the United States has a **federal** system of government. In a federal system, power is divided among a central, national government and smaller self-governing political units such as states. The central government cannot take power from the smaller units. Citizens vote in elections to choose leaders of both the executive and legislative branches.

Parliamentary

Most nations do not have a federal system. Some have a **parliamentary** system. Citizens elect representatives to the parliament, or national legislature. The legislature is the strongest part of the government. The political party with the most members in the parliament elects the nation's leader.

6. INTERPRETING

Identify the systems of government shown in the graphic organizer below.

Ways Governments Distribute Power

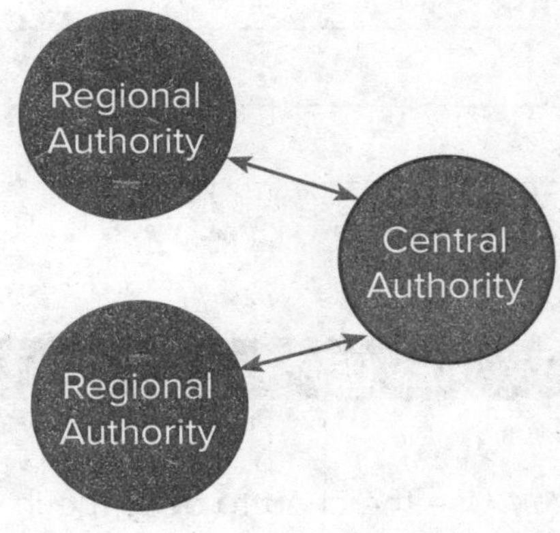

____

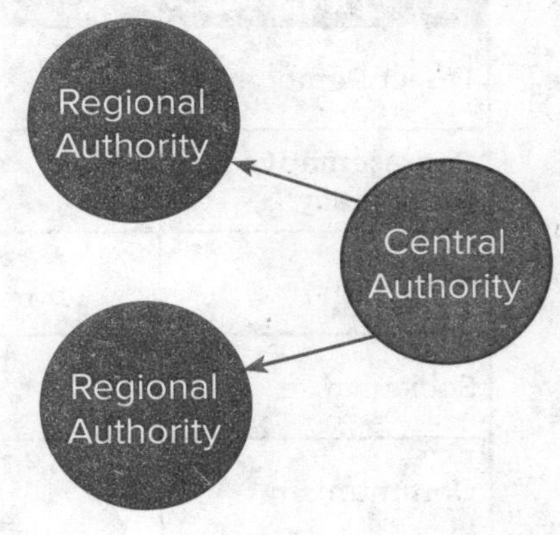

____

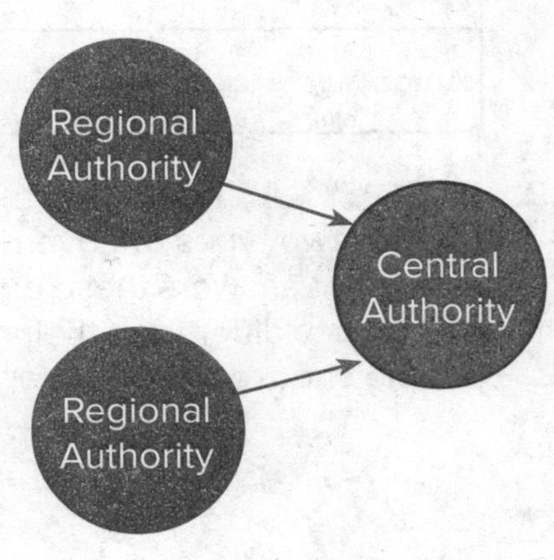

____

7. CONTRASTING

How does the confederal system differ from that of the United States today?

Unitary

Some other nations have **unitary** systems of government. In a unitary system, the central, national government is supreme. It may create smaller administrative units to carry out some of its functions, but they are not protected by a constitution. The central government can give or take power as it sees fit.

Confederal

The United States did not always have a federal system of government. When it achieved its independence, it created a **confederation**. In a confederal system of government, member states agree to join together voluntarily. The states or nations create a common body to carry out certain functions, but each retains its own power.

REVIEW LESSON 4

1. Use the chart to describe in your own words the different types of governments.

TYPE OF GOVERNMENT	KEY FEATURES
Direct Democracy	
Representative Democracy	
Monarchy	
Socialism	
Communism	
Oligarchy	
Autocracy	

2. **CONTRASTING** The role of citizens varies in different types of governments. Choose two types of government other than representative democracy. Write an essay that answers these questions: How does the role of citizens in representative democracy differ from their role in the other types of government? Why might people choose to live under those other types of government?

Benchmark Skill Activities

DIRECTIONS: Write your answers on a separate sheet of paper.

LAFS.68.WHST.1.2; SS.7.C.2.3

1. ANALYZING

Use your FOLDABLES to write an essay answering the following:

You have identified two rights or responsibilities of American citizens. Why do you think these are important to the well-being of our democracy? In your essay, explain what might occur if citizens and the government did not carefully observe these rights and responsibilities.

LAFS.68.RH.2.4

2. USING CONTEXT CLUES

Read the excerpt from the Oath of Citizenship taken by all naturalized citizens. Then, write a definition for each of the underlined words. Use the words around these words, or context clues, to help you determine their meaning.

> *"I hereby declare, on oath, that I absolutely and entirely renounce and abjure all allegiance and fidelity to any foreign prince, potentate, state, or sovereignty, of whom or which I have heretofore been a subject or citizen...."*
>
> *—Oath of Citizenship*

LAFS.68.RH.2.6; SS.7.C.3.4

3. IDENTIFYING POINTS OF VIEW

In a federal system of government, there is a balance of power between the federal and state governments. Americans have not always agreed on how that power should be divided.

- Do research on the Internet on the topic of federal vs state powers. Identify the opposing points of view on the issue. Find two primary or secondary sources on each side of the issue.
- Use the sources to write a summary of each position.
- Decide which view you support. Write a closing paragraph giving your reasons for your position.

HE.7.P.8.2

4. USING AND CITING INFORMATION

Do some research on the Internet about the Healthy, Hunger-Free Kids Act of 2010. Then, write a paper in which you describe the purpose of the law. Then explain if you believe this is a proper function of American government.

LAFS.68.RH.1.2; SS.7.C.3.1; SS.7.C.3.2

5. DETERMINING CENTRAL IDEAS

Former British Prime Minister Winston Churchill once said, "Indeed it has been said that democracy is the worst form of government except for all those other forms that have been tried from time to time. . . ." What do you think Churchill meant by this? Was he correct? What are some of the chief weaknesses of democracy?

Benchmark Note Cards

DIRECTIONS: Use these note cards to help you prepare for the test.

SS.7.G.4.1 Use geographic terms and tools to explain cultural diffusion throughout North America.

IMMIGRATION	The United States is a nation of immigrants. People from all over the world have brought their values and traditions to the United States. Once here, they have worked together to build a nation. • The first people to come to North America were from Asia. Today they are called Native Americans. • The Spanish, French, Dutch, and British were among the first Europeans to arrive in North America. • Hundreds of thousands of Africans were forcibly brought to the United States and enslaved here. • In the early-to-mid 1800s, most immigrants to the United States were from western or northern Europe. Some came from Asia, particularly China. • By the end of the 1800s, most immigrants were from southern and eastern Europe. • Today, most immigrants to the United States are from Asia or Latin America.
VALUES	People with different beliefs and values have made lives for themselves in the United States. Americans of all backgrounds share many values, including: • Freedom • Equality • Opportunity • Justice • Democracy
INSTITUTIONS	Our shared values are reflected in the important institutions of American life, such as: • Family • Religious institutions • Schools • Clubs and volunteer groups • Government institutions

SS.7.C.2.1 Define the term "citizen," and identify legal means of becoming a United States citizen.

CITIZENS AND CITIZENSHIP	**Citizens** are members of a community who owe loyalty to a government and, in turn, are entitled to the protection of that government. **Citizenship** involves the rights and duties of citizens. For many years, full U.S. citizenship was limited largely to white men. Over time, full citizenship has been granted to other groups: • 1868: African American men became citizens through the 14th Amendment. • 1920: Women gained the right to vote through the 19th Amendment. • 1924: All Native Americans were granted citizenship.
NATURAL-BORN CITIZENS	A person automatically becomes an American citizen if he or she was born • in any of the 50 states or in the District of Columbia. • in an American territory. • on a U.S. military base overseas. • on American soil to people who are not American citizens. A person born in another country can claim American citizenship in two cases: (1) if both parents are American citizens or (2) if one parent is a citizen who has lived in the United States.
NATURALIZED CITIZENS	A person can become a citizen even if he or she is not a natural-born citizen. To do so, he or she must complete the naturalization process. Immigrants must meet five requirements: • They must be age 18 or older. • They must have been a lawful permanent resident for five years, or three years if married to a U.S. citizen. • They must be able to read, write, and speak English. • They must be of good moral character. • They must show an understanding of U.S. civics. There are four main steps to the naturalization process: 1. Fill out an application with the U.S. Citizenship and Immigration Service (USCIS) 2. Talk with an USCIS official 3. Take a citizenship exam 4. Attend a citizenship ceremony to take an oath of loyalty

SS.7.C.2.2 Evaluate the obligations citizens have to obey laws, pay taxes, defend the nation, and serve on juries.

DUTIES OF AMERICAN CITIZENS

Duties are actions that citizens are required to perform. citizens of the United States have five important duties:

1. Obey laws
2. Pay taxes
3. Defend the nation
4. Serve in court
5. Attend school

SS.7.C.2.3 Experience the responsibilities of citizens at the local, state, or federal levels.

RESPONSIBILITIES OF AMERICAN CITIZENS

Responsibilities are actions that people should choose to do in order to help create a society that works well. American citizens have many important responsibilities to carry out:

- Be an informed and active citizen
- Vote in local, state, and federal elections
- Respect the rights of others by practicing tolerance
- Contribute to the common good
- Volunteer in the community

SS.7.C.3.1 Compare different forms of government (direct democracy, representative democracy, socialism, communism, monarchy, oligarchy, autocracy).

TYPES OF GOVERNMENT

People create governments to establish order, provide security, and accomplish common goals. However, different nations have different forms of government.

- Direct democracy: a government in which all citizens vote directly on all matters of public policy
- Representative democracy: a government in which citizens choose a group of people to represent them, make laws, and govern on their behalf
- Socialism: a government that owns businesses and industries, decides how to use resources and what to pay workers
- Communism: a government where the state owns all natural resources, industries, and businesses and that is run by a single party
- Monarchy: a government with a hereditary ruler
- Oligarchy: a government in which a small group of people holds all the power
- Autocracy: a government in which one person holds all the power

SS.7.C.3.2 Compare parliamentary, federal, confederal, and unitary systems of government.

SYSTEMS OF GOVERNMENT	Governments can be characterized based on how power is shared, or not shared, among the various levels of government. The basic systems of government include: • Federal system: Power is divided among a central, national government and smaller, self-governing units such as states. • Parliamentary system: Citizens elect representatives to parliament, a national legislature. The political party with the most members in parliament elects the nation's leader. • Unitary system: All power is held by the central, national government. It may or may not grant powers to smaller administrative units. • Confederal system: Smaller governmental units join together voluntarily to create a common, national body to carry out certain functions. They retain most political power.

SS.7.C.3.4 Identify the relationship and division of powers between the federal government and state governments.

LEVELS OF GOVERNMENT	The United States has a federal system of government. This means that government power is divided between the federal, or national, government and the state governments. The national government has the highest level of authority. It makes and enforces laws for the entire country. A state or local government cannot make any laws that violate the laws of the national government or the Constitution. Each of the 50 states has its own independent government. These governments decide matters for the people of their state. Powers not given exclusively to the national government belong to the states. States also have the power to set up local governments. Local governments can be found in counties, cities, and towns. They are the level of government closest to citizens. Like state governments, local governments cannot take actions that go against the laws or authority of the national government.

Chapter 3

VISUAL SUMMARY

DIRECTIONS: Complete the graphic organizers below.

U.S. CITIZENSHIP

By Birth	By Naturalization
•	•
•	•
	•
	•
	•
	•
	•

DUTIES AND RESPONSIBILITIES OF U.S. CITIZENS	
Duties	**Responsibilities**
Obey the law.	Be a well-informed citizen.
	Vote.

USING PRIMARY SOURCES

DIRECTIONS: Write your answers on a separate sheet of paper.

ANALYZING INFORMATION At the end of World War I, Communists had overthrown the ruler in Russia. There was much public anxiety in the United States about who was a "good American." This uncertainty—and the desire to define and identify "Americans" – led to a brief period known as the Red Scare. During this time, a nationwide fear of Communists, anarchists, and other "un-American" types ran throughout society. Innocent people were put in jail for expressing their political opinions, some elected officials ignored civil liberties, and many Americans were afraid that a Communist revolution was imminent.

Franklin D. Roosevelt was the Democratic Party's nominee for vice president in 1920. The following is an excerpt from his acceptance speech for the party's nomination. Read the excerpt, then write a paper in which you answer the questions that follow.

> *Much has been said of late about good Americanism. It is right that it should have been said. And it is right that every chance should be seized to repeat the basic truths underlying our prosperity and our national existence itself. But it would be an unusual and much to be wished-for thing, if in the coming presentation of the issue a new note of fairness and generosity could be struck. Littleness, meanness, falsehood, extreme partisanship [firm belief in a party]: these are not in accord with the American spirit. I like to think that in this respect we are moving forward. Let me be concrete. We have passed through a great war. An armed conflict which called forth every resource, every effort, on the part of the whole population. The war was won by Republicans as well as Democrats. Men of all parties served in our armed forces. Men and women of all parties served the government at home. They strived honestly, as Americans, not as mere partisans. Republicans and Democrats alike worked in administrative positions, raised Liberty Loans, administered food control, toiled in munitions plants, built ships. The war was brought to a successful conclusion by a glorious common effort—one which in the years to come will be a national pride. I feel very certain that our children will come to regard our participation as memorable for the broad honor and honesty which marked it; for the absence of unfortunate scandal and for the splendid unity of action which extended to every portion of the nation. It would therefore not only serve little purpose, but would conform ill to our high standards, if any person should, in the heat of political rivalry, seek to manufacture [create] political advantage out of a nationally conducted trouble.*

1. To whom is Roosevelt addressing his remarks?
2. What are Roosevelt's main points?
3. How do you think Roosevelt would define a "good American"?
4. If you were concerned that "Communists" and "foreigners" were threatening the United States, would Roosevelt's words have changed your mind? Why or why not?

Chapter Practice Test

DIRECTIONS: Circle the best answer for each question.

SS.7.G.4.1 (Moderate)

The following passage is from an address by President Barack Obama.

> *My fellow Americans, we are and always will be a nation of immigrants. We were strangers once, too. And whether our forebears were strangers who crossed the Atlantic, or the Pacific, or the Rio Grande, we are here only because this country welcomed them in, and taught them that to be an American is about something more than what we look like, or what our last names are, or how we worship. What makes us Americans is our shared commitment to an ideal—that all of us are created equal, and all of us have the chance to make of our lives what we will.*
>
> *—Barack Obama, November 20, 2014*

What is the main point of this passage?

A Cultural diversity makes the country strong.

B Immigrants to the United States should learn English.

C Certain shared values help unite all Americans.

D All Americans should believe the same things.

SS.7.G.4.1 (Moderate)

Which statement best describes the United States today?

A The United States is a collection of distinct groups with some shared values and many unique ones.

B The United States is a "melting pot" with values developing more or less equally from all the various immigrant groups.

C The United States consists of an assortment of cultures with few common values.

D The United States is a homogeneous culture based exclusively on Western European values.

SS.7.C.2.1 (High)

In this 1871 cartoon, a police officer orders a Native American to "move on" from voting polls around which are clustered stereotyped "naturalized" Americans.

Based on this cartoon, which of the following positions do you believe the artist would most likely have supported?

A Native Americans should be granted full U.S. citizenship.

B Native American land should be given to naturalized citizens.

C Native Americans should be denied voting rights.

D Native Americans, and not immigrants, are the "real" Americans.

SS.7.C.2.1 (Moderate)

Under American law, which of the following would not be considered a United States citizen?

A any baby born in the United States to two foreign parents

B any baby born overseas to non-American citizens

C any baby born in the United States to American parents

D any baby born overseas to American parents

SS.7.C.2.2, SS.7.C.2.3 (High)

> *In all criminal prosecutions, the accused shall enjoy the right to a speedy and public trial, by an impartial jury of the State and district wherein the crime shall have been committed, which district shall have been previously ascertained by law, and to be informed of the nature and cause of the accusation; to be confronted with the witnesses against him; to have compulsory process for obtaining witnesses in his favor, and to have the Assistance of Counsel for his defence.*
>
> *—from the Sixth Amendment to the U.S. Constitution*

Based on this passage, which of the following is correct?

A Serving on a jury is a right of every responsible American citizen.

B Serving on a jury is on a volunteer basis because it is not authorized by state law.

C Serving on a jury is a duty all responsible citizens must perform when asked.

D Serving on a jury is prohibited by the U.S. Constitution.

SS.7.C.2.2, SS.7.C.2.3 (Moderate)

Which statement correctly identifies the most important duty of a citizen?

A Attending school is a citizen's most important duty because democracy requires that all citizens be active.

B Obeying the law is a citizen's most important duty because laws have been established to maintain safety and public order.

C Tolerance is a citizen's most important duty because the United States is a diverse society.

D Voting is a citizen's most important duty because the states rely on elected officials for leadership.

 **SS.7.C.2.3 (High)**

What is the main point of this passage?

> *My friends, we have work to do. There are the homeless, lost and roaming. There are the children who have nothing, no love and no normalcy. There are those who cannot free themselves of enslavement to whatever addiction—drugs, welfare, the demoralization that rules the slums. There is crime to be conquered, the rough crime of the streets. . . . They need our care, our guidance, and our education. . . .*
>
> *The old solution, the old way, was to think that public money alone could end these problems. But we have learned that that is not so. And in any case, our funds are low. . . . We will make the hard choices, looking at what we have and perhaps allocating it differently, making our decisions based on honest need and prudent safety. And then we will do the wisest thing of all. We will turn to the only resource we have that in times of need always grows: the goodness and the courage of the American people. . . .*
>
> *I have spoken of a Thousand Points of Light, of all the community organizations that are spread like stars throughout the Nation, doing good. We will work hand in hand, encouraging, sometimes leading, sometimes being led, rewarding. . . . The old ideas are new again because they're not old, they are timeless: duty, sacrifice, commitment, and a patriotism that finds its expression in taking part and pitching in.*
>
> *—George H.W. Bush, Inaugural Address, January 20, 1989*

A It is the government's responsibility to care for America's poor, sick, and homeless.

B Every American citizen has a duty to help the less fortunate.

C The government has no more money for social programs.

D Volunteerism has a major role to play in solving America's problems.

 **SS.7.C.3.1 (Moderate)**

Which is a defining characteristic of both absolute monarchies and dictatorships?

A Both are ruled by a single national leader.

B Both are ruled by a king or queen.

C Both have a variety of political parties.

D Both allow significant citizen participation in government.

 **SS.7.C.3.4 (High)**

> *This Constitution, and the laws of the United States which shall be made in pursuance thereof; and all treaties made, or which shall be made, under the authority of the United States, shall be the supreme law of the land; and the judges in every state shall be bound thereby, anything in the Constitution or laws of any State to the contrary notwithstanding.*
>
> *—from Article 6 to the U.S. Constitution*

Based on this passage, which of the following is correct?

A The national government of the United States derives its power from the people.

B Powers not delegated to the national government are reserved to the individual states.

C The national government is superior to state and local governments in every respect.

D A state or local government cannot make any laws that would go against the laws of the national government.

 **SS.7.C.3.1 (Moderate)**

In which two types of government do citizens vote for representatives to a national legislature?

A direct democracy and representative democracy

B oligarchy and theocracy

C representative democracy and constitutional monarchy

D constitutional monarchy and absolute monarchy

CHAPTER 4

The American Colonies and Their Government

CHAPTER BENCHMARKS

SS.7.C.1.1 Recognize how Enlightenment ideas including Montesquieu's view of separation of power and John Locke's theories related to natural law and how Locke's social contract influenced the Founding Fathers.

SS.7.C.1.2 Trace the impact that the Magna Carta, English Bill of Rights, Mayflower Compact, and Thomas Paine's "Common Sense" had on colonists' views of government.

SS.7.C.1.3 Describe how English policies and responses to colonial concerns led to the writing of the Declaration of Independence.

SS.7.C.1.4 Analyze the ideas (natural rights, role of the government) and complaints set forth in the Declaration of Independence.

SS.7.C.2.12 Develop a plan to resolve a state or local problem by researching public policy alternatives, identifying appropriate government agencies to address the issue, and determining a course of action.

Chapter Overview

The people who lived in Great Britain's American colonies came from a wide variety of backgrounds and had very different lifestyles. Despite their differences, most were accustomed to and valued the long-standing English traditions of law and limited government. When colonists believed their freedoms had been denied, they protested. America's political leaders gathered to write a document explaining their desire for and right to freedom—the Declaration of Independence.

WHAT I NEED TO KNOW

TERMS

- ☐ democracy
- ☐ direct democracy
- ☐ representative democracy
- ☐ republic
- ☐ limited government
- ☐ legislature
- ☐ social contract
- ☐ natural rights
- ☐ liberty
- ☐ boycott
- ☐ duty
- ☐ delegate

PEOPLE, PLACES, EVENTS

- ☐ Magna Carta
- ☐ English Bill of Rights
- ☐ John Locke
- ☐ Mayflower Compact
- ☐ Stamp Act
- ☐ Declaratory Act
- ☐ Townshend Acts
- ☐ Tea Act
- ☐ Coercive Acts
- ☐ First Continental Congress
- ☐ Second Continental Congress
- ☐ Thomas Paine
- ☐ Thomas Jefferson
- ☐ Declaration of Independence

CHAPTER 4

The American Colonies and Their Government

CHAPTER BENCHMARKS, *continued*

SS.7.C.3.1 Compare different forms of government (direct democracy, representative democracy, socialism, communism, monarchy, oligarchy, autocracy).

SS.7.G.2.3 Explain how major physical characteristics, natural resources, climate, and absolute and relative location have influenced settlement, economics, and inter-governmental relations in North America.

LAFS.68.RH.1.1 Cite specific textual evidence to support analysis of primary and secondary sources.

LAFS.68.RH.2.4 Determine the meaning of words and phrases as they are used in a text, including vocabulary specific to domains related to history/social studies.

LAFS.68.RH.3.8 Distinguish among fact, opinion, and reasoned judgment in a text.

MAFS.K12.MP.6.1 Attend to precision.

The American Colonies and Their Government

Make this Foldable® and label the tabs Colonial Government, Colonial Settlement, and Disagreements. As you read, take notes on what you learn about the American colonies under the appropriate tabs, and make mental connections relating the past to the present. Use what you have learned to summarize two of the main ideas presented in each lesson. Focus on information that you do not know but that you need to know. On the back of the Foldable, describe what motivated America's first political leaders to write the Declaration of Independence.

Step 1
Fold lined paper horizontally to the margin.

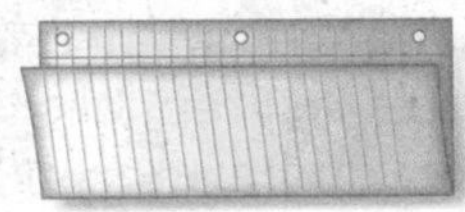

Step 2
Fold the right side and the left side of the paper across the middle to form three equal parts.

Step 3
Cut the two fold lines from the top edge to the bottom fold.

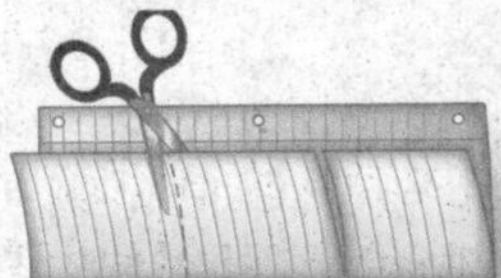

Step 4
Label the tabs as shown.

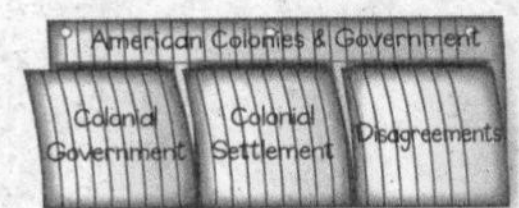

LESSON 1 SUMMARY

Influences on American Colonial Government

1. CONTRASTING

How did government in ancient Athens differ from government in ancient Rome? Which type of government is American government more like?

SS.7.C.1.1, SS.7.C.1.2, SS.7.C.3.1

The Foundations of Democracy

One of the various forms of government is autocracy. In this form of government, a single person holds all the power and is the ruler. In an oligarchy, a small group of people holds the power and makes the rules. In a monarchy, a king, a queen, or an emperor is the supreme ruler. **Democracy**, or rule by the people, is another form of government.

The origins of the American democratic political system can be traced to ancient times. The growth of democracy has not occurred at a steady pace. During some periods, little democracy existed or people were governed by monarchs. At other times, however, the ideas and practices of democracy have grown strong.

Ancient Democracies

The Jewish religion gave the world some of its first democratic ideas. The ancient Jews were ruled by kings, but their religion teaches that every person has worth. This teaching is a basic principle of democracy.

By the 400s B.C., the Greek city-state of Athens had created the world's first direct democracy. In a **direct democracy**, the people govern themselves. All free men over 18 were considered citizens and could participate in the assembly, which made decisions for the community. Direct democracy was possible in Athens because the population was small. However, direct democracy does not work well in places with a large population. Therefore, people choose leaders to govern. The leaders are representatives of the people. Thus, this form of democracy is called **representative democracy**.

The United States is a **republic**. This is a government based on representative democracy. The world's first republic was ancient Rome. In 509 B.C., the Romans overthrew their king. They put government in the hands of a senate. Senators were chosen from among Rome's wealthy upper class. Rome continued as a republic until around 50 B.C. After that time, monarchs called emperors ruled Rome and its empire for another 500 years.

Name ______________________ Date ______________ Class __________

Early English Influences

After the Roman Empire ended, kings and lords ruled most of Europe for the next 700 years. Lords were noblemen who usually inherited land and wealth. Over time, kings gained greater control over the noblemen, and eventually some nobles rebelled. In 1215, English nobles rose up against King John and forced him to sign a document called the Magna Carta (Latin for "Great Charter").

The Magna Carta limited the king's power. It made it illegal for him to place certain taxes on the nobles without their permission. The document gave rights to free men, including equal treatment under the law and trial by one's peers. The Magna Carta also gave nobles the right to rebel if the king broke his part of the agreement. The Magna Carta is important because it established the principle of **limited government**. This is the idea that a ruler or a government is not all-powerful.

The kings of England had a group of nobles and church officials who advised the king. Gradually, this group included representatives of the common people. By the late 1300s, the group was called Parliament. In addition to giving the king advice, Parliament made laws. A lawmaking body like Parliament is called a **legislature**. However, Parliament had only some influence, and kings remained strong. In 1625, King Charles I dismissed Parliament and ruled alone. When he recalled the members in 1628, they forced him to sign the Petition of Right. Like the Magna Carta, this document limited the king's power.

The English Bill of Rights

In 1688, Parliament removed King James II, the son of Charles I, from power. The legislative body then asked James's daughter Mary and her husband, William, to serve as England's monarch. This transfer of power is known as the Glorious Revolution. Before taking power, William and Mary had to agree to the rules set by Parliament. These rules are known as the English Bill of Rights. The Glorious Revolution and the signing of the English Bill of Rights changed English government forever. They also received much notice in England's North American colonies.

2. IDENTIFYING EVIDENCE

Underline the provisions of the Magna Carta. Then, identify which ideas you believe to be the most important and influential on American government. Explain your reasoning.

____

____

____

____

____

____

____

____

____

3. EVALUATING

Which Enlightenment thinkers' ideas seem especially compatible with representative democracy? Do any of their ideas seem anti-democratic? Explain.

ANALYZING VISUALS

4. MAKING INFERENCES

Which Enlightenment thinker do you believe most influenced the Founders' ideas about dividing power among three branches of government in the U.S. Constitution? Explain your answer.

English Bill Of Rights (1689)	
No imprisonment without due process of law	No taxation without Parliament's consent
No loss of property without due process of law	Subjects [people] have the right to bear arms
No cruel punishment	Subjects [people] have the right to petition the king
No standing army in time of peace without Parliament's consent	Freedom of speech in Parliament

Influence of the Enlightenment

The conflict between Parliament and the country's monarch did more than change the ruler. It led to new ideas about the ways people should be governed. These ideas formed part of a large movement in Europe called the Enlightenment. During the 1600s, scientific discoveries led to the belief that God had created an orderly universe. People in this movement began to believe that the laws governing the universe could be discovered through human reason. Many Enlightenment thinkers wanted to apply the laws of nature to people and society. These new ideas greatly changed political thinking in Europe and the Americas.

Enlightenment Thinkers

Many Enlightenment thinkers were influenced by Niccolò Machiavelli (1469–1527), who lived during the time of the Italian Renaissance. In his book *The Prince*, Machiavelli argued that the most effective rulers are feared rather than loved. However, he also wrote that republics were the best form of government.

Thomas Hobbes (1588–1679) was an early English Enlightenment thinker. Hobbes believed that an agreement should exist between government and the people. In this **social contract,** the people give up some freedom and are ruled by government. In return, government protects the people's rights. Hobbes argued that people could not rule themselves well, and therefore they needed a strong leader.

LESSON 1 SUMMARY, *continued*

Englishman John Locke (1632–1704) wrote that all people were born equal, and that they all had certain God-given rights. These rights were called **natural rights**, and they included the rights to life, to freedom, and to own property. Locke also believed in a social contract in which people agreed to give up some rights and to be ruled by a government. If the ruler did not protect the people's rights, Locke argued that the contract between the ruler and the people was broken. When that happened, the people could choose new leaders.

The political ideas of other Enlightenment thinkers are summarized in the following chart. Record the beliefs of Machiavelli, Hobbes, and Locke in the spaces provided.

ENLIGHTENMENT THINKERS		
Name	**Years Lived**	**Beliefs**
Niccolò Machiavelli	1469–1527	
Thomas Hobbes	1588–1679	
John Locke	1632–1704	
Jean-Jacques Rousseau	1712–1778	The legislative power belongs to the people.
Baron de Montesquieu	1689–1755	Separate the parts of government so no one part becomes too powerful
Voltaire	1694–1778	People should have liberty, including freedom of religion and freedom of trade.

Colonists' views about government were shaped by the Enlightenment thinkers. Ideas about a social contract, natural rights, and separation of powers influenced the writers of the Declaration of Independence and the U.S. Constitution.

The First Colonial Governments

England founded colonies in America throughout the 1600s. The early settlers were loyal to England. They believed strongly in democracy and representative government, and the colonists brought these ideas to America.

5. MAKING INFERENCES

Notice the list of rights listed in the chart of the English Bill of Rights. Which of these rights do you have as an American citizen?

6. DIFFERENTIATING

Which early colonial government was more like a republic, Jamestown or Plymouth? Why? How did one differ from the other?

____

____

____

____

____

____

____

____

Jamestown

Jamestown was the first permanent English settlement in North America. It was founded in 1607. At first, the settlement was ruled by a governor and a council appointed by the Virginia Company. Just over 10 years later, in 1619, the company allowed the colony to make its own laws. The colonists began electing leaders, called burgesses, to represent them. This group, called the House of Burgesses, was the first representative government in colonial America.

The Mayflower Compact

In 1620, a group called the Pilgrims sailed to America on a small ship called the *Mayflower* in search of religious freedom. They landed in what is now Massachusetts. This region had no English government, so the men on the *Mayflower* made a list of rules for their new colony. This agreement was called the Mayflower Compact. A compact is a written agreement. The Mayflower Compact established a direct democracy in the new colony of Plymouth. Although only some males could vote, anyone in Plymouth could attend town meetings and express his or her views about issues in the colony.

REVIEW LESSON 1

1. Use the chart below to summarize the main ideas in the Magna Carta, the English Bill of Rights, and the Mayflower Compact. Then, on a separate sheet of paper, write an essay that answers the question that follows.

MAGNA CARTA	ENGLISH BILL OF RIGHTS	MAYFLOWER COMPACT

2. **PREDICTING CONSEQUENCES** The history of colonial North America centers mainly around the struggle of England, France, and Spain to gain control of the continent. Ultimately, England established dominance. Most American colonists grew up valuing the English political traditions described in the chart above. How might colonial government have evolved differently if the colonists had not chosen to follow these traditions and laws? Explain your response.

LESSON 2 SUMMARY

Settlement, Culture, and Government of the Colonies

SS.7.C.1.1, SS.7.C.1.3, SS.7.G.2.3

Settling the English Colonies

Settlers in the English colonies of North America came from many parts of Europe. Many came from England. Others left their homes in Scotland, Ireland, Wales, and Germany for America. The Dutch and Swedes started their own colonies along the Atlantic Coast. In addition, thousands of enslaved Africans were brought to the colonies against their will.

Economic Opportunity

People came to the colonies for different reasons. Many settlers came for land or jobs. Some who wanted to come to America did not have enough money to pay for the trip. They came as indentured servants. American colonists paid to bring these servants to the colonies. Indentured servants promised to work in return for food and shelter. The servants worked from four to seven years. After that, they were free and could work to support themselves.

Religious Freedom

Other people came in search of religious freedom. Some groups of people were treated harshly because of their religious beliefs. Many of these people came from England to America to find a place where they could worship in their own way.

The Puritans founded Massachusetts for religious reasons. The group got its name because members wanted to purify, or reform, the church. A group of Puritans called Pilgrims founded Plymouth colony in 1620. Another group of Puritans started the Massachusetts Bay Colony. The two colonies were close to each other. The Puritans were religious dissenters. This means that they opposed, or did not agree with, official or commonly held views.

The Puritans wanted to worship God in their own way. They could not do this in England. Still, when they came to America, Puritans did not extend that privilege to others. Instead, the Puritans forced people to leave their colony if they had different religious beliefs.

1. REFLECTING

What were some benefits of becoming an indentured servant? What were the costs?

2. MAKING INFERENCES

Were the people of Rhode Island Puritans? Explain.

3. RECOGNIZING RELATIONSHIPS

What factors helped shipping become so important to the economy of the Middle Colonies?

Some colonists who left Massachusetts started other colonies in the Northeast. Rhode Island became known for the freedoms its colonists enjoyed. Settlers in Connecticut developed America's first written constitution. Created in 1639, it is called the Fundamental Orders of Connecticut. This landmark document created an elected assembly of representatives from each town. The representatives had the right to pass laws for the colony. The colonists also were given the right to elect their governor and judges.

Colonial Life

By 1733, England had 13 colonies along the Atlantic Coast of North America. The land and climate of the various colonies were different, influencing each colony's economy and the way colonists lived. Over time, three economic regions developed. Each had its own way of life.

The New England Colonies

The four New England Colonies, Massachusetts Bay, New Hampshire, Connecticut, and Rhode Island, were located in the northeast. Most New Englanders lived in towns. Due to the cold climate and rocky soil in the region, large-scale farming was nearly impossible. As a result, farms were small. Many colonists worked as shopkeepers or in other small businesses. The region's forests provided wood for shipbuilding. Colonists also fished, hunted, and trapped. They traded for furs with Native Americans and shipped the furs to Europe.

The Middle Colonies

Another four colonies were located south of New England. New York, Pennsylvania, New Jersey, and Delaware were called the Middle Colonies. The climate and soil in these colonies were well suited for farming. Farmers in this region raised wheat and other cash crops. These crops were products grown in large quantities for sale, not just to feed a farmer's family. Cash crops were often sold overseas. As a result of the growing trade, New York City and Philadelphia became busy port cities. The Middle Colonies were also rich in natural resources such as lumber, metals, and natural harbors. Because of these natural resources, sawmills, mines, and other businesses developed in this region.

Name ______________________ Date ______________ Class __________

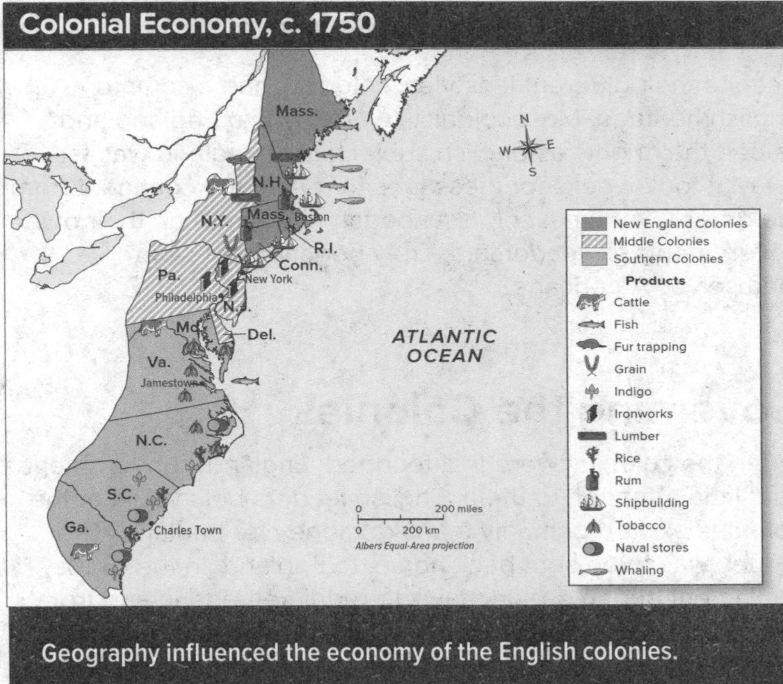

Geography influenced the economy of the English colonies.

The Southern Colonies

A warm climate, a long growing season, and rich soil made large-scale agriculture successful in the Southern Colonies. These colonies included Maryland, Virginia, North Carolina, South Carolina, and Georgia. Cash crops of tobacco and rice grew well along the region's low, flat coastal plains. As a result, large farms called plantations developed in this region. Many people were needed to tend the crops grown on the plantations. At first, indentured servants did much of this work. Over time, however, plantation owners began to depend on enslaved Africans for labor.

Further inland, the soil was poorer. This resulted in smaller farms where farmers grew mainly what they needed to feed their families. These Southerners depended less on enslaved labor than plantation owners.

Southern plantation owners grew wealthy and powerful, and they began to control the region's government. Plantation owners also had greater influence over the economy in the region. Due in part to their influence, few large towns and little industry developed in the Southern Colonies.

ANALYZING MAPS

4. For which colonies was whaling especially important? Ironworking?

____

____

____

____

5. EVALUATING

Which colonial region's economy was most dependent on agriculture? Which was least dependent? Why was this so?

____

____

____

____

____

____

____

____

____

____

____

____

____

____

____

Name ______________________ Date ____________ Class ________

6. EVALUATING EVIDENCE

For a democratic government to work, people must accept their leaders and obey laws. What were the features of the government in the colonies that the colonists most readily accepted? Which did they most resent? Explain your answer.

7. DETERMINING CENTRAL IDEAS

How might John Locke have argued that the British government broke its social contract with its American colonists?

Colonial Government

Despite their different lifestyles, colonists had a common English heritage. Most colonists were loyal to England and valued their rights as English subjects. Yet England was far away. It took weeks for messages to reach one continent from the other. Over time, colonists began to depend on their own governments for leadership. They began to consider themselves Americans.

Governing the Colonies

When the colonies were first founded, England's government paid little attention to them. English leaders believed that the colonies existed primarily to make money for England. The money was to be sent back home, to England. In the 1650s, Parliament began passing laws to regulate trade in and from the colonies. However, England found it difficult to enforce these new laws. In the colonies south of New England, few people lived near the coast. Ships could load and unload goods without being seen. This helped colonists ignore English trade laws.

Eventually the king appointed governors for the majority of the colonies. The appointed royal governor took orders from the English king and Parliament. The governor's job was to enforce England's laws in his colony. Local laws governing a colony were still in effect. These laws were usually passed by an elected assembly consisting of colonists.

A Time of Change

As time passed, the colonists' elected assemblies took more power. This resulted in conflict when elected colonial assemblies and royal governors fought for control. The assemblies had the power to tax. They also got to say how the money would be spent. They used these powers to weaken the royal governors.

By the mid-1700s, colonists were used to governing themselves. Many agreed with the views of John Locke, who said that governments existed to serve the people. Many colonists believed that the royal governors put British interests ahead of their own. Colonists had fewer rights than people living in Great Britain, and they did not like the situation.

Name ______________________ Date ____________ Class __________

REVIEW LESSON 2

1. Use the chart to describe the characteristics of the three colonial regions. Then, on a separate sheet of paper, write an essay that answers the question that follows.

NEW ENGLAND COLONIES	MIDDLE COLONIES	SOUTHERN COLONIES

2. **MAKING INFERENCES** Based on the differences you have identified in the chart, do you believe the governments in some colonial regions might have been more democratic than others? Explain.

LESSON 3 SUMMARY

Disagreements With Great Britain

SS.7.C.1.1, SS.7.C.1.2, SS.7.C.1.3, SS.7.C.1.4

1. COMPARING

In what ways was the Great Awakening similar to the Enlightenment?

Social and Political Changes in the Colonies

From the 1740s through the 1760s, a religious movement called the Great Awakening swept across the colonies. Preachers rejected the teachings of church leaders. They urged people to build a direct relationship with God. Colonists began to question traditional religious authority. Enlightenment leaders urged people to question accepted political authority. Together, these social and political movements made colonists want more **liberty,** or personal freedom. More and more colonists believed that they should have the same rights as people in Great Britain.

Colonists believed that it was Parliament's job to protect the rights of British people. However, it was the king and Parliament that made laws for the colonists, and they believed that royal governors favored British interests. Colonists began to think that they should select their own leaders. By the 1760s, colonial resentment against British rule was growing.

The French and Indian War

By the 1750s, British colonists were moving west into areas claimed by France. The increasing tensions soon led to war. In 1754, French forces joined with some Native American groups to drive British colonists from land west of the Appalachian Mountains. The conflict was called the French and Indian War.

Britain sent troops to the colonies and by 1763 had defeated France. Britain gained French lands all the way to the Mississippi River. The colonists wanted to move into those lands now that the French were gone. But British king George III had other plans for the colonies.

New Laws and Taxes

King George wanted to end the fighting in America. The French were gone, but Native Americans remained in the region. He issued a proclamation, or an official statement, making it illegal for colonists to settle in the lands won from

Name ______________________ Date ______________ Class __________

The Proclamation Line of 1763

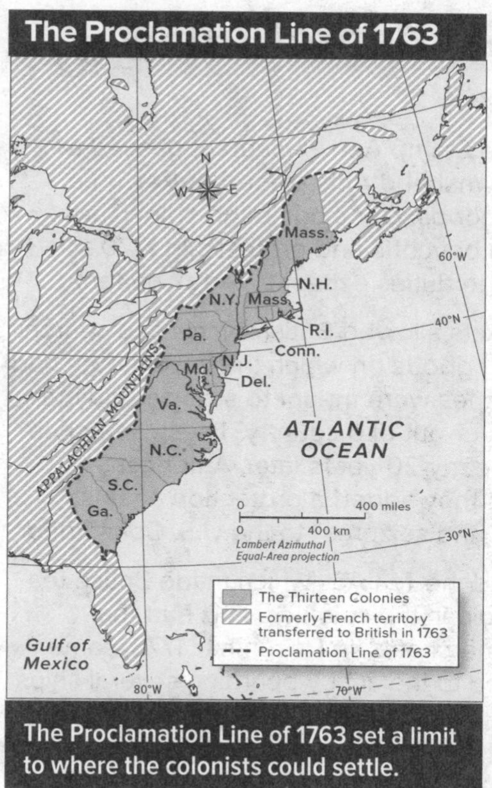

The Proclamation Line of 1763 set a limit to where the colonists could settle.

France. He placed more than 10,000 British troops in the colonies to keep order. Colonists were enraged. Many believed they would never be able to own their own land. Others thought the king was trying to limit the economic growth of the colonies.

King George wanted Parliament to tax the colonies. The French and Indian War had been long and costly. It left Britain deep in debt. The colonists had caused the war by moving west, so the king decided they should pay for it. In 1765, Parliament passed the Stamp Act to pay for the war. The law required colonists to buy and place tax stamps on documents such as newspapers.

The colonies protested this tax. They claimed that only their elected representatives had the right to tax them. Colonial leaders called on the colonists to **boycott** British goods. This meant that they refused to buy them. They also organized a Stamp Act Congress to write a protest to Parliament and the king. In 1766, Parliament repealed, or canceled, the Stamp Act. The same day, however, it passed the Declaratory Act. This law stated that Parliament had the right to tax the colonies and make decisions for them "in all cases whatsoever."

ANALYZING MAPS

2. What physical feature did the Proclamation Line follow?

____

____

3. EVALUATING EVIDENCE

Review and underline the actions that Great Britain took toward the colonies at the end of the French and Indian War. Do you believe Britain was justified in taking these actions? Cite evidence from the text to support your answer.

____

____

____

____

____

____

____

____

____

4. IDENTIFYING CAUSE AND EFFECT

Fill in the flowchart to show how the repeal of the Stamp Act led to the passage of the Coercive Acts.

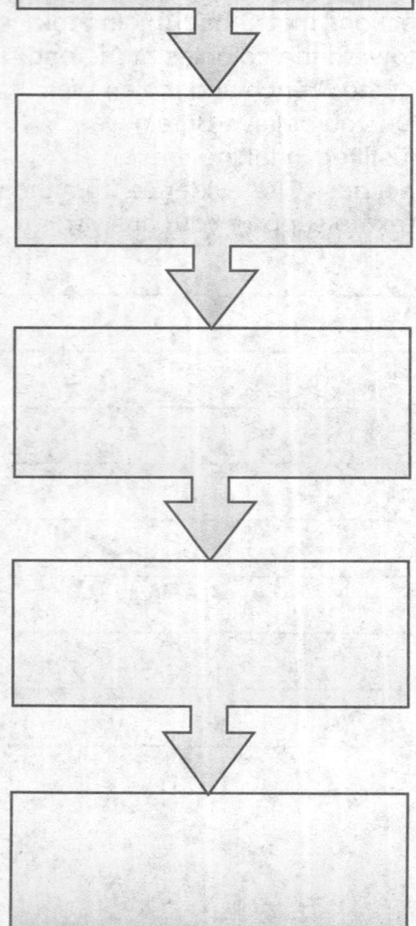

Parliament passes the Declaratory Act, stating that it can tax the colonies and make all decisions for them.

Colonial Dissatisfaction Grows

A year after repealing the Stamp Act, Parliament passed a new set of taxes. The Townshend Acts placed **duties** on a wide range of imported goods. Once again the colonists resisted these taxes with boycotts and protests. In 1770, Parliament repealed all the duties except for a tax on tea.

One of the Townshend Acts allowed British officials to search any business or home for goods on which the import duty had not been paid. The searches were meant to stop smuggling—illegally moving goods in or out of a country. These searches angered the colonists. Nearly 20 years later, Americans remembered them when they added a protection against "unreasonable searches and seizures" to the U.S. Constitution.

In 1773, Parliament passed the Tea Act, which made British tea cheaper than other tea sold in the colonies. This hurt the business of colonial tea merchants. In December 1773, some angry colonists responded to the act by boarding several ships in Boston Harbor. They dumped the ships' cargoes of tea into the harbor. This protest became known as the Boston Tea Party.

Parliament responded by passing laws called the Coercive Acts to punish Massachusetts—and especially Boston—for resisting Great Britain's rule. The Coercive Acts were so harsh that the colonists called them the Intolerable Acts. Some of the laws violated the English Bill of Rights that the colonists held so dear.

Steps Toward Independence

Parliament thought the Coercive Acts would frighten the colonists into respecting British rule. Instead, the reverse occurred. The other colonies banded together to help Massachusetts and challenge British authority.

The First Continental Congress

In September 1774, representatives from 12 of the 13 colonies met in Philadelphia to develop a united response to the Coercive Acts. This meeting was called the First Continental Congress. They decided to send a letter to King George. They asked that Britain respect the colonists' rights as British citizens. The **delegates** also organized a boycott of British goods and a ban on all trade with Britain. They agreed to meet again in the spring if British policies had not improved.

King George's response was not what the colonists wanted. He sent more soldiers to the colonies. He believed that the governments in New England were rebelling. He also said that a fight might be on the way. The colonists would have to decide whether to be loyal British citizens or independent.

The Second Continental Congress

The delegates met again in May 1775. In April, British troops and colonial militiamen had fought at Lexington and Concord, in Massachusetts. Congress had to decide whether to continue working toward peace or to split with Great Britain. The discussion lasted for months. Some delegates wanted independence, but others did not. While the debate continued, the Congress acted as a governing body for the colonies.

At the same time, support for independence was growing. In January 1776, Thomas Paine published a pamphlet titled *Common Sense*. Paine used the ideas of John Locke to make the case for independence. He argued that "common sense" called for the colonists to rebel against the king's "violent abuse of power." Paine stated that the problems in America were seen throughout the world. He went on to argue that the colonists had the power to organize a revolt. More than 500,000 copies of *Common Sense* were sold in 1776. By spring more than half the delegates of the Second Continental Congress favored independence.

The Declaration of Independence

The Congress chose a committee to explain to the world why the colonies should be free. The committee chose Thomas Jefferson to write the document. His thinking was influenced by John Locke. A passage in the second paragraph of the Declaration was inspired by Locke's ideas about natural rights.

> "We hold these truths to be self-evident, that all men are created equal, that they are endowed by their Creator with certain unalienable Rights, that among these are Life, Liberty, and the pursuit of Happiness."

Then, drawing on Locke's views about the social contract, Jefferson wrote:

> "[T]o secure these rights, Governments are instituted among Men, deriving their just powers from the consent of the governed, That whenever any form of government becomes destructive of these ends, it is the Right of the People to alter or abolish it, and to institute new Government."

5. MAKING CONNECTIONS

Which ideas of John Locke did Thomas Paine draw on in his pamphlet, *Common Sense*?

______

6. MAKING GENERALIZATIONS

What was the main complaint against the British government put forth in the Declaration of Independence?

______

7. DETERMINING CENTRAL IDEAS

According to the Declaration of Independence, why do people form a government?

Later in the Declaration, Jefferson put together a long list of ways that King George had abused his power. It was evidence that the social contract had been broken.

Greek ideas about democracy, as well as other Enlightenment thinkers, also influenced Jefferson's writing. Jean-Jacques Rousseau wrote that if a government did not protect its people's freedom, it should not exist. Voltaire believed that people had a right to liberty. The Declaration of Independence reflected many of these old and new beliefs.

The Second Continental Congress approved the Declaration of Independence on July 4, 1776. The Declaration of Independence was a revolutionary document. No other government at that time was based on the principles of government by consent of the governed. Since 1776, many other nations have used the Declaration as a model in their own efforts to gain freedom.

REVIEW LESSON 3

1. Use the chart to compare the First and Second Continental Congresses. Then, on a separate sheet of paper, write an essay that answers the question that follows.

FIRST CONTINENTAL CONGRESS	SECOND CONTINENTAL CONGRESS

2. **DRAWING CONCLUSIONS** The First Continental Congress did not advocate a break from Great Britain. Less than two years later, the Second Continental Congress adopted the Declaration of Independence. How do you account for this change among the congressional delegates?

Benchmark Skill Activities

DIRECTIONS: Write your answers on a separate piece of paper.

LAFS.68.RH.3.8

1. DISTINGUISHING FACT FROM OPINION

Use your FOLDABLES to write an essay.

Think about this statement: *It was inevitable that American colonists would declare their independence from Great Britain*. Is this an opinion or a fact? Do you agree or disagree? Explain your reasoning.

LAFS.68.RH.2.4; SS.7.C.1.1

2. USING DEFINITIONS ACCURATELY

Turn to the "Terms" list on the first page of Chapter 4. Select at least three words to include in a paragraph that summarizes the ideas that would later influence Thomas Jefferson's writing of the Declaration of Independence.

LAFS.68.WHST.1.1; SS.7.C.2.12

3. SUGGESTING A SOLUTION

John Locke taught that the purpose of government is to serve the people and protect their natural rights. Do library or online research to identify a problem in your community where government could be doing a better job of carrying out this responsibility. Develop a plan to address the problem. Your plan should include a course of action that government could take and should identify the appropriate government agency responsible for implementing the action.

MAFS.K12.MP.6.1; SS.7.G.2.3

4. CREATING CHARTS

APPROXIMATE PERCENTAGE OF PEOPLE IMMIGRATING WHO WERE LISTED AS INDENTURED SERVANTS, 1773–1776			
New England	**Middle Colonies**	**Chesapeake**	**Lower South**
3%	60%	95%	15%

The information in the table above shows the number of people immigrating to America as indentured servants between 1773 and 1776. Create a pie chart or a bar graph to communicate this information in a different way. Label your chart carefully and precisely, and calculate the sections of the chart accurately.

LAFS.68.RH.1.1

5. ANALYZING VISUALS

This cartoon, "The Horse America, Throwing His Master," was published in London in August 1779. Cite evidence from the text to interpret this cartoon.

THE HORSE AMERICA, throwing his Master.

Benchmark Note Cards

DIRECTIONS: Use these note cards to help you prepare for the test.

SS.7.G.2.3 Explain how major physical characteristics, natural resources, climate, and absolute and relative location have influenced settlement, economics, and inter-governmental relations in North America.

THREE COLONIAL REGIONS

New England Colonies

- Most New Englanders lived in towns.
- Cold climate and rocky soil made large-scale farming difficult.
- Farms were small and located near towns.
- Trade and industry flourished.

Middle Colonies

- Temperate climate and more fertile soil encouraged agriculture, especially cash crops.
- Trade helped New York City and Philadelphia become busy port cities.
- The region was rich in natural resources such as lumber, metals, and natural harbors.
- Sawmills, mines, and other businesses grew in the region.

Southern Colonies

- Warm climate, a long growing season, and rich soil made large-scale agriculture successful.
- Large plantations developed, eventually depending on the labor of enslaved Africans.
- Further inland, the soil was poorer and farms were smaller.
- Wealthy, powerful plantation owners dominated the region's government and economy.
- The region had few large towns and little industry.

SS.7.C.1.1 Recognize how Enlightenment ideas including Montesquieu's view of separation of power and John Locke's theories related to natural law and how Locke's social contract influenced the Founding Fathers.

JOHN LOCKE

- Locke believed that all people were born equal with certain God-given rights (called natural rights), such as the rights to life, freedom, and property ownership.
- He believed that a social contract existed between the people and government: People agreed to give up some rights and in return received protection from the government.
- Locke thought that if the government failed to protect the peoples' rights, the social contract was broken and the people could choose new leaders.

OTHER ENLIGHTENMENT THINKERS	• Niccolò Machiavelli—Wrote that rulers should be feared not loved, but supported republics • Thomas Hobbes—Introduced the idea of the social contract; thought people needed strong rulers because they were too weak to govern themselves • Baron de Montesquieu—Advocated separation of powers so no single branch of government could become too powerful • Jean-Jacques Rousseau—Thought that legislative power should belong to the people • Voltaire—Believed that people should have liberty; supported freedom of religion and freedom of trade

SS.7.C.1.2 Trace the impact that the Magna Carta, English Bill of Rights, Mayflower Compact, and Thomas Paine's "Common Sense" had on colonists' views of government.

DOCUMENTS THAT INFLUENCED AMERICAN GOVERNMENT	• Magna Carta—Limited monarch's power, established the rule of law • English Bill of Rights—Set out rights of English citizens that no monarch could violate; established Parliament as leading force in English government • Mayflower Compact—Established self-governance and a direct democracy in colonial America • Thomas Paine's *Common Sense*—Used the ideas of John Locke to make the case for independence

SS.7.C.1.3 Describe how English policies and responses to colonial concerns led to the writing of the Declaration of Independence.

COLONISTS OBJECT TO BRITISH POLICIES	Colonists were angered by British policies instituted following the French and Indian War. • Proclamation of 1763—Prohibited colonists from settling west of the Appalachian Mountains • Stamp Act—Colonial tax meant to help pay British debts incurred during French and Indian War • Declaratory Act—Parliament had the right to tax the colonies and make all decisions for the colonies • Townshend Act—Placed duties on a wide range of imported goods; attempted to combat colonial smuggling • Tea Act—Hurt colonial tea merchants by making British tea cheaper than other tea sold in the colonies • Coercive Acts—Laws meant to punish colonists for the Boston Tea Party and for resisting British rule

FIRST AND SECOND CONTINENTAL CONGRESSES	In September 1744, colonial representatives met to plan a united response to the Coercive Acts. Though still loyal to Britain, delegates to this First Continental Congress asked Britain to respect colonists' rights. They organized a total boycott of British goods. Britain responded by sending troops to the colonies, and fighting between those troops and colonial militiamen broke out. A Second Continental Congress was called in May 1775. More delegates advocated independence. By July 1776, a formal Declaration of Independence had been drafted and approved by the Congress.

SS.7.C.1.4 Analyze the ideas (natural rights, role of the government) and complaints set forth in the Declaration of Independence.

THE DECLARATION OF INDEPENDENCE	Thomas Jefferson, author of the Declaration of Independence, was clearly influenced by John Locke's ideas about natural rights: As Jefferson drafted the Declaration, he drew upon John Locke's ideas about the social contract between government and the people. Jefferson emphasized the idea that all men are created equal and that they have the unalienable rights of life, liberty, and the pursuit of happiness.

SS.7.C.3.1 Compare different forms of government (direct democracy, representative democracy, socialism, communism, monarchy, oligarchy, autocracy).

DIFFERENT FORMS OF DEMOCRACY	• Direct democracy—Government in which all citizens vote directly on all matters of public policy • Representative democracy—Government in which citizens choose a group of people to represent them, make laws, and govern on their behalf

Chapter 4

VISUAL SUMMARY

DIRECTIONS: Complete the graphic organizer below.

Ancient influences:

Early English and colonial influences:

Enlightenment thinkers:

Geography affects the development of the American colonies:

★ Subsistence farming and commerce in New England

★ An economy based on cash crops, industry, and trade in the Middle Colonies

★ A farming economy dependent on slavery in the Southern Colonies

A distinctly American culture begins to develop during the colonial period:

★ Colonists began to see themselves as Americans rather than English subjects

★ By the mid-1700s, colonists had become accustomed to governing themselves

The American Colonies and Their Government

Disagreements With Great Britain

To pay for French and Indian War, Great Britain ______________________________

____

Colonists responded to the new laws by organizing __________ of British goods. Tensions rose, culminating in the Boston Tea Party.

The ____________________ met to draft a letter to the British king asking that he respect the colonists' rights as British citizens.

Fighting erupted between British Troops and colonial militia.

While the fighting continued, the Second Continental Congress approved the

______________________ on July 4, 1776.

USING PRIMARY SOURCES

COMPARE AND CONTRAST Below are two sources about the social contract. The first is taken from the Mayflower Compact. The second was written by John Locke. On another sheet of paper, summarize the two pieces. In your writing, compare and contrast what they say about the social contract between rulers and those governed.

In the Name of God, Amen. We, whose names are underwritten, the Loyal Subjects of our dread Sovereign Lord King James . . . Having undertaken for the Glory of God, . . . and the Honour of our King and Country, a Voyage to plant the first Colony in the northern Parts of Virginia; Do by these Presents [the people who signed the document], solemnly and mutually, in the Presence of God and one another, covenant [pledge] and combine ourselves together into a civil Body Politick, for our better Ordering and Preservation, and Furtherance of the Ends aforesaid: And by Virtue hereof do enact, constitute, and frame, such just and equal Laws, Ordinances, Acts, Constitutions, and Officers, from time to time, as shall be thought most meet and convenient for the general Good of the Colony; unto which we promise all due Submission and Obedience. In Witness whereof we have hereunto subscribed our names at Cape-Cod the eleventh of November, in the Reign of our Sovereign Lord King James, of England, France, and Ireland, the eighteenth, and of Scotland, the fifty-fourth, Anno Domini, 1620.

—The Mayflower Compact

... whenever the legislators endeavor [try] to take away, and destroy the property of the people, or to reduce them to slavery under arbitrary [unpredictable] power, they put themselves into a state of war with the people, who are thereupon absolved [set free] from any farther obedience, and are left to the common refuge, which God hath provided for all men, against force and violence. Whensoever therefore the legislative shall transgress [break] this fundamental [basic] rule of society; and either by ambition, fear, folly or corruption, endeavor [try] to grasp themselves, or put into the hands of any other, an absolute power over the lives, liberties, and estates of the people; by this breach [break] of trust they forfeit [give up] the power the people had put into their hands for quite contrary ends, and it devolves [goes back] to the people, who have a right to resume their original liberty, and, by the establishment of a new legislative, (such as they shall think fit) provide for their own safety and security, which is the end for which they are in society.

—*Two Treatises of Government*, John Locke

Chapter Practice Test

DIRECTIONS: Circle the best answer for each question.

SS.7.C.1.2 (High)

> *In the Name of God, Amen. We, whose names are underwritten, the Loyal Subjects of our dread Sovereign Lord King James, by the Grace of God, of Great Britain, France, and Ireland, King, Defender of the Faith, etc. Having undertaken for the Glory of God, and Advancement of the Christian Faith, and the Honour of our King and Country, a Voyage to plant the first Colony in the northern Parts of Virginia; Do by these Presents, solemnly and mutually, in the Presence of God and one another, covenant [pledge] and combine ourselves together into a civil Body Politick, for our better Ordering and Preservation, and Furtherance of the Ends aforesaid: And by Virtue hereof do enact, constitute, and frame, such just and equal Laws, Ordinances, Acts, Constitutions, and Officers, from time to time, as shall be thought most meet [fitting] and convenient for the general Good of the Colony; unto which we promise all due Submission and Obedience. In Witness whereof we have hereunto subscribed our names at Cape-Cod the eleventh of November, in the Reign of our Sovereign Lord King James, of England, France, and Ireland, the eighteenth, and of Scotland, the fifty-fourth, Anno Domini, 1620.*
>
> —The Mayflower Compact

What facts in the document support the argument that the Pilgrims believed in democracy?

A They promised to establish universal suffrage.

B They pledged to use force to resist the monarch.

C They agreed to abide by decisions voted upon.

D They strongly upheld the principles of freedom of religion.

2 **SS.7.C.3.1 (Low)**

Which type of government does the United States have?

A oligarchy

B confederation

C direct democracy

D representative democracy

---

3 **SS.7.C.1.2 (Moderate)**

> *. . . that it is the right of the subjects to petition the king and all commitments and prosecutions for such petitioning are illegal. . .*
>
> —English Bill of Rights (1689)

Which of the following best explains this sentence?

A If people complain to the king, they will be punished.

B Only British citizens can complain to the king and Parliament.

C People have the right to complain to the king without fear of punishment.

D People can send complaints to the king, but complaints are limited to certain topics.

SS.7.C.1.3 (Moderate)

Why was the French and Indian War a critical event in American colonists' relationship with Great Britain?

A The war caused Britain to grant more power to colonial legislatures.

B The war prevented the colonies from trading with Britain.

C The war led Britain to increase taxes on the colonies.

D The war resulted in a restriction on immigration to the colonies.

5 **SS.7.C.3.1 (High)**

> *It is Ordered, sentenced, and decreed, that there shall be yearly two General Assemblies or Courts, the one . . . in April, the other the second . . . in September . . . the first shall be called the Court of Election, wherein shall be yearly chosen from time to time, so many Magistrates [judges] and other public Officers as shall be found requisite [needed]: Whereof one to be chosen Governor for the year ensuing and until another be chosen, and no other Magistrate to be chosen for more than one year: provided always there be six chosen besides the Governor, which being chosen and sworn according to an Oath . . . shall have the power to administer justice according to the Laws here established, . . . and do cohabit [live] within this Jurisdiction having been admitted Inhabitants by the major part of the Town wherein they live. . . .*
>
> — Fundamental Orders of Connecticut (1639)

What is the best term to describe the government established by the Fundamental Orders of Connecticut?

A autocracy

B democracy

C oligarchy

D monarchy

---

6 **SS.7.C.1.1 (High)**

Leaders of colonial independence in the 1760s and 1770s began to speak about "natural rights" rather than talking about "English liberties." What is the best explanation for this?

A Their language reflected the growing racial and ethnic diversity of the American colonies in the eighteenth century.

B Many colonial assemblies passed laws to protect the civil rights of ethnic minorities.

C More and more colonists had been exposed to the ideas advocated by Enlightenment thinkers.

D Independence leaders advocated that government take steps to improve the lives of minorities.

7 **SS.7.G.2.3 (Moderate)**

In which colony would one be most likely to find enslaved Africans working on large plantations?

A Massachusetts

B Rhode Island

C Virginia

D New York

---

8 **SS.7.C.1.3 (Moderate)**

What was the main reason Great Britain established the Proclamation Line of 1763?

A to end Britain's war with France over disputed territory

B to force American colonists to pay for the French and Indian War

C to prevent American industrial development of the Ohio River Valley

D to avoid conflicts between American colonists and Native Americans

---

9 **SS.7.C.1.3 (Moderate)**

What was the significance of the Stamp Act?

A It was the first direct British tax on American colonists.

B It prohibited westward settlement.

C It banned slave trade from the colonies.

D It made town meetings illegal unless the British gave written consent.

SS.7.C.1.1; SS.7.C.1.4 (Moderate)

That whenever any Form of Government becomes destructive of these ends, it is the Right of the People to alter or to abolish it, and to institute new Government, laying its foundation on such principles and organizing its powers in such form, as to them shall seem most likely to effect their Safety and Happiness.

—Declaration of Independence

What is the main idea of this paragraph?

A When people do not agree with their leaders, they can ask someone else to lead.

B Governments must ensure happiness and safety of the people.

C If people do not like their form of government, they can change it.

D Citizens must continually check to see that their government is working well.

CHAPTER 5

The Constitution

Chapter Overview

American colonists began creating their own plans for government even before the Declaration of Independence was signed. Gradually, leaders in all of the states wrote constitutions. These state governments had similar structures, such as two houses to make laws, a governor, and courts. After winning independence, the first plan for the new country was the Articles of Confederation. However, government under the Articles was weak. Leaders soon realized the new nation needed something all its citizens would respect and follow.

Leaders met to create a new plan that all states would accept. After long discussions and differences of opinion, they reached several compromises, and eventually the Constitution was ratified. This important document includes a preamble, articles, and amendments. The Constitution contains the beliefs of the nation and the foundation of the government. These include the principles of popular sovereignty, limited government and the rule of law, separation of powers, checks and balances, and federalism.

CHAPTER BENCHMARKS

SS.7.C.1.1 Recognize how Enlightenment ideas including Montesquieu's view of separation of power and John Locke's theories related to natural law and how Locke's social contract influenced the Founding Fathers.

SS.7.C.1.2 Trace the impact that the Magna Carta, English Bill of Rights, Mayflower Compact, and Thomas Paine's "Common Sense" had on colonists' views of government.

SS.7.C.1.5 Identify how the weaknesses of the Articles of Confederation led to the writing of the Constitution.

SS.7.C.1.6 Interpret the intentions of the Preamble of the Constitution.

SS.7.C.1.7 Describe how the Constitution limits the powers of government through separation of powers and checks and balances.

SS.7.C.1.8 Explain the viewpoints of the Federalists and the Anti-Federalists regarding the ratification of the Constitution and inclusion of a bill of rights.

WHAT I NEED TO KNOW

TERMS

- ☐ bicameral
- ☐ confederation
- ☐ Articles of Confederation
- ☐ Ordinance of 1785
- ☐ Northwest Ordinance
- ☐ Great Compromise
- ☐ Three-Fifths Compromise
- ☐ Electoral College
- ☐ Federalist
- ☐ federalism
- ☐ Anti-Federalist
- ☐ Preamble
- ☐ article
- ☐ amendment
- ☐ popular sovereignty
- ☐ limited government
- ☐ separation of powers
- ☐ checks and balances
- ☐ enumerated powers
- ☐ reserved powers
- ☐ concurrent powers
- ☐ supremacy clause

PEOPLE, PLACES, EVENTS

- ☐ Northwest Territory
- ☐ Shays's Rebellion
- ☐ Constitutional Convention
- ☐ Independence Hall
- ☐ George Washington
- ☐ James Madison
- ☐ The Virginia Plan
- ☐ William Paterson
- ☐ The New Jersey Plan
- ☐ Roger Sherman
- ☐ Alexander Hamilton
- ☐ John Jay

CHAPTER 5

The Constitution

CHAPTER BENCHMARKS, *continued*

SS.7.C.1.9 Define the rule of law and recognize its influence on the development of the American legal, political, and governmental systems.

SS.7.C.3.3 Illustrate the structure and function (three branches of government established in Articles I, II, and III with corresponding powers) of government in the United States as established in the Constitution.

SS.7.C.3.4 Identify the relationship and division of powers between the federal government and state governments.

SS.7.C.3.5 Explain the Constitutional amendment process.

SS.7.G.1.3 Interpret maps to identify geopolitical divisions and boundaries of places in North America.

SS.7.G.2.1 Locate major cultural landmarks that are emblematic of the United States.

LAFS.68.WHST.1.1 Write arguments focused on discipline-specific content.

LAFS.7.SL.1.1 Engage effectively in a range of collaborative discussions (one-on-one, in groups, and teacher-led) with diverse partners on grade 7 topics, texts, and issues, building on others' ideas and expressing their own clearly.

LAFS.7.SL.1.2 Analyze the main ideas and supporting details presented in diverse media and formats (e.g., visually, quantitatively, orally) and explain how the ideas clarify a topic, text, or issue under study.

ELD.K12.ELL.SS.1 English language learners communicate information, ideas and concepts necessary for academic success in the content area of Social Studies.

The Constitution

Create the Foldable® below and write the chapter title on the cover tab. Label four of the tabs with the lesson titles. Label the fifth tab The Constitution Today. Under the appropriate tabs, summarize the main ideas presented in each lesson. Focus on information that you do not currently know or understand. Under The Constitution Today tab, explain how a group of men living more than two hundred years ago were able to write a constitution based upon principles that are still relevant today.

Step 1
Use three sheets of notebook paper.

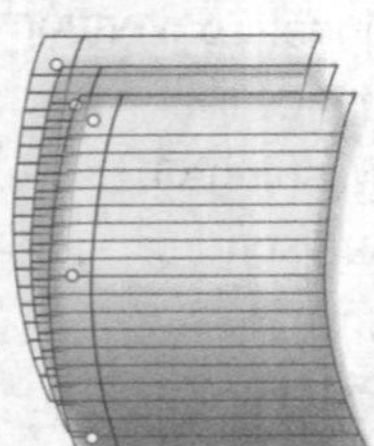

Step 2
Stack the three sheets of paper but align them so the middle sheet is about an inch below the bottom sheet, and the top sheet is about an inch below the middle sheet.

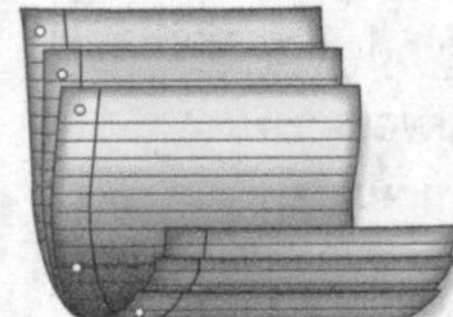

Step 3
Fold the bottom part of the stack up to create five equal tabs. Staple at the bottom and label as directed.

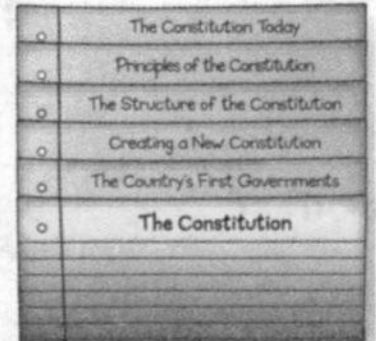

LESSON 1 SUMMARY

The Country's First Governments

SS.7.C.1.2, SS.7.C.1.5, SS.7.G.1.3

State Constitutions

American colonists wanted independence even before the signing of the Declaration of Independence. The Second Continental Congress told the colonists to begin forming governments. In January 1776, New Hampshire became the first colony to organize as a state. Its leaders created a constitution, which is a detailed, written plan for government. Soon, the other colonies did the same.

State Governments

All the state constitutions had similarities. Each had a legislature to make laws. Most were **bicameral,** or divided into two houses. Each state had a governor who was elected by the legislature or its citizens. The governor's role was to carry out the laws. Each state also had courts. Court judges decided what the laws meant and how to apply them.

Bill of Rights

State governments used the Declaration of Independence as a model. They included American ideals such as a person's rights to "life, liberty, and the pursuit of happiness." Most states also added a bill of rights that guaranteed basic freedoms and legal protections for their citizens. These rights included trial by jury and protection of personal property. The Magna Carta, the English Bill of Rights, the Mayflower Compact, and Thomas Paine's *Common Sense* all influenced the colonists' ideas for governing.

1. ANALYZING

Why do you think the state leaders believed they should have written constitutions?

ANALYZING VISUALS

2. IDENTIFYING

What main ideas from the documents listed in the chart were reflected in state constitutions?

PRINCIPLES FOUND IN DOCUMENTS THAT INFLUENCED COLONISTS			
Magna Carta	English Bill of Rights	Mayflower Compact	*Common Sense*
Required king to protect basic rights and limited his powers	Listed rights for citizens, including consent of the people, right to bear arms, right to jury trial, and right to petition the monarch	Created laws that were fair and equal and based on majority rule	Advocated for independence, the sovereignty of the people, a written constitution, and checks and balances

3. ANALYZING

Do you think a plan of government that establishes a "league of friendships" among states would be effective? Explain.

____

____

____

____

____

____

4. IDENTIFYING POINTS OF VIEW

Underline the details that confirm the idea that each state guarded its state sovereignty at the expense of national power. Then, in a small group explain why this attitude might lead to problems for the United States. Be sure to build on others' ideas and to express your ideas clearly. After the discussion, write your viewpoint in three sentences or less.

____

____

____

____

____

____

____

The Articles of Confederation

Once the colonies declared their independence, they had to be ready to govern themselves. They realized that certain things, such as raising and supporting a large army, could not be taken on by individual states. How could 13 small, separate forces hope to fight against the mighty British army? Colonial leaders knew they needed a single, strong army under central control to win the war.

The Second Continental Congress decided to create a confederation of states. A **confederation** is a group of individual state governments that unite for a common purpose. The Congress wrote the first constitution of the United States in 1777. Named the **Articles of Confederation,** it established a "league of friendships" among the states. The articles were approved, or ratified, by the 13 states by 1781. Each state had only one vote in a one-house legislature. The states also kept their own powers and freedoms. They only came together for issues related to defense and dealing with foreign countries.

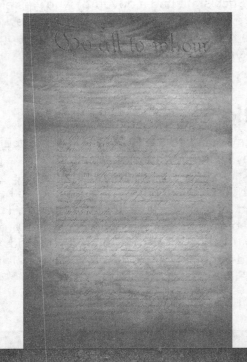

The Articles of Confederation established a legislature, known as the Confederation Congress.

National Archives and Records Administration (301687)

The Northwest Ordinances

The Confederation Congress passed two ordinances, or laws, about the Old Northwest. This region included present-day Ohio, Indiana, Illinois, Michigan, Wisconsin, and part of Minnesota.

The Ordinance of 1785

- set up a plan for surveying western lands (This plan is still used today.)
- described how western lands were to be sold
  - divided the land into townships six miles square
  - divided each township into 36 sections, each one mile square

The Northwest Ordinance

- passed in 1787
- set up a government for the Northwest Territory
- became a model for organizing governments in other new territories
- provided a plan for admitting new states
- stated that slavery and involuntary servitude would not be allowed in the territory

These ordinances had a major effect on U.S. history. They helped people settle the Northwest Territory in an orderly way. During the American Revolution, only a few thousand settlers lived there. By the 1790s, the population had grown to about 120,000.

Northwest Territory, 1785

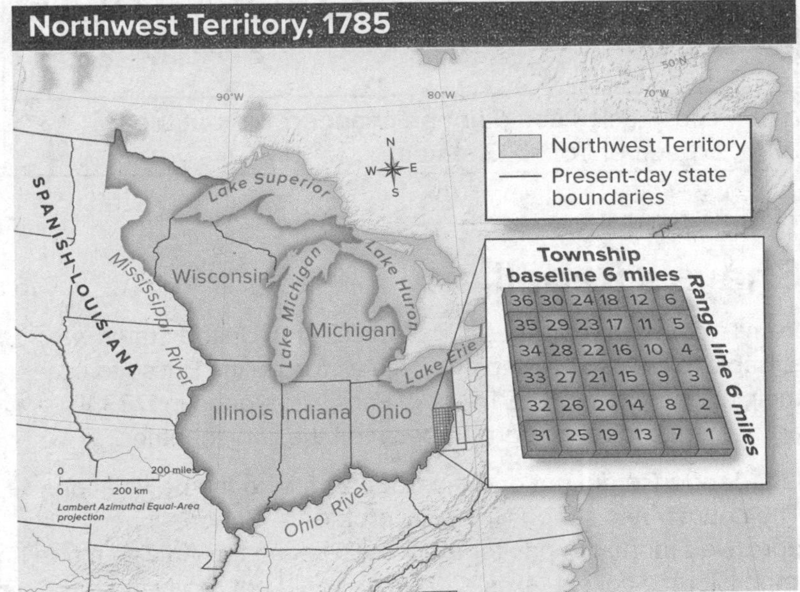

ANALYZING MAP

5. Look at the map of the Northwest Territory in 1785. What formed the southern boundary of the Northwest Territory? What formed its western boundary?

____

____

____

____

In what way did setting these territorial borders in this manner affect the future states in this region?

____

____

____

____

____

____

6. CREATING VISUALS

Look at the Weaknesses of the Articles of Confederation chart. Then, create a chart below to show changes that leaders needed to make to fix those weaknesses.

FIXING WEAKNESSES OF THE ARTICLES
Lack of Power and Money
Lack of Central Power
Rules Too Rigid

Weaknesses of the Articles

While the two Northwest Ordinances were important laws, the Confederation Congress did not accomplish much more. There are several reasons for this. It could not pass a law unless nine states voted for it. Also, if it wanted to amend, or change, the Articles, all 13 states had to agree. These rules made it nearly impossible for Congress to get anything done.

In addition, the Confederation Congress had limited powers. The colonists did not want strong rule. They did not like what they had already experienced with Britain. The Congress could pass laws, but it did not have the power to enforce them. Because there was neither a governor nor an executive, there was no one to ensure that laws were obeyed.

The Congress also did not have the power to tax. The Articles said Congress could ask the states for money, but they did not have to comply. As it turned out, under the Articles, Congress could not require the states to do anything.

WEAKNESSES OF THE ARTICLES OF CONFEDERATION
Lack of Power and Money
• Congress had no power to collect taxes.
• Congress had no power to regulate trade.
• Congress had no power to enforce its laws.
Lack of Central Power
• No single leader or group directed government policy.
• No national court system existed.
Rules Too Rigid
• Congress could not pass laws without the approval of nine states.
• The Articles could not be changed without the agreement of all 13 states.

Shays's Rebellion

In spite of the weaknesses in the Articles, the United States was still able to take some steps. The states forced the British to accept their independence. The Treaty of Paris was signed in 1783. This agreement ended the fighting between the two countries.

Independence did not end the troubles facing the new nation. The country had serious financial problems. Congress had borrowed money to pay for the war. Because the Articles made it impossible to collect taxes, Congress could not repay the debt.

LESSON 1 SUMMARY, *continued*

State governments as well had fallen into debt. They started to tax their citizens heavily to raise needed funds.

At the same time, trade decreased. Many people lost their jobs. Farmers could not sell their crops and had to take on debt. Some even lost their lands. In addition, states had taxed goods imported from other states and countries. These taxes hurt trade, so merchants and businesspeople suffered even more. The Confederation Congress could not fix any of these problems.

Americans did not believe the government could protect them. This led to riots in several states during 1786 and 1787. One riot, known as Shays's Rebellion, took place in Massachusetts. Daniel Shays, a farmer, owed money because of heavy state taxes. The courts in Massachusetts threatened to take his farm to pay his debts. Shays did not believe the state had the right to punish him. Other people agreed with him. Shays led about 1,200 protestors, including some free African Americans, in an attack on a federal arsenal. The state militia was sent to end the rebellion.

Shays's Rebellion served as a warning to the country. Many people saw the need for a stronger national government. They wanted a government that could maintain law and order. In 1787, delegates from 12 of the states attended a meeting in Philadelphia. Their goal was to change the Articles of Confederation.

7. IDENTIFYING ALTERNATIVES

What actions other than organizing a riot could Shays have used to communicate his needs?

REVIEW LESSON 1

1. Complete the chart below to list the failures of the Articles of Confederation.

FAILURES OF THE ARTICLES OF CONFEDERATION	
Economic Issues	
Leadership Issues	
Legislative Issues	

2. **DETERMINING CENTRAL IDEAS** Write an essay to answer the following questions: How did the Articles of Confederation fail as a plan of government? Why would the states purposely create such a document? Give specific examples from the text. Use a separate sheet of paper for your essay.

LESSON 2 SUMMARY

Creating a New Constitution

1. MAKING INFERENCES

Underline in the text the different occupations of the delegates.

Why do you think people with these occupations were chosen to become delegates?

____

____

____

____

____

____

2. ORGANIZING

Use the Internet to locate and research Independence Hall. With a partner, create a brochure for recent immigrants using a question-and-answer format. Make sure to explain the symbolic importance of both Independence Hall and the Liberty Bell.

SS.7.C.1.5, SS.7.C.1.8, SS.7.G.2.1

The Constitutional Convention

Fifty-five delegates from all states except Rhode Island gathered in Independence Hall in Philadelphia, Pennsylvania. This meeting, the Constitutional Convention, began on May 25, 1787. The delegates wanted to fix the Articles of Confederation to give the country a stronger plan of government. Most of these men were well educated and had held political office. They included lawyers, merchants, college presidents, physicians, governors, generals, and planters. Eight delegates had signed the Declaration of Independence. Forty-one of them were or had been members of the Continental Congress. Those delegates had first-hand experience of the failure of the Articles of Confederation.

Some groups were not represented in the meeting. Women, Native Americans, and African Americans could not serve as delegates to the Convention.

Independence Hall, the building in which the delegates met, was the same building where the Declaration of Independence had been signed. After the Declaration of Independence was complete, the Liberty Bell was used to call people to hear the first official public reading of the document on July 8, 1776.

Independence Hall remains an important symbol of the country.

The First Decisions

George Washington was put in charge of the convention. He was highly respected because of his role during the American Revolution. Washington kept the delegates focused on the task at hand. He understood that establishing a better plan of government was vital for the new country.

The delegates agreed that each state would have just one vote. They also agreed that decisions would be made with a simple majority vote. It would take seven votes for an issue to pass. The delegates wanted to discuss the issues freely among themselves. They agreed, however, to keep the work of the convention secret. The public could not attend meetings. Delegates could not discuss what happened in the meetings with anyone other than fellow delegates. Because of this last agreement, there were few written records of the convention. James Madison, a Virginia delegate, did keep a notebook. The most detailed account comes from it.

The original purpose of the convention was to revise the Articles of Confederation. However, as the delegates began their work, they agreed that the current government was too weak. They decided to write a new plan of government—a new constitution. The meeting in Philadelphia became known as the Constitutional Convention.

3. CONTRASTING

Contrast the voting process to change laws under the Articles of Confederation with the voting process at the Constitutional Convention.

____

____

____

____

____

____

____

____

____

____

____

____

Compromising for a Constitution

The delegates knew that they had a difficult task. They wanted every state to accept the new government plan. People understood that state acceptance would mean the difference between failure and success. However, delegates from different states had different ideas.

The Virginia Plan

James Madison of Virginia presented a plan for a strong national government. It became known as the Virginia Plan, and it was similar to today's federal government. Madison wanted a president, courts, and a congress with two houses. He also believed that a state's population should determine the number of representatives in each house. That meant larger states would have more votes than smaller states.

Four states with large populations—Massachusetts, Pennsylvania, Virginia, and New York—liked the plan. However, delegates from states with smaller populations were opposed to the Virginia Plan. They were concerned that the larger states would ignore their interests.

4. CONSTRUCTING AN ARGUMENT

Explain how the Virginia Plan and the New Jersey Plan differed regarding the executive leadership of the nation. Then, choose one of the plans and write an argument supporting it that could have been presented at the Constitutional Convention.

____
____
____
____
____
____
____
____
____
____
____
____

The New Jersey Plan

The Virginia Plan sparked two weeks of debate with no end in sight. Then, William Paterson of New Jersey suggested a different plan. He based the New Jersey Plan on the Articles of Confederation, but there were major differences. Paterson proposed a one-house congress. Each state would have one vote in the congress. Congress would have the power to levy taxes and control trade. These were major things that the congress could not do under the Articles. The New Jersey Plan called for a less powerful committee, named by Congress, to carry out laws. There was no president and no strong single leader.

Smaller states—Maryland, Delaware, and New Jersey—backed the New Jersey Plan. They would have the same power as the large states. Delegates from larger states were not in favor of the plan. They believed states with more people should have more say in deciding issues.

The Great Compromise

Roger Sherman of Connecticut headed a committee to solve the problem of the opposing plans. The committee proposed that

- Congress would have two houses—a Senate and a House of Representatives
- each state would have two members in the Senate
- the number of seats in the House of Representatives would reflect a state's population.

THE GREAT COMPROMISE	
Senate	2 members per state
House of Representatives	Number of members based on population of state

Smaller states were happy about the equal numbers of senators. Larger states were pleased about the seats in the House, where they would have greater representation. Although neither group was completely satisfied, they could all accept the plan. Sherman's plan became known as the **Great Compromise.** A compromise is an agreement between two or more sides, each gives up something in order to get something it wants. Without the Great Compromise, the Constitution might never have been created.

The Three-Fifths Compromise

The delegates also had other difficult issues to resolve. Slavery was prominent in the South. Southern states wanted to count enslaved African Americans as part of their populations. This would give these states more votes in the House of Representatives. At the time, there were more than 550,000 enslaved African Americans. Counting them would add many representatives. The North, however, had few enslaved persons. Enslaved people could not vote or participate in government. Therefore, Northern delegates argued that enslaved African Americans should not be counted for representation.

The compromise for this issue is called the **Three-Fifths Compromise.** Every five enslaved persons would equal three free persons. So, three-fifths of the enslaved population in each state would count for representation in Congress. This rule applied for assessing taxes on the states as well.

Other Compromises

The North and the South also had very different opinions on trade. The North thought Congress should have the power to regulate foreign trade and trade between the states. Southern delegates began to worry that Congress would tax exports. This would hurt the Southern economy, which depended upon exports of tobacco, rice, and other products. The South also thought that Congress might stop traders from bringing enslaved people. The South's agricultural economy relied heavily on this labor. The only way to settle these issues was through compromise.

Southern delegates agreed to allow Congress to regulate trade if the North agreed that Congress could not tax exports. Congress also could not ban the slave trade before 1808.

The delegates also compromised on the process of electing a president. Some thought that the people should elect the president. Others believed that this should be Congress's job. Finally, the delegates decided on an **Electoral College.** The College would consist of electors named by each state legislature. This group of electors would then select the president and vice president. The Electoral College continues today. However, voters in each state now choose the electors.

5. PRIORITIZING

Underline the sentences in the text that describe the four compromises the delegates made at the Constitutional Convention.

Now, rank the compromises according to how important you think each was in helping to create a new constitution. Explain your reasoning for the compromise you ranked as most important.

____
____
____
____
____
____
____
____
____
____
____
____
____
____

6. CONSTRUCTING AN ARGUMENT

Which side would you support, the Federalists or the Anti-Federalists? Write an argument for or against ratifying the Constitution. Provide evidence to support your argument.

Federalists and Anti-Federalists

After many months, the Constitution finally was ready to be ratified. The delegates had decided that each state would set up a ratifying convention to vote "yes" or "no." At least nine of the 13 states were required to ratify the Constitution. Only then would it become the supreme law of the land.

Who Were the Federalists?

Americans who supported the proposed Constitution were known as **Federalists.** This group wanted a government in which power is divided between the federal government and the states. Federal law, however, takes precedence, or is supreme, over state law. This system is called **federalism.**

Federalists argued that the United States had to have a strong national government to survive. A strong government could protect property rights and would solve the nation's problems at home. It could also defend U.S. interests in foreign countries.

Alexander Hamilton, James Madison, and John Jay led the Federalists in the fight for ratification. The three men wrote essays called *The Federalist Papers* to defend the Constitution.

Who Were the Anti-Federalists?

Anti-Federalists opposed the Constitution. They argued that the major problem with the Constitution was that it had no bill of rights. Therefore, individual freedoms were not protected. Some state conventions refused to ratify the Constitution because it did not have a bill of rights. Many supporters of the New Jersey Plan were Anti-Federalists.

VIEWPOINTS OF FEDERALISTS AND ANTI-FEDERALISTS	
Federalists	**Anti-Federalists**
A strong national government will: • protect property rights • solve the country's problems • defend the country's interests in foreign countries	A strong national government will: • destroy individual liberties won in the American Revolution • ignore the states' rights • favor the wealthy over common people

Launching a New Nation

The Federalists agreed to add a bill of rights to the Constitution. When nine of the 13 states had ratified the Constitution, it took effect. The four remaining states also ratified it. In June 1788, the 13 independent states became one nation, the United States of America.

REVIEW LESSON 2

1. Use the chart below to identify the compromises made during the creation of the United States Constitution.

	ISSUES	COMPROMISE
Great Compromise	• Small states wanted a one-house Congress with each state having one vote. • Large states wanted a state's population to determine representatives in each house.	
Three-Fifths Compromise	• Southern delegates wanted enslaved people counted in their population for representation. • North wanted enslaved people counted for taxes but not representation.	
Election of President	• Some delegates wanted Congress to elect the president. • Some delegates thought the people should elect the president.	
Trade	• South did not want Congress to tax exports or stop the trade of enslaved people. • North wanted Congress to regulate foreign trade and trade between the states.	

2. **RECOGNIZING RELATIONSHIPS** What makes the Constitution a document filled with compromises? Using the chart above, write an essay that explains how compromises ensured its creation. Write your essay on a separate sheet of paper.

LESSON 3 SUMMARY

The Structure of the Constitution

SS.7.C.1.6, SS.7.C.1.7, SS.7.C.3.3, SS.7.C.3.5

The Parts of the Constitution

The Constitution of the United States provides a plan of government for the country. It is the basic law of the United States. It establishes the three branches of the federal government and describes the powers of each branch. The Constitution also outlines our nation's basic ideals, including personal liberty and democracy.

The Constitution features three parts as shown below.

Preamble	This part tells the goals and purpose of the United States government.
Articles	This is the major part of the Constitution. It explains how the government is set up.
Amendments	There are 27 amendments. They are additions and changes.

The Preamble

The Preamble is just a single sentence, but it is a powerful one.

"We the People of the United States, in Order to form a more perfect Union, establish Justice, insure domestic Tranquility, provide for the common [defense], promote the general Welfare, and secure the Blessings of Liberty to ourselves and our Posterity, do ordain and establish this Constitution for the United States of America."

—Preamble of the U.S. Constitution

The words of the Preamble clearly indicate that the power of the government comes from the people. This one sentence includes six purposes of government:

1. To unite the states so they can act together for the good of all
2. To make sure that all citizens are treated equally
3. To provide order and keep citizens safe
4. To protect the country from attack
5. To help people live their lives in the best way possible
6. To guarantee that all present-day and future Americans have basic rights

1. INTERPRETING

In the original document, which phrase in the U.S. Constitution is written much larger than any other? What basic idea does the phrase represent?

______

______

______

______

______

______

2. DETERMINING CENTRAL IDEAS

Underline the phrase in the Preamble that you think is most important. Explain why you think that phrase was included.

______

______

______

______

______

______

______

______

______

______

Name ________________ Date ________________ Class ________________

THE ARTICLES OF THE CONSTITUTION
Article I: Outlines the powers of the legislative branch
Article II: Outlines the powers of the executive branch
Article III: Outlines the powers of the judicial branch
Article IV: Describes how the state and national governments work together
Article V: Tells the ways the Constitution can be changed
Article VI: Declares that the Constitution is the "supreme law"
Article VII: Describes how the Constitution was to be ratified

The Seven Articles

The Constitution contains seven articles, or sections. Article I provides details about the lawmaking powers of Congress, the legislative branch. Congress consists of the Senate and House of Representatives. Article I also tells the states how members of both houses of Congress are to be chosen. It then gives rules lawmakers must follow.

Article II describes the executive branch, which is the law-enforcing part of government. The executive branch is led by the president and vice president. Article II tells how these leaders will be elected and how they can be removed from office. It also lists presidential powers.

Article III relates to the judicial branch of government—the nation's courts. The judicial branch interprets laws and ensures that they are applied fairly. Article III establishes the Supreme Court and lower courts as determined by Congress. It lists the powers of federal courts and the cases the courts may hear.

Amending and Interpreting the Constitution

A change to the Constitution is called an amendment. Many amendments have been suggested during the nation's more than 200-year history. However, only 27 amendments have been approved in all that time. The first ten amendments, called the Bill of Rights, were added when the Constitution was first written.

There is an important reason for so few amendments. The Framers purposely made it difficult to change the supreme law of the land. They had spent much time balancing and fine-tuning the plan for government. Even small changes could have significant effect. The Framers wanted to make sure that most people supported any amendments.

3. DRAWING CONCLUSIONS

The powers of the legislative branch make up one article. What does this indicate about the importance of the legislative branch under the Constitution compared to its importance under the Articles of Confederation?

____

____

____

____

____

____

____

____

____

____

4. CREATING CHARTS

On a separate sheet of paper, make a graphic organizer that identifies the three branches of government and explains the function of each.

5. ANALYZING

Why do you think only two-thirds of the states are needed to propose an amendment compared to three-quarters of the states needed to ratify an amendment?

6. HYPOTHESIZING

What issues do you think are important enough for states to call a constitutional convention?

However, the Framers realized that over time changes would be needed. They had seen how difficult it was to change the form of government under the Articles of Confederation. Some adjustments to the structure of the government might be needed in the future. Changing social, political, and cultural ideas might bring about the need for amendments. For example, it took an amendment to free enslaved African Americans and to grant them the right to vote. The increasing demand for women's rights resulted in a constitutional amendment granting women the right to vote.

Formal and Informal Amendments

The Constitution outlines two steps to amending the Constitution: proposal and ratification. An amendment can be proposed in one of two ways:

- by an act of Congress (A vote of two-thirds of the members of both houses of Congress is required.)
- by a national convention called by Congress when requested by two-thirds of the state legislatures

Three-fourths of the states must ratify, or approve, any proposed amendment before it can become a law. There are two ways to do this. The most common way for states to ratify an amendment is through a vote by their state legislature. They may also organize a state convention to vote on the amendment. Only the Twenty-first Amendment has been ratified through state conventions.

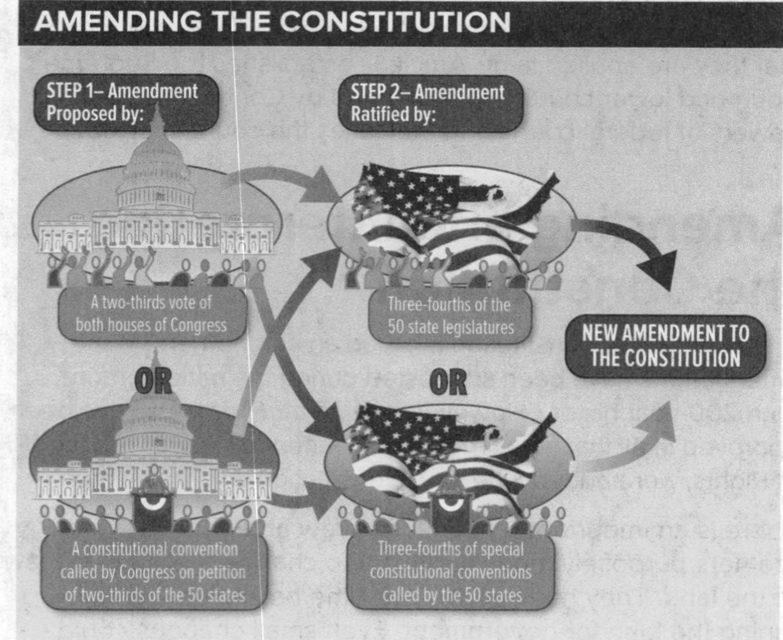
AMENDING THE CONSTITUTION
STEP 1– Amendment Proposed by:
STEP 2– Amendment Ratified by:
A two-thirds vote of both houses of Congress
OR
A constitutional convention called by Congress on petition of two-thirds of the 50 states
Three-fourths of the 50 state legislatures
OR
Three-fourths of special constitutional conventions called by the 50 states
NEW AMENDMENT TO THE CONSTITUTION

Amendments are formal, or official, changes to the Constitution. Sometimes, presidents have made informal, or unofficial, changes to it. The death of President William Henry Harrison brought up an unforeseen issue. As the Constitution allowed, the vice president assumed, or accepted, the role. Yet, it was not clear if he was just an acting president or a true president. In 1967, the Twenty-fifth Amendment made it clear that the vice president does become president in such a case.

7. SPECULATING

Because the Constitution permits Congress to use its implied powers, what modern topics is Congress able to address?

____

____

____

____

____

____

____

Interpreting the Constitution

The delegates writing the Constitution took deliberate action to prevent the abuse of power. For example, they separated the powers of government among the three branches. They also put into place a system of checks to make sure no single group gained too much power. Yet they also tried to keep the Constitution as simple as possible by leaving some matters open for future interpretation, or explanation. For example, Congress could use "implied powers" in addition to those specifically stated in the Constitution. An implied power is something that is understood and does not need to be stated.

REVIEW LESSON 3

1. Complete the chart below to explain the meaning of phrases included in the Preamble to the Constitution.

POLITICAL UNIT	DESCRIPTION
"form a more perfect Union"	
"establish Justice"	
"promote the general Welfare"	
"secure the Blessings of Liberty to ourselves and our Posterity"	

2. **DETERMINING CAUSE AND EFFECT** The Framers of the Constitution relied on past experiences to help them build a better government. Think about what you have already learned about American history. What role did historical events play in determining what the delegates included in the Constitution's Preamble?

LESSON 4 SUMMARY

Principles of the Constitution

SS.7.C.1.1, SS.7.C.1.7, SS.7.C.1.9, SS.7.C.3.4

Major Principles of Government

Like people, countries have principles, or basic beliefs that guide their governments. The U.S. Constitution outlines the most important principles of the United States. People have sacrificed their lives for these principles. The five important principles of the Constitution are described below. They are the foundation for our government.

FIVE BASIC PRINCIPLES OF GOVERNMENT
1. Popular sovereignty
2. Limited government and rule of law
3. Separation of powers
4. Checks and balances
5. Federalism

Popular Sovereignty

The Framers described the shape of the new government in Article IV of the Constitution. They called this new way of ruling a "Republican Form of Government." The delegates who wrote the Constitution used the term *republic* to mean a representative democracy. This is a government where the people have a voice in government. However, they do not have a direct say in every decision. Instead they elect representatives to make the decisions of government.

This kind of government is very different from a monarchy, which was common at the time of the American Revolution. In a monarchy, a king or queen inherits the right to rule and makes the decisions of government. The early English colonists had wanted a say in government. A republic was an ideal way for the new nation to be governed.

1. MAKING CONNECTIONS

How does a republican form of government relate to popular sovereignty?

______

______

______

______

______

______

2. DRAWING CONCLUSIONS

Underline the words that describe how citizens choose leaders in a representative democracy.

Why do you think the Framers of the Constitution wanted a representative democracy rather than direct democracy?

______

______

______

______

______

______

______

LESSON 4 SUMMARY, *continued*

The writers of the Constitution based many of their ideas and principles on the beliefs of Enlightenment thinkers. These thinkers had sought to find ways to apply laws of nature to government. For example, John Locke's idea of people having natural rights, such as the right to life, to freedom, and to own property, was important to the Framers. Locke's idea of a social contract, or agreement, between government and people also influenced the Framers. It called for government to protect people's rights.

The Framers wanted the American people to have sovereignty, or the right to rule. The idea that the power of government rests with the people is known as **popular sovereignty.** The Constitution addresses the idea of popular sovereignty from the beginning with the phrase *We the People*. Later, the Constitution describes elections, which is one way that citizens are able to influence government decisions. For example, citizens decide who will represent them in Congress. They also choose the president and vice president through the system called the Electoral College. Elected officials are always responsible to the people. Regular elections allow the people to replace representatives who do not serve them well.

Limited Government and the Rule of Law

The writers of the Constitution knew that they needed a stronger national government than the one specified in the Articles of Confederation. However, they did not want to make the government too powerful. That is why they included the principle of **limited government** in the Constitution. A limited government is one that can do only what the people allow. The federal government and the state governments are restricted in what they can and cannot do. The Constitution also limits the national government by the rule of law. Everyone, including government leaders, must follow the established law.

Together, limited government and rule of law ensure that no one person or group can take freedoms away from the American people. These two ideas have helped guide the development of the government of the United States since its beginnings.

3. CITING EVIDENCE

Underline in the text the words that offer a definition of the term *rule of law*.

Do you think the rule of law applies in your school? Explain, including an example of how it works.

____

____

____

____

____

____

____

____

4. REASONING

How were the Framers influenced by each of the Enlightenment ideas that they incorporated into the U.S. Constitution?

____

____

____

____

____

____

____

____

____

5. MAKING CONNECTIONS

What idea of Baron de Montesquieu inspired the writers of the Constitution? How did the Framers incorporate his idea?

6. HYPOTHESIZING

As a U.S. senator, describe three ways that you might have checked the power of the executive or the judicial branch during your term. Provide specific examples.

Separation of Powers

The Framers took another step to prevent the misuse of power. They divided the national government into three branches and assigned different jobs to each. The writers of the Constitution borrowed this idea from the French thinker Baron de Montesquieu. He believed that a division of power could protect people's freedoms. In fact, he suggested having a separate legislative, executive, and judicial branch. Today, this division of authority is known as **separation of powers.**

The Framers believed that this separation of powers would limit the ability of any one branch from becoming too powerful. People serving in each branch would work to prevent another branch from broadening its power.

Checks and Balances

The Framers used separation of powers as a way to prevent leaders from having unlimited authority. Yet they still worried that one of the three branches of government could try to exert too much power over the others. They needed to find a way to prevent this from happening. They came up with a plan referred to as **checks and balances.** This system allows each branch to "check," or limit, the power of the other branches in different ways. Look at the following chart to see the system of checks and balances in action.

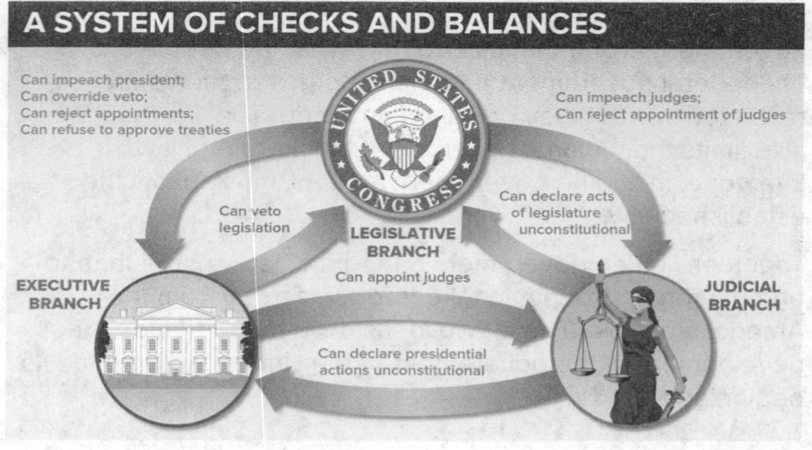
A SYSTEM OF CHECKS AND BALANCES
Can impeach president;
Can override veto;
Can reject appointments;
Can refuse to approve treaties
UNITED STATES CONGRESS
Can impeach judges;
Can reject appointment of judges
Can veto legislation
LEGISLATIVE BRANCH
Can declare acts of legislature unconstitutional
EXECUTIVE BRANCH
Can appoint judges
JUDICIAL BRANCH
Can declare presidential actions unconstitutional

Federalism

Federalism is the system of sharing power between the national and state governments. Each level of government has some authority over people at the same time. The national government holds some powers. Other powers are limited to the states. A few powers are shared by both.

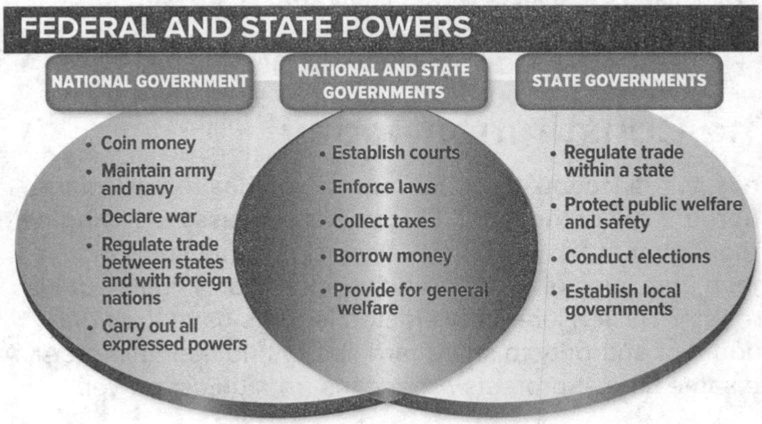

FEDERAL AND STATE POWERS

NATIONAL GOVERNMENT	NATIONAL AND STATE GOVERNMENTS	STATE GOVERNMENTS
• Coin money • Maintain army and navy • Declare war • Regulate trade between states and with foreign nations • Carry out all expressed powers	• Establish courts • Enforce laws • Collect taxes • Borrow money • Provide for general welfare	• Regulate trade within a state • Protect public welfare and safety • Conduct elections • Establish local governments

Three Types of Power

The writers of the Constitution divided the powers of government into three types. These are enumerated, reserved, and concurrent.

Enumerated powers are powers that are directly granted to the national government. This is easy to remember because the word *enumerated* means "listed." Another term for enumerated powers is *expressed powers*.

The Constitution specifically denies the national government some powers. These powers are called **reserved powers** because they are set aside, or reserved, for the states. Regulating trade within state borders and setting up schools are reserved powers.

Both the national and state governments have similar authority in some cases. These **concurrent powers** are powers that both levels of government are allowed to carry out. For example, both the national and state governments can collect taxes. They can also establish their own courts and prisons. In addition, both are permitted to borrow money.

ANALYZING IMAGES

7. EVALUATING

Why do you think only the national government is able to coin money?

____

____

____

____

8. GIVING EXAMPLES

Provide three specific examples of the powers of government at work in your state and in the nation.

State

____

____

____

____

____

____

National

____

____

____

____

____

____

9. PARAPHRASING

Describe the supremacy clause of the U.S. Constitution in your own words.

____

____

____

____

____

____

The Supremacy Clause

Sometimes national laws and a state law may conflict with one another. The delegates writing the Constitution were aware that this might happen and came up with a solution. They included the **supremacy clause** in Article VI. This statement says the Constitution and any law or treaty created by the national government is "the supreme law of the land." In other words, a state law cannot remain in effect if it contradicts a national law or the U.S. Constitution.

The Constitution Today

Since its ratification, the U.S. Constitution has remained the "supreme law of the land." Much of its success as a living plan of government lies with the five principles that support it. These principles give the government not only limits but also strength. This ensures that elected leaders have the right amount of authority to safeguard liberty and maintain order. At the same time, it protects Americans from unjust power.

REVIEW LESSON 4

1. Complete the chart below to describe ideas found in the U.S. Constitution. Include two to three details for each idea.

Separation of Powers
Checks and Balances
Federalism

2. **DIFFERENTIATING** On a separate sheet of paper, write an essay explaining how the principles of the separation of powers and checks and balances each limit the power of government. Why did the Framers use both methods?

Benchmark Skill Activities

DIRECTIONS: Write your answers on a separate piece of paper.

LAFS.68.WHST.2.4

1. GATHERING EVIDENCE

Use your FOLDABLES to write an essay.

Many historians have said that the U.S. Constitution is flexible. Read Clause 18 from Article I, Section 8:

> *"To make all Laws which shall be necessary and proper for carrying into Execution the foregoing Powers, and all other Powers vested by this Constitution in the Government of the United States, or in any Department or Officer thereof."*
>
> —Article I, Section 8, Clause 18 of the U.S. Constitution

In your essay, explain how this clause supports the idea that the Constitution is flexible. You may need to conduct outside research to find specific examples to support your position. Be sure to include references to specific Supreme Court cases you have learned about.

LAFS.68.RH.2.4

2. PARAPHRASING A PRIMARY SOURCE

Read the Preamble of the Constitution below. Paraphrase the Preamble in your own words. Then, explain what you think the purpose of the Preamble was and why it was included in the Constitution.

> *"We the People of the United States, in Order to form a more perfect Union, establish Justice, insure domestic Tranquility, provide for the common [defense], promote the general Welfare, and secure the Blessings of Liberty to ourselves and our Posterity, do ordain and establish this Constitution for the United States of America."*
>
> —U.S. Constitution

LAFS68.WHST.1.1; LAFS.68.WHST.1.2, LA.FS.68.WHST.2.4

3. WRITING AN EXPLANATORY LETTER

Write a letter to the editor of a newspaper in which you explain your reasons for supporting ratification of the Constitution or working against it. You may use a graphic organizer to help plan your letter. List your ideas either in support of ratification or against it. Think about ways the Constitution could be improved, and list them. Then, write your letter.

LAFS.68.RH.2.4; ELD.K12.ELL.SS.1

4. USING DEFINITIONS ACCURATELY

Write a paragraph that explains how the Constitution limits the powers of government through the principles of separation of powers and checks and balances. Use these terms in your paragraph: *legislative branch, executive branch, judicial branch, separation of powers,* and *checks and balances.*

LAFS.7.SL.1.1; LAFS.7.SL.1.2

5. CONSTRUCTING AN ARGUMENT

Imagine that you are a delegate to the Constitutional Convention. In a small group, decide who will be Federalists and who will be Anti-Federalists. Take time to research your viewpoint and take notes on the specific points you wish to emphasize. Then, gather in your group to take turns presenting your positions. Afterward, discuss your ideas as a group, ask questions of other group members, and respond to their questions. Before closing the discussion, provide time for anyone who has changed their position to explain their reasons for doing so.

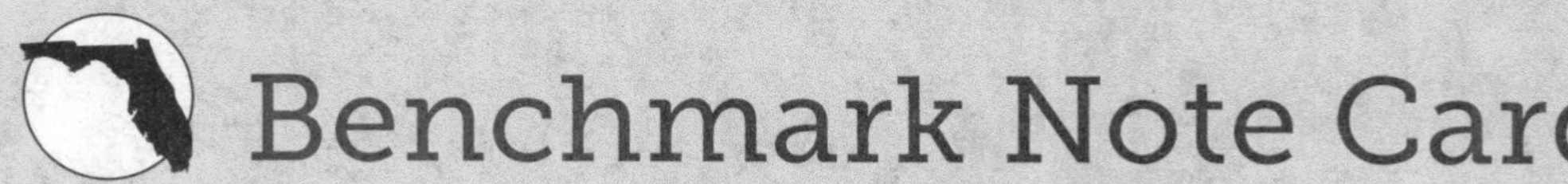

Benchmark Note Cards

DIRECTIONS: Use these note cards to help you prepare for the test.

SS.7.C.1.1 Recognize how Enlightenment ideas including Montesquieu's view of separation of power and John Locke's theories related to natural law and how Locke's social contract influenced the Framers.

ENLIGHTENMENT IDEAS AND THE CONSTITUTION

The Framers of the Constitution based many of their ideas about government on the beliefs of Enlightenment thinkers. These thinkers looked for ways to apply laws of nature to government. Enlightenment thinkers included the Baron de Montesquieu and John Locke.

Locke's ideas involved natural rights, such as the rights to life, to freedom, and to own property. The idea of dividing government into three branches and assigning different jobs to each branch came from Montesquieu. In his writings, Montesquieu suggested having a separate legislative, executive, and judicial branch. The Framers took this idea and created a legislative, an executive, and a judicial branch. This is known as separation of powers.

The Framers wanted the American people to have sovereignty, another idea of the Enlightenment. The Preamble begins with the phrase, *We the People*. With these three words, the Framers emphasized the idea of popular sovereignty.

SS.7.C.1.2 Trace the impact that the Magna Carta, English Bill of Rights, Mayflower Compact, and Thomas Paine's *Common Sense* had on colonists' views of government.

IMPACT OF HISTORICAL DOCUMENTS ON VIEWS OF GOVERNMENT

The Colonists' ideas about government were influenced by both English and colonial documents.

- Magna Carta—required the king to protect basic rights and limited his powers
- English Bill of Rights—listed the rights of citizens, including consent of the people, right to bear arms, right to a jury trial, and right to petition the monarch
- Mayflower Compact—created laws that were fair and equal and based on majority rule
- *Common Sense* by Thomas Paine—advocated for independence, the sovereignty of the people, a written constitution, and checks and balances

SS.7.C.1.5 Identify how the weaknesses of the Articles of Confederation led to the writing of the Constitution.

ARTICLES OF CONFEDERATION	• Was the first constitution of the United States, ratified in 1781 • Established a "league of friendships" among the states • The league had no single executive or governor • Created a one-house legislature, the Confederation Congress • Gave each state one vote in the legislature • Allowed states to keep their own powers and freedoms • National government did not have supremacy over the states • Stated that states would come together for issues dealing with defense and dealing with foreign countries

SS.7.C.1.5 Identify how the weaknesses of the Articles of Confederation led to the writing of the Constitution.

WEAKNESSES OF THE ARTICLES OF CONFEDERATION	The Articles of Confederation formed the first constitution of the United States, ratified in 1781. The Articles established a "league of friendships" among the states. Each state had one vote in the one-house legislature, the Confederation Congress. Congress could deal with defense and foreign countries. The Confederation Congress had limited powers. It could not pass a law unless nine states voted for it and changes to the Articles required approval of all states. The Congress could not enforce laws it passed. It also did not have the power to tax or regulate trade. The government lacked a governor or executive to lead the nation. The Articles also did not include a national court system. Shays's Rebellion showed that the government could not maintain law and order and that a stronger national government was needed.

CONSTITUTIONAL CONVENTION	• Delegates from 12 states met in Philadelphia to fix the Articles because the country needed a stronger plan of government. • Although the original plan had been to revise the Articles, the delegates agreed to start anew and write a new constitution.

SS.7.C.1.6 Interpret the intentions of the Preamble of the Constitution.

THE PREAMBLE OF THE CONSTITUTION	The Preamble is a powerful, single sentence. It states the goals and lists the six purposes of the U.S. government: • unite the states so they act together for the good of all • make sure that all citizens are treated equally • provide order and keep citizens safe • protect the country from attack • help people live their lives in the best way possible • guarantee the basic rights of all Americans

SS.7.C.1.7 Describe how the Constitution limits the powers of government through separation of powers and checks and balances.

LIMITING THE POWERS OF GOVERNMENT	• The Framers deliberately tried to prevent abuse of power. • They divided the national government into legislative, executive, and judicial branches and assigned different jobs to each. This is called separation of powers. • They put into place a system of checks and balances, which allows each branch to "check," or limit, the power of the other branches. • The Framers left some matters open for future interpretation as when they said that Congress could use "implied powers" in addition to those stated. • The Framers included the principle of limited government. This means that the government can do only what the people allow. Both the national government and state governments are restricted in what they can and cannot do.

SS.7.C.1.8 Explain the viewpoints of the Federalists and the Anti-Federalists regarding the ratification of the Constitution and inclusion of a bill of rights.

FEDERALISTS	Federalism is the system of government in which power is divided between the national government and the states. Federalists supported the Constitution. They argued that the nation had to have a strong government to survive. They believed that a strong government would protect property rights and defend the country's foreign interests. James Madison, Alexander Hamilton, and John Jay were leaders of the Federalists. James Madison presented the Virginia Plan at the Constitutional Convention. Many Federalists supported this plan, which proposed a president, courts, and a congress with two houses. Madison also proposed that each state's population should determine the number of representatives in each house of the congress. Madison, Hamilton, and Jay wrote *The Federalist Papers,* in support of ratification of the Constitution.

ANTI-FEDERALISTS	The Anti-Federalists opposed the Constitution. Many favored the New Jersey Plan, suggested by William Paterson of New Jersey. Paterson proposed a one-house congress. Each state would have one vote in congress. Paterson proposed a committee to carry out laws and said the congress could set taxes and control trade. Anti-Federalists argued that the new Constitution would destroy the liberties won in the revolution. They also believed that the new government might be so powerful that it would ignore states' rights. They believed the new Constitution would favor the wealthy over the common people. Finally, the Constitution had no bill of rights to protect individual rights. Anti-Federalists would not ratify it without the promise of a bill of rights.

HOW FEDERALISTS AND ANTI-FEDERALISTS COMPROMISED	• The Great Compromise dealt with some of the differences between Federalists and Anti-Federalists. Its ideas included:
	  o Congress would have two houses—a Senate and a House of Representatives.
	  o Each state would have two members in the Senate.
	  o The number of seats in the House would reflect the state's population.
	• The Three-Fifths Compromise solved the issue of counting the enslaved population for representation and taxation so that every five enslaved persons equaled three free persons.
	• Other compromises included that Congress would regulate foreign trade but it would not tax exports, would not ban slave trade before 1808, and that there would be an Electoral College to select a president and vice president.

SS.7.C.1.9 Define the rule of law and recognize its influence on the development of the American legal, political, and governmental systems.

THE RULE OF LAW	The Constitution limits the national government by the rule of law. Everyone, even a leader, must follow the established law. Rule of law ensures that no one person or group can take freedoms away from the American people.

SS.7.C.3.3 Illustrate the structure and function (three branches of government established in Articles I, II, and III with corresponding powers) of government in the United States as established in the Constitution.

ARTICLES I, II, AND III	Articles I, II, and II of the Constitution set up the three branches of government.
	• Article I outlines the powers of the legislative branch:
	  ◦ Explains that Congress—the Senate and House of Representatives—has all the lawmaking authority for the nation
	  ◦ Describes how members of both houses are chosen
	  ◦ Explains rules lawmakers must follow
	• Article II outlines the powers of the executive branch:
	  ◦ States that the executive branch will be led by the president and vice president
	  ◦ Tells how these leaders are elected
	  ◦ Explains how leaders can be removed from office
	  ◦ Lists presidential powers, including leading armed forces and making treaties with other nations
	• Article III outlines the powers of the judicial branch:
	  ◦ Explains that this branch interprets laws and sees that laws are applied fairly
	  ◦ Sets up a supreme court and lower courts as Congress determines
	  ◦ Lists powers of federal courts
	  ◦ Describes cases the courts may hear

SS.7.C.3.4 Identify the relationship and division of powers between the federal government and state governments.

FEDERALISM	Under federalism, the national government and the states share power. No one level of government has too much authority. The Constitution grants three types of power: • Enumerated powers, or expressed powers, are powers granted to the national government. Only the national government can make treaties with foreign nations. The national government alone has the power to declare war. • Reserved powers are those set aside for the states. These include regulating trade within state borders. They also include setting up schools within a state. • Concurrent powers are those given to both the national and state governments. Both states and the national government can collect taxes. They can both establish courts. They can both borrow money.

THE SUPREMACY CLAUSE	The supremacy clause in Article VI says that the Constitution and any law or treaty created by the national government is "the supreme Law of the land." In other words, a state law cannot stand if it contradicts a national law or the Constitution.

SS.7.C.3.5 Explain the Constitutional amendment process.

AMENDING THE CONSTITUTION	• Amendments are additions and changes to the Constitution.
	• There are only 27 amendments because it is difficult to change the Constitution.
	• Amendments to the Constitution can be proposed in one of two ways:
	  ○ by an act of Congress (A vote of two-thirds of the members of both houses of Congress is required.)
	  ○ by a national convention called by two-thirds of the state legislatures
	• Three-fourths of the states must approve any proposed amendment before it can become a law. This can be done through a vote by their state legislature or by a state convention.

SS.7.G.1.3 Interpret maps to identify geopolitical divisions and boundaries of places in North America.

THE NORTHWEST ORDINANCES	The Confederation Congress passed two ordinances, or laws, about the Old Northwest. This area included present-day Ohio, Indiana, Illinois, Michigan, Wisconsin, and part of Minnesota. These ordinances helped settle the Northwest Territory in an orderly way. • The Ordinance of 1785 set up a plan for surveying western lands and described how western lands were to be sold. • The Northwest Ordinance set up a government for the Northwest Territory, became a model to organize governments for other new territories, provided a plan for admitting new states, and stated that slavery and involuntary servitude would not be allowed in the territory.

SS.7.G.2.1 Locate major cultural landmarks that are emblematic of the United States.

INDEPENDENCE HALL AND THE LIBERTY BELL	The Liberty Bell and Independence Hall in Philadelphia, Pennsylvania, play a special role in the history of the United States. The Liberty Bell symbolizes liberty and freedom. It is a cultural and historical landmark because it called people to hear the reading of the Declaration of Independence. Independence Hall is the site where the Declaration of Independence was adopted and where the Constitutional Convention was held.

Chapter 5

VISUAL SUMMARY

DIRECTIONS: Complete the graphic organizer below.

The Articles of Confederation served as the first constitution for the United States. Because of the problems caused by the Articles, a Constitutional Convention was held. A new constitution, which we use today, was written in 1787 and took effect in 1788.

ARTICLES OF CONFEDERATION	CONSTITUTIONAL CONVENTION	UNITED STATES CONSTITUTION
Established weak central government and strong state governments	Headed by George Washington and held in Philadelphia	Created federal system that divided powers between national government and state governments
Set up "league of friendship" among states; each state kept its own powers and freedoms	Every state would have one vote regardless of number of delegates that represented that state	Became "the supreme Law of the land"
One-house congress that could conduct foreign affairs and maintain an army; could not	Simple majority would decide	Congress was able to issue taxes, regulate trade, declare war and raise an army, and pass laws to carry out its responsibilities.
No chief executive; rule by	Issues included:	Three branches of government set up to provide a system of checks and balances and separation of powers:
		Two-house Congress 1. Senate: 2. House of Representatives:
		Both the House and Senate must approve a bill for it to become law. President may approve or veto it.

USING PRIMARY SOURCES

DIRECTIONS: Write your answers on a separate sheet of paper.

INTERPRETING Below are two views about the Constitution. One was written by George Mason, and the other by James Madison. Determine who wrote each statement, and explain how you came to that conclusion. Then, summarize the two opinions about the Constitution. Use examples from each excerpt to support your position.

Document A

In the first place, it is to be remarked that, however small the republic may be, the representatives must be raised to a certain number, in order to guard [protect against] against the cabals [secret plots] of a few; and that, however large it may be, they must be limited to a certain number, in order to guard against the confusion of a multitude. . . .

In the next place, as each representative will be chosen by a greater number of citizens in the large than in the small republic, it will be more difficult for unworthy candidates to practice with success the vicious arts by which elections are too often carried and, the suffrages [votes] of the people being more free, will be more likely to center in men who possess the most attractive merit and the most diffusive [wide-spread] and established characters.

It must be confessed that in this, as in most other cases, there is a mean [average], on both sides of which inconveniences will be found to lie. By enlarging too much the number of electors, you render the representative too little acquainted with all their local circumstances and lesser interests; as by reducing it too much, you render him unduly [too much] attached to these and too little fit to comprehend and pursue great and national objects. The federal Constitution forms a happy combination in this respect; the great and aggregate [sum total] interests being referred to the national, the local, and particular to the state legislatures.

—Federalist Paper #10

Document B

There is no Declaration of Rights, and the laws of the general government being paramount [superior] to the laws and constitution of the several States, the Declarations of Rights in the separate States are no security. Nor are the people secured even in the enjoyment of the benefit of the common law.

In the House of Representatives there is not the substance but the shadow only of representation; which can never produce proper information in the legislature, or inspire confidence in the people; the laws will therefore be generally made by men little concerned in, and unacquainted with their effects and consequences.

The Senate have the power of altering all money bills, and of originating appropriations of money, and the salaries of the officers of their own appointment, in conjunction with the president of the United States . . .

The President of the United States has no Constitutional Council, a thing unknown in any safe and regular government. He will therefore be unsupported by proper information and advice, and will generally be directed by minions and favorites; or he will become a tool to the Senate—or a Council of State will grow out of the principal officers of the great departments; the worst and most dangerous of all ingredients for such a Council in a free country; From this fatal defect has arisen the improper power of the Senate in the appointment of public officers, and the alarming dependence and connection between that branch of the legislature and the supreme Executive.

—Objections to the Constitution

CIVICS 153

Chapter Practice Test

DIRECTIONS: Circle the best answer for each question.

SS.7.C.1.2 (Low)

Look at the diagram below. It relates to the influence of these historical documents on the colonists' views of government.

Mayflower Compact	Self-government
Magna Carta	Limited monarchy
English Bill of Rights	?

Which idea is missing from the diagram?

A Checks and balances

B Rights of citizens

C Economic freedom

D Written plan of government

SS.7.C.3.5 (High)

The excerpt below is part of a speech given by George Mason at the Constitutional Convention.

> *"There is no Declaration of Rights, and the laws of the general government being paramount to the laws and constitution of the several States, the Declarations of Rights in the separate States are no security. Nor are the people secured even in the enjoyment of the benefit of the common law."*
>
> —George Mason

Based on the excerpt, which action would George Mason want included in the Constitution?

A a way to amend the Constitution to include a bill of rights

B a way to amend the Constitution to protect the rights of government officials

C making the Constitution difficult to change to protect its integrity

D making the Constitution easy to change to allow for differences of opinion

3

SS.7.C.1.6 (Moderate)

Read the Preamble of the Constitution below.

> *"We the People of the United States, in Order to form a more perfect Union, establish Justice, insure domestic Tranquility, provide for the common [defense], promote the general Welfare, and secure the Blessings of Liberty to ourselves and our Posterity, do ordain and establish this Constitution for the United States of America."*
>
> —U.S. Constitution

Which phrase best indicates the Framers' intent that the Constitution should provide for peace throughout the United States?

A "to form a more perfect Union"

B "establish Justice"

C "insure domestic Tranquility"

D "promote the general Welfare"

4

SS.7.C.1.1 (Moderate)

What could be said about Montesquieu's ideas on separation of powers?

A They were based on traditional forms of government.

B They presented common British thinking of the time.

C They were based on ideas from the American colonies.

D They presented a forward-thinking way of governing.

5 **SS.7.C.1.5 (Moderate)**

How did the Constitution deal with a weakness of the Articles of Confederation?

A It created an executive branch to carry out the laws.

B It provided for a legislature to make the laws.

C It allowed each state to have sovereignty over its laws.

D It limited the powers of government through checks and balances.

---

6 **SS.7.C.3.4 (Moderate)**

Which statement accurately reflects the information in the diagram?

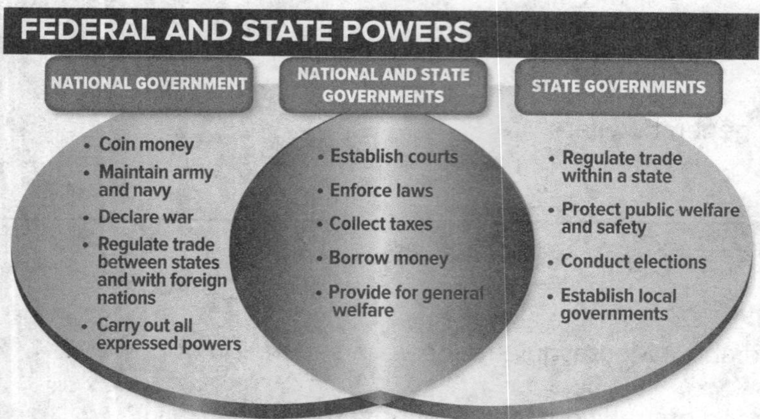
FEDERAL AND STATE POWERS
NATIONAL GOVERNMENT
NATIONAL AND STATE GOVERNMENTS
STATE GOVERNMENTS
• Coin money
• Maintain army and navy
• Declare war
• Regulate trade between states and with foreign nations
• Carry out all expressed powers
• Establish courts
• Enforce laws
• Collect taxes
• Borrow money
• Provide for general welfare
• Regulate trade within a state
• Protect public welfare and safety
• Conduct elections
• Establish local governments

A State governments can operate under expressed powers.

B Both levels of government get funding from taxes.

C State governments set rules about trade with other states.

D Both levels of government provide military protection.

7 **SS.7.C.1.7 (High)**

Read the excerpt below.

> *"If men were angels, no government would be necessary. If angels were to govern men, neither external nor internal controls on government would be necessary. In framing a government which is to be administered by men over men, the great difficulty lies in this: you must first enable the government to control the governed; and in the next place oblige it to control itself."*
>
> —James Madison, *Federalist* #52

To what principle of the Constitution does this excerpt best relate?

A states' rights

B popular sovereignty

C separation of powers

D establishment of a judicial branch

SS.7.C.1.9 (Moderate)

Impeachment proceedings were held against President Andrew Johnson, President Richard Nixon, and President Bill Clinton. Which part of the Constitution do these actions demonstrate?

A enumerated powers

B executive privilege

C supremacy clause

D the rule of law

SS.7.C.1.8 (Moderate)

Which statement best demonstrates the view of the Anti-Federalists regarding ratification of the Constitution?

A The national government should take precedence over state governments and be the "supreme Law of the land."

B The individual liberties of the people must be protected from abuses by the federal government.

C A strong national government will prevent another Shays's Rebellion from occurring.

D State government should have some powers, but they must not be in opposition to those of the national government.

SS.7.C.3.3 (High)

The chart below shows the articles of the Constitution dealing with the three branches of government.

Article I	Legislative branch
Article II	Executive branch
Article III	Judicial branch

Which article(s) of the Constitution would be involved if the president asked Congress to declare war on a foreign country?

A Article I

B Article II

C Articles I and II

D Articles I, II, and III

CHAPTER 6

The Bill of Rights

Chapter Overview

The first 10 amendments to the U.S. Constitution are called the Bill of Rights. These amendments identify rights that are considered fundamental to our way of life. In later years, these rights were expanded upon with more amendments that focused on specific groups in society, such as Africans Americans and women.

CHAPTER BENCHMARKS

SS.7.C.2.4 Evaluate rights contained in the Bill of Rights and other amendments to the Constitution.

SS.7.C.2.5 Distinguish how the Constitution safeguards and limits individual rights.

SS.7.C.2.6 Simulate the trial process and the role of juries in the administration of justice.

SS.7.C.2.10 Examine the impact of media, individuals, and interest groups on monitoring and influencing government.

SS.7.C.3.6 Evaluate Constitutional rights and their impact on individuals and society.

SS.7.C.3.7 Analyze the impact of the 13th, 14th, 15th, 19th, 24th, and 26th amendments on participation of minority groups in the American political process.

LAFS.68.RH.2.4 Determine the meaning of words and phrases as they are used in a text, including vocabulary specific to domains related to history/social studies.

LAFS.68.RH.2.5 Describe how a text presents information (e.g., sequentially, comparatively, causally).

WHAT I NEED TO KNOW

TERMS

- ☐ civil liberty
- ☐ free speech
- ☐ petition
- ☐ restriction
- ☐ accused
- ☐ probable cause
- ☐ search warrant
- ☐ indictment
- ☐ double jeopardy
- ☐ self-incrimination
- ☐ due process
- ☐ bail
- ☐ black codes
- ☐ suffrage
- ☐ poll tax

PEOPLE, PLACES, EVENTS

- ☐ grand jury
- ☐ militia
- ☐ Civil War

CHAPTER BENCHMARKS, *continued*

LAFS.68.WHST.2.4 Produce clear and coherent writing in which the development, organization, and style are appropriate to task, purpose, and audience.

LAFS.68.WHST.3.9 Draw evidence from informational texts to support analysis, reflection, and research.

LAFS.7.SL.1.1 Engage effectively in a range of collaborative discussions (one-on-one, in groups, and teacher-led) with diverse partners on grade 7 topics, texts, and issues, building on others' ideas and expressing their own clearly.

The Bill of Rights

Make this three-pocket Foldable® and label the pockets with the titles of the three lessons. Use quarter sheets of notebook paper or notecards as information cards. Number notecards to correspond to the lesson pocket in which they are sorted and stored. As you read the chapter, write terms, names, dates, and events relating to the Bill of Rights on the front of each notecard. On the back of each card, write notes regarding what is featured on the front. When possible, include a quick sketch to strengthen your recall.

Step 1
Place a legal-size piece of paper (8.5" x 14") lengthwise on your desk. Fold the bottom edge of the paper up 2 inches to create a flap.

Step 2
Fold the left and right sides of the paper to create three equal sections.

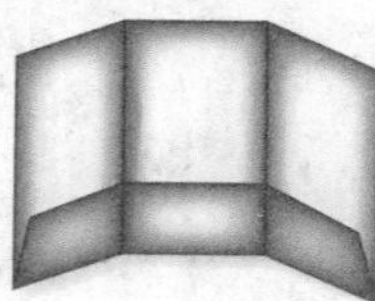

Step 3
Tape or staple the open right and left sides of the pockets.

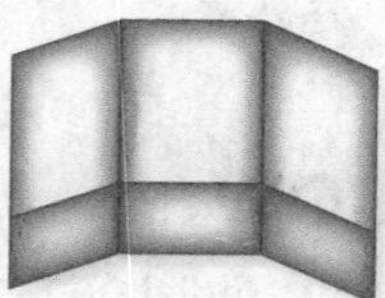

Step 4
Label the pockets and use notecards or cut notebook paper for notes.

LESSON 1 SUMMARY

The First Amendment

SS.7.C.2.4, SS.7.C.2.5, SS.7.C.2.10

Guaranteeing Civil Liberties

The Constitution guarantees that we have basic freedoms. We can think and act freely without fear. The government cannot interfere with our freedom or provide unfair legal treatment. These freedoms are our **civil liberties**. They are called civil liberties because they are connected with being a citizen.

The Bill of Rights protects many of these civil liberties. The Bill of Rights is the first 10 amendments to the Constitution. The First Amendment is especially important. It protects our freedom to believe as we choose and to express ourselves. This amendment includes five specific freedoms. These are freedom of religion, freedom of speech, freedom of the press, freedom of assembly, and freedom to petition the government.

Freedom of Religion

There are two ways that the First Amendment protects freedom of religion. The first way is called the establishment clause. It says that Congress cannot establish, or set up, any religion as the official religion of the United States. The First Amendment is the reason the United States does not have an official religion as Iran and Egypt do.

The First Amendment also protects how people express their religion. Americans have the right to practice their faith however they choose. This amendment prevents the government from making any laws that would stop people from worshipping the way they want. In some nations, such as the People's Republic of China, the government puts limits on some religions.

1. DRAWING CONCLUSIONS

According to the First Amendment, is prayer allowed in public schools? Explain.

2. PARAPHRASING

Restate Justice Fortas's statement in your own words.

______

3. REASONING

Do school newspapers have the right to criticize the principal and school board? Explain.

______

Freedom of Speech

In the United States, the First Amendment guarantees our right of **free speech**. We can state our opinions, in public or in private, without fear of being punished by the government.

Free speech includes what we say in speeches, meetings, and conversations. It also includes what is said on radio and television. The Supreme Court has decided that "speech" can mean more than just words. Its decision means that Internet messages, art, music, and even clothing are protected. Supreme Court Justice Abe Fortas addressed this issue in *Tinker* v. *Des Moines School District* when he stated: "It can hardly be argued that either students or teachers shed their constitutional rights to freedom of speech or expression at the schoolhouse gate."

Freedom of the Press

Freedom of the press prevents the government from censoring news reports. Censorship means banning printed materials or films because they have alarming or offensive ideas. Our government cannot stop the press from publishing or broadcasting information. In some other countries, reporters do not have this protection. Their government officials can remove what they do not approve of or even arrest reporters.

Freedom of the press means the media have the right to criticize the government. A free press is one way we can prevent the government from misusing its power.

The phrase "the press" used to mean only printed materials such as newspapers, magazines, and books. Today it has a broader meaning. It includes radio, television, and the Internet. Americans are able to hear many different views on public issues, all because of freedom of the press.

Freedom of Assembly

Because of the First Amendment, Americans have the right to come together in groups. We can assemble, or gather, together for any reason, but we must be peaceful. This right protects us in meetings, parades, and celebrations. The government cannot ban these activities. However, it can make rules about when and where they are held.

This right also includes the freedom of association. We have the right to create and join groups. Examples include political parties, labor unions, and clubs.

Peaceful protest marches are protected by freedom of assembly guaranteed in the First Amendment.

Freedom to Petition

The First Amendment grants Americans the right to send petitions to the government. A **petition** is a formal request for the government to do something. A petition can be a written document signed by hundreds or thousands of people. It can also be an e-mail or a letter from one person. A petition is another way that Americans can express themselves to the government.

Limits on Civil Liberties

The First Amendment gives several key rights to Americans. However, those rights do not allow citizens to do anything they please. Civil liberties must be used responsibly. When people exercise their rights, they should not interfere with the rights of others or the rights of the community. Doing so could cause conflict. The rights of the community to peace and safety often come first.

ANALYZING VISUALS

4. DESCRIBING

Which First Amendment rights are being exercised in this image?

____

____

____

____

____

____

____

5. GIVING EXAMPLES

Which of the following are examples of the freedom to petition?

- ☐ Calling your congressperson
- ☐ Writing a letter to the governor
- ☐ Attending a candidates' debate
- ☐ Voting for school board president
- ☐ Speaking at a town council meeting
- ☐ Posting a comment on a political blog
- ☐ Writing a letter to the editor of a newspaper

6. MAKING CONNECTIONS

What limits govern the gathering shown in the photograph on the previous page?

____

____

____

____

____

Restrictions, or limits, can be put on free speech rights. Those limits must be reasonable. Americans have the right to criticize public officials. Yet no one has the right to spread lies that will harm a person's reputation. If a person speaks such lies, it is a crime called slander. Lies that appear in print are considered a crime of libel.

There are other limits on free speech. For example, there is no right to speak or write in a way that directly leads to criminal acts. Also, people do not have the right to make a speech that will lead to efforts to overthrow the government by force. These kinds of speech are illegal.

REVIEW LESSON 1

1. Use the concept web below to identify and describe the rights protected by the First Amendment.

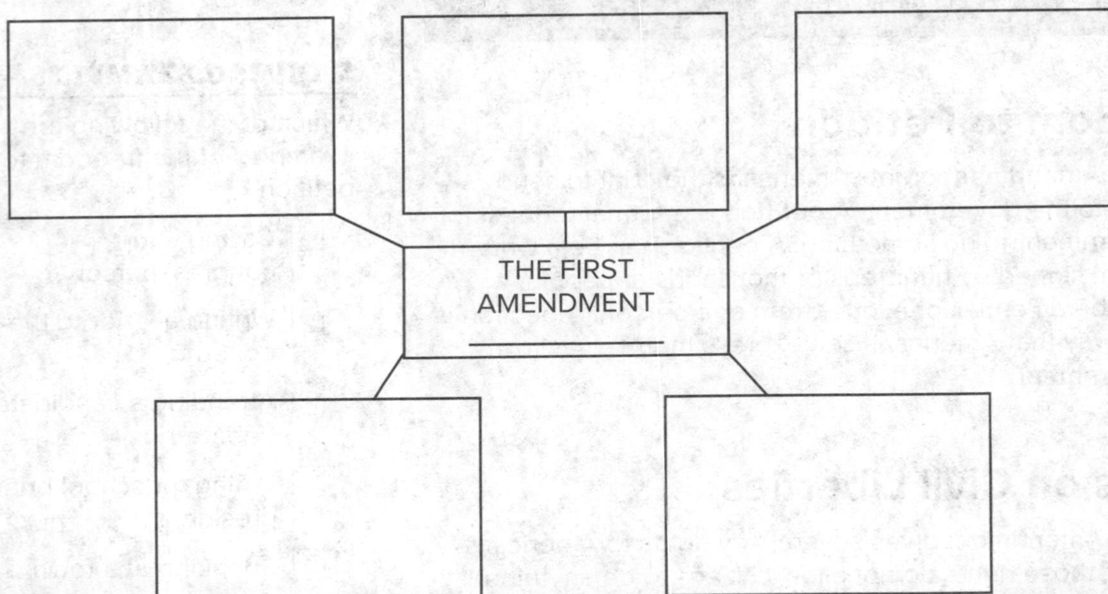

2. **EVALUATING** The First Amendment protects our most basic freedoms. These freedoms protect us as well as our democratic system of government. Which First Amendment right is most important for democracy to function effectively? On a separate piece of paper, write an essay that states and defends your opinion.

LESSON 2 SUMMARY

Other Bill of Rights Protections

SS.7.C.2.4, SS.7.C.2.5, SS.7.C.2.6, SS.7.C.3.6

Rights of the Accused

The Bill of Rights guarantees the right to fair treatment in the legal system. Four amendments protect the rights of the **accused,** people officially charged with crimes.

The Fourth Amendment

The Fourth Amendment protects Americans against "unreasonable searches and seizures." Law enforcement officials cannot search a person's property or take his or her possessions unless they follow certain requirements. First, they must have **probable cause,** or strong reasons to think that the person or property was involved in a crime. Then they must convince a judge to give them a **search warrant**. A search warrant allows officers to search a suspect's home, business, or other property. The search warrant allows officers to take items listed in the warrant as evidence.

The Fifth Amendment

The Fifth Amendment protects a person accused of a crime. First, it states that no one can be tried for a serious crime without an indictment by a grand jury. An **indictment** is a document formally charging someone with a crime. All the evidence against an accused person is presented to a grand jury. The grand jury issues an indictment if they think the accused might have committed the crime. A trial decides the accused's guilt or innocence.

The amendment also provides protections against **double jeopardy** and **self-incrimination,** the right to **due process,** and protection of property rights by limits on eminent domain.

1. SEQUENCING

Number the events in the order in which they lead to a trial.

_____ The accused is brought to trial.

_____ The judge issues a search warrant.

_____ The grand jury issues an indictment.

_____ The police search the accused's property.

_____ The evidence is presented to the grand jury.

_____ The police find probable cause against a suspect.

ANALYZING VISUALS

2. EXPLAINING

If a grand jury fails to issue formal charges, does the double jeopardy rule apply? Explain.

____

____

____

____

THE FIFTH AMENDMENT PROTECTIONS				
Grand Jury Indictment	**Double Jeopardy**	**Self-Incrimination**	**Due Process**	**Eminent Domain**
No one can be tried for a serious crime unless a grand jury has reviewed the evidence and issued formal charges against him or her.	People cannot be tried for a crime if they were previously found innocent of that crime.	People cannot be made to testify against themselves or forced to confess to a crime they did not commit.	Certain legal procedures must be followed. The laws governing those procedures must be reasonable.	The government has the right to take private property for public use, but they must pay a fair price for the property.

3. MAKING INFERENCES

A man is accused of a crime. Can his friends and family serve on the jury in his trial? Explain.

4. ASSESSING

A woman has been indicted for vandalism for putting graffiti on a wall. This is the second time she's been accused of this crime. She earns $12 an hour at her job. Which bail is a judge most likely to assign her?

Explain your reasoning.

$10

$5,000

$1,000,000

The Sixth Amendment

The Sixth Amendment guarantees additional rights of the accused. First, it requires that persons be clearly told the charges against them.

It also requires that the accused be allowed a trial by jury. However, the accused may choose a trial by a judge instead. A jury trial must be public and must take place quickly. It should be held in the community where the crime happened, if possible. The persons in the jury must act fairly.

The Sixth Amendment also gives the accused certain rights related to witnesses at the trial. The accused has the right to hear and question all witnesses against him or her and to call witnesses in his or her defense. Finally, the accused has the right to a lawyer. If the accused cannot afford a lawyer, the government must pay for one.

The Eighth Amendment

The Eighth Amendment establishes guidelines for before and after a trial. It provides pre-trial protection against excessive bail, or bail that is too high. **Bail** is a sum of money paid by the accused as a promise to appear at the trial in exchange for being let out of jail. When the accused attends the trial, the bail is returned. If the person fails to appear, he or she loses the money. A judge decides the bail amount by considering the crime committed, the accused person's record, and the likelihood that he or she will appear in court. If a judge thinks the accused will try to run away, bail will be denied.

The amendment's post-trial protections relate to punishment. When a person is found guilty of a crime, he or she cannot be punished too harshly or charged with fines that are too high.

The Eighth Amendment also forbids "cruel and unusual punishments." Many Americans agree that punishment should fit the crime committed. However, people disagree strongly about whether the death penalty is cruel and unusual punishment.

Additional Protections

The Founders remembered the British government's abuses of power that had led to the American Revolution. When they wrote the Bill of Rights, they wanted to prevent similar abuses by the American government.

The Second Amendment

The Second Amendment says, "A well regulated Militia being necessary to the security of a free State, the right of the people to keep and bear Arms shall not be infringed." To infringe a right is to put limits on it.

When the Founders wrote the Bill of Rights, a state's militia was made up of people who served as soldiers when needed. Today, people disagree on the meaning of the Second Amendment. Some think it means that states should allow members of state militias to carry firearms. Others believe that it gives all individuals the right to own firearms. However, the government can pass laws to control gun ownership. State and federal governments can establish rules for who can have a license to own firearms.

The Third Amendment

The British had required colonists to house and feed British soldiers. The Third Amendment bans that practice in peacetime. It says that in peacetime, soldiers may not stay in people's homes unless the homeowner gives permission.

The Seventh Amendment

The Seventh Amendment deals with civil cases. These are lawsuits that happen when people's rights are in conflict. This amendment guarantees the right to a jury trial in most civil cases heard in the federal courts. It applies to disagreements about property worth more than $20. Nearly all such disputes involve greater amounts. The Seventh Amendment also establishes the roles for judges and juries in civil cases. However, if both sides in a conflict agree, the trial can be held with a judge hearing the evidence and deciding the verdict.

ROLES IN CIVIL CASES	
Judge	**Jury**
• Solves issues of law, such as whether certain evidence is allowed	• Listens to evidence • Considers the facts presented • Reaches a verdict, or decision

5. SUMMARIZING

How has the meaning of the Second Amendment changed over time?

______

6. REASONING

Thea fails to repay Beth for a movie ticket. Beth files a civil lawsuit against Thea. Can Thea ask for a jury trial? Explain.

______

ANALYZING VISUALS

7. INFERRING

Why does the judge and not the jury solve issues of law in a civil case?

______

Name ______________________ Date ______________ Class __________

8. CONTRASTING

How do the Ninth and Tenth Amendments differ from the other Bill of Rights amendments?

The Ninth Amendment

The Ninth Amendment states that all other rights not explained in the Constitution are kept by the people. This amendment makes it clear that citizens have other rights besides those listed in the Constitution and that those rights may not be taken away.

The Tenth Amendment

The Tenth Amendment recognizes that the federal government's power is limited. It states that any powers the Constitution does not specifically give to the federal government belong to the states or the people. The purpose of this amendment is to prevent Congress and the president from becoming too strong. The government of the United States only has the powers the people give it.

REVIEW LESSON 2

1. Of the nine amendments covered in this lesson, select three that you consider most important. Use the chart to summarize the content of those three. Below each summary, add a sentence to explain why you chose the amendment.

AMENDMENT	RIGHTS AND PROTECTIONS

2. **PROBLEM-SOLVING** A lawyer goes to the jail to visit a man accused of stealing a car. The man tells the lawyer that he isn't sure why he was arrested, that the police searched his home and garage, that he cannot afford a lawyer, and that bail was set at $1 million. Write an essay that answers the question: What should the lawyer ask or discuss with the accused to find out whether any of his rights, under which amendments, have been violated?

LESSON 3 SUMMARY

Furthering Civil Liberties

SS.7.C.3.6, SS.7.C.3.7

Civil War Amendments

Since the ratification of the Bill of Rights, 17 other amendments have been added to the Constitution. Three from the mid-1800s are known as the Civil War Amendments.

Before 1865, many African Americans were enslaved. They had almost no rights. Northern states and southern states were divided over slavery. When 11 southern states tried to create a new nation, their action led to the Civil War. When the war ended in 1865, slavery also ended.

The Civil War Amendments were meant to protect the rights of African Americans. However, unfair treatment of African Americans continued. They were not able to fully enjoy these rights until the late 1900s.

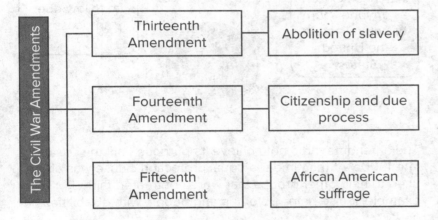

The Civil War Amendments	
Thirteenth Amendment	Abolition of slavery
Fourteenth Amendment	Citizenship and due process
Fifteenth Amendment	African American suffrage

The Thirteenth Amendment

The Thirteenth Amendment was approved in 1865. By outlawing slavery, it freed enslaved African Americans. It also banned forced labor, or forcing someone to work. However, forced labor is allowed as punishment for committing a crime. Prisoners can be made to work in prison. Judges can also order people who break the law to do community service.

1. REASONING

Why was it necessary to pass the Thirteenth Amendment before the other Civil War Amendments?

Name ______________________ Date ______________ Class __________

2. MAKING GENERALIZATIONS

What effect did the Fourteenth Amendment have on the power of the Bill of Rights?

____

____

____

____

____

____

____

____

____

____

3. PREDICTING CONSEQUENCES

What other ways might states find to deny African Americans the right to vote under the Fifteenth Amendment?

____

____

____

____

____

____

The Fourteenth Amendment

The Thirteenth Amendment did not guarantee full rights for African Americans. Many Southern states soon passed laws known as **black codes**. These laws limited the rights of African Americans related to jobs, property, and other areas.

The purpose of the Fourteenth Amendment was to protect African Americans from those laws. It had four main parts: citizenship, equal protection, interference, and due process.

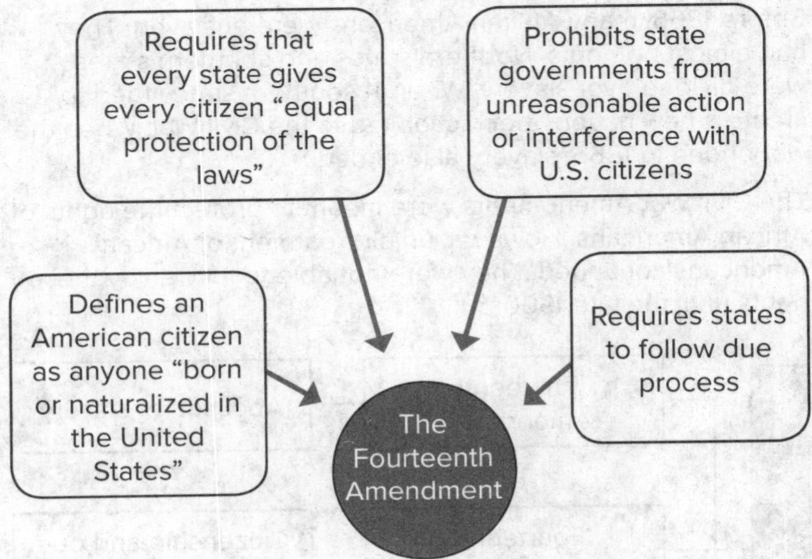
Requires that every state gives every citizen "equal protection of the laws"
Prohibits state governments from unreasonable action or interference with U.S. citizens
Defines an American citizen as anyone "born or naturalized in the United States"
Requires states to follow due process
The Fourteenth Amendment

The amendment did not achieve its purpose until the late 1900s. At that time the equal protection clause was also used to help other groups that were not treated fairly. For example, it also helped women and people with disabilities.

Originally, the Bill of Rights applied only to federal law. However, the courts have used the "due process" wording to extend the Bill of Rights to the states. In 1925, the Supreme Court ruled that states had to respect the rights of free speech and freedom of the press. Since then, the Supreme Court has applied other rights to the states. This means that all citizens in the country have the same basic rights no matter where they live.

The Fifteenth Amendment

The Fifteenth Amendment says that no state can use race as a reason to deny a person the right to vote. The amendment was meant to guarantee **suffrage**—the right to vote—for African American men. Still, many states found other ways to keep African Americans from voting.

Electoral Process and Voting Rights

During the 1900s, voting and elections changed due to new amendments. As a result, the people gained more power.

The Nineteenth Amendment

Under the Constitution, women did not have the right to vote. Many Americans believed women should not have the same rights as men. As early as the 1840s, women campaigned to gain suffrage. Finally in 1920, the Nineteenth Amendment was approved. It protected the right of women to vote in all national and state elections.

This cartoon illustrates how families might need to adjust on Election Day. Many opponents of women's suffrage believed that it threatened the natural order of society.

The Twenty-fourth Amendment

African American men had gained the right to vote with the Fifteenth Amendment. However, Southern states found ways to block them from voting. One way was by requiring a **poll tax,** a fee people had to pay in order to vote. The fee had to be paid for the current year and for previous unpaid years. Many African Americans and poor whites could not afford to pay the tax. For that reason, they could not vote.

ANALYZING VISUALS

4. IDENTIFYING POINT OF VIEW

Does the political cartoon support or oppose the Nineteenth Amendment? Explain your reasoning.

5. MAKING CONNECTIONS

With which Civil War Amendment is the Twenty-fourth Amendment most closely connected? How is it connected?

The Twenty-fourth Amendment made poll taxes illegal in national elections. Two years later, the Supreme Court banned poll taxes in state elections.

The Twenty-sixth Amendment

In the past, most states had set the minimum voting age at 21. In 1971, younger Americans were fighting in the Vietnam War. However, they could not vote for the leaders who sent them to war. That same year, the Twenty-sixth Amendment was approved. It established 18 as the minimum voting age.

REVIEW LESSON 3

1. Use the chart below to note the content of each amendment and its effect(s).

AMENDMENT	CONTENT	EFFECT
THIRTEENTH		
FOURTEENTH		
FIFTEENTH		
NINETEENTH		
TWENTY-FOURTH		
TWENTY-SIXTH		

2. **DETERMINING CAUSE AND EFFECT** Study your chart above. How did these amendments change American democracy? On a separate sheet of paper, write an essay that answers the question and incorporates details from your chart.

Benchmark Skill Activities

DIRECTIONS: Write your answers on a separate piece of paper.

LAFS.68.WHST.2.4

1. EVALUATING

Use your FOLDABLES® to write an essay.

The U.S. National Archives considers the Bill of Rights to be one of the nation's Charters of Freedom. A charter is a contract. In what ways is the Bill of Rights a charter or contract? How do the other civil liberties amendments relate to this contract? Explain.

LAFS.68.RH.2.4

2. DETERMINING WORD MEANINGS

Read the excerpt below from the Sixth Amendment. Then write a definition for each of the underlined words. Use context clues and your prior knowledge of the amendment to help you determine their meaning.

> "In all criminal prosecutions, the accused shall enjoy the right to a speedy and public trial, by an impartial jury . . . ; to be confronted with the witnesses against him; to have compulsory process for obtaining witnesses in his favor, and to have the Assistance of Counsel for his defence."
>
> —U.S. Constitution, Sixth Amendment

LAFS.7.SL.1.1

3. ASSESSING

The Florida Constitution specifically protects the right to privacy, but privacy is not mentioned anywhere in the Bill of Rights or other amendments to the U.S. Constitution. Should the U.S. Constitution be amended to include the guarantee of a right to privacy? Why or why not?

Discuss the question with your classmates. Use details from your reading in this chapter and from your own knowledge and experiences to support your opinion.

LAFS.68.RH.2.5

4. ANALYZING INFORMATION

Analyze the organization of information in this chapter. How were the amendments grouped together? Would the chapter have been more effective or less effective if the amendments had been presented in numerical order? Explain.

LAFS.68.WHST.3.9

5. REFLECTING

Write an essay or a journal entry that explains which amendment is most important to you and your life. Why is that amendment so important to you?

Benchmark Note Cards

DIRECTIONS: Use these note cards to help you prepare for the test.

SS.7.C.2.4 Evaluate rights contained in the Bill of Rights and other amendments to the Constitution.

THE BILL OF RIGHTS	**Civil Liberties** • The First Amendment (freedoms of religion, speech, press, assembly, and petition) **Rights of the Accused** • The Fourth Amendment (no unreasonable searches and seizures) • The Fifth Amendment (grand jury indictment for serious crimes, protection against double jeopardy, protection against self-incrimination, right to due process, limits on eminent domain) • The Sixth Amendment (right to be informed of charges, right to a speedy and public trial by jury, the right to a fair jury, the right to a lawyer, the right to confront and call witnesses) • The Eighth Amendment (protections against excessive bail, high fines, harsh punishment, and cruel and unusual punishments) **Other Protections** • The Second Amendment (right to bear arms) • The Third Amendment (no housing soldiers in peacetime without permission) • The Seventh Amendment (right to a jury trial in civil cases, separate roles for judge and jury in civil cases) • The Ninth Amendment (rights not specified in the Constitution belong to the people) • The Tenth Amendment (powers not specifically given to the federal government in the Constitution belong to the states or the people)

OTHER AMENDMENTS TO THE CONSTITUTION	**Civil War Amendments** • The Thirteenth Amendment (made slavery illegal) • The Fourteenth Amendment (defined citizenship, guaranteed equal protection of the laws, prohibited state interference with citizens, required states to follow due process) • The Fifteenth Amendment (granted suffrage to African American men) **Electoral Process and Voting Rights** • The Nineteenth Amendment (granted suffrage to women) • The Twenty-fourth Amendment (prohibited poll taxes in national elections) • The Twenty-sixth Amendment (lowered minimum voting age to 18)

SS.7.C.2.5 Distinguish how the Constitution safeguards and limits individual rights.

INDIVIDUAL RIGHTS	The Bill of Rights protects individual rights, such as freedom of speech and freedom of assembly, but the exercise of those rights cannot infringe upon the rights of others or the rights of the community. For example, the press can criticize government officials but it cannot spread lies about the officials. People can express their opinions but they cannot encourage others to commit violent acts.

SS.7.C.2.6 Simulate the trial process and the role of juries in the administration of justice.

THE TRIAL PROCESS	• The accused must be informed of the charges against him or her. • The accused chooses trial by jury or trial by judge. • The judge sets bail. • During the trial, the accused or the lawyer of the accused questions and calls witnesses. • If the accused is convicted, the judge issues a sentence, but it cannot be excessively harsh, cruel, or unusual. It might include a sentence of forced labor.

THE ROLE OF JURIES	• Jurors must be fair. • In civil cases, jurors listen to the evidence, consider the facts, and reach a verdict.

SS.7.C.2.10 Examine the impact of media, individuals, and interest groups on monitoring and influencing government.

MONITORING AND INFLUENCING GOVERNMENT	• Freedom of the press allows the media to act as a government watchdog and call out any abuses of power. • Freedoms of speech, assembly, and petition help make the government more responsive to the will of the people.

SS.7.C.3.6 Evaluate Constitutional rights and their impact on individuals and society.

THE IMPACT OF CONSTITUTIONAL RIGHTS	• Constitutional rights place limits on the power of government. • Constitutional rights guarantee fair treatment and protection against government abuses.

SS.7.C.3.7 Analyze the impact of the 13th, 14th, 15th, 19th, 24th, and 26th amendments on participation of minority groups in the American political process.

THE IMPACT OF THE 13TH, 14TH, 15TH, 19TH, 24TH, AND 26TH AMENDMENTS	• The 13th, 14th, 15th, and 24th Amendments helped encourage the participation of African Americans in the American political process by giving them freedom, recognizing their citizenship, granting suffrage, and eliminating the poll tax that prevented many from voting. • The 19th Amendment gave women the right and means to participate in the political process by granting them suffrage. • The 26th Amendment increased the number of eligible voters by lowering the minimum voting age from 21 to 18.

Chapter 6

VISUAL SUMMARY

DIRECTIONS: Complete the graphic organizer below.

THE BILL OF RIGHTS

CIVIL LIBERTIES

1st Amendment Freedoms

★ Speech

★ ______

★ ______

★ ______

★ ______

Limits

★ ______

★ ______

RIGHTS OF THE ACCUSED

★ 4th—No unreasonable searches and seizures.

★ 5th— ______

★ 6th— ______

★ 8th— ______

OTHER PROTECTIONS

★ 2nd— ______

★ 3rd— Soldiers may not stay in a person's home without permission.

★ 9th— ______

★ 10th— ______

FURTHER CIVIL LIBERTIES

CIVIL WAR AMENDMENTS

★ 13th—Ended slavery

★ 14th—Defined citizenship

______

★ 15th— ______

VOTING RIGHTS AND ELECTORAL PROCESS

★ 19th— ______

★ 24th— ______

★ 26th— ______

USING PRIMARY SOURCES

ANALYZE PRIMARY SOURCES Below is a selection from a speech by President Ronald Reagan to citizens of the Soviet Union in 1988. He spoke about the rights and freedoms enjoyed by U.S. citizens. Read the excerpt, and then answer the questions.

> *We Americans make no secret of our belief in freedom. In fact, it's something of a national pastime. Every 4 years the American people choose a new President, . . . But freedom doesn't begin or end with elections.*
>
> *Go to any American town, to take just an example, and you'll see dozens of churches, representing many different beliefs—in many places, synagogues and mosques—and you'll see families of every conceivable nationality worshiping together. Go into any schoolroom, and there you will see children being taught the Declaration of Independence, that they are endowed by their Creator with certain unalienable rights—among them life, liberty, and the pursuit of happiness—that no government can justly deny; the guarantees in their Constitution for freedom of speech, freedom of assembly, and freedom of religion. Go into any courtroom, and there will preside an independent judge, beholden [indebted] to no government power. There every defendant has the right to a trial by a jury of his peers, usually 12 men and women—common citizens; they are the ones, the only ones, who weigh the evidence and decide on guilt or innocence. In that court, the accused is innocent until proven guilty, and the word of a policeman or any official has no greater legal standing than the word of the accused. Go to any university campus, and there you'll find an open, sometimes heated discussion of the problems in American society and what can be done to correct them. Turn on the television, and you'll see the legislature conducting the business of government right there before the camera, debating and voting on the legislation that will become the law of the land. March in any demonstration, and there are many of them; the people's right of assembly is guaranteed in the Constitution and protected by the police. Go into any union hall, where the members know their right to strike is protected by law. . . .*
>
> *But freedom is more even than this. Freedom is the right to question and change the established way of doing things.*
>
> —President Ronald Reagan, speech at Moscow State University, 1988

1. ANALYZING PRIMARY SOURCES Which amendments does Reagan refer to in his speech? What rights are mentioned that are not included in the Bill of Rights?

2. HYPOTHESIZING Reagan gave this speech in the USSR, where civil liberties were not recognized. What might have been his purpose for giving this speech?

Chapter Practice Test

DIRECTIONS: Circle the best answer for each question.

1 **SS.7.C.3.6, SS.7.C.3.7 (High)**

How does this photo illustrate the effects of later amendments to the Constitution?

A It shows people paying a poll tax, which Southern states instituted in response to the Fifteenth Amendment.

B It shows poor people voting, which they could not have done before the Twenty-fourth Amendment repealed the poll tax.

C It shows women, an African American, and a young person voting, which would not have been possible without the Fifteenth, Nineteenth, and Twenty-sixth Amendments.

D It shows women and African Americans receiving due process and equal protection of the laws in a state election, which were guaranteed in the Fourteenth Amendment.

2 **SS.7.C.2.10, SS.7.C.3.6 (High)**

Thomas Jefferson, the third president of the United States, once made a statement about the press. He said he would choose newspapers without a government over a government without newspapers. With which of the following statements would Jefferson most likely agree?

A Freedom of the press is a basic and fundamental right.

B A government cannot function in a society without media.

C Freedom of the press is more important than freedom of speech.

D A government must be able to control the media to control the country.

3 **SS.7.C.2.5 (Moderate)**

In this cartoon, titled "Church and State—No Union Upon Any Terms," members of various faiths appeal for the support of the woman who represents the U.S. government. Which First Amendment principle is illustrated by this cartoon?

A the right to freedom of worship

B the right to assemble in protest

C the prohibition against censorship of the media

D the prohibition against establishing an official religion

SS.7.C.2.4 (Moderate)

Which First Amendment right is being exercised by the people in this photograph?

A freedom of religion

B freedom of the press

C freedom of assembly

D freedom to petition the government

SS.7.C.2.6 (Moderate)

Mark was arrested for a crime. The evidence against him has been presented to the grand jury, and he was indicted. A judge has informed Mark of the charges against him.

According to the Eighth Amendment, what should happen next?

A The judge sets reasonable bail.

B Mark calls witnesses in his defense.

C Mark questions the witnesses against him.

D The judge sentences Mark with an appropriate punishment.

SS.7.C.2.4, SS.7.C.2.5 (Moderate)

Which scenario violates the rights of the accused as spelled out in the Bill of Rights?

A A city uses eminent domain to buy a house.

B A suspect is jailed indefinitely without a trial.

C The accused waives his or her right to a jury trial.

D The accused does not testify on his or her own behalf.

SS.7.C.2.10 (High)

Which scenario would most likely result if the Bill of Rights did not protect freedom of the press?

A Citizens would be unable to express their opinions of government policies.

B Media could use their power to shape and influence government elections.

C Media could slander or libel government officials without fear of punishment.

D Citizens would have access only to the information that the government wants them to have.

SS.7.C.2.4, SS.7.C.2.5 (Moderate)

President Thomas Jefferson once referred to the establishment clause of the First Amendment as a "wall of separation between church and state."

How does the establishment clause create this wall?

A It prevents the government from setting up a state or official religion.

B It guarantees people the right to form and join religious organizations.

C It guarantees people the right to worship in ways of their own choosing.

D It prevents the government from censoring religious publications.

SS.7.C.3.7 (Moderate)

> *The right of citizens of the United States to vote shall not be denied or abridged by the United States or by any state on account of race, color, or previous condition of servitude.*
>
> —Fifteenth Amendment to the United States Constitution

Which statement suggests the Fifteenth Amendment's purpose was not initially fulfilled?

A Many African American men were prevented from voting through the use of poll tax laws.

B African American women did not gain suffrage until passage of the Nineteenth Amendment.

C African American teenagers did not gain suffrage until passage of the Twenty-sixth Amendment.

D Many Southern states restricted the rights of African Americans by passing laws called black codes.

SS.7.C.3.6 (High)

In this letter, Thomas Jefferson talks about the separation of church and state.

> *Believing with you that religion is a matter which lies solely between Man & his God, that he owes account to none other for his faith or his worship, that the legitimate powers of government reach actions only, & not opinions, I contemplate with sovereign reverence that act of the whole American people which declared that their legislature should "make no law respecting an establishment of religion, or prohibiting the free exercise thereof," thus building a wall of separation between Church & State.*
>
> —President Thomas Jefferson,
> Letter to the Danbury Baptists, January 1, 1802

Which right, besides freedom of religion, does he refer to as a basis for separation of church and state?

A freedom of assembly

B freedom to petition the government

C freedom of speech

D freedom to exercise civil liberties

CHAPTER 7
The Legislative Branch

Chapter Overview

Congress is the lawmaking, or legislative, branch of the federal government. It makes the federal laws that affect all Americans. Congress is made up of the Senate and the House of Representatives. The Framers of the Constitution gave Congress many powers. However, the Framers also placed limits on those powers.

The work of Congress is important because its members have the responsibility of serving their constituents and the nation as a whole. Members of Congress perform different tasks to get their job completed. The process they must follow to make laws is complex.

CHAPTER BENCHMARKS

SS.7.C.1.7 Describe how the Constitution limits the powers of government through separation of powers and checks and balances.

SS.7.C.2.10 Examine the impact of media, individuals, and interest groups on monitoring and influencing government.

SS.7.C.3.3 Illustrate the structure and function (three branches of government established in Articles I, II, and III with corresponding powers) of government in the United States as established in the Constitution.

SS.7.C.3.8 Analyze the structure, functions, and processes of the legislative, executive, and judicial branches.

SS.7.C.3.9 Illustrate the law making process at the local, state, and federal levels.

SS.7.G.4.2 Use maps and other geographic tools to examine the importance of demographics within political divisions of the United States.

LAFS.68.RH.1.1 Cite specific textual evidence to support analysis of primary and secondary sources.

LAFS.68.RH.1.2 Determine the central ideas or information of a primary or secondary source; provide an accurate summary of the source distinct from prior knowledge or opinions.

WHAT I NEED TO KNOW

TERMS

- ☐ Senate
- ☐ House of Representatives
- ☐ expressed powers
- ☐ enumerated powers
- ☐ implied powers
- ☐ elastic clause
- ☐ nonlegislative powers
- ☐ impeach
- ☐ lobbyist
- ☐ special-interest group
- ☐ joint resolution
- ☐ rider
- ☐ filibuster
- ☐ cloture
- ☐ pocket veto

CHAPTER 7

The Legislative Branch

CHAPTER BENCHMARKS, *continued*

LAFS.68.RH.1.3 Identify key steps in a text's description of a process related to history/social studies (e.g., how a bill becomes law, how interest rates are raised or lowered).

LAFS.68.RH.2.4 Determine the meaning of words and phrases as they are used in a text, including vocabulary specific to domains related to history/social studies.

LAFS.68.RH.3.7 Integrate visual information (e.g., in charts, graphs, photographs, videos, or maps) with other information in print and digital texts.

LAFS.68.WHST.1.1 Write arguments focused on discipline-specific content.

LAFS.68.WHST.1.2 Write informative/explanatory texts, including the narration of historical events, scientific procedures/experiments, or technical processes.

LAFS.68.WHST.2.4 Produce clear and coherent writing in which the development, organization, and style are appropriate to task, purpose, and audience.

LAFS.68.WHST.2.6 Use technology, including the Internet, to produce and publish writing and present the relationships between information and ideas clearly and efficiently.

LAFS.68.WHST.3.9 Draw evidence from informational texts to support analysis, reflection, and research.

LAFS.7.SL.1.2 Analyze the main ideas and supporting details presented in diverse media and formats (e.g., visually, quantitatively, orally) and explain how the ideas clarify a topic, text, or issue under study.

MAFS.K12.MP.5.1 Use appropriate tools strategically.

The Legislative Branch

Create the Foldable® below and write the chapter title on the cover tab. Label four of the tabs with the lesson titles. Label the fifth tab Current Congressional Issues. Under the appropriate tabs, identify three or more important ideas presented in each lesson. Focus on concepts that you do not know but that you need to know. On the fifth section, identify, research, and summarize one or more critical issues currently being debated in Congress. How do you think it will be decided?

Step 1
Use three sheets of notebook paper.

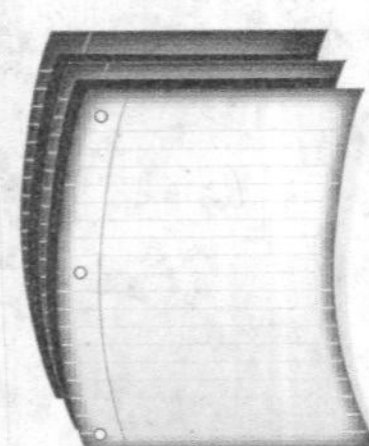

Step 2
Stack the three sheets of paper but align them so the middle sheet is about an inch below the bottom sheet, and the top sheet is about an inch below the middle sheet.

Step 3
Fold the bottom part of the stack up to create five equal tabs. Staple at the bottom and label as directed.

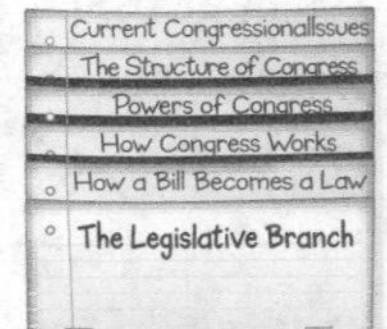

LESSON 1 SUMMARY

Structure of Congress

SS.7.C.3.3, SS.7.C.3.8, SS.7.G.4.2

The Two Houses of Congress

Congress is the legislative, or lawmaking, branch of the government of the United States. Congress contains two houses: the Senate and the House of Representatives. Both houses have their own structure, rules, and procedures, or ways of conducting business.

The Framers of the Constitution knew that a separate legislative branch was necessary. However, there was much debate about how Congress would function. Delegates from smaller states wanted equal representation. Delegates from larger states thought representation should be based on a state's population. This would give larger states more lawmaking power.

The two sides compromised. The U.S. Congress was created as a bicameral, or two-part, body. Every state sends two representatives to the **Senate.** This means that every state has equal representation there. In contrast, the number of members for each state in the **House of Representatives** is based on its population.

The Framers purposely addressed the structure and function of the legislative branch first. They did this to stress the importance of Congress. Article I of the Constitution outlines the responsibilities, duties, and processes of this branch of government.

Congress's main responsibility is to make laws for the entire nation. Each year, 100 elected senators and 435 elected representatives meet in Washington, D.C., to serve their states and the nation.

1. CREATING CHARTS

Fill in the chart to show the structure of the lawmaking branch of the U.S. government.

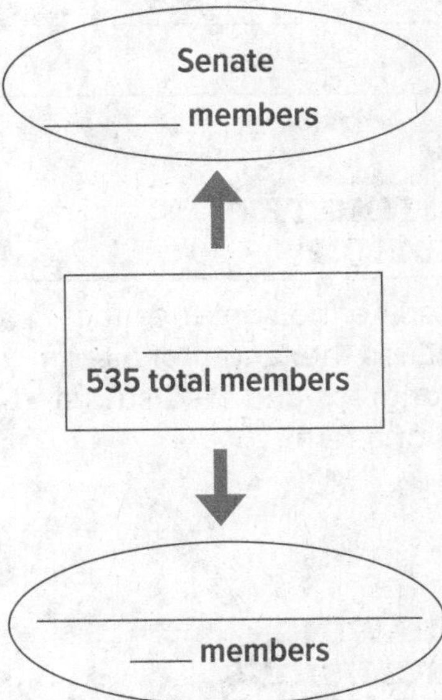

ANALYZING VISUALS

2. DRAWING CONCLUSIONS

Why might the Senate and the House of Representatives meet in the same building?

3. CITING TEXT EVIDENCE

Underline the sentence that identifies the length of a term of Congress and the usual start date of a term.

4. DRAWING CONCLUSIONS

Why might someone say that every session of Congress will be different?

Members of Congress meet in the U.S. Capitol building in the nation's capital city of Washington, D.C. The Senate and the House of Representatives each has its own meeting room where they discuss and vote on proposed laws.

Terms and Sessions

Congressional terms last for two years usually beginning on January 3 of an odd-number year. Each term of Congress is numbered. For example, the 2015–2016 term was the 114th Congress. Congressional terms are divided into two sessions, or meetings, with one held during each year of the two-year term. A session usually runs from January through November or December. Sometimes the Senate and House meet together in special joint sessions. These may take place in times of crisis or simply to hear the president give a speech.

The House of Representatives

The 435 members of the House of Representatives are elected for two-year terms. The number of representatives for each state is determined in a certain way. Every 10 years, the Census Bureau takes a census, or a count of the population. The number of representatives for each state increases or decreases based on the size of its population.

LESSON 1 SUMMARY, *continued*

Each state is divided into congressional districts. The boundaries for these districts are determined by the state legislatures. Districts must be divided so that each contains about the same number of people, or constituents. Voters in each district elect their representative for the House.

Congressional Apportionment

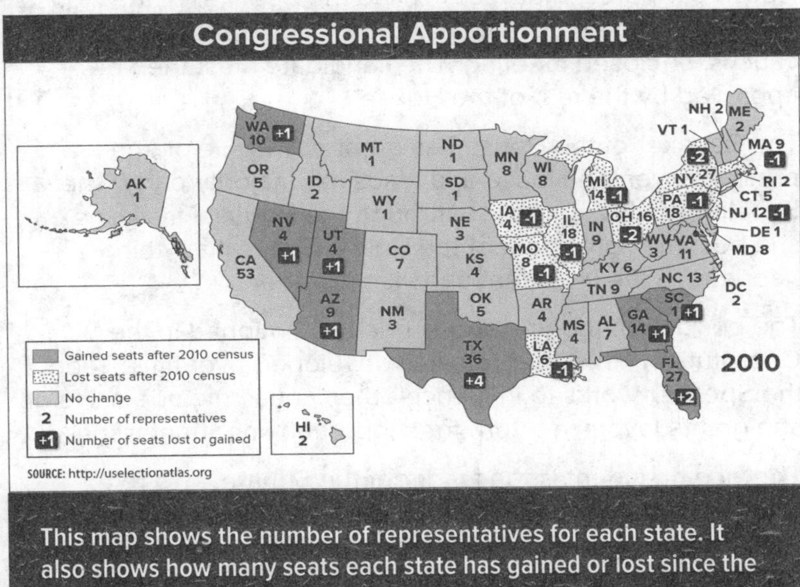

This map shows the number of representatives for each state. It also shows how many seats each state has gained or lost since the previous census.

ANALYZING MAPS

5. Which parts of the country gained representatives? Where were representatives lost? How might these changes affect the states' influence in Congress?

____

____

____

____

____

____

____

____

The Senate

Unlike representatives, the two senators from each state represent their entire state. Senators serve six-year terms, but not all senators are elected at the same time. No more than one-third of the senators run for reelection at any one time. This staggering of elections means that the Senate will not experience drastic changes following an election.

Sometimes a senator might not be able to complete his or her term. State law determines how a senator is replaced. In most states, the governor appoints a temporary replacement until the next scheduled election.

6. MAKING CONNECTIONS

Why is the election of senators held every six years, but the election cycle for representatives is only two years?

____

____

____

____

____

____

____

____

____

Congressional Leadership

Both political parties are represented in both houses of Congress. The majority party is the party to which more than half of the members in a house belong. The other party is the minority party. At the start of each new Congress, each party's members in each house choose the party's leader who will direct its activities. In this way a majority leader and a minority leader are selected.

7. COMPARING AND CONTRASTING

How are the leadership structures of the House and the Senate similar and different?

Each leader speaks out for the interests of his or her party. For example, the leader tries to get enough votes to pass bills his or her party supports. An assistant leader called a "whip" helps each party leader.

Each house also has one presiding officer. The leader of the House of Representatives is called the Speaker of the House. Members of the majority party choose the Speaker at a caucus, or closed meeting. The candidate must then be approved by the rest of the House.

The Speaker of the House has great power. He or she presides over the House and leads the majority party. The Speaker guides legislation through the House. Finally, he or she becomes president of the United States if anything happens to the president and vice president.

The position of the Speaker is briefly mentioned in the Constitution. His or her role has developed over time. Today the Speaker works to influence other House members. He or she grants favors in return for support on important issues.

The vice president is the leader of the Senate. This role requires running Senate sessions and keeping order during these sessions. Unlike the Speaker of the House, the vice president is only allowed to vote on issues when there is a tie. A temporary officer fills in when the vice president is not available. That officer is the president pro tempore. This role is usually given to the member of the majority party who has served in the Senate the longest.

8. ANALYZING PRIMARY SOURCES

Reread the quote by Woodrow Wilson. What important information does it reveal about committees?

The Committee System

Thousands of bills, or proposed laws, flow through each house of Congress in a single session. A committee system has been established in each house to make the workload of Congress easier. Each committee carefully reviews an issue that Congress must address.

President Wilson said this about the role of committees:

> "It is not far from the truth to say that Congress in session is Congress on public exhibition, whilst Congress in its committee rooms is Congress at work."
>
> —Woodrow Wilson, *Congressional Government,* 1885

Name ______________________ Date ______________ Class ________

LESSON 1 SUMMARY, *continued*

Types of Committees

Congress has three types of committees. Standing committees are permanent committees that remain in place from one congressional term to the next. Each standing committee concentrates on a different area of government work. For example, both houses have standing committees that focus on agriculture, commerce, and veterans' affairs. In contrast, temporary committees meet for a limited amount of time. They are formed to address a specific issue and end when the issue is resolved. Sometimes the Senate and the House form a joint committee where members of both houses discuss a specific issue. Four committees in Congress are joint committees.

CONGRESSIONAL COMMITTEES		
House of Representatives—Standing Committees		
• Agriculture • Appropriations • Armed Services • Budget • Education and Labor • Energy and Commerce • Financial Services	• Foreign Affairs • Homeland Security • House Administration • Judiciary • Natural Resources • Oversight and Government Reform	• Rules • Science and Technology • Small Business • Standards of Official Conduct • Transportation and Infrastructure • Veterans Affairs • Ways and Means
Senate—Standing Committees		
• Agriculture, Nutrition, and Forestry • Appropriations • Armed Services • Banking, Housing, and Urban Affairs • Budget	• Commerce, Science, and Transportation • Energy and Natural Resources • Environmental and Public Works • Finance • Foreign Relations	• Health, Education, Labor, and Pensions • Homeland Security and Governmental Affairs • Judiciary • Rules and Administration • Small Business and Entrepreneurship • Veterans Affairs
Joint Committees		
• Economic • Printing	• Taxation • Library	

Serving on Committees

Newly elected senators and representatives try to get placed on committees that affect the people who elected them. A member from a farm area would likely want to join an agricultural committee. It is up to the party leaders to decide who serves on which committee. They think about members' interests and experience. They also consider seniority, or years of service.

ANALYZING VISUALS

9. HYPOTHESIZING

Select a standing committee from the Congressional Committees chart and explain what you think members of that committee are currently discussing.

____

____

____

____

____

____

____

Why is the committee system structured to include similar committees in both houses?

____

____

____

____

____

____

____

____

____

10. CREATING CHARTS

On a separate sheet of paper, create a chart that lists three committees on which you think your representatives should serve with an explanation of why you think it is important to have your state represented in each. Include specific state-related issues you think should be brought up.

Chairpersons of committees often gain much power. This position usually goes to the longest-serving committee member from the majority party. Chairpersons usually decide when a committee will meet, which bills will be studied, and who will serve on subcommittees.

The longest-serving committee member of the minority party is called the ranking minority member. He or she leads the minority party members on the committee.

People disagree about whether the seniority system is a good idea. Some say that it makes sure that chairpersons have enough experience. Others argue that the most qualified individuals might not get the best jobs for them.

REVIEW LESSON 1

1. Complete the chart below to describe each listed component of Congress.

THE LEGISLATIVE BRANCH	
Structure of the House of Representatives	
Leaders of the House	
Structure of the Senate	
Leaders of the Senate	
Types of Committees	
Committee Leadership	

2. **Evaluating** In an essay on a separate piece of paper, evaluate the strengths and weaknesses of the committee system in Congress. Address these questions: Does having different types of committees help or hinder the work of Congress? Is seniority the best basis for choosing committee chairs? Is it a good idea for party leaders to decide who serves on committees?

LESSON 2 SUMMARY

Powers of Congress

SS.7.C.1.7, SS.7.C.3.3, SS.7.C.3.8

Legislative Powers

You might not realize it, but the decisions of Congress affect your day-to-day life. After all, Congress makes the laws for the entire country. For example, there are laws that deal with the food you eat. Almost everything you consume must pass health or safety requirements established by law.

The decisions of Congress affect not only you and your family but also the nation's society and economy as a whole. Good citizens need to know and understand the powers given to Congress. They also need to know and understand the limits on the powers of Congress.

Expressed Powers

Article I, Section 8 of the Constitution describes most of the powers granted to Congress. Because these powers are clearly stated in the document they are called the **expressed powers** or the **enumerated powers** of Congress. There are 18 constitutional clauses listing the powers given to Congress.

Implied Powers

Congress has also been given some powers that are not specifically stated in the Constitution. Article I, Section 8, Clause 18 authorizes this practice. It states that Congress has the power to do whatever is "necessary and proper" to carry out its expressed powers. These additional powers are called **implied powers.**

1. DETERMINING WORD MEANINGS

Underline the sentence that offers a definition of *expressed powers.* Circle another term for expressed powers.

2. DRAWING CONCLUSIONS

Why do you think the Framers did not include more expressed powers?

Clause 18 has been given the nickname the **elastic clause.** It allows Congress to "stretch" its powers to meet new needs. Congress has the expressed power to support the armed forces. However, the Constitution does not explain how it should do this. One way is to create jobs in the Defense Department. The elastic clause gives Congress the power to create those jobs.

POWERS OF CONGRESS	
Selected Expressed Powers	**Selected Implied Powers**
Money Powers	
• Levy and collect taxes • Borrow money • Coin, print, and regulate money	• Levy and collect taxes implies the power to support public schools, public housing, etc. • Borrow money implies the power to maintain the Federal Reserve Board
Commerce Powers	
• Regulate foreign and interstate commerce	• Regulate commerce implies the power to prohibit discrimination in restaurants, hotels, and other public accommodations
Military and Foreign Policy Powers	
• Declare war • Raise, support, and regulate an army and navy • Punish acts committed on international waters and against the laws of nations	• Raise and support an army implies the right to draft people into the armed forces
Other Legislative Powers	
• Establish laws of naturalization • Establish post offices • Create lower federal courts • Govern Washington, D.C.	• Establish laws of naturalization implies the power to limit the number of immigrants coming into the United States

3. PREDICTING CONSEQUENCES

What do you think might happen if Congress stretched its implied powers too far?

______

______

______

______

______

______

ANALYZING VISUALS

4. DRAWING CONCLUSIONS

What expressed power of Congress allows lawmakers to adjust the minimum wage or protect workers from harm?

______

______

______

5. INTERPRETING

What implied powers would Congress likely have because of the expressed power to establish post offices?

______

______

______

______

______

Lawmaking Powers

Most congressional powers relate to making laws. The expressed lawmaking powers outlined in Article I, Section 8 deal with money, commerce, or foreign policy.

The Constitution not only grants Congress the power to raise money but also the power to spend money. An important way that Congress raises money is by requiring citizens to pay taxes. Congress is allowed to spend money to provide services to citizens and help with other national needs. Congress is also permitted to regulate, or manage, interstate commerce. Commerce is the buying and selling of goods and services. In addition, Congress has the power to make laws related to foreign issues. It can create laws to defend the country, wage war, and build and maintain the armed forces. Did you know that only Congress has the power to declare war?

Other Powers and Limits

Congress also has duties and responsibilities not related to the making of laws. These congressional powers are known as **nonlegislative powers.**

Nonlegislative Powers

Suggesting amendments to the Constitution is one nonlegislative power that Congress has employed over the years. More often, Congress uses its nonlegislative powers to check the other branches of government. Some of these checks are specified in the Constitution, but others have come about over time.

Congress checks the power of the executive branch in several ways. For example, the Senate has the power to approve or reject the president's nominees for various offices, including Supreme Court justices and ambassadors. This keeps the nation's executive leader from becoming too powerful.

6. CITING TEXT EVIDENCE

Underline two nonlegislative powers of Congress.

7. HYPOTHESIZING

What might happen if Congress did not have nonlegislative powers?

____

____

____

____

____

____

____

8. REASONING

Why do you think only a majority vote is necessary to impeach a federal official, but a 2/3 vote is required to convict him or her?

The Constitution also grants Congress the power to remove from office a federal official involved in serious wrongdoing. The House has the power to **impeach,** or accuse officials of misconduct in office. To do this, a majority vote is needed. After impeachment, the Senate conducts a trial in which it decides the official's guilt or innocence. Convicting and removing an official from office requires a two-thirds vote in the Senate.

Impeachment Process

House of Representatives votes to impeach (requires a majority vote). → Senate holds a trial. Senators act as the jury. → 2/3 vote "guilty" → Removed from office

→ less than 2/3 vote "guilty" → Remains in office

9. DRAWING CONCLUSIONS

Why does the Constitution say that Congress cannot block the writ of habeas corpus in most cases?

In which cases do you think Congress is allowed to block a writ of habeas corpus?

Limits on Congressional Powers

The Constitution also describes what the lawmakers cannot do. Some limits are outlined in the Bill of Rights. In fact, the purpose of the Bill of Rights was to ensure that the federal government could not interfere with personal freedoms.

Article I, Section 9 outlines other limits on congressional power. Among other limits, Congress is not allowed to favor one state over another, tax interstate commerce, or tax exports. Section 9 also provides for the protection of the legal rights of individuals:

- Congress cannot block writs of habeas corpus in most cases. This type of writ directs the police to bring a prisoner before the court and explain the charges against the person.
- Congress cannot pass bills of attainder. Such laws would allow citizens to be punished without a trial.
- Congress cannot pass an ex post facto law. This type of law would say that an act is a crime *after* the act has been committed.

Name ______________________ Date ______________ Class __________

The Constitution limits the powers of Congress in another way. Some powers are expressly reserved for the state governments. One such power is the right to regulate public schools.

Congress's powers are also limited through the separation of powers. Both the executive branch and the judicial branch have the authority to check the power of Congress. The Supreme Court has the power to declare laws passed by Congress unconstitutional. The president can veto, or turn down, laws that Congress has passed. Likewise, Congress can check the power of the other branches. For example, it can override a presidential veto by a two-thirds vote.

10. DRAWING CONCLUSIONS

On a separate sheet of paper, answer: Why is it necessary to limit Congress through checks and balances even though the Constitution places other limits on Congress?

REVIEW LESSON 2

1. Complete the chart below to describe the powers and limits of Congress.

	WHAT IT MEANS	EXAMPLE
Expressed Powers		
Implied Powers		
Lawmaking Powers		
Nonlegislative Powers		
Limits on Congressional Powers		
Limits Because of Separation of Powers		

2. **EVALUATING** Write an essay in which you evaluate whether Congress has the right amount of power. Begin by explaining the powers of Congress as well as its limits. Then, explain why you think Congress has the right amount of power, too much power, or too little power. Write your essay on a separate sheet of paper.

LESSON 3 SUMMARY

How Congress Works

SS.7.C.2.3, SS.7.C.2.10, SS.7.C.3.8

1. EVALUATING

How fair do you think the media is to the members of Congress who represent you?

2. HYPOTHESIZING

Imagine that you will be voting in the next election. What factors would you consider in selecting the best candidate to send to the Senate or House of Representatives? What factors would you likely not consider?

Qualifications and Staffing

Being a member of Congress is not easy. As citizens, members have taken on the enormous responsibility of helping to run the national government. They make hard decisions every day. They also have the responsibility of meeting the needs of their constituents. They need to be informed about current events and the workings of government. Meetings can last into the night. Not only that, members are always in the spotlight, with the media and others tracking their every movement. They need to be accountable for every action they take. Also, most understand the importance of responding to communications from citizens. Finally, they need to accept the fact that they may be voted out of office when their term is over.

Requirements and Benefits

Candidates for the Senate and House of Representatives must meet certain requirements. Senators must be at least 30 years old, while representatives must be at least 25. All must live in the state they represent. Senators must have been American citizens for at least nine years, while for Representatives the requirement is just seven years.

Besides these formal qualifications, there are also informal qualifications that help candidates gain office. A law degree helps but is not essential. Being outgoing and involved in the community are also beneficial. So too is leadership experience. Many senators and representatives have had careers in local or state politics before moving to the national level. This helps explain why senators in the 114th Congress had an average age of 61 and House members an average age of 56.

PROFILE OF THE 114TH CONGRESS

GENDER

House: 350 Men, 85 Women

Senate: 80 Men, 20 Women

PARTY AFFILIATION

House of Representatives: 247 Republican, 188 Democrat

Senate: 54 Republican, 44 Democrat, Independent 2

In the 114th Congress, more women than ever before served and the Republican Party was the majority party in both houses.

3. HYPOTHESIZING

What do you think the make-up of the next Congress will be like? Explain your answer.

____

Members of Congress are eligible for many benefits besides their salaries. The federal government pays for their offices and trips back home. These benefits make the work for members not only easier but also possible.

Congressional Staffs

It would be hard for members of Congress to handle all their responsibilities without assistance. That is why they hire a staff. A typical staff may include clerks, secretaries, and special assistants. Together, these assistants handle a wide variety of tasks, including those listed in the chart on the next page.

4. EXPLAINING

Identify two qualifications of congressional staff. Why do you think these two qualifications are so important?

____

____

____

____

____

____

____

____

CONGRESSIONAL STAFF RESPONSIBILITIES
Gather information on new bills and issues
Schedule and organize meetings and events
Handle requests from constituents
Deal with news reporters and lobbyists
Make contacts to influence policymaking
Work in reelection campaigns (on their own time as required by law)

Lobbyists contact lawmakers so that they can try to influence them to help support their ideas. **Lobbyists** are people who represent special-interest groups. A **special-interest group** is an organization made up of people with a common interest. These types of groups work to ensure that their stands on issues become national policy. Sometimes, lobbyists or special-interest groups use propaganda to create the public attitude they want.

The mass media has encouraged the use of propaganda in advertising and politics. It is spread through newspapers, radio, television, the Internet, billboards, and every other form of mass communication.

Dealing with news reporters, lobbyists, and constituents is a critical task for congressional assistants. Media, individuals, and special-interest groups all monitor and influence government. A senator or representative's staff makes sure that these people's needs are addressed. For example, staff members want to make sure that the media reports about their member of Congress are positive. Also, good relationships with lobbyists can help the senator or representative succeed or gain reelection.

In addition to paid staff, many members of Congress hire students from their districts to work as volunteers. As volunteers, these students experience the responsibility of citizens at the national level. They also gain skills that will help them in later life, particularly if they pursue jobs in government.

In addition to their staff, members of Congress have access to several congressional agencies that support their work.

Name ______________________ Date ______________ Class __________

AGENCIES OF CONGRESS
The Library of Congress
• Is the largest library in the world, with at least one copy of every book ever published in the United States • Is an important source of information for members of Congress and their staff
The Government Accountability Office (GAO)
• Examines financial matters for Congress • Reviews spending by federal agencies to ensure that government money is well spent • Examines federal programs to ensure they work properly • Makes suggestions for the best use of funds • Studies problems and analyzes possible solutions to help lawmakers decide the best actions to take
The Congressional Budget Office (CBO)
• Provides necessary information for Congress to create the government's budget • Helps Congress develop and follow a budget • Analyzes costs and benefits of possible actions • Makes suggestions for the best use of funds

Congress at Work

Addressing the needs of more than 310 million people might seem overwhelming. However, that is the task of the 535 members of Congress. Each member of Congress is responsible for looking out for the needs of the constituents he or she represents.

Making Laws

Because Congress is the legislative branch of government, it makes sense that the main task of its members is to make laws. Throughout each congressional session, the lawmakers introduce and consider bills, or proposed laws, on a variety of topics. This process includes many different tasks, such as investigating and addressing issues, writing proposals for laws, promoting bills to ensure passage, and evaluating the strengths and weaknesses of proposed bills.

5. PRIORITIZING

Imagine that you are a U.S. senator about to vote on a law related to the environment. List four sources you might refer to or consult with. Then, rank your sources from most important to least important. Explain the criteria you used to determine your rankings.

6. VISUALIZING

Draw a political cartoon about pork-barrel projects on a separate sheet of paper. If possible, relate the cartoon to your state or community. Then on the lines below, explain the meaning of your cartoon.

____

____

____

____

____

7. MAKING CONNECTIONS

Think about a project that could be built in your community with federal funds. Tell where and why this project should be built.

____

____

____

____

Doing Casework

Sometimes constituents need assistance dealing with the federal government. This help is called casework. For example, constituents may not have received a Social Security check or may need help completing a government form. Often, they turn to their senators or representatives for help and guidance.

The lawmakers are usually willing to assist for several reasons. It helps them gain voter supprt, it helps them gauge how well the government is working, and it provides citizens with the help they need and expect.

Helping the District or State

Members of Congress are elected by citizens of their states and districts. Therefore, lawmakers do everything they can to help their home area prosper. They work to bring federal government projects to their districts and states which helps create jobs for the area.

Some of these projects paid for by the federal government mainly benefit a member of Congress's home district or state. These types of projects are referred to as pork-barrel projects. How did this kind of project get such an unusual name? Think of the federal treasury being the "pork barrel." A lawmaker dips into the barrel and pulls out a piece of "fat." This fat is actually a juicy federal project for his or her district.

Some people criticize this longtime practice as wasting taxpayer money. Many lawmakers think of it as a way to help fill a need in their district or state. They want their constituents to benefit from government spending.

Congress passes public works bills each year that set aside billions of dollars for local projects. It allocates money for building military bases, veterans' hospitals, highways, bridges, and dams. Many workers are needed to construct these projects, bringing both jobs and money to wherever they are built. Often, even more jobs are created when the projects are up and running.

Name ______________________ Date ______________ Class __________

Senators and representatives do not have the direct power to grant projects to their districts. However, they are able to take other actions to help bring projects home. They can try to influence the agency in charge of making decisions about the project. For example, they can encourage constituents to contact agency leaders. Members of Congress can also add wording to bills to set aside funds for a certain project. These additions to bills are known as "earmarks." If the bill passes both houses of Congress, that project is approved, too.

Many grants and contracts are available through the federal budget. Just a small part of the money set aside for projects can help a state or district's economy grow.

8. SEQUENCING

What steps might a citizen take to make sure the project becomes a reality? What steps might a member of Congress take to gain federal funds for the project?

____

____

____

REVIEW LESSON 3

1. Complete the chart below to organize your thoughts about the interactions lawmakers have with others.

	EXPLANATION
Why is being a member of Congress more than a 9 to 5 job?	
What people skills do you think members of Congress need?	
Why is it important for members of Congress to have a good relationship with their staff and with their constituents?	
Why are reporters and lobbyists interested in meeting with members of Congress?	
When might constituents get in touch with a member of Congress?	

2. **DETERMINING CAUSE AND EFFECT** Using a separate sheet of paper, write an essay in which you describe how members of Congress are influenced by outside forces and how members of Congress in turn influence those forces.

LESSON 4 SUMMARY

How a Bill Becomes a Law

1. IDENTIFYING

Read each example. Then, complete the chart by indicating whether the example represents a bill or a joint resolution and explaining why.

Example	What is it and why?
Allocate money to pay for president's inauguration	☐ joint resolution ☐ bill Explain:
DREAM (Development, Relief, and Education for Alien Minors) Act	☐ joint resolution ☐ bill Explain:
Making the last Thursday in November the official date of Thanksgiving	☐ joint resolution ☐ bill Explain:
Use of armed forces in the Middle East	☐ joint resolution ☐ bill Explain:
American Jobs Act	☐ joint resolution ☐ bill Explain:

SS.7.C.1.7, SS.7.C.2.10, SS.7.C.3.8, SS.7.C.3.9

Types of Bills

As a legislature, the major job of Congress is to pass laws. It is no surprise that Congress deals with many bills, or proposals for new laws. There are more than 10,000 bills proposed each session! However, only a few hundred of those bills actually become law. The process for a bill becoming a law is complicated. That is what the Framers intended. The process was set up that way to make sure that bills are thought through carefully.

Bills are divided into two categories, or types: public bills and private bills.

PUBLIC BILLS	PRIVATE BILLS
have to do with the entire nation	have to do with individual people or places
involve general matters such as taxation, farm policy, or highway building	involve people's claims against the government

In addition to bills, Congress is also charged with the task of considering resolutions. Resolutions are formal statements that express lawmakers' opinions or decisions. Unlike a bill, a resolution may have to do with Congress or one of its houses. Certain resolutions may relate to how one of the houses operates. Other resolutions may express the overall opinion of the House of Representatives or the Senate on a public policy issue.

Joint resolutions must be passed through both houses of Congress. Unlike other resolutions, they have the same effect as bills. If the president signs a joint resolution, it will become law. Congress passes joint resolutions to solve a limited or a temporary problem. Joint resolutions may propose constitutional amendments, designate money for a special purpose, or establish commemorative days. The main difference between a joint resolution and a bill is that a joint resolution usually has to do with one subject.

From Bill to Law

All bills begin as ideas. These ideas come from three main sources:

- private citizens
- the president
- special-interest groups

Regardless of the source of the bill, only a member of Congress can submit it. That member of Congress is known as the bill's sponsor. It is possible for a bill to have several sponsors. After it has been submitted, the bill is given a title and a number. The first bill introduced during the first session of Congress is called S. 1 in the Senate and H.R. 1 in the House of Representatives.

Committee Action

Once introduced, a bill is sent to a standing committee. The standing committee it goes to depends on the subject of the bill and whether it was introduced in the Senate or the House. For example, a bill on forest health introduced by a representative would first go to the House Committee on Natural Resources.

The standing committees will decide whether the bill will continue. If the committee approves the bill, it will go to the floor for a vote by the full House or Senate.

Committee members may hold hearings to gather information about a bill they think is worth considering. Then the committee members discuss the bill.

The committee will then take one of the following actions:

- pass the bill, which sends it to the full House or Senate
- make changes to the bill and then pass it and send it to the full House or Senate
- replace the original bill with a new bill on the same subject
- "pigeonhole," or ignore, the bill and let it die in committee
- kill the bill outright with a majority vote against it

2. GIVING EXAMPLES

What types of special-interest groups do you think might exist in the United States today?

____

____

____

____

____

____

3. MAKING CONNECTIONS

Think about what you might do when you want people to know your ideas or opinions. How do you think special-interest groups might get their messages to Congress?

____

____

____

____

____

____

Name ______________________ Date ______________ Class __________

ANALYZING VISUALS

4. INTERPRETING
On a separate piece of paper, explain in your own words the steps of how a bill introduced in the Senate becomes a law.

Debating a Bill

Once a bill passes the committee, the full House or Senate holds a floor debate. Members of the House or Senate argue for or against the bill and consider possible amendments. The House only considers amendments that are related to the bill. However, the Senate allows unrelated amendments, or **riders,** to be added.

HOW A BILL BECOMES A LAW

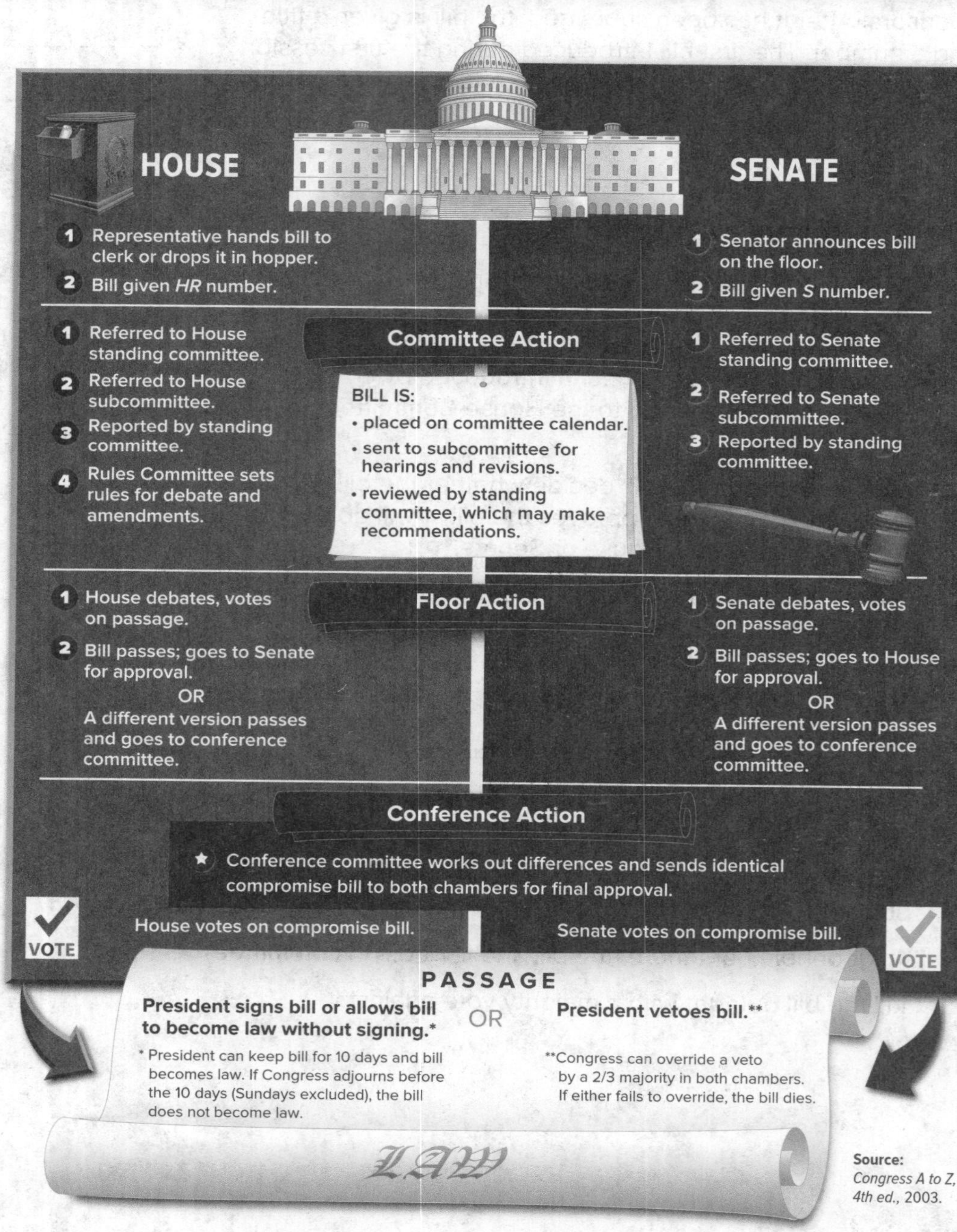

HOUSE

1. Representative hands bill to clerk or drops it in hopper.
2. Bill given *HR* number.

SENATE

1. Senator announces bill on the floor.
2. Bill given *S* number.

Committee Action

House:

1. Referred to House standing committee.
2. Referred to House subcommittee.
3. Reported by standing committee.
4. Rules Committee sets rules for debate and amendments.

BILL IS:
- placed on committee calendar.
- sent to subcommittee for hearings and revisions.
- reviewed by standing committee, which may make recommendations.

Senate:

1. Referred to Senate standing committee.
2. Referred to Senate subcommittee.
3. Reported by standing committee.

Floor Action

House:

1. House debates, votes on passage.
2. Bill passes; goes to Senate for approval.
OR
A different version passes and goes to conference committee.

Senate:

1. Senate debates, votes on passage.
2. Bill passes; goes to House for approval.
OR
A different version passes and goes to conference committee.

Conference Action

★ Conference committee works out differences and sends identical compromise bill to both chambers for final approval.

VOTE House votes on compromise bill.

Senate votes on compromise bill. VOTE

PASSAGE

President signs bill or allows bill to become law without signing.* OR **President vetoes bill.****

* President can keep bill for 10 days and bill becomes law. If Congress adjourns before the 10 days (Sundays excluded), the bill does not become law.

**Congress can override a veto by a 2/3 majority in both chambers. If either fails to override, the bill dies.

LAW

Source: *Congress A to Z, 4th ed.*, 2003.

Name ______________________ Date ______________ Class __________

Each house follows different rules for their debates. In the House, the Rules committee sets the debate terms. There is usually a time limit on the discussion. The Senate has fewer rules so senators can speak longer. Sometimes in the Senate, a senator will speak for many hours. When Senators speak against a bill, or talk a bill to death, this is called a **filibuster.** A filibuster is meant to delay a bill's vote until the bill's sponsor withdraws the bill. The only way to end a filibuster is for three-fifths of the Senate to vote for cloture. **Cloture** limits the amount of time a senator may speak to no more than one hour.

Voting and Vetoes

Once the debate is over, the bill is voted on. Both the House and Senate have several methods of voting: recorded vote, voice vote, standing vote, and roll-call vote.

VOTING METHODS

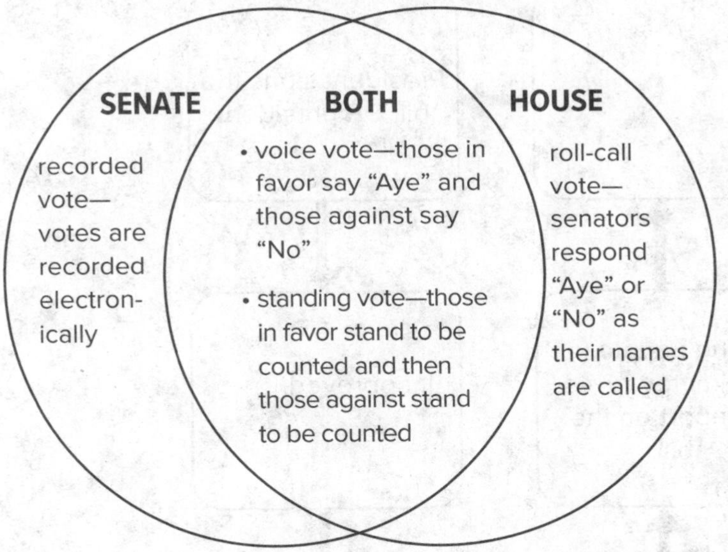

SENATE	BOTH	HOUSE
recorded vote—votes are recorded electronically	• voice vote—those in favor say "Aye" and those against say "No" • standing vote—those in favor stand to be counted and then those against stand to be counted	roll-call vote—senators respond "Aye" or "No" as their names are called

A simple majority of all members who are present is needed for a bill to pass. After a bill passes in one house, it is sent to the other house. However, if one house rejects a bill, it dies.

Both the Senate and the House must pass a bill in exactly the same form. If each house has its own version, then a conference committee made up of members from both houses meets. They compromise and make changes to the bill. Then both houses must accept it or reject it.

ANALYZING VISUALS

5. INTERPRETING

Refer to the illustration that shows how a bill becomes a law. What happens if the president vetoes the bill?

6. POSING QUESTIONS

Write two or three questions that you would ask a senator after he or she has publicly announced the decision to use a filibuster.

LESSON 4 SUMMARY, *continued*

7. MAKING INFERENCES

Why might a president kill a bill using a pocket veto?

Once both houses approve a bill, it is sent to the president. If the president signs it, the bill becomes a law. However, the president may veto, or refuse to sign, it. The president may also do nothing for 10 days. If Congress is in session after that time, the bill becomes law without the president's signature. But if Congress is not in session after those 10 days, the bill dies. When a bill is killed in this way, it is called a **pocket veto.**

What happens if the president vetoes the bill? Congress has a chance to save it. Members can override the veto with a two-thirds majority vote in each house. This is difficult to do. Between 1789 and July 2010, Congress overturned only 109 out of 2,560 vetoes. If the bill was killed as a pocket veto, Congress cannot override the veto. The bill is dead.

REVIEW LESSON 4

1. Complete the chart below to explain the role both houses of Congress have in turning a bill into a law. You may assume that the bill is the same in both houses.

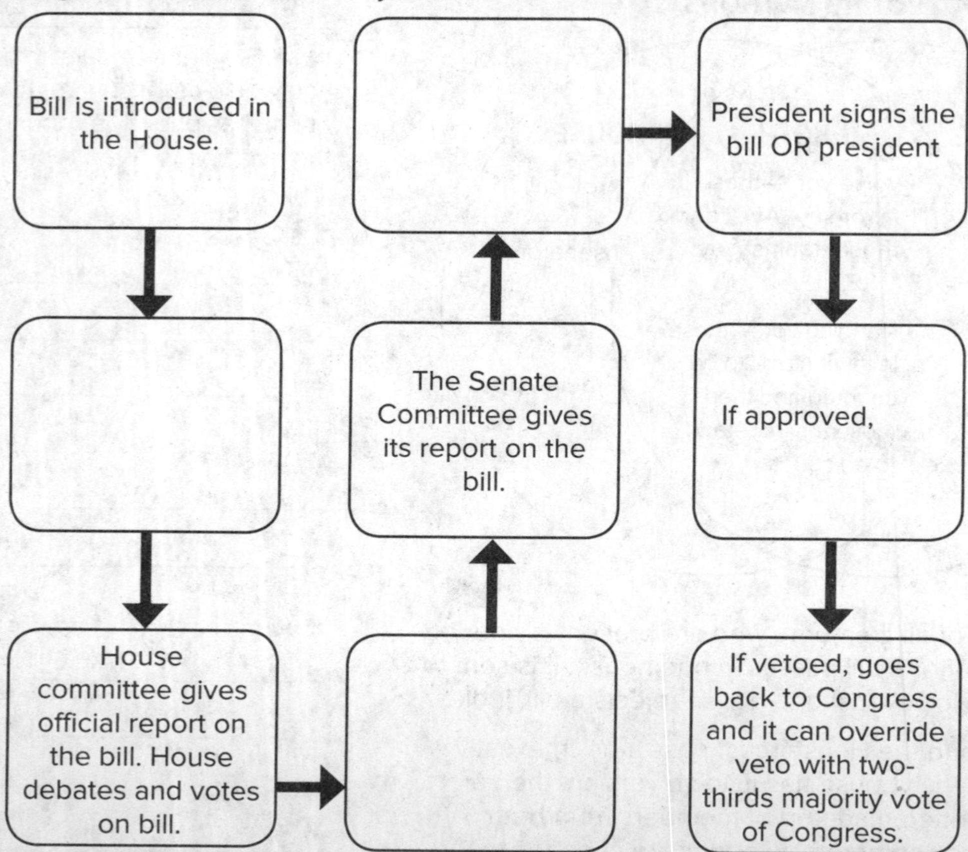

2. **DETERMINING CENTRAL IDEAS** What role does Congress have in making a bill into a law? On a separate piece of paper, write an essay in which you explain the role and the process Congress follows to achieve it.

Benchmark Skill Activities

DIRECTIONS: Write your answers on a separate piece of paper.

LAFS.68.WHST.1.2, LAFS.68.WHST.3.9

1. GATHERING EVIDENCE

Use your FOLDABLES to write an essay.

Consider one of the critical issues currently being debated in Congress that you researched and summarized. In your essay, explain how one or more special-interest groups might affect the outcome of the issue being debated. Include your ideas about how lobbying might be used in relation to the issue.

MAFS.K12.MP.5.1

2. MAKING GRAPHS

Use the Internet to find out the percentage of bills that actually became laws during the last session of Congress. Identify whether the president and the majority in Congress were from the same party or different parties. Create a graph to show the information.

Now find information from the past when the president was from one party and the majority in Congress was from the other party and when the president and the majority of Congress were from the same party. Create a graph for each set of data that shows the percentage of bills that actually became laws during these times. Compare the rates of passage and draw a conclusion based on your three graphs. Write three questions that someone could answer using your graphs. Show your graphs to a partner and have him or her answer your questions while you answer his or her questions.

LAFS.68.RH.2.4, LAFS.68.WHST.1.2

3. USING DEFINITIONS ACCURATELY

Write a paragraph that explains the nonlegislative powers of Congress and limits on congressional powers. Use these words in your paragraph: *nonlegislative powers, impeach, writ of habeas corpus, bill of attainder,* and *ex post facto law.*

Benchmark Note Cards

DIRECTIONS: Use these note cards to help you prepare for the test.

SS.7.C.1.7 Describe how the Constitution limits the powers of government through separation of powers and checks and balances.

SEPARATION OF POWERS AND CHECKS AND BALANCES

The Constitution provides for a separation of powers by dividing power between the three branches of government. The branches are kept separate to prevent the abuse of power.

The legislative branch makes laws.
The executive branch implements and enforces the laws.
The judicial branch renders judgment in cases involving laws.

Checks and balances means any branch has duties that check, or limit, the power of the other two branches. The executive branch can veto bills passed by the legislative branch, but the legislative branch can override the veto. The judicial branch can declare a law or a presidential order unconstitutional, but members of the Supreme Court are appointed by the executive branch and approved by the legislative branch.

SS.7.C.2.10 Examine the impact of media, individuals, and interest groups on monitoring and influencing government.

IMPACT AND INFLUENCE ON GOVERNMENT

Media

Media exposure can be positive, keeping constituents informed of issues and activities of government. This can keep elected officials accountable for their actions. Negative exposure can also be informative, but on occasion may distract attention to unrelated matters.

Individuals

Individuals have an influence on government through voting and through staying informed on government activities. Writing letters and emails to officials is an easy and effective way to make them aware of issues important to the public. Casework is one way in which senators or representatives and their staffs assist individuals in dealing with the government.

Interest Groups

Interest groups of many types work to ensure that their stands on issues become national policy. Lobbyists are people who represent special-interest groups, and they contact lawmakers to try to influence the leaders to support their ideas. Good relationships with lobbyists can help the senator or representative succeed or gain reelection.

SS.7.C.3.3 Illustrate the structure and function (three branches of government established in Articles I, II, and III with corresponding powers) of government in the United States as established in the Constitution.

STRUCTURE AND FUNCTION OF CONGRESS

Organization of Congress

- lawmaking branch of the government
- addresses most important issues
- 100 senators, 2 from each state
- 435 representatives, based on state population, updated with census every 10 years

Requirements or Qualifications to Be in Congress

- Senators must be at least 30 and a citizen for at least 9 years.
- Representatives must be at least 25 and a citizen for at least 7 years.
- A law degree is helpful.
- Leadership experience, an outgoing personality, and being involved in the community are helpful.

Legislative Powers of Congress

- Article I, Section 8 clearly states congressional powers. These are expressed, or enumerated, powers.
- Article I, Section 8, Clause 18 describes implied powers, which are powers given to Congress though not clearly stated. Congress has the power to do whatever is "necessary and proper" to carry out its expressed powers.
- Clause 18 is called the elastic clause because it allows Congress to "stretch" its powers to meet its needs.

CONGRESSIONAL LEADERSHIP

Both political parties are represented in both houses of Congress, but the party with more than half of the members is considered the majority party. The other party is the minority party. At the start of each new Congress, each party elects a party leader to direct its activities.

Each house also has one presiding officer. The Speaker of the House presides over the House of Representatives, guides legislation, and becomes the next president of the United States if anything happens to the president and vice president.

The Vice President is leader of the Senate, running Senate sessions and keeping order. The Vice President is allowed to vote only when there is a tie. If the Vice President is absent, a temporary officer, called president pro tempore, fills in.

COMMITTEES IN CONGRESS	• Committees set up to make workload easier • Standing committees: permanent committees that stay in place from one congressional session to another; each concentrates on a different area of government • Temporary committees: formed to address special issues and end when issues are resolved • Party leaders decide who serves on which committee; this is sometimes based on seniority. • Chairpersons have power to decide when committees meet, which bills are studied, and who will be on subcommittees.

LAWMAKING POWERS OF CONGRESS	• Raises money by requiring citizens to pay taxes • Spends moneys to provide services • Regulates interstate commerce • Makes laws related to foreign issues • Creates laws that deal with defending the country, waging war, and building and maintaining armed forces **Nonlegislative Powers** • Suggests amendments

SS.7.C.3.9 Illustrate the lawmaking process at the local, state, and federal levels.

BILLS AND HOW THEY BECOME LAW	Bills start with ideas from private citizens, special-interest groups, or even the president, but only a congressional member can submit a bill. The bill then goes to a standing committee, which decides whether it will be introduced in the House or Senate. The committee holds hearings to discuss the bill, and can pass it on, make changes to it, replace it, ignore it, or kill it. If the bill passes the committee, the full House or Senate debates it. After debate, the bill is voted on, and a simple majority will pass it. Then the bill is sent to the other house. Both houses must pass a bill in exactly the same form. Then it is sent to the president for signing. The signed bill becomes law. If the president vetoes (refuses to sign) the bill, Congress can override the veto with a two-thirds majority vote. If the president ignores the bill for ten days and Congress is in session, the bill becomes law. If the president ignores the bill for ten days and Congress in adjourned, the bill is killed. This is called a pocket veto.

Chapter 7

VISUAL SUMMARY

DIRECTIONS: Complete the graphic organizers below.

TWO HOUSES OF CONGRESS	
Senate	**House of Representatives**
Members:	Members:
Term:	Term:

LEADERSHIP IN CONGRESS	
Majority Party	**Minority Party**
Senate Leadership	**House Leadership**
Three types of committees in Congress:	

LEGISLATIVE POWERS	
Most important duty of Congress is	
Expressed Powers	**Implied Powers**
Elastic clause:	
How Framers prevent Congress from abusing power:	

CONGRESSIONAL MEMBERSHIP REQUIREMENTS	
Senate	**House**
Age:	Age:
Citizen:	Citizen:
Congressional Staffs include:	
Agencies of Congress include: ★ : largest library in world ★ : looks into financial matters for Congress ★ : provides information to develop the government's budget	
Members of Congress help people from They also try to bring federal government projects to their districts and states. These projects are called	

HOW A BILL BECOMES A LAW			
1. Ideas come from:	2. Bill is written in House or Senate, submitted, and given number.	3. Bill goes to and subcommittees for hearings.	4. Approved bill:
5.	6.	7. President	8. An approved bill becomes law.

USING PRIMARY SOURCES

INTERPRET Below is a primary source that involves the issue of earmarking in Congress. Read the excerpt and answer the questions that follow on a separate sheet of paper.

> *Given the deficits that have mounted up over the past decade, we can't afford to make these investments unless we're also willing to cut what we don't need. That's why I've submitted to Congress a plan for a three-year budget freeze, and I'm prepared to offer additional savings. But as we work to reform our budget, Congress should also put some skin in the game. I agree with those Republican and Democratic members of Congress who've recently said that in these challenging days, we can't afford what are called earmarks. These are items inserted into spending bills by members of Congress without adequate review.*
>
> *Now, some of these earmarks support worthy projects in our local communities. But many others do not. We can't afford Bridges to Nowhere like the one that was planned a few years back in Alaska. Earmarks like these represent a relatively small part of overall federal spending. But when it comes to signaling our commitment to fiscal responsibility, addressing them would have an important impact.*
>
> *As a Senator, I helped eliminate anonymous earmarks and created new measures of transparency so Americans can better follow how their tax dollars are being spent. As President, time and again, I've called for new limitations on earmarks. We've reduced the cost of earmarks by over $3 billion. And we've put in place higher standards of transparency by putting as much information as possible on earmarks.gov. In fact, this week, we updated the site with more information about where last year's earmarks were actually spent, and made it easier to look up Members of Congress and the earmarks they fought for.*
>
> *Today, we have a chance to go further. We have a chance to not only shine a light on a bad Washington habit that wastes billions of taxpayer dollars, but take a step towards restoring public trust. We have a chance to advance the interests not of Republicans or Democrats, but of the American people; to put our country on the path of fiscal discipline and responsibility that will lead to a brighter economic future for all. And that's a future I hope we can reach across party lines to build together.*
>
> —President Barack Obama, Weekly Address, November 13, 2010

1. What is the main idea expressed in the primary source?
2. Why does President Obama agree with members of Congress who say earmarks should be eliminated?
3. What does President Obama mean by the expression "put some skin in the game"?
4. Why would addressing earmarks signal fiscal responsibility to the American people?
5. Do you think President Obama is trying to make members of Congress more accountable for their actions? How do you know?
6. Why do you think President Obama is urging Congress to reach across party lines?

Chapter Practice Test

DIRECTIONS: Circle the best answer for each question.

SS.7.C.1.7 (Low)

Under the system of checks and balances, how can Congress limit the power of the president?

A can appoint federal officials to enforce the laws

B can overturn a presidential veto with a two-thirds vote

C can rule that presidential actions are unconstitutional

D can amend the Constitution to overturn court decisions

SS.7.C.3.9 (Moderate)

This diagram shows some of the steps involved in how a bill becomes a law. Which answer completes the diagram?

A The bill is sent to the Senate, debated, and then approved.

B Congress overturns the president's veto by a two-thirds vote.

C The Senate passes its own version of the bill.

D The bill goes to a conference committee for revision.

3 **SS.7.C.2.10 (Low)**

What is the main purpose of lobbying?

A to safeguard and limit the powers of government

B to reduce the budget by doing away with earmarks

C to speed up the process of a bill becoming a law

D to influence legislation on behalf of special-interest groups

---

4 **SS.7.C.3.3, SS.7.C.3.8 (High)**

Read the statement from the U.S. Constitution.

> *Congress shall have power . . . to make all laws which shall be necessary and proper for carrying into execution the foregoing power.*
>
> —The United States Constitution

To what does this statement refer?

A an executive privilege

B the elastic clause

C nonlegislative powers

D limits on governmental power

5 **SS.7.G.4.2 (Moderate)**

Based on the map, which statement is true about the change in representation in the House of Representatives after the 2010 census?

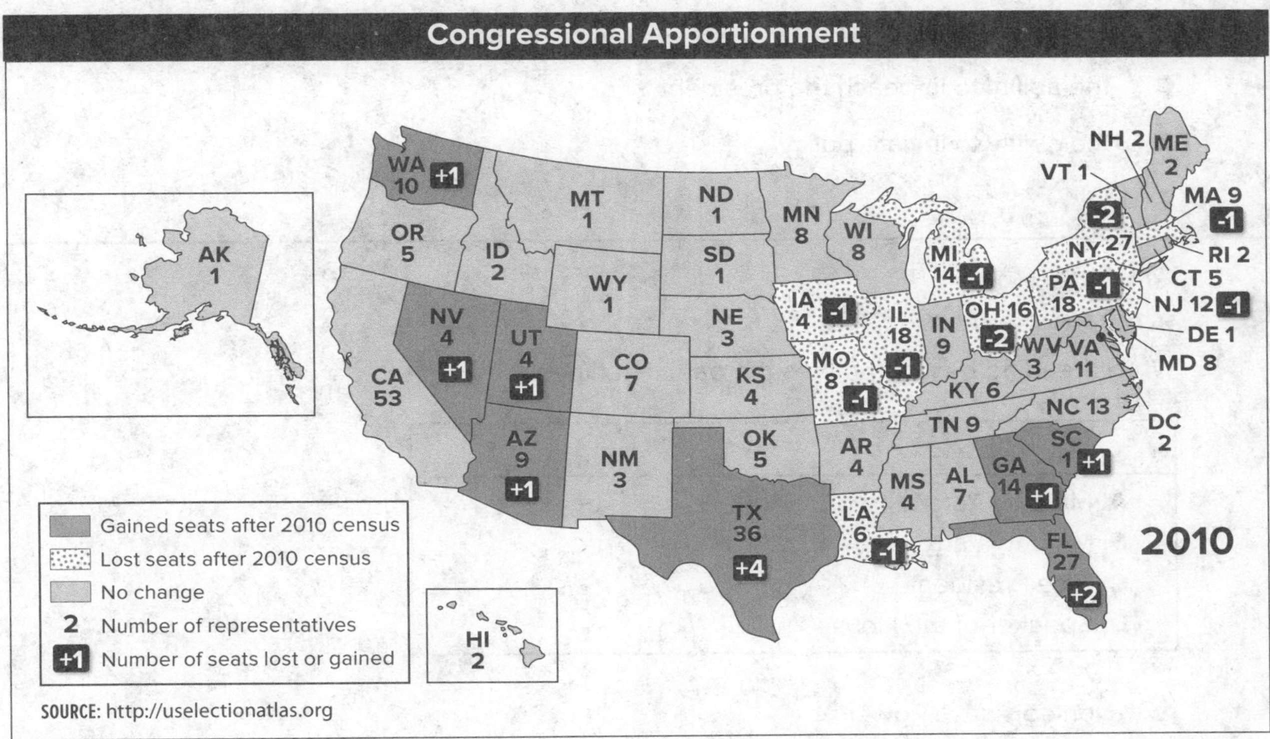

A The number of representatives in southern and western states remained the same.

B The total number of representatives increased due to population growth.

C As a result of population changes, ten states had fewer representatives and eight states gained representatives.

D An increase in representation occurred in the northern and eastern states due to population changes.

6 **SS.7.C.3.3 (Moderate)**

Which of the following is a power held only by members of the Senate?

A the ability to override a veto

B the ability to filibuster

C the ability to impeach the president

D the ability to initiate policy

---

7 **SS.7.C.3.3 (Moderate)**

Which heading best completes the partial outline?

I.
A. Majority Party **B.** Minority Party **C.** Vice President **D.** Speaker of the House

A Nonlegislative Powers

B The Committee System

C Congressional Staff

D Congressional Leadership

SS.7.C.3.8 (Moderate)

What is the primary responsibility of congressional committees?

A to save time for members of Congress

B to track decisions and communicate with constituents

C to monitor earmarks by members of Congress

D to study bills and make recommendations

9 **SS.7.C.3.3, SS.7.C.3.8 (High)**

Which statement provides evidence that Congress is fulfilling its responsibilities as the legislative branch of government?

A A bill vetoed by the president is sent back to a conference committee.

B A one-month recess is announced to allow members of Congress to complete needed paperwork.

C A bill to provide funds for repairs to interstate highways is passed and sent to the president.

D A mass mailing is sent to constituents to ask for campaign donations.

SS.7.C.3.3, SS.7.C.3.8 (High)

Read the statement from the U.S. Constitution.

> *"The privilege of the Writ of Habeas Corpus shall not be suspended, unless when in Cases of Rebellion or Invasion the public Safety may require it."*
>
> —The United States Constitution

What does this statement represent?

A a legislative power of Congress

B a limit on congressional powers

C a nonlegislative power of Congress

D a limit on congressional earmarks

CHAPTER 8
The Executive Branch

CHAPTER BENCHMARKS

SS.7.C.1.7 Describe how the Constitution limits the powers of government through separation of powers and checks and balances.

SS.7.C.3.3 Illustrate the structure and function (three branches of government established in Articles I, II, and III with corresponding powers) of government in the United States as established in the Constitution.

SS.7.C.3.8 Analyze the structure, functions, and processes of the legislative, executive, and judicial branches.

SS.7.C.4.3 Describe examples of how the United States has dealt with international conflicts.

LAFS.68.RH.2.4 Determine the meaning of words and phrases as they are used in a text, including vocabulary specific to domains related to history/social studies.

LAFS.68.WHST.2.4 Produce clear and coherent writing in which the development, organization, and style are appropriate to task, purpose, and audience.

LAFS.68.WHST.3.7 Conduct short research projects to answer a question (including a self-generated question), drawing on several sources and generating additional related, focused questions that allow for multiple avenues of exploration.

MAFS.K12.MP.3.1 Construct viable arguments and critique the reasoning of others.

Chapter Overview

The president of the United States arguably has the most important job in the world. As head of the executive branch of the federal government, the president has a wide variety of powers and duties. Some are spelled out by the Constitution, while others have developed over time. Making foreign policy is one of a president's most important functions. In this, as in all other duties, the president is aided by an extensive array of agencies, advisers, and departments.

WHAT I NEED TO KNOW

TERMS

- ☐ elector
- ☐ executive order
- ☐ foreign policy
- ☐ ambassador
- ☐ national security
- ☐ treaty
- ☐ executive agreement
- ☐ trade sanctions
- ☐ federal bureaucracy
- ☐ executive agency
- ☐ government corporation
- ☐ regulatory commission
- ☐ political appointee
- ☐ civil service system

The Executive Branch

FOLDABLES®

The Executive Branch

Create the Foldable® below and label the tabs with the lesson titles. Under each tab, outline the key points presented in each lesson and give a brief description if a memory aid is needed. On the back of the Foldable, describe who currently holds the offices of president and vice president of the United States. Explain why the president is a symbol of the people and the federal government.

Step 1
Use a piece of paper and fold the right side of the paper over, leaving a vertical margin on the left side.

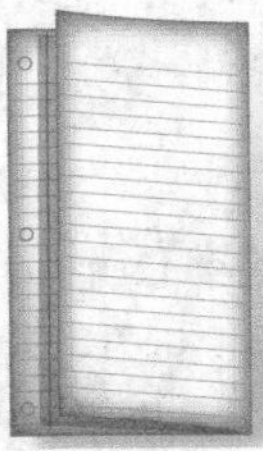

Step 2
Cut a horizontal line across the top flap, dividing it into two equal parts. Make an additional horizontal cut dividing each of the two sections.

Step 3
Label the tabs as shown.

LESSON 1 SUMMARY

The President and Vice President

1. IDENTIFYING EVIDENCE

Underline the constitutional requirements for becoming president. Write a sentence on each requirement to explain why you think the Founders included it.

2. REFLECTING

What qualities should voters look for in a presidential candidate? Military service? Political experience? A business background or college degree? Explain.

SS.7.C.3.3, SS.7.C.3.8

Office of the President

The legislative branch makes laws for the nation, but those laws do not mean much if no one follows them. That is the primary purpose of the executive branch. This arm of the federal government is responsible for making sure that federal laws are enforced. The president of the United States is the head of the executive branch.

The U.S. Constitution lists only three rules for being president. A president must be at least 35 years old. He or she must be a native-born American citizen. Finally, he or she must have lived in the United States for at least 14 years.

Characteristics of Presidents

Most U.S. presidents have been white Protestant men from states with large populations. Most have had a college education. Some were lawyers, others were military leaders. In recent years, presidential candidates have been more diverse in both race and religion. In the 1984 and 2008 elections, there was a woman running for vice president.

Electing a President

Presidential elections are held every four years. During a presidential election, voters cast votes for their candidates, but these votes do not choose the president. Instead, these votes choose **electors,** or members of the Electoral College. These members meet in December after the election and vote for president. The number of electors for each state equals the number of congressional seats for that state. The District of Columbia also has three members. Thus, the Electoral College has 538 members.

Name ______________________ Date ____________ Class ________

Electoral College

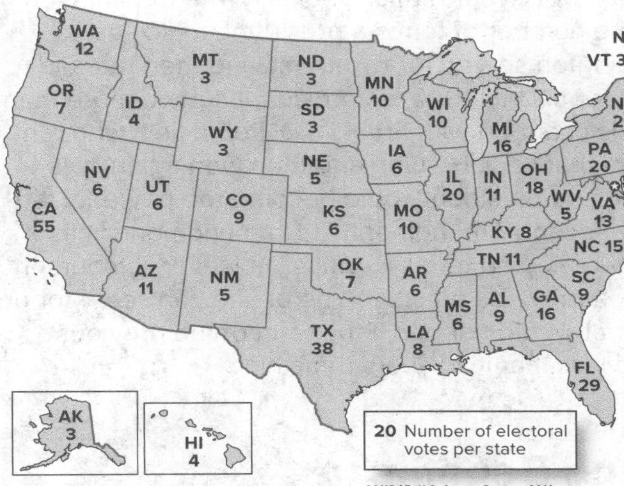

20 Number of electoral votes per state

SOURCE: U.S. Census Bureau, 2010 census

Each state has a specified number of electors, based upon the number of representatives and senators in the state. These figures are recalculated after every census. This map shows electors based on the 2010 census data.

Most states give all of their electoral votes to the candidate who wins the most popular votes. This happens even if the candidate wins by a small margin. A small number of voters can have a big effect. To win the election, a candidate must win more than half of the 538 electoral votes. This means the winner must have at least 270 votes. In a close election, a few small states can decide the result. If no candidate has a majority of the electoral votes, the House of Representatives chooses the president. In this case, each state has only one vote.

Election results are not official until the Electoral College votes, even though the winning candidate is usually known on election night. Congress counts the Electoral College votes the following January. A candidate is then officially declared winner of the election.

ANALYZING MAPS

3. Which region of the United States has the larger number of electoral votes—the area east of the Mississippi River or the area west of the Mississippi River? How might this affect a presidential candidate's campaign?

____

____

____

____

____

____

4. EVALUATING

Which feature of the Electoral College system do you think is a problem? Are any parts of it worth keeping?

____

____

____

____

____

____

____

____

____

____

5. ASSESSING

Do you believe the president should be limited to two terms? Why or why not?

____

____

____

____

____

____

____

____

____

Term of Office

Presidents serve four-year terms. Originally, the Constitution did not limit the number of terms a president could serve. George Washington served for two terms and then refused to run for a third term. Until 1940, no president served more than two terms. This changed with Franklin D. Roosevelt, who ran for a third term that year. He won and then won again in 1944. The concern that a president could become too powerful led to the Twenty-second Amendment. This amendment limits a president to two elected terms in office. However, if a person takes over for a previous president, he or she can serve for up to 10 years. That would happen if the term of the previous president had less than two years remaining.

Salary and Benefits

The president receives an annual salary of $400,000 as well as money for personal costs and travel. The White House is not only where the president works, but also where he or she lives. When traveling, the president uses a fleet of special cars, helicopters, and airplanes.

The Vice President

The vice president is elected with the president. He or she is also chosen by the Electoral College. The rules for becoming vice president are the same as those for the presidency.

The Constitution gave the vice president little power. He or she leads the Senate but can only vote to break a tie. The vice president becomes president if the president dies, is removed from office, becomes seriously ill, or leaves office.

Presidential Succession

In 1841, President William Henry Harrison died while in office. This was the first time something like this had happened. The Constitution stated that the vice president would take on the "powers and duties" of the presidency. But the document did not explain whether the vice president was to perform the duties of the president or become president. It also did not say whether the country was to hold a special election to replace the president.

Name ______________________ Date ______________ Class ________

After President Harrison's death, Vice President John Tyler declared himself president and took the oath of office. Since Tyler's time, eight other vice presidents have taken over the presidency after a president has either died or left office.

The Presidential Succession Act

In 1947, Congress passed the Presidential Succession Act. The law spelled out who would become president after the vice president, and in what order. The line of succession provides 18 possible replacements for the president. A line of succession is the order in which officials are expected to succeed, or follow, another person to an office. The chart below shows the first 10. If the first person on the list is unable to serve, the next person on the list becomes president.

ORDER OF PRESIDENTIAL SUCCESSION	
1	Vice President
2	Speaker of the House
3	President *pro tempore* of the Senate
4	Secretary of State
5	Secretary of the Treasury
6	Secretary of Defense
7	Attorney General
8	Secretary of the Interior
9	Secretary of Agriculture
10	Secretary of Commerce

The Twenty-fifth Amendment

The Twenty-fifth Amendment, which was ratified in 1967, addressed other issues regarding presidential succession. This amendment makes it clear that if the president dies or leaves office, the vice president becomes president. Then the new president chooses a new vice president. Both the Senate and the House of Representatives must approve the choice.

The Twenty-fifth Amendment also allows the vice president to serve as acting president if the president becomes very ill or needs to have surgery. The vice president serves as acting president until the president can resume his or her duties.

6. THEORIZING

Why do you think the Speaker of the House is second in line for presidential succession? What potential political problems could this create for the party in the White House?

____

____

____

____

____

____

____

____

____

____

7. IDENTIFYING STEPS IN A PROCESS

Complete the flowchart to show the process of choosing a new vice president after the sitting vice president succeeds to the presidency.

Sitting vice president becomes new president

↓

[ ]

↓

[ ]

REVIEW LESSON 1

1. Use the chart below to list information about the office of the president.

OFFICE OF THE PRESIDENT	
Purpose of the executive branch	
Constitutional requirements	
Electoral votes needed	
Term of office	
Who are the first three to succeed to the presidency?	

2. **CONSTRUCTING AN ARGUMENT** Does the line of presidential succession make sense? Should it be changed in any way, or is it sufficient to ensure competent leadership during a crisis? Explain your reasoning in an essay on a separate sheet of paper.

LESSON 2 SUMMARY

The President's Powers and Roles

SS.7.C.3.3, SS.7.C.3.8, SS.7.C.4.3

Presidential Powers

The president's powers are established in the Constitution. As the head of the executive branch, the president's primary role is to carry out the laws passed by Congress. Additionally, the Constitution gives the president the following specific powers:

- He or she can veto, or reject, bills passed in Congress.
- He or she can call Congress into special session.
- He or she serves as commander in chief of the armed forces.
- He or she receives leaders and other officials of foreign countries.
- He or she can make treaties with other countries, which then need approval by the Senate.
- He or she names the heads of executive agencies, judges of the federal court, ambassadors, and other top government officials. These appointments need Senate approval.
- He or she can pardon or reduce the penalties against people convicted of federal crimes.

The Constitution also states that the president must tell Congress about the "state of the union." Each year, the President gives a speech to discuss the nation's most important issues and his or her plans to deal with these issues. The speech is called the State of the Union address.

Presidential Roles

The president's primary role is as leader of the executive branch. As the nation has grown, the office of the president has taken on other roles.

Chief Executive

One person alone cannot carry out the laws of the entire nation. For that reason, the president has the assistance of 15 cabinet departments and many executive agencies.

1. PRIORITIZING

Rank the items in the bulleted list of presidential powers in order of importance from 1 to 7. Then, use the space below to explain the reasons behind your number one choice.

2. HYPOTHESIZING

How important are the meetings that the president holds with his cabinet and senior advisers? Why is it critical that the president hear different viewpoints about policy and national security issues?

Name ______________________ Date ______________ Class ________

3. INTERPRETING

Some people have argued that issuing executive orders is unconstitutional. Do you agree? Explain.

____
____
____
____
____
____
____
____
____
____

4. ASSESSING

Do you think the president should have the power to grant pardons, reprieves, or amnesty? Should Congress have the power to approve or deny them? Explain your reasoning.

____
____
____
____
____
____
____
____
____

The president names people to head the departments and the agencies, but the Senate must approve the choices. The president meets frequently with the heads of the 15 cabinet departments and senior staff members.

To carry out laws, presidents use **executive orders.** These rules, or commands, have the same power and force as laws. Presidents use executive orders to tell government agencies details about how laws should be enforced. Many executive orders relate to the usual work of the executive branch. However, some have much broader effects. One example is an executive order issued by President Harry S. Truman in 1948. It ended the separation of the races in the armed forces.

As chief executive, the president can nominate justices to the Supreme Court and judges of other federal courts. Because Supreme Court justices decide constitutional issues and serve for life, this is an important presidential power.

The president can grant pardons, issue a reprieve, or grant amnesty. A pardon declares forgiveness and freedom from punishment. A reprieve delays punishing a person until a higher court can hear the case. Amnesty is a pardon for a large group of people.

Chief Diplomat

The president leads American foreign policy. **Foreign policy** is a nation's plan for dealing with other nations. It is the president who decides how the United States will act toward other countries. The president names people to serve as ambassadors. An **ambassador** is an official who represents the United States government in another nation.

Head of State

As head of state, the president represents the American people. The president greets leaders from other countries when they visit the United States. He also represents all Americans at important ceremonies and events.

Commander in Chief

The Constitution makes the president commander in chief of the nation's armed forces. This allows the president to use force when he or she needs it for foreign policy decisions. The commanders of the army, navy, air force, marines, and coast guard all obey the orders of the president.

President Barack Obama made several trips to meet with American soldiers stationed in foreign lands.

The president shares power to make war with Congress. However, only Congress has the constitutional power to declare war on another country. It is the president, though, who can order troops into battle. In the past, presidents have done so more than 150 times. Congress, however, has declared war only five times.

In 1973, after the Vietnam War, Congress passed the War Powers Resolution. This law says that the president must let Congress know within 48 hours when troops are sent into battle. Unless Congress approves their use or declares war, those troops must be brought home after 60 days.

Legislative Leader

As leader of the executive branch, the president not only works to enforce congressional law but is also expected to propose new laws. Every president has goals and suggests new laws for Congress to pass. Then he or she makes speeches to build support for these laws and works with Congress to get them passed.

Many times however, the president and Congress disagree over what laws should pass or how they should be written. The disagreement happens because the president represents the interests of the entire nation, but members of Congress represent the interests of their states or districts. Local interests may not be the same as national interests.

ANALYZING VISUALS

5. DRAWING CONCLUSIONS

What role is the president performing in this image?

Why do you think this role is important?

6. ASSESSING

Do you believe someone without military experience can be an effective commander in chief? Why or why not?

7. POSING QUESTIONS

Write two questions you would ask a president about how best to improve the economy of the United States.

1. ____________________

____

____

2. ____________________

____

____

Economic Leader

Every president tries to help the economy grow. Voters expect the president to solve problems such as unemployment, rising prices, and high taxes. The president meets with budget officials and members of Congress to decide which programs to support and which to cut.

Party Leader

One final role of the president is as the leader of his or her political party. He or she supports other party members when they are running for political office. The president also helps the party raise money.

REVIEW LESSON 2

1. In the chart below, write a brief description in your own words of each role the president must perform.

PRESIDENTIAL ROLE	DESCRIPTION
Chief Executive	
Chief Diplomat	
Head of State	
Commander in Chief	
Legislative Leader	
Economic Leader	
Party Leader	

2. **ASSESSING** Use the information from your chart to write an essay that answers this question: Has the job of president become too complex for one person to carry out? Explain your reasoning. Write your essay on a separate sheet of paper.

LESSON 3 SUMMARY

Making Foreign Policy

SS.7.C.1.7, SS.7.C.3.3, SS.7.C.3.8, SS.7.C.4.3

1. IDENTIFYING EVIDENCE

Underline the goals of American foreign policy. Then, explain how those goals compete with and reinforce one another.

____

____

____

____

____

____

____

____

____

____

____

____

____

____

____

The President and Foreign Policy

American foreign policy has four main goals. The first and most important goal is **national security.** This means keeping the nation safe from harm or attack. The second goal is building trade with other nations to ensure a strong economy. The third foreign policy goal is promoting world peace. The final goal is to advance democracy around the world. Worldwide democracy and the protection of human rights in other countries encourage peace and make the nation safer.

The Foreign Policy Team

In order for the president to successfully lead the nation's foreign policy, he or she must know about and understand global events. The president is advised by close aides like the National Security Advisor. A large team of experts also works on foreign policy. This team includes the following executive agencies:

- State Department
- Defense Department
- National Security Council
- Office of the Director of National Intelligence (ODNI)
- Central Intelligence Agency (CIA)

The president takes the information from these agencies and uses it to make foreign policy decisions. The foreign policy team then carries out the president's policies.

Congress Versus the President

The president is the chief diplomat, but Congress also plays a part in foreign policy. For example, only Congress can declare war. The War Powers Resolution allows Congress to stop the president from using the armed forces in certain ways. Congress also has the power to decide how much money should be spent on defense.

2. EVALUATING

Regarding foreign policy, do you believe power is adequately balanced between the executive branch and the other branches of government? Explain.

______

3. MAKING GENERALIZATIONS

What types of knowledge and experiences do you believe are needed by a U.S. ambassador to a foreign nation?

______

The Constitution does not spell out how the legislative and executive branches should work together. Over the years, the balance of power has shifted back and forth. The War Powers Resolution is an example of Congress taking more control. With the war on terrorism, the balance has shifted back toward the president.

The Tools of Foreign Policy

The executive and legislative branches use many different "tools" to carry out the foreign policy of the United States. One important tool is making agreements with other countries and sending ambassadors. Other tools are foreign aid, trade policy and, when needed, military force.

Treaties and Executive Agreements

A formal agreement between the governments of two or more countries is called a **treaty.** Treaties can cover different issues, including trade, human rights, and defense or security. The North Atlantic Treaty Organization (NATO) is an example of a military treaty. In this pact, the United States, Canada, and many nations in Western Europe promised to defend one another if attacked.

The Senate must approve any treaty by a two-thirds vote. If unable to get Senate approval, the president can make an **executive agreement** with the leader of another country.

Appointing Ambassadors

About 150 ambassadors represent the government of the United States in other nations. These officials are appointed by the president and then confirmed by the Senate. They only go to countries with governments that our country believes have a right to exist. If the government of a country has gained political power illegally, the president can refuse to recognize it.

Name ______________________ Date ______________ Class ________

Foreign aid helps sustain lives in many impoverished and war-torn regions of the world. This camp in North Darfur, Sudan, was set up to help people whose homes and way of life had been destroyed.

USAID

Foreign Aid

Foreign aid is another powerful foreign policy tool. The United States sends many types of aid to countries in need. This aid may consist of money, food, military help, or other supplies.

International Trade

One of the ways the president can work to keep the nation's economy growing is by making trade agreements with other countries. One example is the North American Free Trade Agreement (NAFTA). A trade agreement allows the United States to join a free-trade group. In a free-trade group, members agree to trade with one another without import taxes, or tariffs.

When there is a foreign policy problem, the president can use **trade sanctions,** which stop or slow trade between the United States and another nation. The United States might also join an embargo, which is an agreement by a group of countries to stop trading with a certain nation.

Congress plays a role in the nation's economy as well. It must approve the treaties that allow the United States to join a trade group. It also can set tariffs for countries without trade agreements.

Military Force

As commander in chief, a president sometimes decides that military force is necessary to carry out a foreign policy decision. There have been many times when a president has sent American troops to another country to help prevent an invasion or perhaps to calm a civil conflict. This has been done even when Congress has not declared war.

ANALYZING VISUALS

4. CONSTRUCTING AN ARGUMENT

Examine the image of the mother and child. What evidence can you see to support the position that the United States should participate in international efforts to provide food and shelter for refugees?

____

____

____

____

____

____

____

____

____

5. SPECULATING

How might a free trade agreement such as NAFTA contribute to national security?

____

____

____

____

____

____

____

____

Name ______________________ Date ______________ Class __________

Complete the chart to describe the tools a president can use to carry out the nation's foreign policy. In the left column, write the tool. Then, in the right column, give an example of a situation for which each tool might be appropriately used.

FOREIGN POLICY TOOL	EXAMPLE OF APPROPRIATE USE

REVIEW LESSON 3

1. Use the chart below to identify major departments that make up the president's foreign policy team and the role they play in advising the president.

THE FOREIGN POLICY TEAM	ROLE IN ADVISING THE PRESIDENT

2. **SPECULATING** On a separate sheet of paper, write an essay to explain the role that Congress and the foreign policy team would play if the president wanted to send American forces to join in an international peacekeeping mission.

How the Executive Branch Works

SS.7.C.3.3, SS.7.C.3.8

Executive Office Agencies

The third president Thomas Jefferson had a very small staff to help him: a few advisers, a messenger, and a part-time secretary. In 1939, President Franklin D. Roosevelt created the Executive Office of the President (EOP). Today, the EOP has nearly 2,000 employees and an annual budget of almost $400 million. The EOP consists of many different agencies.

The White House Office

The president's chief of staff oversees the EOP. He or she also is in charge of the president's schedule and decides who can meet with the president. The chief of staff, deputy chiefs of staff, and senior advisers are the president's closest advisers.

The core of the EOP is the president's home office—the White House Office. The 500 people who work here help the president communicate with the public and Congress. They also help the president develop policy. Regardless of their jobs, they work directly for the president.

Office of Management and Budget

The Office of Management and Budget (OMB) works with the president to prepare the federal budget. This proposal shows the president's spending plans for the coming year. The OMB also monitors how executive agencies spend their money.

National Security Council

For issues of defense and security, the president seeks advice from the National Security Council (NSC). The National Security Advisor, appointed by the president, heads the NSC. Other members include the vice president, the secretaries of state and defense, and the chairperson of the Joint Chiefs of Staff. The top commanders of the four parts of the armed services form the Joint Chiefs of Staff. The Director of National Intelligence also is a member. Intelligence is the gathering of information about action and plans of other governments.

1. MAKING INFERENCES

Franklin Roosevelt is sometimes called the founder of the "modern presidency." Use the information on this page to explain why.

2. ASSESSING

The size of the Executive Office of the President has grown considerably since its beginnings in 1939. Has it grown too big? Explain your answer.

Name ______________________ Date ______________ Class __________

3. EXPLAINING

The Senate must approve all presidential cabinet appointees. Why is such approval necessary?

____

____

____

____

____

____

Council of Economic Advisers

The president appoints people to the Council of Economic Advisers (CEA). Once these members are confirmed by the Senate, they work to advise the president on economic issues such as job growth and trade.

The President's Cabinet

The executive branch also includes 15 executive departments that employ thousands more people. The president chooses the heads of these departments with the Senate's approval. They form the group of presidential advisers called the cabinet. The chart below lists the cabinet departments.

THE CABINET	
Department	**Role**
Department of State (1789)	Manages the nation's foreign policy
Department of Treasury (1789)	Manages the nation's financial resources
Department of Defense (1789 as War Department; renamed in 1949)	Manages the nation's armed forces
Department of Justice (1870; originally created in 1789 as the Office of the Attorney General)	Oversees the nation's legal affairs
Department of the Interior (1849)	Protects public lands and natural resources; oversees relations with Native Americans
Department of Agriculture (1889)	Develops conservation programs; assists farmers and consumers of farm products
Department of Commerce (1903)	Supervises trade; promotes the nation's business and tourism
Department of Labor (1913)	Deals with worker safety and wages of U.S. workers
Department of Health and Human Services (1953)	Oversees public health and social services
Department of Housing and Urban Development (1965)	Ensures equal housing opportunities; helps make mortgage money available for buying homes
Department of Transportation (1966)	Regulates all aspects of the nation's transportation needs—air travel, railroads, highways, and mass transit
Department of Energy (1977)	Plans energy policy; researches and develops energy technology
Department of Education (1979)	Coordinates federal assistance programs for schools; oversees programs for students with special needs
Department of Veterans Affairs (1989)	Administers hospitals and programs for veterans
Department of Homeland Security (2002)	Controls government organizations that protect the nation against terrorist attacks

The Constitution in Article II, Section 2, states that the president may require "in writing" the opinion of the heads of each of the executive departments. It does not mention a cabinet, though. The cabinet is a tradition that began with the first president. President Washington held regular meetings with the heads, or secretaries, of the then four executive departments. Other presidents continued these meetings. Over time, the cabinet grew as more departments were added.

4. IDENTIFYING PROBLEMS

What problems might derive from the sheer size and complexity of the federal bureaucracy?

Cabinet Responsibilities

The president relies on his or her cabinet secretaries for advice relating to the departments they lead. He or she decides when and how often the cabinet meets. Often, the vice president and other top aides join the meeting. Cabinet secretaries are then responsible for carrying out the president's plans within their departments. Before they can begin their posts, they must be approved by the Senate.

The Federal Bureaucracy

The executive branch has hundreds of agencies helping to make government policy. These agencies are known as the **federal bureaucracy.** About 3 million people work in executive branch agencies performing three basic kinds of tasks.

First, some agencies make new laws work. The laws that Congress passes are often written in general terms. The agencies take the laws' guidelines and form them into more detailed and specific rules. Then people and businesses know how to follow the law.

Second, departments and agencies carry out the day-to-day activities of the federal government. These federal workers are in charge of delivering mail, collecting taxes, and taking care of national parks.

Third, federal agencies regulate certain activities. One agency watches over banks to make sure they are using people's money appropriately. Another agency tests products to see whether they are safe to use. Yet another agency sets rules that protect our health and our environment. However, none of these executive agencies could exist without a congressional law giving them the power to do their work.

ANALYZING VISUALS

5. MAKING COMPARISONS

Why do you think independent agencies exist? Do you think they should be more closely tied to the president?

Independent Agencies

The executive branch also has three types of independent agencies. They are called independent because they do not belong to a cabinet department. The three types of independent agencies with examples are listed in the chart.

INDEPENDENT AGENCIES	
Executive Agencies	Executive agencies deal with certain specific areas within the government. They report to the president. • The National Aeronautics and Space Administration (NASA) directs the space program. • The Central Intelligence Agency (CIA) gathers intelligence information for use by the government. • The Environmental Protection Agency (EPA) sets and enforces regulations to protect people's health and the environment.
Government Corporations	These are nonprofit businesses owned and run by the government. They offer goods and services for sale. However, they are not supposed to make a profit. They report to the president. • The United States Postal Service (USPS) provides mail services and supplies. • The Tennessee Valley Authority sells energy to people in its region.
Regulatory Commissions	These commissions protect the public by making and enforcing rules for certain industries or groups. The president names people to head these commissions. However, they do not report to the president, and only Congress can remove them. • The Federal Communications Commission (FCC) makes rules for television and radio stations. • The U.S. Consumer Product Safety Commission sets safety standards for consumer products.

Government Workers

After a president is elected, he or she appoints specific people to fill certain positions in departments or agencies. Only the top government jobs usually go to these **political appointees.** Some of them have experience in the work they will do. Others get their job because they supported the president during the election. However, when the president leaves office, these people leave the appointed jobs as well.

During the early years, government workers were given jobs using the spoils system. Each new president fired many government workers and replaced them with political supporters.

Name ______ Date ______ Class ______

Because the spoils system workers weren't always qualified for their jobs, Congress passed the Civil Service Reform Act of 1883. This law created the **civil service system,** which required the government to hire people based on their skills and how well they do on competitive examinations.

About 90 percent of federal government workers are civil service workers. Unlike political appointees, civil service workers usually have permanent jobs. They might be clerks, lawyers, or park rangers who are hired through the civil service system.

The Office of Personnel Management (OPM) directs the civil service system today. It sets standards for federal jobs. It also gives tough tests to people who want those jobs.

6. DRAWING CONCLUSIONS

How has the establishment of the civil service impacted the federal government?

______

REVIEW LESSON 4

1. Use the chart below to fill in key agencies in the Executive Office of the President.

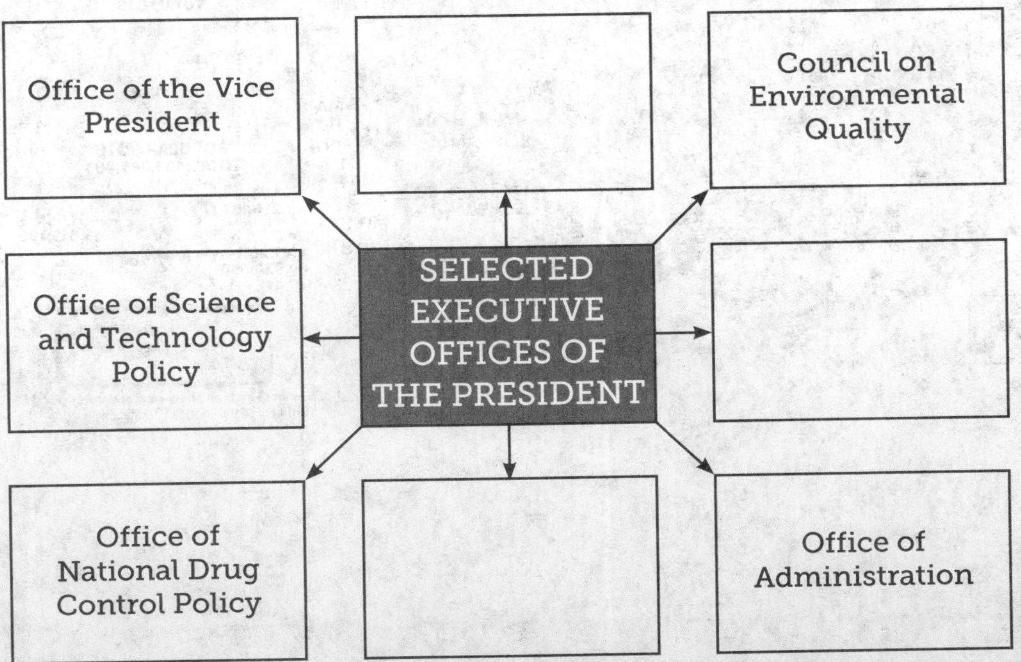

2. **EXPLAINING** On a separate sheet of paper, explain the roles of the Executive Office of the President and the White House staff.

Benchmark Skill Activities

DIRECTIONS: Write your answers on a separate sheet of paper.

LAFS.68.WHST.2.4

1. REFLECTING

Use your FOLDABLES to write an essay.

Many Americans look to the president to take the lead in solving the nation's problems. In your opinion, what makes a presidency successful? Give specific examples.

MAFS.K12.MP.3.1

2. ANALYZING MAPS

Using the map of the 2012 presidential election results, describe a scenario by which Mitt Romney could have defeated Barack Obama.

Presidential Election of 2012

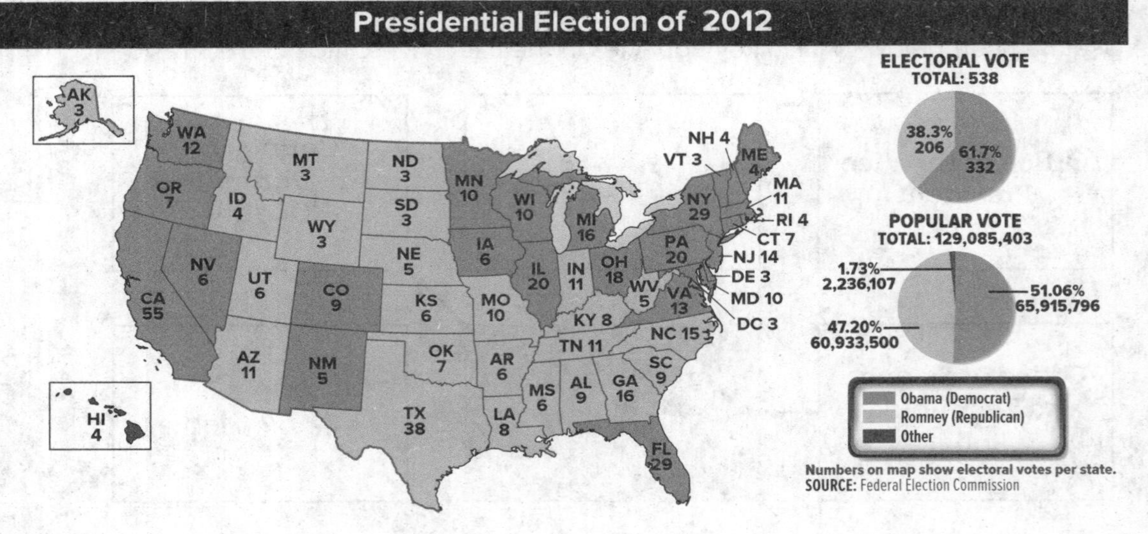

LAFS.68.RH.2.4

3. USING CONTEXT CLUES

Read the following oath of office for president of the United States. The U.S. Constitution, Article II, Section 1, includes the oath and says that the president shall take the oath before taking office. Then, write a definition for each of the underlined words. Use a dictionary or the Internet to help you determine their meanings.

> *"I do solemnly swear (or affirm) that I will faithfully execute the office of President of the United States, and will to the best of my ability, preserve, protect, and defend the Constitution of the United States."*
>
> —Constitution of the United States

LAFS.68.WHST.1.1

4. CONSTRUCTING AN ARGUMENT

A line-item veto is the power of an executive to cancel specific provisions of a bill—particularly a spending bill—without vetoing the entire legislative package. Though most states give their governors some form of line-item veto power, the president does not have it. Should the president have this power? Explain why or why not.

LAFS.68.WHST.2.6, LAFS.68.WHST.3.7

5. USING AND CITING INFORMATION

The actions of regulatory commissions often impact individual citizens. Do research on the Internet to investigate the actions of a particular regulatory commission during the past 12 to 24 months. Explain what the commission has been doing. Then describe how it has affected the quality of American life. Write at least two questions about the commission's work. Cite the sources you used in your research.

Benchmark Note Cards

DIRECTIONS: Use these note cards to help you prepare for the test.

SS.7.C.1.7 Describe how the Constitution limits the powers of government through separation of powers and checks and balances.

SEPARATION OF POWERS: THE PRESIDENT AND CONGRESS, WAR POWERS	The U.S. Constitution says that the president is the commander in chief, but it also gives Congress certain war powers. • Only Congress can declare war. • Only Congress can spend or hold back money for defense. • The War Powers Resolution allows Congress to stop the president from using the armed forces in certain ways.

SS.7.C.3.3 Illustrate the structure and function (three branches of government established in Articles I, II, and III with corresponding powers) of government in the United States as established in the Constitution.

CONSTITUTIONAL QUALIFICATIONS FOR PRESIDENT	The U.S. Constitution lists only three rules for being president. A president must • be at least 35 years old • be a native-born American citizen • have lived in the United States for at least 14 years

ELECTING A PRESIDENT	The Constitution requires the president to be elected by a group called the Electoral College. Each state has the same number of electors as it has members of Congress. In addition, the District of Washington has three electors. To win the election, a candidate must win more than half of the 538 electoral votes. Most states give all of their electoral votes to the candidate who wins the popular vote in the state.

TERM OF OFFICE	Presidents serve four-year terms. The Twenty-second Amendment of the Constitution (ratified in 1951) limits a president to two elected terms in office. Originally, the Constitution did not limit the number of terms a president could serve.

PRESIDENTIAL SUCCESSION

The Twenty-fifth Amendment to the Constitution makes it clear that, if the president dies or leaves office, the vice president becomes president. The new president chooses a new vice president, who is subject to the approval of Congress.

The amendment also allows the vice president to serve as acting president if the president becomes unable to do the job, or if the president becomes very ill or needs to have surgery.

PRESIDENTIAL POWERS

Article II of the Constitution makes the president's main job carrying out the laws passed by Congress. The Constitution gives the president several specific powers. The president

- can veto, or reject, bills passed in Congress
- can call Congress into special session
- serves as commander in chief of the armed forces
- receives leaders and other officials of foreign countries
- makes treaties with other countries, although they need approval by the Senate
- names the heads of executive agencies, judges of the federal courts, ambassadors, and other top government officials with Senate approval
- can pardon or reduce the penalties against people convicted of federal crimes

PRESIDENTIAL ROLES

As the United States has grown, the president has taken on a variety of roles:

- Chief executive
- Chief diplomat
- Head of state
- Commander in chief
- Legislative leader
- Economic leader
- Party leader

SS.7.C.3.8 Analyze the structure, functions, and processes of the legislative, executive, and judicial branches.

THE PRESIDENT AS CHIEF EXECUTIVE	The president can write executive orders—regulations about how laws are to be carried out. They have the same power and force as laws. The president can nominate justices to the Supreme Court and judges to other federal courts. The president can grant pardons, forgiving someone of a crime or excusing someone from punishment. The president can grant a reprieve, delaying punishment until a case goes to a higher court. A president can grant amnesty, which is like a pardon granted to a group of people instead of individuals. The president appoints members of the Cabinet, heads of 15 executive departments in the federal government who advise him. Individuals the president chooses must be confirmed, or approved, by the Senate.
EXECUTIVE OFFICE AGENCIES	The Executive Office of the President (EOP) has nearly 2,000 employees to help the president carry out his or her duties. The EOP consists of several agencies, including the • White House Office • Office of Management and Budget • National Security Council • Council of Economic Advisers
THE FEDERAL BUREAUCRACY	The various agencies that help the government run are part of the federal bureaucracy. They perform three basic kinds of tasks: • Making new laws work • Carrying out daily activities of the federal government • Regulating certain activities Three types of independent agencies are important parts of the federal bureaucracy: • Executive agencies—deal with specific areas of the government • Government corporations—businesses owned by the government • Regulatory commissions—agencies that protect the public

GOVERNMENT WORKERS	Most federal government workers are civil service workers. They must pass rigorous examinations in order to get their jobs. Top government jobs usually go to political appointees, who are people chosen by the president because of their expertise or because they are political supporters of the president. Most civil service workers have permanent jobs. Appointees usually leave office when the president does.

SS.7.C.4.3 Describe examples of how the United States has dealt with international conflicts.

FOREIGN POLICY GOALS	A nation's plan for dealing with other nations is called its foreign policy. The United States has four main foreign policy goals: • Maintaining national security • Building trade with other nations • Promoting world peace • Advancing democracy around the world A large team of experts helps the president with foreign policy decisions, including people from the State Department, National Security Council, Central Intelligence Agency, and others.

THE TOOLS OF FOREIGN POLICY	The Constitution divides foreign policy powers between the president and Congress so that both share in the making of foreign policy. They can use the following tools: • Treaties and executive agreements • Appointing ambassadors • Foreign aid • International trade • Military force

Chapter 8

VISUAL SUMMARY

DIRECTIONS: Complete the graphic organizer below.

According to the Constitution, to qualify for the presidency a person must...

★ ______________________

★ ______________________

★ ______________________

The president has a wide variety of roles to play:

★ Chief executive

★ Chief diplomat

★ Head of state

★ ______________________

★ ______________________

★ ______________________

★ ______________________

THE EXECUTIVE BRANCH

Many agencies and departments are needed to help the executive branch run smoothly.

★ Executive Office of the President
- o White House Office
- o Office of the Vice President
- o Office of Management and Budget
- o National Security Council
- o Council of Economic Advisers
- o Council on Environmental Quality
- o Office of Administration
- o Office of National Drug Control Policy
- o Office of Science and Technology Policy

★ Cabinet

★ Federal Bureaucracy
- o Executive agencies
- o Government corporations
- o Regulatory commissions

U.S. Foreign Policy Goals

★ ______________________

★ ______________________

★ ______________________

★ ______________________

Tools of Foreign Policy

★ Treaties and executive agreements

★ Appointing ambassadors

★ Foreign aid

★ International trade

★ Military force

USING PRIMARY SOURCES

DETERMINE CENTRAL IDEAS The following passage is from Barack Obama's first Inaugural Address given on January 20, 2009. Use this passage to answer the questions that follow. Write your answers on a separate sheet of paper.

> *For as much as government can do and must do, it is ultimately the faith and determination of the American people upon which this nation relies. It is the kindness to take in a stranger when the levees break, the selflessness of workers who would rather cut their hours than see a friend lose their job, which sees us through our darkest hours. It is the firefighter's courage to storm a stairway filled with smoke, but also a parent's willingness to nurture a child, that finally decides our fate.*
>
> *Our challenges may be new. The instruments with which we meet them may be new. But those values upon which our success depends—hard work and honesty, courage and fair play, tolerance and curiosity, loyalty and patriotism—these things are old. These things are true. They have been the quiet force of progress throughout our history. What is demanded then is a return to these truths. What is required of us now is a new era of responsibility—a recognition, on the part of every American, that we have duties to ourselves, our nation, and the world, duties that we do not grudgingly accept but rather seize gladly, firm in the knowledge that there is nothing so satisfying to the spirit, so defining of our character, than giving our all to a difficult task.*
>
> *This is the price and the promise of citizenship.*
>
> *This is the source of our confidence: the knowledge that God calls on us to shape an uncertain destiny.*
>
> *This is the meaning of our liberty and our creed, why men and women and children of every race and every faith can join in celebration across this magnificent mall, and why a man whose father less than 60 years ago might not have been served at a local restaurant can now stand before you to take a most sacred oath.*
>
> —Barack Obama, Inaugural Address, January 20, 2009

1. What is the general theme of this passage?
2. Which executive roles is President Obama fulfilling by delivering this message to the American people?
3. Why do you think President Obama is saying these things to the American people?
4. How do you think public opinion affects the power of the president, and how can presidents use public support to carry out their roles?

Chapter Practice Test

DIRECTIONS: Circle the best answer for each question.

SS.7.C.3.3 (Moderate)

The following passage is from Article II, Section 1 of the U.S. Constitution.

> *No Person except a natural born Citizen, or a Citizen of the United States at the time of the Adoption of this Constitution, shall be eligible to the Office of President; neither shall any person be eligible to that Office who shall not have attained to the Age of thirty five Years, and been fourteen Years a Resident within the United States.*
>
> —Constitution of the United States

According to this passage, what is required of a presidential candidate?

A The candidate must have been honorably discharged from the military.

B The candidate must be at least 35 years old.

C The candidate must have prior legislative experience.

D The candidate must be a naturalized citizen of the United States.

SS.7.C.3.3 (Moderate)

Which of the following would result from the direct election of presidential candidates?

A The Electoral College would become much more influential.

B Voter turnout on Election Day would almost certainly fall dramatically.

C Each vote would count equally in determining which candidate won the election.

D Party loyalty would be weakened after a presidential election.

SS.7.C.3.3 (High)

In this 1832 cartoon, President Andrew Jackson is depicted as a king holding a vetoed bill and trampling on the U.S. Constitution.

What does the cartoonist accuse President Jackson of doing?

A refusing to fulfill his duties as chief executive

B supporting states' rights over the U.S. Constitution

C attempting to turn the United States into a monarchy

D exceeding the constitutional limits of his authority

SS.7.C.1.7 (Moderate)

What was the primary purpose of the War Powers Resolution?

A to limit the power of the president to send troops into combat

B to allow for a more rapid response to a military attack

C to help the president effectively carry out the role of commander in chief

D to force the president to use diplomacy rather than military action

SS.7.C.3.3 (High)

The following passage is from Article II, Section 2 of the U.S. Constitution.

> *The President shall be Commander in Chief of the Army and Navy of the United States, and of the Militia of the several States, when called into the actual Service of the United States.*
>
> —Constitution of the United States

In which of the following scenarios is the president carrying out the role described in the passage?

A The president orders troops into a foreign country.

B The president entertains a foreign leader at the White House.

C The president asks Congress for an increase in defense spending.

D The president appoints the Secretary of Defense.

SS.7.C.3.8 (Moderate)

What is the main reason for the creation of independent regulatory commissions?

A to maintain the system of checks and balances in the federal government

B to provide extra support to cabinet-level departments

C to oversee certain industries to protect the public

D to give government jobs to the president's political supporters

7 **SS.7.C.4.3 (High)**

The following passage is from the 1961 Inaugural Address of President John F. Kennedy.

> *. . . Let every nation know, whether it wishes us well or ill, that we shall pay any price, bear any burden, meet any hardship, support any friend, oppose any foe to assure the survival and the success of liberty.*
>
> —John F. Kennedy, Inaugural Address, 1961

Which conclusion is best supported by this quotation?

A Kennedy understood the limitations of power, even for a strong nation like the United States.

B Kennedy encouraged a strong American presence in foreign policy.

C Kennedy believed that foreign aid is the best way to encourage world peace.

D Kennedy thought that the United States should avoid involvement with other nations.

---

8 **SS.7.C.4.3 (Moderate)**

Who plays the dominant role in shaping the foreign policy of the United States?

A the National Security Council

B the cabinet

C the Congress

D the president

9 **SS.7.C.3.8 (High)**

The following passage is from the concurring opinion of Supreme Court Justice Robert Jackson in *Youngstown Sheet and Steel Company* v. *Sawyer* (1952). In the passage, Justice Jackson formulates a three-tier test for evaluating claims of presidential power.

> *When the president acts pursuant to [according to] an express or implied authorization of Congress, his authority is at its maximum, for it includes all that he possesses in his own right plus all that Congress can delegate. . . . When the President acts in absence of either a congressional grant or denial of authority, he can only rely upon his own independent powers, but there is a zone of twilight [unclear area] in which he and Congress may have concurrent authority, or in which its distribution is uncertain. . . . When the President takes measures incompatible with [or defying] the expressed or implied will of Congress, his power is at its lowest ebb [lowest point], for then he can rely only upon his own constitutional powers minus any constitutional powers of Congress over the matter.*
>
> —Justice Robert Jackson, 1952

According to Jackson, in which of the following instances is a president's authority least legitimate?

A in cases where the president is defying congressional orders

B in cases where the president acts with approval from Congress

C in cases where Congress has been silent on an issue

D in cases where the public has expressed strong sentiment

---

10 **SS.7.C.3.8 (Low)**

Which presidential power is not granted by the Constitution?

A appointing justices to the Supreme Court

B submitting a treaty to the Senate for ratification

C suspending a session of Congress

D granting amnesty to convicted criminals

CHAPTER 9

The Judicial Branch

Chapter Overview

The judicial branch of government interprets the law and settles disputes among states. The Constitution established a national Supreme Court. Later, Congress created lower federal courts, which exist alongside 50 separate state court systems and try cases that involve federal law and constitutional issues.

The U.S. Supreme Court has the power of judicial review. It can decide whether laws passed by the legislative branch or actions taken by the executive branch are constitutional. This power is an important check on the other branches of government. Over its history, the Court has issued many landmark decisions that have greatly impacted life in the United States.

CHAPTER BENCHMARKS

SS.7.C.1.7 Describe how the Constitution limits the powers of government through separation of powers and checks and balances.

SS.7.C.2.10 Examine the impact of media, individuals, and interest groups on monitoring and influencing government.

SS.7.C.3.3 Illustrate the structure and function (three branches of government established in Articles I, II, and III with corresponding powers) of government in the United States as established in the Constitution.

SS.7.C.3.8 Analyze the structure, functions, and processes of the legislative, executive, and judicial branches.

SS.7.C.3.11 Diagram the levels, functions, and powers of courts at the state and federal levels.

SS.7.C.3.12 Analyze the significance and outcomes of landmark Supreme Court cases including, but not limited to, *Marbury* v. *Madison, Plessy* v. *Ferguson, Brown* v. *Board of Education, Gideon* v. *Wainwright, Miranda* v. *Arizona, in re Gault, Tinker* v. *Des Moines, Hazelwood* v. *Kuhlmeier, United States* v. *Nixon,* and *Bush* v. *Gore.*

WHAT I NEED TO KNOW

TERMS

- ☐ dual court system
- ☐ jurisdiction
- ☐ exclusive jurisdiction
- ☐ concurrent jurisdiction
- ☐ original jurisdiction
- ☐ appellate jurisdiction
- ☐ ruling
- ☐ opinion
- ☐ precedent
- ☐ litigant
- ☐ tenure
- ☐ subpoena
- ☐ judicial review
- ☐ constitutional
- ☐ nullify
- ☐ writ of certiorari
- ☐ docket
- ☐ caseload
- ☐ brief
- ☐ stare decisis
- ☐ concurring opinion
- ☐ dissenting opinion
- ☐ unanimous opinion

ACTIONS AND CONCEPTS

- ☐ Judiciary Act of 1789
- ☐ *Marbury* v. *Madison*

The Judicial Branch

CHAPTER BENCHMARKS, *continued*

LAFS.68.RH.3.7 Integrate visual information (e.g., in charts, graphs, photographs, videos, or maps) with other information in print and digital texts.

LAFS.68.WHST.2.5 With some guidance and support from peers and adults, develop and strengthen writing as needed by planning, editing, revising, rewriting, or trying a new approach, focusing on how well purpose and audience have been addressed.

LAFS.68.WHST.3.8 Gather relevant information from multiple print and digital sources, using search terms effectively; assess the credibility and accuracy of each source.

MAFS.K12.MP.3.1 Construct viable arguments and critique the reasoning of others.

The Judicial Branch

Make this Foldable® and label the tabs *Federal Courts* and *Supreme Court.* Under each tab, list important terms and note significant individuals, events, or responsibilities relating to these courts. Record a phrase, write a short sentence, or sketch something next to each to help you remember what you read. On the back of your Foldable, describe what you think the nation would be like if there were no court systems.

Step 1
Use an 11" x 17" sheet of paper arranged horizontally. Fold the left side of the paper over to the right edge and fold the paper in half.

Step 2
While the paper is folded in half horizontally, fold the top of the paper down to the bottom to fold in half vertically.

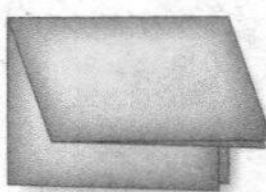

Step 3
Unfold paper and cut the horizontal fold from the left edge to the center of the paper.

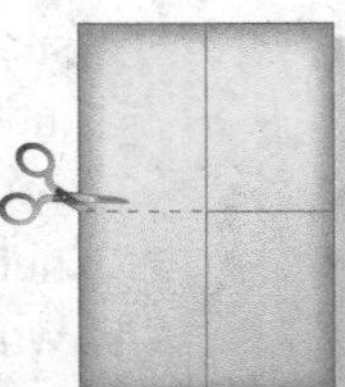

Step 4
Fold the shutters down and label as directed.

LESSON 1 SUMMARY

Federal Courts

SS.7.C.3.3, SS.7.C.3.8, SS.7.C.3.11

Role of the Federal Courts

Courts make up the judiciary, or the judicial branch of government. The judiciary has two main jobs. The first is to make sure laws are fairly enforced. The second is to interpret the laws. Courts hear two types of cases: criminal and civil.

In criminal cases, people accused of crimes appear in court for a trial. In a criminal trial, witnesses present evidence. A jury or a judge listens to the evidence and then decides whether the accused person is innocent or guilty.

In civil cases, courts use laws to settle civil disputes. A civil dispute is a conflict between parties that believe their rights have been harmed. Such civil disputes can be between:

- two private parties (people, companies, or organizations)
- a private party and the government
- the U.S. government and a state or local government
- state governments

Both sides present their positions in court. The court applies the law to those facts and decides in favor of one side or the other.

Origin of the Federal Court System

Under the Articles of Confederation, there was no national court system. Each state had its own laws and its own courts. There was no guarantee that people would receive equal justice in all the states. To solve these problems, the Founders created a federal judiciary. Article III of the Constitution established a national Supreme Court and gave Congress the power to make lower federal courts. Congress passed the Judiciary Act of 1789. This legislation established two types of lower federal courts: district courts and circuit courts. The district courts were trial courts for specific geographic areas. These courts heard minor civil and criminal cases. Circuit courts took more serious cases. They also heard appeals from district courts. In 1891, Congress determined that circuit courts would only hear appeals.

The structure of the federal courts has remained the same over time. The 94 district courts at the lower level are trial courts. The 13 circuit courts are appeals courts. The Supreme Court, the court of final appeal, is at the top.

1. EVALUATING

Determine whether each case below is a civil case or a criminal case.

A home owner sues a contractor for not living up to a construction contract.

Criminal ☐ Civil ☐

A motorist is arrested for drunk driving and running a red light.

Criminal ☐ Civil ☐

An individual is caught trying to rob a pharmacy.

Criminal ☐ Civil ☐

A customer slips on the icy sidewalk in front of a store and sues the store owner for compensation.

Criminal ☐ Civil ☐

2. ANALYZING

Why do you think the Articles of Confederation did not include a national court system? What problems resulted from this?

____

____

____

____

____

____

____

Name ______________________ Date ______________ Class ________

3. ANALYZING INFORMATION

Complete the graphic organizer showing the hierarchy of the federal court system.

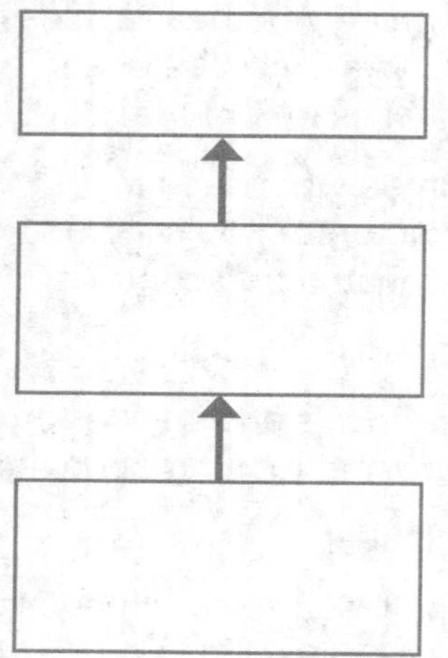

4. REFLECTING

In your opinion, how well do U.S. courts live up to the ideal of "equal justice under the law"? Explain your answer.

____

____

____

____

____

____

____

____

____

Dual Court System

The United States has a **dual court system.** The federal court system represents the nation. Each of the 50 states has its own court system and laws. Federal courts get their powers from the U.S. Constitution and laws passed by Congress. State courts get their powers from their state constitutions and state laws.

DUAL COURT SYSTEM	
Federal Courts	**State Courts**
Three levels: trial, appeals, Supreme	Three levels: trial, appeals, supreme (structure and names of courts vary by state)
Derive powers from U.S. Constitution and federal laws	Derive powers from state constitutions and state laws
Hear cases involving federal law	Hear cases involving state law
Most judges appointed for life	Most judges elected or appointed for set terms
U.S. Supreme Court: appeals from state supreme courts allowed	State appeals courts: no cases that originate in federal courts

The Goal of the Court System

Our legal system is based on the ideal of equal justice under the law. The goal of the courts is to treat every person the same. Each person accused of a crime is considered innocent until proven guilty. To achieve equal justice, the Constitution gives accused people the right to a public trial. If the accused cannot afford a lawyer, the court will provide one.

Equal justice is difficult to achieve. Judges and juries sometimes have their own viewpoints and prejudices. Wealthy people and corporations can spend more money for legal defense teams than poor people. Nonetheless, American courts try very hard to ensure equal justice for all.

Name ______________________ Date ____________ Class ________

Federal Court Jurisdiction

Most court cases involve state laws and are tried in state courts. Article III of the Constitution gives federal courts **jurisdiction**—the authority to hear and decide a case—only in certain kinds of cases. This way, federal courts do not interfere with state courts. See the table below for cases in which federal courts have jurisdiction.

FEDERAL COURT JURISDICTION
the Constitution and constitutional rights
federal crimes such as kidnapping, tax evasion, and counterfeiting
disputes between the states
disputes between citizens of different states
accidents or crimes that occur at sea
disputes between the U.S. government and foreign governments and diplomats

Types of Jurisdiction

In most of the areas listed above, federal courts have **exclusive jurisdiction.** This means that only federal courts have the authority to hear those cases. When state law is involved, the case is heard in a state court.

In some cases, however, both federal and state courts have jurisdiction. This is called **concurrent jurisdiction.** For example, if someone is accused of a crime that breaks both federal and state law, the trial can be held in either federal or state court.

5. RECOGNIZING BIAS

Why do you think federal courts have jurisdiction on disputes involving the states? Give an example of such a case.

6. REASONING

If a civil case has concurrent jurisdiction, how do you believe the person who brings the suit would choose whether to use a federal court or a state court?

REVIEW LESSON 1

1. Complete this Venn diagram on types of jurisdiction.

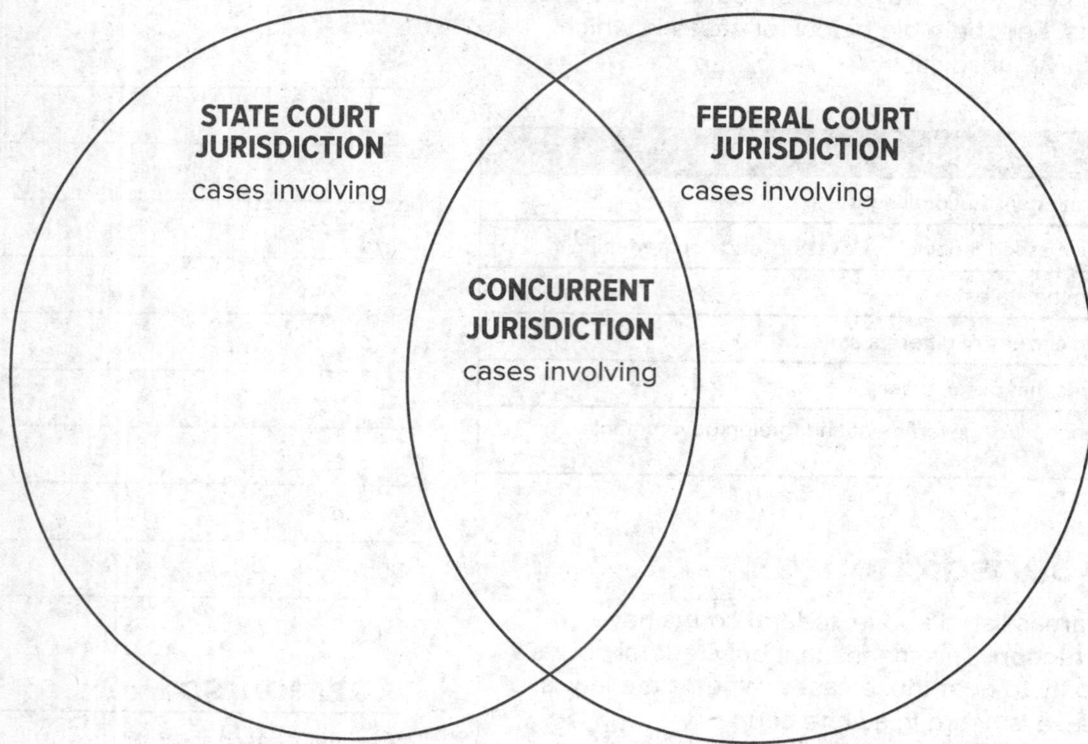

2. **MAKING INFERENCES** Write an essay to explain why the Constitution gives federal courts the power to hear cases involving foreign diplomats. Use a separate sheet of paper for your essay.

LESSON 2 SUMMARY

The Federal Court System

SS.7.C.1.7, SS.7.C.2.10, SS.7.C.3.3, SS.7.C.3.8, SS.7.C.3.11

The Lower Courts

The federal court system has three levels, each with its own purpose and structure. At the top of the federal system is the U.S. Supreme Court. District courts and circuit courts of appeals make up the lower federal courts. Each has its own role in the judicial system.

District Courts

The U.S. district courts are the lowest level of the federal system. These courts typically have **original jurisdiction.** This means that these courts have the authority to hear cases for the first time. There are 94 district courts. Every state has at least one. Some states have more. Most federal cases begin in a U.S. district court.

District courts take both criminal and civil cases. District courts are the only federal courts in which witnesses testify and juries hear cases and reach verdicts.

Circuit Courts of Appeals

The next level in the federal court system consists of the circuit courts of appeals. These courts are also called federal appeals courts, courts of appeals, or appellate courts. A court of appeals is not a trial court. These courts do not decide on a person's guilt or innocence or which party should win a lawsuit. Instead, they have **appellate jurisdiction,** which is the authority to review a lower court case. Appeals courts may also review the decisions of a federal regulatory agency if a party says that the agency acted unfairly.

Lawyers appeal a case when they believe that the district court judge has made a mistake during the trial. The appeal is based on how the judge in the lower court applied the law in that particular case. Appeals can also be based on how the judge in the lower court interpreted the law. Sometimes a person found guilty might think that the judge was wrong to allow certain evidence to be used. The losing side in a case is the side that appeals. In a criminal case, only the accused person who has been found guilty can file an appeal. If the prosecution in the criminal case loses, there can be no appeal.

1. EVALUATING

Decide which court would hear each case below. Write DC if the case would be heard by a U.S. District Court. Write CC if it would be heard by a U.S. Circuit Court.

Person A is charged with counterfeiting $20 bills.

____

Person A is convicted of counterfeiting and wants to appeal. _______

The Environmental Protection Agency fines a U.S.-based company for polluting. The company believes the fine is too high. _______

An employer prohibits Miriam from hanging a poster with a political message at her desk. Miriam believes her free-speech rights are being violated.

____

2. DETERMINING CENTRAL IDEAS

Why is the government prohibited from appealing a case if the defendant is found not guilty?

____

____

____

____

____

Name ______________________ Date ______________ Class __________

3. SEQUENCING

Number each event (either 1, 2, or 3) to place the three events in the correct chronological order.

_____ The Court of Appeals remands the case.

_____ A new trial begins.

_____ A decision from a district court is appealed.

There are 12 circuit courts of appeals. Each court has jurisdiction over a specific geographic area called a *circuit*. In 1981, Congress added a 13th appeals court to hear special cases involving international trade, patent laws, or other civil cases brought against the United States. This court is called the Court of Appeals for the Federal Circuit. It is based in Washington, D.C., but it can hear cases everywhere in the United States.

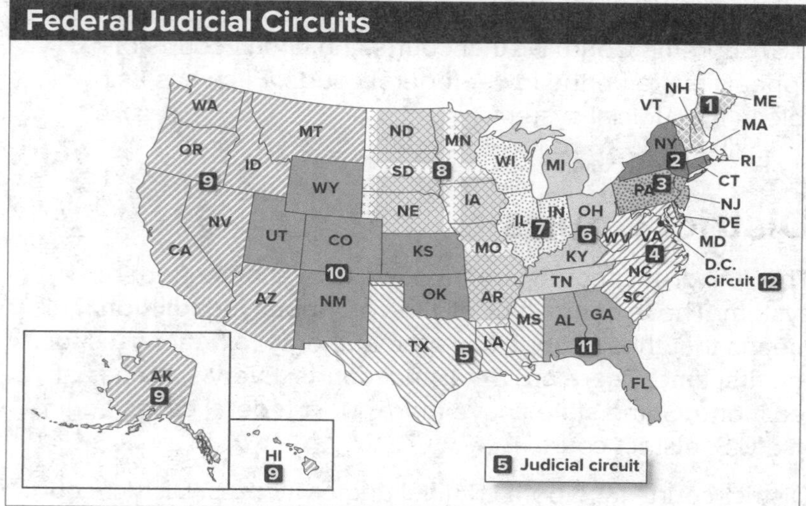

Rulings

Appeals courts do not hold trials or decide on guilt or innocence. Instead, a panel of three or more judges reviews the case. This panel of judges also listens to arguments made by lawyers for both sides. Then the panel meets and decides whether the original trial was fair. The panel's decision is known as a **ruling.** A ruling is an official decision that settles a case and helps establish the meaning of the law. There are three ways that judges can decide a case.

- They can uphold the result of the trial. The verdict in that trial remains unchanged.
- They can reverse the result of the trial. Judges will take this step if they think the original judge made an error in procedure or in interpreting the law.
- They can remand the case. This means that they send the case back to the lower court to be tried again. Judges will remand a case when they think there was some kind of problem in the original trial.

Decisions of the courts of appeals can be appealed. Without an appeal, however, the decisions are final. Any appeals are made to the U.S. Supreme Court.

LESSON 2 SUMMARY, *continued*

Opinions

When an appeals court makes a ruling, only one judge will write the opinion on that case for the court. The **opinion** explains in detail the legal thoughts on which the judges based their decision. The opinion also sets an example to be followed by other judges in their district. This example is called a **precedent.** Judges use precedents to help make decisions in future cases that are similar. A precedent does not have the force of law. However, precedents are used as a basis for legal arguments in future cases. Judges and courts almost always follow precedents as they make their decisions.

4. MAKING GENERALIZATIONS

What are the advantages of the doctrine of judicial precedent? Are there any disadvantages?

____

____

____

____

____

____

____

Principles of the Legal System

Federal courts have followed certain principles, or guiding ideas, since the early days of the nation's founding. An important principle is that no federal court can decide a question of law by seeking out a lawsuit. Federal courts cannot ask for cases to be brought to them. The courts must wait for **litigants,** or parties involved in a lawsuit, to bring a suit to them.

The decisions of the highest court are binding on all lower courts. This means that if the Supreme Court decides a case, that decision is binding on all courts in the country. Likewise, if a state supreme court decides an issue, that decision is binding on all lower courts in the state.

Federal Judges

The federal court system has more than 650 district court judges. Each district court has at least two judges. In areas with large populations, the district court may have more than two judges. More cases will be heard, and therefore more judges are needed. Each appeals court has from 6 to 28 judges. The Supreme Court has nine judges. Supreme Court judges are called *justices.*

Use the graphic organizer to identify the number of judges in each level of the federal court system.

FEDERAL COURT	NUMBER OF JUDGES
U.S. Supreme Court	
U.S. Circuit Court of Appeals	
U.S. District Court	

Name ______________________ Date ______________ Class __________

Appointing Federal Judges

Article II, Section 2 of the Constitution gives the president the power to appoint all federal judges. However, a majority of U.S. senators must approve these judicial appointments. Presidents often use senatorial courtesy when they appoint judges to district courts. This means that the president will tell senators from a nominee's home state about the choice before making the choice public. If a senator from that home state objects to the president's choice, the president usually chooses a different nominee. Senatorial courtesy usually only applies to the naming of district court judges.

The appointment process begins when a judge resigns, retires, or dies. The Constitution does not list specific qualifications for federal judges. Presidents usually appoint judges who have similar ideas about justice and the law. Presidents are also careful to choose candidates who are likely to be approved by the Senate.

Other groups weigh in on judicial appointments. The Justice Department may offer its opinion of the nominee. The American Bar Association often submits its own opinion or rating of the nominee's past legal decisions. Other interest groups will often review the opinions of a nominee and provide their views about the nominee as well.

Term of Office

Federal judges have their jobs for life. The Framers gave this right to judges for a specific reason. They believed that the right to hold their office, or **tenure,** for life would shield judges from public or political pressures when they hear cases. It is not easy to remove a federal judge. It can be done, however, through the process of impeachment.

Other Court Officials

Judges have staffs consisting of clerks, secretaries, and court reporters. In addition, three key officials serve in each district court. Magistrate judges help district court judges by doing much of the routine work. For example, a magistrate judge can issue search warrants and hear preliminary, or introductory, evidence. Then the magistrate judge decides whether a case should be brought to trial. Magistrates also make decisions about whether people under arrest can be released on bail or if they should be kept in jail. A magistrate judge may also try minor cases. Magistrate judges are appointed by a majority of the federal judges in a district. They typically serve terms of eight years and can be reappointed.

5. RECOGNIZING RELATIONSHIPS

How does the nomination process for federal judges reflect the principle of separation of powers?

____

____

____

____

6. ASSESSING

Do you think that the senators from a judicial nominee's state should be able to approve or reject a nominee before the nomination is made public?

____

____

____

____

____

____

7. CONSTRUCTING AN ARGUMENT

Life tenure for federal judges was intended to foster judicial independence. As life expectancy grows, critics have called for a reconsideration of tenure on the grounds that the work of older judges may begin to suffer. On a separate sheet of paper, write an essay that takes a position on this issue.

Name ______________________ Date ______________ Class ________

LESSON 2 SUMMARY, *continued*

Each district has a U.S. attorney and one or more deputies. These are the lawyers who prosecute people accused of breaking federal law. This legal team also represents the government of the United States in civil cases. The president appoints U.S. attorneys, and they serve four-year terms. Their appointments must be approved by the Senate.

In addition to the U.S. attorney, each federal judicial district also has a U.S. Marshal. Their jobs, however, are very different. Marshals and their staffs make arrests, collect fines, and transport convicted persons to prison. It is the job of the marshals to protect jurors, to keep order in federal courts, and to deliver subpoenas. A **subpoena** is a court order that requires a person to appear in court.

8. PREDICTING CONSEQUENCES

What might happen if a subpoena is ignored?

REVIEW LESSON 2

1. Use the Venn diagram below to decide whether each description fits district courts only, courts of appeals only, or both. Write the letter of the description in the correct part of the diagram. The first one is done for you.

A. hear civil cases

B. might have a jury trial

C. do not decide a defendant's guilt or innocence

D. hear criminal cases

E. review verdicts to check for errors

F. usually have a panel of judges

G. usually have original jurisdiction

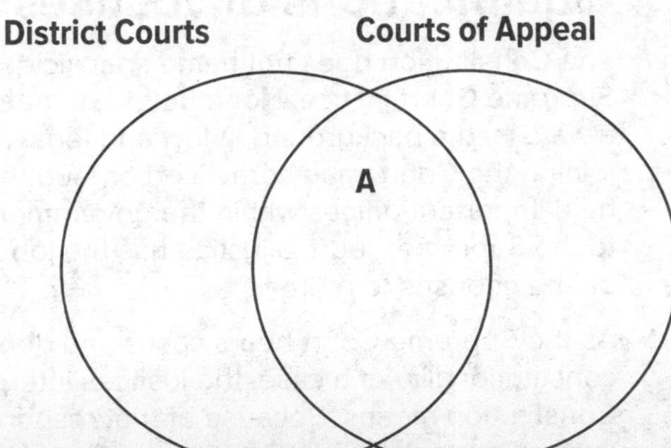

2. **IDENTIFYING CENTRAL ISSUES** Use the information from this diagram to answer the following question: Why is appellate jurisdiction important? Write your essay on a separate sheet of paper.

LESSON 3 SUMMARY

The Supreme Court

1. DISTINGUISHING FACT FROM OPINION

Suppose a classmate tells you that the Supreme Court is "mainly a trial court." Is this accurate? Explain.

2. REFLECTING

What qualifications and personal characteristics do you think are needed by Supreme Court justices? Explain.

SS.7.C.1.7, SS.7.C.3.3, SS.7.C.3.8, SS.7.C.3.11, SS.7.C.3.12

Jurisdiction and Duties

The primary role of the Supreme Court is to decide whether laws are constitutional. The Court has just nine justices. The Court's leader is called the chief justice, and the others are associate justices. While the Constitution sets up the court system, the number of justices is set by Congress.

The Supreme Court has original jurisdiction in only two types of cases: those involving disputes between two or more states and those involving diplomats from foreign countries. All other Supreme Court cases come from appeals from lower courts. The Court has final authority in cases involving the Constitution, acts of Congress, and treaties with other nations. All other courts must follow the decisions made by the Supreme Court.

Every year, the Court is asked to review thousands of cases. The justices choose to hear only a small percentage of those cases. When the Court decides not to hear a case, the decision of the lower court will stand.

Qualifications of Justices

The Constitution does not name specific qualifications for a Supreme Court justice. Nonetheless, to date justices have always had a background in law and legal training. Before joining the Court, many practiced or taught law. Many have held important offices within the government. Once appointed to the Supreme Court, a justice has the job for life or until he or she chooses to retire.

As the Supreme Court hears cases and decides upon the constitutionality of a case, the justices interpret what the Constitution means. Because of that responsibility, a nominee to the Court is carefully scrutinized. Past decisions are examined to see how a nominee has ruled in various cases.

As with other federal judge appointments, presidents want a justice who shares similar ideas about the law. Presidents also choose nominees carefully so that the Court nominees win approval in the Senate. Other interest groups offer their point of view and commendation or reasons for rejection as well.

Name ______________________ Date ______________ Class ________

Powers and Limits

Article III of the Constitution created the judicial branch. The Constitution, however, does not provide a thorough description of the judiciary. Over the years, Congress has established most of the rules that give the Supreme Court its powers and organization. The constitutional system of checks and balances limits the power of the Supreme Court, as it does the entire federal court system.

3. MAKING INFERENCES

Nine justices serve on the U.S. Supreme Court. The number nine is an odd number. Is having an odd number of justices important to the makeup of the Court?

Judicial Review

The Supreme Court has the power to review any federal, state, or local law or action. It is the Court's job to see that these laws and actions are in accord with the Constitution. This power to review laws is known as **judicial review.** A law that is **constitutional** follows the Constitution and can remain in effect. If the Court decides that a law is unconstitutional, it can **nullify,** or cancel, that law.

The Supreme Court uses its power of judicial review as a check on the legislative and executive branches. Congress and the president must follow the rulings of the Supreme Court. Judicial review also applies to state and local laws. If the Supreme Court finds a state or local law to be unconstitutional, it cannot stand. Government at every level must follow the decisions of the Supreme Court.

Marbury v. *Madison*

The power of judicial review is not spelled out in the Constitution. The Judiciary Act of 1789 gave the Court this power, and at the time, judicial review was limited to acts of state governments. The 1803 Supreme Court case *Marbury* v. *Madison* is considered a landmark case. The ruling in this case made it clear that the Court had the same power in regard to acts of Congress.

Chief Justice John Marshall described the power of judicial review when he said:

"It is emphatically [strongly] the province [function] and duty of the judicial department to say what the law is. Those who apply the rule to particular cases, must of necessity expound [explain] and interpret that rule. If two laws conflict with each other, the courts must decide on the operation of each."

—Chief Justice John Marshall, *Marbury* v. *Madison* (1803)

4. IDENTIFYING CENTRAL ISSUES

Critics of Supreme Court rulings sometimes characterize the Court's decisions as "unconstitutional." On a separate sheet of paper, answer the following questions: Can a Supreme Court ruling be unconstitutional? When the Court rules on a constitutional issue, do those who disagree have any recourse? Explain.

The opinion in *Marbury* v. *Madison* sets three principles of judicial review:

- The Constitution is the supreme law of the land.
- If there is a conflict between the Constitution and any other law, the Constitution rules.
- The judicial branch has a duty to uphold the Constitution. It must be able to nullify laws that are found to be unconstitutional.

Limits on the Supreme Court

Just as with the other two branches of government, there are limits to the power of the Supreme Court. For example, the Court can only hear and rule on cases that are referred directly to the Court for review. No person or organization can simply ask the Court to decide whether a law is constitutional. The Court will only rule on a law or action that has been challenged on appeal from a lower court. Furthermore, the Court can only hear cases that involve a federal question.

Traditionally, the Court has avoided dealing with political matters. However, after the 2000 presidential election, the court did hear two cases of a political nature. Both of these cases involved recounting of votes in Florida.

The Supreme Court does not have the power to enforce its rulings. This too limits the power of the Court. It depends on the executive branch and on state and local officials to carry out its rulings.

If Congress disagrees with a Court ruling, it can pass a new law or change a law that has been ruled unconstitutional. Congress can also try to undo a Court ruling by amending the Constitution. For example, in *Dred Scott* v. *Sandford* (1857), the Court said that African Americans could not be U.S. citizens. The Fourteenth Amendment, approved in 1868, overturned that part of the Court's decision.

ANALYZING VISUALS

5. IDENTIFYING CENTRAL ISSUES

Study the Landmark Cases of the Supreme Court chart. Which cases addressed the issue of free speech? Which addressed the rights of the accused?

____

____

____

____

____

____

LANDMARK CASES OF THE SUPREME COURT
***Marbury* v. *Madison* (1803)**
In this landmark case the Supreme Court held that it is the Court itself that has the final say on what the Constitution means. The Supreme Court also has the final say in whether an act of government violates the Constitution.
***Plessy* v. *Ferguson* (1896)**
When it came to the doctrine of "separate but equal" used by Southern states to practice segregation, the Supreme Court held that the equal protection clause of the Fourteenth Amendment did not require equal access to the same facilities, just equal public facilities for the two races.
***Brown* v. *Board of Education* (1954)**
This case overruled *Plessy* v. *Ferguson* and abandoned the "separate but equal" doctrine in public schools. The Court held that racial segregation violates the equal protection clause of the Fourteenth Amendment. The Court's holding in this case has been extended beyond public education to nearly all public accommodations and activities.
***Gideon* v. *Wainwright* (1963)**
The Supreme Court ruled in this case that poor defendants facing criminal charges have the right to a state-paid attorney under the Sixth Amendment.
***Miranda* v. *Arizona* (1966)**
This landmark case held that a person in police custody cannot be questioned unless told that • he or she has the right to remain silent • he or she has the right to an attorney, at public expense if the person is unable to pay • anything the person says after acknowledging that he or she understands these rights can be used as evidence of guilt at trial
***In re Gault* (1967)**
This case was brought by parents on behalf of their 15-year-old-son, Gerald Gault, who was charged and convicted in juvenile court without representation by an attorney. The Supreme Court ruled that juveniles are entitled to the same due process as adults.
***Tinker* v. *Des Moines* (1969)**
The Supreme Court held that public schools could not violate the First Amendment rights of students. The case involved students who were suspended for wearing armbands as a symbol of opposition to the Vietnam War.
***Hazelwood School District* v. *Kuhlmeier* (1988)**
In this case, the Supreme Court decided that students' First Amendment rights do not include deciding what will and will not be published in a school newspaper that is part of school curriculum.
***United States* v. *Nixon* (1974)**
When President Richard Nixon resisted a court order on the basis of presidential confidentiality, the Supreme Court disagreed. The Court held that not all presidential communications are protected from a judicial order of disclosure.
***Bush* v. *Gore* (2000)**
When the presidential election of 2000 was close to a tie in the state of Florida, the state supreme court ordered a recount. Lawyers for Republican candidate George W. Bush appealed the case to the U.S. Supreme Court, which ordered the recount to stop. The reason was because across Florida, different counties used different methods of voting, and every ballot would not be treated equally. As a result, Bush became president.

REVIEW LESSON 3

1. Use the chart below to identify the three principles of judicial review.

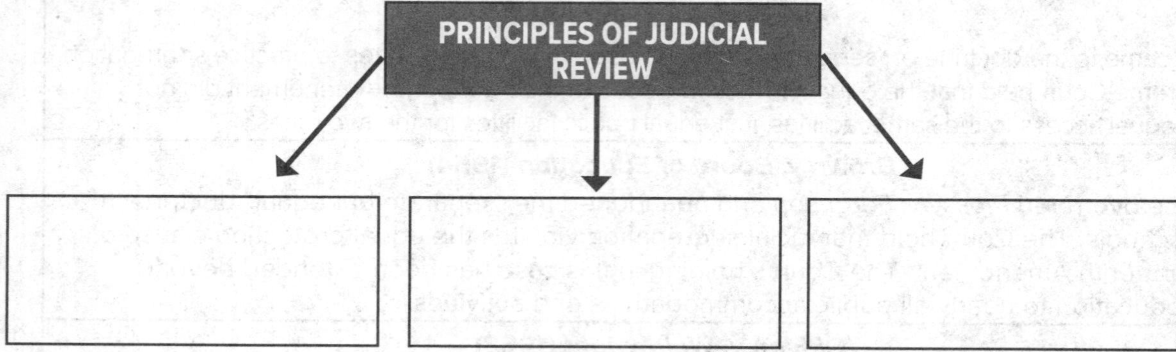

2. **EVALUATING** Using the graphic organizer above, write an essay on a separate sheet of paper about the Supreme Court's ruling in *Marbury* v. *Madison*. Some have called it the most important decision in the history of the Supreme Court. Would you agree? Explain why or why not.

Supreme Court Procedures and Decisions

SS.7.C.3.3, SS.7.C.3.8, SS.7.C.3.11, SS.7.C.3.12

Court Procedures

The Supreme Court meets each year for about nine months. The Court begins each of its terms on the first Monday in October. That term usually ends in early summer of the next year. Terms are named after the year in which they begin, so the 2016 term began in October 2016 and ended in 2017. Sometimes special Court sessions are called to handle urgent matters. When hearing cases, justices follow specific procedures.

Most cases reach the Supreme Court after a decision is made by a lower court. A case comes to the Court by a request for a writ of certiorari. A **writ of certiorari** is an order that the higher court, in this case the Supreme Court, issues to a lower court. The lower court is instructed to send its records for a particular case to the higher court. The Supreme Court will then review the lower court records for that case. The Court receives about 10,000 petitions, or requests for writ of certiorari, each term but grants only about 75 to 80 of them. The Court accepts a case when four of the nine justices agree to do so. Accepted cases go on the Court **docket,** or calendar. The number of cases the Court hears each session is called the **caseload.**

Complete the flowchart to show what happens when the Supreme Court receives a request to hear a case.

PATH TO THE SUPREME COURT

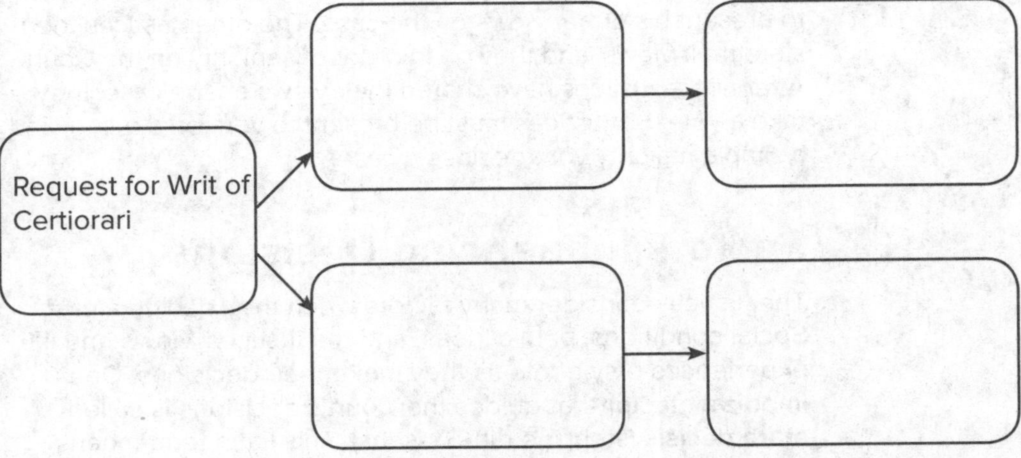

1. POSING QUESTIONS

Suppose you are a Supreme Court justice trying to decide whether the Court should hear a certain case. Write three questions you would ask about the case to make your determination.

Name ______________________ Date ______________ Class __________

2. ASSESSING

How long does each side in a Supreme Court case have to make its oral argument? Do you think this is enough time to make a case? Explain.

3. IDENTIFYING EVIDENCE

Underline the factors influencing Supreme Court decisions. Then, on a separate sheet of paper, explain which factor you believe a justice should consider first when making a decision about a case, and why.

The decision about which cases to hear is a critical one. The Court tends to select cases that involve important constitutional questions or that the justices deem to be critical to the nation. Such cases may involve constitutional issues like freedom of speech, equal protection of the laws, and fair trials. Justices also take cases when courts of appeal have made different decisions on the same point of law.

How the Court's Rulings Are Made

Once the Court announces that it will take a case, lawyers for each side write a brief. A **brief** is a document that explains one side's position on the case. The two opposing parties in the case can study each other's briefs and give a second brief to the Court. The second briefs are shorter. They address the arguments made in the first briefs. Groups that are interested in the case can also write briefs in support of one side or the other and submit their briefs to the Court. After all the briefs are filed, the justices examine them and develop questions.

Next, lawyers for each side present oral arguments to the Court. Each side gets only 30 minutes for its arguments. The party that appealed the case goes first. During oral arguments, the justices ask the lawyers questions about their side of the case. Questions asked by the justices tend to be demanding, and the argument proceedings can be grueling for both sides.

Conference

The justices meet once a week during the Court's term to discuss the cases they have heard. These meetings are held in secret. There are no official meeting minutes, and no audience is allowed to attend, The Chief Justice presides and is the first to present his or her views on the case. The other justices then state their views, and they go in order of seniority on the Court. After all the justices have shared their views on the case, they take a vote. Six justices must be present to vote on a ruling, and a simple majority vote decides a case.

Factors Influencing Decisions

The justices consider many factors when they decide a case. Social conditions, public ideas, and the justices' views and life experiences play a role as they make their decisions. One important factor that guides the Court's decisions is called **stare decisis** (stehr•ee dih•SY•suhs). This Latin term means "let the decision stand." In other words, follow precedent.

However, the body of law governing the nation and its people must also be able to change with the times. Social conditions change. Technology and innovation bring new challenges. New laws are needed to deal with the changing times, and the laws must follow the Constitution. As the highest U.S. court, the Supreme Court can overturn precedents and interpret laws in new ways. For example, in *Brown* v. *Board of Education* (1954), the Court overturned earlier decisions that supported racial segregation. In *Miranda* v. *Arizona* (1966) the Court ruled that at the time of arrest, suspects could not be questioned until they were informed of their rights.

Writing Opinions

After the Court has made a decision about a case, at least one justice writes the opinion for the majority. The majority opinion states the facts, gives the ruling, and explains how the Court reached its decision. The reasoning often draws on the precedents set by earlier decisions. These written opinions from the Supreme Court set a precedent for lower courts.

4. REFLECTING

Review the *Miranda* case. One of the Miranda rights is the right to remain silent, which means that the police must advise a suspect that he or she has the right to remain silent during questioning. Why do you think this is an important right in the judicial system?

____

____

____

____

____

____

LANDMARK SUPREME COURT DECISIONS

CIVIL LIBERTIES

- ***Brown v. Board of Education* (1954)** overturned ***Plessy v. Ferguson* (1896)**, which said African Americans could be provided with "separate but equal" public facilities; began school integration
- ***Reed v. Reed* (1971)** held that a state law that discriminated against women was unconstitutional
- ***Roe v. Wade* (1973)** legalized a woman's right to an abortion under certain circumstances
- ***Bush v. Gore* (2000)** ruled that Florida recount of presidential votes violated Fourteenth Amendment; recount stopped and Bush became president

FIRST AMENDMENT RIGHTS

- ***Brandenburg v. Ohio* (1969)** expanded the protection of political speech unless it is linked to immediate lawless behavior
- ***Near v. Minnesota* (1931)** ruled against censorship of information, defining "prior restraint" of written material as unconstitutional
- ***DeJonge v. Oregon* (1937)** reinforced peaceable assembly and association protection of the First Amendment
- ***Engel v. Vitale* (1962)** held that a public school district's practice of starting the day with prayer violates the establishment clause
- ***United States v. Eichman* (1990)** struck down Federal Flag Protection Act; held that flag burning is expressive speech

FEDERAL POWER

- ***Marbury v. Madison* (1803)** established the Supreme Court's power of judicial review
- ***McCulloch v. Maryland* (1819)** ruled that in a conflict between national and state power, the national government is supreme
- ***Gibbons v. Ogden* (1824)** established that Congress has sole authority to regulate interstate commerce

RIGHTS OF THE ACCUSED

- ***Gideon v. Wainwright* (1963)** declared that a person accused of a major crime had the right to legal counsel during a trial
- ***Miranda v. Arizona* (1966)** ruled that at the time of arrest suspects cannot be questioned until informed of their rights
- ***Hamdan v. Rumsfeld* (2006)** ruled that special military courts for foreign prisoners violated U.S. military law and international laws

5. DRAWING CONCLUSIONS

How can a dissenting opinion influence judicial precedent? Explain.

Sometimes a justice agrees with the majority decision but has different reasons for supporting the Court's decision. That justice can write a **concurring opinion.** In that opinion, the justice will lay out the differing legal reasons for agreement with the majority. Justices who disagree with the Court's decision in the case can choose to write **dissenting opinions.** In these opinions, justices often cite precedents to explain and support their views. If all the justices agree on the decision in a case, the Court issues a **unanimous opinion.** These decisions are especially powerful.

Opinions are first drafted and justices on each side, majority and minority, review the opinion for their side. When all the justices' opinions have been written, reviewed, and revised, the Court announces its decision. These written opinions guide rulings in new cases before the Supreme Court and other courts around the country.

REVIEW LESSON 4

1. Use the chart below to show the sequence of a Supreme Court case.

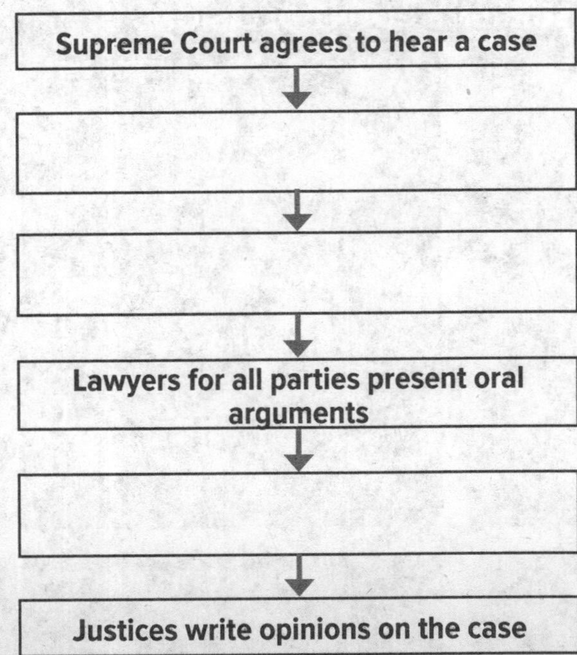
Supreme Court agrees to hear a case
Lawyers for all parties present oral arguments
Justices write opinions on the case

2. **CONSTRUCTING AN ARGUMENT** From the roughly 10,000 petitions it receives each year, the Supreme Court selects only about 75 cases. Explanations for the Court's decisions are almost never given. Should they be? Should the Court indicate how individual justices voted in the selection process? Why or why not? On a separate sheet of paper, write an essay answering these questions.

Benchmark Skill Activities

DIRECTIONS: Write your answers on a separate piece of paper.

LAFS.68.WHST.2.5

1. REFLECTING

Use your FOLDABLES to write an essay.

You have described what you think the United States would be like without a court system. Exchange Foldables with a classmate. Read your classmate's reflections, edit as needed, and make comments that you think would improve your classmate's writing. Then, return Foldables to their owners. Write a final essay on this topic, taking into account your classmate's revisions. Turn in your final essay and your original reflections.

LAFS.68.RH.3.7

2. MAKING INFERENCES

There are 13 circuits in the U.S. circuit courts of appeals; 12 are shown on the map below. Do you think the 9th Circuit or the 10th Circuit has the heavier caseload? Explain.

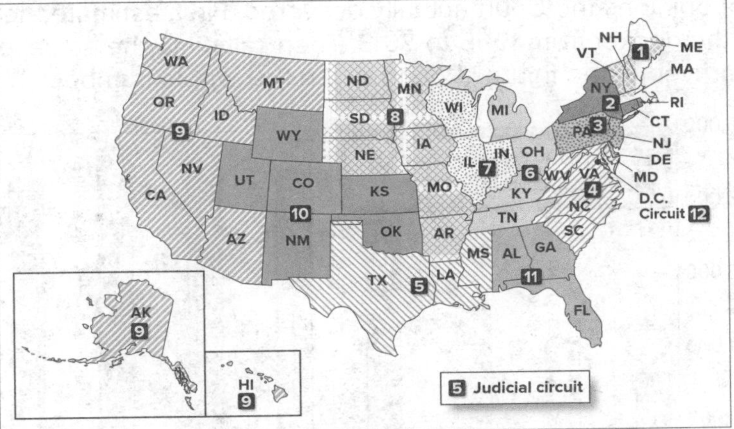

LAFS.68.RH.2.4, SS.7.C.3.11

3. COMPARING AND CONTRASTING

Compare and contrast the various types of federal jurisdiction.

LAFS.68.WHST.3.8

4. JUDGING RELIABILITY

In June 2012, the Supreme Court made an important ruling about the Affordable Care Act (sometimes referred to as Obamacare). Use the Internet to find at least six sources that discuss the potential impact of the Court's decision and evaluate the credibility and accuracy of each.

For each source you find, list the author, publication/Web site, and publication date. Then, briefly summarize the information in the source. Finally, rank the source's credibility and accuracy on a scale of 1 (completely credible and accurate) to 5 (not at all credible and accurate). Write a sentence for each source explaining how you arrived at your ranking.

MAFS.K12.MP.3.1

5. ANALYZING GRAPHS

The graph compares the number of requests for the Supreme Court to hear a case to the number of opinions the Court actually delivered. First, estimate the percent of increase in cases on the docket from 1965 to 2013. Then calculate the actual percent and explain how you arrived at the figure. (Round to the first whole number.)

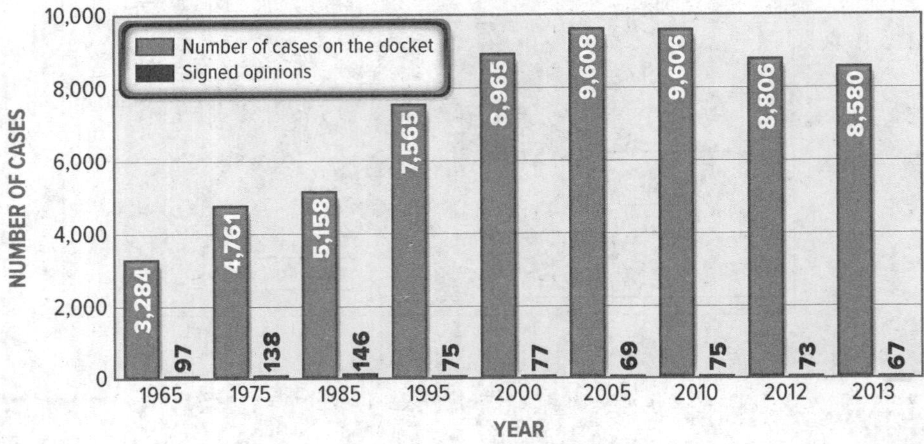

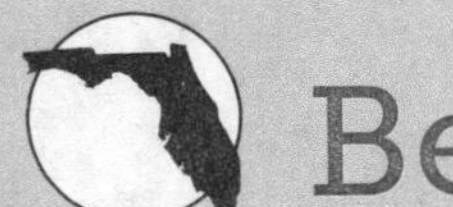

Benchmark Note Cards

DIRECTIONS: Use these note cards to help you prepare for the test.

SS.7.C.1.7 Describe how the Constitution limits the powers of government through separation of powers and checks and balances.

POWERS OF THE SUPREME COURT	Supreme Court Justices interpret what the Constitution means. Like all federal justices, they have their jobs for life. They can be removed from office only through the process of impeachment. That gives the Supreme Court great power. Judicial review is the power of the Supreme Court to declare any federal, state, or local law unconstitutional. This prevents the legislative and executive branches of government from straying too far from the Constitution. Congress and the president must follow the Constitution and the Court's rulings.

CHECKS ON THE SUPREME COURT	The system of checks and balances puts limits on the power of all federal courts, including the Supreme Court: • The Court cannot enforce its rulings. • The Court can rule only on cases before it. • Congress can change laws the Court has ruled unconstitutional.

SS.7.C.3.3 Illustrate the structure and function (three branches of government established in Articles I, II, and III with corresponding powers) of government in the United States as established in the Constitution.

STRUCTURE OF FEDERAL COURT SYSTEM

U.S. SUPREME COURT
(Judges/No Jury)
Jurisdiction: Limited original jurisdiction and appellate jurisdiction

↑

U.S. COURTS OF APPEALS
(Judges/No Jury)
Jurisdiction: Appellate

↑

U.S. DISTRICT COURT
(Judges and Juries)
Jurisdiction: Original

SS.7.C.3.8 Analyze the structure, functions, and processes of the legislative, executive, and judicial branches.

FUNCTIONS OF THE JUDICIAL BRANCH	Courts make up the judicial branch of government, and have two main jobs: to make sure laws are fairly enforced and to interpret laws. Courts hear civil cases, conflicts between people who believe their rights have been violated. Courts also hear criminal cases in which people accused of crimes are judged guilty or not guilty. A ruling is an official decision that settles a case and helps establish the meaning of the law. Previous rulings are used as examples to be followed by other judges. Such an example is called a precedent. Judges and courts almost always follow precedents.

ROLE OF THE FEDERAL COURTS	Article III of the Constitution gives federal courts jurisdiction only in certain kinds of cases. Federal courts have jurisdiction in cases involving: • the Constitution and constitutional rights • federal laws such as kidnapping, tax evasion, and counterfeiting • disputes between the states • disputes between citizens of different states • disputes involving the federal government • accidents or crimes that occur at sea • disputes between the U.S. government and foreign governments and diplomats

THE DUAL COURT SYSTEM

DUAL COURT SYSTEM	
Federal Courts	**State Courts**
Three levels: trial, appeals, Supreme	Three levels: trial, appeals, Supreme (structure and names of courts vary by state)
Derive powers from U.S. Constitution and federal laws	Derive powers from state constitutions and state laws
Hear cases involving federal law	Hear cases involving state law
Most judges appointed for life	Most judges elected or appointed for set terms
U.S. Supreme Court: appeals from state supreme courts allowed	State appeals courts: no cases that originate in federal courts

SS.7.C.3.12 Analyze the significance and outcomes of landmark Supreme Court cases including, but not limited to, *Marbury* v. *Madison*, *Plessy* v. *Ferguson*, *Brown* v. *Board of Education*, *Gideon* v. *Wainwright*, *Miranda* v. *Arizona*, *in re Gault*, *Tinker* v. *Des Moines*, *Hazelwood* v. *Kuhlmeier*, *United States* v. *Nixon*, and *Bush* v. *Gore*.

MARBURY V. MADISON

In 1803, the Supreme Court used the case of *Marbury* v. *Madison* to establish the power of judicial review in regard to acts of Congress. The opinion sets three principles of judicial review:

- The Constitution is the supreme law of the land.
- If there is a conflict between the Constitution and any other law, the Constitution rules.
- The judicial branch has a duty to uphold the Constitution. It must nullify laws that are unconstitutional.

Chapter 9

VISUAL SUMMARY

DIRECTIONS: Complete the graphic organizers below.

FEDERAL COURT SYSTEM

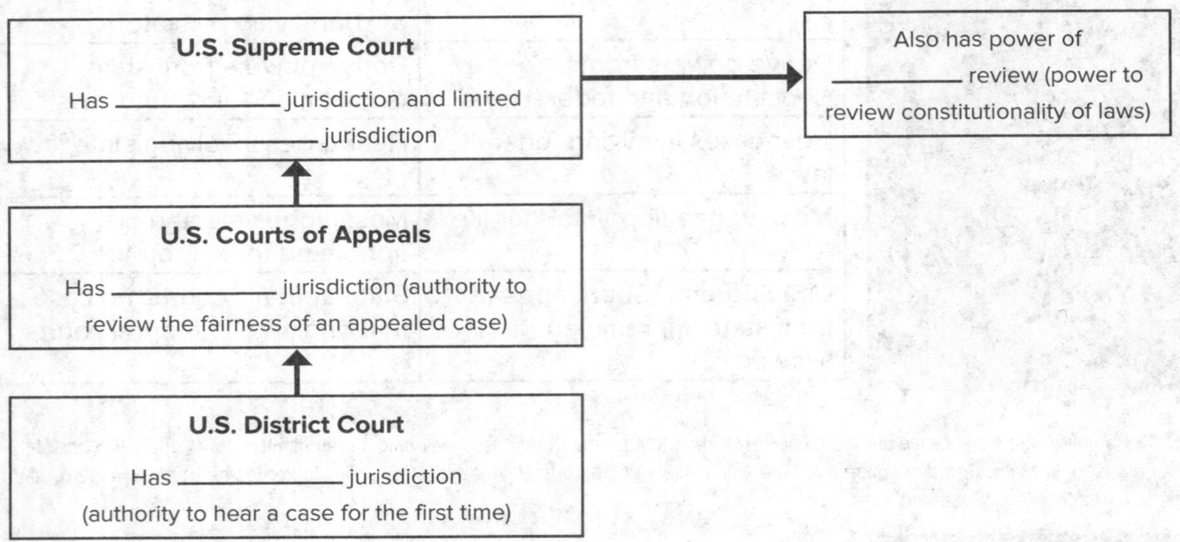

U.S. Supreme Court
Has ____________ jurisdiction and limited ____________ jurisdiction
Also has power of ____________ review (power to review constitutionality of laws)
U.S. Courts of Appeals
Has ____________ jurisdiction (authority to review the fairness of an appealed case)
U.S. District Court
Has ____________ jurisdiction (authority to hear a case for the first time)

APPEALS PROCESS

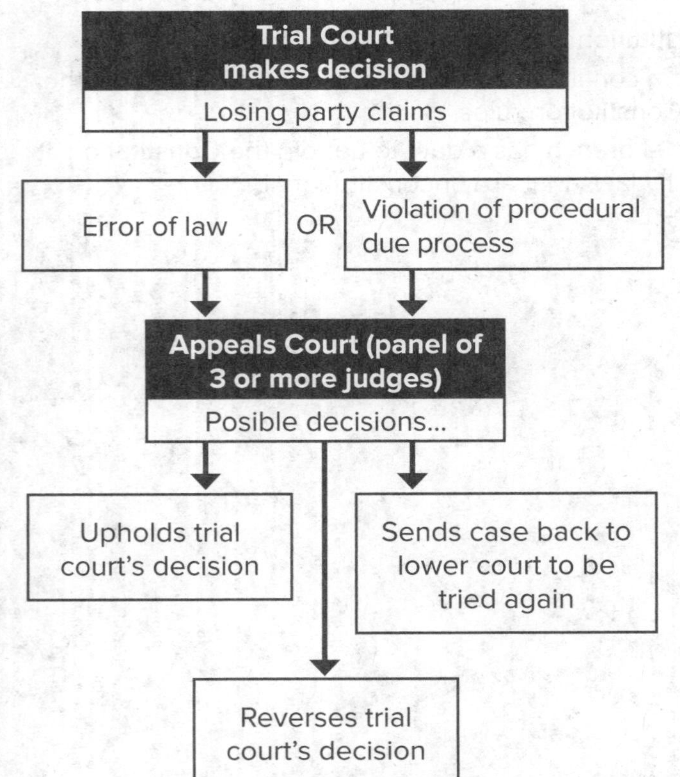

Trial Court makes decision
Losing party claims
Error of law
OR
Violation of procedural due process
Appeals Court (panel of 3 or more judges)
Posible decisions...
Upholds trial court's decision
Sends case back to lower court to be tried again
Reverses trial court's decision

Appeals court can issue various opinions about the case:

- ____________ opinion—explains how most of the judges or justices reached their decision
- ____________ opinion—written when a judge or justice agrees with the court's decision, but for different reasons
- ____________ opinion—written when a judge or justice disagrees with the court's opinion
- ____________ opinion—written when all judges or justices agree on the case

USING PRIMARY SOURCES

IDENTIFY POINTS OF VIEW Use the passage below to answer on a separate sheet of paper the questions that follow.

1. Some critics of the *Marbury* v. *Madison* decision argue that, because the states created the Constitution, the states are the rightful judges of whether a law is constitutional. What evidence might be given in support of this position?
2. What evidence would John Marshall give in response?

It is emphatically [strongly] the province [function] and duty of the judicial department to say what the law is. Those who apply the rule to particular cases must, of necessity, expound [explain] and interpret that rule. If two laws conflict with each other, the courts must decide on the operation of each.

So if a law be in opposition to the Constitution; if both the law and the constitution apply to a particular case, so that the court must either decide that case conformably to the law, disregarding the Constitution; or conformably to the Constitution, disregarding the law; the court must determine which of these conflicting rules governs the case. This is of the very essence of judicial duty.

If, then, the courts are to regard the Constitution, and the Constitution is superior to any ordinary act of the legislature, the Constitution, and not such ordinary act, must govern the case to which they both apply. . . .

From these, and many other selections which might be made, it is apparent that the framers of the Constitution contemplated that instrument as a rule for the government of courts, as well as of the legislature.

It is also not entirely unworthy of observation that, in declaring what shall be the supreme law of the land, the Constitution itself is first mentioned; and not the laws of the United States generally, but those only which shall be made in pursuance of the Constitution, have that rank.

Thus, the particular phraseology [wording] of the Constitution of the United States confirms and strengthens the principle, supposed to be essential to all written constitutions, that a law repugnant [offensive] to the Constitution is void; and that courts, as well as other departments, are bound by that instrument.

—Supreme Court Chief Justice John Marshall, *Marbury* v. *Madison* (1803)

Chapter Practice Test

DIRECTIONS: Circle the best answer for each question.

SS.7.C.3.8 (Moderate)

> *SECTION 1. Be it enacted by the Senate and House of Representatives of the United States of America in Congress assembled, That the supreme court of the United States shall consist of a chief justice and five associate justices, any four of whom shall be a quorum, and shall hold annually at the seat of government two sessions, the one commencing the first Monday of February, and the other the first Monday of August. That the associate justices shall have precedence according to the date of their commissions, or when the commissions of two or more of them bear date on the same day, according to their respective ages.*
>
> —Judiciary Act of 1789

How is the modern Supreme Court different than the court as established by the Judiciary Act of 1789?

A The order of seniority is based solely on the judges' dates of birth.

B A greater number of justices sit on the modern Court.

C There is no longer an age restriction on modern justices.

D Modern justices must have a law degree.

SS.7.C.3.3 (Moderate)

In which of the following cases does the Constitution grant exclusive jurisdiction to federal courts?

A A divorced couple in Montana cannot agree how to share financial support for their children.

B A motorist in Florida is charged with reckless driving after running over a fire hydrant.

C The states of Missouri and Illinois are in dispute over water rights on the Mississippi River.

D A senator from Ohio is accused of robbing a jewelry store in Cleveland.

3 **3. SS.7.C.3.8 (High)**

> *"Justices have come from countries around the world and visited here and they've said, 'We can't do important work the way you do because we have to decide three thousand cases a year.' They spend a lot of time pushing paper and making sure individual cases that don't have a lot of impact are correctly decided. We don't. We try to focus on the ones that are going to be important for how our system of government functions."*
>
> —The Supreme Court: A C-SPAN Book, Featuring the Justices in Their Own Words

Based on this excerpt, which of the following best reflects the caseload of the U.S. Supreme Court?

A The Court takes on only as many cases as it thinks it can thoroughly hear during a term.

B The Court takes on more cases than foreign supreme courts during its term.

C The Court takes on only those cases that are of highest national interest.

D Foreign supreme courts and the U.S. Supreme Court hear about the same number of important cases.

---

4 **SS.7.C.1.7 (Low)**

Who must approve all appointments of federal judges?

A president

B Senate

C House of Representatives

D Supreme Court

SS.7.C.3.8 (Moderate)

> *"What Daniel Webster termed 'the miracle of our Constitution' is not something that happens in every generation. But every generation in its turn must accept the responsibility of supporting and defending the Constitution, and bearing true faith and allegiance to it."*
>
> —Chief Justice John G. Roberts, Jr.

What is the main point of this quote?

A Only the Supreme Court should concern itself with constitutional issues.

B All Americans have a duty to keep the Constitution strong.

C The Constitution is no longer relevant to most Americans.

D Americans should be required to swear a loyalty oath to the Constitution.

SS.7.C.3.8 (Moderate)

Which set of events is in correct chronological order?

A A criminal defendant is found guilty. The court of appeals overturns the verdict. The defense appeals the case.

B The Supreme Court nullifies a law. Congress passes a law. The Supreme Court hears a case about the law.

C Evidence is presented to the jury. Members of a jury are chosen. The jury returns a verdict.

D Trial is held in district court. An appeal is made to the court of appeals. The Supreme Court agrees to hear the case.

SS.7.C.3.3 (High)

> *The judicial Power of the United States, shall be vested in one Supreme Court, and in such inferior Courts as the Congress may from time to time ordain and establish. The Judges, both of the supreme and inferior Courts, shall hold their Offices during good Behavior, and shall, at stated Times, receive for their Services a Compensation [payment] which shall not be diminished during their Continuance in Office.*
>
> —Article III, Section 1 of the U.S. Constitution

What is the best summary of this passage?

A The passage grants judicial power to federal courts, establishes a Supreme Court, grants life tenure to federal judges, and prohibits decreasing their salaries.

B The passage guarantees the Supreme Court the power of judicial review, allows the Supreme Court to establish inferior courts, and gives judges the right to appoint court officials.

C The passage grants all judicial power in the United States to the Supreme Court, requires all judges to be of strong moral character, and promises judges a fair salary.

D The passage allows the Supreme Court to determine the salary of members of Congress, based on the good behavior they exhibit as legislators.

SS.7.C.3.12 (Moderate)

Why was the Court's decision in *Marbury* v. *Madison* especially important?

A It established the federal court system in the United States and gave the Supreme Court exclusive jurisdiction over certain cases.

B It affirmed the Supreme Court's authority to examine executive or legislative acts and to invalidate any that contradict constitutional principles.

C It expanded the constitutional rights of individuals accused of crimes.

D It overturned earlier decisions that validated racial segregation and declared invalid the "separate but equal" doctrine.

9 **SS.7.C.1.7 (High)**

> *It is . . . rational to suppose, that the courts were designed to be an intermediate body between the people and the legislature, in order, among other things, to keep the latter within the limits assigned to their authority.*
>
> —from *Federalist* No. 78 by Alexander Hamilton (1788)

This passage can best be interpreted as a description of the process of

A appellate jurisdiction.

B exclusive jurisdiction.

C stare decisis.

D judicial review.

---

10 **SS.7.C.3.8 (Low)**

What term is used to describe a legal case establishing a principle or rule that a court adopts when deciding later cases with similar issues or facts?

A unanimous opinion

B ruling

C precedent

D writ of certiorari

CHAPTER 10

POLITICAL PARTIES

Chapter Overview

Political parties did not exist when the United States was founded, but they have become an essential part of American government. Parties help run the government as well as help citizens participate in the political process.

Today, the political system in the United States has two major parties and some smaller third parties. They differ in their ideas about the role of government.

Other countries also have political parties. The party systems, however, differ from country to country.

CHAPTER BENCHMARKS

SS.7.C.2.8 Identify America's current political parties, and illustrate their ideas about government.

SS.7.C.2.10 Examine the impact of media, individuals, and interest groups on monitoring and influencing government.

SS.7.C.3.1 Compare different forms of government (direct democracy, representative democracy, socialism, communism, monarchy, oligarchy, autocracy).

LAFS.68.RH.1.2 Determine the central ideas or information of a primary or secondary source; provide an accurate summary of the source distinct from prior knowledge or opinions.

LAFS.68.RH.2.4 Determine the meaning of words and phrases as they are used in a text, including vocabulary specific to domains related to history/social studies.

LAFS.68.RH.2.6 Identify aspects of a text that reveal an author's point of view or purpose (e.g., loaded language, inclusion or avoidance of particular facts).

LAFS.68.WHST.1.1 Write arguments focused on discipline-specific content.

LAFS.68.WHST.4.10 Write routinely over extended time frames (time for reflection and revision) and shorter time frames (a single sitting or a day or two) for a range of discipline-specific tasks, purposes, and audiences.

WHAT I NEED TO KNOW

TERMS

- ☐ political party
- ☐ two-party system
- ☐ third party
- ☐ platform

PEOPLE, PLACES, EVENTS

- ☐ Democratic Party
- ☐ Republican Party
- ☐ single-issue party
- ☐ multiparty system
- ☐ one-party system
- ☐ grassroots movement
- ☐ opposition party

Political Parties

Political Parties

Create this Foldable® like a small booklet. Label the front Political Parties. Open the Foldable and label the top left section Past and the top right section Present. On the left side, sequence key events from the development of political parties to their rise in modern politics. On the right side, sequence the events involved in selecting political candidates to represent the major parties. On the back of the folded booklet, explain the importance of political parties.

Step 1
Arrange a piece of paper horizontally and fold in half from left to right.

Step 2
Label the inside of your booklet as shown.

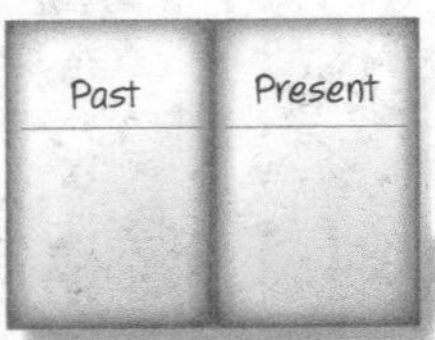

LESSON 1 SUMMARY

History of Political Parties

SS.7.C.2.8, SS.7.C.3.1

Growth of American Parties

One way Americans participate in our government is by joining political parties. A **political party** is a group of people with broad, shared interests. They come together to support candidates they like in order to help them win elections. They also use their combined strength to shape government policy.

The United States has a **two-party system.** That means two major parties compete for power. While there have been two major parties since shortly after the United States was formed, the names and political ideas of those parties have changed over time.

Today's Major Parties Form

The first parties took shape because people had different ideas on how to govern the United States. Several parties were created and disappeared in the early decades. Since the 1850s, the Republicans and the Democrats have been our nation's major parties. The Democratic Party formed in 1828. It emphasized its ties to common people. The Republican Party was formed in 1854 by people who opposed slavery.

In the late 1800s and early 1900s, the Republican Party dominated national politics. The Great Depression of the 1930s made the Democrats more popular. Since 1968, though, Republicans have won the presidency more often than the Democrats. Today, the Republican Party is considered to be more conservative in its views about government than the Democratic Party.

Third Parties

Throughout American history, smaller political parties known as **third parties** have competed against the two main parties. These smaller parties usually do not gain much support. They can have influence over the country, though. Third parties often promote ideas that gain popularity and sometimes become law. For example, during the 1890s the Populist Party wanted senators to be directly elected by the people instead of being chosen by a state's legislature. This led to the Seventeenth Amendment in 1913. Since then, senators are directly elected by the people in each state.

1. THEORIZING

Why do the power and popularity of political parties change over time?

2. REFLECTING

Which type of third party do you think would be most successful? Why?

____

____

____

____

____

____

____

____

3. EVALUATING

On a separate sheet of paper, rank the party systems, including the two-party system, from most to least democratic. Then, write an essay explaining your rankings, using details about each system to support your analysis.

Types of Third Parties

The Prohibition Party that formed in 1872 had one main purpose. It wanted to prohibit, or ban, the sale of alcohol. It represents one type of third party, single-issue political parties. They form around a specific cause. Another example is the Green Party USA. It is focused on "green" issues such as ecology. Single-issue parties usually disappear when the issue is no longer important or a major party takes it over as one of its ideas.

Other third parties form around an ideology, or set of beliefs, about government. The Communist Party USA, for example, promotes the idea that the government or workers should own all resources and businesses. Parties based on specific beliefs can exist for long periods of time.

Some third parties form to support a strong, independent leader. For example, Ross Perot founded the Reform Party, but he lost two presidential elections. The Reform Party is weaker today. These parties often do not survive that leader's defeat.

TYPES OF THIRD PARTIES			
	Single Issue	**Ideological**	**Strong Leader**
Definition	Party formed around a specific cause	Party formed around an ideology	Party formed around a leader
Example	Green Party USA	Communist Party USA	Ross Perot's Reform Party

Third parties often struggle to compete against the major parties. In many states, the names of candidates from major parties are always placed on the ballots. Candidates from third parties, however, often must overcome many hurdles. They must gather signatures from a large number of voters in order to appear on the ballot. Because they are less known, they often cannot raise enough money to campaign effectively.

Other Party Systems

Most nations have political parties. Party systems and the roles parties play vary from country to country, though.

Many democracies have multiparty systems with three or more parties. In these countries, one party rarely wins enough support to control the government. As a result, several parties must work together to govern the country.

Some nations have a one-party system. Such systems typically appear under a communist form of government. These systems are not democratic. No other parties are allowed, and elections are often for show.

OTHER PARTY SYSTEMS	
Multiparty Systems	**One-Party Systems**
Canada (3 major parties) France (more than 8 major parties) Israel (more than 20 parties)	People's Republic of China Democratic People's Republic of Korea (North Korea)

Party Differences

The Republicans and the Democrats of today have different ideas about the role of government in the economy and in citizens' lives.

Republicans favor less government involvement overall. They believe that a hands-off approach to the economy will bring about more prosperity. The Democrats think that the government should regulate the economy. They also believe that the government should help the poor in regard to housing, income, education, and jobs. Both parties agree, however, that a healthy economy will provide more jobs, which in turn would help the unemployed find jobs.

Both parties are national parties. Throughout the country, Democratic and Republican candidates run for office. However, some areas of the United States tend to support one party more than the other. Republican support is strong in the South. The Democrats do better in the Northeast and on the West Coast.

Differences between the parties sometimes may seem small. The views of both parties on specific issues may seem similar. Often this is because both parties try to take a moderate view. Other times, Americans may agree on an issue, so the parties would share those views as well.

Still, there are ways that citizens can determine how the parties are different. Every four years, each party writes a platform when it nominates a presidential candidate. The **platform** is a written document that explains the party's basic beliefs. It also describes its positions on various issues. People can read each party's platform to learn about their differences.

4. HYPOTHESIZING

What proposals might a Republican business owner want included in the Republican Party platform?

Name ________________ Date ________________ Class ________________

LESSON 1 SUMMARY, *continued*

REVIEW LESSON 1

1. Use the chart below to describe current political parties in the United States.

MAJOR POLITICAL PARTIES IN THE UNITED STATES		
Democratic Party	Republican Party	Third Parties in the United States
Founded in ________ **Originally emphasized** ________ ________ **Ideas about role of government** ________ ________ ________ ________	**Founded in** ________ **Originally emphasized** ________ ________ **Ideas about role of government** ________ ________ ________	**Types of third parties** ________ ________ ________ **Contribution to politics** ________ ________ ________
Differences can be identified by ________ ________		
Both parties agree that ________ ________		

2. **EVALUATING** Review the information about parties in your chart. On a separate sheet of paper, write an essay that answers these questions: What is the main difference between the two major parties? Do you think government regulations play a positive or negative role for businesses? For individual citizens? Give reasons for your answer.

LESSON 2 SUMMARY

Political Parties Today

SS.7.C.2.8, SS.7.C.2.10

Organization of Political Parties

Political parties want their candidates to win, and they want to win as many offices as possible. Both the Republican and Democratic Parties are organized at the national, state, and local levels to help accomplish these goals and spread their ideas. They also rely on the participation of citizens.

Becoming Involved in a Political Party

Joining a political party is one way citizens can participate in politics and influence government. Political parties welcome anyone who wishes to participate. Members can do volunteer work, such as registering citizens to vote or helping citizens get to the polls on election day. Very active members can help shape the party's platform. Volunteers often enjoy the feeling of being involved in something that matters to them.

Other Political Party Functions

Even though the main purpose of political parties in the United States is to elect candidates to office, parties serve other functions as well. They help people govern themselves. They also provide a way for citizens to talk with their government leaders. Finally, they ensure that the government remains responsive to the needs of the people.

Communicating With the People

Parties help citizens influence government, in part by providing a way for voters and candidates to exchange ideas. Candidates tell voters where they stand on issues and listen to what citizens have to say on the issues. The media plays a role in this process. News reports, articles, or interviews may present an issue or feature a candidate. Candidates often run campaign advertisements in the media to reach large numbers of voters.

1. DRAWING CONCLUSIONS

Political parties are organized at local, state, and national levels. How does that help individuals monitor and influence government?

2. PREDICTING CONSEQUENCES

A grassroots movement calls for free community college for people who have low incomes. Which political party is most likely to adopt this idea? Why?

3. DETERMINING CAUSE AND EFFECT

How do political parties influence the running of government?

Sometimes citizens feel strongly about an issue and want to communicate that to government leaders. They may form a grassroots movement. If the movement gains enough support, it can influence the political process when a political party or candidate adopts these ideas. Other times, the movement can lead to the creation of a third party.

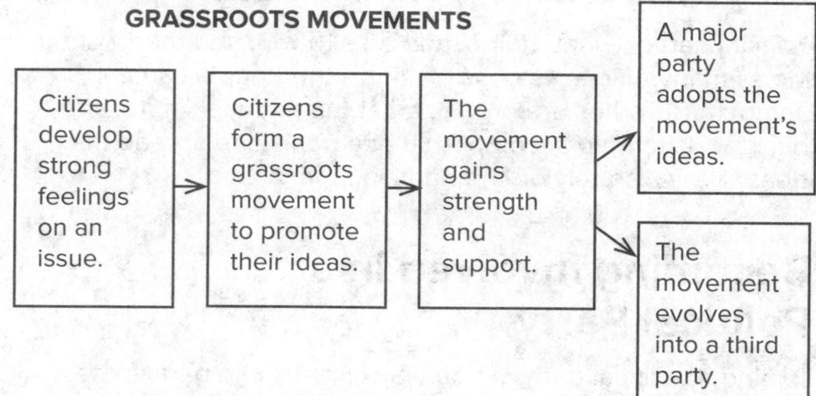
GRASSROOTS MOVEMENTS
Citizens develop strong feelings on an issue.
Citizens form a grassroots movement to promote their ideas.
The movement gains strength and support.
A major party adopts the movement's ideas.
The movement evolves into a third party.

Running Different Parts of Government

Political parties shape the way government runs. Legislatures, including Congress, are organized around party membership. Legislators try to make sure their fellow party members support the party's position on any new bills. That support is needed before a bill can be passed and become a law.

Parties play a role in the executive branch as well. The president, governors, and mayors often appoint individuals to government jobs based on party membership and support. This way the leaders can be sure their policies are carried out.

Linking Different Levels of Government

Political parties encourage cooperation among officials at different levels of government. If a mayor and a governor belong to the same party, they likely share goals and ideas. This can make it easier for them to work together to address problems that affect both the city and the state. The same is true across branches of government. If a majority of the legislature belongs to the same party as the chief executive, they are more likely to agree on the kinds of bills to pass.

Name ______________________ Date ______________ Class __________

LESSON 2 SUMMARY, *continued*

Acting as a Watchdog

Political parties also help to monitor the government. When a political party loses elections for most government seats, it is considered out of power. An out-of-power party is often called the opposition party.

The opposition party monitors the performance of the party in power. It tries to make sure that the governing party does not misuse or abuse its power. It also tries to ensure that the governing party pays attention to the ideas of people who disagree with it.

4. MAKING CONNECTIONS

Is a third party more likely to be an opposition party or a party in power? Explain.

____

____

____

____

REVIEW LESSON 2

1. Use the graphic organizer below to summarize the roles of political parties.

POLITICAL PARTIES

Main Purpose:

Help government function	Help citizens monitor and influence government
1.	1.
2.	2.
3.	3.
	4.

2. **ASSESSING** Use the information in your graphic organizer to write an essay that answers this question: Are political parties a good way for citizens to monitor and influence government? Write your essay on a separate sheet of paper.

Benchmark Skill Activities

DIRECTIONS: Write your answers on a separate piece of paper.

LAFS.68.RH.1.2

1. SUMMARIZING

Use your FOLDABLES to write an essay that summarizes the role of political parties in the government of the United States.

LAFS.68.RH.2.4

2. DETERMINING WORD MEANINGS

Read the excerpt below from an editorial by Theodore Roosevelt. Then, write a definition for each of the underlined words. Use the words around these words, or context clues, to help you determine their meanings.

> *"A party should not contain utterly incongruous elements, radically divided on the real issues, and acting together only on false and dead issues insincerely painted as real and vital. . . . It should be so composed that there should be a reasonable agreement in the actions taken by it both in the Nation and in the several States."*
>
> —Theodore Roosevelt, "Platform Insincerity"

LAFS.68.RH.2.6

3. IDENTIFYING POINT OF VIEW

In his Farewell Address, President George Washington said the following about political parties:

> *"The alternate domination of one faction [dissenting group] over another, sharpened by the spirit of revenge, natural to party dissension, which in different ages and countries has perpetrated the most horrid enormities [hardships], is itself a frightful despotism [rule by a dictator]. But this leads at length to a more formal and permanent despotism."*
>
> —George Washington, Farewell Address, 1796

Based on this excerpt, how did George Washington feel about political parties? Which words and phrases best illustrate his opinion?

LAFS.68.WHST.1.1

4. CONSTRUCTING AN ARGUMENT

Write an argument that supports or opposes this statement: Political parties are essential to the function of American democracy. In your argument, clearly state your claim and provide supporting reasons and relevant evidence.

LAFS.68.WHST.4.10

5. REFLECTING

Find the official Web sites for the Republican and Democratic Parties and navigate to their platforms. Read each party's position on issues that are important to you. Do the same for a third party, such as the Green Party or the Libertarian Party.

Write a paragraph or two explaining which party you would be most likely to support. Be sure to include specific examples.

Benchmark Note Cards

DIRECTIONS: Use these note cards to help you prepare for the test.

SS.7.C.2.8 Identify America's current political parties, and illustrate their ideas about government.

MAJOR POLITICAL PARTIES	**Democratic Party** • The Democratic Party was founded in 1828. • In its beginnings, the party stressed its ties to common people. • Today, the party believes the government should become directly involved in regulating the economy. It also believes the government should provide job, housing, and other assistance to the poor. **Republican Party** • The Republican Party was founded in 1854. • Originally, the party was founded by people who opposed slavery. • Today, the party believes the government should have minimal involvement in the economy.
THIRD PARTIES	• These parties can be formed around a single issue, an ideology, or a leader with a strong personality. • Third parties have difficulty competing against major parties for inclusion on the ballot and fundraising. • Third parties can have their ideas adopted by one of the major parties, if their ideas gain enough public support.

SS.7.C.2.10 Examine the impact of media, individuals, and interest groups on monitoring and influencing government.

MONITORING AND INFLUENCING GOVERNMENT	• The media helps citizens and candidates exchange ideas. • The opposition party, or party out of power, acts as a watchdog. It monitors the party in power to make sure it does not abuse its power or ignore differing viewpoints. • Citizens can influence government through grassroots movements that either become third parties or contribute ideas to a major party. • Political parties provide a way for citizens to influence government through voting in elections and volunteering for a party. • Political parties influence how government works because most legislatures are organized around party membership.

SS.7.C.3.1 Compare different forms of government (direct democracy, representative democracy, socialism, communism, monarchy, oligarchy, autocracy).

POLITICAL SYSTEMS	The role of political parties varies with each nation's political system. Countries with democratic forms of government have two-party systems or multiparty systems. Other nations have only one party. This system is usually found in communist nations, where only one political party is allowed.

Chapter 10

VISUAL SUMMARY

DIRECTIONS: Complete the graphic organizers below.

POLITICAL PARTIES IN THE UNITED STATES	
Who They Are	**What They Do**
Democratic Party	Citizen Involvement
Republican Party	Government Influence
Third Parties	Acting as a Watchdog

PARTY SYSTEMS
Two-Party System
Multiparty System
One-Party System

USING PRIMARY SOURCES

In 1912, Theodore Roosevelt wrote the editorial below about political parties. He mentions "party machines," which are also called political machines. These are local party organizations that have become very strong. As a result, they can control votes by helping or giving jobs to voters. Read the excerpt, and then answer the questions on the following page.

Introduction

Judged by these standards, both of the old parties break down. Neither can longer be trusted to do the work so urgently needed by the country. . . .

The bosses of the Democratic party and the bosses of the Republican party alike have a closer grip than ever before on the party machines in the States and in the Nation. This crooked control of both the old parties by the beneficiaries of political and business privilege renders it hopeless to expect any far-reaching and fundamental service from either.

It is in large part a sequel [something that happens after] to this crooked control that there has been so long a record of failure on the part of both the old parties to redeem [make better] their platform pledges. I very earnestly hope that the Progressive party will bear this fact in mind when it comes to building its platform. Not only should the platform be right, but it should be so clearly drawn as to make the intentions of those who draw it perfectly understood by the average man; it should deal wisely and boldly with the new issues confronting our people; and, finally, it should scrupulously [with great care to be correct] refrain from promising anything that cannot be performed, and should clearly show that it intends as a matter of honorable obligation to carry out every promise made. To make a promise which cannot be carried out or which would hopelessly damage the country if carried out is equivalent to announcing in advance that, not only this promise, but all the other promises in the platform, are meant to be broken, and are for campaign uses only. No party, and no candidate, should receive the support of the people if the platform shows on its face the corrupt insincerity of those making it.

The present conditions in the two old parties, and the platforms put forth by both of them and judged by the standards outlined above, show that it is hopeless to get anything good out of them. ...

—Theodore Roosevelt, "Platform Insincerity"

DIRECTIONS: Write your answers to these questions.

1. MAKING INFERENCES What type of party is the Progressive Party? How do you know?

2. DETERMINING CENTRAL IDEAS According to Roosevelt, what is wrong with the platforms of the major parties?

3. IDENTIFYING POINT OF VIEW Based on this excerpt, does Roosevelt support the two-party system?

4. DISTINGUISHING FACT FROM OPINION Is Roosevelt's editorial mostly fact or mostly opinion? Does this strengthen or weaken Roosevelt's argument?

5. MAKING COMPARISONS Do Roosevelt's criticisms of the major parties still apply today? Explain.

Chapter Practice Test

DIRECTIONS: Circle the best answer for each question.

SS.7.C.2.8 (Moderate)

> *"[P]riorities remain clear: to provide a tax cut for working families, to promote policies that produce jobs and economic growth, and to assist millions of our fellow Americans who have lost their jobs through no fault of their own."*
>
> —Representative Nancy Pelosi (California), 2010 press release

Based on this quotation, which political party does Pelosi most likely belong to?

A Green Party USA

B Democratic Party

C Republican Party

D Communist Party USA

SS.7.C.2.8 (Moderate)

Imagine that these are signs being held up by delegates at a political party's national convention.

We want a shorter workweek	Five Days is TOO MANY	Less time at work; more time with family	Work Smarter—Fewer Days

Based on the signs, what can you conclude about the party?

A It is likely a third party.

B It is likely a grassroots party.

C It is likely an opposition party.

D It is likely a single-issue party.

3 **SS.7.C.2.8 (High)**

The United States experiences an economic decline. Unemployment goes up. Housing prices go up. Salaries go down.

Which recommendation is the Republican Party most likely to make in response to this crisis?

A The government should take a direct action to fix the economy.

B The government should provide assistance to the unemployed.

C The government should take a minor action to fix the economy.

D The government should purchase all businesses and resources.

4 **SS.7.C.3.1 (Moderate)**

These charts show the percentage of legislative seats held by each party in four different countries.

COUNTRY A	
Party 1	2%
Party 2	1%
Party 3	50%
Party 4	47%

COUNTRY B	
Party 1	25%
Party 2	20%
Party 3	18%
Party 4	37%

COUNTRY C	
Party 1	12%
Party 2	28%
Party 3	32%
Party 4	28%

COUNTRY D	
Party 1	33%
Party 2	30%
Party 3	5%
Party 4	22%

Which country most likely has a two-party political system?

A Country A

B Country B

C Country C

D Country D

5 **SS.7.C.3.1 (Moderate)**

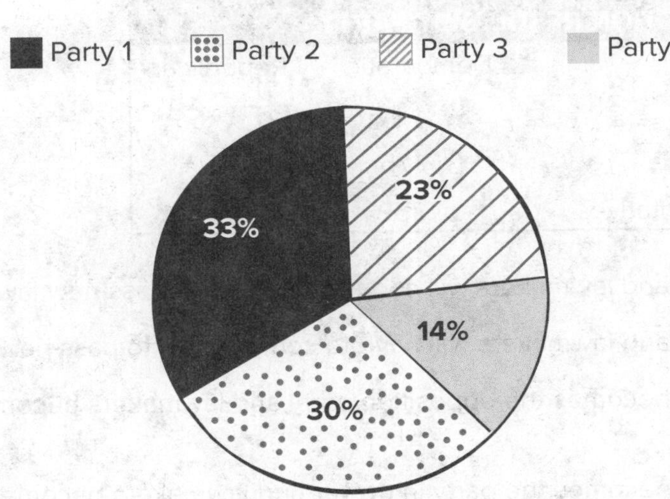

Which form of government does Country X likely have?

A reform

B communist

C single ruler

D democracy

---

6 **SS.7.C.2.10 (High)**

Ellen thinks her local schools are being neglected. Many of her neighbors agree with her. They want the government to provide more money and attention to the school system.

What is Ellen's best course of action?

A form a third party

B vote in a primary election

C join a major political party

D form a grassroots movement

SS.7.C.2.10 (High)

What is the most likely effect of these election results?

ELECTION RESULTS BY PARTY		
	Democratic	Republican
President		X
Senate	75	25
House of Representatives	359	76

A The president and lawmakers will cooperate easily to pass new laws.

B The president and lawmakers will have to compromise to pass new laws.

C The president becomes the opposition party and lawmakers become the party in power.

D The president becomes the party in power and lawmakers become the opposition party.

SS.7.C.2.10, SS.7.C.3.1 (High)

Which scenario is most likely in a system without an opposition party?

A The party in power seeks ideas from other parties.

B The party in power passes laws in its own best interest.

C The party in power responds to the wishes of the people.

D The party in power cooperates with other levels of government.

SS.7.C.2.8 (High)

Which statement best describes the cartoon shown here?

A The Populist Party is gaining strength over the Democratic Party.

B The Populist Party is gaining control over the nation.

C The Republican Party is not strong enough to enter the fight between the other two parties.

D The Democrats and the Republicans are in a bitter fight for power.

10

SS.7.C.2.8, SS.7.C.2.10 (High)

What is most likely to happen to a popular grassroots movement demanding lower taxes and smaller government?

A The movement becomes a new major party.

B The movement becomes an ideological third party.

C The movement's ideas are adopted by the Democratic Party.

D The movement's ideas are adopted by the Republican Party.

CHAPTER 11

Voting and Elections

CHAPTER BENCHMARKS

SS.7.C.2.3 Experience the responsibilities of citizens at the local, state, or federal levels.

SS.7.C.2.5 Distinguish how the Constitution safeguards and limits individual rights.

SS.7.C.2.7 Conduct a mock election to demonstrate the voting process and its impact on a school, community, or local level.

SS.7.C.2.9 Evaluate candidates for political office by analyzing their qualifications, experience, issue-based platforms, debates, and political ads.

SS.7.C.2.10 Examine the impact of media, individuals, and interest groups on monitoring and influencing government.

SS.7.C.2.11 Analyze media and political communications (bias, symbolism, propaganda).

SS.7.C.3.6 Evaluate Constitutional rights and their impact on individuals and society.

SS.7.C.3.7 Analyze the impact of the 13th, 14th, 15th, 19th, 24th, and 26th amendments on participation of minority groups in the American political process.

SS.7.C.3.8 Analyze the structure, functions, and processes of the legislative, executive, and judicial branches.

Chapter Overview

Voting is both a right and a privilege given to American citizens by the Constitution. When people vote in an election, they determine the shape of their government. They choose their leaders and decide important issues. Over time, voting rights have been expanded to include African Americans, Native Americans, and women. Many barriers to voting have been removed as well to make it easier for people to participate.

Throughout the United States, different types of elections take place, including primary, general, and special elections. Every four years, citizens vote in presidential elections, which involves the Electoral College. All across the United States, thousands of people run for political office by planning campaigns, getting donations, and reaching out to voters in their towns, cities, and states.

WHAT I NEED TO KNOW

TERMS

- ☐ suffrage
- ☐ polling place
- ☐ ballot
- ☐ voter turnout rate
- ☐ apathy
- ☐ issue
- ☐ referendum
- ☐ initiative
- ☐ recall
- ☐ popular vote
- ☐ winner-take-all system
- ☐ canvass
- ☐ political action committee (PAC)

PEOPLE, PLACES, EVENTS

- ☐ Fifteenth Amendment
- ☐ Nineteenth Amendment
- ☐ Twenty-fourth Amendment
- ☐ Twenty-sixth Amendment
- ☐ *Bush* v. *Gore*
- ☐ primary election
- ☐ general election
- ☐ special election
- ☐ presidential election

CHAPTER 11

Voting and Elections

CHAPTER BENCHMARKS, *continued*

SS.7.C.3.12 Analyze the significance and outcomes of landmark Supreme Court cases including, but not limited to, *Marbury* v. *Madison, Plessy* v. *Ferguson, Brown* v. *Board of Education, Gideon* v. *Wainwright, Miranda* v. *Arizona, in re Gault, Tinker* v. *Des Moines, Hazelwood* v. *Kuhlmeier, United States* v. *Nixon,* and *Bush* v. *Gore.*

LAFS.68.RH.1.1 Cite specific textual evidence to support analysis of primary and secondary sources.

LAFS.68.RH.1.2 Determine the central ideas or information of a primary or secondary source; provide an accurate summary of the source distinct from prior knowledge or opinions.

LAFS.68.RH.1.3 Identify key steps in a text's description of a process related to history/social studies (e.g., how a bill becomes law, how interest rates are raised or lowered).

LAFS.68.RH.2.6 Identify aspects of a text that reveal an author's point of view or purpose (e.g., loaded language, inclusion or avoidance of particular facts).

LAFS.68.RH.3.7 Integrate visual information (e.g., in charts, graphs, photographs, videos, or maps) with other information in print and digital texts.

LAFS.68.RH.3.8 Distinguish among fact, opinion, and reasoned judgment in a text.

LAFS.68.WHST.1.2 Write informative/explanatory texts, including the narration of historical events, scientific procedures/ experiments, or technical processes.

LAFS.68.WHST.2.4 Produce clear and coherent writing in which the development, organization, and style are appropriate to task, purpose, and audience.

LAFS.68.WHST.3.9 Draw evidence from informational texts to support analysis reflection, and research.

LAFS.68.WHST.4.10 Write routinely over extended time frames (time for reflection and revision) and shorter time frames (a single sitting or a day or two) for a range of discipline-specific tasks, purposes, and audiences.

Voting and Elections

Create the Foldable® below. Label the tabs with the lesson titles. Under the left tab, sequence key events in the history of voting in the United States. On the right side, explain the different types of elections. On the back of the Foldable, apply what you have learned in Lesson 2 to describe how you might help a candidate run his or her campaign for president.

Step 1
With the paper arranged horizontally, fold the left side over to the right edge and fold paper in half.

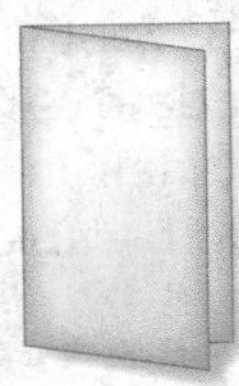

Step 2
While the paper is folded in half, fold the top of the paper down to the bottom to fold in half again.

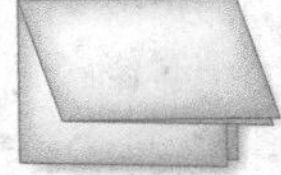

Step 3
Unfold the paper and cut the horizontal fold from the left edge to the center of the paper.

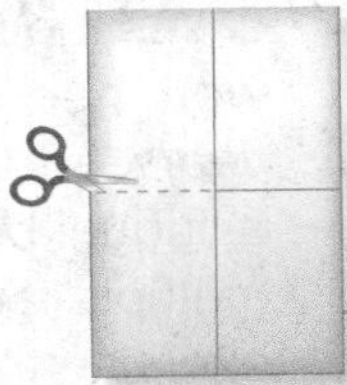

Step 4
Fold shutters down and label as directed.

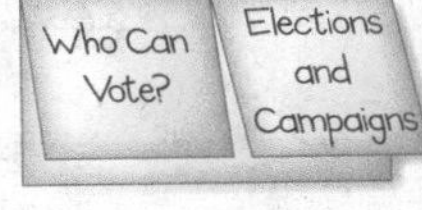

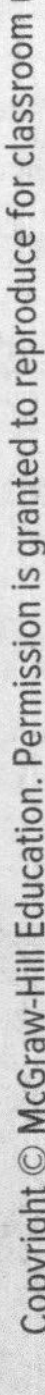

LESSON 1 SUMMARY

Who Can Vote?

SS.7.C.2.3, SS.7.C.2.5, SS.7.C.2.11, SS.7.C.3.6, SS.7.C.3.7, SS.7.C.3.12

Qualifying to Vote

One characteristic of early civilizations is that people lived under rulers like kings, queens, and emperors. These rulers inherited their positions. The people could not choose them.

The same was true of the American colonies until the colonists fought for independence. Then people began voting for their leaders. That is how it remains today. Voting is considered one of our most precious rights. It forms the basis of being an American citizen. Most adults remember casting a vote in their first election.

1. IDENTIFYING POINTS OF VIEW

Use the Internet to learn about colonists' attitudes about who should vote. Then, on a separate sheet of paper, write a paragraph that explains the colonists' beliefs and attitudes that supported this limitation.

Expanding Suffrage

Did you know that when the Constitution was written, most states only allowed white male property owners to vote? While the Declaration of Independence may have said that "All men are created equal," that principle, or basic belief, did not apply to everyone. The right to vote, or **suffrage,** in many states was restricted to a small group of white, male landowners.

PEOPLE ONCE BARRED FROM VOTING
• Adult white males who did not own property
• Women
• African American males
• Native American males
• People under 21 years of age

Suffrage, however, has changed in the United States over time. People who once could not express their voice about government, are now able to vote.

Groups once denied the right to vote were given suffrage when amendments were added to the Constitution. In some cases though, government acts and Supreme Court decisions were needed to help enforce these amendments. Over the years, additional changes have been made to mandate bilingual ballots, voting assistance, and voting materials in multiple languages so that all minority voters would be able to exercise their right to vote.

2. EVALUATING

How is extending the right to vote related to the basic ideas and principles of the Constitution?

Name ______________________ Date ______________ Class ________

SUFFRAGE AMENDMENTS	
Amendment/What it Said	**Its Impact**
Fifteenth (1870): No person can be denied the right to vote because of race or color.	• This amendment extended suffrage to African Americans who were recently freed from slavery. • Laws throughout the South were passed to prevent African Americans from voting. Beginning in the 1950s, a series of civil rights and voting rights laws were enacted to ensure African Americans true suffrage. • In 1944, the Supreme Court ruled in *Smith* v. *Allwright* that prohibiting African Americans from voting in primary elections is unconstitutional.
Nineteenth (1920): Prohibited the denial of the right to vote because of gender	• This amendment extended suffrage to all American women. • Women had been fighting for suffrage since about 1848.
Twenty-fourth (1964): Eliminated the poll tax (and any other tax) as a condition for voting	• Some people who did not have the money to pay poll taxes were effectively denied the right to vote. • This amendment ensured that whether rich or poor, everyone could vote.
Twenty-sixth (1971): No state can set the minimum age for voting at more than 18 years of age.	• Before this amendment, the voting age in most states was 21. • This amendment provided younger people with a voice in government.

Voting Requirements Today

The Constitution gives the states the power to set suffrage qualifications. States cannot go against the Constitution in setting their requirements. For example, in the 1975 Supreme Court case *Hill* v. *Stone,* the Court found that the Texas constitution could not declare that only those people who owned taxable property could vote in city bond elections. This was an unreasonable requirement that was prohibited by the Fourteenth Amendment's Equal Protection Clause.

However, most states still have the right to deny the vote to certain groups: people with certain kinds of mental illness, people convicted of serious crimes, and people who have immigrated to the United States but are not yet citizens.

Steps in the Voting Process

Voting sounds simple, but it is a three-step process with responsibilities that citizens must fulfill. These responsibilities are registering, preparing, and then casting a ballot.

Registering to Vote

The first step is to register, or sign up, to vote. Why is this a responsibility of citizens? Registration helps the government ensure that each eligible voter only votes once per election.

The steps for registration are not difficult:

- Fill out a form with personal information, including name, address, and age or birthday. You can give your political party or register as an independent voter.

3. REASONING

Just as voting requirements are set by each state, so is voter registration. This means some of the rules vary. For example, the state of North Dakota is the only state that does not require voters to register. Why do you think voter registration is required by the other 49 states? Do you think it should be standardized across the country? Explain your reasoning.

____

____

____

____

____

____

____

____

____

Name ________________ Date ________________ Class ________________

4. DRAWING CONCLUSIONS

President Obama used the slogan "Yes We Can" during his 2008 campaign. Why do you think this campaign slogan was effective?

5. EVALUATING

It is important for voters to evaluate each candidate's qualifications, experience, position on issues, statements in debates, and political ads. List three additional questions you might ask a candidate.

- Provide a driver's license, birth certificate, or other valid form of identification to prove citizenship and age.

Some states, including Florida, allow registration by mail, when renewing a driver's license, or in libraries.

Preparing to Vote

Registering does not mean you are ready to vote. You now have to prepare for an upcoming election. You do this by being informed about public issues and current events.

Many good sources of information are available. They include Web sites, television, radio, newspapers, books, and magazines. Another way to prepare is by reading letters, pamphlets, and ads. However, political parties and special-interest groups distribute many of these materials. Citizens must read carefully to avoid propaganda and bias. Propaganda is meant to persuade people to think a certain way. Bias means good or bad feelings about a person or group that affect judgment. Bias is based on opinions rather than solid facts.

After reading and preparing, voters can decide where they stand on the issues and choose the candidates they want to support. It is helpful to ask questions such as these:

- Does the candidate stand for the things I think are important?
- Is the candidate reliable and honest?
- Does the candidate have the relevant past experience?
- Will the candidate be effective in office?
- Does the candidate have a real chance of winning?

Casting Your Vote

Many states allow early voting and voting by mail. This helps people who are traveling or members of the military living out of state. Each state sets its own requirements and rules.

On Election Day, people go to a **polling place** to vote. Polling places are set up in schools, community centers, or other public buildings. Each voter shows some identification. Officials check the list of registered voters to be sure he or she is eligible to vote. The voter then signs in and goes into the voting booth. Each booth has a barrier, such as a curtain or a divider. The barrier provides privacy so each person can vote in secret.

In the booth, voters cast their **ballots** for the candidates they want in office and the issues they want approved. A ballot is a list of candidates' names with their political party and the office they seek. Ballots may also list issues, such as a tax increase, for people to vote on.

Name ______________________ Date ______________ Class ________

Each state determines the ballot's form. It may be a sheet of paper with check boxes. Some states use punch cards to put in a machine that punches a hole next to the candidate voted for. Many states have ballots on computer touch screens.

After voting, some people wear "I voted!" stickers as a sign that they have met their civic responsibility. As soon as the polling places close, officials begin counting the votes and then announce the results.

Why Your Vote Counts

Just as the law applies equally to everyone, so does voting. Everyone's vote is counted the same and has the same value.

Reasons to Vote

Citizens vote because it is both a right and a responsibility. Voting gives people the opportunity to choose their leaders. It enables people to show whether they are happy or unhappy with those in office who are running for reelection. Lastly, voting provides people with a voice in how things are run. People who vote generally are positive about government. They have exercised their right to be part of the process.

Understanding Voter Participation

Voting gives citizens power. Why then is the percentage of eligible voters who actually vote, or **voter turnout rate,** so low? Some people are not interested in voting. This **apathy,** or disinterest, accounts for a voter turnout rate in the United States that is often below 50 percent.

Bush v. *Gore*

After the outcome of the 2000 presidential election was decided by the Supreme Court, many people became concerned about the fairness of American elections, the Electoral College, and the Supreme Court's powers. Here are the events that led to those concerns:

- The election between George W. Bush and Al Gore was close. Whoever won Florida's electoral votes would be the next president. Only a few hundred votes separated the two candidates in Florida.
- Many of Florida's paper ballots were damaged or improperly marked. Florida's state supreme court said that each ballot that showed the intent of the voter should be recounted.

6. SUGGESTING A SOLUTION

Voter participation in the United States is fairly low. This is especially true for years without presidential elections. What could be done to increase voter participation? Make suggestions and explain them.

Name ____________________ Date ____________ Class ________

7. POSING QUESTIONS

On a separate sheet of paper, write three questions that you would ask the Supreme Court justices who ruled for Bush in *Bush* v. *Gore*. Then, write three questions for the justices who ruled against Bush.

- Bush's lawyers said it was impossible to tell a voter's intent on a mismarked ballot. They appealed to the U.S. Supreme Court.
- The U.S. Supreme Court ruled for Bush in a 5-4 decision. The Court stated that the damaged ballots made it impossible for the same equal and fair standards to be applied to every ballot across the state. The recount was stopped, and Bush won Florida by 537 votes. He had enough electoral votes to win the Electoral College and become president.

Many people believed that the Supreme Court went beyond its authority and that the decision should have been made by the state of Florida. To this day, *Bush* v. *Gore* remains a controversial decision.

REVIEW LESSON 1

1. Use the chart below to explain how the expansion of voting rights in the United States impacted individuals and society.

HOW VOTING HAS EXPANDED IN THE UNITED STATES	
Changes	**Impact on Minority Groups and Society**
Fifteenth Amendment	
Nineteenth Amendment	
Twenty-fourth Amendment	
Twenty-sixth Amendment	
Civil Rights Acts/Voting Rights Acts/Supreme Court Decisions	
Bilingual Ballots, Voting Assistance, Voting Materials in Multiple Languages	

2. **IDENTIFYING EVIDENCE** Use the chart to write an essay on a separate sheet of paper about the expansion of voting in the United States. How have these changes impacted minority groups and society in general?

LESSON 2 SUMMARY

Elections and Campaigns

SS.7.C.2.7, SS.7.C.2.9, SS.7.C.2.10, SS.7.C.2.11, SS.7.C.3.8

Types of Elections

The Constitution outlines the structure, functions, and processes of the legislative and executive branches of the national government. All of this would be meaningless without people to serve as leaders. These leaders carry out the duties of government. The nation's citizens also play an important role. After all, they choose the candidates who will represent them. To do this, they must carefully evaluate each candidate's strengths and weaknesses.

Primary and General Elections

Most states hold two kinds of elections during the election process. These consist of a primary election and a general election.

- **Primary elections:** Voters from each party choose one candidate running for election. To do this they consider the candidates' qualifications, experience, position on issues, and other factors. In the 1800s, party leaders chose their party's nominees. Today, citizens can vote in the primary election and have the opportunity to influence who will lead their country. Florida holds separate primary elections for presidential candidates in March, and primaries for local and state candidates in August.
- **General elections:** Candidates selected by the opposing parties during the primary election face off against each other in a general election.

Initiatives, Referendums, and Special Elections

Voting for leaders is one way that individuals can monitor and influence government. Citizens also can vote on **issues,** or topics of public interest. For example, citizens might vote on whether to build a new park or stadium or fund a new kind of transportation.

Two special processes allow individuals to have a direct impact on government. A **referendum** gives voters the chance to accept or reject a law passed by state or local lawmakers.

1. DRAWING CONCLUSIONS

How do general elections affect the structure and makeup of Congress and its ability to make laws?

2. COMPARING AND CONTRASTING

How are referendums and initiatives alike and different?

3. DISTINGUISHING FACT FROM OPINION

Tell whether each statement is a fact or an opinion.

1. Some states hold recall elections to give voters a chance to decide whether a leader should stay in office.

   ____

2. The Electoral College should be replaced because it does not always honor the popular vote.

   ____

3. Citizens must take action to abolish the winner-take-all system for choosing electors.

   ____

4. Citizens do not directly determine the result of a presidential election.

   ____

An **initiative** lets citizens propose new laws or amendments to the state constitution. This process takes two steps: People who want a new law gather signatures from other voters. Enough signatures means a place on the ballot. People then vote on the proposed law, called a proposition.

Individuals can monitor government by deciding whether leaders stay in office. They can do this by either voting for or against a leader in the next election. Another way to do this is through a **recall** election. Enough demand for a leader's removal can lead to a special election to decide whether the leader stays in office.

Presidential Elections

Citizens do not directly elect the president of the United States. Instead, they influence the process through their votes. The vote directly cast by the people is known as the **popular vote.** The popular vote decides how their state will be represented by electors in the Electoral College. Citizens of a state are voting on whether they think Republican or Democratic electors should go to the Electoral College.

THE ELECTORAL COLLEGE PROCESS

TUESDAY AFTER FIRST MONDAY IN NOVEMBER

- On Election Day, voters cast ballots for a slate of electors pledged to a particular presidential candidate.

MONDAY AFTER SECOND WEDNESDAY IN DECEMBER

- Winning electors in each state meet in their state capitals to cast their votes for president and vice president.
- A statement of the vote is sent to Washington, D.C.

JANUARY 6

- Congress counts electoral votes. A majority of electoral votes is needed to win (270 out of 538).

JANUARY 20

- The candidate receiving majority of electoral votes is sworn in as president of the United States.

The process of electing a president is more complicated than one might first think. This flowchart shows what happens after citizens cast their votes.

ANALYZING VISUALS

4. ANALYZING INFORMATION About how long after Election Day does it take to know the official results of the election? Why is the media usually able to predict the next president on Election Day or soon after? Why does the media take on this task?

____

____

____

____

____

Most states, including Florida, use a **winner-take-all system.** This means that the candidate who wins the popular vote in a state election gets all the state's electoral votes. It is possible that a candidate could win the national popular vote but lose the Electoral College vote. This has happened four times in our nation's history. Most recently, in the 2000 presidential election, Al Gore won the popular vote, but George W. Bush won the Electoral College vote. Critics say that the Electoral College system lessens the impact citizens can have on influencing the decisions of the executive branch.

The basic structure and function of the Electoral College are described in the Constitution. The idea resulted from a compromise over the issue of how much direct control over government the American people should have.

5. EVALUATING

Use the Internet to locate a campaign advertisement from a past local or state election. Analyze the ad for examples of bias and propaganda. Then, on a separate sheet of paper, write a summary and an explanation of the bias and propaganda you found. Explain why they are biased or propaganda.

Running for Office

Candidates for office launch campaigns to convince voters to support them. Citizens must carefully evaluate candidates in order to cast their votes thoughtfully. To do so, voters should

- think about the candidates' qualifications and experience. Has their career prepared them for the office?
- learn about the candidates' stands on important issues. Listening to speeches and interviews are good ways to learn about candidates' ideas.
- listen to debates and decide who does the best job.
- look closely at political ads. Separate facts from opinions and learn to recognize bias as well as propaganda.
- carefully consider the role of the media. What media sources provide the most trustworthy information? Are media sources covering the campaign fairly?

Citizens often do more than just vote for candidates. They might tell candidates what they think about issues and ask questions. They might write letters or blog entries in support of their candidate. They might inform others about important issues. Some citizens volunteer to help a candidate. They might go door-to-door, or **canvass,** to gather support. Also, they might help run the local campaign office or make phone calls.

Name ______________________ Date ______________ Class ________

ANALYZING VISUALS

6. EVALUATING News organizations pledge to be objective and balanced. However, some citizens and political leaders dispute that claim. What is the interviewer's role in the panel discussion in this image? Why might some people think that a program such as this could be biased?

7. CONTRASTING

How does the impact of individual and special-interest group campaign contributions differ?

The media monitors and influences government as it reports on candidates and their campaigns.

A good way to prepare for the responsibility of voting is to take part in a mock election. For example, the students in your school could model the process of holding a national election:

- Several students can take on the roles of presidential candidates.
- Candidates can form committees and debate one another.
- Other students can work on the campaigns of the candidates.
- Still other students can serve as online and print reporters.
- Then the whole class can vote.

Campaign Finance

Campaigns are expensive because candidates want to reach and convince as many voters as possible to vote for them. To do this, they buy print and online advertisements, visit a variety of states or cities and towns, and pay for key staffers. Often they get support from individuals and groups who want to influence government by making sure their preferred candidate gets elected. Such groups include **political action committees (PACs).** PACs are created by special-interest groups to raise funds for candidates' campaigns. They are willing to invest money to help candidates who will in turn support their ideas and beliefs.

McGraw-Hill Education/Jill Braaten, photographer

Name ______________________ Date ______________ Class ________

LESSON 2 SUMMARY, *continued*

REVIEW LESSON 2

1. Use the chart below to describe the role of citizens in the election process.

TOPIC	ROLE OF CITIZENS
Election of Members of Congress	
Election of President	
Stands on Issues	
Choosing the Best Candidate	
Supporting a Candidate	
Judging Ads and News Reports	

2. **IDENTIFYING CENTRAL IDEAS** Congratulations! You are 18 years old and about to vote for the first time. Using the chart, write an essay to describe the role you think you and other good citizens should take in the election process. Write your essay on a separate sheet of paper.

Benchmark Skill Activities

DIRECTIONS: Write your answers on a separate piece of paper.

LAFS.68.WHST.1.2, LAFS.68.WHST.2.4

1. GATHERING EVIDENCE

Use your FOLDABLES to write an essay.

Imagine that you feel strongly about a candidate and want to join his or her campaign. In your essay, explain how you think you can help the campaign. Include what types of jobs you might want to do for the campaign and ideas you have for campaign posters, slogans, and so on.

LAFS.68.RH.1.2, LAFS.68.RH.2.4

2. USING DEFINITIONS ACCURATELY

Look at the Terms list on the first page of this chapter. Choose at least four words to include in a paragraph that summarizes the election process for a presidential campaign.

LAFS.68.WHST.2.4, LAFS.68.WHST.3.9

3. GIVING EXAMPLES

Imagine that you have just turned 18 and are now able to vote in the upcoming presidential election. You have prepared for the election by learning about the candidates and the issues. Some of your friends are planning to vote too, but they haven't taken the time to prepare for it. A few just like the campaign slogan for a specific candidate because it sounds fun. What steps could you take to help your friends be better prepared and more knowledgeable voters? How might you help them understand propaganda and bias in campaign materials? Write a plan to help them know their responsibilities. Describe three ways you would use to inform your friends about the candidates, the issues, and what to watch out for when preparing to vote.

LAFS.68.RH.1.2

4. FINDING THE MAIN IDEA

Read the excerpt from the Voting Rights Act of 1965. Then, in your own words, rewrite the excerpt and explain its main idea.

> SEC. 3. (b) If in a proceeding instituted by the Attorney General under any statute to enforce the guarantees of the fifteenth amendment in any State or political subdivision the court finds that a test or device has been used for the purpose or with the effect of denying or abridging the right of any citizen of the United States to vote on account of race or color, it shall suspend the use of tests and devices in such State or political subdivisions as the court shall determine is appropriate and for such period as it deems necessary. . . .
>
> —Voting Rights Act of 1965

SS.7.C.2.7, SS.7.C.3.8, LAFS.68.RH.1.3

5. IDENTIFYING STEPS IN A PROCESS

You want to hold a mock election for mayor of your community in your school. On a separate sheet of paper create a flow chart that outlines steps you might take to hold a successful election.

Benchmark Note Cards

DIRECTIONS: Use these note cards to help you prepare for the test.

SS.7.C.2.3 Experience the responsibilities of citizens at the local, state, or federal levels.

RESPONSIBILITIES OF CITIZENS FOR VOTING	Voting is both a right and a responsibility for citizens. It consists of three steps: • Registering makes citizens eligible to vote in each election. • Being prepared to vote involves getting informed about issues, current events, and candidates. • Casting a ballot lets citizens choose the candidates they want in office and the issues they approve.

SS.7.C.2.5 Distinguish how the Constitution safeguards and limits individual rights.

SAFEGUARDS OF THE CONSTITUTION	• States have the power to set suffrage qualifications, but they cannot go against the Constitution in setting their requirements. • When amendments to expand suffrage were passed, the Constitution safeguarded these rights. • Congress has the right to add legislation to further protect people's right to vote.

SS.7.C.2.7 Conduct a mock election to demonstrate the voting process and its impact on a school, community, or local level.

MOCK ELECTION PROCEDURES	A good way to prepare for the responsibility of voting is to take part in a mock election. Students in your school can model the process of holding a national election. • Several students can take on the roles of presidential candidates. • Candidates can form committees and debate one another. • Other students can work on the campaigns of the candidates. • Still other students can serve as online and print reporters. • Then the whole class can vote.

SS.7.C.2.9 Evaluate candidates for political office by analyzing their qualifications, experience, issue-based platforms, debates, and political ads.

EVALUATE CANDIDATES

Before voting, voters must carefully evaluate candidates in order to cast their votes thoughtfully. Citizens should

- think about the candidates' qualifications and experience and whether their career has prepared them for the office.
- learn about the candidates' stands on important issues.
- listen to debates and decide who does the best job.
- look closely at political ads and separate facts from opinions and learn to recognize bias as well as propaganda techniques.
- carefully consider the role of the media and whether it provides the most trustworthy information and is covering the campaign fairly.

SS.7.C.2.10 Examine the impact of media, individuals, and interest groups on monitoring and influencing government.

IMPACT OF MEDIA, INDIVIDUALS, AND SPECIAL-INTEREST GROUPS ON GOVERNMENT

The media monitors and influences government by informing the public about government actions, issues, and candidates. Individuals influence government by supporting candidates, voting, and communicating with their leaders through letters, email, and phone calls. Political action committees (PACs) are created by special-interest groups to raise funds for candidates' campaigns. The PACs are willing to invest money to help candidates who support their ideas and beliefs win the election.

SS.7.C.2.11 Analyze media and political communications (bias, symbolism, propaganda).

PROPAGANDA AND BIAS IN POLITICAL COMMUNICATIONS

- Propaganda is meant to persuade you to think a certain way. Bias is based on opinions rather than solid facts.
- Letters, pamphlets, and ads may contain propaganda and bias because they are distributed by political parties or special-interest groups eager to sway support for their view.

SS.7.C.3.6 Evaluate Constitutional rights and their impact on individuals and society.

RIGHTS AND THEIR IMPACT	
	• Expanding suffrage made it possible for more people to be eligible to vote, including African Americans, women, Native Americans, and people between the ages of 18 and 21. • New and amended voting rights laws have mandated bilingual ballots, voting assistance, and voting materials in multiple languages be made available so that all minority voters are able to exercise their right to vote.

SS.7.C.3.7 Analyze the impact of the 13th, 14th, 15th, 19th, 24th, and 26th amendments on participation of minority groups in the American political process.

IMPACT OF SUFFRAGE AMENDMENTS	
	• The Fifteenth Amendment extended suffrage to African Americans who were recently freed from slavery. Southern states passed laws to prevent this, and it took years for African Americans to gain suffrage. • The Civil Rights Acts and Voting Rights Acts were passed to ensure African Americans received true suffrage. • The Nineteenth Amendment extended suffrage to all American women so they now had a voice in government and could participate in politics. • The Twenty-fourth Amendment eliminated poll taxes ensuring that people could vote even if they could not afford to pay a poll tax. • The Twenty-sixth Amendment extended voting to those who were 18, 19, and 20 years old. This gave younger people a say in government.

SS.7.C.3.8 Analyze the structure, functions, and processes of the legislative, executive, and judicial branches.

STRUCTURE, FUNCTIONS, AND PROCESSES OF VOTING	• In primary elections, voters from each party choose one candidate to run for election. Candidates elected in the primary face off against each other in a general election. • Citizens do not directly elect the president of the United States. Instead, they vote for electors who cast their votes in the Electoral College based on the popular vote in that state. • Two special processes allow individuals to have a direct impact on government. A referendum gives voters the opportunity to accept or reject a law. An initiative is the process by which citizens propose new laws.

SS.7.C.3.12 Analyze the significance and outcomes of landmark Supreme Court cases including, but not limited to, *Marbury* v. *Madison, Plessy* v. *Ferguson, Brown* v. *Board of Education, Gideon* v. *Wainwright, Miranda* v. *Arizona, in re Gault, Tinker* v. *Des Moines, Hazelwood* v. *Kuhlmeier, United States* v. *Nixon*, and *Bush* v. *Gore*.

SUPREME COURT CASES RELATED TO VOTING	• *Smith* v. *Allwright* ruled that prohibiting African Americans from voting in primary elections is unconstitutional. • The 1975 Supreme Court case *Hill* v. *Stone* found that the Texas constitution could not declare only those people who owned taxable property eligible to vote in city bond elections. The Court said this was an unreasonable requirement and was prohibited by the Fourteenth Amendment's Equal Protection Clause. • In *Bush* v. *Gore* the U.S. Supreme Court reversed a Florida supreme court decision to allow a recount of the state's presidential election ballots. The Court stated that a recount could not be done consistently in each county. This did not allow equal and fair treatment and was unconstitutional.

Chapter 11

VISUAL SUMMARY

DIRECTIONS: Complete the graphic organizer below.

Voting and Elections

SUFFRAGE EXPANDS

- Fifteenth Amendment: ______________________ ______________________.
- __________ Amendment: ______________________
- Twenty-fourth Amendment: outlaws poll taxes
- __________ Amendment: ______________________

THE VOTING PROCESS

Registering

You: ______________________

Why? ______________________ ______________________

Preparing

You: ______________________

Why? ______________________ ______________________ ______________________

Casting Ballot

You: ______________________

Why? to pick your candidate and make your voice heard

CANDIDATES AND CITIZENS

Before voting, citizens should consider:

- ______________________ ______________________
- ______________________

Voters should look closely at political ads. They should:

- ______________________
- ______________________ ______________________
- ______________________

Citizens can volunteer to help a candidate or help the campaign.

TYPES OF ELECTIONS

Primary Elections: Voters from each party choose one candidate running for elections from their party.

General Elections: Voters ______________________

Referendums: Voters ______________________

Initiative: Voters ______________________ ______________________ ______________________

Presidential Elections: ______________________ ______________________ ______________________

USING PRIMARY SOURCES

INTERPRET The following excerpts from two speeches relate to extending suffrage to different groups of Americans. Read each and answer a few short questions. Then, on a separate sheet of paper, write an essay comparing and contrasting the two documents. Include examples of supporting details, persuasive language, and reasoning used in each document.

Document A

The history of mankind is a history of repeated injuries and usurpations [taking by force] on the part of man toward woman, having in direct object [purpose] the establishment of an absolute tyranny over her. To prove this, let facts be submitted to a candid [open-minded] world.

He has never permitted her to exercise her inalienable right to the elective franchise [voting].

He has compelled her to submit to laws, in the formation of which she had no voice.

He has withheld from her rights which are given to the most ignorant and degraded men—both natives and foreigners. . . .

He has taken from her all right in property, even to the wages she earns. . . .

He has so framed the laws of divorce, as to what shall be the proper causes of divorce; in case of separation, to whom the guardianship of the children shall be given; as to be wholly regardless of the happiness of women—the law, in all cases, going upon the false supposition of the supremacy of man, and giving all power into his hands. . . .

Resolved, That woman is man's equal—was intended to be so by the Creator, and the highest good of the race demands that she should be recognized as such. . . .

Resolved, That it is the duty of the women of this country to secure to themselves their sacred right to the elective franchise.

—Seneca Falls Declaration, 1848

1. The Seneca Falls Declaration is similar to which historical document?

____

2. What words or phrases reveal the point of view in the Seneca Falls Declaration?

____

____

Document B

I believe the time has come to lower the voting age in the United States, and thereby to bring American youth into the mainstream of our political process. To me, this is the most important single principle we can pursue as a nation if we are to succeed in bringing our youth into full and lasting participation in our institutions of democratic government. . . .

First, our young people today are far better equipped—intellectually, physically, and emotionally—to make the type of choices involved in voting than were past generations of youth. Many experts believe that today's 18 year-old is at least the equal, physically and mentally, of a 21 year-old of his father's generation, or a 25 year-old of his grandfather's generation.

The contrast is clear in the case of education. Because of the enormous impact of modern communications, especially television, our youth are extremely well informed on all the crucial issues of our time, foreign and domestic, national and local, urban and rural. . . .

. . . Our 18 year-olds today are a great deal more mature and more sophisticated than former generations at the same stage of development. Their role in issues like civil rights, Vietnam and the environment is as current as today's headlines. Through their active social involvement and their participation in programs like the Peace Corps and Vista, our youth have taken the lead on many important questions at home and overseas. In hundreds of respects, they have set a far-reaching example of insight and commitment for us to emulate.

Second, by lowering the voting age to 18, we will encourage civic responsibility at an earlier age, and thereby promote lasting social involvement and political participation for our youth. . . .

. . . [T]here can be no question that we must do more to improve the political participation of our youth, especially our young adults.

—*Senator Edward "Ted" Kennedy, Testimony Before the Senate Subcommittee on Constitutional Amendments, 1970*

3. What details does Senator Kennedy use to support his main idea? Circle the first detail. Draw a box around the second detail.

4. Find one example Senator Kennedy uses to support his ideas.

Chapter Practice Test

DIRECTIONS: Circle the best answer for each question.

SS.7.C.2.9 (High)

The boxes below show political campaign flyers for two candidates in a mock election for governor.

Who Will Make the Best Governor? **LACEY NORTH** • 12 Years in Florida Senate • 6 Years Mayor of Tampa • 2 Years City Council Member **You Can Trust Lacey** **She Has Always Worked Hard for Florida**	**A MODERN-DAY GOVERNOR** **VOTE FOR CHIP RENWALD** • Born in 1990 • Loves Florida • Supports local universities and sports teams • Knows just what our state needs for the future **A vote for Chip is a vote for today!**

Why might Lacey North be more qualified to be governor?

A She is older than Chip Renwald.

B She has experience in government.

C She is trustworthy.

D She works hard for Florida.

SS.7.C.2.7 (Moderate)

Your school is holding a mock election. How can you ensure that the mock election is similar to the actual voting process?

A Voters cast their votes by a show of hands.

B Everyone writes slogans for their favorite candidate.

C Each eligible voter casts only one vote.

D People vote according to their political party.

3 **SS.7.C.3.6 (High)**

> *The right of citizens of the United States, who are 18 years of age or older, to vote, shall not be denied or abridged by the United States or any state on account of age.*
>
> —Section 1, Twenty-sixth Amendment to the Constitution

What is one possible long-term result of the Twenty-sixth Amendment?

A African Americans gain more representation in their states.

B Women speak out against practices that pay women less than men.

C Minority groups petition the government for increased rights.

D College students become more involved in political campaigns.

SS.7.C.2.3 (High)

Suppose that a state constitution says the following about electors:

> *Every eligible citizen who is 18 or older and resides permanently in the state and is registered, is an elector of the county in which the citizen registered.*

Based on the above information, which statement is correct?

A Registering to vote is only for electors of a county.

B Registering to vote is a guarantee of the state constitution.

C Registering to vote is a responsibility that allows a person to vote.

D Registering to vote is an action that is required for every eligible citizen.

5 **SS.7.C.2.5 (Low)**

What right did the Nineteenth Amendment grant to women?

A the right to vote

B right to equality before the law

C right to free speech

D the right to protest

---

6 **SS.7.C.2.11 (High)**

Look at the image below.

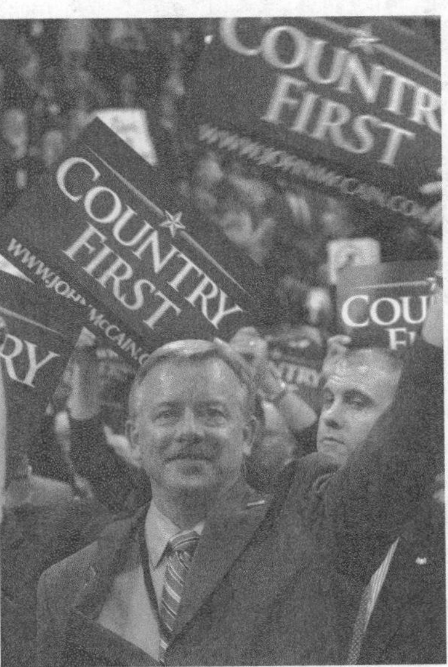

This image shows supporters of John McCain, the Republican presidential candidate in 2008. Why is this an example of propaganda?

A McCain is reminding people that he served in Vietnam and was a prisoner of war.

B McCain is implying that the Republican candidate thinks of the country before any political considerations.

C McCain is stating that the Democratic candidate cares more about winning than about the country.

D McCain is letting people know that when he becomes president, he will focus on domestic affairs.

7 **SS.7.C.3.12 (Moderate)**

What were the issues at stake in the Supreme Court case *Bush* v. *Gore*?

A Florida's election laws setting a deadline for announcing final results and a recount of all ballots

B a violation of the U.S. Constitution and the improper marking of some ballots

C whether the U.S. Supreme Court had the right to rule on a recount of Florida's votes and name a winner

D a recount of votes and who would become president of the United States

---

8 **SS.7.C.3.7 (Moderate)**

A newspaper notice in 1948 might have looked something like this:

> **Don't Forget!**
>
> **Pay Your Poll Tax**
>
> The deadline is January 25.
>
> On Election Day, you must bring a receipt to prove your poll tax is paid or you will not be allowed to vote.

Which constitutional amendment made such notices no longer necessary?

A the Fifteenth Amendment

B the Nineteenth Amendment

C the Twenty-fourth Amendment

D the Twenty-sixth Amendment

9 **SS.7.C.2.10 (Moderate)**

What is the main purpose of political action committees (PACs)?

A to raise campaign funds to support challengers

B to support participation in campaigns by the general electorate

C to raise campaign funds to support favored candidates

D to support policies that improve domestic relations

---

10 **SS.C.3.8 (Moderate)**

Why does a referendum enable voters to have a direct impact on government?

A It allows voters to have a say in which officials receive political appointments.

B It determines whether voters support an action by their state lawmakers.

C It begins the long process of removing elected officials from public office.

D It provides a way for a candidate to be chosen if no candidate receives a majority.

CHAPTER 12

Public Opinion and Government

CHAPTER BENCHMARKS

SS.7.C.2.3 Experience the responsibilities of citizens at the local, state, or federal levels.

SS.7.C.2.10 Examine the impact of media, individuals, and interest groups on monitoring and influencing government.

SS.7.C.2.11 Analyze media and political communications (bias, symbolism, propaganda).

SS.7.C.2.12 Develop a plan to resolve a state or local problem by researching public policy alternatives, identifying appropriate government agencies to address the issue, and determining a course of action.

SS.7.C.2.13 Examine multiple perspectives on public and current issues.

SS.7.C.3.12 Analyze the significance and outcomes of landmark Supreme Court cases including, but not limited to, *Marbury* v. *Madison*, *Plessy* v. *Ferguson*, *Brown* v. *Board of Education*, *Gideon* v. *Wainwright*, *Miranda* v. *Arizona*, *in re Gault*, *Tinker* v. *Des Moines*, *Hazelwood* v. *Kuhlmeier*, *United States* v. *Nixon*, and *Bush* v. *Gore*.

LAFS.68.RH.1.1 Cite specific textual evidence to support analysis of primary and secondary sources.

LAFS.68.RH.1.2 Determine the central ideas or information of a primary or secondary source; provide an accurate summary of the source distinct from prior knowledge or opinions.

Chapter Overview

In a democracy, the people are the source of political power. Elected leaders need to be aware of the public's views in order to carry out the will of the people. The media is one of the strongest influences on public opinion in America, informing people about issues and linking the people to elected officials. People in government also rely heavily on special-interest groups to make public policy and legislation. Interest groups allow individual citizens to join together to work toward common policy goals.

WHAT I NEED TO KNOW

TERMS

- ☐ public opinion
- ☐ mass media
- ☐ public opinion poll
- ☐ pollster
- ☐ public agenda
- ☐ leak
- ☐ watchdog
- ☐ prior restraint
- ☐ shield law
- ☐ malice
- ☐ public-interest group
- ☐ nonpartisan

CHAPTER 12

Public Opinion and Government

Public Opinion and Government

Make this Foldable® and label the three sections *Public Opinion, Mass Media,* and *Interest Groups*. As you read the lessons, list main ideas in the columns of your Foldable. On the back of the Foldable, give examples of ways in which politicians, the mass media, and special interest groups try to influence public opinion. How do you think public opinion influences the decisions politicians make?

Step 1
Arrange a piece of notebook paper vertically. Fold the the left and right sides once each to create three equal columns.

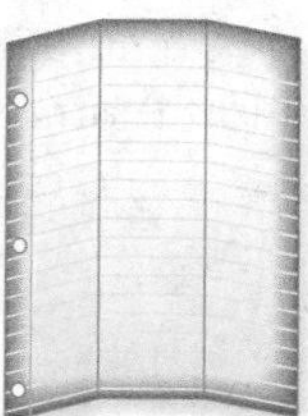

Step 2
Unfold the paper and label the columns as directed.

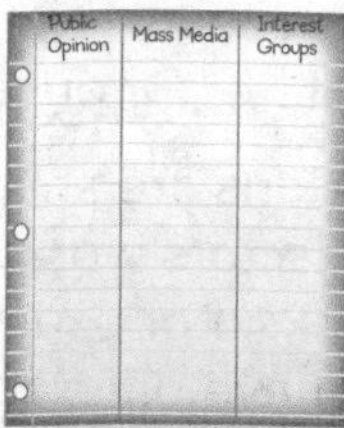

Forming Public Opinion

1. EXPLAINING

Why is public approval such a valuable resource for a president?

2. GIVING EXAMPLES

Underline three major influences on public opinion. Then, identify which of these you think would be most important for a person who is running for public office for the first time. What might be the most important for someone who is voting for the first time?

SS.7.C.2.3, SS.7.C.2.10

Public Opinion

Government leaders often talk about "the public." In the United States, the public—all the people in our country—is the source of political power. This is why government leaders want to know what the public thinks. The term for the attitudes of all Americans is *public opinion*. **Public opinion** means the ideas and views people have toward various issues or elected officials.

Public opinion is important in a democracy. For one thing, elected officials—including the president—must understand what the people want them to do. When enough people hold an opinion, government officials listen to them. Public opinion can also help determine how successful elected officials can be. Government leaders are more likely to get the political support they need to carry out their programs if their plans are popular with the public.

Sources of Public Opinion

Americans often have different opinions about matters of public policy. Several factors influence their attitudes and viewpoints. These include a person's background, the mass media, and interest groups.

People's opinions are shaped by their life experiences. A number of factors work together to influence how each individual thinks. For example, a retired person in a small town will probably have different opinions on education than a working mother who lives in a city.

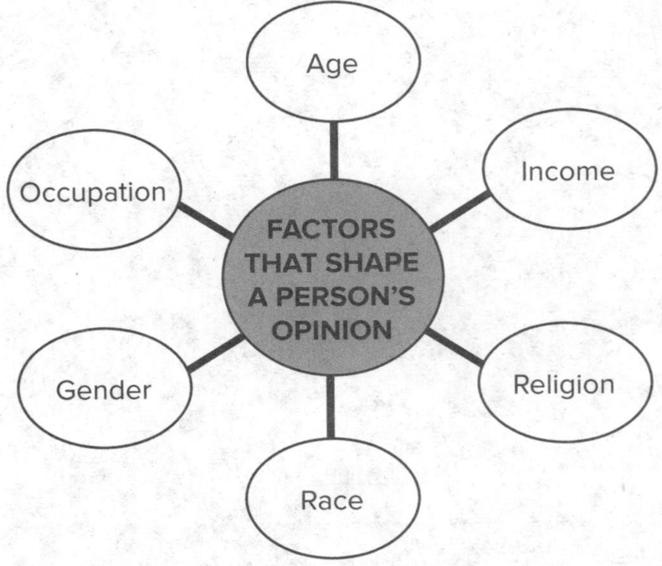

A major factor shaping public opinion is the **mass media.** The mass media include all the types of communication that reach large audiences. People use information from the mass media to form their opinions. The more stories the media publish about an issue, the more people will view it as important. Editorials and blogs also can shape opinions.

TYPES OF MASS MEDIA
Television
Radio
Internet Web sites
Newspapers
Magazines
Books
Recordings
Movies, including documentaries

Interest groups are formed by people who have the same opinion about an issue. People in a particular interest group share a common goal. They come together to support their views and to persuade others—government leaders as well as other citizens—to agree with them. Interest groups are sometimes called pressure groups because they put pressure on leaders to act in ways the group wants.

Features of Public Opinion

People often use three factors to describe public opinion: direction, intensity, and stability.

Direction refers to whether public opinion on a topic is positive or negative. For example, do people agree or disagree with a tax cut? In most cases, direction is mixed, but one side can be stronger than the other.

Intensity refers to the strength of a person's or group's opinion. When people feel strongly about an issue, they are often more inclined to pay attention to it. They are also more likely to take action. To do so, they may join an interest group, work on an election campaign, or try to solve a problem with a public action.

Stability tells how firmly people hold their opinions. Opinions based on strong beliefs are usually very stable. For example, most people don't change their views about civil rights, but their opinions about political candidates change more easily.

3. REFLECTING

If you were an elected official, to which would you pay the most attention: the direction, intensity, or stability of your constituents' opinions on issues? Explain.

4. JUDGING RELIABILITY

Do you believe public opinion polls are reliable indicators of Americans' true political beliefs? Why or why not?

____

____

____

____

____

____

____

____

____

____

Public Opinion Polls

Public opinion can be measured. One way is by examining election results. If voters elect a candidate, they probably agree with many of the candidate's ideas. However, election results give only a general idea of public opinion. Voters support candidates for many reasons. They may not agree with all of the candidate's views. Elections also don't happen often, so they might not provide current results.

Polls Measure Public Opinion

A better way to measure public opinion is to ask people what they think about important issues. A **public opinion poll** is a survey with questions about a particular issue or person. Such polls combine many people's answers to measure the public's opinion. Hundreds of groups conduct public opinion polls. Elected officials use polls to stay in touch with public opinion. They also use them to help win elections.

A person who conducts polls is called a **pollster.** Pollsters have different ways of selecting the people they survey. A valid poll is based on an unbiased sample of people. That means that there should be a variation in the group in age, gender, race, and socioeconomic status. Often such a sample is a smaller version of the U.S. population. People polled are picked at random. In addition, a certain number of people are needed in order to obtain valid results in any poll. Polls that are based on random sampling are known as scientific polls.

Pollsters must word questions carefully to get accurate responses. The way a question is asked can change the way a person answers it. A good poll uses unbiased questions. Responsible pollsters do not want to influence the answers they receive. Polls that are written to shape a person's answers are called push polls. When looking at poll results, citizens should ask themselves whether the questions were fair and unbiased. The questions asked in push polls are not.

Name ______________________ Date ______________ Class __________

Pros and Cons of Polls

Polls can be taken on any issue. Common topics include crime, education, or a leader's performance. Some people believe that public opinion polls are useful. They believe that polls help elected leaders recognize what citizens want and need, which can guide their decisions. Some polls are broken down by groups, such as working people and retired people. This way leaders can find out how certain groups think.

Others, however, argue that polls cause elected leaders to focus on pleasing the vocal members of the public rather than making wise decisions that benefit everyone. Many also believe that polls unfairly affect election results. For example, if the media report that polls indicate a candidate is a "sure winner," then people might not bother to vote.

5. MAKING GENERALIZATIONS

How do public opinion polls make government more democratic? Less democratic?

____

____

____

____

____

____

____

____

REVIEW LESSON 1

1. Public opinion can influence elected officials, and elected officials try to shape public opinion. In the chart below, write *P* next to examples of citizens attempting to influence public policy. Write *E* next to examples of elected officials attempting to influence public opinion.

A senator holds a press conference about a foreign policy issue.	
A voter writes a letter to the newspaper criticizing the president.	
A citizen joins an environmental interest group.	
A mayor answers questions about the city budget at a town hall meeting.	

2. **MAKING GENERALIZATIONS** Can citizens more effectively impact the actions of elected leaders on an individual basis or on a collective basis? Explain.

LESSON 2 SUMMARY

The Mass Media

ANALYZING VISUALS

1. DESCRIBING

According to the graph, which media format is most popular among people aged 65 and older? Which is least popular?

____

____

2. EVALUATING

Does the media have too much power over the setting of the public agenda?

____

____

____

____

____

____

____

____

____

____

SS.7.C.2.3, SS.7.C.2.10, SS.7.C.2.13, SS.7.C.3.12

The Influence of the Media

In the United States, the mass media play an important role in informing people about issues. They also influence government and connect citizens to their elected officials. There are two types of mass media sources: print (newspapers, magazines, newsletters, and books) and electronic (radio, television, and the Internet). Most media outlets are private businesses, which means they want to make a profit. Often, media managers choose topics that are popular and will allow them to make more money on advertisements. Such selections can shape what the media cover.

AMERICA'S USE OF MASS MEDIA

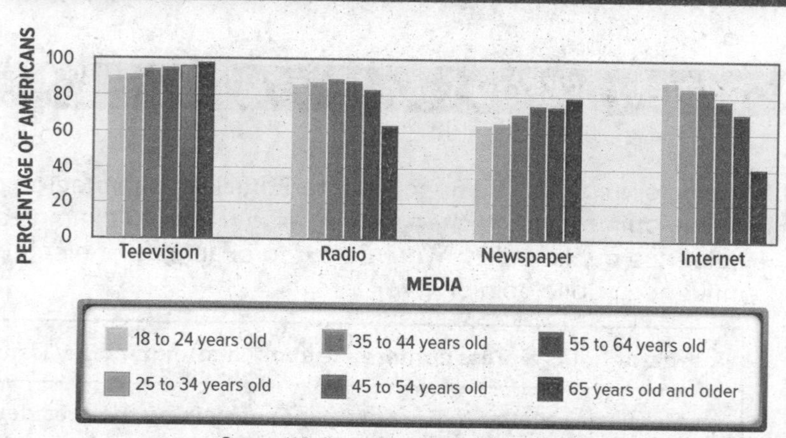

Source: U.S. Census Bureau; *Statistical Abstract of the United States*, 2009.

Influencing the Public Agenda

The government deals with many problems and issues. Those problems and issues that receive the most time, money, and effort from government leaders make up what is often called the **public agenda.** The media can influence which problems officials consider important. People begin to notice a problem when the media focus on it. Then they often demand action.

Name ______________________________ Date ______________ Class __________

Covering Candidates and Officials

The mass media can also impact who runs for office. Usually candidates are experienced politicians. Some, however, are people who became famous in another field, such as movies or sports. When candidates are already well known, they often get extra attention from the media.

Reporters and politicians have a complicated relationship. Reporters need information to write articles, and elected officials need media coverage to publicize their ideas. Sometimes officials **leak,** or secretly pass on, information to reporters to find out whether the public will like the idea before officially committing to it. At the same time, the media sometimes reports information that embarrasses the government or a politician. Reporters sometimes ask questions that make elected officials look bad. Politicians occasionally try to avoid answering reporters' questions, but they are usually criticized for doing so.

Watchdog Role

The mass media also play a crucial **"watchdog"** role by closely monitoring what politicians are doing. For example, reporters often write stories about government waste and political corruption. This serves the public interest by exposing wrongdoing by elected officials.

Media and National Security

Americans have a responsibility to be informed citizens. At the same time, the government has a responsibility to keep Americans safe. Sometimes the government must keep secrets for national security reasons. Reporters are not allowed to see this information.

The government attempts to shape the news in other ways. For example, some journalists accompanied American troops going into battle in Iraq. Some critics charged that the government was trying to control what the media was reporting about the war.

3. ANALYZING

Elected officials often hold official, scheduled press conferences. They also meet with the press at other public events. Do you believe elected officials have an obligation to meet regularly with the press?

____

____

____

____

____

____

____

____

4. EXPRESSING AN OPINION

Do you believe the media should be allowed to report on the actions of the U.S. military during times of war? Explain.

____

____

____

____

____

____

____

____

____

5. MAKING CONNECTIONS

How does the media help Americans fulfill their duties and responsibilities as citizens?

6. EVALUATING

Do you agree with the Court's ruling in *New York Times Co.* v. *Sullivan?* Why or why not?

Protecting the Press

The Founders knew that democracy depends on a free flow of information and ideas. Citizens need information in order to understand public issues. This is why freedom of the press is one of the first freedoms in the Bill of Rights. The press refers to both electronic and print media. Because of the First Amendment, the media are free from prior restraint. **Prior restraint** is when the government censors material before it is published. Journalists in the United States are generally free to write what they want to write, even if it is unpopular.

The media have some other protections as well. For example, sometimes people give information to reporters anonymously. This means they do not want their names made public. Because of this, most states have **shield laws** that allow reporters to keep their sources secret.

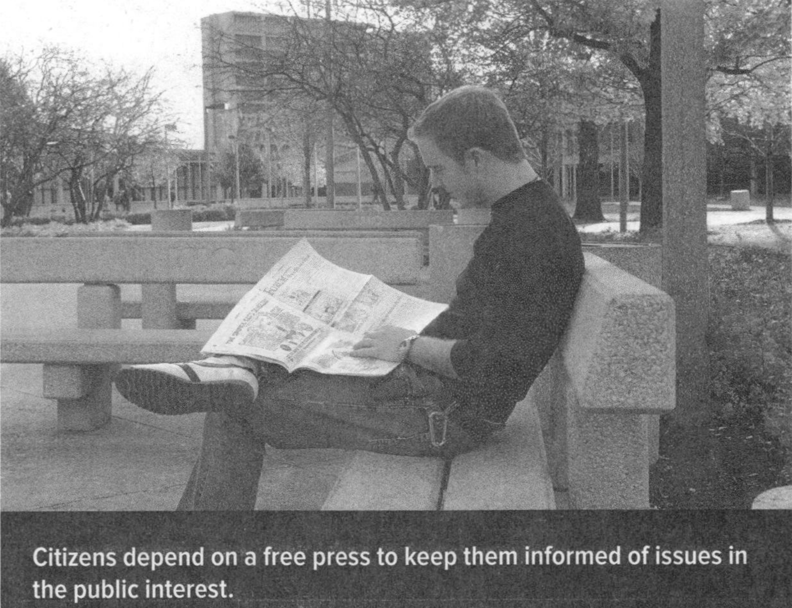

Citizens depend on a free press to keep them informed of issues in the public interest.

Freedom Within Limits

There are some limits on freedom of the press. For example, the media cannot publish false information that harms someone's reputation. This is called libel. Government officials rarely win libel lawsuits, however. In *New York Times Co.* v. *Sullivan* (1964), the Supreme Court said that public officials must prove actual **malice,** or evil intent, to win a libel suit. The official must show that the publisher knew the information was false and published it anyway.

Name ______________________ Date ______________ Class __________

Regulating the Media

The federal government controls some aspects of broadcast media. The airwaves available for radio and TV broadcasting are limited, so the government decides who can use them. The government also requires broadcasters to spend part of their airtime covering public affairs. In addition, the Federal Communications Commission (FCC) makes rules about what can and cannot be said on TV and radio. It can punish stations that break its rules.

7. DRAWING CONCLUSIONS

Do you believe the current president would have been elected without the modern media? Why or why not?

____

____

____

____

____

____

REVIEW LESSON 2

1. Use the chart below to identify several important roles the media play.

IMPORTANT MEDIA ROLES

2. **EVALUATING** Look at the roles of media in your chart. Do you believe the media has too much influence over public opinion in the United States? On a separate sheet of paper, write an essay to explain your answer.

LESSON 3 SUMMARY

Interest Groups and Lobbying

SS.7.C.2.3, SS.7.C.2.10, SS.7.C.2.11, SS.7.C.2.13

1. REFLECTING

Would you ever consider becoming an active member of an interest group? Why or why not?

2. SPECULATING

Why do some interest groups seem to have more power and influence than others?

Interest Groups

Elected officials are interested in your opinions. You can contact them by phone or in writing by letter or electronically through social media sites, Web sites, and e-mail. You have the right to contact them. You also have the right to join with others to make your voice heard. This right is guaranteed in the First Amendment. When people join together on issues, they become more influential. Interest groups are one way citizens can join with others to influence public policy. Interest groups can be broken down into various types.

Business and Labor Groups

Some interest groups are based on shared economic goals. For example, the U.S. Chamber of Commerce promotes overall business interests. Some interest groups act for particular kinds of businesses. They try to persuade the government to act in ways that benefit their industries. The National Automobile Dealers Association, for example, works on behalf of companies that sell cars and trucks.

Other interest groups, such as labor unions, are formed by workers. Labor unions work for better wages and working conditions for their members. The American Federation of Labor and Congress of Industrial Organizations (AFL-CIO) is the largest labor union in the United States.

Other Interest Groups

Another type of interest group works for people who share similar characteristics or interests. For example, the National Association for the Advancement of Colored People (NAACP) works for the rights of African Americans. The U.S. Chamber of Commerce speaks up on behalf of small business owners.

Public-interest groups want to do more than promote only their members' interests. They support causes that affect most Americans. One example is the League of Women Voters. This **nonpartisan** organization does not work for any political party. It exists to inform voters about candidates and issues. There are also public-interest groups that support consumer rights.

Name ________________________________ Date ________________ Class __________

Being Active in Elections

Interest groups use four main types of actions to influence the decisions that leaders make. The first action is being active in elections. Many interest groups try to get people elected who support their goals. Some have formed political action committees (PACs). PACs collect money from group members and donate that money to help candidates who agree with their views and support their positions on the issues they care about. They can also spend money to oppose candidates they want to see defeated.

Working Through the Courts

The second way interest groups can affect public policy is by bringing cases to court. For instance, an interest group might help a disabled person sue a company because of unfair treatment. A group may also try to convince a court that a law or policy is unconstitutional.

Directly Influencing Officials

Lobbying is the third, and perhaps most important, way interest groups try to shape policy. Interest groups hire lobbyists to contact elected officials on their behalf. They try to convince lawmakers at all levels of government to support their ideas. Lobbyists supply government leaders with information about issues and suggest solutions to problems. They sometimes write drafts of bills and testify at hearings. They may work to make sure that laws are enforced in their favor once they are passed. However, lawmakers must keep in mind that the information lobbyists supply can be biased. It may only present one side of an issue.

Shaping Public Opinion

Lastly, interest groups want to shape public opinion and to do so try to attract new members to support their efforts. Many use e-mail, direct mail, and even advertising to do so. They also hold protests and organize public events to gain media coverage and more attention for their cause.

When interest groups communicate, they can provide important information. They can also reveal a group's bias. A bias is an attitude that favors one way of thinking or acting over any other. For example, campaign workers communicate their bias toward their chosen candidate. They try to persuade others to vote for him or her.

3. SUGGESTING A SOLUTION

Some people have argued that limiting the amount of money that can be spent by a PAC is an unconstitutional limit on free speech. Others worry about the unfair influence wealthy PACs might have over decision makers. How might these two concerns be reconciled?

____

____

____

____

____

____

____

4. IDENTIFYING EVIDENCE

Underline one of the four actions used by interest groups to reach political leaders and influence public opinion. Then explain which way you think is most likely to sway decision makers, and why.

____

____

____

____

____

____

____

ANALYZING VISUALS

5. IDENTIFYING

Suppose an animal welfare group ran an advertisement featuring a famous actor urging you to adopt an animal. Which propaganda technique would that represent?

6. CONSTRUCTING AN ARGUMENT

Should foreign governments be prohibited from lobbying Congress? Should they be prohibited from hiring ex-legislators? Explain.

Interest groups may use propaganda to promote their ideas. Propaganda consists of ideas or statements that are stated in a specific way or exaggerated in order to promote a particular viewpoint. Sometimes propaganda involves symbols, such as when a candidate wears a patriotic symbol in order to project an image of patriotism. In addition to symbolism, there are many other ways to spread propaganda.

PROPAGANDA TECHNIQUES

THE BANDWAGON

"Polls show our candidate is pulling ahead, and we expect to win in a landslide."

NAME-CALLING

"Candidate A is a dangerous extremist."

ENDORSEMENT

Popular beauty queen says, "I'm voting for Candidate B and so should you."

TRANSFER

Associating a patriotic symbol with a candidate.

GLITTERING GENERALITY

"Candidate B is the one who will bring us peace and prosperity."

JUST PLAIN FOLKS

"My parents were ordinary, hardworking people, and they taught me those values."

STACKED CARDS

"Candidate C has the best record on the environment."

Interest groups sometimes use propaganda to influence public opinion. These propaganda techniques are similar to those that companies use to promote their products to consumers.

Regulating Interest Groups

Although the Constitution protects the right of all Americans to join interest groups, laws regulate what these groups can do. For example, some laws limit how much money PACs can give to candidates. Others require lobbyists to register with the government and disclose who hired them and how they spend money related to their work. In addition, former government officials must wait for a period of time after leaving office before they can become lobbyists. Such laws try to restrain the influence of lobbyists on the government.

Name ______________________ Date ______________ Class ________

LESSON 3 SUMMARY, *continued*

Some people believe that interest groups are too influential. They believe that interest groups should not affect public policy more than ordinary voters. Others defend interest groups, arguing that they make the government address people's concerns. They think that interest groups allow more Americans to participate in government.

REVIEW LESSON 3

1. Use the chart below to identify various propaganda techniques.

PROPAGANDA TECHNIQUES	
Technique	**Example**
	"Join our team, we're going to win!"
	"My opponent is a dangerous radical."
	Famous athlete says, "I'm voting to re-elect our senator!"
	"Our candidate has the best record on the economy."
	"Our candidate cares about peace and prosperity."
	"I learned the value of hard work from my mom and dad."
	A candidate's ad is full of images of American flags.

2. **ASSESSING** Which propaganda technique do you think is usually the most effective? The least effective? On a separate sheet of paper, write an essay to explain your choices.

Benchmark Skill Activities

DIRECTIONS: Write your answers on a separate piece of paper.

LAFS.68.WHST.3.8; SS.7.C.2.10

1. REFLECTING

Use your FOLDABLES to write an essay.

Which do you think most influences elected officials: public opinion, the mass media, or special-interest groups? Which do you think *should* influence them the most? Explain your answers.

LAFS.68.WHST.2.4; SS.7.C.2.12

2. SUGGESTING A SOLUTION

Write a letter or an e-mail to one of your elected officials about an issue of public policy that you care about. In your letter, explain the issue and why you are interested. Suggest a course of action that should be taken. Share the official's response with your classmates.

LAFS.68.RH.3.7; SS.7.C.2.13

3. EXAMINING POINTS OF VIEW

Think of issues on which people you know have differing opinions: organic food versus commercially prepared food, a student's right to privacy versus school safety, or some other topic. Choose one issue and research opposing viewpoints. Design two posters using propaganda techniques, each promoting one of the opposing viewpoints. Make notes indicating the point of view each one represents. Label the propaganda technique you used.

LAFS.68.RH.1.2, LAFS.68.WHST.3.8

4. USING AND CITING INFORMATION

The table below shows the top ten interest groups in spending during the 2010 midterm elections. Select one of the groups and conduct online research about it. Investigate the following points:

- What is the purpose of the group you selected?
- What issues does it support and oppose? How does it defend those positions?
- What legislation has it supported and opposed in recent years?
- Which political candidates has the group endorsed? Why?

After you have gathered this information, explain whether you support the group's goals. Cite reasons for your views.

INTEREST GROUP
Chamber of Commerce
American Action Network
American Crossroads
Crossroads Grassroots Policy Strategies
Service Employees International Union
American Federation of Employees
American Future Fund
Americans for Job Security
Club for Growth
National Rifle Association

LAFS.68.RH.2.4

5. USING DEFINITIONS ACCURATELY

Write at least two paragraphs describing the importance of the First Amendment. Correctly use at least three vocabulary words from the Chapter 12 Terms list in your description.

Benchmark Note Cards

DIRECTIONS: Use these note cards to help you prepare for the test.

SS.7.C.2.3 Experience the responsibilities of citizens at the local, state, or federal levels.

CITIZENS AND PUBLIC POLICY	Americans often have different opinions about matters of public policy. Several factors influence their attitudes: • Personal background—Factors such as age and gender, race, religion, occupation, and income all work together to influence how each individual views public issues. • Mass media—Citizens have a responsibility to stay informed about the workings of government. The media provide the information citizens need to understand public issues. • Interest groups—An interest group consists of people who have the same opinion about a public policy issue. When people join together in an interest group, they can influence public policy.

SS.7.C.2.10 Examine the impact of media, individuals, and interest groups on monitoring and influencing government.

IMPACT OF THE MEDIA ON GOVERNMENT	The mass media play many important roles. They • inform people about issues • connect citizens to their elected officials • monitor the actions of government leaders • influence the public agenda

IMPACT OF INDIVIDUALS ON GOVERNMENT	When all the opinions of individuals are collected and viewed together, it is called public opinion. Public opinion helps elected officials understand what the people want them to do. In addition, public opinion can help determine how successful elected officials can be. Government leaders are more likely to get the political support they need to carry out their programs if their plans are popular with the public.

IMPACT OF INTEREST GROUPS ON GOVERNMENT	Interest groups influence public policy by • being active in elections • working through the courts • working directly with lawmakers • trying to shape public opinion

SS.7.C.2.11 Analyze media and political communications (bias, symbolism, propaganda).

MEDIA AND POLITICAL COMMUNICATIONS	Communicating about government often involves promoting a particular point of view. Such a view, or slant, is bias. Taking the bias of a writer into account helps the reader interpret and evaluate the message. Interest groups sometimes use propaganda to promote their ideas. Propaganda is delivering information in a biased manner in order to elicit a response.

SS.7.C.2.13 Examine multiple perspectives on public and current issues.

PROS AND CONS OF POLLS	Some citizens believe that polls can guide the decisions of elected leaders by helping them understand what the people want and need. Others argue that polls cause elected leaders to focus on pleasing the vocal members of the public rather than making wise decisions that benefit everyone. Many also believe that polls unfairly affect election results.

PROS AND CONS OF INTEREST GROUPS	Some people believe that interest groups are too influential. They believe that interest groups should not affect public policy more than ordinary voters. Others argue that interest groups make the government address people's concerns and allow more Americans to participate in government.

SS.7.C.3.12 Analyze the significance and outcomes of landmark Supreme Court cases including, but not limited to, *Marbury* v. *Madison, Plessy* v. *Ferguson, Brown* v. *Board of Education, Gideon* v. *Wainwright, Miranda* v. *Arizona, in re Gault, Tinker* v. *Des Moines, Hazelwood* v. *Kuhlmeier, United States* v. *Nixon, and Bush* v. *Gore.*

NEW YORK TIMES CO. V. SULLIVAN	In *New York Times Co.* v. *Sullivan* (1964), the Supreme Court held that public officials must prove actual malice, or evil intent, to win a libel suit. The official must show that the publisher knew the information was false and published it anyway. This decision protects the media from false charges of libel.

Chapter 12

VISUAL SUMMARY

DIRECTIONS: Complete the graphic organizer below.

ROLE OF MEDIA
Inform people about issues
Influence public agenda
Connect citizens to elected officials
Play watchdog role over government activities

STRATEGIES OF INTEREST GROUP

Public Opinion and Government

FACTORS INFLUENCING THE VIEW OF INDIVIDUALS
Gender
Occupation
Age

USING PRIMARY SOURCES

ANALYZE VISUALS Propaganda is frequently used by interest groups to promote their agendas. Governments and political campaigns also use propaganda for a simliar purpose. Shown here are a Barack Obama 2008 campaign button and a poster issued by the federal government during World War II that promotes the cause of the Allies (United States, United Kingdom, Soviet Union, France, and others). Examine the objects, and then on a separate sheet of paper write an essay that answers the questions that follow.

- What is the desired effect of each object? For whom are the objects intended?
- What emotions do the images convey? Are any words chosen for impact?
- In what way are the objects the same? How are they different?
- Which propaganda techniques do the objects use?
- How successful do you believe the objects were?

Chapter Practice Test

DIRECTIONS: Circle the best answer for each question.

 1

SS.7.C.2.10 (Moderate)

The passage below is from the First Amendment to the U.S. Constitution.

> *Congress shall make no law respecting an establishment of religion, or prohibiting the free exercise thereof; or abridging the freedom of speech, or of the press; or the right of the people peaceably to assemble, and to petition the Government for a redress of grievances.*
>
> —U.S. Constitution

What civil right is guaranteed by the text?

A the right to join an interest group

B the right to have a fair and speedy trial

C the right to libel elected officials

D the right to avoid excessive punishments

 2

SS.7.C.2.10 (Moderate)

Which of the following questions is most likely from a push poll?

A What is your opinion about U.S. troop involvement in Iraq?

B Do you favor or oppose sending additional troops into Iraq?

C Do you believe the United States should remove troops from Iraq and let the terrorists win?

D What is your opinion about the president's decision to send troops into Iraq?

SS.7.C.2.3 (High)

Which of the following is most helpful to a president who wants congressional support for a program?

A donations from interest groups in favor of the program

B statements of support from former presidents

C opinions of advisers who agree with the president

D expressions of strong public support for the program

SS.7.C.2.3 (High)

During the Vietnam War, a chemical called Agent Orange was used to kill vegetation in battle areas. Many Americans expressed their concerns about its possible effects.

Which of the following shows how public opinion on Agent Orange influenced government?

A The American Medical Association organized seminars to educate doctors about Agent Orange.

B Citizens' groups created Web sites to communicate the dangers of using Agent Orange.

C Public television made a documentary film about the use of Agent Orange.

D Congress passed a law to provide treatment to veterans with illnesses linked to Agent Orange.

5 **SS.7.C.2.10 (Moderate)**

The passage below was written by James Madison in 1787.

> *AMONG the numerous advantages promised by a well-constructed Union, none deserves to be more accurately developed than its tendency to break and control the violence of faction. . . .*
>
> *By a faction, I understand a number of citizens, whether amounting to a majority or a minority of the whole, who are united and actuated [moved to action] by some common impulse of passion, or of interest, adverse to [opposed to] the rights of other citizens, or to the permanent and aggregate interests of the community. . . .*
>
> *There are . . . two methods of removing the causes of faction: the one, by destroying the liberty which is essential to its existence; the other, by giving to every citizen the same opinions, the same passions, and the same interests.*
>
> —*Federalist Paper,* No. 10 (1787)

What was James Madison's opinion of interest groups?

A He believed they should be free from all government restraint.

B He viewed them as dangerous but unavoidable.

C He thought they should be replaced by political parties.

D He believed they should be banned from political activity.

---

6 **SS.7.C.2.11 (High)**

Which of the following is an example of bias?

A A public university organizes a study of the sources citizens use to get information about candidates for election.

B A political party hires a polling organization to conduct a national poll on voters' attitudes on an issue.

C A national broadcasting company televises a panel discussion with three candidates from the same political party.

D A statewide interest group publishes a guide to candidates and issues on the ballot for Election Day.

7 **SS.7.C.2.13; SS.7.C.3.12 (High)**

In a 5 to 4 ruling, the Supreme Court decision in *Citizens United* v. *FEC* (2010) declared that the government restriction on independent political spending by corporations and unions was unconstitutional. This decision overturned precedent that allowed the government to regulate such spending.

> *At bottom, the Court's opinion is thus a rejection of the common sense of the American people, who have recognized a need to prevent corporations from undermining self government since the founding, and who have fought against the distinctive corrupting potential of corporate electioneering since the days of Theodore Roosevelt. It is a strange time to repudiate that common sense. While American democracy is imperfect, few outside the majority of this Court would have thought its flaws included a dearth of corporate money in politics.*
>
> —Opinion of Supreme Court Justice John Paul Stevens

What did Justice Stevens think of the decision?

A He believed that money should be kept completely out of politics.

B He strongly disagreed with the Court's ruling.

C He argued that corporations have the same rights as individuals.

D He voted with the majority on this case.

SS.7.C.2.10 (Moderate)

In which of the following instances is the media carrying out its role as watchdog?

A A magazine interviews a senator about her views regarding the minimum wage.

B Major TV and radio stations broadcast the president's State of the Union message.

C A newspaper prints an article about the corrupt practices of an elected official.

D A television station provides live coverage of a major snowstorm.

SS.7.C.2.11 (Moderate)

Examine the poster below of "Uncle Sam" issued by the government of the United States during World War II to encourage support of the war effort.

Which propaganda technique does the poster use?

A just plain folks

B transfer

C glittering generality

D name-calling

SS.7.C.2.10 (Moderate)

What is the primary function of political action committees?

A to promote public awareness of important issues

B to shape public policy by bringing cases to court

C to raise funds to support favored candidates

D to consult with Congress regarding domestic policy

Library of Congress Prints and Photographs Division [LC-USZC4-595]

CHAPTER 13

State Government

Chapter Overview

State governments are similar to the federal government in structure and function. They are divided into three branches: legislative, executive, and judicial. State legislatures make laws for the state. State executives make sure state laws are carried out. State courts decide the guilt of criminals and settle disputes in civil cases.

State governments share some powers with the federal government. However, states also have their own powers separate from the federal government. Each state has its own constitution that explains the state government and lists the rights guaranteed to state citizens. Many state constitutions also establish rules for state budgets.

CHAPTER BENCHMARKS

SS.7.C.2.10 Examine the impact of media, individuals, and interest groups on monitoring and influencing government.

SS.7.C.3.4 Identify the relationship and division of powers between the federal government and state governments.

SS.7.C.3.7 Analyze the impact of the 13th, 14th, 15th, 19th, 24th, and 26th amendments on participation of minority groups in the American political process.

SS.7.C.3.9 Illustrate the law making process at the local, state, and federal levels.

SS.7.C.3.11 Diagram the levels, functions, and powers of courts at the state and federal levels.

SS.7.C.3.13 Compare the constitutions of the United States and Florida.

SS.7.C.3.14 Differentiate between local, state, and federal governments' obligations and services.

SS.7.E.2.1 Explain how federal, state, and local taxes support the economy as a function of the United States government.

LAFS.68.RH.1.1 Cite specific textual evidence to support analysis of primary and secondary sources.

WHAT I NEED TO KNOW

TERMS

- ☐ federal system
- ☐ reserved powers
- ☐ concurrent powers
- ☐ supremacy clause
- ☐ grants-in-aid
- ☐ unfunded mandate
- ☐ extradition
- ☐ legislator
- ☐ special session
- ☐ legislative referendum
- ☐ popular referendum
- ☐ governor
- ☐ line-item veto
- ☐ trial court
- ☐ criminal case
- ☐ misdemeanor
- ☐ civil case
- ☐ plaintiff
- ☐ defendant
- ☐ felony
- ☐ appellate court

CHAPTER BENCHMARKS, *continued*

LAFS.68.RH.1.3 Identify key steps in a text's description of a process related to history/social studies (e.g., how a bill becomes law, how interest rates are raised or lowered).

LAFS.68.RH.2.4 Determine the meaning of words and phrases as they are used in a text, including vocabulary specific to domains related to history/social studies.

LAFS.68.WHST.1.2 Write informative/explanatory texts, including the narration of historical events, scientific procedures/ experiments, or technical processes.

LAFS.68.WHST.2.6 Use technology, including the Internet, to produce and publish writing and present the relationships between information and ideas clearly and efficiently.

MAFS.K12.MP.6.1 Attend to precision.

State Government

Make this Foldable® and label the three tabs *Legislative*, *Executive*, and *Judicial*. On the back of the Foldable, describe how the federal system allows national and state governments to share power. Under the tabs, describe what you learn about the powers and responsibilities of the legislative, executive, and judicial branches of state government. Relate what you read to your state government and current officials.

Step 1
Fold lined paper horizontally to the margin.

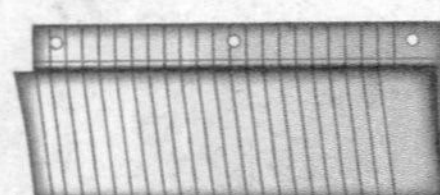

Step 2
Fold the right side and the left side of the paper across the middle to form three equal parts.

Step 3
Cut the two fold lines from the top edge to the bottom fold.

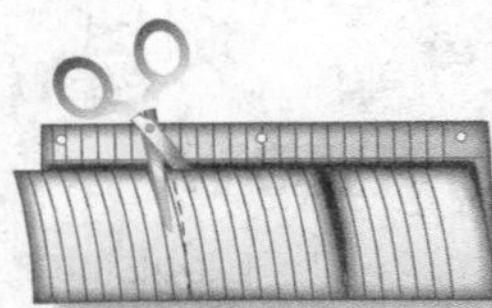

Step 4
Label the tabs as shown.

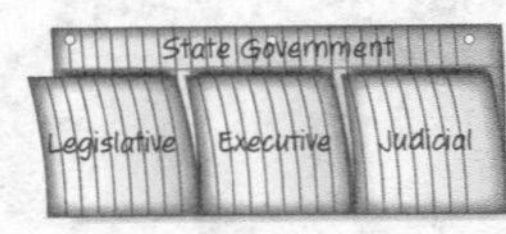

LESSON 1 SUMMARY

The Federal System

SS.7.C.3.4, SS.7.C.3.7, SS.7.C.3.13, SS.7.C.3.14, SS.7.E.2.1

Federal and State Powers

The United States has a **federal system** of government. That means powers are shared by and divided between the national government and the state governments. Some powers belong to state governments. Some powers belong to the federal government. Some powers are shared by both.

States in the Constitution

The federal system was created by the Framers of the Constitution. When they wrote the Constitution, they set limits on state power. They also provided the states with certain protections. For example, the Constitution says:

- Each state must respect legal actions taken by other states.
- Each state will treat the people of other states equally.
- A state's area is guaranteed. Land cannot be taken from any state to make a new state without its approval. Two states cannot be combined into a new state unless they agree.
- Each state is promised a republican form of government. That government will be protected against an enemy attack or a revolt.

Sharing and Dividing Powers

The federal system means different powers are assigned in different ways. The federal government has three kinds of power.

- *Expressed* powers are those specifically listed in the Constitution.
- *Implied* powers are not listed in the Constitution but can be based on it.
- *Inherent* powers are the kinds of powers a government has simply because it is a government.

Powers given only to the states are called **reserved powers.** These powers come from the Tenth Amendment in the Bill of Rights.

Powers shared by the national and state governments are called **concurrent powers.** Even though concurrent powers are not in the Constitution, both levels of government need these powers in order to function.

1. SPECULATING

Why might citizens benefit from state and local governments having different powers than the federal government?

2. MAKING CONNECTIONS

Why did the Framers of the Constitution put limits on the powers of the states?

They did this so that the states wouldn't have too much power, like they did under the Articles of Confederation.

Name ______________________ Date ______________ Class __________

ANALYZING VISUALS

3. DIFFERENTIATING

Identify each of the powers listed below as federal, reserved (state), or concurrent. Use "F" for federal, "S" for reserved (state), and "C" for concurrent.

F Print new $20 bills

C Make ballots for the presidential election

C Appoint judges

C Approve city charters

S Administer high school exit exams

F Negotiate a foreign trade agreement

S Set speed limits

C Provide police and fire services

4. ASSESSING

Which of the following actions are allowed under the federal system? Check all that apply.

- [ ] Maine declaring war on Canada
- [x] Ohio passing laws against age discrimination
- [ ] Iowa passing a law contradicting federal agricultural policy
- [ ] Arizona setting immigration quotas
- [x] Georgia creating a new fuel tax

THE FEDERAL SYSTEM		
Federal Powers	**Shared (Concurrent) Powers**	**Reserved (State) Powers**
Expressed Powers • regulate interstate and international commerce • coin and regulate money • declare war • raise and support a military • create lower federal courts **Implied Powers** • deploy the military • build highways • create national parks **Inherent Powers** • issue executive orders	• collect taxes • set up courts • build highways • create laws • enforce laws	• establish local governments • administer elections • protect public welfare and safety • establish school systems • regulate commerce within the state

Federalism works because of the manner in which the Constitution assigns powers.

Limits on State Power

The Constitution limits the powers of the states. States are not allowed to declare war, issue their own money, impose import taxes, or make treaties with other countries.

The Fourteenth Amendment also limits state power. It requires states to apply due process of law and requires states to provide "equal protection of the laws" to all citizens. Courts have used the Fourteenth Amendment to stop states from limiting or taking away people's rights.

The Constitution's **supremacy clause** also limits state power. The clause states that the Constitution and all federal laws "shall be the supreme Law of the Land." That means, if a state law conflicts with the Constitution or a federal law, the state law is thrown out.

Working Together

The federal and state governments also work together. Every year the states receive **grants-in-aid** from the federal government. These grants are used to meet goals set by Congress in areas such as education and health care. These can be general goals or come with specific guidelines.

Sometimes Congress directs states to do something without helping to pay for it. These laws are called **unfunded mandates.** Some people think these mandates are unfair.

States do not always agree with federal laws. One example is the Real ID Act of 2005. The law set strict standards for driver's licenses. Congress said the new law would help national security, but half of the states protested the law.

State governments work with each other, too. They collaborate on issues such as energy policy or income taxes for people who live in one state and work in another. Many states also cooperate through a legal process called **extradition.** In this process, a person charged with a crime who has fled to another state is returned to the state where the crime was committed.

5. HYPOTHESIZING

Why might some people think unfunded mandates are unfair?

____

____

____

____

____

____

____

The State Constitutions

Like the federal government, each state government is guided by a constitution. However, these constitutions vary from state to state.

Similarities in State Constitutions

Each state constitution describes the structure of the state government. State governments, like the federal government, are organized into executive, legislative, and judicial branches. State constitutions also list the rights guaranteed to citizens. Florida's list is called the Declaration of Rights. It is nearly three times longer than the Bill of Rights.

Differences Among State Constitutions

State constitutions differ in age. Florida, for example, has had six constitutions. The current one was ratified in 1968.

State constitutions also vary in length. Florida's constitution is about 57,000 words, making it 50,000 words longer than the U.S. Constitution. One reason Florida's constitution is longer is because it includes far more details.

State constitutions differ in the number of amendments, too. Florida has more than 100 amendments. The U.S. Constitution, by comparison, has only 27 amendments.

Name ______________________ Date ______________ Class ________

The Constitution of Florida

Florida's constitution begins with a list of citizens' rights. Many of these rights are included in the Bill of Rights. However, Florida's constitution also includes the right to privacy, the rights of crime victims, a taxpayer bill of rights, and a definition of marriage.

Another difference is that Florida's constitution addresses campaign funding and spending limits. These issues are covered in the article about voting and elections.

THE FLORIDA CONSTITUTION	
Article I	Lists the rights guaranteed to citizens Guarantees equality before the law Guarantees individual rights Defines marriage
Article II	Defines state boundaries Establishes state capital Makes English the official language Sets rules for public officials Protects Florida's natural resources
Article III	Describes the legislative branch
Article IV	Describes the executive branch
Article V	Describes the judicial branch
Article VI	Describes voting and election rules, including funding and spending limits
Article VII	Sets tax rules for state and local governments
Article VIII	Describes organization and powers of local governments
Article IX	Creates public schools and state universities
Article X	Covers a variety of topics, including lotteries, minimum wage, animal cruelty, conservation of resources, and the need for a monorail
Article XI	Sets rules for reviewing and amending the state constitution every 20 years
Article XII	Describes the process for implementation of the new (1968) constitution

The Florida Constitution has five more articles than the U.S. Constitution.

6. CONTRASTING

List five differences between the Florida state constitution and the U.S. Constitution. On a separate sheet of paper, write at least one conclusion you can draw from these differences.

1. ______________________

____

2. ______________________

____

3. ______________________

____

4. ______________________

____

5. ______________________

____

ANALYZING VISUALS

7. GIVING EXAMPLES

Which articles of the Florida Constitution describe reserved powers? Which describe concurrent powers?

____

____

____

____

____

Name ________________ Date ________________ Class ________

Article XI explains that Florida's constitution must be reviewed every 20 years to make sure it still meets the state's needs. During the review, the state legislature, the review commission, or the citizens of Florida can suggest amendments or revisions. Amendments must be approved by 60 percent of the state's voters in order to take effect.

Florida's constitution has been reviewed twice since it was enacted. The review in the late 1990s resulted in 12 new amendments. The next review is scheduled for 2017.

8. SPECULATING

On a separate piece of paper, describe amendments that might be proposed during the next review of the Florida Constitution. Explain your choices.

REVIEW LESSON 1

1. Use the chart below to describe where state governments get their power and responsibilities.

The Federal System	**State Constitutions**
Powers of the States	Similarities with U.S. Constitution
Limits to State Powers	Florida's Constitution
Cooperation	

STATE GOVERNMENT

2. **RECOGNIZING RELATIONSHIPS** Is the relationship between the federal and state governments more of a parent-child relationship or a sibling relationship? Use details from your chart above to support your answer.

The State Legislative Branch

SS.7.C.2.10, S.7.C.3.9, SS.7.E.2.1

1. REASONING

Think about how the presiding officer is chosen in different legislative chambers. Which leader do you think is most effective in managing the lawmaking process? Explain your reasons.

How Legislatures Function

Most states have a legislative branch similar to that of the federal government. Every state except Nebraska has a two-house legislature, like Congress. The upper house is called the senate. The lower house is usually called the house of representatives.

Legislators and Leaders

The leaders in each house of a state legislature help set the schedule for legislation. They also schedule the discussion of new bills by **legislators,** or the members of the legislature.

Each house has a presiding, or supervising, officer. In the lower chamber, the presiding officer is often a speaker chosen by members of the body. In the senate, it is sometimes the state's lieutenant governor. Each house also has a majority leader and minority leader.

These leadership positions are based on party membership. Members of each party choose someone to serve as their party's leader in each house.

Legislatures at Work

The meeting of a legislature is called a legislative session. Most legislative sessions last a few months, but they can be extended. During a time of crisis, the legislature can meet in a **special session** to address the emergency.

The main job during a legislative session is to make laws. The following diagram illustrates the procedure.

Name ______________________ Date ______________ Class __________

Making State Laws

A new law is suggested by a citizen, the governor, or a legislator.

↓

A legislator introduces the bill to his or her chamber of the legislature.

↓

A committee reviews, revises, and votes on the bill.

↓

If the bill is approved by the committee, the full chamber discusses and votes on it.

↓

If the bill wins a majority of votes in the chamber, it goes to the other house of the legislature.

↓

The bill goes through another committee review and full vote.

↓

When both houses have approved the bill, it goes to the governor to be signed into law.

↓

If the governor vetoes the bill, the legislature can override by a two-thirds majority in each house.

The process for making state laws is similar to the process for making federal laws.

ANALYZING VISUALS

2. DETERMINING CAUSE AND EFFECT What happens to a bill if a committee does not approve it?

____

____

____

____

____

____

____

Citizen Power

Citizens can influence the lawmaking process through a referendum. In a **legislative referendum,** the legislature asks voters to approve a law it has passed. Some states require a legislative referendum for borrowing money or raising taxes. In most states, voters must approve changes to the state constitution.

3. CONTRASTING

How is a legislative referendum different from a popular referendum?

In some states, citizens also have the option of a **popular referendum.** This type of referendum is a petition that citizens can use if they dislike a law and want it repealed, or reversed.

State Economic Issues

Most states are required to have a balanced budget. This means that states cannot spend more money than they collect. They are also not allowed to borrow money to pay their regular expenses. Therefore, if a state's income is less than expected, that state's government must decide how it is going to balance the budget. Often, this means spending cuts.

State Revenues and Spending

Taxes are a state's chief source of income. Two-thirds of state revenue comes from income taxes and sales taxes. People pay sales taxes when they purchase goods. Most state sales taxes are between 3 percent and 8 percent. In most states people pay income taxes on the money they earn from working or get from other sources. Florida does not have an income tax.

ANALYZING VISUALS

4. IDENTIFYING PROBLEMS What does this image reveal about economic conditions? What would be the negative effects on the state and its residents?

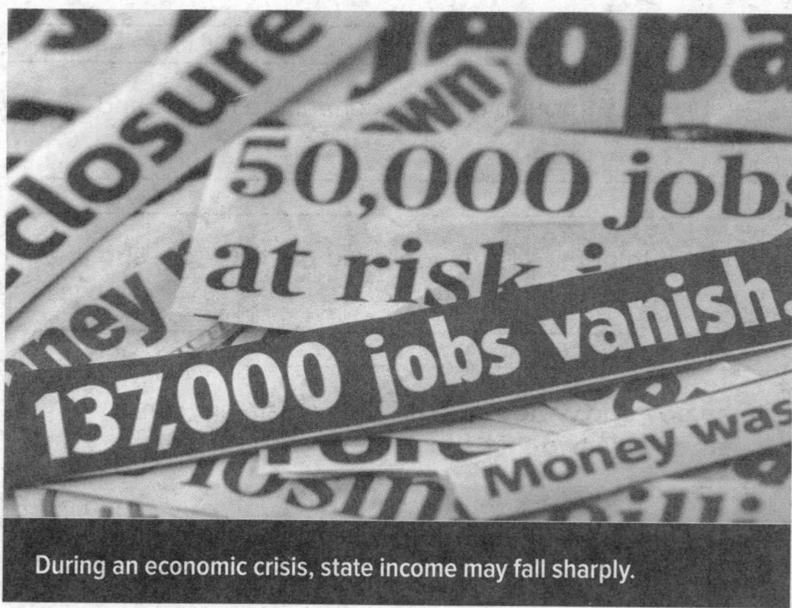

During an economic crisis, state income may fall sharply.

States also get income from fees. People pay state fees for marriage licenses, driver's licenses, fishing licenses, and other official documents. Road tolls are also a type of fee.

States spend most of their money providing services, such as assistance to the poor and disabled, health care, and schools. States also need money in order to provide police services, repair roads, and maintain state parks.

Name ______________________ Date ______________ Class __________

Budget Crunch

When states lose income, balancing the budget can be difficult. When the American economy slowed during the late 2000s, many people lost their jobs and reduced their spending. As a result, states lost tax income.

At the same time, states faced an increase in expenses. More people depended on state unemployment payments or required help with health care.

Many states responded to the crisis by making deep budget cuts. Other states increased taxes. Higher taxes meant that people had less money to spend on other things. The federal government helped by giving the states extra money, but it was not always enough to close the gap in the state budgets.

5. POSING QUESTIONS

What are three questions a state legislator might ask when deciding how to deal with a budget crunch?

1. ______________________
2. ______________________
3. ______________________

REVIEW LESSON 2

1. Use the diagram below to describe how state legislatures work.

STATE LEGISLATURES → MAKE LAWS

STATE LEGISLATURES → MANAGE BUDGETS

2. **MAKING CONNECTIONS** How are the lawmaking and budgeting responsibilities of state legislatures connected? Using a separate sheet of paper, write an essay explaining the connection. Support your answer with details from your chart.

LESSON 3 SUMMARY

State Executive Branch

SS.7.C.3.9

1. SEQUENCING

What role does the governor play at the start of the lawmaking process? What role does he or she play at the end?

2. INTERPRETING

What do you think are the advantages of a line-item veto? What are the disadvantages?

The Governor

Governors are the heads of their states. Like the president, a governor has a variety of roles. These roles include chief executive, commander in chief, legislative leader, judicial leader, party leader, and ceremonial leader.

The Chief Executive

Similar to the president, a governor serves as the head of the executive branch of state government. It is his or her job to make sure that state laws are carried out. Most governors also write the budgets for their states. They present their budgets to the legislature. Legislators must approve the budget for it to take effect. Governors also choose a person to fill a U.S. Senate seat for their state if it becomes vacant. In addition, they head the state's National Guard.

Other Roles of the Governor

Governors have legislative responsibilities. Every year, they outline their goals for the state in a State of the State message. These goals help the governor determine what bills to send to the legislature.

Governors can also veto bills. Most governors have the option of using a **line-item veto.** This means they can veto part of a bill rather than the whole law. If a governor uses his or her veto power, lawmakers can override the veto by passing the bill again.

Finally, governors have some judicial power. They can appoint judges and change criminal sentences so that people have their sentences removed or serve less time in prison.

Name ______________________ Date ______________ Class ________

State Executive Departments

To help the governor carry out laws, state governments have a number of executive departments, agencies, and boards. Some have federal counterparts, such as departments of labor, justice, and agriculture. Others relate specifically to state needs and powers. These include departments of health and public works and highways.

Major Executive Officials

Most states have five major executive officials. The titles of these officials are different in each state. No matter what they are called, though, they carry out important activities. In most states, these officials are elected and are independent of the governor.

Secretary of State	• Oversees elections • Records and publishes laws • Keeps official records
Attorney General	• Acts as state's chief lawyer • Leads team that represents state in legal matters
State Treasurer	• Handles and tracks state revenue and spending
State Auditor	• Makes sure state departments and officials are honest and efficient • Makes sure tax dollars are used properly
Commissioner of Education	• Sometimes called "superintendent of education" • Supervises the state's public schools

Executive officials advise the governor and help carry out the state's laws.

State Cabinets

In most states, the governor is assisted by a cabinet. The cabinet is made up of executive department officials. They meet regularly with the governor to give advice and share information. Each official brings special knowledge when discussing issues.

3. MAKING INFERENCES

Why are some state executive departments different from those in the federal government?

____

____

____

____

____

____

____

ANALYZING VISUALS

4. ASSESSING Which executive officials are most closely associated with the lawmaking process? Explain.

____

____

____

____

____

____

____

____

____

____

____

Name ______________________ Date ______________ Class ________

REVIEW LESSON 3

1. Use the diagram below to explain the role of the state executive branch in the lawmaking process.

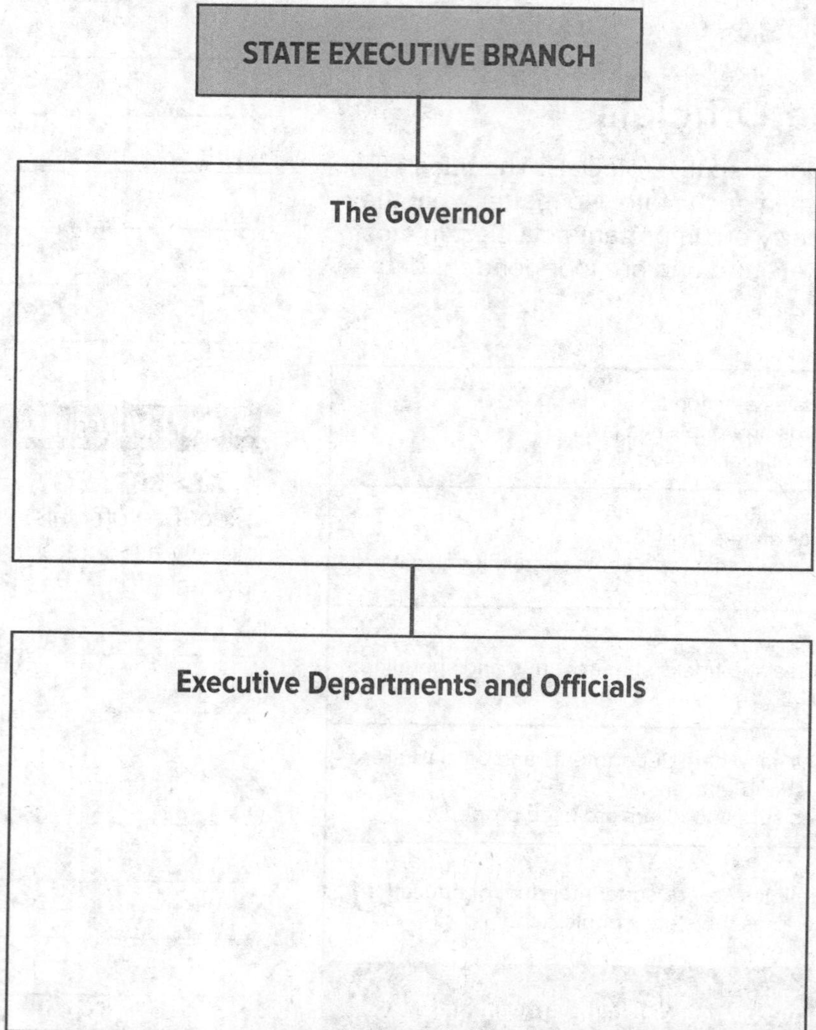

2. **IDENTIFYING STEPS IN A PROCESS** Summarize how state laws are made, including the role of the executive branch in the lawmaking process. Write your answer on a separate piece of paper.

LESSON 4 SUMMARY

State Judicial Branch

SS.7.C.3.11

The Structure of State Courts

Every state has its own court system, but all of the systems are organized in a similar way. There are two types of state courts: lower courts and higher courts. Each level handles different kinds of cases.

Lower Courts

The lower courts are **trial courts.** In a trial court, a judge or a jury examines evidence and decides in favor of one party in the case. Lower trial courts may be called justice courts, district courts, or municipal courts. These lower courts deal with both criminal and civil cases.

Criminal cases determine the guilt or innocence of a person accused of a crime. Those who are found guilty are issued a punishment. Lower courts handle only simple criminal cases, such as traffic violations or misdemeanors. **Misdemeanors** are the least serious of crimes. They include theft of a small sum of money or trespassing. Punishment is usually a fine or a short stay in a local jail rather than in a prison. Judges often decide misdemeanor cases instead of a jury.

Civil cases are also heard in lower courts. **Civil cases** involve disputes between two parties in which one claims to have been harmed by the other. The **plaintiff** is the person claiming harm. The **defendant** is the person who supposedly caused the harm. These cases often involve failure to uphold a contract, or an agreement, and involve small sums of money.

Use the Venn diagram below to compare and contrast the types of cases heard in lower state courts.

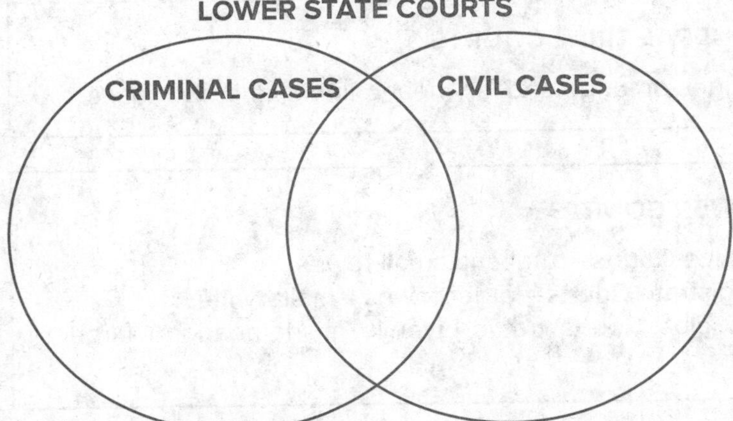

1. CONTRASTING

What do you think is the difference between cases handled by lower courts and those handled by higher courts?

2. MAKING CONNECTIONS

Person A owns a roofing company and is contracted to replace Person B's roof. After the work is done, Person B's roof still leaks. When Person B sues Person A for damages, what type of case would it be?

While the case is being heard, what would Person B be called?

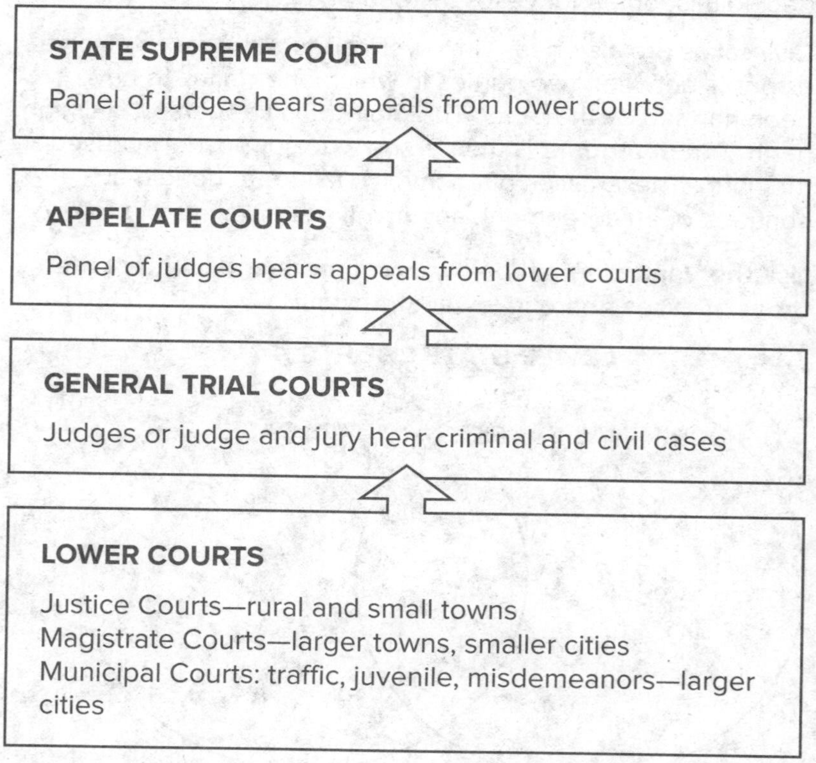

3. ANALYZING INFORMATION

Could a case appear in both a higher trial court and an appellate court? Explain.

____

____

____

____

____

ANALYZING VISUALS

4. DIFFERENTIATING

Which level of the state court structure would deal with each situation described below?

1. A person driving to work is issued a ticket for running a red light.

   ____

2. A person is arrested for breaking into a business and stealing goods.

   ____

3. A person convicted of a civil crime wants the conviction to be overturned.

   ____

Higher Courts

State higher courts can be either trial courts or appellate courts. Higher-level trial courts handle felonies. **Felonies** are more serious crimes, such as assault, robbery, kidnapping, and murder. In these cases, an accused person can ask that the judge, not a jury, decides guilt or innocence.

Higher trial courts also handle serious civil cases. These cases may involve large sums of money. As with criminal cases, they can be decided by either a judge or a jury.

In an **appellate court,** the party who lost the case asks a judge to review and reverse the case decision. The party who appeals often claims that the case included legal errors. The appellate court decides whether errors occurred. The courts of appeal deal only with cases that have been decided by another court.

Most states have two levels of appellate courts. The first level is an intermediate court called the court of appeals. In this court, a group of judges hears a case and decides whether to overturn the previous court's ruling.

Courts in one state do not have to respect the rulings of another state's courts. However, they might consult similar cases from other states when making a decision.

STATE COURT STRUCTURE

STATE SUPREME COURT

Panel of judges hears appeals from lower courts

↑

APPELLATE COURTS

Panel of judges hears appeals from lower courts

↑

GENERAL TRIAL COURTS

Judges or judge and jury hear criminal and civil cases

↑

LOWER COURTS

Justice Courts—rural and small towns
Magistrate Courts—larger towns, smaller cities
Municipal Courts: traffic, juvenile, misdemeanors—larger cities

Name ______________________ Date ______________ Class __________

State Supreme Court

At the top of each state court system is the state supreme court. This court hears appeals of civil and criminal cases from the intermediate appellate courts. State supreme courts write out their rulings to guide judges in future cases.

In state law, state supreme courts are the final step. However, if someone believes a state court ruling violated his or her rights under the U.S. Constitution, he or she can appeal to the U.S. Supreme Court. The U.S. Supreme Court, however, is not required to hear the case.

REVIEW LESSON 4

1. Use the diagram below to describe the levels, functions, and powers of the state judicial branch.

U.S SUPREME COURT

State Supreme Court

State Higher Courts

State Lower Courts

2. **IDENTIFYING STEPS IN A PROCESS** A person is caught painting graffiti in a park. On a separate sheet of paper, describe the sequence of events as the case goes through the state court system all the way to the state supreme court.

Benchmark Skill Activities

LAFS.68.WHST.1.2

1. SUMMARIZING

Use your FOLDABLES to write an essay.

Write an explanation of the structure and functions of state government. Include in your explanation at least one chart or diagram that supports your text.

LAFS.68.RH.2.4

2. DETERMINING WORD MEANINGS

Read the excerpt below from the Florida Constitution. Then, write a definition for each of the underlined words. Use the words around these words, or context clues, to help you determine their meaning.

> "(c) **Special Sessions** (1) The governor, by proclamation stating the purpose, may convene the legislature in special session during which only such legislative business may be transacted as is within the purview [aim] of the proclamation. . . .
> (d) **Length of Sessions** A regular session of the legislature shall not exceed sixty consecutive days."
>
> —Florida Constitution, Article III, Section 3

MAFS.K12.MP.6.1

3. USING DEFINITIONS ACCURATELY

Refer to the Chapter 13 Terms list. In a paragraph, summarize the federal system using at least three words from the list.

LAFS.68.RH.1.3, LAFS.68.WHST.2.6

4. IDENTIFYING STEPS IN A PROCESS

Create a slideshow or video presentation that teaches how a bill becomes a state law. Use a combination of text and images to effectively convey the information.

LAFS.68.RH.1.1

5. ANALYZING NEWS MEDIA

Find a news story about state government. It can be about a state law, the state legislature, the state executive branch, or the state courts. Compare the news story with what you have read in Chapter 13. Did the story accurately describe state government? What information did it leave out? Give specific examples to support your analysis.

Benchmark Note Cards

DIRECTIONS: Use these note cards to help you prepare for the test.

SS.7.C.3.4 Identify the relationship and division of powers between the federal government and state governments.

THE FEDERAL SYSTEM	Powers are shared by and divided between the national government and state governments. • The Constitution gives the federal government expressed, implied, and inherent powers. These include regulating interstate commerce (trade), coining and regulating money, and declaring war. • The Tenth Amendment gives reserved powers to the states, such as establishing local governments and running elections. • Concurrent powers are shared by the national and state governments and include the powers to tax, set up courts, and make laws. • The supremacy clause in the Constitution means that a state law cannot conflict with a federal law.

SS.7.C.3.7 Analyze the impact of the 13th, 14th, 15th, 19th, 24th, and 26th amendments on participation of minority groups in the American political process.

THE FOURTEENTH AMENDMENT	The Fourteenth Amendment limits state powers by making the Bill of Rights apply to the states. • States cannot take away citizens' rights without due process of law. • States must guarantee every citizen equal protection of the laws.

SS.7.C.3.9 Illustrate the law making process at the local, state, and federal levels.

LAWMAKING AT THE STATE LEVEL

Step 1: The governor, a legislator, or a citizen proposes a bill.

Step 2: A legislator introduces the bill to one chamber of the legislature.

Step 3: A committee reviews and revises the bill. If they approve it, it goes to the full chamber.

Step 4: The full chamber votes on the bill. If it passes by a majority vote, it goes to the other chamber of the legislature.

Step 5: Another committee reviews and revises the bill. If they approve it, it goes to the full chamber.

Step 6: The second chamber votes on the bill.

Step 7: Once both chambers have passed the bill, the bill goes to the governor.

Step 8: If the governor signs the bill, it becomes law.

Step 9: If the governor vetoes the bill, the legislature can override by a two-thirds majority in each house.

SS.7.C.3.11 Diagram the levels, functions, and powers of courts at the state and federal levels.

THE STATE COURT SYSTEM

State courts have two levels: lower courts and higher courts.

Lower courts are trial courts. They hear civil and criminal cases, but deal only with less serious matters.

Higher trial courts deal with serious criminal and civil cases. They can be trial courts or appellate courts.

- Appellate courts review cases that have already been decided. Judges look for legal errors and can keep the original verdict or overturn it.
- There are two levels of state appellate courts: an intermediate court called the court of appeals and the state supreme court.

People who believe the state court decision violated their rights under the U.S. Constitution can appeal to the U.S. Supreme Court.

SS.7.C.3.13 Compare the constitutions of the United States and Florida.

THE U.S. AND FLORIDA CONSTITUTIONS	
	The Florida Constitution is younger and longer than the U.S. Constitution. Like the U.S. Constitution, the Florida Constitution lists the rights it protects and defines the executive, legislative, and judicial branches. The Florida Constitution specifies rights that are not included in the U.S. Constitution or the Bill of Rights, such as the right to privacy, the rights of crime victims, and a taxpayer bill of rights. The Florida Constitution addresses campaign funding and spending limits, which the U.S. Constitution does not address. Unlike the U.S. Constitution, the Florida Constitution must be reviewed every 20 years. At that time, the state constitution can be revised or amended to better meet the state's needs.

SS.7.C.3.14 Differentiate between local, state, and federal governments' obligations and services.

STATE OBLIGATIONS AND SERVICES	
	• Each state must respect legal actions taken by other states. • Each state must treat the people of other states equally. • As part of their reserved powers, states are responsible for running elections, protecting the public, and establishing schools. States are also responsible for establishing local governments. • Under state constitutions, most states have to maintain a balanced budget.

SS.7.E.2.1 Explain how federal, state, and local taxes support the economy as a function of the United States government.

STATE TAXES	
	• Most state income comes from taxes. • Income taxes are taxes people pay on the money they earn. • Sales taxes are taxes people pay on the goods and services that they buy. • Tax income allows the state government to provide services such as education, benefits to the poor and disabled, and health care. • When the economy slows, state income slows but demand for state services can increase. States must then find a way to balance their budgets by cutting spending or raising tax rates.

Chapter 13

VISUAL SUMMARY

DIRECTIONS: Complete the graphic organizer below.

FEDERAL GOVERNMENT

POWERS
- Expressed ______
- Implied ______
- Inherent ______

SUPREMACY CLAUSE ______

STATE GOVERNMENTS

POWERS
- Reserved: ______
- Concurrent: ______

CONSTITUTIONS
- Describe three-branch structure of state government
- List rights guaranteed to state citizens, such as in Florida's Declaration of Rights

ECONOMIES
- Must have a balanced budget in most states
- Income: ______
- Spending: ______

STATE LEGISLATIVE BRANCH	STATE EXECUTIVE BRANCH	STATE JUDICIAL BRANCH
Most states have two-house legislatures.	Governor is state chief executive.	States have two levels of courts.

USING PRIMARY SOURCES

ANALYZE PRIMARY SOURCES Segregation, the forced legal separation of African Americans, was once widely practiced in Southern states. In 1957, a U.S. Supreme Court decision called for an end to segregation in public schools. This led to conflict in Little Rock, Arkansas. Below are excerpts from two documents related to this conflict: one from the President of the United States and one from the Governor of Arkansas. Read both excerpts. Then answer the questions that follow.

Document 1

". . .WHEREAS the command contained in that Proclamation has not been obeyed and wilful obstruction of enforcement of said court orders still exists and threatens to continue:

NOW, THEREFORE, by virtue of the authority vested in me by the Constitution and Statutes of the United States, . . . It is hereby ordered as follows:

SECTION 1. I hereby authorize and direct the Secretary of Defense to order into the active military service of the United States as he may deem appropriate to carry out the purposes of this Order, any or all of the units of the National Guard of the United States and of the Air National Guard of the United States within the State of Arkansas to serve in the active military service of the United States for an indefinite period and until relieved by appropriate orders.

SEC. 2. The Secretary of Defense is authorized and directed to take all appropriate steps to enforce any orders of the United States District Court for the Eastern District of Arkansas for the removal of obstruction of justice in the State of Arkansas with respect to matters relating to enrollment and attendance at public schools in the Little Rock School District, Little Rock, Arkansas. In carrying out the provisions of this section, the Secretary of Defense is authorized to use the units, and members thereof, ordered into the active military service of the United States pursuant to Section 1 of this Order.

SEC. 3. In furtherance of the enforcement of the aforementioned orders of the United States District Court for the Eastern District of Arkansas, the Secretary of Defense is authorized to use such of the armed forces of the United States as he may deem necessary.

SEC. 4. The Secretary of Defense is authorized to delegate to the Secretary of the Army or the Secretary of the Air Force, or both, any of the authority conferred upon him by this Order.

THE WHITE HOUSE,
September 24, 1957.

—President Dwight D. Eisenhower, Executive Order 10730

Document 2

Last year, I stated during the September crisis that I was not elected Governor of Arkansas to surrender all our rights as citizens to an all-powerful federal autocracy. . . . It is my responsibility, and it is my purpose and determination, to defend the constitutional rights of the people of Arkansas to the full extent of my ability. . . .

I am fully aware of the deep concern of the parents for the continued proper education of their children, and I am fully aware of the inconvenience to the students in the interruption of the proper educational processes. To them, both parents and students, I express my sympathy and understanding.

To the students who are concerned, I say that in the years to follow, when you have come to realize the importance of maintaining our form of government, and the importance of preserving the great freedoms and privileges which we have known, you will be happy and proud to remember that you suffered inconvenience and personal sacrifice, and thereby made a worthwhile contribution to the maintenance of our dual system of government.

—Arkansas Governor Orval E. Faubus, September 18, 1958

1. **MAKING CONNECTIONS** What part of the Constitution gives President Eisenhower the right to use the U.S. military to enforce a court order against a state? What does that part of the Constitution say?

2. **APPLYING** How does the concept of reserved powers apply to Governor Faubus's argument?

3. **ASSESSING** Based on your understanding of the federal system and state government, who is "right" in this conflict? Explain.

Chapter Practice Test

DIRECTIONS: Circle the best answer for each question.

SS.7.C.3.4 (Moderate)

> *"Although states may exercise their police power in a manner that has an incidental or indirect effect on aliens [immigrants], a state may not establish its own immigration policy or enforce state laws in a manner that interferes with the federal immigration laws. The Constitution and the federal immigration laws do not permit the development of a patchwork of state and local immigration policies throughout the country."*
>
> —U.S. Department of Justice, July 6, 2010

Which part of the federal system is illustrated by this excerpt?

A inherent powers

B due process of law

C the supremacy clause

D equal protection of the laws

SS.7.C.3.4, SS.7.C.3.14 (Moderate)

Mr. Hernandez wants his name on the ballot for the presidential election.

Who is responsible for setting the guidelines Mr. Hernandez needs to follow?

A the governor

B the U.S. Congress

C the Electoral College

D the state government

3 **SS.7.C.3.11 (Moderate)**

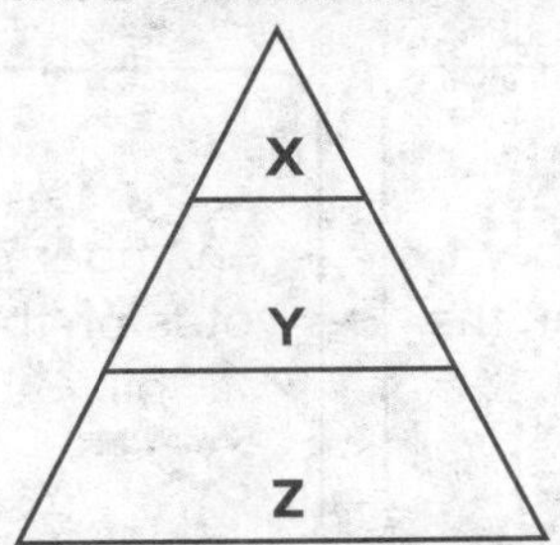

Which court is represented by section Y of the diagram?

A traffic court

B municipal court

C court of appeals

D state supreme court

4 **SS.7.E.2.1 (High)**

A state decides to lower its income tax rate. What is the most likely outcome of this decision?

A The state will have to increase spending on its programs and services.

B The state will have to increase its quantity of unfunded mandates.

C The federal government will have to reduce its grants-in-aid to the state.

D The citizens of the state will have more money to spend on goods and services.

5 **SS.7.C.3.9 (Moderate)**

STATE LAWMAKING PROCESS

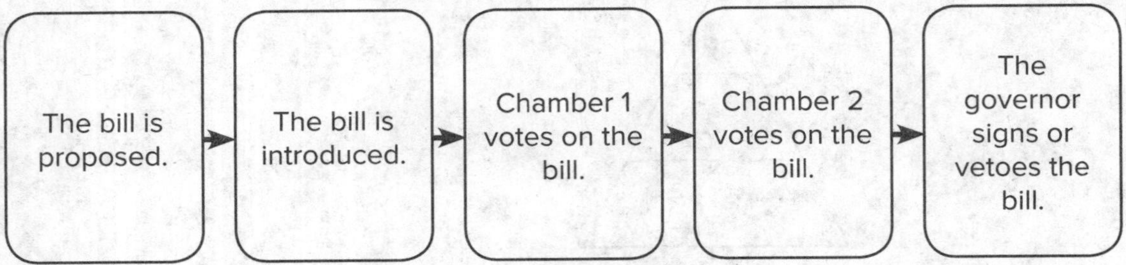
The bill is proposed.
The bill is introduced.
Chamber 1 votes on the bill.
Chamber 2 votes on the bill.
The governor signs or vetoes the bill.

Which statement identifies an error in the diagram?

A It does not show the review by committees in each chamber.

B It does not include the funding of the bill by the state treasurer.

C It does not include repeal of the bill through popular referendum.

D It does not show the calling of a special session to consider the bill.

---

6 **SS.7.C.3.13 (Moderate)**

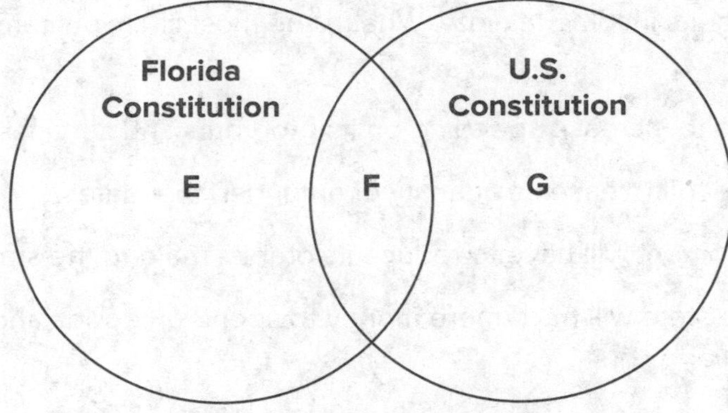
Florida Constitution
U.S. Constitution
E
F
G

Which right belongs in section F of the diagram?

A the right to privacy

B the right to a fair trial by jury

C the right of a taxpayer to fair treatment

D the right of a crime victim to know about his or her case

7 **SS.7.C.3.4 (High)**

In 1971, the U.S. Constitution set the minimum voting age at 18. The Florida state legislature wants to lower the minimum voting age to 16.

What is the most likely outcome of this scenario?

A The voting age issue is postponed until the next review of the Florida Constitution.

B The voting age is lowered in Florida because managing elections is a reserved power.

C The state legislature is forced to keep the voting age of 18 because of the U.S. Constitution's supremacy clause.

D The state legislature calls for a legislative referendum to determine public support for the change in voting age.

---

8 **SS.7.C.3.4 (Moderate)**

> *"In order to achieve excellence through teaching students, advancing research and providing public service for the benefit of Florida's citizens, their communities and economies, the people hereby establish a system of governance for the state university system of Florida."*
>
> —Article IX, Florida Constitution

Which type of power is being described in this excerpt?

A implied power

B reserved power

C expressed power

D concurrent power

9 **SS.7.C.3.7 (Moderate)**

Why is the state of Florida prohibited from giving special privileges or protections to any one group of people?

A The supremacy clause requires states to obey the U.S. Constitution.

B The U.S. Constitution reserves that power for the federal government.

C The Fourteenth Amendment requires states to follow due process of law.

D The Fourteenth Amendment requires states to guarantee equal protection of the laws.

---

10 **SS.7.C.3.11 (High)**

STATE COURT SYSTEM

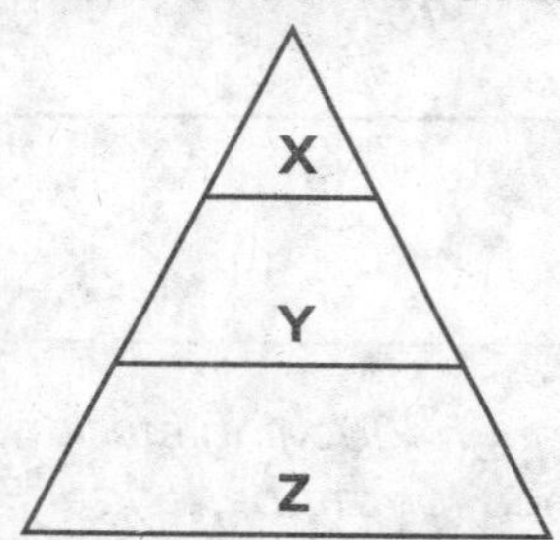

Which case is most likely to be heard by a court represented by section Z of the diagram?

A Mary is accused of breaking a $500 contract.

B Carrie is accused of stealing her neighbor's car.

C Anna is accused of owing her landlord $7,000 in rent.

D Sarah is accused of a hit-and-run accident in her car.

Local Government

Chapter Overview

Like the federal and state governments, local governments have obligations and provide services to their citizens. However, local governments can be organized in different ways. The organization of a city, county, town, township, or village sometimes depends on the size of the community. In many instances, the organization depends on the manner in which citizens want their government to be organized. Regardless of the structure, or organization, local governments serve the people and get their powers from the state.

CHAPTER BENCHMARKS

SS.7.C.2.3 Experience the responsibilities of citizens at the local, state, or federal levels.

SS.7.C.3.9 Illustrate the law making process at the local, state, and federal levels.

SS.7.C.3.14 Differentiate between local, state, and federal governments' obligations and services.

LAFS.68.RH.1.1 Cite specific textual evidence to support analysis of primary and secondary sources.

LAFS.68.RH.1.2 Determine the central ideas or information of a primary or secondary source; provide an accurate summary of the source distinct from prior knowledge or opinions.

LAFS.68.RH.2.4 Determine the meaning of words and phrases as they are used in a text, including vocabulary specific to domains related to history/social studies.

LAFS.68.RH.3.8 Distinguish among fact, opinion, and reasoned judgment in a text.

LAFS.68.WHST.2.4 Produce clear and coherent writing in which the development, organization, and style are appropriate to task, purpose, and audience.

WHAT I NEED TO KNOW

TERMS

- ☐ incorporate
- ☐ city charter
- ☐ home rule
- ☐ ordinance
- ☐ special district
- ☐ metropolitan area
- ☐ county
- ☐ county seat
- ☐ levy
- ☐ town
- ☐ township
- ☐ town meeting
- ☐ village

Local Government

Local Government

Make this Foldable® and label the three columns of the chart *City, County,* and *Town, Township, Village*. Before you read the chapter, review what you know about each type of government. Write questions that you have in the columns of your Foldable. Search for answers as you read and record any new questions that arise. On the back of your Foldable, draw a large circle and label it *Federal*. Draw a medium-sized circle in the large circle and label it *State*. Draw a smaller circle in the medium circle and label it *County*. Compare the different types of government. What additional circle could be added?

Step 1

Arrange a piece of notebook paper vertically. Fold the left and right sides once each to create three equal columns.

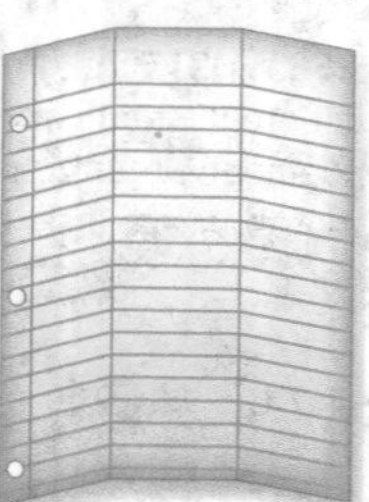

Step 2

Unfold the paper and label the columns as directed.

City Governments

SS.7.C.3.9, SS.7.C.3.14

How City Governments Are Created

State constitutions usually outline the powers and duties of local governments, such as city governments. City governments make laws its citizens must follow. They also provide citizens with many services. These services include upkeep of roads and schools as well as fire and police protection. Local governments get much of the money they need to pay for services through state and federal grants. Local taxes, fees, and fines are other sources of income.

Becoming a City

The official name for a city is a "municipality." The state creates a municipality by allowing it to **incorporate,** or become an organized government. States frequently establish certain requirements for incorporated places. For example, the state may require that a place have a certain number of people to be considered a city. If a place fulfills the state's requirements for incorporation, the citizens living in an area can ask for a city charter. A **city charter** is a document granting power to the local government.

A city charter usually outlines the structure, functions, and authority of the new government. A typical charter outlines the basic laws of the city and describes how the city creates laws. It is like a constitution for a city. Some states including Florida practice **home rule.** In other words, citizens can write their own charters and choose their own form of local government. Municipalities usually have one of these main forms of government: mayor-council, commission, or council-manager.

The Mayor-Council Form

For many years, almost all cities in the United States had the mayor-council form of government. Many still do. This form of government is structured to ensure separation of powers. The mayor takes on the role of chief executive. The council serves as the lawmaking body. It is responsible for passing city laws, or **ordinances.**

1. DETERMINING CENTRAL IDEAS

Why do you think states require cities to have charters?

2. HYPOTHESIZING

What details might you expect to find in a city charter?

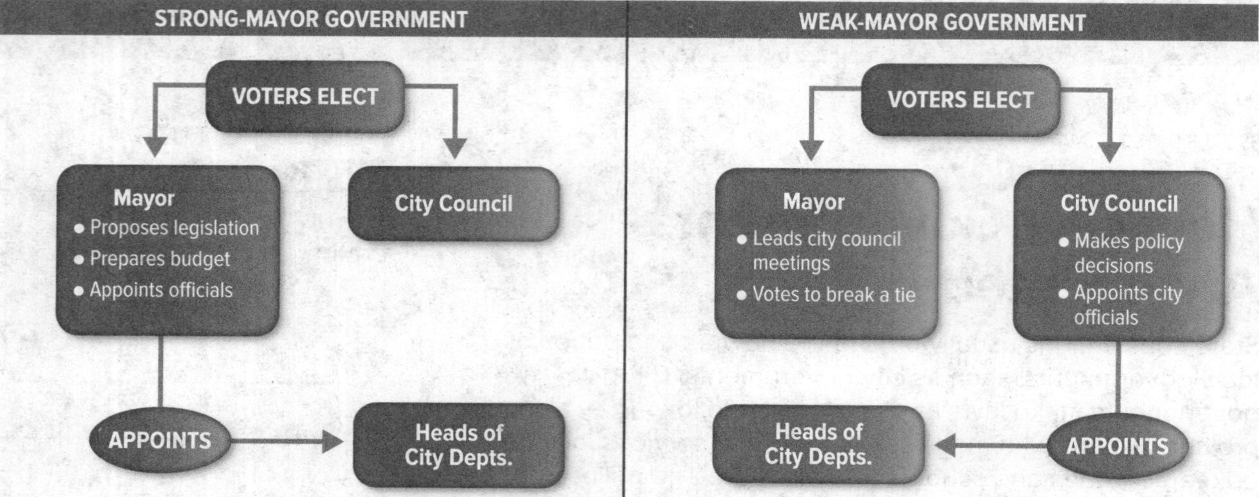

3. DRAWING CONCLUSIONS

Why might a city or town choose a weak-mayor form of government?

____

____

____

____

____

____

____

ANALYZING VISUALS

4. IDENTIFYING Look at the strong-mayor and weak-mayor diagrams. Whom would citizens most likely want to contact to change a law in a weak-mayor government?

____

____

Strong Mayors and Weak Mayors

You might have heard the terms *strong mayor* and *weak mayor*. These terms do not apply to the ability or personality of a city's chief executive. Instead, they name the two types of mayor-council government.

As its name implies, the chief executive in a strong-mayor system has a great deal of power. Just as a governor runs a state, the mayor runs his or her city. Strong mayors have the authority to plan the city's budget and to select department leaders. They also oversee the everyday workings of city government. The city council serves as the lawmaking body, but strong mayors have some influence over lawmaking. For example, they can propose new laws and can veto laws passed by the city council.

The strong-mayor system of government is most often found in large cities. For example, Jacksonville, Orlando, Miami, and Tampa all have a strong-mayor system of government. About 40 more Florida cities have strong mayors.

Strong mayors have more power because they usually work full time and have a large staff. Council members tend to work part time and cannot spend as much time working on issues. Also, in larger cities council members tend to be elected by wards, or parts of a city. They focus more on issues that are important to their wards.

In contrast, the chief executive in a weak-mayor system has less power. The city council takes on many of the duties of government. Weak mayors usually do not appoint the heads of departments or create budgets. They also cannot veto laws. Often, the mayor votes on issues only when the city council is tied. More than 75 Florida cities have weak mayors.

Name ______________________ Date ______________ Class ____________

Council-Manager and Commission Governments

Two other forms of city government can be found throughout much of the country. They are the council-manager form and the commission form.

The Council-Manager Form

In a council-manager form of city government, the city council remains responsible for passing laws. However, it appoints a city manager to oversee specific duties such as the following:

- creating the city budget
- directing city departments
- handling day-to-day issues of government

Smaller cities with managers often hold at-large elections for council members. That way, all council members will think of the entire city as they pass laws and vote on issues. About 250 cities in Florida have council-manager governments.

The Commission Form

The commission form of government merges legislative and executive powers. This type of government has departments that specialize in certain tasks, such as police, fire, or finance. Together the department heads, or commission, act as a legislature. They pass ordinances and make decisions about government. In Florida, only the cities of Bascom, El Portal, and South Pasadena currently have commission governments.

ANALYZING VISUALS

5. COMPARING Look at the diagrams on this page. Who makes laws in the council-manager form of government, the city council or the city manager?

____

Which form of government gives citizens a more direct say in selecting department heads?

____

According to the diagrams, how are the two forms similar?

____

____

____

____

____

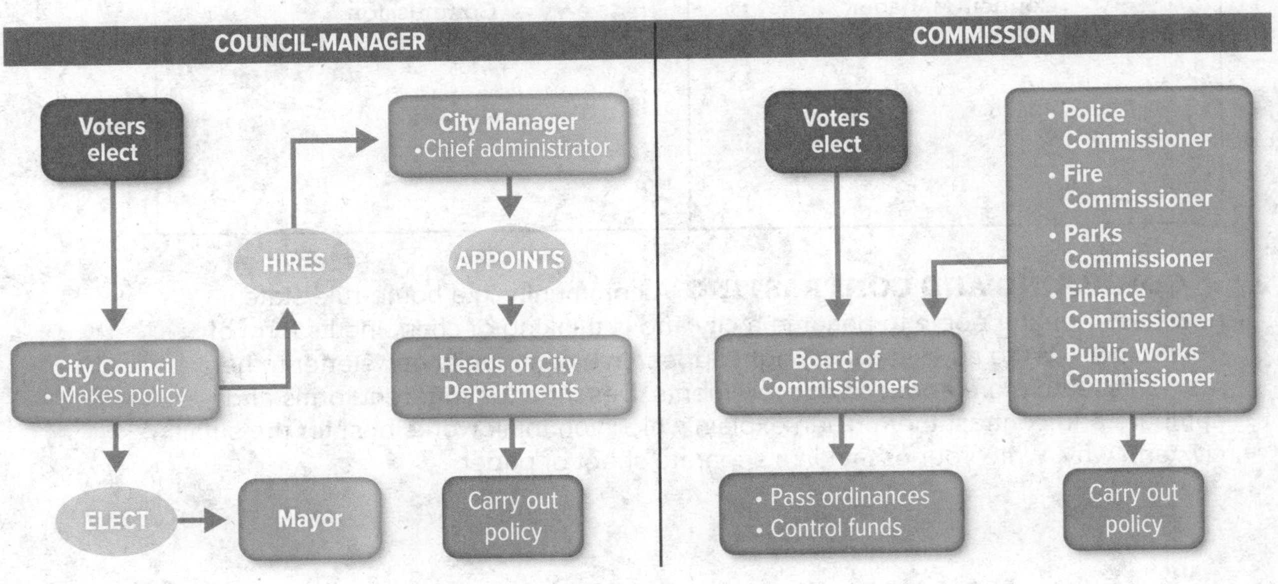

6. DRAWING CONCLUSIONS

What issues might be discussed in a metropolitan-area council for a large city in your state? Name at least five issues.

____

____

____

____

____

Other Units of Government

States may have two other types of municipal governments. A **special district** is formed to handle a specific task, such as education or transportation. For example, a city or county may create a local school district. A board or commission runs the day-to-day operation of the district. Board members can be elected or appointed.

A **metropolitan area** consists of a large city and its surrounding suburbs. Sometimes it also includes small towns that are close enough to be affected by the large cities. In some cases, more people live in the area around a city than actually live in it. Sometimes, large cities and nearby towns join together to address common problems, such as traffic and crime. They create councils that make decisions affecting the entire metropolitan area.

REVIEW LESSON 1

1. Use the chart below to list the main characteristics of each form of city government.

FORMS OF CITY GOVERNMENT	
Mayor-Council Form: Strong Mayor	Mayor-Council Form: Weak Mayor
Council-Manager	Commission

2. **COMPARING AND CONTRASTING** A community in a home-rule state now has enough people to become a city and is thinking of changing its form of government. Write an essay that might appear in a community newsletter to help residents learn more about city governments. Describe the different forms and compare and contrast them. Then explain which you think works best for the small city, and why. Write your essay on a separate sheet of paper.

LESSON 2 SUMMARY

County Governments

SS.7.C.3.9, SS.7.C.3.14

How County Governments Are Organized

You live in a state *and* you live in a county. A **county** is a state's largest territorial and political unit. County government is the part of government that takes care of different types of services. Some of these services, such as the fire department, you only use in an emergency. Other services, such as water and sewer services, fill a specific need. The United States has more than 3,000 counties, and Florida has 67 counties.

County Seats

A **county seat** is the town or city where the county courthouse is located. The county seat is usually in a central location in the county so it is easy for all county residents to reach.

The Functions of County Government

Just as the federal government has an obligation to provide services to its citizens, so do state and county governments. Counties are created by the state to administer state laws within their borders. Counties also are required to perform state duties related to public safety, property assessment, road maintenance, peacekeeping, education, elections, and trials. In addition, county government administers county laws. Other county functions and obligations vary from state to state and county to county. The chart below lists some county obligations.

MOST COMMON SERVICES OF COUNTIES	
Maintain jails and other correctional facilities	Assess property for tax purposes
Build and repair roads, bridges, and other public works	Record deeds, mortgages, marriage licenses, and other documents
Collect taxes and allocate funds	Maintain schools
Administer state courts and supervise elections	Issue licenses
OTHER COUNTY SERVICES	
Provide water and sewer services	Provide safety and medical services
Operate mass-transit systems	Enforce zoning, regulate land use

1. CITING TEXT EVIDENCE

Underline the details that explain why states create counties.

ANALYZING VISUALS

2. PRIORITIZING Look at the chart of the services provided by counties. Identify the top five services you think counties provide and rank them in order from most important to least important. Give reasons for your choice of the most important service.

ANALYZING VISUALS

3. IDENTIFYING Look at the "Organization of County Government" chart. Circle the positions that are related to the legislative process of county government.

What is the relationship between the county sheriff and the county prosecutor?

______

______

______

______

Who Runs a County?

The governing body of a county is usually a county board of elected officials. These officials, called commissioners or supervisors, are elected to four-year terms. The commissioners or supervisors serve as the county's legislature and pass county ordinances. They are also responsible for the county's budget, so they need to **levy,** or collect, taxes.

Forms of County Government

County officials have a wide range of responsibilities. A typical county government includes a governing body, a board of commissioners, appointed officials, and elected officials. Some county governments have a strong commission government. Other counties have a commission-manager or commission-elected executive form of government.

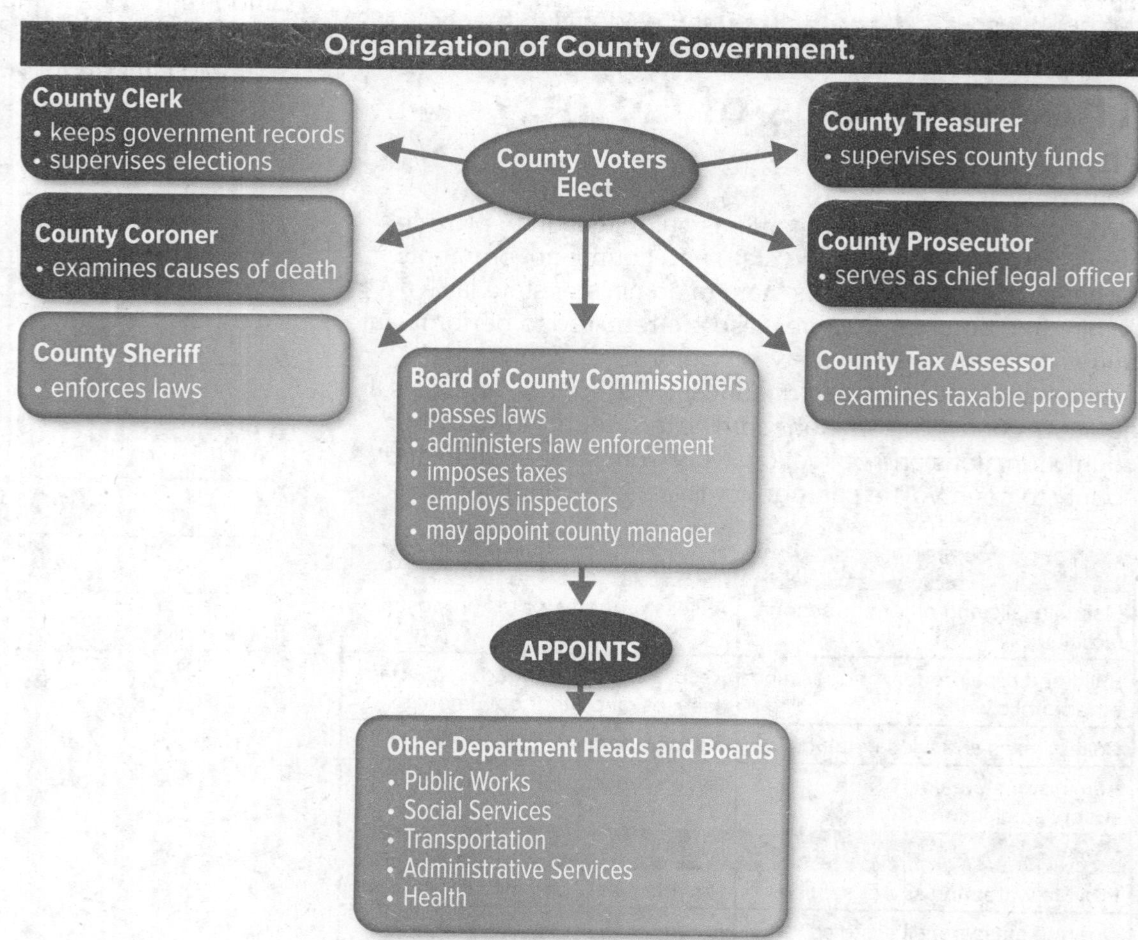

Name ____________________ Date ____________ Class ________

A strong commission form of government has four primary characteristics:

- It has both legislative and executive authority.
- It passes and carries out laws.
- It works with other county officials to do some executive work.
- It oversees the work of appointed officials.

Some counties have limited their county boards to act only as a legislature. In those counties, the executive power is then handled in one of the following ways:

COMMISSION-MANAGER	COMMISSION-ELECTED EXECUTIVE
Has a board-named county manager	Has an elected office called the county executive
DUTIES OF COUNTY MANAGER OR COUNTY EXECUTIVE	
• Carries out the laws for the county • Manages county government • Appoints top officials	

Sheriffs, DAs, and More

Did you know that a sheriff is an elected official? People support an effective sheriff by reelecting him or her. The sheriff plays an important role in the county because he or she enforces the law.

The district attorney (DA), or county prosecutor, is also an elected official. He or she investigates crimes and brings charges against those suspected of breaking the law. The district attorney must prove his or her case in a trial court before a judge and jury.

The assessor, the county treasurer, and the auditor handle the finances for the county. These officials are responsible for valuing property, collecting taxes, paying the county's bills, and making sure money is spent according to state and local laws.

Two other officials are the county clerk and the county coroner. The county clerk keeps official government records and may conduct elections. The coroner investigates deaths that were not due to natural causes.

County governments have grown in recent years. Today, more than 2 million people work for counties across the United States.

4. CONTRASTING

How is a county with a strong commission different from a county with a commission-manager or commission-elected executive?

____

____

____

____

____

____

5. THEORIZING

Why do you think three different officials handle a county's finances?

____

____

____

____

____

____

Name ______________________ Date ______________ Class __________

LESSON 2 SUMMARY, *continued*

REVIEW LESSON 2

1. Use the chart below to identify the obligations and services provided by county governments.

COUNTY GOVERNMENT OBLIGATIONS AND SERVICES TO CITIZENS	
Legislative and Executive Functions	
Public Safety and Welfare	

2. **DETERMINING CAUSE AND EFFECT** Use the information from the chart to write an essay that explains why county governments are best at providing the services listed. Write your essay on a separate piece of paper.

LESSON 3 SUMMARY

Towns, Townships, and Villages

SS.7.C.3.9, SS.7.C.3.14

Towns and Town Meetings

If you belong to a school club, you are probably familiar with meetings. People hold meetings to discuss issues, solve problems, and work to get things done. Towns hold meetings for the same reasons.

Towns, Townships, and Counties

Counties are the state's largest political divisions. Sometimes, counties are further divided into smaller political units called towns. A **town** is a political unit that is larger than a village but smaller than a city. Other counties may be divided into townships. A **township** is a smaller area of a county that can include several smaller communities. Towns and townships are similar to county and city governments because they all receive their powers from the state.

The various regions of the United States have different ways of organizing their local governments, as shown in the following chart.

NEW ENGLAND	MID-ATLANTIC STATES AND THE MIDWEST	SOUTH AND WEST
Town governments are in charge of most government duties of small communities.	Township government is important.	Usually have no townships.
Counties are judicial districts that organize the local courts.	County and township governments share powers.	County government is more important.

ANALYZING VISUALS

1. CONTRASTING
Look at the chart. How is the way that the South and West generally organize their government different from the way the Mid-Atlantic and Midwest states organize?

____

____

____

____

____

____

____

____

2. MAKING GENERALIZATIONS

Do you think a national direct democracy would be possible in the United States? Why or why not?

New England Town Meetings

Town meetings began in New England during colonial times and still continue today. A **town meeting** is a gathering of local citizens to discuss and vote on important issues. This type of meeting is one of the oldest forms of democracy. Town meetings are a form of direct democracy. This differs from the rest of the United States, which follows the form of democracy known as representative democracy.

Town meetings are held just once a year, so they are not an effective way to make daily government decisions. Therefore, each New England town elects a group of officials to run the government. In some towns, the people discuss ordinances and the budget during the yearly town meeting. They also discuss local issues and set up what the town government will do for the next year. Some larger towns have changed to representative town meetings. Only representatives elected by the town's voters may vote. Other towns have stopped town meetings and use a town council to run local government.

Townships and Villages

New York, New Jersey, and Pennsylvania have towns and township governments that serve people in urban areas. Townships in Indiana, Kansas, Nebraska, and Ohio serve people in rural communities.

Townships

Townships came about as settlers moved westward after the American Revolution. These units of government continue today. A small body of elected officials called a township committee, board of supervisors, or board of trustees makes laws for the township. They hold regular meetings in which citizens can voice their opinions about the services and policies of their government. Some counties and townships work together to provide local services.

Village Government

Villages form the smallest unit of local government. They generally lie within a township or a county. Because villages are small, most depend on county or township governments for their services.

What happens if the people in a village decide that the services being provided by the county do not meet their needs? Perhaps they want their own school system or fire and police departments. Because only the state can decide these kinds of issues, the village needs state permission to set up a village government.

Village governments consist of a small board of elected trustees or an elected executive. Some may also hire a city manager. Village governments have the power to collect taxes and spend money on services that benefit the community such as maintaining streets, sewer and water systems, or a public library.

The following chart lists the benefits and a drawback to forming a village government.

BENEFITS OF VILLAGE GOVERNMENT	DRAWBACK OF VILLAGE GOVERNMENT
Receive better services	Might have higher taxes to support government
May be more attractive to visitors, new residents, and businesses	
Have more control over local affairs	

3. DRAWING CONCLUSIONS

Why might citizens work together to form a village government?

______

ANALYZING VISUALS

4. SPECULATING

Look at the chart. Do you think the benefits of having a village government outweigh the drawback? Why?

______

Name ______________________ Date ______________ Class __________

REVIEW LESSON 3

1. Use the chart below to note the differences among a town, township, and village form of government.

POLITICAL UNIT	DESCRIPTION
Town	
Township	
Village	

2. **IDENTIFYING CENTRAL IDEAS** How do towns, townships, and villages govern? Use the chart to write an essay that explains and distinguishes among these types of local governments. Write your essay on a separate sheet of paper.

Benchmark Skill Activities

DIRECTIONS: Write your answers on a separate piece of paper.

LAFS.68.WHST.2.4

1. REASONING

Use your FOLDABLES to write an essay.

A state gets its powers from the U.S. Constitution. However, city, county, town, township, and village governments get their powers from the state government. In your essay, explain why it is necessary for state governments to oversee and control local governments.

LAFS.68.RH.3.8

2. DISTINGUISHING AMONG FACT, OPINION, AND REASONED JUDGMENT

Read the statements below. On the lines, indicate whether each statement is a fact (F), an opinion (O), or a reasoned judgment (J).

1. ________ Citizens in Florida can write their own charters and choose their own form of government because Florida practices home rule.

2. ________ The mayor-council form of government most likely was used for many years by most cities in the United States because it was structured to ensure separation of powers.

3. ________ Cities with special districts have much better schools than those run by county government.

4. ________ The two most important obligations city or county governments have to their citizens are overseeing elections and trials.

5. ________ During colonial times, a town meeting probably was held yearly because people lived far from the center of town.

6. ________ Commissioners or supervisors make up the governing body of a county.

LAFS.68.RH.2.4, LAFS.68.WHST.2.4

3. USING DEFINITIONS ACCURATELY

Turn to the Terms list for this chapter. Choose at least three words and include them in a paragraph that summarizes city or county government.

LAFS.68.WHST.1.2, LAFS.68.WHST.2.4

4. REFLECTING

Review the various forms of local government and their powers and obligations. If you could choose, in which type of local government would you, as a citizen, want to live? Explain your choice.

LAFS.68.WHST.1.2, LAFS.68.WHST.2.4

5. SPECULATING

Imagine that you would like to work as a local government official. In which type of local government would you like to serve? Which local government job would you like to have?

Benchmark Note Cards

DIRECTIONS: Use these note cards to help you prepare for the test.

SS.7.C.2.3 Experience the responsibilities of citizens at the local, state, or federal levels.

RESPONSIBILITIES OF CITIZENS AT THE LOCAL LEVEL

- People elect mayors, commissioners, and other officials to represent and work for them in counties, cities, towns, townships, and villages.
- Citizens have a responsibility to make their voices heard and to constructively take part in government.
- At town meetings, people vote on important issues and have the opportunity to say what they want about issues in their community.
- People in a village may decide that the services being provided do not meet their needs and may ask the state for permission to form a village government.

SS.7.C.3.9 Illustrate the law making process at the local, state, and federal levels.

LAWMAKING IN A CITY, SPECIAL DISTRICT, OR METROPOLITAN AREA

In an incorporated city, a city charter grants power to the city government. The government can take different forms.

- The mayor-council form ensures separation of powers. A mayor is the chief executive, and a council serves as the city's lawmakers.
    - In a strong-mayor system, a mayor runs the city, plans the budget, selects leaders, and oversees everyday workings of city government. The city council is the chief lawmaker, although the mayor may propose new laws or veto them.
    - In a weak-mayor system, the city council takes on most of the duties including lawmaking. The mayor may vote only if the city council is tied and does not have veto power.
- In a council-manager form, the city council is responsible for passing laws. A city manager creates the budget, directs city departments, and handles day-to-day issues.
- The commission form merges legislative and executive powers. Department heads act as a legislature to pass ordinances and make decisions about government.
- Special districts handle specific tasks and are overseen by the city or county government.
- Metropolitan areas consist of a large city and its surrounding area. These areas may join together to address common problems by creating councils to make decisions.

LAWMAKING IN A COUNTY	Counties usually are run by a county board of elected officials known as commissioners or supervisors. The county board passes ordinances, or laws, levies taxes, and determines the county's budget. A strong commission has both legislative and executive authority. It works with other county officials to do executive work and oversees the work of appointed officials. Some counties have limited their county boards to act only as a legislature. Either a commission-manager or a commission-elected executive has executive power and carries out the laws, manages county government, and appoints top officials.

LAWMAKING IN TOWNS, TOWNSHIPS, OR VILLAGES	• Towns, townships, and villages are smaller political units in a county with their own government. • Some towns hold yearly town meetings to discuss ordinances, taxes, and budgets. Such meetings are a direct democracy because the people are directly involved in government. Other towns have representative town meetings where only elected representatives vote. Towns elect officials to run local government on a daily basis. • Townships usually have a small body of elected officials who make laws and provide services. • Village governments may have a small board of elected trustees or an elected executive who is responsible for collecting taxes and providing services.

SS.7.C.3.14 Differentiate between local, state, and federal governments' obligations and services.

OBLIGATIONS AND SERVICES OF CITY GOVERNMENTS	• City government services include upkeep of roads and schools as well as fire and police protection. • Special districts are often created to handle tasks related to services such as education or transportation.
OBLIGATIONS AND SERVICES OF COUNTY, TOWN, AND VILLAGE GOVERNMENTS	Counties perform state-required duties as a political subdivision of the state. These include • maintaining jails and courts • assessing property and collecting other taxes • building and repairing roads • issuing and recording licenses and other documents • maintaining schools • providing water and sewer services as well as police and fire • operating airports and mass-transit systems Village governments also provide services that benefit the community such as maintaining streets, sewer and water systems, or a public library. They depend on county or township governments for some services.

Chapter 14

VISUAL SUMMARY

DIRECTIONS: Complete the graphic organizer below.

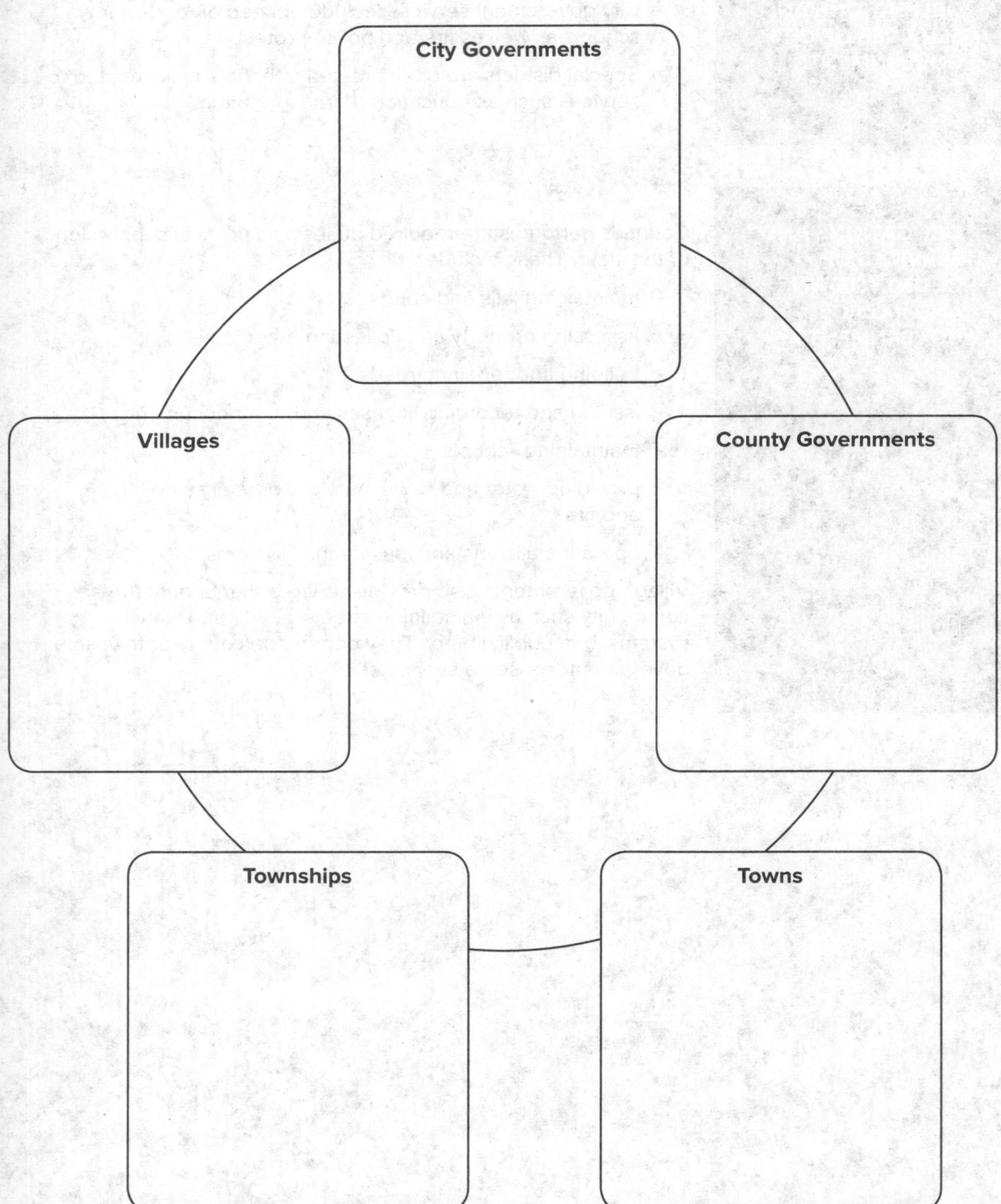

USING PRIMARY SOURCES

EVALUATE Below are two statements related to a rule that was passed in New York City. Read both statements and then answer the questions that follow on a separate sheet of paper.

Document A

"The link between sugary drinks and obesity is no longer in question. What we do need to question is the beverage industry's continued promotion of these unhealthy products in communities most burdened by obesity and diabetes. The rule capping sugary drinks at 16 ounces is a necessary and important step toward improving the health of New Yorkers regardless of their zip code. We are confident the rule will be upheld and that New York City will continue to innovate and work to protect all New Yorkers from the illnesses that threaten the health of our population."

—Mary T. Bassett, M.D., M.P.H., Commissioner,
New York City Department of Health and Mental Hygiene

Document B

We hold that the New York City Board of Health, in adopting the "Sugary Drinks Portion Cap Rule," exceeded the scope of its regulatory authority. By choosing among competing policy goals, without any legislative delegation or guidance, the Board engaged in law-making and thus infringed upon the legislative jurisdiction of the City Council of New York. . . ."

—Judge J. Pigott, Opinion of the New York Court of Appeals,
June 26, 2014

1. How are Documents A and B related?
2. Do you think Document A was written to inform, persuade, or entertain? Why?
3. Why was Document B written?
4. What words or phrases does the writer of Document A use to reveal point of view? Underline them.
5. What words or phrases does the writer of Document B use to reveal point of view? Underline them.
6. What justification for the rule is found in Document A? Summarize it in your own words.
7. What was the opinion of the court? Summarize it in your own words.
8. Do you think both statements are valid? Explain.

Chapter Practice Test

DIRECTIONS: Circle the best answer for each question.

SS.7.C.3.9 (Moderate)

The diagram below provides details about city governments.

Which detail is missing from the diagram?

A Municipality receives a city charter.

B Services include upkeep of roads.

C State creates council-manager government.

D Local governments get money from taxes.

SS.7.C.3.9 (Moderate)

What makes a commission form of city government different from a mayor-council or council-manager form of government?

A It has a weak mayor who votes on issues when there is a tie.

B It is structured to ensure separation of powers.

C It merges legislative and executive powers.

D It has a city manager who creates budgets.

3 **SS.7.C.3.14 (Moderate)**

Look at the diagram below about some services provided by county governments.

Assess property	?
Build and repair roads and bridges	Collect taxes

Which service could be added to the diagram?

A Regulate banks

B Coin currency

C Make treaties

D Create police departments

---

4 **SS.7.C.3.9 (Moderate)**

From where do local governments derive their power?

A federal government

B state governments

C the county

D citizens

5 **SS.7.C.2.3 (Moderate)**

Which of the local government forms below is an example of direct democracy?

A town meeting

B council-manager

C commission

D mayor-council

6 **SS.7.C.2.3 (High)**

A group of village residents are unhappy because their garbage has not been regularly picked up for several weeks. Their calls for service have been ignored by the county. Which of the following represents a responsible action these citizens could take?

A They could stop paying their county taxes.

B They could petition the state to set up a village government.

C They could set up their own trash collection.

D They could demand a special election to elect a new county manager.

7 **SS.7.C.3.9 (High)**

Read the following newspaper headline.

> **Newly Named County Manager**
> **Reorganizes Government—No Jobs Lost**

The county represented in the newspaper headline most likely has which form of county government?

A strong commission

B commission-elected executive

C township committee

D commission-manager

---

8 **SS.7.C.3.9 (Moderate)**

Read the following section of the Florida Constitution.

> *"Municipalities shall have governmental, corporate and proprietary powers to enable them to conduct municipal government, perform municipal functions and render municipal services, and may exercise power for municipal purposes except as otherwise provided by law."*
>
> —Article VIII, Section 2(b), Florida Constitution

To what does this part of the Florida Constitution refer?

A the formation of a county seat

B a city's home rule powers

C the levying of taxes by a city

D the creation of a township

9 **SS.7.C.3.14 (High)**

Look at the partial outline below.

A. ______________________________

1. Recording deeds and mortgages
2. Enforcing zoning and other land-use regulations
3. Maintaining schools
4. Supervision of elections

Which heading best completes the outline?

A Ways to govern a city

B Services provided by the federal government

C Agenda of a town meeting

D Obligations and services of county governments

---

10 **SS.7.C.3.14 (High)**

Read the statement below.

Counties may pass laws to assess risks to public water sources.

What conclusion can be drawn from this statement?

A It is necessary for the county to enforce laws that make it illegal to dump waste materials.

B It is necessary for the county to enact ordinances related to consumption of resources.

C It is necessary for the county to protect its citizens from contaminated water supplies.

D It is necessary for the county to create management programs for available water.

CHAPTER 15

Citizens and the Law

Chapter Overview

Laws are created to keep citizens safe. They allow people to live together in a peaceful, orderly society. Our legal system has evolved from ancient codes of behavior to the statutes and regulations that are on the books today. In the United States, the Constitution is the most important source of law. The Constitution establishes many important rights concerning individuals and the law.

CHAPTER BENCHMARKS

SS.7.C.2.2 Evaluate the obligations citizens have to obey laws, pay taxes, defend the nation, and serve on juries.

SS.7.C.2.4 Evaluate rights contained in the Bill of Rights and other amendments to the Constitution.

SS.7.C.2.5 Distinguish how the Constitution safeguards and limits individual rights.

SS.7.C.3.6 Evaluate Constitutional rights and their impact on individuals and society.

SS.7.C.3.10 Identify sources and types (civil, criminal, constitutional, military) of law.

SS.7.C.3.12 Analyze the significance and outcomes of landmark Supreme Court cases including, but not limited to, *Marbury* v. *Madison, Plessy* v. *Ferguson, Brown* v. *Board of Education, Gideon* v. *Wainwright, Miranda* v. *Arizona, in re Gault, Tinker* v. *Des Moines, Hazelwood* v. *Kuhlmeier, United States* v. *Nixon,* and *Bush* v. *Gore.*

LAFS.68.WHST.2.6 Use technology, including the Internet, to produce and publish writing and present the relationships between information and ideas clearly and efficiently.

LAFS.68.WHST.3.8 Gather relevant information from multiple print and digital sources, using search terms effectively; assess the credibility and accuracy of each source.

WHAT I NEED TO KNOW

TERMS

- ☐ common law
- ☐ precedent
- ☐ statute
- ☐ lawsuit
- ☐ constitutional law
- ☐ case law
- ☐ administrative law
- ☐ writ of habeas corpus
- ☐ due process
- ☐ presumption
- ☐ exclusionary rule
- ☐ Miranda Warning

CHAPTER 15

Citizens and the Law

Citizens and the Law

Create this Foldable® like a small booklet. Label the front *Citizens and the Law*. Open the Foldable and label the top of the two inside sections with the lesson titles. On the left side, sequence and describe early legal systems that influence our laws today. On the right side, sequentially describe the amendments that protect citizens accused of a crime. On the back of the folded booklet, list and explain the different types of laws described in Lesson 1.

Step 1
Arrange a piece of paper horizontally and fold it in half from left to right.

Step 2
Label the inside of your booklet as shown.

LESSON 1 SUMMARY

Sources and Types of Law

SS.7.C.2.2, SS.7.C.3.10

Why We Have Laws

Laws are sets of rules. They allow people to live together peacefully. Laws establish which actions are permissible and which are not. If you break the law, you can expect to be punished or penalized. Society punishes lawbreakers in the hope of discouraging people from breaking laws.

Some laws are better than others. The following table shows the four main characteristics of good laws.

Fair	Fair laws treat people equally. Fair laws do not make different rules for different groups of people.
Reasonable	A reasonable law must not be too harsh. For example, it would not be reasonable for death to be a punishment for stealing.
Understandable	Laws must be easy to understand. Otherwise, people might not realize they are disobeying the law.
Enforceable	Good laws are ones that authorities are able to enforce. The government can enforce laws better when people are willing to obey them.

1. EVALUATING

In the table, circle the characteristics of a good law. Can you think of a law that you believe is important for people to obey? Explain how obeying that law has a positive impact on the community or nation.

The most important laws to obey are the basic laws that everyone knows like don't steal from or kill another person. It's good to follow these laws because laws help people live in peace

Development of the Legal System

The American legal system is based on ideas, traditions, and laws that have been passed down from generation to generation. Some are thousands of years old.

Code of Hammurabi

In about 1760 B.C., King Hammurabi (ha•muh•RAH•bee) of Babylonia created the first written code of law, known as the Code of Hammurabi. It included laws related to the family, marriage and adoption, slavery, and business. It also set prices for goods and services. Compared to laws today, the penalties were harsh.

2. CONTRASTING

How are laws today different from the Code of Hammurabi?

Today, the punishment for breaking laws are alot more reasonable than the laws in the Hammurabi's code.

3. SPECULATING

Why do you think Justinian I wanted to reorganize Roman laws into a new group of rules?

I think he did this so that the laws in the Roman Empire were more understandable

4. DETERMINING CENTRAL IDEAS

Why is precedent so important to a common law system?

The common law system is based on previously ruled court cases

Israelite Law

Like the Babylonians, the ancient Israelites also lived in the Middle East. They followed a set of written laws that prohibited actions such as murder and theft. Many of these actions are still considered crimes today.

Roman Law

The most important laws that developed in the Western world came from ancient Rome. The first Roman laws were published in 450 B.C. As the Roman Empire grew, its laws spread to parts of Europe, Africa, and Asia. In A.D. 533, Justinian I—ruler of the Eastern Roman Empire—simplified the Roman laws into a body of rules called the Justinian Code. This code influenced laws of the Roman Church, known as canon laws, as well as the laws of many European countries.

Napoleonic Code

The Justinian Code was updated in 1804 by the French emperor Napoleon Bonaparte. This major reform was called the Napoleonic Code. Napoleon spread these laws to all the lands he conquered. The Louisiana Territory had been under French control before the United States bought it in 1803. As a result, Louisiana still has laws based on the Napoleonic Code.

English Common Law

The most important influence on the American legal system is English common law. **Common law** is based on court decisions rather than on a legal code. This form of law developed after 1066, when Norman conquerors from France took control of England. Judges were sent throughout England to hear cases. They based their rulings on **precedents,** or the rulings set forth earlier in similar cases. Because it is based on the decisions of judges, common law is considered judge-made law.

The English blended Roman law and canon law into common law. Basic principles of individual rights, such as the idea that a person is innocent until proven guilty, became part of common law. Eventually, the English Parliament also gained the power to create laws. Laws made by a legislature are called **statutes.**

LESSON 1 SUMMARY, *continued*

When English settlers came to North America in the 1600s and 1700s, they brought their traditions of common law and individual rights. These became important parts of the judicial system of the United States.

Types of Laws

There are three basic types of laws: public, criminal, and civil. Public laws regulate how people deal with government. Criminal laws seek to protect public safety. Civil laws handle disagreements between people and groups.

Criminal Law

Criminal laws deal with acts that prevent people from living together peacefully. There are two basic types of crimes: felonies and misdemeanors.

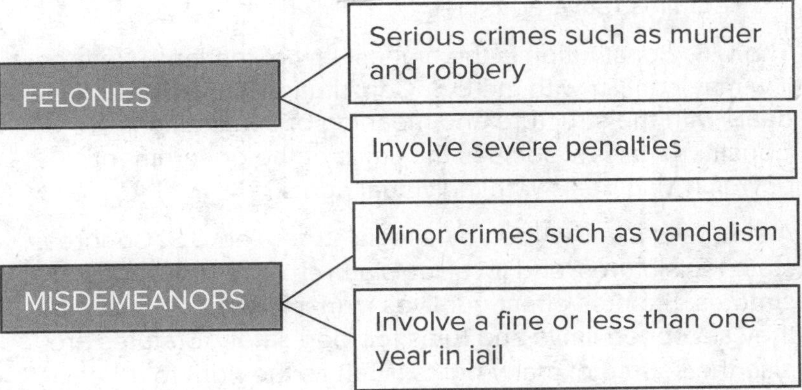
FELONIES
Serious crimes such as murder and robbery
Involve severe penalties
MISDEMEANORS
Minor crimes such as vandalism
Involve a fine or less than one year in jail

Crimes against property are the most common type of crime. They do not involve force or the threat of force against the victim. These include crimes in which property is destroyed, damaged, or stolen.

Civil Law

Civil law deals with disputes between people or groups. Many civil cases involve a broken contract. For example, if you do not receive an item that you have purchased online, the company has broken a contract with you. You could sue the company in court to get your money back. A court case is called a **lawsuit.** People who think they have been harmed in a dispute must file a lawsuit themselves. The government cannot bring such a case.

5. GIVING EXAMPLES

Give three examples each of situations involving criminal law and civil law.

Criminal Law

1. Students spray paint on school without permission
2. A regular shoplifter pickpockets a citizen
3. A detective is murdered with a frozen lamb leg.

Civil Law

1. A student is promised a class that he never gets
2. You wait 2 hours in a restaurant and don't receive your food.
3. ____________

6. COMPARING

Which source of law is most like common law: statutes, case law, or administrative law? Explain.

7. REFLECTING

Citizens have a responsibility to uphold the law. What should they do if they believe a law is unjust? Do people have a duty to oppose such laws? Explain.

Military Law

Military law is a special set of statutes that people serving in the U.S. armed forces must follow in addition to civil law. Civilians who work for the military also must follow these laws. Military laws refer to actions like disobeying a superior officer and mutiny. People accused of serious offenses may end up at court-martial, which is a military court.

Sources of Law

Criminal and civil laws come from several sources, including

- the U.S. Constitution
- state constitutions
- statutes
- case law
- administrative agencies

The U.S. Constitution is the highest law of the land. No other law may conflict with the U.S. Constitution. **Constitutional law** deals with the structure and meaning of constitutions. Constitutional law decides the limits of the government's power. It also deals with individual rights.

A statute is a law written by a legislature. The U.S. Congress, state legislatures, and local legislatures write thousands of statutes. Statutes affect our lives in many ways. For example, they set speed limits and rules for food safety. Statutes are also the source of many rights, such as the right to a free public education.

Case Law

Case law is law that is based on earlier decisions by judges. Some cases cannot be decided by a statute. In these cases, judges make rulings based on precedent. These rulings have the same weight as statutes.

Administrative Law

Administrative law involves all the rules and regulations created by the executive branch. The federal and state constitutions give legislatures the power to form administrative agencies. These agencies create rules and regulations that have the same weight as statutes passed by legislatures.

Name ______________________ Date ______________ Class __________

REVIEW LESSON 1

1. Use the chart below to identify various types of laws.

TYPE OF LAW	DESCRIPTION
	Type of law that seeks to protect public safety
	Type of law that handles disagreements between people and groups
	Set of statutes that must be followed by people serving in or working for the U.S. armed forces
	Laws that deal with the structure and meaning of constitutions
	Law that is based on precedent
	Rules and regulations set up by the executive branch

2. **DETERMINING CENTRAL IDEAS** On a separate sheet of paper, write an essay to answer the question, "What are the sources of our laws?" Identify and describe at least three sources of laws in the United States.

The American Legal System

1. IDENTIFYING

Is there a constitutional protection available to a person in jail who believes there is not enough evidence to hold him? If so, what is that right?

____

____

____

____

ANALYZING VISUALS

2. MAKING CONNECTIONS Why did the Fourteenth Amendment guarantee due process when the Fifth Amendment had already done so almost 100 years earlier?

____

____

____

____

____

____

____

____

SS.7.C.2.4, SS.7.C.2.5, SS.7.C.3.6, SS.7.C.3.12

Basic Legal Rights

The U.S. Constitution includes many important protections for American citizens. These protections prohibit the government from using laws unfairly. One of the most important protections is found in Article I. An accused person has the right to ask for a **writ of habeas corpus.** This is a court order that requires police to bring a prisoner to court to explain why the person is being held. The judge decides whether the imprisonment was lawful. This protection stops officials from jailing people for no reason.

Article I also prevents the government from issuing bills of attainder and ex post facto laws. A bill of attainder is a law that punishes a person without a trial. An ex post facto law is a law that would allow a person to be punished for an act that was not illegal when it was committed. *Ex post facto* means "after the fact."

The Constitution also ensures that the government respects our individual rights as it carries out the law. The Fourteenth Amendment says that states must treat all people equally under the law. It bans unequal treatment based on factors such as gender, race, and religion. Over the years, the equal protection clause has been used to win rights for minorities and women.

The Fourteenth Amendment and its equal protection clause also strengthen the Fifth Amendment right of due process. **Due process** means following established legal procedures. The government cannot take our lives, liberty, or property without following the law.

DUE PROCESS CLAUSES IN THE U.S. CONSTITUTION	
Fifth Amendment	"No person shall. . . be deprived of life, liberty, or property, without due process of the law."
Fourteenth Amendment	"No state shall. . . deprive any person of life, liberty, or property, without due process of law."

The Rights of the Accused

The Constitution guarantees that people accused of crimes are treated fairly. They must have a chance to defend themselves. These rights are based on the **presumption** of innocence. A person is believed to be innocent until proven guilty in a court of law.

Fourth Amendment Rights

The Fourth Amendment protects citizens against "unreasonable searches and seizures." This means a police officer cannot search your home or take your property without having a good reason for doing so. Police must obtain a search warrant before searching someone's home or property. A search warrant is a court document allowing a search. Police must tell a judge exactly what they are searching for, and why.

If police find evidence of a crime without a search warrant, the evidence may not be used in court. This rule is known as the **exclusionary rule.** The 1961 Supreme Court case *Mapp* v. *Ohio* ruled that illegally obtained evidence will be excluded, or banned, from a state court trial. Such evidence had already been banned from a federal court trial.

Fifth Amendment Rights

The Fifth Amendment states that no person can be forced "to be a witness against himself" in a criminal case. This means that people do not have to answer questions that might show they committed a crime. Before the 1960s, police often pressured suspects to confess to a crime. This practice ended in 1966 with the Supreme Court case *Miranda* v. *Arizona*. The Court ruled that police must issue a **Miranda Warning** to accused suspects who are in police custody.

The Miranda Warning tells suspects that

- they have the right to remain silent
- anything they say may be used against them as evidence in court
- they have the right to an attorney, and if they cannot afford an attorney, the court will provide one

The Fifth Amendment also protects the accused from double jeopardy. This means that a person who is tried for a crime and found not guilty may not be tried again for the same crime.

3. IDENTIFYING PROBLEMS

What arguments might be made against the exclusionary rule?

____

____

____

____

____

____

____

____

4. MAKING CONNECTIONS

Based on the Fifth Amendment, what questions does a person accused of burglary not have to answer?

____

____

____

____

____

____

Name ______________________ Date ______________ Class ________

5. DIFFERENTIATING

What is the difference between a grand jury and a trial jury?

Under the Fifth Amendment, people accused of a federal crime have the right to bring their case before a grand jury. A grand jury is a group of 12 to 23 citizens that decides whether the government has enough evidence to hold a trial. If there is enough evidence, the grand jury indicts, or formally charges, the suspect.

Sixth Amendment Rights

The Sixth Amendment states that defendants are entitled to representation by a lawyer. In the 1963 Supreme Court case *Gideon* v. *Wainwright*, the Court said that the amendment means that if a defendant cannot afford a lawyer, the state must provide one. The Sixth Amendment also says that accused people

- have a right to know the charges against them
- can question their accusers
- have the right to a speedy public trial
- have the right to be tried by an impartial, or fair, jury

6. THEORIZING

Though jurors are usually chosen from the area where a crime was committed, sometimes a trial is moved to a different location. This is called a change of venue. Why might a judge grant a defendant a change of venue?

EXAMPLES OF VIOLATIONS OF CONSTITUTIONAL RIGHTS

Scenario	Right Violated
Person A is wearing a T-shirt that reads "Laws Limit Freedom!" A police officer stops him and demands to search A's backpack because he doesn't like A's T-shirt.	Fourth Amendment Right
Person B was tried last year for shoplifting. A jury found her not guilty. Today, the prosecutor has charged her with the same crime. He vows he will continue to bring B to trial until she is convicted.	Fifth Amendment Right
Person C was arrested six months ago for running a stop sign. She has been in jail ever since then, waiting for a trial.	Sixth Amendment Right
Person D is found guilty of breaking his neighbor's window on purpose. This is the first time D has been convicted of a crime. A judge orders D to serve 20 years in jail.	Eighth Amendment Right

Name ______________________ Date ______________ Class __________

Eighth Amendment Rights

The Eighth Amendment prohibits "cruel and unusual punishments." In other words, the punishment must fit the crime. For example, a life sentence for shoplifting would be excessive.

In *Furman* v. *Georgia* (1972), the Supreme Court ruled that the death penalty as then carried out was unconstitutional. The Court did not rule that the death penalty itself was cruel, but that it was being applied unequally. It unfairly targeted African Americans and the poor. This violated the Fourteenth Amendment. After the *Furman* decision, states revised their death penalty laws to meet the Court's guidelines.

The Eighth Amendment also prohibits excessive bail. In setting the amount of the bail, the judge looks at the seriousness of the crime, the criminal record of the accused, and the ability of the accused to pay bail.

7. PRIORITIZING

This lesson identifies four important Supreme Court rulings regarding the rights of accused persons. List these cases in order from the one you consider most important to the one you consider least important. Then, explain your reasoning on a separate sheet of paper.

1. ______________________
2. ______________________
3. ______________________
4. ______________________

REVIEW LESSON 2

1. Use the chart below to identify the constitutional sources for the rights listed.

SOURCE	RIGHTS
	• Forbids cruel and unusual punishments • Prohibits excessive bail
	• Right to counsel • Right to a speedy public trial before an impartial jury
	• Requires states to treat all people equally under the law • Guarantees due process
	• Guarantees due process • Protects against self-incrimination
	• Habeas corpus • Protects against ex post facto laws
	• Protects against unreasonable searches and seizures

2. **SPECULATING** Imagine what life in the United States would be like without the protections identified in the chart. For each article or amendment listed, describe one possible outcome if that safeguard were not included in the Constitution. Write your answers on a separate sheet of paper.

Benchmark Skill Activities

DIRECTIONS: Write your answers on a separate sheet of paper.

LAFS.68.WHST.2.4, SS.7.C.3.6

1. CONSTRUCTING AN ARGUMENT

Use your FOLDABLES to write an essay.

Some critics of the criminal justice system have argued that defendants have more rights than crime victims. Do you believe the system needs to be "rebalanced" in favor of crime victims? In what ways does the current system benefit victims as well as defendants?

LAFS.68.WHST.2.4

2. ASSESSING

The following passage is from the 1963 Supreme Court ruling in the *Gideon* v. *Wainwright* case.

> *"In our . . . system of justice, any person . . . too poor to hire a lawyer, cannot be assured a fair trial unless counsel is provided for him. This seems to us to be an obvious truth. . . . [L]awyers in criminal courts are necessities, not luxuries."*
>
> *—Gideon* v. *Wainwright*, 1963

What does this passage—and the Court's ruling in the case—say about the commitment to justice in U.S. courts?

LAFS.68.WHST.3.8, LAFS.68.WHST.3.9

3. DIFFERENTIATING

Do some library and Internet research to understand how the Napoleonic Code makes Louisiana law different from that in other states. As you review the results of your research, distinguish between fact, opinion, and reasoned judgments in the sources you use. Report your findings in a brief essay or visual presentation.

LAFS.68.WHST.2.6

4. ORGANIZING

Examine the following time line:

Events Contributing to Equal Protection

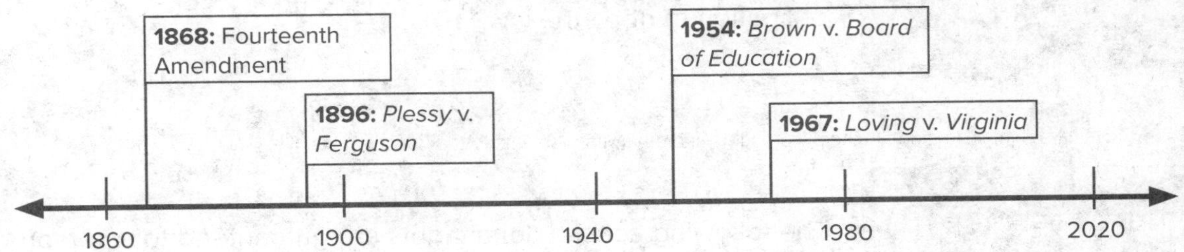

Conduct Internet research to learn more about each event shown on the time line. Use that information to create a multimedia presentation about the development of equal protection guarantees. End your presentation with a brief prediction about how you believe equal protection will continue to evolve in the years ahead.

LAFS.68.RH.1.2, SS.7.C.3.10

5. DRAWING CONCLUSIONS

Burden of proof is a duty of the prosecution or plaintiff to prove a disputed fact. The proof must reach a certain standard or level. In civil cases, the burden of proof is a "preponderance [a greater amount] of the evidence." That is, the plaintiff will win if just a little more than 50 percent of the evidence is in his or her favor.

The burden of proof in a criminal case is "beyond a reasonable doubt." That means that there must be convincing evidence that the person is guilty of the crime. While there is no numerical figure for reasonable doubt, it is *much* greater than 50 percent.

In other words, a great deal of convincing evidence is needed to obtain a conviction in a criminal case. Less is needed in a civil case. Why do you think the burden of proof is higher in a criminal case than in a civil case?

Benchmark Note Cards

DIRECTIONS: Use these note cards to help you prepare for the test.

SS.7.C.2.2 Evaluate the obligations citizens have to obey laws, pay taxes, defend the nation, and serve on juries.

WHY WE HAVE LAWS	Laws are created to keep citizens safe. They allow people to live together in a peaceful, orderly society. Citizens have an obligation to obey the law.

SS.7.C.2.4 Evaluate rights contained in the Bill of Rights and other amendments to the Constitution.

RIGHTS OF THE ACCUSED

The following constitutional rights are guaranteed to a person accused of a crime.

- Article I guarantees a writ of habeas corpus. It also protects against both bills of attainder and ex post facto laws.
- The Fourth Amendment protects against unreasonable searches and seizures.
- The Fifth Amendment guarantees due process and protects against both self-incrimination and double jeopardy. The amendment also provides for grand juries in the case of federal crimes.
- Sixth Amendment rights include the right to counsel, to know the accusations, to a speedy public trial, to confront the accuser, and to be tried by an impartial jury.
- The Eighth Amendment forbids cruel and unusual punishments and prohibits excessive bail.
- The Fourteenth Amendment requires states to treat all people equally under the law and guarantees due process.

SS.7.C.2.5 Distinguish how the Constitution safeguards and limits individual rights.

BASIC LEGAL RIGHTS	The U.S. Constitution includes many important protections for American citizens. These protections prohibit the government from using laws unfairly. • **Writ of habeas corpus—**Officials must explain to a judge why someone has been arrested. The judge decides whether the accused was lawfully imprisoned. • **Bills of attainder—**Laws that punish a person without a trial are prohibited. • **Ex post facto laws—**Laws that would allow a person to be punished for an act that was legal when it was committed are prohibited. • **Due process—**The government cannot take our lives, liberty, or property without following the law.

SS.7.C.3.6 Evaluate Constitutional rights and their impact on individuals and society.

IMPACT OF CONSTITUTIONAL RIGHTS	The Constitution guarantees that people accused of crimes are treated fairly. They must also have a chance to defend themselves. These rights are based on the presumption of innocence. A person is believed to be innocent until proven guilty in a court of law.

SS.7.C.3.10 Identify sources and types (civil, criminal, constitutional, military) of law.

SOURCES OF LAW	Criminal and civil laws come from several sources, including • the U.S. Constitution • state constitutions • statutes • case law • administrative agencies

TYPES OF LAW

- **Criminal law**—deals with the types of crimes that prevent people from living together peacefully
- **Civil law**—handles arguments that arise between people or groups
- **Military law**—set of statutes that must be followed by people serving in or working for the U.S. armed forces
- **Constitutional law**—composed of the laws that deal with the structure and meaning of constitutions
- **Case law or common law**—law that is based on legal precedents and prior judicial decision
- **Administrative law**—refers to the body of rules and regulations set up by the executive branch to carry out its job

SS.7.C.3.12 Analyze the significance and outcomes of landmark Supreme Court cases including, but not limited to, *Marbury* v. *Madison, Plessy* v. *Ferguson, Brown* v. *Board of Education, Gideon* v. *Wainwright, Miranda* v. *Arizona, in re Gault, Tinker* v. *Des Moines, Hazelwood* v. *Kuhlmeier, United States* v. *Nixon*, and *Bush* v. *Gore*.

KEY SUPREME COURT CASES

Mapp* v. *Ohio—Illegally obtained evidence will be excluded, or banned, from a state court trial.

Miranda* v. *Arizona—Police must issue a warning to accused suspects advising them of their Fifth Amendment rights.

Gideon* v. *Wainwright—If a defendant cannot afford a lawyer, the state must provide one.

Furman* v. *Georgia—The death penalty as then carried out was unconstitutional because it was applied unequally by targeting African Americans and the poor.

Chapter 15

VISUAL SUMMARY

DIRECTIONS: Complete the graphic organizer below.

Characteristics of Good Laws	Sources of U.S. Law	Types of U.S. Law
• • • •	• • • • •	• • • •

American Legal System

CONSTITUTIONAL PROTECTIONS AND GUARANTEES	
From Article 1	
From Fourth Amendment	
From Fifth Amendment	
From Sixth Amendment	
From Eighth Amendment	
From Fourteenth Amendment	

USING PRIMARY SOURCES

COMPARE AND CONTRAST When the Supreme Court decided the *Miranda* v. *Arizona* case, the justices split their vote. Five justices voted in support of Miranda. Four justices voted in opposition to the majority decision. In its ruling in this case, the Court held that the Fifth Amendment requires law enforcement officials to advise suspects in custody of their right to remain silent and their right to obtain an attorney.

Below are excerpts from the Court's opinions. Chief Justice Earl Warren wrote the majority opinion. Justice Byron White wrote a dissenting opinion. Read each excerpt, and determine which person wrote each statement. On a separate sheet of paper, explain how you came to that conclusion. Then, use examples from each excerpt to summarize Warren's and White's opinions about the Fifth Amendment.

Opinion 1

The proposition [statement] that the privilege [right] against self-incrimination forbids in-custody interrogation without the warnings . . . and without a clear waiver of counsel has no significant support in the history of the privilege or in the language of the Fifth Amendment. . . .

I have no desire whatsoever to share the responsibility for any such impact on the present criminal process.

In some unknown number of cases, the Court's rule will return a killer, . . . or other criminal to the streets and to the environment which produced him, to repeat his crime whenever it pleases him. As a consequence, there will not be a gain, but a loss, in human dignity.

Opinion 2

To be sure, the records do not evince [show signs of] overt physical coercion [force] or patent psychological ploys [obvious mental moves to gain advantage]. The fact remains that in none of these cases did the officers undertake to afford [give] appropriate safeguards [protections] at the outset [beginning] of the interrogation [questioning] to insure that the statements were truly the product of free choice.

It is obvious that such an interrogation environment is created for no purpose other than to subjugate [bring under control] the individual to the will of his examiner. This atmosphere carries its own badge of intimidation. To be sure, this is not physical intimidation, but it is equally destructive of human dignity. . . .

If the individual indicates in any manner, at any time prior to or during questioning, that he wishes to remain silent, the interrogation must cease. . . . If the individual states that he wants an attorney, the interrogation must cease until an attorney is present. At that time, the individual must have an opportunity to confer [meet and talk] with the attorney and to have him present during any subsequent [further] questioning.

Chapter Practice Test

DIRECTIONS: Circle the best answer for each question.

SS.7.C.3.10 (Moderate)

> *". . . [W]e must see to it that the man made free by the Constitution . . . is a freeman indeed; that he can go where he pleases, work when and for whom he pleases . . . go into schools and educate himself and his children; that the rights and guarantees of the good old common law are his, and that he walks the earth, proud and erect in the conscious dignity of a free man."*
>
> —The Congressional Globe

What is the legal basis for this passage?

A civil case law

B the Napoleonic code

C English common law

D Roman law

SS.7.C.3.10 (Moderate)

Which of the following would involve civil law, but not criminal law?

A assault inside a restaurant

B an incorrect charge on a hospital bill

C vandalism of a school

D jaywalking

3 **SS.7.C.3.12 (Moderate)**

Person X drives his car 45 miles per hour in a school zone.

↓

A police officer pulls the driver over because the driver is speeding. The officer then notes that the car has been reported as stolen.

↓

Under police questioning, the driver admits that he stole the car and is immediately arrested.

↓

The officer transports the driver to county jail.

Based on the information in the diagram, which of the following statements is accurate?

A The officer should have read Person X the Miranda Warning as soon as the driver pulled over.

B A Miranda Warning was not required because the driver was initially stopped for speeding.

C The officer should have read Person X the Miranda Warning as soon as Person X was questioned.

D A Miranda Warning was not required because of the exclusionary rule.

SS.7.C.2.2 (High)

Why would a law that required a shoplifter to be jailed for 25 years not be considered a "good" law?

A There is no precedent for such a law.

B Such a law would not be enforceable.

C The Napoleonic Code does not specify such a law.

D Such a law would not be reasonable.

SS.7.C.2.5 (Moderate)

The following passage is taken from the U.S. Constitution.

> *The Privilege of the Writ of Habeas Corpus shall not be suspended [temporarily stopped], unless when in Cases of Rebellion or Invasion the public Safety may require it.*
>
> —U.S. Constitution

Based on this passage, what can the government not do?

A seize a person's property without first paying for it

B hold a prisoner indefinitely without showing cause

C discriminate against citizens based on gender or race

D declare a person guilty of a crime without allowing a trial

---

SS.7.C.3.6 (Moderate)

Why is the Supreme Court decision in *Gideon* v. *Wainwright* important?

A It protects against self-incrimination.

B It guarantees the right to legal representation.

C It guarantees due process.

D It assures a speedy trial.

7 **SS.7.C.3.6 (High)**

In May 2015, the U.S. Senate debated the USA Freedom Act. The following excerpt is from remarks made by Senator Patrick Leahy regarding the bulk collection of phone records by the U.S. government.

> *We all know that the NSA has for years been using section 215 of the USA PATRIOT Act to sweep up phone records of innocent Americans without any connection to terrorism. . . . The American people oppose this indiscriminate dragnet [planned actions to catch criminals] collection of their records—not only that, the courts do, too.*
>
> —Senator Patrick Leahy

What is Senator Leahy's main concern?

A Eighth Amendment prohibitions against cruel and unusual punishments

B Sixth Amendment promises of a fair and speedy jury trial

C Fifth Amendment guarantees of grand jury proceedings

D Fourth Amendment protections against unreasonable searches and seizures

---

8 **SS.7.C.3.10 (Moderate)**

Which type of law relies extensively upon precedents?

A administrative law

B military law

C case law

D statutory law

SS.7.C.2.4 (Moderate)

> *In all criminal prosecutions, the accused shall enjoy the right to a speedy and public trial, by an impartial jury of the state and district wherein the crime shall have been committed, which district shall have been previously ascertained by law, and to be informed of the nature and cause of the accusation; to be confronted with the witnesses against him; to have compulsory process for obtaining witnesses in his favor, and to have the assistance of counsel for his defense.*
>
> —U.S. Constitution

This passage is taken from which constitutional amendment?

A Fourth Amendment

B Sixth Amendment

C Eighth Amendment

D Fourteenth Amendment

SS.7.C.3.6 (Moderate)

A police officer enters a person's home without a search warrant and sees stolen goods lying on the table. The stolen goods cannot be used as evidence against the person. Why?

A the exclusionary rule

B the doctrine of double jeopardy

C prohibitions against ex post facto laws

D the lack of a Miranda Warning

CHAPTER 16

Civil and Criminal Law

Chapter Overview

Both civil law and criminal law can lead to court cases. Civil law involves disputes over contracts, property issues, family issues, and personal injury. The court may award money to help the person who has been harmed.

Criminal law involves offenses against society's rules. Criminal law offenses are separated into serious and less serious offenses. Being convicted in court can lead to jail or prison time.

Most of the time, juveniles are treated in a different way than adults. After the police take a juvenile into custody, a social worker helps determine what happens next. The court system also helps juveniles who are neglected or abused.

CHAPTER BENCHMARKS

SS.7.C.3.6 Evaluate Constitutional rights and their impact on individuals and society.

SS.7.C.3.8 Analyze the structure, functions, and processes of the legislative, executive, and judicial branches.

SS.7.C.3.10 Identify sources and types (civil, criminal, constitutional, military) of law.

SS.7.C.3.11 Diagram the levels, functions, and powers of courts at the state and federal levels.

LAFS.68.RH.1.1 Cite specific textual evidence to support analysis of primary and secondary sources.

LAFS.68.RH.1.2 Determine the central ideas or information of a primary or secondary source; provide an accurate summary of the source distinct from prior knowledge or opinions.

LAFS.68.RH.1.3 Identify key steps in a text's description of a process related to history/social studies (e.g., how a bill becomes law, how interest rates are raised or lowered).

LAFS.68.RH.2.4 Determine the meaning of words and phrases as they are used in a text, including vocabulary specific to domains related to history/social studies.

WHAT I NEED TO KNOW

TERMS

- ☐ contract
- ☐ tort
- ☐ negligence
- ☐ damages
- ☐ plaintiff
- ☐ defendant
- ☐ summons
- ☐ discovery
- ☐ penal code
- ☐ misdemeanor
- ☐ felony
- ☐ sentence
- ☐ prosecution
- ☐ plea bargaining
- ☐ cross-examination
- ☐ juvenile delinquent
- ☐ delinquent offender
- ☐ status offender
- ☐ custody
- ☐ detention hearing
- ☐ adjudication hearing
- ☐ disposition hearing

CHAPTER 16
Civil and Criminal Law

CHAPTER BENCHMARKS, *continued*

LAFS.68.WHST.1.2 Write informative/explanatory texts, including the narration of historical events, scientific procedures/experiments, or technical processes.

LAFS.68.WHST.2.4 Produce clear and coherent writing in which the development, organization, and style are appropriate to task, purpose, and audience.

LAFS.68.WHST.2.6 Use technology, including the Internet, to produce and publish writing and present the relationships between information and ideas clearly and efficiently.

LAFS.68.WHST.3.7 Conduct short research projects to answer a question (including a self-generated question), drawing on several sources and generating additional related, focused questions that allow for multiple avenues of exploration.

LAFS.68.WHST.3.8 Gather relevant information from multiple print and digital sources, using search terms effectively; assess the credibility and accuracy of each source; and quote or paraphrase the data and conclusions of others while avoiding plagiarism and following a standard format for citation.

LAFS.68.SL.2.4 Present claims and findings, emphasizing salient points in a focused, coherent manner with pertinent descriptions, facts, details, and examples; use appropriate eye contact, adequate volume, and clear pronunciation.

Civil and Criminal Law

Create the Foldable® below and write the chapter title on the cover tab. Label the three tabs below the title with the three lesson titles. As you study the chapter, record important terms and main ideas that will help you describe types of civil and criminal law. Under the third tab, summarize past and present treatment of juvenile offenders. On the back of the Foldable, outline the legal procedures in a criminal law case.

Step 1
Begin with two sheets of lined paper.

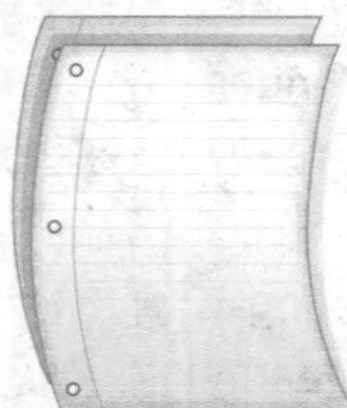

Step 2
Stack the two sheets of paper, but align them so one sheet is about an inch below the other sheet.

Step 3
Fold the bottom part of the stack up to create three equal tabs. Flip over. Staple at the fold and label as directed.

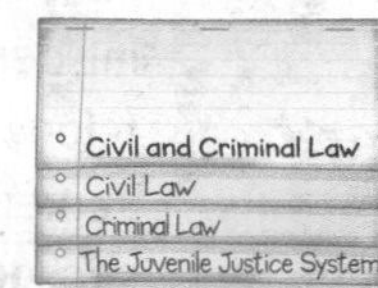

LESSON 1 SUMMARY

Civil Law

SS.7.C.3.6, SS.7.C.3.8, SS.7.C.3.10, SS.7.C.3.11

Types of Civil Law

Civil law deals with disputes, or disagreements. These disputes can involve individuals, groups of individuals, companies, or the government in any combination. For instance, if a person is injured in a car accident with the driver of a business, he or she can sue the driver who might have caused the accident or the business for which the driver works.

In civil law, the people involved might have to go to court. Court cases can involve four different branches of civil law: contract law, property law, family law, and personal injury law. In the Florida court system, they will be heard at one of these levels:

- County Courts—hear civil cases involving disputes of $15,000 or less
- Circuit Courts—hear civil cases involving disputes of more than $15,000, family law matters, and appeals from county courts
- District Courts of Appeal—hear appeals from lower courts

Contract Law

You agree to give your friend a baseball card in exchange for another baseball card. You and your friend have entered into a contract. A **contract** is an agreement between two or more parties to exchange something of value. Both parties involved are obligated to honor the agreement. A contract can be a written or an oral agreement. Before signing any contract, you should read it carefully. Once you sign it, you have agreed to do what it says.

Property Law

Property law covers buying, selling, and renting land or buildings. Just as there are rules for contract law, there are rules related to property law. One important law is that a person cannot sell property without proof of legal ownership.

1. SUMMARIZING

What are civil laws? What makes them different from criminal laws?

2. COMPARING AND CONTRASTING

How are contract law and property law similar? How are they different?

Name ______________________ Date ______________ Class __________

3. CONTRASTING

Family law and personal injury law deal with different types of cases. What is another key difference between them?

____

____

____

____

____

Property law protects both property owners and renters. For example, a renter is responsible for any intentional damages made to an apartment. The renter would have to pay to repair the damages. The same legal protection exists for the renter. An apartment owner cannot hide problems such as mold from a renter.

Many times, however, property issues are not clear-cut. That is when disputes happen. An apartment owner is responsible for repairing a broken water heater. A renter did not tell the owner about the water heater problem until the heater was beyond repair and needed to be replaced. Is the owner still responsible or should the renter pay? When the owner and renter cannot come to an agreement, a court must decide.

ANALYZING VISUALS

4. MAKING INFERENCES

Study the chart on this page. Which branch of civil law would be involved if a person agrees to purchase a bicycle and then is unable to pay for it?

____

Which branch of civil law would be involved if a person riding a bicycle hits and injures a pedestrian?

____

Family Law

As the name suggests, family law concerns matters relating to families. Such matters include marriages, birth, adoptions, divorces, and death. Much of family law is not based on ending a disagreement. For example, if a couple wants to adopt a child, they must go to court. The court legally sets up a parent-child relationship for the new family.

Personal Injury Law

The remaining branch of civil law works with personal injury disputes. Sometimes a person commits an act that is not illegal but that causes harm to another person or property. The person who is harmed has the right to sue. This type of case is called a **tort.** Throwing a rock through a window could be a tort, especially if someone inside the house is hit by flying glass. If the person throwing the rock did this on purpose, it is an intentional tort.

Torts also deal with harmful acts caused by careless or reckless behavior. This is called **negligence.** Playing ball near a window and accidentally breaking it would be a negligent act.

BRANCHES OF CIVIL LAW	
Contract Law	involves not honoring a written or an oral agreement to exchange something of value
Property Law	involves buying, selling, or transferring property and the rights of owners and renters of property
Family Law	involves matters related to birth, marriage, divorce, adoption, and death
Personal Injury Law	involves wrongful actions that cause injury to another person or damage to property

Name ______ Date ______ Class ______

The Legal Process in Civil Cases

A civil lawsuit begins when the plaintiff's lawyer files a complaint. This statement lists the wrong that the plaintiff says the defendant committed and the harm that was done. Most complaints ask the court to award **damages,** a sum of money, to repay the plaintiff for losses. The complaint might also ask for a contract to be honored.

Disputes often lead to lawsuits, usually with two parties. The **plaintiff** is the injured person who files a lawsuit. The **defendant** is the person thought to be responsible for the injury. Civil lawsuits follow specific steps and procedures. These steps satisfy the right to due process required by the Constitution.

Once a complaint is filed, the court issues a summons to the defendant. The **summons** is a document telling a person he or she is being sued. It also gives details about the court hearing.

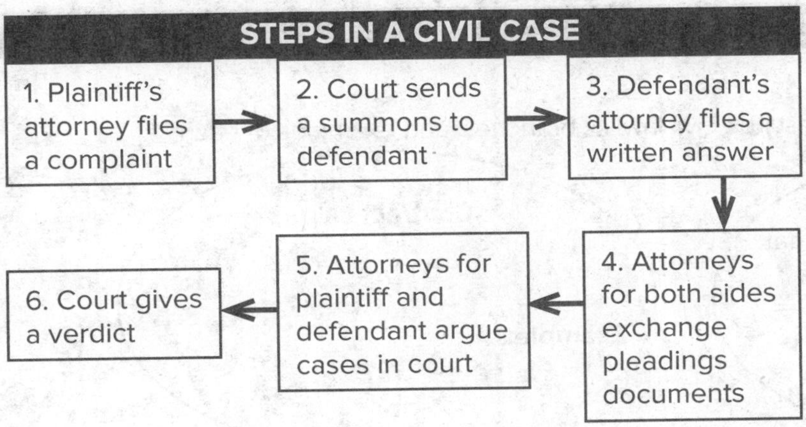

STEPS IN A CIVIL CASE

1. Plaintiff's attorney files a complaint →
2. Court sends a summons to defendant →
3. Defendant's attorney files a written answer ↓
4. Attorneys for both sides exchange pleadings documents →
5. Attorneys for plaintiff and defendant argue cases in court →
6. Court gives a verdict

Before the Trial

The defendant's lawyer may file an answer to the complaint. The next step is **discovery,** when attorneys on both sides check facts and gather evidence.

A trial can be expensive. One way of avoiding high court costs is for the plaintiff and defendant to reach a settlement. Such a settlement can occur at any time during the process. Many civil cases are settled this way.

The Trial

If there is no settlement, the parties go to trial. In a trial, a judge or jury will settle the case. The judge's role also includes keeping order and making sure that both parties receive equal treatment under the law. During a trial, both parties present evidence and their lawyers might question witnesses. The judge or jury then issues a verdict.

ANALYZING VISUALS

5. ANALYZING INFORMATION Review the graphic organizer on this page. What role does the court play in civil law?

______

6. EVALUATING

How does the process in civil law help protect the constitutional rights of the individual?

______

7. DRAWING CONCLUSIONS

Why do you think the losing party is allowed to appeal to a higher court?

A trial has several possible outcomes:

- The defendant proves he or she was not at fault. The plaintiff gets nothing and might have to pay court costs.
- The plaintiff proves the defendant was at fault. The defendant must pay for any damages in the amount set by the judge or jury.

Appeals and Other Actions

Regardless of the outcome, the losing party can appeal the case to a circuit court, and then a district court of appeal. An appeals court might look at whether an error occurred during the trial. It might also lower the amount of damages to be paid. A plaintiff might also have to ask for the court's help if the defendant does not pay damages.

REVIEW LESSON 1

1. Complete the diagram below to describe civil law, its branches, and examples of each.

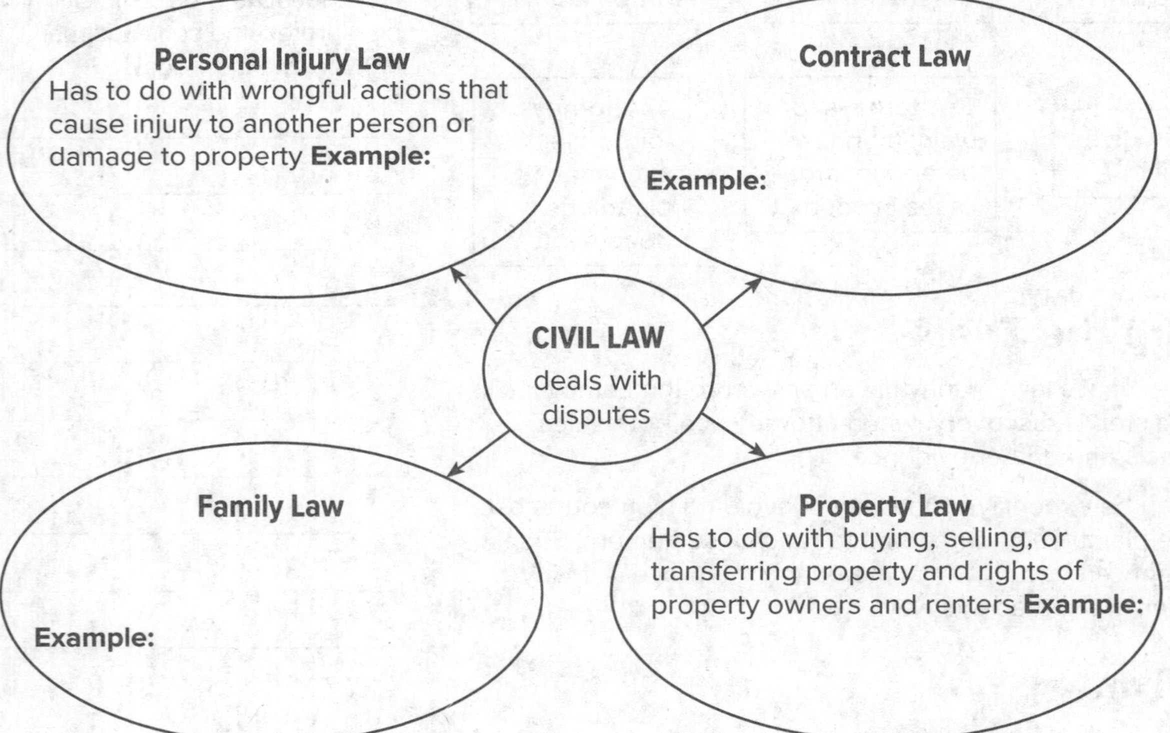
Personal Injury Law
Has to do with wrongful actions that cause injury to another person or damage to property Example:
Contract Law
Example:
CIVIL LAW
deals with disputes
Family Law
Example:
Property Law
Has to do with buying, selling, or transferring property and rights of property owners and renters Example:

2. **COMPARING AND CONTRASTING** On a separate sheet of paper, write an essay in which you explain civil law and its different branches. Give examples of each branch.

LESSON 2 SUMMARY

Criminal Law

SS.7.C.3.6, SS.7.C.3.8, SS.7.C.3.10, SS.7.C.3.11

Crime and Punishment

A crime is any act that harms people or society. Each state has a list of criminal laws and the punishments for each crime. This set of laws is called the **penal code.**

Most crimes are tried in state courts. However, some criminal acts are federal crimes. Examples of federal crimes include acts of terrorism, identity theft, immigration fraud, computer hacking, drug trafficking, and mail fraud. Federal crimes are tried in federal court based on the federal penal code. Criminals who commit federal crimes serve time in a federal prison.

Types of Crime

A crime can be a misdemeanor or a felony. A **misdemeanor** is a minor crime for which a person can be fined a small sum of money or jailed for up to one year. A **felony** is a more serious crime that is punishable by more than one year in prison. Some types of crime like theft can be either a misdemeanor or a felony depending on the amount of damage.

There are crimes against property and crimes against people. If someone steals a purse from a store, that is most likely a misdemeanor. If someone grabs a purse from another person by force or threat, that crime is a felony. It is also a violent crime because it is a crime against a person.

TYPES OF CRIMES	
Misdemeanor	**Felony**
Theft of something worth less than $100	Grand theft, robbery
Simple assault, threatening to or trying to attack someone	Murder or manslaughter, aggravated [more severe] assault
Driving with a suspended license	Repeated driving while intoxicated convictions

1. HYPOTHESIZING

Do you think that criminal laws are necessary at both the state and federal levels? Explain your answer.

ANALYZING VISUALS

2. EXPLAINING Look at the information in the chart. Based on the information, write your own definitions for *misdemeanor* and *felony*. Contrast the two types of crimes.

ANALYZING VISUALS

3. IDENTIFYING STEPS IN A PROCESS Look at the chart. At what step is it possible for a defendant to accept a plea bargain? What must the defendant do for the prosecutor to agree to that plea bargain?

____

____

____

____

____

____

____

____

Punishment for Crimes

Criminal laws generally give harsher punishment to more serious crimes. Most criminal laws also have a range of penalties for the same crime. Judges can look at the circumstances for each crime. They then decide which level of **sentence,** or punishment, best fits the crime. Some prisoners may be paroled after they serve part of their sentence. They must report regularly to a parole officer for the remaining time of their sentence.

The Purposes of Punishment

The main purpose of prison sentences is punishment, but there are other purposes, too. Keeping a dangerous person locked up protects the rest of society. It may keep others from committing crimes. In addition, it may help prisoners change their behavior. Services such as counseling, job training, and education give them valuable skills for life after prison.

Criminal Case Procedure

The Bill of Rights protects the rights of a person suspected or accused of a crime. The government is the plaintiff in criminal cases and is called the **prosecution.** Because the law must treat everyone fairly, the government follows the rules of due process. In fact, the law protects an individual accused of a crime at every step of the criminal case procedure.

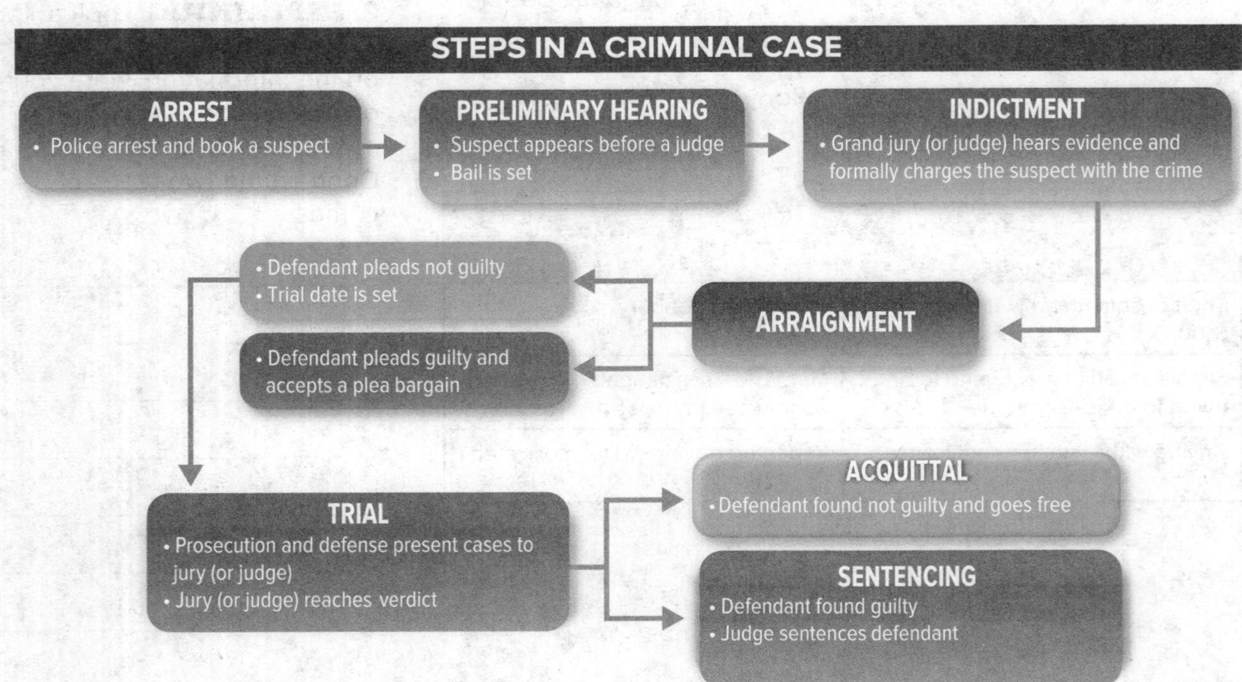

STEPS IN A CRIMINAL CASE
ARREST
• Police arrest and book a suspect
PRELIMINARY HEARING
• Suspect appears before a judge
• Bail is set
INDICTMENT
• Grand jury (or judge) hears evidence and formally charges the suspect with the crime
ARRAIGNMENT
• Defendant pleads not guilty
• Trial date is set
• Defendant pleads guilty and accepts a plea bargain
TRIAL
• Prosecution and defense present cases to jury (or judge)
• Jury (or judge) reaches verdict
ACQUITTAL
• Defendant found not guilty and goes free
SENTENCING
• Defendant found guilty
• Judge sentences defendant

Arrest and Booking

When a crime has been committed, the police need evidence before they can arrest a person. The evidence must convince a judge to issue an arrest warrant. During the arrest, the police must tell the accused person of the right to remain silent and the right to an attorney.

The police then take the suspect to the police station for booking. Booking includes making a record of the arrest and taking the person's photograph and fingerprints.

The Preliminary Hearing

The police cannot keep a suspect in custody without further action. The suspect has a preliminary hearing with a judge. At this hearing, the prosecution, or government, must show the judge that there is probable cause, or good reason, to believe that the suspect committed the crime. The judge then explains the charges to the suspect. If the suspect cannot afford a lawyer, the court provides one at this time.

For a misdemeanor, the suspect can either enter a guilty or a not guilty plea. With a guilty plea, the judge gives a sentence. If the plea is not guilty, the judge sets a trial date.

For a felony, the suspect does not enter a plea. The judge sets a hearing date to learn more. The judge may keep the suspect in jail or release him or her. The judge might also set bail. Bail allows the suspect to leave jail with the promise to return to court for the hearing.

Indictment, Arraignment, and Pleas

Before a person can be tried for a crime, he or she must be indicted, or charged with the crime. In some states, a grand jury does this. In other states, a judge fulfills this responsibility. If the evidence is not strong enough, the case will be dismissed.

If the case has strong evidence, the next step is arraignment. The accused either enters a plea of guilty or not guilty. If the suspect pleads guilty, he or she is sentenced. If the suspect states that he or she is not guilty, the judge sets a trial date.

To avoid a trial, the lawyers for the prosecution and defense may enter into **plea bargaining.** During this step, a prosecutor will agree to charge the defendant with a lesser crime in return for a guilty plea. Plea bargaining saves time and money. The defendant likely will receive a lighter sentence than after a trial. Most criminal cases end this way.

4. MAKING CONNECTIONS

How does the criminal case procedure reflect the values on which the nation was founded?

____

____

____

____

____

____

____

____

____

____

____

____

5. DRAWING CONCLUSIONS

Why might the judge rather than the jury be responsible for sentencing?

____

____

____

____

____

____

6. SEQUENCING

On a separate sheet of paper, make a graphic organizer that lists the steps in the criminal case process that are set up to protect an individual's rights.

The Trial

A defendant can choose a trial by judge or jury. Most choose a judge. In a trial by jury, the jurors would be chosen next.

Like a civil trial, a criminal trial begins with an opening statement by both lawyers. The prosecution always begins. Both sides then present evidence and witnesses. Each side is also allowed to ask questions of the other side's witnesses. This is called **cross-examination.** At the end of the trial, each side summarizes their case in a closing statement. If there are jurors, the judge explains to them how the law applies to the case.

The Verdict, Sentencing, and Appeals

In a jury trial, the jury will review the evidence, discuss the case, and vote on the defendant's guilt. This takes place in secret in a separate room. Under American law, a person is innocent until proven guilty beyond a reasonable doubt. The 1894 U.S. Supreme Court decision, *Coffin* v. *United States*, formally made this concept a part of the constitutional principle of due process. As a result, the jury must be certain beyond a reasonable doubt that the defendant committed the crime. In fact, most states require the jury vote to be unanimous. That means that all the jury members must vote for the guilty verdict. Federal court requires a unanimous decision as well.

If a jury cannot come to a decision, the judge is required to call a mistrial. This means no decision could be made on guilt or innocence. The prosecution has to decide whether to try the defendant again.

If the defendant is found to be not guilty, he or she is free. This is called an acquittal. However, if the judge or jury found the defendant guilty, a date is set for sentencing. If the crime is serious, the judge may hold a hearing to learn about the defendant's history, previous criminal record, and other factors to help decide sentencing. Victims of crimes can make statements at this hearing.

Like civil cases, criminal cases can be appealed to a higher court. The appeals court does not retry the case. Instead, the higher court reviews whether the defendant's rights were violated or whether errors were made during the trial.

REVIEW LESSON 2

1. Complete the chart below. Identify the steps involved in criminal arrests, the powers given to the court, and the ways the rights of the accused are protected.

1 - Arrest	Police gather evidence. Judge issues warrant. Accused is advised of Miranda Warning.
2 - Preliminary Hearing	
3 -	
4 -	
5 -	
6- Acquittal or Sentencing	Sentencing is based on guidelines. Convicted person can appeal.

2. **INTERPRETING** Choose three points from the chart above. On a separate sheet of paper, explain why each of those steps or protections is important in the American legal system.

LESSON 3 SUMMARY

The Juvenile Justice System

1. ASSESSING

Do you think trying to rehabilitate juvenile offenders is a more effective way to deal with them than punishing them? Explain your answer.

2. REFLECTING

Do you think the "considerations" listed for the juvenile justice system today are fair? Why or why not?

SS.7.C.3.6, SS.7.C.3.8, SS.7.C.3.10, SS.7.C.3.11

Juvenile Justice

Today, most juveniles who commit crimes are not treated in the same manner as adults who commit the same crimes. At one time, however, juveniles were treated like adult criminals.

During the mid-1800s, a group of reformers blamed the family when children committed crimes. These reformers were able to change the way juvenile offenders were treated by the justice system. A new court was set up—juvenile court. The juvenile court system worked to rehabilitate, or correct, a young person's behavior. However, the system still punished some juvenile offenders.

Changes to the System

By the 1960s, people started to think that the punishment juveniles received was too harsh. At times it was even harsher than the punishment adults received for the same crime. Over time, the U.S. Supreme Court ruled that children were entitled to the same legal rights as adults.

These rights included being told of the charges, having an attorney, having an attorney cross-examine witnesses against them, and remaining silent when being questioned. In addition, just like adults, juveniles have to be "guilty beyond a reasonable doubt."

Over time, the crime rates of young offenders began to rise. In the 1990s, the public demanded more severe penalties for juvenile offenders. Many state legislatures passed laws allowing juveniles to be tried as adults when they commit certain crimes.

Juvenile Justice Today

Young people who commit crimes are called **juvenile delinquents.** Although every state has its own laws regarding juveniles, here are some basic considerations:

- Anyone under 18 is a juvenile (in some states, the age is 16).
- A person over the cutoff age is tried as an adult.
- A person below the age is treated as a juvenile.
- A juvenile charged with a felony such as murder can be charged as an adult. In some states, this is automatic. In other states, a judge or prosecutor makes the decision.

Juvenile Offenders

Some crimes committed by juveniles are minor, or less serious. However, there are juveniles who commit armed robbery, murder, and other felonies.

The justice system divides juvenile delinquents into two categories: delinquent offender and status offender. A **delinquent offender** is a young person who has committed an act that would also be a crime if committed by an adult. A **status offender** is a young person who has committed an act that would not be a crime if done by an adult. Such acts include skipping school or running away from home.

3. INFERRING

Why do you think a category for status offenders makes sense?

The Juvenile Court System

Juvenile courts deal with two types of cases concerning juveniles. Cases of neglect involve young people whose caregivers abuse them or do not take care of them properly. When this happens, courts have the power to remove children from their homes and place them under the care of others. Delinquency cases deal with juveniles who have committed crimes.

4. EVALUATING

Is it a good idea to release juveniles to their caregivers or refer them to counseling? Explain your answer.

The Intake Process

Delinquency cases follow a process. Police can take **custody** of a young person. Taking custody means officially taking charge of someone. If a juvenile is caught committing a minor offense, the police can give a warning and release the youth to his or her caregiver. Sometimes the police think the juvenile needs help, such as counseling. Police can then refer the case to a social service agency.

When a youth has committed a felony, he or she will most likely go to juvenile court. A social worker will do a review called an intake and decide what to do. About a third of the cases are dismissed, moved to adult court, or moved to diversion. Diversion means that the youth receives services such as counseling or drug treatment.

The Hearing Process

Juveniles whose cases remain in the juvenile court system have several hearings. A **detention hearing** is like a preliminary hearing. During a detention hearing, the state has to prove it has good reason to think that the juvenile committed the crime.

An **adjudication hearing** is like an adult trial. This hearing has no jury, but evidence is presented, witnesses are called, and witnesses are cross-examined. At the end of the hearing, the judge decides whether the youth is innocent or delinquent.

If a juvenile is found to be delinquent, a **disposition hearing** takes place. This hearing is similar to sentencing. For minor offenses, a youth may be given probation. During this time, the juvenile must follow rules set by the judge. The charges will be dropped and will not appear on the juvenile's record if the youth adheres to the rules. For serious crimes, it is likely the youth will be sent to an institution for young offenders. Most serve for from one to three years.

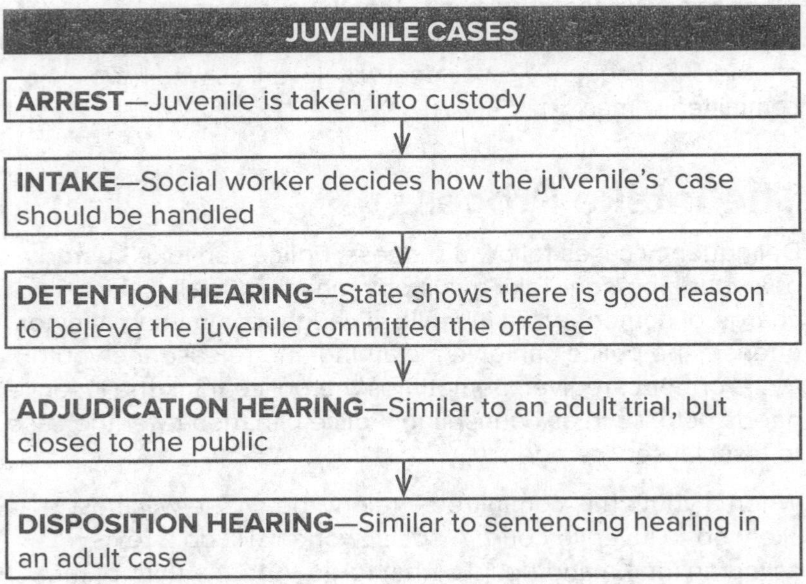

JUVENILE CASES

ARREST—Juvenile is taken into custody

↓

INTAKE—Social worker decides how the juvenile's case should be handled

↓

DETENTION HEARING—State shows there is good reason to believe the juvenile committed the offense

↓

ADJUDICATION HEARING—Similar to an adult trial, but closed to the public

↓

DISPOSITION HEARING—Similar to sentencing hearing in an adult case

5. THEORIZING

Do you think that dropping charges and placing juveniles on probation is a good idea? Explain your answer.

____

____

____

____

____

____

____

____

ANALYZING VISUALS

6. IDENTIFYING Look at the chart. What happens during the detention hearing? What step is it similar to in the criminal process for an adult?

____

____

____

____

____

____

____

Name ______________________ Date ______________ Class __________

REVIEW LESSON 3

1. Complete the chart below to identify the ways the juvenile justice system operates.

THE JUVENILE COURT SYSTEM	
Delinquency Cases What They Are: Who They Are:	**Procedures for Delinquency Cases** The Intake Process: For Misdemeanor: For Felony:
Juveniles' Rights:	**The Hearing Process** Detention Hearing: Adjudication Hearing: Disposition Hearing for Minor Offenses: Disposition Hearing for Felony:

2. **IDENTIFYING CENTRAL IDEAS** On a separate sheet of paper, write an essay in which you explain whether you believe juvenile delinquents are treated fairly by the juvenile court system. Provide evidence from the lesson to support your ideas.

Benchmark Skill Activities

DIRECTIONS: Write your answers on a separate piece of paper.

LAFS.68.WHST.1.2, LAFS.68.WHST.2.4, SS.7.C.3.8, SS.7.C.3.10

1. COMPARING AND CONTRASTING

Use your FOLDABLES to write an essay.

There are some similarities and differences between civil law procedures and criminal law procedures. In your essay, compare and contrast the procedures.

LAFS.68.RH.1.2, LAFS.68.RH.1.3, SS.7.C.3.10

2. ANALYZING TO DETERMINE ESSENTIAL MESSAGE

Make a poster that summarizes the information about one of the three types of law covered in this chapter. Be sure to show how the procedures protect constitutional rights. Also include the powers of the courts and the judicial branch.

LAFS.68.RH.2.4, LAFS.68.WHST.2.4, SS.7.C.3.10

3. USING DEFINITIONS ACCURATELY

Turn to the terms list for this chapter. Choose at least three words to include in a paragraph that summarizes civil law, criminal law, or the juvenile justice system.

LAFS.68.RH.2.4

4. DETERMINING WORD MEANINGS

Read the sentences below. Look at the underlined word in each sentence. Use context clues to help you determine the meaning of each word. Then, write the definitions of the underlined words.

The court said that Jenny had to pay damages in the amount of $3,000 because her cat bit her neighbor.

Steve's attorney was able to uncover a witness during discovery who was able to prove Steve was innocent of all the charges.

The police officially took custody of the young children and took them to child services for safety.

LAFS.68.WHST.2.6, LAFS.68.WHST.3.7, LAFS.68.WHST.3.8, LAFS.68.WHST.3.9, LAFS.68.SL.2.4

5. ANALYZING DATA

At one time, juveniles who were thought to have committed crimes had no rights and were treated, in some cases, more severely than adult offenders. Conduct outside research to find information that traces the treatment of juveniles from the 1800s to the present. Look for both written and visual sources that provide this information. Be sure to assess the credibility of your sources for accuracy.

If possible, make copies of the sources you find. Then, organize your information into a visual presentation using presentation software. Write your information and ideas clearly and efficiently. Include primary or secondary source information in your presentation, but be sure to paraphrase anything that you do not use as a direct quotation. Draw conclusions about what you learned as it relates to the juvenile justice system in general.

Then, present your findings to the class. Be sure to use appropriate eye contact, adequate volume, and clear pronunciation.

Benchmark Note Cards

DIRECTIONS: Use these note cards to help you prepare for the test.

SS.7.C.3.6 Evaluate Constitutional rights and their impact on individuals and society.

CONSTITUTIONAL RIGHTS	The U.S. Constitution grants people many protections. These protections apply to both civil and criminal law. In civil law, the plaintiff and the defendant and their attorneys follow specific procedures. These procedures are based on constitutional rights. They include a trial by jury and the right to appeal. In criminal law, the suspect also has rights guaranteed by the Constitution. Police, prosecutors, and defense attorneys must protect these rights as they do their jobs during a criminal case. The U.S. Supreme Court ruled that juveniles are entitled to the same legal rights as adults. These rights include having an attorney and having to be proven "guilty beyond a reasonable doubt."

SS.7.C.3.8 Analyze the structure, functions, and processes of the legislative, executive, and judicial branches.

PROCESSES IN CIVIL LAW	Civil law cases involve disputes that arise when people think they have been harmed by someone else's actions. They follow these steps: • The plaintiff's attorney files a complaint. The court sends a summons to the defendant. The defendant's attorney may respond. During discovery, the attorneys for both sides check facts, question witnesses, and gather evidence. • Attorneys for the plaintiff and the defendant argue the case in court. This can be a trial by judge or by jury. The court gives a verdict. • At any time in this process, the parties may agree to a settlement. • Either party can appeal to a higher court.

PROCESSES IN CRIMINAL LAW

Criminal law deals with acts that harm people or society and break a criminal law. They follow these steps:

- Police gather evidence for a judge to issue a warrant. During arrest, an accused person is advised of the right to remain silent and the right to a lawyer. At the police station during booking, a record is created and the suspect is photographed and fingerprinted.
- During the preliminary hearing, the suspect of a misdemeanor may plead guilty and is sentenced. If the suspect pleads not guilty, a trial date is set. For a felony, a judge may set bail until a grand jury hears a case and formally charges the suspect. During arraignment, the suspect may plead guilty and is sentenced. For a not guilty plea, a trial date is set.
- The prosecution and defense present the case to a jury or judge during trial. The defendant will be acquitted if found innocent. A judge will sentence the defendant if found guilty. Sentencing is determined based on guidelines.
- A convicted person may appeal to a higher court.

PROCESSES IN JUVENILE JUSTICE

Juvenile courts deal with neglect and delinquency involving children and teenagers under the age of 18. The courts can remove children from homes if the children are neglected or abused. Juvenile delinquents may be categorized as delinquent offenders or status offenders. The juvenile court system follows these procedures:

- Police take custody of a juvenile accused of committing a crime. For a misdemeanor, the police can give a warning and release the youth to his or her caregiver. For a felony, the youth goes to juvenile court. During intake, a social worker decides how the case should be handled.
- Juveniles staying in the system face three different hearings. A detention hearing is like a preliminary hearing for adults. An adjudication hearing is like an adult trial. A disposition hearing is like sentencing. Judges may give juveniles probation with rules to follow. At the end of probation, the charges can be dropped and the record remains clean. Juveniles who commit a serious crime may be sent to an institution for young offenders. Some juveniles may be tried as adults for certain crimes.

SS.7.C.3.10 Identify sources and types (civil, criminal, constitutional, military) of law.

BRANCHES OF CIVIL LAW	Civil law has to do with disputes. It has the following branches: • Contract law—relates to written or oral agreements to exchange something of value • Property law—relates to buying, selling, transferring of property, and rights of owners and renters • Family law—relates to issues of birth, marriage, divorce, adoption, and death • Personal injury law—relates to torts, wrongful actions that cause injury to another person or damage to property (intentional or negligent)

TYPES OF CRIMINAL LAW	A misdemeanor is a minor crime for which a person can be fined a small sum of money or jailed for up to a year. A felony is a serious crime that is punishable by more than one year in prison. Some crimes can be either a misdemeanor or a felony, depending on the amount of damage or the amount of money stolen. A crime against property is likely to be a misdemeanor, while a crime against a person is a violent crime and is likely to be a felony.

SS.7.C.3.11 Diagram the levels, functions, and powers of courts at the state and federal levels.

COURTS IN CIVIL LAW	Florida's civil court system includes county courts, circuit courts, and district courts of appeal. County courts hear civil cases involving disputes over amounts of $15,000 or less. Circuit courts hear civil cases involving disputes over amounts of more than $15,000, family law matters, and appeals from county courts. District courts of appeal hear appeals from lower courts.

Chapter 16

VISUAL SUMMARY

DIRECTIONS: Complete the graphic organizers below.

CIVIL LAW PROCESS					
Plaintiff's attorney files a complaint.		Attorney for defendant files a written answer.			

CRIMINAL LAW PROCESS

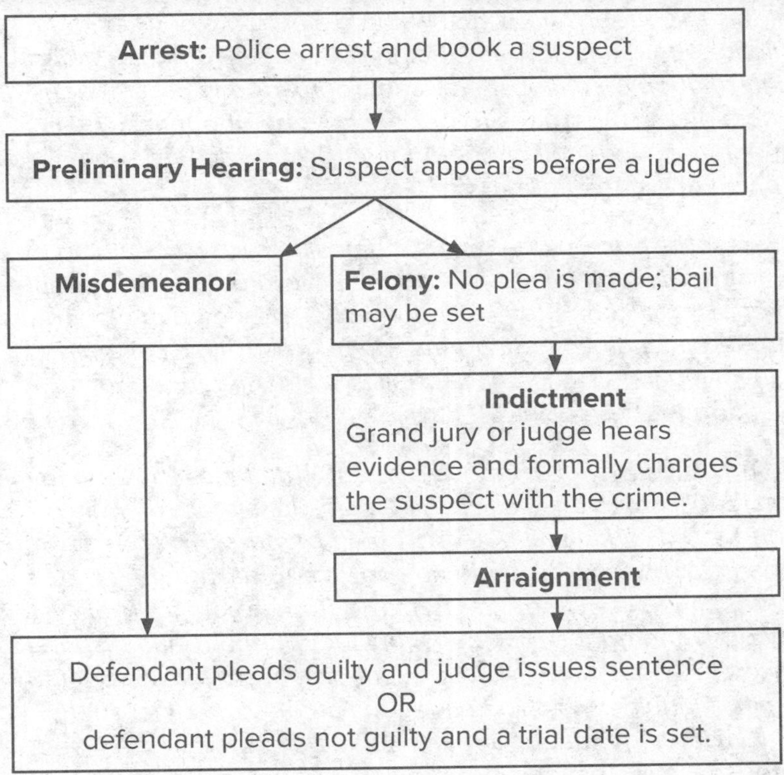

Arrest: Police arrest and book a suspect
Preliminary Hearing: Suspect appears before a judge
Misdemeanor
Felony: No plea is made; bail may be set
Indictment
Grand jury or judge hears evidence and formally charges the suspect with the crime.
Arraignment
Defendant pleads guilty and judge issues sentence
OR
defendant pleads not guilty and a trial date is set.

JUVENILE JUSTICE PROCESS				
Arrest		**Detention Hearing**	**Adjudication Hearing**	
	Social workers decide how the juvenile's case should be handled.			

USING PRIMARY SOURCES

INTERPRET Below are two primary sources related to the law. Read both documents. Then, answer the questions that follow on a separate sheet of paper.

Document A

In order to have a fair and lawful trial, there are rules that all jurors must follow. A basic rule is that jurors must decide the case only on the evidence presented in the courtroom. You must not communicate with anyone, including friends and family members, about this case, the people and places involved, or your jury service. You must not disclose [make public] your thoughts about this case or ask for advice on how to decide this case.

I want to stress that this rule means you must not use electronic devices or cell phones to communicate about this case, including tweeting, texting, blogging, e-mailing, posting information on a website or chat room, or any other means at all. Do not send or accept any messages to or from anyone about this case or your jury service. In addition, your cell phone or electronic device must be turned completely off while you are in the courtroom.

You must not do any research or look up words, names, [maps], or anything else that may have anything to do with this case. This includes reading newspapers, watching television or using a computer, cell phone, the Internet, any electronic device, or any other means at all, to get information related to this case or the people and places involved in this case. This applies whether you are in the courthouse, at home, or anywhere else.

All of us are depending on you to follow these rules, so that there will be a fair and lawful resolution [decision] to this case. Unlike questions that you may be allowed to ask in court, . . . if you investigate, research or make inquiries on your own outside of the courtroom, the trial judge has no way to assure they are proper and relevant [apply] to the case. . . . That is contrary to our judicial system, which assures every party the right to ask questions about and rebut [dispute] the evidence being considered against it and to present argument with respect to that evidence. Non-court inquiries and investigations unfairly and improperly prevent the parties from having that opportunity our judicial system promises. Any juror who violates these restrictions jeopardizes [threatens] the fairness of these proceedings, and a mistrial could result that would require the entire trial process to start over. A mistrial is a tremendous expense and inconvenience to the parties, the court, and the taxpayers. If you violate these rules, you may be held in contempt [disrespect] of court, and face sanctions [punishments], such as serving time in jail, paying a fine or both.

If you become aware of any violation of these instructions or any other instruction I give in this case, you must tell me by giving a note to the [court deputy] [bailiff].

—Florida State Supreme Court, Standard Jury Instructions, Criminal Cases

Document B

Amendment IV
The right of the people to be secure [safe] in their persons, houses, papers, and effects, against unreasonable searches and seizures [taking], shall not be violated, and no Warrants [authorization] shall issue, but upon probable cause, supported by Oath or affirmation [declaration], and particularly describing the place to be searched, and the persons or things to be seized.

Amendment V
No person shall be held to answer for a capital, or otherwise infamous crime, unless on a presentment [charge] or indictment of a Grand Jury, except in cases arising in the land or naval forces, or in the Militia, when in actual service in time of War or public danger; nor shall any person be subject for the same offence to be twice put in jeopardy of life or limb; nor shall be compelled [forced] in any criminal case to be a witness against himself, nor be deprived of life, liberty, or property, without due process of law; nor shall private property be taken for public use, without just compensation [payment].

Amendment VI
In all criminal prosecutions, the accused shall enjoy the right to a speedy and public trial, by an impartial [fair] jury of the State and district wherein the crime shall have been committed, which district shall have been previously ascertained [made sure] by law, and to be informed of the nature and cause of the accusation; to be confronted with the witnesses against him; to have compulsory [forced] process for obtaining witnesses in his favor, and to have the Assistance of Counsel for his defence.

Amendment VIII
Excessive [too much] bail shall not be required, nor excessive fines imposed [set], nor cruel and unusual punishments inflicted.

—U.S. Constitution

1. How are Documents A and B related?
2. What is the purpose of Amendment IV of Document B?
3. Reread the first paragraph in Document A. Underline the detail that tells how jurors must decide the case. Why is this a necessary rule? To which part of Document B do these details most closely relate?
4. Reread the fourth paragraph in Document A. Underline the details related to the action that would be in violation of the proper functioning of the judicial system.
5. Paraphrase Amendment IV from Document B. Then, indicate which part of the criminal law process relates to this amendment.
6. Why do you think Amendment VIII of Document B is necessary?

Chapter Practice Test

DIRECTIONS: Circle the best answer for each question.

---

1 **SS.7.C.3.11 (Moderate)**

The diagram below shows some of the steps involved in a civil law case.

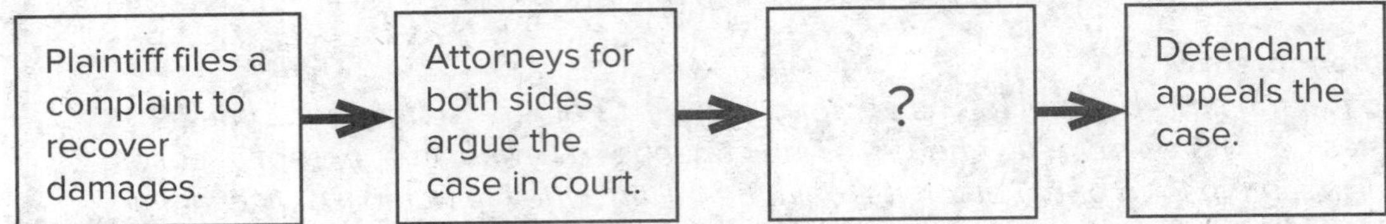

Plaintiff files a complaint to recover damages.
Attorneys for both sides argue the case in court.
?
Defendant appeals the case.

Which step is missing from the diagram?

A Accused has a bail hearing.

B Court gives a verdict.

C Attorney is appointed.

D Defendant is arrested.

---

2 **SS.7.C.3.6 (High)**

What amendment protects from illegal searches and seizures?

A Amendment IV

B Amendment V

C Amendment VI

D Amendment VIII

3 **SS.7.C.3.8 (High)**

Read the scenario below.

Jamie ordered books and a bookcase. When the goods arrived, they were damaged so Jamie did not pay the bill. The company filed a complaint against Jamie.

What will happen next?

A The court will issue an arrest warrant based on the evidence.

B Jamie will have to pay for the books and the bookcase.

C The court will issue a summons for Jamie to appear in court.

D Jamie will appeal the court's decision because it was unjust.

---

4 **SS.7.C.3.10 (Moderate)**

Which is an example of a status offense?

A spray painting graffiti on a bus

B driving too fast in a school zone

C shoplifting from a grocery store

D running away from home

5 **SS.7.C.3.8 (Moderate)**

Read the scenario below.

A tree from your yard fell on your neighbor's house. The cost to repair the house is $8,000. Your neighbor decides to sue you for damages.

Which Florida court will hear the case?

A circuit court

B county court

C federal court

D district court of appeals

SS.7.C.3.8 (High)

How did the U.S. Supreme Court affect the juvenile justice system during the 1960s and 1970s?

A It refused to hear cases on the matter, saying that juvenile offenders were the responsibility of the state.

B It ruled that due process rights for juveniles are the same as those for adults.

C It ruled that juvenile offenders were to be treated as they had been treated in the past.

D It set up programs meant to rehabilitate juvenile offenders so the courts would be less crowded.

7 **SS.7.C.3.10 (Moderate)**

Read the scenario below.

A man is seen on a videotape robbing a convenience store. He is arrested and then has a trial. The jury finds him guilty of burglary. The judge sentences him to seven years in prison.

Which type of law is being followed?

A juvenile

B civil

C criminal

D appeals

---

8 **SS.7.C.3.6 (High)**

Read the excerpt below.

> *"In all criminal prosecutions, the accused shall enjoy the right to a speedy and public trial, by an impartial [fair] jury of the State and district wherein the crime shall have been committed, which district shall have been previously ascertained [made sure] by law, and to be informed of the nature and cause of the accusation; to be confronted with the witnesses against him; to have compulsory [forced] process for obtaining witnesses in his favor, and to have the Assistance of Counsel for his defence."*
>
> —Amendment VI of the U.S. Constitution

Which of these does Amendment VI specifically prohibit?

A setting an immediate date for a trial

B selecting jurors who are biased

C allowing witnesses to testify

D holding a trial in the defendant's district

9

SS.7.C.3.10 (Moderate)

Which of the following punishments would most likely be given to an adult convicted of committing a felony?

A a fine of $100

B six months in prison

C five years in prison

D community service

SS.7 .C.3.11 (High)

Read the excerpt below.

> *"The Supreme Court of Florida has said that the legislature intended the State's electors to "participat[e] fully in the federal electoral process . . ." That statute, in turn, requires that any controversy [dispute] or contest that is designed to lead to a conclusive [definite] selection of electors be completed by December 12. That date is upon us, and there is no recount procedure in place under the State Supreme Court's order that comports [agrees] with minimal constitutional standards. Because it is evident that any recount seeking to meet the December 12 date will be unconstitutional for the reasons we have discussed, we reverse the judgment of the Supreme Court of Florida ordering a recount to proceed."*
>
> —*Bush* v. *Gore*, 2000

What conclusion can be drawn from this excerpt?

A An appeal was made to a higher court to change a ruling made by a lower court.

B The requirement to recount votes in a presidential election is not a legal process.

C A lower court was not capable of making a fair decision within a specific time frame.

D A higher court made a decision that impacted the laws in the state of Florida.

Introduction to Economics

Chapter Overview

People in every society must balance their wants and needs with what they have available. They must answer some important questions: What will be produced? How will these things be produced? Who will use them? The study of how societies do this is called economics.

There are different ways to make choices. This results in different economic systems. The economy of the United States depends on the interaction between consumers and producers in a market system and the choices each group makes.

CHAPTER BENCHMARKS

SS.7.E.1.1 Explain how the principles of a market and mixed economy helped to develop the United States into a democratic nation.

SS.7.E.1.3 Review the concepts of supply and demand, choice, scarcity, and opportunity cost as they relate to the development of the mixed market economy in the United States.

SS.7.E.1.5 Assess how profits, incentives, and competition motivate individuals, households, and businesses in a free market economy.

LAFS.68.RH.1.1 Cite specific textual evidence to support analysis of primary and secondary sources.

LAFS.68.RH.1.3 Identify key steps in a text's description of a process related to history/social studies (e.g., how a bill becomes law, how interest rates are raised or lowered).

LAFS.68.WHST.2.5 With some guidance and support from peers and adults, develop and strengthen writing as needed by planning, revising, editing, rewriting, or trying a new approach, focusing on how well purpose and audience have been addressed.

MAFS.K12.MP.1.1 Make sense of problems and persevere in solving them.

MAFS.K12.MP.6.1 Attend to precision.

WHAT I NEED TO KNOW

TERMS

- ☐ want
- ☐ resource
- ☐ scarcity
- ☐ traditional economy
- ☐ market economy
- ☐ command economy
- ☐ mixed market economy
- ☐ trade-off
- ☐ opportunity cost
- ☐ revenue
- ☐ fixed cost
- ☐ variable cost
- ☐ total cost
- ☐ marginal cost
- ☐ marginal revenue
- ☐ marginal analysis
- ☐ benefit-cost analysis
- ☐ consumer
- ☐ demand
- ☐ producer
- ☐ supply
- ☐ market
- ☐ competition
- ☐ equilibrium price
- ☐ surplus
- ☐ shortage

Introduction to Economics

Introduction to Economics

Make this three-pocket Foldable® and label the pockets *Economics*, *Economic Decisions*, and *Market Economy*. Use quarter sheets of notebook paper or note cards as information cards. Label note cards to correspond to the pocket in which they are sorted and stored. As you read the chapter, write terms, names, dates, and events on the front of each note card. On the back of each card, write a description of the term listed on the front. When possible, include a quick sketch to strengthen your recall.

Step 1
Take a legal sized piece of paper (8.5" x 14") and place it lengthwise on your desk. Fold the bottom edge of the paper one-third of the way up the page.

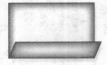

Step 2
Fold the left and right sides of the paper to create three equal sections.

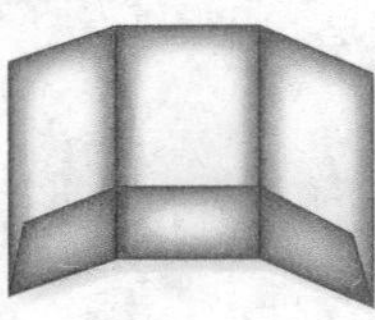

Step 3
Tape or staple the open right and left sides of the pockets.

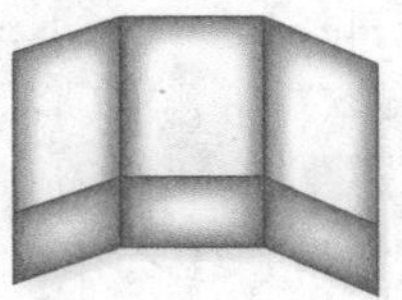

Step 4
Label the pockets and use note cards or cut notebook paper for notes.

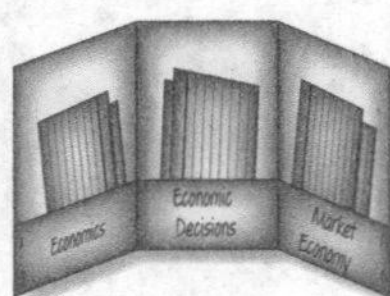

LESSON 1 SUMMARY

What Is Economics?

SS.7.E.1.1, SS.7.E.1.3, SS.7.E.1.6

Our Wants and Resources

Wants are desires people have that can be fulfilled by getting a product or a service. Because most people have a limited amount of money, they must choose between wants. For example, you might want to buy two different items in a store, but you have money to buy only one. Most people have long lists of wants. That is why we say wants are unlimited.

Economists separate wants into two categories: goods and services. Goods are physical objects, or things we can touch. Services are work or actions, such as being examined by a doctor or getting a haircut.

Limited Resources

Unlike wants, resources are limited. **Resources** are all the things that can be used to provide goods or services. Economics is the study of how people use limited resources to satisfy their unlimited wants. There are three basic types of resources: natural resources, labor, and capital.

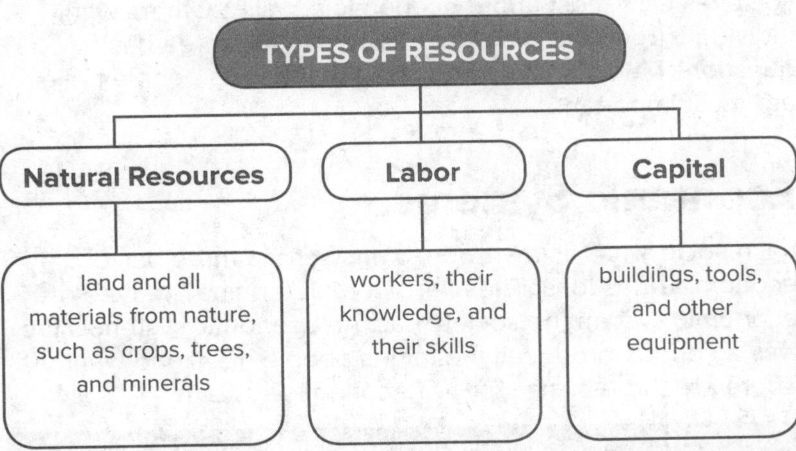

The Basic Economic Problem

Everyone must choose between competing wants. At the same time, no one—whether a person, an organization, or a government—has all of the resources it wants. This creates **scarcity.** In economic terms, scarcity happens when we do not have all the resources we need to satisfy all the wants we have. The purpose of economics is to look at how individuals and societies deal with this basic economic problem.

ANALYZING VISUALS

1. DIFFERENTIATING

Mark each of the following resources as natural resources, labor/human resources, or capital resources. Use N for natural resources, L for labor/human resources, and C for capital resources.

_________ timber

_________ minerals

_________ office building

_________ woodworking

_________ truck

_________ teacher

2. COMPARING

What economic problem do both individuals and countries face?

____

____

____

____

____

Name ______________________ Date ______________ Class __________

3. THEORIZING

A country has large natural gas and petroleum deposits. How is it likely to answer the three basic economic questions?

____

____

____

____

____

____

____

____

____

____

____

ANALYZING VISUALS

4. ASSESSING In which economic system would it be easiest to create and sell a new invention? Explain your choice.

____

____

____

____

____

____

____

____

____

Societies and Economic Choices

Scarcity forces all societies to make choices. These economic choices are guided by three questions: What goods and services will be produced? How will they be produced? Who will consume, or use, them?

Each society must decide *what* goods and services to produce. Countries take into account their natural, labor, and capital resources when they make these decisions. For example, a nation with a lot of fertile land and a long growing season is likely to use its land for farming.

Once a society has decided what goods and services to produce, it must decide *how* to produce them. For example, the society must decide if goods are better produced by large manufacturing companies or by small businesses.

Once the goods and services are produced, a society must decide *who* gets them. The choices made about distributing goods affect how the goods are consumed. Should the goods be made available to everyone? Or should they be reserved for certain groups?

A society's economic decisions are determined by more than their resources. The society's values are also a factor. Some societies care most about economic equality. Others want individual freedom. Different answers to the three basic questions help a society promote the ideas its people believe are most important.

Economic Systems

Each society has its own way to answer the three basic economic questions. These answers determine the type of economic system the society has. An economic system is the way a country produces the things people need and want. There are three basic types of economic systems.

BASIC ECONOMIC SYSTEMS		
Traditional Economy	**Market Economy**	**Command Economy**
• Habit or custom answers the economic questions. • These economies are less productive and less likely to change their ways of doing things.	• Individuals and businesses use profit and price to answer the economic questions. • Choices are based on how to make the most profit.	• Government answers the economic questions. • Government makes economic decisions. Individuals and businesses have limited input.

The American Economy

The United States has a **mixed market economy,** combining elements of all three economic systems. Just like in a market economy, businesses compete for profit. Individuals and businesses decide what to produce. Prices determine who consumes the products. However, the government is involved in the economy, making sure that businesses act fairly and honestly. Government makes rules about the treatment of workers. It also provides services, such as education, national defense, and disaster relief. A bit of a traditional economy is found in the United States, too. It is not unusual, for example, for people to work in the same industry as their parents.

5. MAKING CONNECTIONS

In what way is the mixed market economy of the United States a democratic system?

REVIEW LESSON 1

1. Use the diagram below to identify key economic ideas and concepts.

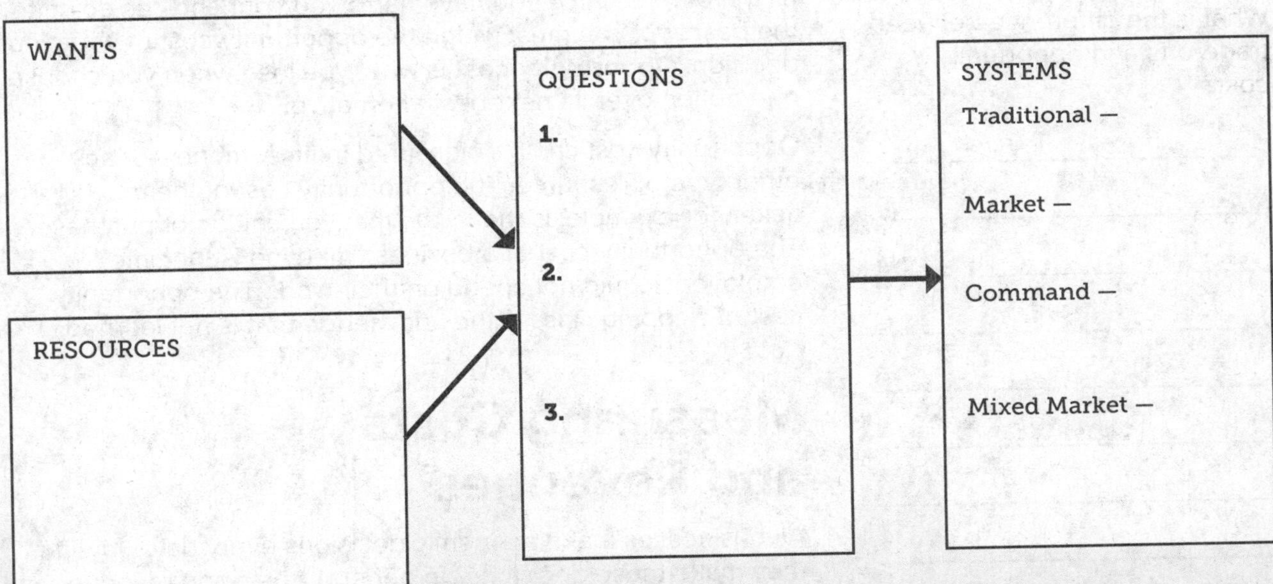

2. **PROBLEM SOLVING** Adrian wants to open a business. Write an essay to explain the decisions Adrian will need to make as he prepares his plans. Use a separate sheet of paper for your essay.

LESSON 2 SUMMARY

Economic Decisions

1. DRAWING CONCLUSIONS

What is the opportunity cost if a city builds an office building instead of a park?

2. CONTRASTING

What is the difference between trade-offs and opportunity cost?

SS.7.E.1.3, SS.7.E.1.5

Trade-Offs

When you choose between wants, you are making a trade-off. A **trade-off** is giving up one good or service for another. When you buy a movie ticket, you are giving money in exchange for the service of seeing a film. The trade-off is that you cannot use that same money to buy music. Trade-offs apply to more than just money. They also apply to how you spend your time. When you decide to do your homework instead of playing a video game, you are making a trade-off.

Businesses and governments also make trade-offs. Every choice they make about where and how to spend their money is a trade-off. Money spent on advertising cannot be used to hire workers. Money spent on schools cannot be spent on the military.

Opportunity Costs

When you make a trade-off, you are choosing one option over all the others. Once you have narrowed your choices down to the best two, you must weigh the opportunity cost of your final decision. **Opportunity cost** is what you lose when you choose one option over its next-best alternative.

Opportunity cost can be measured in time, money, or any other type of resource. The opportunity cost of the movie ticket, for example, is the music that you could not purchase. The opportunity cost of a business meeting is the time employees could not spend on their work. The opportunity cost of skipping class is the knowledge that is not learned.

Measuring Costs and Revenues

All businesses make economic decisions every day. How do they make these decisions? In general, costs and revenue determine what economic decisions a business makes. Costs are money spent. **Revenue** is money earned.

Assessing Costs

Businesses have different types of costs. **Fixed costs** are expenses that do not change no matter how much a business produces. Rent and insurance are fixed costs. Expenses that depend on how much a business produces are called **variable costs.** Labor and supplies are variable costs. **Total cost** is the combination of fixed and variable costs.

When businesses think about making a decision, they usually consider increasing or decreasing activities in small amounts. What would it cost to stay open one more hour? What would it cost to make one more cabinet in a day? The increase in expenses to produce one more unit of something is called **marginal cost.**

Different Types of Revenues

Revenue is the total amount of money a business collects from selling its goods or services. In making business decisions, however, businesses must consider marginal revenue rather than total revenue. **Marginal revenue** is the additional income each additional unit of sales brings to the business.

Marginal Analysis

Marginal analysis compares marginal revenue with marginal cost. If the additional revenue is greater than what it costs to produce more of it, the rule is to make the change. If the additional cost is equal to or greater than the additional revenue, the rule is to keep things the same.

3. MAKING INFERENCES

During economic downturns, what costs would a business cut? Why?

______

______

______

______

______

______

______

______

______

______

Name ______________________ Date ______________ Class ________

ANALYZING VISUALS

4. INTERPRETING

Based on the graph on Tony's tables, what would happen if Tony increased production by four tables?

____

____

____

____

____

____

ANALYZING VISUALS

5. CALCULATING

Study the Benefit-Cost Analysis chart. What is the benefit-cost ratio for an additional option, Option D, with revenue of $120 and cost of $75? Which of the four options should the business choose? Why?

____

____

____

____

____

____

____

____

____

____

For example, Tony wants to increase production at his table company. This graph illustrates the marginal costs and revenues involved in producing more tables. For each additional table, the marginal cost goes up and the marginal revenue goes down. For two additional tables, the benefits are still higher than the cost, so Tony will make the tables. At the third table, marginal cost and benefit are the same. From here on out, Tony sees no benefit, so he won't make more tables.

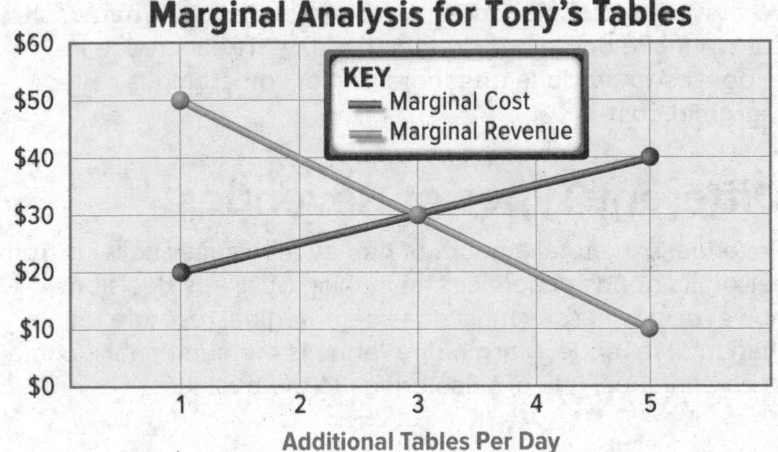

Benefit-Cost Analysis

Marginal analysis is useful for making a single decision. For more complex situations, benefit-cost analysis can be more helpful. **Benefit-cost analysis** uses a ratio to compare benefit and cost.

To calculate the benefit-cost ratio, the size of the benefit is divided by the size of the cost. Businesses use these ratios to choose among two or more options. The option with the highest ratio is the best choice. The chart shows how this is calculated.

BENEFIT-COST ANALYSIS			
	Benefit (Revenue)	Cost	Benefit-Cost Ratio
Option A	$140	$95	140/95 = 1.47
Option B	$125	$80	125/80 = 1.56
Option C	$100	$65	100/65 = 1.54

Thinking Like an Economist

Most everyday decisions cannot be thought of in money terms. However, marginal analysis can still be applied. This is called "thinking like an economist." Suppose you are thinking about sleeping past your alarm in the morning. A line graph of this marginal benefit would slope downward the longer you oversleep. Then there is the opportunity cost of the other things you could not do because you were sleeping. The longer you sleep, the greater the marginal cost would be.

6. MAKING CONNECTIONS

How can thinking like an economist help you better manage your money?

____

____

____

____

____

____

REVIEW LESSON 2

1. Use the chart to make notes about the different ways to make economic decisions.

OPPORTUNITY COST	
MARGINAL ANALYSIS	
BENEFIT-COST ANALYSIS	

2. **PROBLEM SOLVING** Alma is a tutor and charges $25 an hour. She meets with each of her three clients for one hour a week. Alma wants to take on a fourth client. What is the opportunity cost for Alma? What is the marginal analysis? Write an essay explaining which choice Alma should make, and why. Use a separate sheet of paper.

LESSON 3 SUMMARY

Demand and Supply in a Market Economy

1. RECOGNIZING RELATIONSHIPS

Are the words *consumers* and *producers* synonyms or antonyms? What about *demand* and *supply*? How do you know?

2. REASONING

Why does demand have so many parts to its definition?

SS.7.E.1.1, SS.7.E.1.3, SS.7.E.1.5

Demand and Supply Make Markets

In a command economy, the government decides what is produced and how. It also sets the prices for most goods and services. In market economies, such as we have in the United States, the forces of demand and supply determine prices.

Consumers are the people who buy goods and services. They determine demand. **Demand** measures how much consumers are willing and able to buy at various prices during a given time period. This definition has four different parts:

- *How much*—Demand measures the amount, or number of items, consumers will buy at different prices.
- *Willingness to buy*—Consumers must want to buy a good or service.
- *Ability to buy*—Consumers must have the money available to buy a good or service.
- *Price*—Consumers demand more when prices are low and demand less when prices are high.

Producers are the people or businesses that provide goods and services. They determine supply. **Supply** is a measure of how much producers are willing and able to sell. When prices rise, producers tend to provide more. When prices drop, they tend to provide less.

Markets and Competition

Charts called schedules can be used to show the amount of an item demanded or supplied at each price. This information can then be put in lines on a graph. The lines are called the *demand curve* and *supply curve*. An example is shown on the next page. It shows the demand and supply for crude oil. Crude oil is used to make gasoline, heating oil, jet fuel, and a variety of other products.

Name ______________________ Date ______________ Class ________

Demand and Supply for Crude Oil

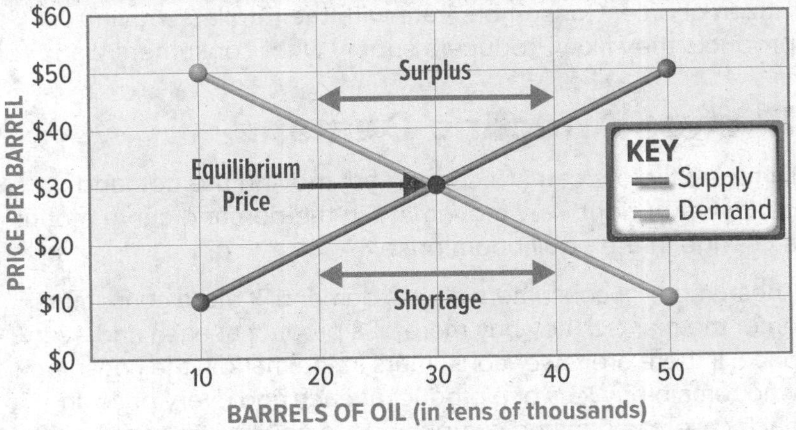

Each line in the schedule is shown as a point on the line graph. The demand curve shows the amount demanded at different prices. It curves down to the right because people tend to buy more when the price is low and less when the price is high. The supply curve shows the quantity supplied at different prices. It curves the opposite way because producers tend to supply more when the price is high and less when the price is low.

The graph shows a *market*. A **market** is where buyers and sellers of a good or service meet. It can be a physical location or a Web site. To work effectively, markets need competition. **Competition** is the struggle among sellers to attract buyers. This struggle helps control prices. If there are too few sellers, prices might stay too high. For that reason, the United States has laws that protect competition.

How Prices Are Set

A free market sets its own prices based on demand and supply. This makes free markets efficient. Look at the graph "Demand and Supply for Crude Oil." The point where the demand curve and supply curve meet is called the **equilibrium price.** That is the price the market sets for a good or service. At this price, the amount consumers want to buy equals the amount producers are willing to provide.

When producers provide more than consumers are willing to buy, it is called a **surplus.** A surplus tends to cause prices to fall until they reach the equilibrium level. When consumers want more than producers have provided, it is called a **shortage.** A shortage causes prices to rise until they reach the equilibrium level.

ANALYZING VISUALS

3. INTERPRETING Look at the Demand and Supply for Crude Oil graph. What happens to demand as supply increases? What happens to supply as demand increases?

____

____

____

____

____

4. PREDICTING CONSEQUENCES

Would the equilibrium price increase or decrease if the number of consumers grew? Why?

____

____

____

____

____

____

____

____

____

____

5. POSING QUESTIONS

Marco makes furniture. He is thinking about making and selling a new style of chair. What questions should he ask to determine if this is a good decision?

Markets are essential to the economy of the United States. Like American democracy, a market economy is based on citizen choice. Consumers vote with their dollars, buying products they like. Producers supply what consumers want.

Factors Affecting Demand

Different factors can affect demand, moving the demand curve left or right. Any movement in the demand curve means a change in the equilibrium price.

The number of consumers affects demand. If more consumers enter the market, they buy more of a product at each and every price. If there are fewer consumers in the market, the consumers who remain buy less of a product at each and every price. In each case, the demand curve—and the equilibrium price—shifts.

Changes in consumer income also affect demand. When people earn more, they have more money to spend. Demand goes up, resulting in a rise in the equilibrium price. When people earn less, they have less money to spend. The equilibrium price drops.

Changes in consumer interest are the third factor affecting demand. If more consumers like and buy a product, the equilibrium price increases. If consumers lose interest in a product, the equilibrium price decreases.

Factors Affecting Supply

Supply can also change, usually because of the number of suppliers and the costs of production. More suppliers mean more products in the market. As the quantity of products available in the marketplace increases, the price goes down. If the number of suppliers drops, however, the quantity of products available decreases, and prices go up. When consumers have fewer choices, producers can charge more.

Costs of production also affect supply. When costs increase, producers supply less, and the equilibrium price rises. If producers find ways to reduce their costs, they can supply more. This will drive the equilibrium price down.

The Economic Role of Prices

Prices drive the markets for goods and services in a market economy. They measure value, help consumers and producers make economic decisions, and help answer the three basic economic questions. First, prices help producers decide what to produce. High consumer demand for a product drives the price of that product up. Businesses produce more to meet demand. The reverse is also true. Lower consumer demand means lower prices and less production.

LESSON 3 SUMMARY, *continued*

Second, prices influence how goods and services are produced. Producers look for ways to keep their costs low. They hope they can make goods at a price consumers are willing to pay. Third, prices help answer the question, "Who will use the product?" Goods and services are provided for consumers—but only those consumers who can and will buy them at a certain price.

Prices serve as a measure of value. In a market economy, every good and service has a price. That price determines the value of that good or service on that day. Consumers and producers then use the prices to measure the value of what they buy. They also use prices to compare the values of various goods and services available.

Prices work as signals, too. Consumers will not buy items whose prices are too high. Producers must lower prices for these items if they expect to sell them. The reverse is also true. When consumers cannot buy a product at the low price they want, they must realize that producers are not able to provide the product at that price. Consumers must be willing to pay a higher price or do without the product.

6. PRIORITIZING

Which role of prices do you think is most important? Explain.

REVIEW LESSON 3

1. Use the chart to make notes about demand, supply, and prices in a market economy.

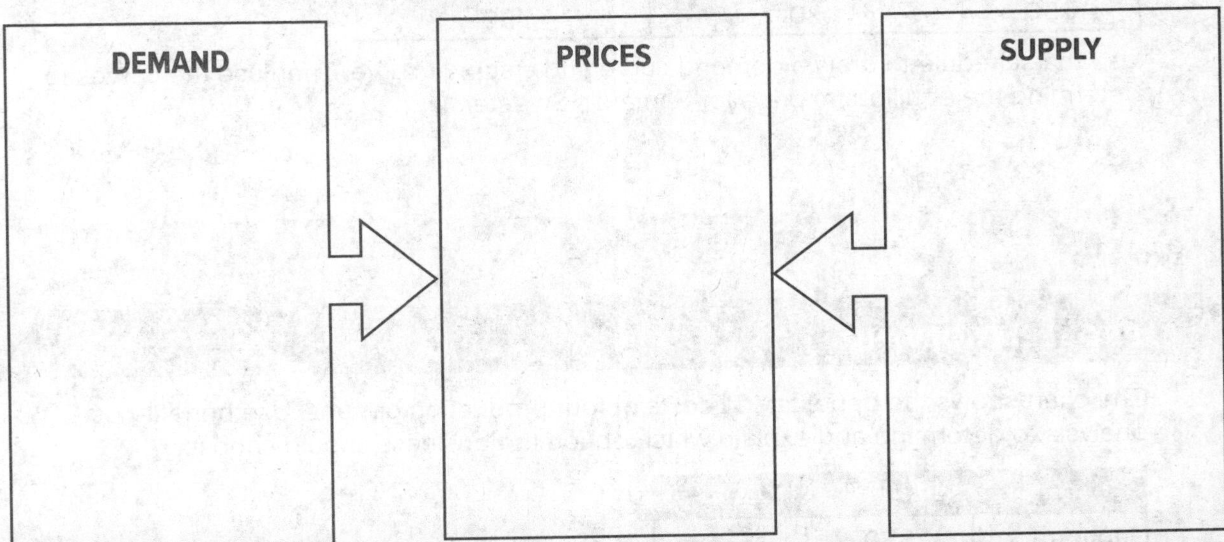

2. **PREDICTING CONSEQUENCES** An average laptop computer sells for about $500. What would happen to that price if consumers stopped buying laptops? What would happen to that price if more companies began making more laptops? On a separate sheet of paper, write an essay to explain each scenario.

Benchmark Skill Activities

DIRECTIONS: Write your answers on a separate piece of paper.

LAFS.68.RH.1.3

1. IDENTIFYING STEPS IN A PROCESS

Use your FOLDABLES to write an essay explaining how a market economy works. Include how decisions are made and how prices are set.

MAFS.K12.MP.6.1

2. CREATING GRAPHS

The chart is a demand and supply schedule for Samara's Sweaters.

PRICE	QUANTITY DEMANDED	QUANTITY SUPPLIED
$10	100	30
$20	80	60
$30	60	90
$40	40	120
$50	20	150

Use the schedule to draw a demand curve and a supply curve. Then use the curves to determine the equilibrium price for Samara's Sweaters.

MAFS.K12.MP.1.1

3. PROBLEM SOLVING

The chart shows the benefits and costs of four production options. Use benefit-cost analysis to determine and explain which option the business should choose.

	BENEFIT	COST
Option 1	$90	$35
Option 2	$75	$30
Option 3	$60	$25
Option 4	$45	$20

LAFS.68.WHST.2.5

4. INFORMATIVE/EXPLANATORY

Create a graphic novel that teaches the information from Lesson 1 of this chapter. Use a storyboard to plan the text and images. Trade rough drafts with a partner to edit plans before submitting the final version.

LAFS.68.RH.1.1

5. ANALYZING PRIMARY SOURCES

In 1933, President Franklin D. Roosevelt announced a plan to help end the Great Depression by creating jobs. Read his announcement. Then write an essay to explain how Roosevelt's plan would affect demand, supply, and prices. Cite specific details from the excerpt to support your explanation.

> *First, we are giving opportunity of employment to one-quarter of a million of the unemployed, especially the young men who have dependents [children or others they support], to go into the forestry and flood prevention work. This is a big task because it means feeding, clothing and caring for nearly twice as many men as we have in the regular army itself. In creating this civilian conservation corps we are killing two birds with one stone. We are clearly enhancing [improving] the value of our natural resources and second, we are relieving [making less painful] an appreciable [considerable] amount of actual distress [hardship]. This great group of men have entered upon their work on a purely voluntary basis, no military training is involved and we are conserving not only our natural resources but our human resources. One of the great values to this work is the fact that it is direct and requires the intervention [involvement] of very little machinery. Second, I have requested the Congress and have secured action upon a proposal to put the great properties owned by our Government at Muscle Shoals to work after long years of wasteful inaction, and with this a broad plan for the improvement of a vast area in the Tennessee Valley. It will add to the comfort and happiness of hundreds of thousands of people and the incident benefits will reach the entire nation.*
>
> —President Franklin D. Roosevelt, Fireside Chat, May 7, 1933

Benchmark Note Cards

DIRECTIONS: Use these note cards to help you prepare for the test.

SS.7.E.1.1 Explain how the principles of a market and mixed economy helped to develop the United States into a democratic nation.

DEMOCRATIC PRINCIPLES	Market and mixed-market economies depend on consumer choice to drive the market. Consumer choice is similar to democracy because the people hold the power. Just like citizens vote for leaders on a ballot, consumers vote for products with their spending dollars.

SS.7.E.1.3 Review the concepts of supply and demand, choice, scarcity, and opportunity cost as they relate to the development of the mixed market economy in the United States.

SUPPLY	• the amount producers are willing and able to sell at a certain price • influenced by the number of producers and production costs • goes up when prices go up, and goes down when prices drop

DEMAND	• the amount consumers are willing and able to buy at a certain price • influenced by the number of consumers, the amount consumers have to spend, and consumer interest • goes up when prices go down, and goes down when prices rise

CHOICE	Choices about how to answer the three basic economic questions determine a nation's economic system. These basic economic questions are • What goods and services will be produced? • How will they be produced? • Who will consume them? Consumers and producers have limited resources. They must make choices about what to buy or what to produce. These choices determine the market.

SCARCITY	People, businesses, and governments have unlimited wants but limited resources. This is called *scarcity.* Because of scarcity, choices and trade-offs must be made. These choices and trade-offs determine the market.

OPPORTUNITY COST	• what is lost when one option is chosen over its next-best alternative • can be measured in time, money, or other resources

SS.7.E.1.5 Assess how profits, incentives, and competition motivate individuals, households, and businesses in a free market economy

MOTIVATIONS IN A FREE MARKET ECONOMY	• Consumers—individuals and households—seek to buy goods and services at a price they can afford. • Producers—people and businesses—seek to supply goods and services at a price that will attract consumers and cover their costs. • Competition ensures that prices do not get too high and that consumers have a range of producers to choose from.

Chapter 17

VISUAL SUMMARY

DIRECTIONS: Complete the graphic organizers below.

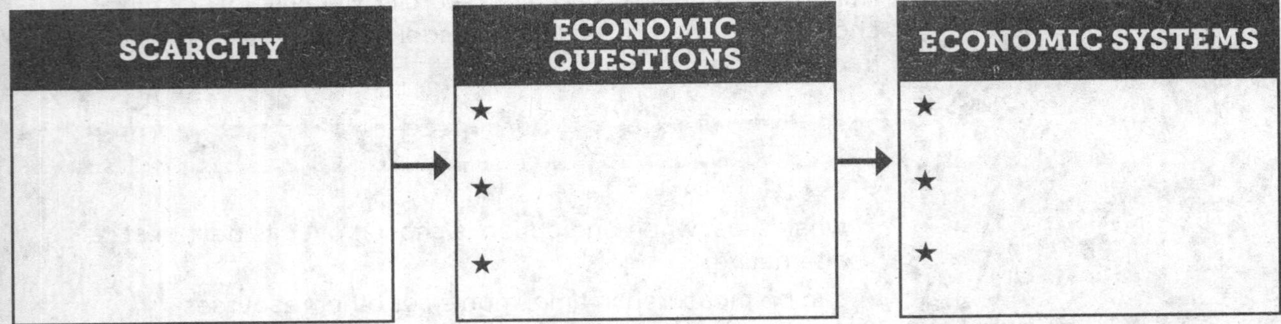

CHOICES IN A MARKET ECONOMY

Trade-Offs and Opportunity Cost

Marginal Analysis

Benefit-Cost Analysis

MARKET SYSTEMS

Demand

Supply

Competition

Prices

USING PRIMARY SOURCES

COMPARE AND CONTRAST Below are two explanations of economics. On another sheet of paper, write an essay that paraphrases and compares the explanations. Also identify the major economic concepts they address. Then explain how these concepts embody the idea of "thinking like an economist."

Explanation 1

Economics is, at root, the study of incentives [encouragements]: how people get what they want, or need, especially when other people want or need the same thing. . . . An incentive is simply a means of urging people to do more of a good thing and less of a bad thing. But most incentives don't come about organically [naturally]. Someone—an economist or a politician or a parent—has to invent them. Your three-year-old eats all her vegetables for a week? She wins a trip to the toy store. A big steelmaker belches too much smoke into the air? The company is fined for each cubic foot of pollutants over the legal limit.

—Steven Levitt and Stephen Dunbar, *Freakonomics*

Explanation 2

It keeps cropping up all over the place. There is an economics of money and trade, of production and consumption, of distribution and development. . . . There is an economics of war and an economics of power. There is even an economics of love. Economics seems to apply to every nook and cranny of human experience. It is an aspect [part] of all conscious [mindful] action. Whenever alternatives exist, life takes on an economic aspect. It has always been so. But how can it be?

—Robert Mundell, *Man and Economics*

Chapter Practice Test

DIRECTIONS: Circle the best answer for each question.

SS.7.E.1.3 (Moderate)

> *"The market price of every particular commodity [good or service] is regulated by the proportion [relationship] between the quantity which is actually brought to market, and the demand of those who are willing to pay the natural price of the commodity."*
>
> —Adam Smith, *The Wealth of Nations*

Which economic concept is Smith explaining?

A surplus

B shortage

C equilibrium price

D capital resources

SS.7.E.1.5 (Moderate)

In which situation would a new producer be most likely to enter the market?

A when demand is high and supply is low

B when supply is greater than demand

C when prices and demand are low

D when prices are high and demand is low

3 **SS.7.E.1.3 (High)**

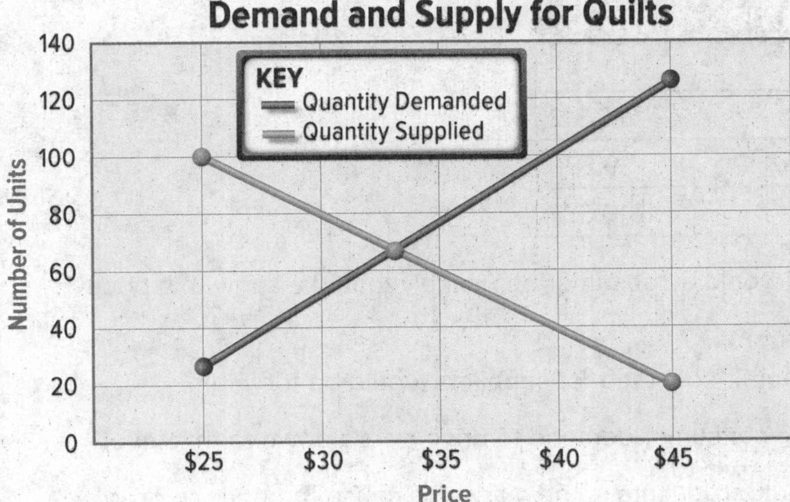

What would happen to the graph if more consumers entered the market?

A The equilibrium price would move down.

B The equilibrium price would move to the left.

C The equilibrium price would move straight up.

D The equilibrium price would move to the right.

---

4 **SS.7.E.1.3 (Moderate)**

What is the opportunity cost of choosing to take the bus instead of riding a bicycle to school?

A the money spent on bus fare

B the exercise of riding a bicycle

C the time saved by traveling by bus

D the conversations with friends on the bus

5 **SS.7.E.1.5 (High)**

VEHICLE PRODUCTION COSTS	
Producer 1	$10,545
Producer 2	$9,312
Producer 3	$9,879
Producer 4	$10,637

Based on the chart, why would a consumer be unlikely to find a car with a price of $10,000 or less?

A At that price, the benefit-cost ratio for suppliers would be too high.

B There is not enough consumer demand to drive prices down to that level.

C There are not enough producers in the market to cause the price to drop that low.

D At that price, producers would not earn enough revenue to cover their productions costs.

 **SS.7.E.1.3 (Moderate)**

Wish List	**Available Funds**
shoes	$20 in wallet
sweater	$32 in change jar
new skateboard	
new phone	
new game console	

Which economic concept is illustrated above?

A scarcity

B markets

C competition

D opportunity cost

7

SS.7.E.1.1 (Moderate)

How is a market economy similar to a democracy?

A Both rely on government planners.

B Both are based on shared customs.

C Both are driven by people's choices.

D Both rely on formal election processes.

8

SS.7.E.1.3, SS.7.E.1.5 (Moderate)

> *"We realized from the facts of the case that the important competition was between the superstores. They played a special role, and if one were to be eliminated—prices were likely to go up, [Stephen Calkins] said."*
>
> —MSNBC, June 12, 2007

Based on information in the excerpt, why would prices go up?

A The number of suppliers in the market would increase.

B The number of suppliers in the market would decrease.

C The number of consumers in the market would increase.

D The number of consumers in the market would decrease.

9 **SS.7.E.1.3 (Moderate)**

What would cause demand to decline?

A an increase in consumers

B an increase in producers

C a drop in equilibrium price

D a drop in consumer income

---

10 **SS.7.E.1.3 (High)**

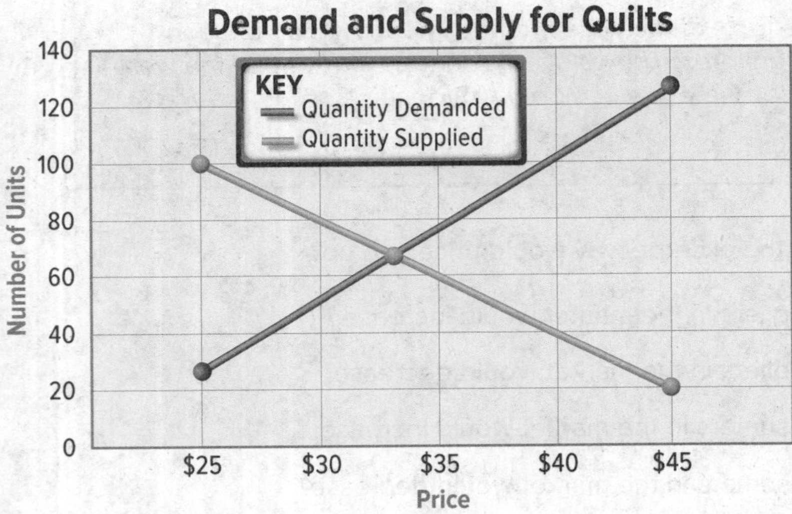

What would happen to the graph if some suppliers left the market?

A The demand curve would move down.

B The supply curve would move down.

C The equilibrium price would move left.

D The supply curve would move up.

CHAPTER 18

The American Economy

Chapter Overview

A nation's economy is made up of many different elements. Each nation has businesses that create and sell products. Businesses also develop and sell services. People and businesses form the consumer group. They buy the goods and services that are offered in the marketplace. These exchanges promote economic growth. As a nation's economy grows, the nation gains wealth. This wealth leads to a higher standard of living and better lives for all citizens.

The United States has a free enterprise economy. Individuals and groups have the freedom to start new businesses and run them with little government involvement. Citizens, not the government, make most of the economic decisions. The free enterprise system has enabled the United States to grow the largest economy in the world.

CHAPTER BENCHMARKS

SS.7.E.1.1 Explain how the principles of a market and mixed economy helped to develop the United States into a democratic nation.

SS.7.E.1.3 Review the concepts of supply and demand, choice, scarcity, and opportunity cost as they relate to the development of the mixed market economy in the United States.

SS.7.E.1.5 Assess how profits, incentives, and competition motivate individuals, households, and businesses in a free market economy.

SS.7.E.2.1 Explain how federal, state, and local taxes support the economy as a function of the United States government.

SS.7.E.2.4 Identify entrepreneurs from various gender, social, and ethnic backgrounds who started a business seeking to make a profit.

SS.7.E.3.4 Compare and contrast the standard of living in various countries today to that of the United States using gross domestic product (GDP) per capita as an indicator.

SS.7.G.6.1 Use Geographic Information Systems (GIS) or other technology to view maps of current information about the United States.

WHAT I NEED TO KNOW

TERMS

- ☐ product
- ☐ Gross Domestic Product (GDP)
- ☐ entrepreneur
- ☐ GDP per capita
- ☐ standard of living
- ☐ circular flow model
- ☐ factor market
- ☐ product market
- ☐ economic growth
- ☐ productivity
- ☐ specialization
- ☐ division of labor
- ☐ human capital
- ☐ capitalism
- ☐ free enterprise
- ☐ voluntary exchange
- ☐ profit
- ☐ profit motive
- ☐ competition
- ☐ private property rights
- ☐ laissez-faire economics

CHAPTER 18

The American Economy

CHAPTER BENCHMARKS, *continued*

LAFS.68.RH.2.4 Determine the meaning of words and phrases as they are used in a text, including vocabulary specific to domains related to history/social studies.

LAFS.68.RH.2.6 Identify aspects of a text that reveal an author's point of view or purpose (e.g., loaded language, inclusion or avoidance of particular facts).

LAFS.68.WHST.2.4 Produce clear and coherent writing in which the development, organization, and style are appropriate to task, purpose, and audience.

LAFS.68.WHST.2.5 With some guidance and support from peers and adults, develop and strengthen writing as needed by planning, revising, editing, rewriting, or trying a new approach, focusing on how well purpose and audience have been addressed.

LAFS.68.WHST.3.8 Gather relevant information from multiple print and digital sources, using search terms effectively; assess the credibility and accuracy of each source.

MAFS.K12.MP.3.1 Construct viable arguments and critique the reasoning of others.

The American Economy

Make this Foldable® and label the three tabs with the lesson titles. Before reading each lesson, find and record the guiding questions presented. Under the tabs, take notes that will help you discuss and answer each question. On the back of the Foldable, relate what you learn to economic choices you make today and will make in the future.

Step 1
Fold lined paper horizontally to the margin.

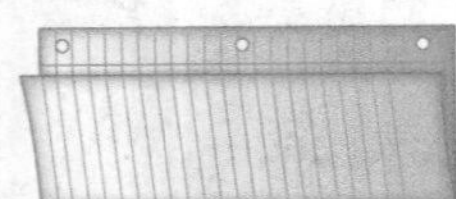

Step 2
Fold the right side and the left side of the paper across the middle to form three equal parts.

Step 3
Cut the two fold lines from the top edge to the bottom fold.

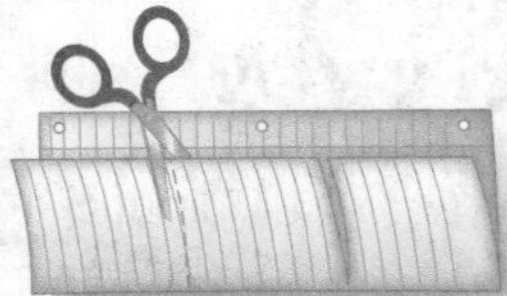

Step 4
Label the tabs as shown.

LESSON 1 SUMMARY

Gross Domestic Product

SS.7.E.1.3, SS.7.E.1.5, SS.7.E.3.4

Why GDP Is Important

The economy of the United States produces a wide variety of products. A **product** can be either a *good* or a *service*. Goods are physical things you use, like laptop computers, shoes, or eyeglasses. Services are jobs that others do for you, like repairing a car or cutting hair.

The production of goods and services makes up the **Gross Domestic Product (GDP).** GDP is the total market value of all final products a country produces in one year. In 2014, the GDP of the United States totaled about 17 *trillion* dollars. This makes the United States the largest economy in the world. It produces about one-fifth of all the goods and services produced in the world. China is the second-largest economy. In 2014, China's GDP was about $10.3 trillion.

Purchases that consumers, businesses, and the government make are all included in GDP. When people produce these goods and provide services, they earn income. This income also is included in GDP. Thus, GDP is a way to measure the nation's income.

Many people are needed to make a product. For example, factory workers who assemble an automobile are paid for their labor. So are workers who mine the metal, mix the paint, and produce the tires. Later, when the automobile is taken to a garage for service, the mechanics who fix it also earn income.

Factors of Production

People called entrepreneurs are important to an economy. An **entrepreneur** (ahn•truh•pruh•NUHR) is someone who takes a risk and starts a new business. The risk is that the business might not succeed. If the business is successful, though, the entrepreneur will earn money.

1. IDENTIFYING

Select an item in the room you are in right now. Make a list of all the workers who were needed to produce that item. Be sure to include the workers who created the component parts of the item.

2. EXPLAINING

What is an entrepreneur? Why do entrepreneurs go into business?

An entrepreneur is one of the four factors of production. Entrepreneurs bring together the other three factors of production: natural resources, labor, and capital. When a product like an automobile is produced, *all* of the factors of production earn income—not just labor. For example, the auto manufacturer must pay companies that own natural resources like metal and rubber. They must also pay companies that provide capital such as machinery and tools that are used to produce the automobiles.

ANALYZING VISUALS

3. POSING QUESTIONS

Ask four questions relating to the four factors of production of a product featured in the photograph. Identify each factor of production.

1.

2.

3.

4.

This girl is shopping for some new clothes. The four factors of production were all used to make the garments that she is considering.

Measuring GDP

It is difficult to measure GDP because countries produce so many different goods and services each year. The table below shows an example of how to calculate GDP: price x number produced = total for one product. Adding the total of all goods produced by a nation each year gives the total GDP. This is a simple version of the kind of math that economists use to calculate the GDP of a nation.

CALCULATING GROSS DOMESTIC PRODUCT (GDP)			
Final Product	**Price**	**Number Produced**	**Total**
Bicycles	$200	10	$2,000
Computers	$1,500	10	+ $15,000
Watches	$100	10	+ $1,000
GDP			$18,000

GDP Only Includes Final Products

GDP does not include all goods and services. It only includes *final* goods and services that are produced and sold. A final good or service is something that is sold directly to its final user. A book you purchase in a bookstore is a final good. The ink and paper used to make the book are not final goods and are not part of GDP. These are called *intermediate goods.*

Intermediate goods are things that go into making a final good. They are not counted in GDP because the final price of the book includes their value. Used goods are not counted either; their value was counted when they were first sold. Re-selling them does not involve new production. GDP also does not include housework or chores performed by family members—even if you are paid to do them.

Products such as books, automobiles, and haircuts are called consumer goods and services. To *consume* means "to use as a customer." The products businesses use to make consumer goods—like machines or office supplies—are called producer goods. They are also known as investment goods or capital goods, and they are counted in a country's GDP.

Complete the chart below. If the item listed in the table is included in GDP, write *Yes*. If it is not included, write *No*.

ACTIVITY	INCLUDED IN GDP?
A woman has her nails done in a salon.	
A boy buys a new bike at a bike shop.	
A man cuts his son's hair at home.	
A woman takes her family out to lunch at a local diner.	
A man pays his neighbor $10 to shovel snow from his sidewalk.	
A girl buys a book at a used book store.	

4. DETERMINING CENTRAL IDEAS

Suppose a bakery buys a bag of flour, uses that flour to bake bread, then sells the bread to customers. What is included in GDP? Explain.

5. DRAWING CONCLUSIONS

China has the second-largest national economy in the world, but more than 100 countries have a larger GDP per capita than China. What is a possible explanation for this difference? How would you compare China's economic health to that of the United States?

Name ______________________ Date ______________ Class ________

ANALYZING VISUALS

6. COMPARING The GDP per capita of the United States is about nine times that of which nation shown in the table? How do you think the standard of living in that nation compares to the standard of living in the United States?

____

____

____

____

7. ANALYZING MAPS

If your school has access to Geographic Information Systems (GIS), find maps comparing the GDP per capita of countries over several decades. Look at how the GDP has changed over time, and summarize your findings in a chart or by making notes on a world map.

8. SPECULATING

Is it possible for a country to have a relatively low GDP per capita yet still have a relatively high standard of living? Explain.

____

____

____

____

____

GDP Per Capita

GDP tells how large a country's economy is. When we compare countries, however, it is better to measure **GDP per capita.** *Per capita* means "per person." GDP per capita is a better comparison because the populations and economies of countries differ in size. GDP per capita gives the share of GDP each person in the country would get if GDP were divided equally. To find GDP per capita, divide the country's GDP by its population. The result states GDP in terms of each person in the country. The table below shows the rankings of various countries in terms of their GDP per capita.

GDP PER CAPITA

Rank	Country	GDP per capita
1	Qatar	$145,000
11	Norway	$68,400
19	United States	$56,300
56	Czech Republic	$31,500
85	Panama	$20,900
112	China	$14,300
158	India	$6,300
212	Ethiopia	$1,700

Source: *CIA World Factbook*, 2015 estimates

The Standard of Living

Economists also use standard of living to compare economic development among countries. The **standard of living** is the quality of life for the people in a country. It is based on how well people are able to meet their needs and wants. GDP does not measure standard of living because it is a total number. If the GDP of a nation is high, that does not necessarily mean that all citizens are doing well. Other conditions are also examined when measuring standard of living. For example, China has a strong economy but also suffers from heavy pollution, which lowers the standard of living.

Name ______________________ Date ______________ Class __________

REVIEW LESSON 1

1. Use the chart below to describe GDP.

GROSS DOMESTIC PRODUCT (GDP)	
GDP is	
Included in GDP are	
GDP does not include	
GDP per capita means	
To calculate GDP per capita	
Standard of living means	
GDP is not a measure of the standard of living because	

2. **COMPARING AND CONTRASTING** Economists use GDP to compare and contrast the economic activity of different nations. They may also use GDP per capita to help determine the standard of living in a nation. Use the information from your chart to write an essay that answers these questions: How are GDP per capita and standard of living related? How is the standard of living in the United States similar to and different from the standard of living in China? Use GDP per capita to compare and contrast.

LESSON 2 SUMMARY

Economic Flow and Economic Growth

1. RECOGNIZING RELATIONSHIPS

In the product market, which sector of the circular flow model is the demand side? Which is the supply side? What about in the factor market?

2. MAKING CONNECTIONS

From which market—product or factor—would economic activity be included as a part of Gross Domestic Product (GDP)? Explain.

SS.7.E.1.3, SS.7.E.2.1

The Circular Flow Model

Economists often use models to demonstrate how the economy functions. A model is a graph or diagram that helps explain something. The **circular flow model** shows how resources, goods and services, and money flow between businesses and consumers in a circular path. It is in a circle because there is no beginning or end. The model has four main parts. Two parts are markets where buying and selling occur. The other two parts are sectors that show the main groups taking part in the markets: consumers and businesses.

The Factor and the Product Markets

The **factor market** is where factors of production are bought and sold. When people take a job, they are selling their labor in the factor market. Machines, tools, and natural resources like oil and timber are also part of the factor market. The **product market** is where businesses sell goods and services. The product market is like one giant store where all goods and services are sold.

The Consumer Sector and Business Sector

The consumer sector is made up of everyone in the economy who gets paid and who purchases goods and services. This sector is active in both the factor and the product markets. Employees sell their labor in the factor market and are paid for the work they perform. Then they use that money to buy goods and services in the product market.

The business sector includes all the companies that produce goods and services. Businesses are also active in both markets. They sell goods and services in the product market. They then use the money they earned to purchase factors of production in the factor market.

Name ______________________ Date ______________ Class ________

CIRCULAR FLOW OF ECONOMIC ACTIVITY

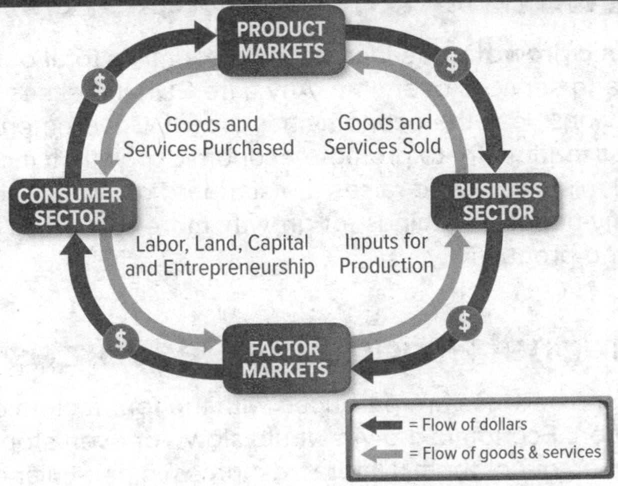

The Circular Flow

In the circular flow diagram, money always flows in a clockwise direction. Looking at the model, money flows from the consumer sector through the product market to the business sector. The money then continues through the factor market back to consumers. By contrast, the loop representing goods, services, and factors of production flows in a counterclockwise direction.

The model shows what happens in real life: The money that is spent and the products that are purchased flow in different directions. For example, if you buy a pair of sunglasses at a department store, you give the clerk money and the clerk gives you the glasses. Money flows in one direction, the glasses in the other. The model also shows that markets link the consumer and business sectors.

The Government and Foreign Sectors

Two other sectors are also involved in economic flow: the government and foreign sectors. For simplicity, the model above does not show these sectors. The government sector consists of federal, state, and local governments. They buy goods and services in the product market just as people in the consumer sector do. Governments also sell goods and services to earn income. For example, local bus systems charge fares and public parks charge entry fees. Such charges are not enough to pay for all government services, though. Governments also collect taxes and borrow money.

The foreign sector consists of all the people and businesses in other countries that buy and sell goods in both U.S. markets. In recent years, Americans have bought more goods and services from the foreign sector than they have sold to it.

ANALYZING VISUALS

3. ASSESSING Ally works at a sports store and purchases snacks at a grocery store. Using the diagram, explain how Ally takes part in the circular flow model.

____

____

____

____

____

____

____

____

____

4. EXPLAINING

What role do federal, state, and local taxes play in the economy?

____

____

____

____

____

____

5. PREDICTING CONSEQUENCES

As a key natural resource becomes more and more scarce, what effect does this have on the product and factor markets? Why?

6. MAKING INFERENCES

How do specialization and the division of labor help reduce the economic problem of scarcity?

Promoting Economic Growth

Economic growth is the increase in a country's total output of goods and services over time. Any time GDP increases from the previous year, the economy has grown. Government and business leaders try to promote economic growth. It increases the nation's wealth and raises the standard of living. The economy needs two things for growth: more resources and increased productivity.

Additional Productive Resources

Goods and services are produced with the four factors of production. Economic growth would slow—or even stop—if a country ran out of them. Natural resources in particular are often in limited supply. There is only so much land or oil under the ground. A country could use up all of its timber before new trees could grow back.

Increasing Productivity

Economic growth also requires a population that is either growing or becoming more productive. **Productivity** is a measure of how efficiently resources are being used. Productivity increases when more products are made with the same amount of factors of production in the same amount of time. For example, suppose a factory manufactures 1,000 cell phones each day. If the factory begins manufacturing 1,100 phones each day without hiring additional workers, its productivity has increased. Businesses that are productive can make more money than unproductive companies.

Productivity usually improves when businesses and people focus on providing one product or service. This is called **specialization.** Specialization allows people to become experts at what they do. For example, a person who has good mechanical skills might specialize in auto repair. An auto mechanic would be able to repair more cars each day than someone who is not an expert. Specialization helps employees and businesses become more productive.

Specialization leads to **division of labor,** which involves breaking down a large job into smaller tasks. A different worker performs each task. This allows the overall job to be done more quickly and efficiently—improving productivity and increasing economic growth.

Name ______________________ Date ______________ Class __________

LESSON 2 SUMMARY, *continued*

Businesses want to become more productive to make more profit. For example, they may find better methods of building machines. They can also use factors of production that are of higher quality. This is especially true of labor. Economists call this **human capital**–the knowledge, skills, and experience their workers possess. As workers gain training, education, and experience, their work improves. This results in greater productivity. This, in turn, leads to economic growth and a higher standard of living.

REVIEW LESSON 2

1. Complete the information in the circular flow model below.

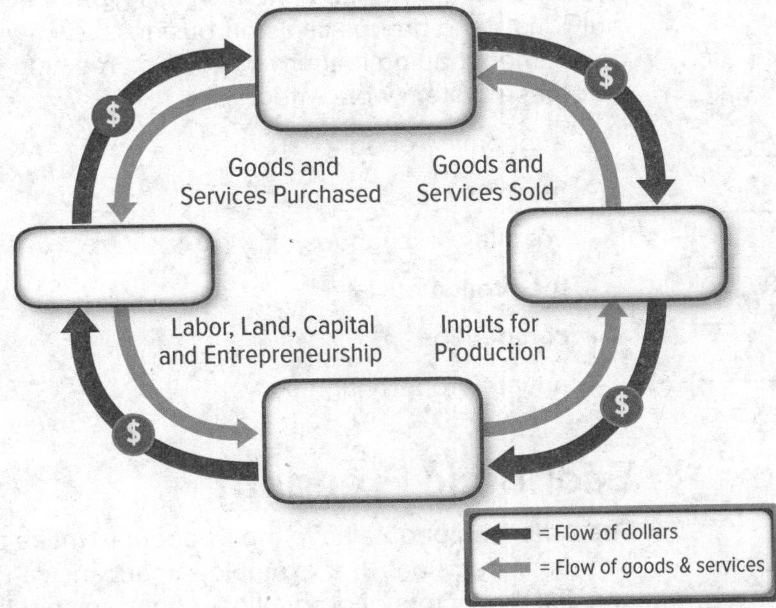

2. **EXPLAINING** Write an essay to explain how resources, goods and services, and money flow in the economy. Why is the diagram called a "circular flow" model? Use a separate sheet of paper for your essay.

LESSON 3 SUMMARY

Capitalism and Free Enterprise

1. GIVING EXAMPLES

What is one specific example of how economic freedom allows the U.S. marketplace to adjust quickly to economic changes?

SS.7.E.1.1, SS.7.E.1.3, SS.7.E.1.5, SS.7.E.2.4

Capitalism in the United States

The American market economy is large. One reason is that citizens, not the government, make most of the economic decisions. They do so in productive ways. This kind of economic system is called capitalism. Under **capitalism,** private individuals own the factors of production and decide how best to use them to make money.

The economic system of the United States is also sometimes called a **free enterprise** system. In this type of economy, individuals and groups can start businesses without government getting in the way. Six features help the free enterprise system work effectively:

- economic freedom
- markets
- voluntary exchanges
- the profit motive
- competition
- private property rights

Economic Freedom

The American people have the freedom to make their own economic decisions. For example, Americans can freely buy and sell the factors of production. They can start businesses and choose what types of goods or services to offer. It is up to entrepreneurs to determine how they want to run their businesses. Workers are free to sell their labor as they choose and decide what jobs they will take. They can also use their money as they wish—to spend it, save it, or invest it.

Economic freedom allows the American marketplace to adjust quickly to changes in economic conditions. This results in a very efficient and productive economy.

Markets

Markets are where buyers and sellers interact. In the United States, the forces of supply and demand drive markets. The government does not tell businesses what to produce or consumers what to buy or sell. Rather, consumers and businesses decide for themselves which products and services will be available in the market. Though there can be problems in markets, over time they have proven to be the best way to bring buyers and sellers together. Markets encourage competition and set prices.

Voluntary Exchange

Voluntary exchange occurs when buyers and sellers freely and willingly choose to take part in an exchange. Buyers give up something—usually money—in order to gain a product or service. Sellers offer goods and services in exchange for money. In a voluntary exchange, both parties are better off than they were before the exchange occurred.

Complete the chart below. If the item listed in the table is an example of a voluntary exchange, write *Yes*. If it is not, write *No*.

You sell your old video game to a friend.	
Your neighbor borrows your lawn mower without asking.	
You buy a candy bar at the drugstore.	
You exchange a football ticket for a concert ticket with your friend.	

The Profit Motive

In our capitalist economy, the desire to make money motivates people to offer goods and services to buyers. Entrepreneurs risk their savings because they think they can make a profit. **Profit** is the money left over from the sale of goods or services after all the costs of production have been paid. The **profit motive** is the desire to earn money by creating and selling goods and services. It inspires people to create new or improved goods and services and encourages productivity. The profit motive is the main force behind the American economy.

2. SPECULATING

Imagine that the government decided which products businesses could produce. How do you think that would affect the economy?

______

3. CONSTRUCTING AN ARGUMENT

Do you believe government should limit the amount of profit a business can earn? Explain.

______

4. EVALUATING

Review the paragraph about entrepreneurs and how they started a business to make a profit. Choose the one you think made the most significant contribution and underline the person's name. Research the person and the business he or she created. On a separate sheet of paper, explain why you think the contribution is most significant.

Many individuals who started businesses observed a need and developed a way to meet it. These entrepreneurs included men and women from various social and ethnic backgrounds. C. J. Walker saw that African American women needed beauty products. Granville T. Woods invented a way for moving trains to communicate with each other in order to avoid collisions and dangers on the tracks. Sarah E. Goode heard people talking about needing beds in small apartments, so she invented a cabinet bed that met their needs. Pedro Flores transformed a kind of weapon into a toy called a yo-yo and mass-produced it in a small factory. These entrepreneurs met a need for others while making a profit for themselves.

Competition

The free enterprise system thrives on competition. **Competition** exists when businesses try to sell similar products at the best prices to attract the most buyers. Businesses with lower prices usually have the most customers. Sometimes, though, a business can win buyers by offering a higher quality product, even if the price is higher than the competition. Competition forces businesses to be more efficient and to offer good quality goods and services. Otherwise, they will lose customers.

5. MAKING INFERENCES

How is a business likely to behave if it has no competition?

Private Property Rights

People and businesses in the United States have **private property rights.** This means they can own and use their property the way they want to. They can even choose to dispose of, or get rid of, that property if they so desire. Private property rights give people the incentive to work because they can keep any profits they earn. These rights also motivate people to take better care of their possessions.

Name ____________________ Date ____________ Class ________

The Origins of U.S. Capitalism

A book called *The Wealth of Nations* greatly influenced the nation's Founders. The author, Adam Smith, was a Scottish philosopher and economist. He wrote that the profit motive and competition resulted in efficiency and a stable society. He argued that market exchanges work best with little government interference.

The writings of Smith and others led to the idea of laissez-faire economics. Laissez-faire means "to let alone." Therefore, **laissez-faire economics** means that the government should not interfere in the economy. Government should act only to make sure that competition can take place.

6. MAKING CONNECTIONS

How do you think the idea of laissez-faire economics relates to the idea of democracy?

____

____

____

____

____

____

____

REVIEW LESSON 3

1. Use the chart below to identify the features of the free enterprise system.

FEATURES OF THE FREE ENTERPRISE SYSTEM

2. **SPECULATING** Using the information in your chart, write an essay to answer the following question: Can a democratic government like the United States exist without a free enterprise economic system? Explain your answer. Use a separate sheet for your answer.

Benchmark Skill Activities

DIRECTIONS: Write your answers on a separate piece of paper.

LAFS.68.WHST.2.4, LAFS.68.WHST.2.5

1. DETERMINING CENTRAL IDEAS

Use your FOLDABLES to write an essay.

Think about five purchases that you have recently made. For each one, tell: (1) if the purchase will be counted in the GDP; (2) in which market and sector of the circular flow model you were participating; and (3) how one of the features of the free enterprise system was involved in the purchase. Develop your writing by planning, revising, editing, and rewriting as necessary to focus on your purpose.

MAFS.K12.MP.3.1

2. DRAWING CONCLUSIONS

The following graph provides data about U.S. Gross Domestic Product from 1960 to 2010.

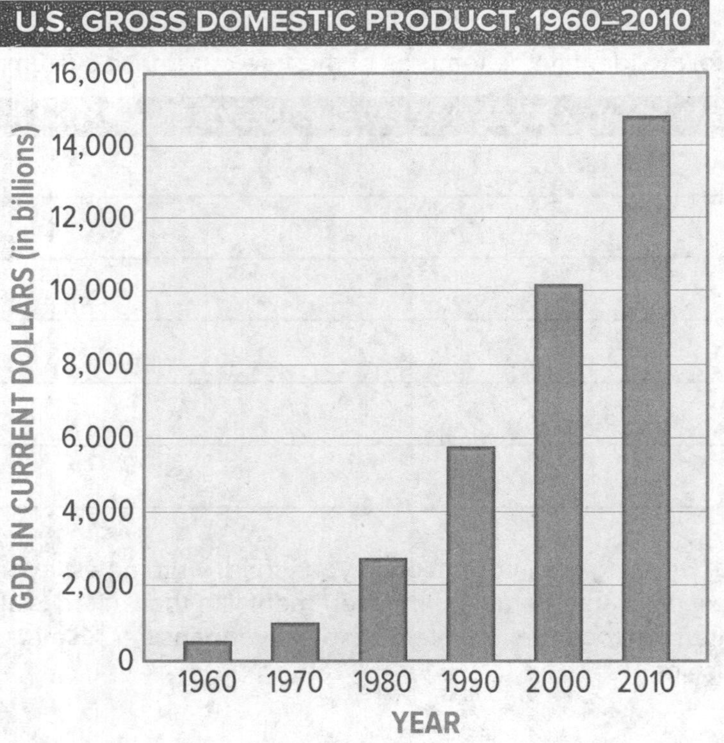

Source: Office of Management and Budget

Based on the data in the graph, what conclusions can you draw about economic growth in the United States during the 1970s? Explain your answer.

LAFS.68.WHST.2.4, LAFS.68.WHST.3.8, SS.7.E.3.4

3. COMPARING AND CONTRASTING

Do research on the Internet to find at least two primary or secondary sources about the standard of living in the United States and in one other nation of your choosing. Include GDP per capita as well as any other factors you believe contribute to a nation's standard of living. Then write an essay comparing and contrasting living standards in both countries. Explain how you decided which factors to use in your analysis.

LAFS.68.RH.2.4

4. DESCRIBING

Turn to the "Terms" list on the first page of this chapter in your workbook. Choose at least three words to include in a paragraph describing the American economy.

LAFS.68.WHST.3.8

5. COMPARING PRIMARY SOURCES

Locate three print or digital articles on how to start a small business. Assess the credibility and accuracy of each source. Combine information from the articles to write a summary of what you learned about starting a small business.

Benchmark Note Cards

DIRECTIONS: Use these note cards to help you prepare for the test.

SS.7.E.1.1 Explain how the principles of a market and mixed economy helped to develop the United States into a democratic nation.

FREE ENTERPRISE AND POLITICAL FREEDOM	Just as the American people enjoy a great deal of political freedom, so do they enjoy the freedom to make their own economic decisions. Six features help the free enterprise system work effectively: • economic freedom • markets • voluntary exchange • the profit motive • competition • private property rights

SS.7.E.1.3 Review the concepts of supply and demand, choice, scarcity, and opportunity cost as they relate to the development of the mixed market economy in the United States.

SPECIALIZATION AND THE DIVISION OF LABOR	Specialization and division of labor help combat the problem of scarcity by allowing businesses to become more efficient and produce more goods.

SS.7.E.1.5 Assess how profits, incentives, and competition motivate individuals, households, and businesses in a free market economy.

ENTREPRENEURS AND THE PROFIT MOTIVE	• An entrepreneur is someone who takes a risk and starts a new business. • Entrepreneurs are one of the four factors of production. They bring together the other three factors of production to create products and services. • The profit motive leads entrepreneurs to start businesses. The profit motive is the desire of a business to make money. It causes businesses to become more efficient and productive.

COMPETITION	Competition exists when businesses try to sell similar products at the best prices to attract the most buyers. It forces businesses to address the wants and needs of customers. Otherwise, they will lose customers and make less profit.

BENCHMARK NOTE CARDS, *continued*

SS.7.E.2.1 Explain how federal, state, and local taxes support the economy as a function of the United States government.

GOVERNMENT SECTOR	• The government sector consists of units of the federal, state, and local governments. • Just like the consumer and business sectors, the government sector participates in the product and factor markets. • The government sector participates in the product market by both purchasing and selling goods and services.

SS.7.E.2.4 Identify entrepreneurs from various gender, social, and ethnic backgrounds who started a business seeking to make a profit.

ENTREPRENEURS FROM VARIOUS BACKGROUNDS	Women and men with different social and ethnic backgrounds have started businesses. They saw a need and created a way to meet it. C. J. Walker developed beauty products for African American women. Granville T. Woods improved railroad safety by inventing a way for trains to communicate. Sarah E. Goode created a cabinet bed for small apartments. Pedro Flores developed a toy called a yo-yo.

SS.7.E.3.4 Compare and contrast the standard of living in various countries today to that of the United States using gross domestic product (GDP) per capita as an indicator.

GROSS DOMESTIC PRODUCT	• Gross Domestic Product (GDP) is the total market value of all final products a country produces in one year. • In 2015 the United States had the largest national GDP in the world. China had the second largest.

GDP PER CAPITA	• GDP per capita gives the share of GDP each person in a country would get if GDP were divided equally. • Other factors besides GDP per capita are examined when a nation's standard of living is assessed. These include quality of available health care and pollution levels.

Chapter 18

VISUAL SUMMARY

DIRECTIONS: Complete the graphic organizer below.

GROSS DOMESTIC PRODUCT

The total market value of all final goods and services produced in one year

FACTORS OF PRODUCTION

The American Economy

CIRCULAR FLOW OF ECONOMIC ACTIVITY

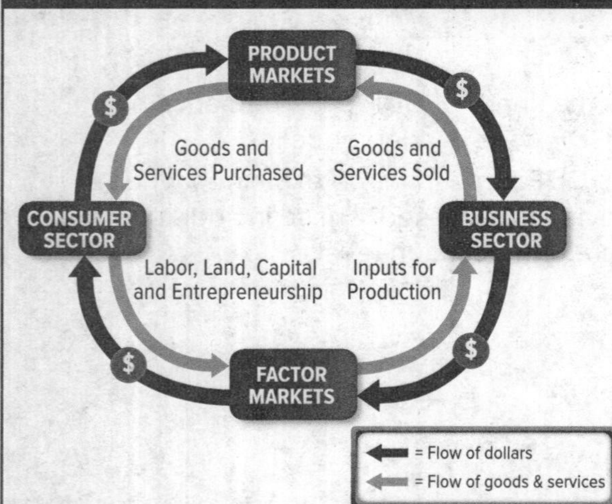

FEATURES OF FREE ENTERPRISE

USING PRIMARY SOURCES

INTERPRET In 1776 Adam Smith, a Scottish Enlightenment thinker, published *An Inquiry Into the Nature and Causes of the Wealth of Nations*. It was a groundbreaking work. Although the word *economics* is never directly mentioned, the book is considered to be a founding work in the field of economics.

The following excerpt is by Adam Smith. After reading it, answer the questions below.

> *"It is the maxim [saying] of every prudent [sensible] master of a family never to attempt [try] to make at home what it will cost him more to make than to buy. The tailor does not attempt to make his own shoes, but buys them of the shoemaker. The shoemaker does not attempt to make his own clothes, but employs a tailor. The farmer attempts to make neither the one nor the other, but employs those different artificers [skilled workers]. All of them find it for their interest to employ their whole industry in a way in which they have some advantage over their neighbors, and to purchase with a part of its produce, or what is the same thing, with the price of a part of it, whatever else they have occasion [need] for.*
>
> *What is prudence [good judgment] in the conduct of every private family can scarce be folly [not be considered foolish] in that of a great kingdom. If a foreign country can supply us with a commodity [product or service] cheaper than we ourselves can make it, better buy it of them with some part of the produce of our own industry employed in a way in which we have some advantage."*
>
> —Adam Smith, *The Wealth of Nations*, 1776

1. What economic concept is Smith describing in this passage? Explain how you determined this.

____

____

____

____

____

____

____

2. Explain why individuals and businesses are motivated to follow the concept Smith is describing.

____

____

____

____

____

Chapter Practice Test

DIRECTIONS: Circle the best answer for each question.

SS.7.E.1.1 (Moderate)

The following excerpt is from the Fifth Amendment to the U.S. Constitution.

> *No person shall be . . . deprived of life, liberty, or property, without due process of law; nor shall private property be taken for public use, without just compensation.*
>
> —U.S. Constitution

This passage touches on which principle of a market economy?

A government taxation

B private property rights

C the profit motive

D competition

SS.7.E.1.3 (Moderate)

Which of the following represents a factor market interaction?

A A retiree buys tickets for a Caribbean cruise.

B A real estate agent sells a home in your neighborhood.

C A local remodeling company hires workers for a painting job.

D A high school senior buys a class ring.

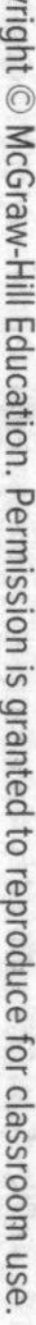

3 **SS.7.E.1.3 (Moderate)**

Examine the model of the circular flow of economic activity.

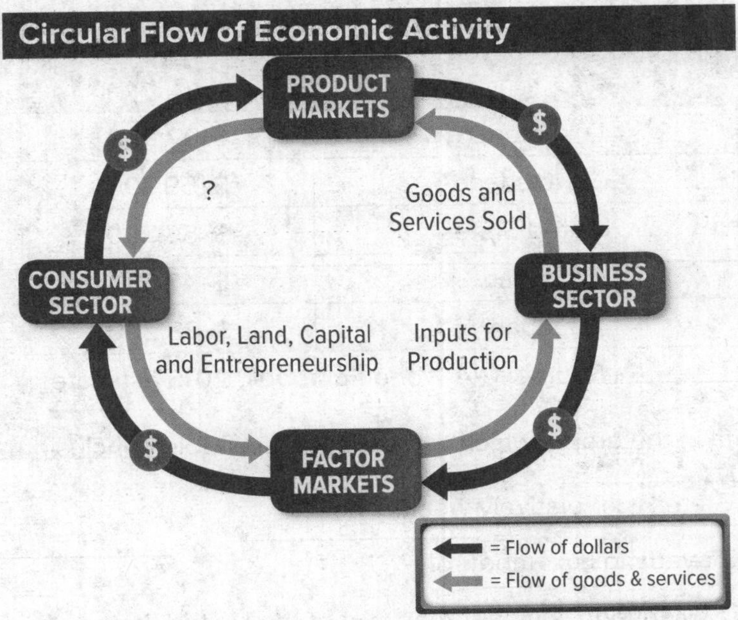

Which of the following best completes the diagram?

A Human Capital

B Government Taxation

C Factors of Production

D Goods and Services Purchased

---

4 **SS.7.E.1.5 (Moderate)**

Which of the following would be in agreement with the philosophy of laissez-faire economics?

A labor unions

B private property ownership

C government corporations, such as Amtrak

D government agencies, such as the Environmental Protection Agency

5 **SS.7.E.3.4 (High)**

Examine the following table.

GDP PER CAPITA FOR SELECTED COUNTRIES		
Rank	**Country**	**GDP Per Capita**
2	Luxembourg	$102,900
16	Switzerland	$ 59,300
19	United States	$ 56,300
28	Taiwan	$ 47,500
42	Japan	$ 38,200

Source: *CIA World Factbook,* 2015 estimates

Based on the data in the graph, which is the most reasonable conclusion?

A The United States is a relatively wealthy nation.

B There is no poverty in Luxembourg.

C The GDP of Switzerland is higher than that of the United States.

D European countries are more prosperous than Asian countries.

---

6 **SS.7.E.2.1 (Moderate)**

Which sector of the economy relies on taxation to participate in product markets?

A the business sector

B the government sector

C the consumer sector

D the foreign sector

SS.E.1.1 (Moderate)

Examine the table below and then identify the missing feature that contributes to an efficient free enterprise system.

FEATURES OF FREE ENTERPRISE SYSTEM
Markets
Voluntary exchange
Profit motive
Competition
Private property rights
?

A Economic freedom

B Entrepreneurs

C Laissez-faire economics

D Factor markets

SS.7.E.1.5 (Moderate)

What is the main reason entrepreneurs begin their own businesses?

A They feel a civic duty to contribute to society.

B They strongly believe in free enterprise.

C They want to provide jobs for people.

D They want to earn a profit for themselves.

9 **SS.7.E.3.4 (High)**

Examine the following economic information for the United States and Ethiopia.

ECONOMIC COMPARISON OF THE UNITED STATES AND ETHIOPIA		
	United States	Ethiopia
GDP	$17.97 trillion (world rank: 3)	$159.2 billion (world rank: 73)
GDP annual growth rate	2.6% (world rank: 114)	8.7% (world rank: 5)
Per capita GDP	$56,300 (world rank: 19)	$1,700 (world rank: 212)

Source: *CIA World Factbook*, 2015 estimates

Which of the following is the best conclusion that can be drawn from the data?

A Ethiopia's economy is stronger than the economy of the United States.

B The economic gap between Ethiopia and the United States is shrinking rapidly.

C An economy's annual growth rate is not a good indicator of the standard of living.

D The population of Ethiopia and the United States is about the same.

---

10 **SS.7.E.1.3 (Moderate)**

Which of the following helps ease the economic problem of scarcity?

A private property ownership

B specialization and division of labor

C competition among businesses

D government participation in the factor market

CHAPTER 19

Personal Finance

Chapter Overview

Personal finance is the study and practice of how individuals manage their money. Money management includes understanding your role as a consumer and being aware of your consumer rights and responsibilities. It means understanding what credit is and how it works, as well as its benefits and dangers. Making and keeping a budget can help you manage your money. Personal finance also includes decisions about saving and investing, from deciding how much to save to knowing which saving or investing option is best for your situation.

CHAPTER BENCHMARKS

SS.7.C.2.11 Analyze media and political communications (bias, symbolism, propaganda).

SS.7.E.1.2 Discuss the importance of borrowing and lending in the United States, the government's role in controlling financial institutions, and list the advantages and disadvantages of using credit.

SS.7.E.1.3 Review the concepts of supply and demand, choice, scarcity, and opportunity cost as they relate to the development of the mixed market economy in the United States.

SS.7.E.1.4 Discuss the function of financial institutions in the development of a market economy.

SS.7.E.1.5 Assess how profits, incentives, and competition motivate individuals, households, and businesses in a free market economy.

SS.7.E.1.6 Compare the national budget process to the personal budget process.

SS.7.E.2.3 Identify and describe United States laws and regulations adopted to promote economic competition.

SS.7.E.2.5 Explain how economic institutions impact the national economy.

ELD.K12.ELL.SI.1 English language learners communicate for social and instructional purposes within the school setting.

WHAT I NEED TO KNOW

TERMS

- ☐ consumerism
- ☐ comparison shopping
- ☐ disposable income
- ☐ discretionary income
- ☐ budget
- ☐ expense
- ☐ balance
- ☐ balanced budget
- ☐ deficit
- ☐ credit
- ☐ credit limit
- ☐ credit card
- ☐ principal
- ☐ debit card
- ☐ stock
- ☐ bond
- ☐ mutual fund

Personal Finance

CHAPTER BENCHMARKS, *continued*

LAFS.68.RH.2.5 Describe how a text presents information (e.g., sequentially, comparatively, causally).

LAFS.7.SL.1.1 Engage effectively in a range of collaborative discussions (one-on-one, in groups, and teacher-led) with diverse partners on grade 7 topics, texts, and issues, building on others' ideas and expressing their own clearly.

LAFS.68.WHST.2.6 Use technology, including the Internet, to produce and publish writing and present the relationships between information and ideas clearly and efficiently.

MAFS.K12.MP.1.1 Make sense of problems and persevere in solving them.

MAFS.K12.MP.6.1 Attend to precision.

Personal Finance

Make this Foldable® and label the three columns of the chart *Consumerism, Budgeting,* and *Saving/Investing*. Before you read the chapter, review what you know about each topic. Skim through each lesson and identify and write key terms in the appropriate columns of your Foldable. Search for definitions as you read and record any new terms that arise. On the back of your Foldable, draw a large circle and label it *Income*. Inside this circle draw smaller circles to represent each of your expenses, savings, and other uses of your income. Write a brief explanation of your diagram that applies at least four terms from the chapter.

Step 1

Arrange a piece of notebook paper vertically. Fold the left and right sides once each to create three equal columns.

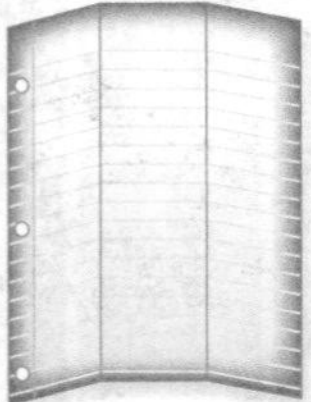

Step 2

Unfold the paper and label the columns as directed.

LESSON 1 SUMMARY

Consumerism

SS.7.C.2.11, SS.7.E.1.3, SS.7.E.1.5, SS.7.E.2.3

Consumer Rights

You have learned that American citizens have rights. Consumers have rights, too. They gained these rights largely through a movement called **consumerism.** It works to educate buyers about goods and services. Consumerism also demands that suppliers provide better, safer products.

Consumer interests are protected by two government agencies: the Food and Drug Administration (FDA) and the Federal Trade Commission (FTC). The FDA oversees the safety of food, drugs, and medical devices. The FTC works to protect consumers against fraud, deception, and unfair business practices.

In 1962, President John F. Kennedy noted that consumers had greater access to more goods than ever before. Additionally, technology had made many goods more complex. Retailers were using more persuasive advertising to sell these goods. All of these things made it more difficult for a buyer to make educated choices.

Kennedy proposed establishing a consumer bill of rights. The original bill listed only four rights. Over time, more rights were added. These rights help protect consumers in a market economy. Today, a private organization called the Better Business Bureau (BBB) helps consumers exercise these rights.

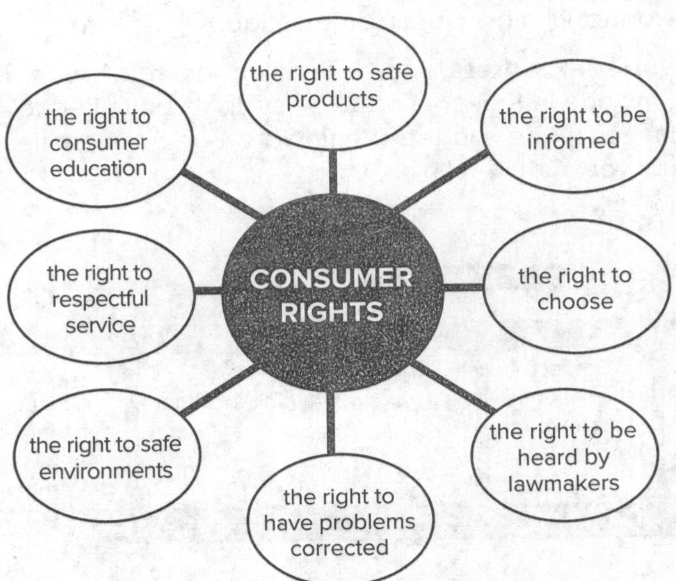

1. MAKING INFERENCES

How does the Federal Trade Commission help promote economic competition?

ANALYZING VISUALS

2. ASSESSING Which consumer right do you think is most important to the functioning of a market economy? Explain your reasoning.

3. DISTINGUISHING FACT FROM OPINION

An advertisement for a snack food contains the following information. Identify each detail as a fact (F) or an opinion (O).

_____ New and Improved!

_____ Now 50% Larger

_____ America's Favorite Treat

_____ Only 100 Calories per Serving

How does this ad try to persuade the consumer to buy the snack?

____

____

____

____

ANALYZING VISUALS

4. SUGGESTING A SOLUTION A person buys a laptop. When she gets home, she finds it won't charge. What should she do?

____

____

____

____

Consumer Responsibilities

Political rights come with responsibilities. So do consumer rights. Consumer responsibilities are also smart purchasing strategies.

Be an Informed Consumer

Smart consumers learn about products before buying them. By reading consumer magazines and Web sites, they can learn about product quality and other consumers' experiences.

They can also use advertisements to learn about products. However, ads tend to use special techniques to persuade people to buy things they do not need. Therefore, consumers must be careful about how they use advertisements.

After deciding on a product, consumers must choose where to buy it. **Comparison shopping** helps consumers take advantage of competition. To comparison shop, compare prices at different stores or companies. Often, this can be done online. Sometimes, a generic good—a less expensive product without a brand name—is a better choice.

Handle Problems Appropriately

If a product or a service is faulty, the consumer has the responsibility to obtain redress, or remedy. If you discover that a good or service is faulty, do not try to fix it yourself. The product might need to be repaired by a qualified technician. It also might be covered by a warranty. A warranty is a manufacturer's or a seller's promise to repair or replace a faulty product within a certain time period.

When you seek redress, keep a detailed record of your efforts. Include in these records the people you talked to or to whom you wrote a letter. The flowchart below identifies the steps you should follow.

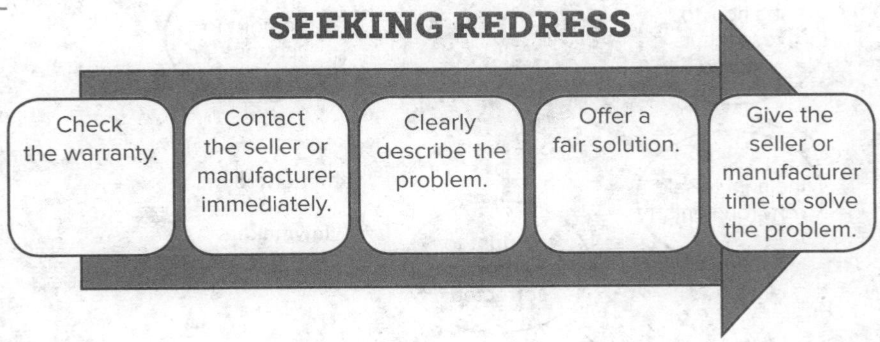

SEEKING REDRESS

Check the warranty. → Contact the seller or manufacturer immediately. → Clearly describe the problem. → Offer a fair solution. → Give the seller or manufacturer time to solve the problem.

You should be honest as you make your claim. For example, if an item broke because you dropped it, you should not claim that it was faulty. The manufacturer and seller should be honest with you, too. If you are not satisfied with the seller's or manufacturer's solution, file a report with your state's consumer protection agency.

Making Purchasing Decisions

Consumers must make decisions about what to buy. This means considering the effects of purchasing decisions.

Avoid Impulse Buying

Responsible consumers protect their budget by controlling impulse buying. Impulse buying happens when a consumer makes an unplanned purchase based on emotion. There are a variety of ways to control impulse spending:

- Make a shopping list and buy only the items on the list.
- When you are tempted to buy, take a break. Walk away from the item. Wait a little while and think about whether you really need the item. Give the urge a chance to pass.
- If you decide to buy the item, take the time to comparison shop. Be careful with online shopping since it is easy to charge purchases to a credit card.
- Pay with cash, and use your credit card only for emergencies.

Prioritize Your Wants

The wants we have are not all the same. Some things are necessary, such as food, clothing, and shelter. Other items are not necessary but make life easier or more pleasurable, like music downloads, books, and electronics. Consumers must decide between these competing wants. Even things that are necessary still require choices. Should food come from the grocery store or a fancy restaurant? Should a family move into an apartment or a mansion? Should a person buy clothing in a department store or a boutique?

After ranking their wants by importance, consumers must then decide how much money to spend on each. They base these decisions on their **disposable income.** Disposable income is the money left from a paycheck after taxes have been paid. It is also called **discretionary income** because consumers can choose how they spend this money.

5. REASONING

You and a friend are at the mall. Your friend sees a display of a new game and wants to buy it. What advice could you give your friend?

______

______

______

______

______

______

6. DETERMINING CAUSE AND EFFECT

Why should consumers prioritize their wants?

______

______

______

______

______

______

Name ______________________ Date ______________ Class ________

Think About Opportunity Cost

Responsible consumers also consider their economic goals when they make buying decisions. This means considering opportunity cost, or considering the value of the next-best choice, before making a purchase. If you buy Item A, what would you *not* be able to buy or do as a result?

REVIEW LESSON 1

1. Use the chart below to identify the elements of being a consumer.

CONSUMER RIGHTS	CONSUMER RESPONSIBILITIES	PURCHASING DECISIONS
• Right to safe products • Right to be informed • • • • • • • Protected by the FDA, FTC, and Better Business Bureau	• Learn about products before buying them • • •	• Control impulse buying • • • •

2. **HYPOTHESIZING** Using the information in your chart, write an essay that answers the question: How does consumerism help shape supply and demand in the U.S. economy? Use a separate sheet of paper to write your essay.

LESSON 2 SUMMARY

Budgeting Your Money

SS.7.E.1.2, SS.7.E.1.3, SS.7.E.1.4, SS.7.E.1.5, SS.7.E.1.6

Using a Personal Budget

A **budget** is an effective tool for managing money. It is a careful record of the money you earn and the money you spend. Keeping such a record makes it easier to reduce impulse spending and to save money.

Budgeting Basics

Personal budgets and government budgets are made up of the same three parts:

1. Income—money earned or received
2. **Expenses**—money spent
3. **Balance**—what is left after expenses are subtracted from income

For any budget, the goal is to maintain a **balanced budget.** This occurs when the amount of income is equal to the amount spent. When you have more income than expenses, you have a **surplus.** This results in a positive balance. The surplus can be saved for emergencies or future expenses. The opposite of a surplus is a **deficit,** or negative balance. A deficit happens when expenses are greater than income.

1. ASSESSING

Label the income, expenses, and balance in the budget shown. Is it a balanced budget? Explain your answer.

Babysitting:	$35.00
Allowance:	$15.00
	$50.00
Movie Ticket:	$10.00
Bus Fare:	$20.00
Lunches:	$30.00
	$60.00
Total:	– $10.00

Name ____________ Date ____________ Class ____________

ANALYZING VISUALS

2. INTERPRETING Circle the items in the monthly budget that had actual amounts different from the planned amounts. What caused this budget to have a deficit?

____

____

____

____

____

____

____

____

____

____

Making a Budget

Making a budget is not difficult. To create a budget, follow these steps:

1. List everything you spend for a period of two weeks.
2. List all the money you receive and where it came from for the same time period.
3. Compare the two lists.

At the end of the two weeks, analyze the information. Did you have a surplus, a deficit, or a balanced budget? If you had a deficit, look for ways to spend less or earn more. If your income equaled your expenses, you had a balanced budget. Decide whether you want to spend less, earn more, or make no changes. If you had a surplus, decide if you want to increase spending or save the extra money.

MONTHLY BUDGET	PLANNED	ACTUAL
Income		
allowance	$60.00	$60.00
babysitting money	$70.00	$60.00
interest from savings	$5.00	$5.00
INCOME TOTAL	$135.00	$125.00
Expenses		
savings deposit	$20.00	$20.00
cell phone	$30.00	$45.00
clothes	$25.00	$20.00
other shopping	$10.00	$15.00
entertainment	$20.00	$27.50
other expenses	$15.00	$10.00
EXPENSES TOTAL	$120.00	$137.50
Balance	+$15.00	–$12.50

Using Credit

Today, most people and businesses use credit to make some purchases. **Credit** is a way of borrowing money. When you use credit, you buy something now but pay for it later. Credit is a helpful tool when it is used responsibly.

Credit Basics

To understand credit, you need to be familiar with the terms shown in the chart below:

CREDIT TERM	MEANING
lender	a person or an organization that gives someone money on a temporary basis for a fee
fee	a cost or charge
interest	fee charged for borrowing money
loan	money lent at interest
borrower	the person or organization who receives the loan
annual percentage rate (APR)	the annual cost of the loan, expressed as a percentage of the amount borrowed
credit rating	an estimate of a borrower's ability to repay a loan
collateral	property used as a promise to repay the loan

Lenders use previous credit history, job history, finances, and other information to determine a person's credit rating. Once credit is approved and the borrower uses it, he or she must pay back the loan by making monthly payments. These payments are made up of part of the purchase price and interest. If the loan is not repaid, the lender can take the borrower's collateral as payment. The collateral can be a house, a car, or some other valuable item.

3. PREDICTING CONSEQUENCES

How might competition affect interest rates on credit?

4. HYPOTHESIZING

What do you think would happen if you failed to repay a loan?

5. DRAWING CONCLUSIONS

Which is a safer place to get credit: a bank or a finance company? Why?

6. PROBLEM SOLVING

How can a person avoid paying interest when using a credit card?

Sources of Credit

Credit can be obtained from different sources, including banks, credit unions, and finance companies. A bank is an institution that offers checking accounts, savings accounts, and loans. A credit union is similar to a bank but is formed by a group with a common bond, such as the workers in one company. Finance companies only make loans. They have fewer government rules to follow, and they charge higher interest rates than banks.

Some stores offer credit to help consumers buy their goods. A store is more likely to offer a low credit limit. A **credit limit** is the maximum amount a borrower can charge.

Cars and houses are expensive items to purchase. Because of the high cost, many consumers use credit to buy them. When making these types of purchases, the buyer must make a down payment. A down payment is a portion of the purchase price that is paid at the time of the purchase. The rest of the purchase price is divided into equal monthly payments.

Credit Cards

Most people and businesses today use **credit cards.** A credit card allows consumers to make purchases using borrowed money. It can be issued by a bank, a credit card company, or a retail store. Credit cards have a spending limit. The limit is determined by a borrower's credit rating.

When using credit, it is important to be aware of the interest rate and fees and the effect they have on your balance. If you pay your entire balance each month by the due date, you might not have to pay interest. If you pay the minimum payment each month, you will be charged interest on the remaining balance. If you do not make your payment by the due date, you will be charged interest on the remaining balance and a late fee. After several late payments, your credit card could be assigned a higher interest rate.

The following example illustrates the dangers of interest. Notice that the borrower in Scenario 2 ended up paying more than 150 percent of the original purchase price because of the accumulated interest.

THE COST OF INTEREST		
	Scenario 1	**Scenario 2**
Purchase Price	$2,000	$2,000
Interest Rate	18%	18%
Monthly Payment	$2,000 (paid in full)	$80 (4% of purchase price)
Interest Owed	$0	$1,142
Total Cost	$2,000	$3,142
Time to Pay in Full	one month	more than 10 years

Benefits and Drawbacks of Credit

Credit can be a valuable tool, if it is used responsibly. Otherwise, it might present dangers. Being aware of the benefits and dangers of credit can help you use credit responsibly.

Benefits include:

- Making purchases without waiting to save all the money needed
- Buying expensive items, such as a car or a house
- Practicing discipline by making monthly payments

Dangers include:

- Borrowing more than can be repaid
- Always being in debt from making only the minimum monthly payments, often at high interest rates

7. RECOGNIZING RELATIONSHIPS

How can using the benefits of credit have negative effects?

8. REASONING

You have compared prices of an item you want to purchase. You use a credit card with a high APR to buy the item at a low price. What problem might develop?

Your Responsibilities as a Borrower

When you borrow money, you promise to make timely payments. It is important to make sure you can afford the payments before taking out a loan or using a credit card.

Payment terms are always included in the credit agreement. Review the agreement and look for the following information:

- the annual percentage rate (APR)
- whether the APR stays the same or changes over time
- payment size, frequency, and length of payment period
- additional fees, such as those for late payments.

Add the costs into your budget. Do you have room in your budget for the payments? Will your income last long enough to pay the full debt? If not, you should not take out the loan or make the purchase.

REVIEW LESSON 2

1. Use the chart below to note the ways a budget and credit can help a consumer.

	BUDGET	CREDIT
What It Is		
How It Works		
How It Helps		

2. **EVALUATING** Use the information in your chart to write an essay that explains how a financially responsible person uses a budget and credit. Use a separate sheet of paper to write your essay.

LESSON 3 SUMMARY

Saving and Investing

SS.7.E.1.2, SS.7.E.1.4, SS.7.E.1.5, SS.7.E.2.5

Saving Money

Consumers are often told to make savings the first expense in their budgets. Saving means setting aside money for later use.

Reasons to Save Money

Saving helps you reach your long-term spending goals. People save so they can make a down payment on a large purchase, such as a house or a car. People save money to pay for vacations or luxury purchases. Savings also allow people to be able to pay emergency expenses, such as medical bills or home repairs.

Saving money helps you and the economy. When you have a savings account, the bank pays you interest on your money. This makes your savings grow. Banks also put your money back into the economy by using it to make loans to other customers.

Savings Accounts Versus Checking Accounts

There are many ways to save money. The most common is a bank account. Banks offer savings accounts and checking accounts. Many people have both. Such accounts are safe and easy to access.

Savings accounts begin with an amount of money called the **principal.** Over time, interest is added to the principal, which makes the account grow. The larger the principal and the longer you keep the account, the more interest you will earn.

Checking accounts are better for spending money than saving it. Like a savings account, a checking account is a place to deposit money. However, checking accounts rarely earn interest. Instead, checking accounts offer two ways to make purchases: with checks or with a **debit card.**

1. IDENTIFYING CENTRAL ISSUES

What are two reasons to save money?

2. REASONING

What is one advantage of using a debit card instead of a credit card?

ANALYZING VISUALS

3. ASSESSING Which is riskier to use: a check or a debit card? Why?

____

____

____

____

____

____

4. DIFFERENTIATING

Lyssa has three years to save for college. Would she be better off opening a money market account or a CD? Why?

____

____

____

____

____

____

A debit card looks like a credit card but works like a check. The money for a debit card purchase comes directly out of your checking account. Whether you write a check or use a debit card, it is important to record the money you spend.

CHECKS
Piece of paper used to pay bills or buy things
Adds a fee if "bounced" (written for an amount greater than the account balance)
Forged check loss limited to $50 by law
Can be used to make purchases
Takes money directly from checking account
DEBIT CARDS
Looks like a credit card
Cannot spend more than what is in the account
Loss or misuse of card is not covered by law

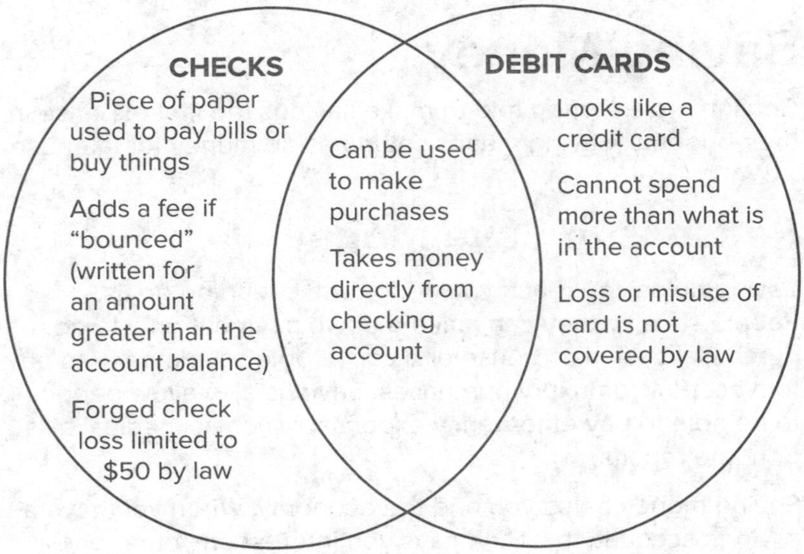

Savings Plans

Savings accounts are a safe and reliable way to save money. However, they do not earn as much interest as other methods of saving.

Money Market Accounts

Money market accounts are like savings accounts, but they require a larger initial deposit. They pay higher interest rates than regular savings accounts. Some money market accounts allow depositors to write checks on the account.

Certificates of Deposit

Another savings option is a certificate of deposit (CD). Unlike savings and money market accounts, CDs have a time limit. You deposit a sum of money for a certain number of months or years. During that time, the account earns interest. However, the interest is not added to the account until the CD reaches the end of the time limit, which is called maturity.

CDs usually offer higher interest rates than savings or money market accounts. However, you cannot easily withdraw money from a CD until maturity. If you close the CD early to withdraw your money, you have to pay a penalty, or fee, for doing so.

Factors to Consider When You Save

Just as with other financial decisions, saving money involves a trade-off. Saving money means you will have more to spend later. However, it also means you will have less to spend now. Nevertheless, it is a good idea to have some sort of savings plan.

HOW MUCH SHOULD I SAVE?
How much do I usually spend on regular expenses?
Why am I saving?
How much interest could my savings earn?
What is my income now?
What will my income be in the future?

Stocks and Bonds

Savings accounts, money market accounts, and CDs are useful ways to save, but investments tend to have a higher return. A return is the amount of interest earned. Investments earn higher returns because they combine money from many different people. However, they also carry some risk. The most common types of investments are stocks and bonds.

Stocks

When you buy **stock,** you buy a piece of ownership in a company. The piece of ownership is called a share. Someone who owns stock is called a shareholder, or a stockholder. The value of stock shares goes up or down depending on how well the company is doing. Shares can be bought and sold at any time. If you sell stock at a price higher than what you originally paid, you make a profit. If you sell it for less, you lose money.

Dividends can increase the profit you make from stock. A dividend is a portion of a company's earnings paid to shareholders based on the number of shares they hold. Dividends are paid regularly, such as every three months.

Stocks generally earn a higher return than other investments because they can be a risk. There is no guarantee that you will make money. You could even lose your money if the company closes down.

ANALYZING VISUALS

5. REFLECTING Do the answers to these questions stay the same or change over time? What does that say about a savings plan?

______

______

______

______

______

______

6. IDENTIFYING CENTRAL ISSUES

What are the benefits and risks of investing in stocks?

______

______

______

______

______

______

______

7. MAKING INFERENCES

Why are U.S. government bonds considered one of the safest investments?

______

______

______

______

______

______

8. SPECULATING

Many financial planners suggest splitting your investments among different types of savings options. Does this sound like a good plan? Explain your answer.

______

______

______

______

______

______

______

Bonds

Bonds are certificates of agreement between borrowers and lenders. The borrowers can be companies or governments. When you buy a bond, you lend money to a company or the government for a specific amount of time, usually several years. Unlike stock, a bond does not give ownership in the company or the government.

Bonds sold by companies are usually in large amounts. Companies use this money to pay for major expenses, such as new equipment. Bondholders earn a fixed rate of interest over a specific period. These bonds are risky, though, because the company might not be able to make all payments.

Federal, state, and local governments also issue bonds. The federal government offers savings bonds in small and large amounts. These bonds are considered one of the safest investments.

Mutual Funds

Mutual funds make it easier and safer to invest in stocks and bonds. **Mutual funds** are companies that sell stock in themselves. They then pool the money to purchase a variety of stocks and bonds in other companies. Because mutual funds spread the investment across many stocks and bonds, they have less risk than individual stocks or bonds. Financial experts decide which stocks or bonds to purchase. Their decisions determine your return.

Investors can track the performances of their stocks, bonds, and mutual funds by checking a stock index, such as the Dow Jones Industrial Average (DJIA) or the Standard and Poor's (S&P) 500.

Name ______________________ Date ______________ Class __________

REVIEW LESSON 3

1. Use the chart below to identify the benefits and drawbacks for each saving or investing option.

OPTION	BENEFITS	DRAWBACKS
Savings Accounts		
Checking Accounts		
Money Market Accounts		
Certificates of Deposit (CD)		
Stocks		
Bonds		
Mutual Funds		

2. **ASSESSING** Use the information in your chart to rank the options from safest to riskiest. On a separate sheet of paper, write an essay that explains your rankings.

Benchmark Skill Activities

DIRECTIONS: Write your answers on a separate sheet of paper.

MAFS.K12.MP.6.1

1. USING DEFINITIONS ACCURATELY

Choose five key terms defined on your FOLDABLES and explain how they are related.

LAFS.68.RH.2.5

2. ANALYZING INFORMATION

The following excerpt was written by the U.S. Securities and Exchange Commission (SEC). The SEC is the government agency that regulates stocks in the United States. Read the excerpt and write a paragraph explaining how the text organizes and presents information. Provide examples to support your analysis.

> What are the best saving and investing products for you? The answer depends on when you will need the money, your goals, and if you will be able to sleep at night if you purchase a risky investment where you could lose your principal.
>
> For instance, if you are saving for retirement, and you have 35 years before you retire, you may want to consider riskier investment products, knowing that if you stick to only the "savings" products or to less risky investment products, your money will grow too slowly—or given inflation [a continual rise in the prices of goods and services] or taxes, you may lose the purchasing power of your money. A frequent mistake people make is putting money they will not need for a very long time in investments that pay a low amount of interest.
>
> On the other hand, if you are saving for a short-term goal, five years or less, you don't want to choose risky investments, because when it's time to sell, you may have to take a loss. Since investments often move up and down in value rapidly, you want to make sure that you can wait and sell at the best possible time.
>
> —from "Determine Your Risk Tolerance," U.S. Securities and Exchange Commission

MAFS.K12.MP.1.1

3. SUGGESTING A SOLUTION

Use the data in the chart to create a budget. Determine whether the budget is balanced, has a deficit, or has a surplus. Based on that determination, recommend a course of action.

ITEM	AMOUNT EARNED	AMOUNT SPENT
Paycheck	$100.00	
New Shoes		$75.00
Babysitting	$60.00	
Music Download		$10.00
Pizza		$15.00
Bus Fare		$7.50
Gym Membership		$20.00

LAFS.7.SL.1.1, ELD.K12.ELL.SI.1

4. EVALUATING

Gather with a small group of your classmates. Use what you know from your life and from the chapter to discuss the question: Do you think it is easier or harder to be financially responsible in today's society? Support your answers with specific examples.

LAFS.68.WHST.2.6

5. ANALYZING INFORMATION

Use the Internet to conduct research on three different credit cards. Take note of the special incentives they offer, the annual percentage rate, and the fees associated with each card. Then compare and contrast the benefits and drawbacks of each card and select the one you think is the best choice for a consumer. Write a short essay describing your findings and supporting your choice.

Benchmark Note Cards

DIRECTIONS: Use these note cards to help you prepare for the test.

SS.7.C.2.11 Analyze media and political communications (bias, symbolism, propaganda).

MEDIA COMMUNICATIONS	Advertisers use special techniques such as playing on people's emotions to get consumers to make impulse purchases.

SS.7.E.1.2 Discuss the importance of borrowing and lending in the United States, the government's role in controlling financial institutions, and list the advantages and disadvantages of using credit.

BORROWING AND LENDING	• Credit is a type of borrowing. It helps people make immediate or large purchases that they would not otherwise be able to afford. • Bonds are also a form of borrowing. They allow companies and governments to borrow money from consumers to pay for expenses and special projects.

GOVERNMENT AND FINANCIAL INSTITUTIONS	• The Federal Trade Commission (FTC) works to protect consumers against fraud, deception, and unfair business practices. • The government regulates banks and credit unions more tightly than it regulates finance companies. • The government provides protection against the use of stolen checks, but not against the use of a lost or stolen debit card.

USING CREDIT	**Advantages** • Can make purchases without waiting • Can buy expensive items, such as a car or a house • Helps practice discipline through the making of timely monthly payments **Disadvantages** • Easy to fall into deep and perpetual debt by borrowing more than can be repaid, making late payments, or paying only the minimum due each month

SS.7.E.1.3 Review the concepts of supply and demand, choice, scarcity, and opportunity cost as they relate to the development of the mixed market economy in the United States.

SUPPLY AND DEMAND	• Consumerism educates buyers about goods and services and demands suppliers provide better, safer products. • The Consumer Bill of Rights ensures consumers use their powers of demand responsibly and that suppliers respect the demands of consumers.

CHOICE, SCARCITY, AND OPPORTUNITY COST	**Choice** • Consumers must choose among competing wants. • Consumers have the right to choose among a variety of goods, according to the Consumer Bill of Rights. • Consumers have a variety of choices for saving and investing. **Scarcity** • Consumers must decide how to use their disposable income to meet their wants. **Opportunity Cost** • When making spending and saving decisions, consumers must consider the opportunity costs of their choices.

SS.7.E.1.4 Discuss the function of financial institutions in the development of a market economy.

FINANCIAL INSTITUTIONS	• Financial institutions provide consumers with a variety of options for managing their money, such as loans, checking accounts, savings accounts, and money market accounts. • Banks, credit unions, and finance companies compete for consumer business.

SS.7.E.1.5 Assess how profits, incentives, and competition motivate individuals, households, and businesses in a free market economy.

PROFITS, INCENTIVES, AND COMPETITION	**Profits** • Consumers use savings accounts, money market accounts, stocks, bonds, and mutual funds to earn a profit on their money. • Investors hope to make a profit when they sell their stocks. **Incentives** • Consumers save to be prepared for emergencies, to be able to afford luxury purchases, to achieve future goals, and to be able to make down payments on large purchases. • Companies and governments offer bonds to get money for expenses and special projects. **Competition** • Consumers can take advantage of competition by comparison shopping before making purchases.

BENCHMARK NOTE CARDS, *continued*

SS.7.E.1.6 Compare the national budget process to the personal budget process.

MAKING A BUDGET	The basics of making a budget are the same for a government as for an individual. • Make and compare lists of expenses and income. • When expenses are greater than income, the budget has a deficit. Expenses must be cut or income increased. • When expenses equal income, the budget is balanced. • When income is greater than expenses, the budget has a surplus. The extra funds can be put into savings.

SS.7.E.2.3 Identify and describe United States laws and regulations adopted to promote economic competition.

PROMOTING COMPETITION	The Federal Trade Commission (FTC) works to protect consumers against fraud, deception, and unfair business practices.

SS.7.E.2.5 Explain how economic institutions impact the national economy.

ECONOMIC INSTITUTIONS AND THE NATIONAL ECONOMY	Savings help the national economy grow. Banks use savings deposits to make loans to other customers. This puts money back into the economy by helping those customers make purchases.

Chapter 19

VISUAL SUMMARY

DIRECTIONS: Complete the graphic organizer below.

PERSONAL FINANCE

CONSUMERISM

Consumers are protected by a consumer bill of rights, the FDA, the FTC, and the BBB.

Consumers have the responsibility to ______________________________

____

Consumers should ______________________________

____

BUDGETING

A budget helps people manage money and plan for the future.

Budgets list and compare ______________________________

A deficit is ______________________________

____

A surplus is ______________________________

____

A balanced budget means ______________________________

USING CREDIT

Credit means buying something now but paying for it later.

The amount owed must be ______________________________

Credit comes from ______________________________

Be aware of ______________________________

Credit helps people buy expensive items, but ______________________________

SAVING AND INVESTING

Saving helps people reach long-term goals and helps the economy.

Savings and checking accounts provide ______________________________

Checks are more protected than ______________________________

Money market accounts offer ______________________________

____

CDs pay higher interest, but ______________________________

Stocks and bonds ______________________________

Mutual funds ______________________________

USING PRIMARY SOURCES

COMPARE AND CONTRAST The Federal Communications Commission (FCC) is the government agency that regulates media. In the 1990s, it pushed for a bill of rights for consumers who used cable television services. The text below is from that campaign.

Write an essay that compares the bill of rights for cable television consumers with the consumer bill of rights in Lesson 1 of this chapter. What do they have in common? What rights are unique to the bill of rights for cable television consumers? What might explain those differences?

> *From your cable company:*
>
> *(1) Consumers should expect a fair deal from their local cable company, with reasonable rates that fairly reflect the costs of doing business.*
>
> *(2) Consumers should expect an explanation from their cable companies whenever rates for the programming service tier are raised, particularly when cable companies attribute price rises to increases in the cost of obtaining programming.*
>
> *(3) Consumers are entitled to write or call their cable companies whenever they have complaints about the cable services being provided on the various channels, or about program cost increases, and they should expect a speedy response.*
>
> *From your local government:*
>
> *(4) Consumers are entitled to file complaints with their local government (i.e., city, town, or county) regarding basic tier cable rate increases and service quality.*
>
> *From the FCC:*
>
> *(5) Consumers are entitled to provide their own inside wiring for cable hookups.*
>
> *(6) Consumers will soon be entitled to purchase and use cable set-top boxes at competitive market prices.*
>
> *—"Cable Consumer Bill of Rights Campaign," March 31, 1999, Federal Communications Commission*

Chapter Practice Test

DIRECTIONS: Circle the best answer for each question.

SS.7.E.1.6 (Moderate)

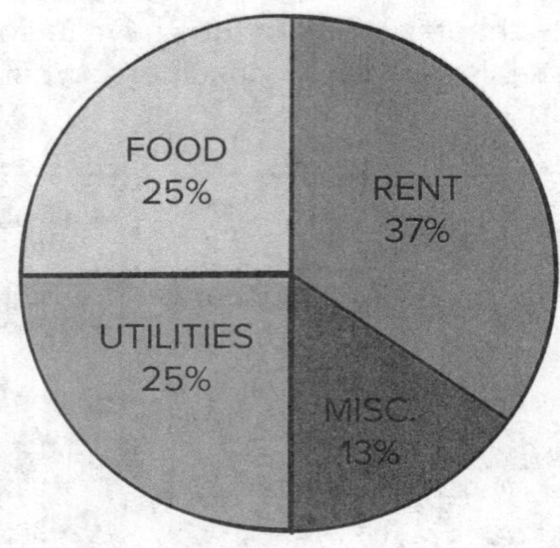

Which part of a budget does this circle graph represent?

A deficit

B income

C surplus

D expenses

SS.7.E.1.2 (Moderate)

STATEMENT SUMMARY **Month of July**	
Previous Balance:	$ 576.34
Payment/Credits:	−$25.00
Purchases:	417.86
Fees Charged:	0.00
Interest Charged:	103.84
New Balance:	$ 1,073.04

What concept is illustrated by this statement summary?

A the danger of excessive fees

B the risk of making only minimum monthly payments

C the benefits of using a debit card

D the rewards of earning interest on a savings account

3 **SS.7.C.2.11 (High)**

Live Your Best Life at Countryside Farms!
New luxury homes starting at $500,000
Community Amenities:
• Olympic-size pool
• Five-mile bicycle path
• Four basketball courts
• Two tennis courts
• Fully equipped gym

How does this advertisement try to persuade consumers to buy a new house?

A It suggests home buyers will lead healthier lives.

B It emphasizes the affordable price of the homes.

C It suggests home buyers will enjoy being farmers.

D It emphasizes the thrill of being first at something.

---

4 **SS.7.E.1.3, SS.7.E.1.6 (Moderate)**

How can comparison shopping help a budget?

A It can help increase income by finding jobs that offer higher paychecks.

B It can help grow income by finding stocks that offer the greatest earnings.

C It can help cover more expenses by finding credit cards with the lowest interest rates.

D It can help keep expenses to a minimum by finding the best prices for goods and services.

 **SS.7.E.1.3, SS.7.E.1.5 (High)**

	SAVINGS ACCOUNT	MONEY MARKET ACCOUNT	CERTIFICATE OF DEPOSIT	U.S. GOVERNMENT BOND
Interest Rate	0.75%	1.5%	2.25%	.25%
Minimum Deposit	$100	$1,000	$5,000	$1,000
Interest Paid	monthly	monthly	after 1 year	once a year

Miller has $1,000 to save, but he needs easy access to his money to pay medical bills. Which savings option is his best choice?

A savings account

B money market account

C certificate of deposit

D U.S. government bond

 **SS.7.E.1.2, SS.7.E.2.3 (Moderate)**

Why are checks safer to use than debit cards?

A Checks are more difficult to steal than debit cards.

B Checks come with greater legal protections than debit cards.

C Checks earn a higher interest rate than debit cards.

D Checks take less money from your account than debit cards.

7 **SS.7.E.1.3 (High)**

Jo has $500 to spend. Which expense should she pay first?

A rent

B vacation

C new shoes

D new phone

---

8 **SS.7.E.1.4, SS.7.E.2.5 (Moderate)**

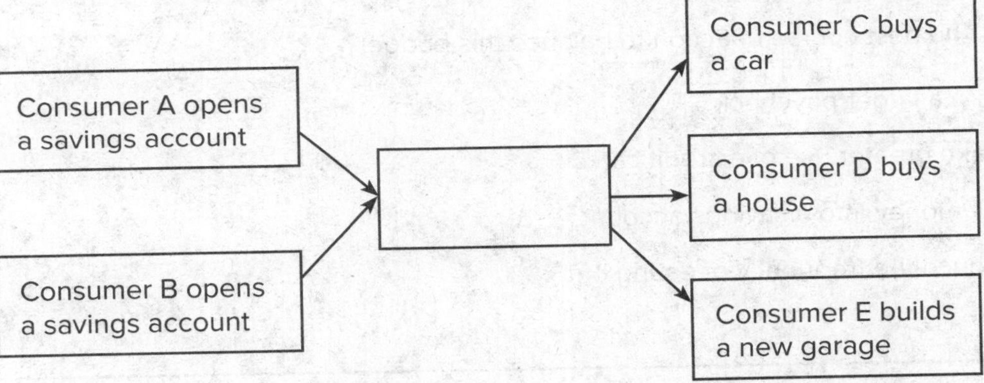

What belongs in the blank box in the diagram?

A Savings accounts earn interest

B Financial expert chooses stocks

C Bank uses savings to make loans

D Financial institution requires collateral

9 **SS.7.E.1.6 (High)**

Budget	
Paycheck:	$200.00
Paycheck:	$200.00
	$400.00
New bike tires:	$50.00
Eating out:	$250.00
Gym membership:	$65.00
Utilities:	$75.00
	$440.00
Total:	—$40.00

What is the best course of action to balance this budget?

A earn a larger paycheck

B make greater use of a credit card

C put money into a savings account

D reduce the frequency of eating out

---

10 **SS.7.E.1.3 (Moderate)**

Why is it to a supplier's advantage to provide good quality products?

A Consumers are more likely to make an impulse purchase of a quality good.

B Consumers are more likely to purchase a generic good if it is made well.

C Consumers are less likely to seek redress if the product is good quality.

D Consumers are less likely to consider opportunity cost if the product is made well.

CHAPTER 20

Business in America

Chapter Overview

Businesses in America come in a wide range of sizes. Some are small and have just one owner or a few partners. Others are large corporations or franchises. Most businesses try to make a profit on the goods they produce or the services they provide. Nonprofit organizations and cooperatives are the exception.

Labor unions work to increase employees' wages and ensure a safe workplace. Unions negotiate on behalf of employees. Sometimes, unions and employers cannot reach agreements. Then they might use tools such as strikes, boycotts, lockouts, and injunctions to reach their goals.

CHAPTER BENCHMARKS

SS.7.E.1.5 Assess how profits, incentives, and competition motivate individuals, households, and businesses in a free market economy.

SS.7.E.2.3 Identify and describe United States laws and regulations adopted to promote economic competition.

LAFS.68.RH.1.2 Determine the central ideas or information of a primary or secondary source; provide an accurate summary of the source distinct from prior knowledge or opinions.

LAFS.68.WHST.1.2 Write informative/explanatory texts, including the narration of historical events, scientific procedures/ experiments, or technical processes

LAFS.68.WHST.2.4 Produce clear and coherent writing in which the development, organization, and style are appropriate to task, purpose, and audience.

LAFS.68.WHST.2.6 Use technology, including the Internet, to produce and publish writing and present the relationships between information and ideas clearly and efficiently.

LAFS.68.WHST.3.7 Conduct short research projects to answer a question (including a self-generated question), drawing on several sources and generating additional related, focused questions that allow for multiple avenues of exploration.

WHAT I NEED TO KNOW

TERMS

- ☐ sole proprietorship
- ☐ liability
- ☐ partnership
- ☐ corporation
- ☐ charter
- ☐ franchise
- ☐ nonprofit organization
- ☐ labor union
- ☐ right-to-work law
- ☐ collective bargaining
- ☐ strike
- ☐ picketing
- ☐ lockout
- ☐ injunction
- ☐ mediation
- ☐ arbitration
- ☐ social responsibility

Business in America

Business in America

Create this Foldable® like a small booklet. Label the front *Business in America.* Open the Foldable and label the top of the left section *Business* and the right section *Labor.* On the left side, describe the three main types of businesses and their role in our nation's economy. On the right side, explain the importance of organized labor. On the back of the folded booklet, explain the social responsibilities of businesses. Give an example of how a local or a national business helps your community.

Step 1
Arrange a piece of paper horizontally and fold in half from left to right.

Step 2
Label the inside of your booklet as shown.

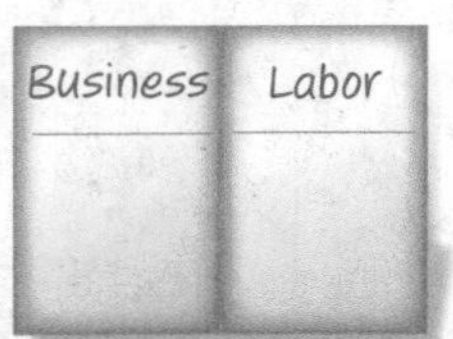

LESSON 1 SUMMARY

How Businesses Are Organized

SS.7.E.1.5

Sole Proprietorships

People are motivated to work for many reasons. An important one is that they want to earn money to pay for a place to live, food to eat, and other wants. People start businesses for this same reason. They want to earn a profit from the services they offer or the products they create.

The free market economy of the United States is based on the idea that individuals and groups have the right to start the business of their choice. The most common form of business is a sole proprietorship. In a **sole proprietorship,** a sole individual—one person—owns the business. That one person supplies the money needed to start and run the business. He or she receives all the profits if the business is successful. However, a sole proprietor also assumes all **liability.** This means that the business owner is totally responsible for the actions of the business. Most sole proprietorships, or simply proprietorships, are small businesses in a local area. Restaurants and auto repair shops often take this form. Proprietorships make up more than 70 percent of all businesses.

The primary incentive for accepting this responsibility is the opportunity to earn a profit. All the money the small business earns is not profit, though. Some of the money pays rent on the building in which the business resides. Money is also needed to buy raw materials and equipment for the business.

SOLE PROPRIETORSHIP	
Advantages	**Disadvantages**
• The owner makes all of the decisions for the business. He or she is the boss. • The owner collects all the profits. • A sole proprietorship is the easiest form of business to start.	• The owner may have a hard time raising money to start or run the business. • There is no limit on liability, or legal responsibility. The owner may have to sell personal property to pay the debts of the business.

1. DRAWING CONCLUSIONS

What incentives, other than profits, might encourage an individual to start a new company?

ANALYZING VISUALS

2. RANKING Look at the chart. Which advantage to a sole proprietorship do you think is most important? Why?

3. MAKING INFERENCES

What might happen if two or more people start a business without signing articles of partnership?

______

______

______

______

______

______

______

______

______

Partnerships

Sometimes two or more people decide to start and operate a business together. They agree to share the start-up costs and then to split any profits. This form of business is called a **partnership.** Pooling money is one reason for creating a partnership. Another may be that people bring different skills into it. A partnership can be small with just two partners. It can also be large, with hundreds of partners in different cities.

It is important for everyone in a partnership to sign a legal document called articles of partnership. This document sets up the rules of the partnership. It usually outlines how any profits will be distributed, when and how people can join, and how the partnership can be ended.

Partnerships can take two different forms. In a general partnership, all partners share the business and responsibility. In a limited partnership, limited partners only have a share in the business and usually provide the money needed. They do not work in or run the business. In turn, they are liable for only the amount of money they invested. The initials *LLP* in a business name show that it is a limited liability partnership.

PARTNERSHIP	
Advantages	**Disadvantages**
• Partnerships are better able to raise money and obtain bank loans than sole proprietorships. • Partnerships can gain additional money by adding new partners. • Partners may have different skills that can help the business.	• In a general partnership, each partner has unlimited liability for business debts. • Multiple owners have to share the profits. • Partners may disagree on how to run the company.

Corporations

People can also form a business as a **corporation.** You can tell that a business is a corporation if the word *Inc.* is a part of the name. *Inc.* is the abbreviation for "incorporated." Corporations are the most complicated form of business. They operate under a state **charter,** which is a document granting permission to form the business. Corporations have the same rights and responsibilities as an individual. They can own property, pay taxes, and enter contracts. Corporations are often very large, and some have annual earnings greater than many countries.

Name ______________________ Date ______________ Class ________

LESSON 1 SUMMARY, *continued*

CORPORATION	
Advantages	**Disadvantages**
• Corporations can easily raise money to buy equipment or expand operations. They do so by selling stocks or issuing bonds. Some corporations are huge, with annual earnings greater than some countries. • Ownership in a corporation can be transferred easily through the buying and selling of stock. A stockholder can pass stock on to heirs when he or she dies. • Owners in a corporation have limited liability. If the corporation is sued, the personal property of stockholders is protected.	• Corporations are subject to more government regulations than other types of businesses. • Corporations are closely observed. They must publish their financial records and hold regular meetings. • Corporations may have to address diverse needs of a large number of stockholders. It can be difficult for stockholders to unite and force changes.

The owners of corporations are groups of people called stockholders. Stockholders supply the money the corporation needs to operate. In return, stockholders receive stocks, or documents showing how much of the company they own. They are entitled to receive a percentage of the company's profits based on the amount of stock they own. Stockholders usually do not play a day-to-day role in the company's operation, though. Instead, during annual meetings they vote for members of a board of directors. A shareholder usually gets one vote for each share of common stock he or she owns. The board hires a president and managers to run the corporation.

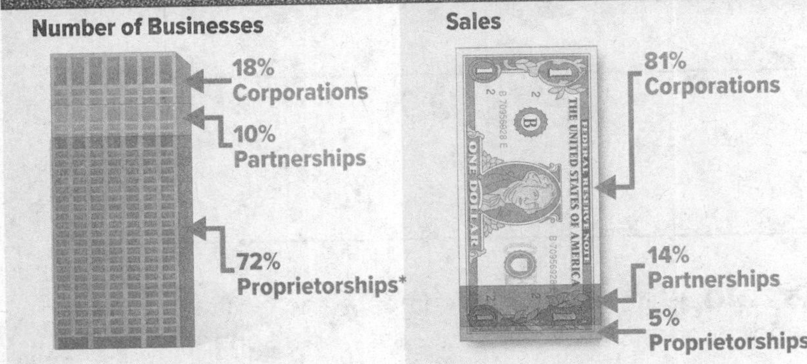

Source: IRS, Statistics of Income Division, November 2012
*Nonfarm Sole Proprietorships

4. IDENTIFYING PROBLEMS

What problem might stockholders have because the people who run the company are chosen by a board of directors?

____
____
____
____
____
____
____
____

ANALYZING VISUALS

5. INTERPRETING Which form of business organization has the highest percentage of sales? Why do you think this is so?

____
____
____
____
____
____
____

Name ____________________ Date ____________ Class ________

LESSON 1 SUMMARY, *continued*

6. GIVING EXAMPLES

Name two examples of nonprofit organizations that have the goal of helping others rather than making a profit.

____

____

____

____

____

____

Other Forms of Business

A **franchise** is a business with the right to be sole seller of a product in a particular place. In exchange for the right to sell, the owner pays a fee and gives the supplier of the product a portion of any profits made. The supplier helps the franchise owner run the business but also often has specific rules the franchise owner must follow.

A **nonprofit organization** is a company that does not work to make a profit. Instead, the goal of a nonprofit is to help others or to promote a cause. Public hospitals and labor unions are nonprofit organizatons.

Sometimes people form a kind of nonprofit organization called a cooperative. Members of a cooperative join together so they can benefit economically. For example, a consumer cooperative buys goods in bulk. This means that members pay less to buy these goods than they would if they bought them somewhere else.

REVIEW LESSON 1

1. Complete the chart below to identify the characteristics of different forms of businesses.

FORMS OF BUSINESSES			
	Sole Proprietorship	Partnership	Corporation
Ownership	A single owner receives profits.	Two or more owners receive profits.	Multiple stockholders receive profits.
Liability			
Financing			

2. **COMPARING AND CONTRASTING** Write an essay to compare and contrast sole proprietorships, partnerships, and corporations. Write your essay on a separate sheet of paper.

LESSON 2 SUMMARY
Labor

SS.7.E.1.5

Organized Labor

The number of people working or looking for work in the United States today is nearly twice what it was in 1970. However, the number of people in labor unions during that same period has decreased by about half. A **labor union** is an organization of workers that tries to improve the wages and working conditions of its members. One reason for the decrease is the shift from manufacturing to service jobs. Fewer service workers tend to join unions. Also, some employers keep unions out. Still, unions remain important.

Types of Unions

Workers can join two types of unions. People who share a skill or a trade join *trade unions*. Bakers and printers are examples. An *industrial union* brings together workers in the same industry regardless of job or skill. An example is the United Auto Workers.

Unions used to exist mostly for workers in manufacturing. Today there are unions for actors, professional athletes, and health-care professionals as well as for workers in other industries. More workers in government join unions than in businesses. The nation's largest unions include the National Education Association of the United States, the International Brotherhood of Teamsters, and the American Federation of State, County and Municipal Employees.

Unions in the Workplace

A union is able to form in a place of business if a majority of the employees agree to it. Some unions set up a *union shop*. The employer can hire anyone in this workplace, but then that person must join the union. Many companies, however, do not want to set up a union shop. This has led some states to pass **right-to-work laws,** which forbid union shops. Some states have modified union shops. Workers are not required to join a union. If they do, they have to remain union members for as long as they have their job. Some workplaces are *agency shops*. Workers who do not join are required to pay a fee to the union because they still benefit from the union's actions.

1. REASONING

What specific issues might the National Education Association of the United States be interested in promoting?

2. DRAWING CONCLUSIONS

Why do so many unions exist for different groups and industries?

3. ASSESSING

There are advantages and disadvantages for workers who go on strike. How might a strike affect the family of a worker who has decided to take part in a strike?

4. EVALUATING

Do you think a lockout is the best solution for dealing with striking workers? Explain.

Labor Negotiations

The job of a union is to help workers gain better wages and working conditions. To do this, unions work with companies in a process called **collective bargaining.** In this process, officials of the union and the company meet to negotiate, or discuss, the terms of employment, or the workers' contract. Topics of these talks often are wages and benefits, such as sick days, holidays, and health insurance. Perhaps, workers want more sick days or another break during the workday. Rules for workers are also discussed. Usually, the unions and companies reach an agreement at the end of their bargaining.

Labor's Tools

If a union and a company cannot agree, the union has several ways to make the company agree to its demands. One way is to call a **strike.** During a strike, all union members refuse to work. The company loses money while it is shut down and may be forced to do what the union wants.

Workers who are on strike often take part in **picketing.** This is a tactic in which striking workers walk with signs that express their grievances. Often, members of the public agree with the picketing workers. When this happens, people may boycott the company and stop buying its products or services. Again, the company loses money.

Just as strikes can create problems for businesses, they can create problems for workers. The union workers receive no pay during a strike. During a long strike, the lack of a paycheck might cause the workers to pressure the union to settle. Sometimes workers don't make any gains. In most cases, however, strikes are settled when the company and the union work out an agreement.

Employers' Tools

Companies have ways to pressure unions, as well. After all, they, too, cannot afford to lose income. A company facing a union strike might institute a **lockout.** During a lockout, the workers cannot enter the workplace. The company then hires replacement workers. An employer who knows the union might strike also can seek an **injunction.** This is a legal order from a court to prevent a certain activity, such as a strike.

Name ____________________ Date ____________ Class ________

Outside Help

Injunctions are not just for employers, though. If the industry is important to the economy, the government may get an injunction so that the company is forced to end its lockout. Also, unions may file for this court order to prevent a lockout.

If unions and companies cannot agree on a contract but want to avoid a strike, they have other options. In **mediation,** a third party tries to lead them to an agreement. In **arbitration,** a third party listens to the arguments of both sides and then makes a decision. Unions and companies agree beforehand to abide by this decision.

The government can intervene in a strike if it threatens the nation. Federal laws allow the president to force workers to return to work during a cooling-off period of no more than 80 days. However, during the cooling-off period, the company and the union must work to reach a settlement. If at the end of the cooling-off period there still is no agreement, the workers can strike. In extreme cases, the government can take over a company or an industry for a short time, but such instances are rare.

NEGOTIATION TOOLS	
Labor Union's Tools	**Employer's Tools**
• Strikes • Picketing • Economic Pressure • Injunctions	• Lockouts • Injunctions
Tools Used by Both Sides	
Collective Bargaining Mediation Arbitration	

5. MAKING INFERENCES

Why might unions and employers agree to arbitration?

____

____

____

____

____

6. IDENTIFYING

Which tool of negotiation guarantees an outcome? Explain.

____

____

____

____

____

____

Name ____________ Date ____________ Class ____________

REVIEW LESSON 2

1. Complete the chart below to describe organized labor and labor negotiations.

ORGANIZED LABOR	LABOR NEGOTIATIONS
A labor union is	Collective bargaining is
Two types of labor unions are	Labor's tools include Employers' tools include
A union shop is	Ways to avoid strikes include
Right-to-work laws are	The government may

2. **CONSTRUCTING AN ARGUMENT** Labor negotiations involve two sides: company officials and union officials. In general, union officials are trying to get better conditions for employees, such as increases in pay or more time off. Company officials are trying to hold costs down in order to remain profitable and competitive. Use the information from your chart to write an essay that answers this question: During labor negotiations, which side do you think has more powerful tools to use? Support your position with logical reasons. Write your essay on a separate sheet of paper.

LESSON 3 SUMMARY

Roles and Responsibilities of Businesses

SS.7.E.1.5, SS.7.E.2.3

The Social Responsibility of Businesses

You might be surprised to learn that most businesses give back to their communities. Some even give back to the nation and the world. They may do this by supporting schools or other organizations that benefit society. While businesses are producers with the goal of making profits, they also take their **social responsibility** seriously. They recognize that they have an obligation to pursue other goals that benefit society as well as themselves.

Other Business Responsibilities

Business owners are required to follow laws and regulations. Some of these laws relate to the responsibilities they have to their consumers, owners, and employees. Regardless of the specific laws or regulations, failure to abide by them might mean legal action. It could also mean less profit because customers might stop doing business with them.

Responsibilities to Consumers

When you buy a product, you expect it to work properly and safely. A business cannot knowingly sell you an inferior product. For example, when you buy milk from the supermarket, you expect it not to be spoiled or contaminated. You also expect your new cell phone to work properly and the auto mechanic to fix a car correctly. Many companies give guarantees on their products or services for a certain amount of time. They will repair or replace items that don't work. Businesses should also tell the truth when they advertise their products. Finally, businesses are expected to treat all customers fairly.

1. EVALUATING

What are some of the benefits that businesses gain from giving back to a community?

2. HYPOTHESIZING

Why do you think businesses have so many responsibilities to consumers?

Name ______________________ Date ______________ Class __________

ANALYZING VISUALS

3. INTERPRETING What generalization can you make to explain the differences between what the law requires companies to do for its employees and what companies may do voluntarily?

____

____

____

____

____

____

____

____

Responsibilities to Owners

Stockholders invest their money in a corporation and become owners of that corporation. They generally do not run the corporation. It is the responsibility of the corporation's managers to provide financial reports regularly. Stockholders can then see how their money is being spent and what profits are being made.

Corporate officers are required by law to sign a document that states that financial statements are correct and honest. They cannot falsify documents or mislead the stockholders about the corporation's financial health. Corporate officers can be prosecuted for these illegal actions.

Responsibilities to Employees

Businesses must follow certain laws related to their employees. However, businesses can choose the types of employee benefits and services they offer. Providing incentives to employees generally helps both the business and the workers. A healthy worker misses fewer days of work and can be more productive.

BUSINESS RESPONSIBILITIES	
Required Responsibilities Related to Workers	• Provide a safe workplace. • Treat all workers fairly and without discrimination based on race, gender, age, religion, or disability. 　◦ Men and women doing the same job must be paid the same wage. 　◦ Workers cannot be fired based on an older age. • Provide health insurance; tax credits for small businesses help make this more affordable.
Possible Benefits or Services for Workers	• Provide child care centers. • Offer fitness centers. • Help pay for college or trade school.

Name ______________________ Date ______________ Class __________

REVIEW LESSON 3

1. Complete the chart below to identify the responsibilities businesses have to consumers, stockholders, and workers.

RESPONSIBILITIES OF BUSINESSES		
To Consumers	To Stockholders	To Workers
• • •	•	• • •

2. **Identifying Central Ideas** Write an essay to answer the following questions: Why are there laws to regulate the responsibilities of businesses? Do they help or hurt businesses? Use the information in the chart above and in the lesson in your essay. Use a separate sheet of paper for your essay.

Benchmark Skill Activities

DIRECTIONS: Write your answers on a separate piece of paper.

LAFS.68.WHST.1.2, LAFS.68.WHST.2.4, SS.7.E.1.5

1. GIVING EXAMPLES

Use your FOLDABLES to write an essay.

Businesses and labor contribute to the economy and quality of life in the United States. In what ways do they each support economic growth and improve people's lives? Include specific examples.

LAFS.68.RH.1.2

2. DETERMINING POINT OF VIEW

Some states have passed right-to-work laws so that workers have the right to have a job in a company whether or not they join a union. Suppose your state is taking a vote on this issue. How will you vote? Use evidence from the chapter to support your opinion.

LAFS.68.RH.2.4, LAFS.68.WHST.2.4

3. USING DEFINITIONS ACCURATELY

Turn to this chapter's Terms list. Choose at least three words to include in a paragraph that explains the relationship between business and labor.

LAFS.68.RH.1.2, LAFS.68.WHST.1.2, LAFS.68.WHST.2.6, LAFS.68.WHST.3.7

4. ANALYZING INFORMATION

You have learned about different actions labor unions and employers can take if they cannot agree during collective bargaining. Do research on the Internet to find information about a disagreement between labor unions and businesses. What actions did either group take to convince the other side? What did they do to resolve the disagreement?

After you analyze the information, use a computer to write a blog entry about the disagreement and its resolution, as well as your opinion about both.

Benchmark Note Cards

DIRECTIONS: Use these note cards to help you prepare for the test.

SS.7.E.1.5 Assess how profits, incentives, and competition motivate individuals, households, and businesses in a free market economy.

PROFITS IN A FREE MARKET ECONOMY	People start businesses to earn a profit from the services they offer or the products they create. In a sole proprietorship, one person receives all the profits if the business is successful. In a partnership, both general and limited partners share profits. In a corporation, stockholders receive a percentage of the company's profits based on the amount of stock they own.

INCENTIVES IN A FREE MARKET ECONOMY	People might have the incentive to start a company to fill a market need, to help the community by creating jobs, or to be an entrepreneur. Businesses can provide incentives to their employees. Some incentives might be helping to pay for college or trade school, providing child care, and having fitness centers.

LABOR'S ROLE IN A FREE MARKET ECONOMY	Unions work to improve the wages and working conditions of its members. Unions often get benefits for employees, such as sick days, holidays, and health insurance.

TOOLS OF LABOR AND EMPLOYERS	• If a union and a company cannot agree, the union can call a strike and picket. • A company facing a strike may request an injunction to prevent the strike. • A company facing a strike may declare a lockout and hire replacement workers. • A union may request an injunction to end a lockout.

SS.7.E.2.3 Identify and describe United States laws and regulations adopted to promote economic competition.

LAWS THAT REGULATE BUSINESSES	• Businesses must treat customers fairly and not discriminate. • Businesses must advertise honestly. • The officers of corporations are required to provide correct and honest financial statements to their stockholders. • Businesses are required to follow laws related to their employees. These include providing a safe workplace and health benefits, and treating all workers fairly and without discrimination.

Chapter 20

VISUAL SUMMARY

DIRECTIONS: Complete the graphic organizers below.

FORMS OF BUSINESS	
Sole Proprietorship	★ Owner gets profits ★ Owner makes all decisions ★ May be difficult to raise money ★ No limits on liability ★ Easiest form of business to start
Partnership	★ ★ ★ ★ ★
Corporation	★ ★ ★ ★ ★ ★

ORGANIZED LABOR

★ Organization of workers

★ Goal: ______

★ Types: ______

★ In the workplace: ______

LABOR NEGOTIATIONS

★ Collective bargaining: ______

★ Disagreement can result in: ______

★ Disagreements can be ended by: ______

RESPONSIBILITIES OF BUSINESS

★ Social responsibilities:

★

★

★

USING PRIMARY SOURCES

COMPARE AND CONTRAST Read the two primary sources related to the structure of businesses. Then, on a separate sheet of paper, answer the questions that follow.

Document A

When you're starting a business, one of the first decisions you have to make is the type of business you want to create. A sole proprietorship? A corporation? . . . This decision is important, because the type of business you create determines the types of applications you'll need to submit. You should also research liability implications [issues] for personal investments you make into your business, as well as the taxes you will need to pay. It's important to understand each business type and select the one that is best suited for your situation and objectives. . . .

Here is a list of the most common ways to structure a business. . . .

Corporation

A corporation is an independent legal entity owned by shareholders. This means that the corporation itself, not the shareholders that own it, is held legally liable for the actions and debts incurred [experienced] by the business. . . .

Partnership

A partnership is a single business where two or more people share ownership. When two or more people decide to join together to carry on a trade or business, their relationship is considered to be a partnership. . . .

—"Incorporating Your Business," U.S. Small Business Administration

Document B

"Much that one man cannot do alone two can do together, and once admit the fact that co-operation, or what is the same thing, combination, is necessary on a small scale, the limit depends solely upon the necessities of business. Two persons in partnership may be a sufficiently large combination for a small business, but if the business grows, or can be made to grow, more persons and more capital must be taken in. The business may grow so large that a partnership ceases [stops] to be a proper instrumentality [means] for its purposes, and then a corporation becomes a necessity. . . ."

—John D. Rockefeller

1. How are Documents A and B similar?
2. What is the purpose of each document?
3. What reasons does each document give for choosing to do business as a corporation?

Chapter Practice Test

DIRECTIONS: Circle the best answer for each question.

---

1 **SS.7.E.1.5 (High)**

The flowchart below shows the possible events in a dispute between a labor union and an employer. Which likely step is missing from the chart?

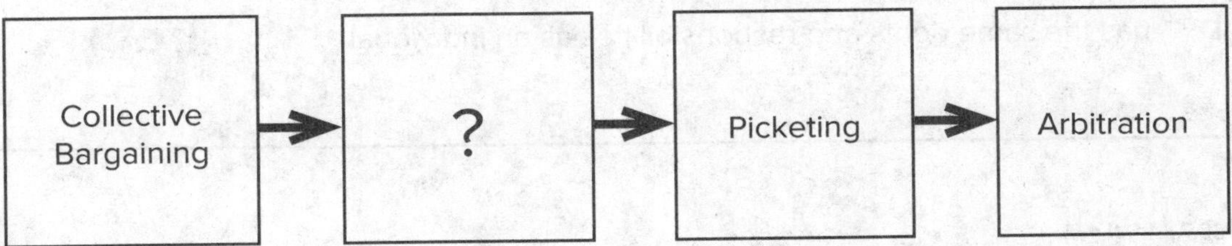

A Lockout

B Strike

C Replacements Hired

D Mediation

2 **SS.7.E.2.3 (Moderate)**

Which of the following is required of businesses?

A They must contribute to charities.

B They must work with unions to help employees.

C They must treat all employees fairly.

D They must publish annual financial reports.

3 **SS.7.E.1.5 (Moderate)**

Which of the following accurately describes a corporation?

A has unlimited liability

B is the easiest form of business to start

C gains financial capital by adding new partners

D has the same rights and responsibilities as an individual

4 **SS.7.E.1.5 (Low)**

The diagram below shows characteristics of one type of business.

- easy to start with few regulations
- does not need to share profits with anyone
- might have to use own money to help struggling company

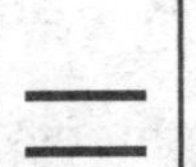

Which type of business completes the diagram?

A sole proprietorship

B partnership

C corporation

D nonprofit organization

5 **SS.7.E.1.5 (Moderate)**

Read the scenario below.

Jesse decides to open a computer repair shop. He uses all the money in his savings account and borrows money from his dad to start the business. Then he hires an assistant.

Which of the following is a disadvantage of Jesse's business?

A He earns all the profit.

B He has unlimited liability.

C He can offer incentives to his assistant.

D He finds it easy to organize his business.

6 **SS.7.E.1.5 (high)**

Read the news item below.

Workers arrived at the company at their usual starting time, but they found that they were unable to enter the building. Company officials were not available to comment on the situation.

What likely happened before the event described in the news item?

A The government declared a cooling-off period.

B A union requested an injunction from the court.

C The company agreed to offer employees health insurance.

D A union suggested to its members to strike.

SS.7.E.1.5 (High)

Read the scenario below.

> *An auto mechanic wants to open his own garage to repair cars. He has a friend who is an accountant who would also like to own a business.*

What advantage would there be for the two of them to form a partnership?

A It would allow them to transfer ownership easily.

B It would provide them with unlimited liability.

C It would be easier to raise financial capital.

D It would enable them to sell stock in the business.

SS.7.E.2.3 (Moderate)

Read the scenario below.

> *Mario is 63 years old and has worked for the same company for 35 years. He has been a loyal employee. He has never received a bad performance review. In fact, at his last review he received a large pay increase and a promotion. Yesterday, Mario was laid off. Five other employees over the age of 50 also were laid off.*

For what reason does it appear that these workers are being laid off?

A They are being treated like other workers doing the same job.

B They are being discriminated against because of their age.

C They are refusing to join the union.

D They are doing a poor job.

9 **SS.7.E.1.5 (Medium)**

How are corporations different from other forms of business?

A They are required to hire minority workers.

B They must ensure that working conditions are safe.

C They are subject to more government regulations.

D They compete with other businesses.

10 **SS.7.E.1.5 (High)**

Read the excerpt below from a statement by Massachusetts governor Calvin Coolidge about a strike by the Boston police.

> *"There is no right to strike against the public safety by anyone, anywhere, any time."*
>
> —Governor Calvin Coolidge

What conclusion can you draw about the excerpt?

A The government intervened because the strike threatened the safety of the city's residents.

B The government got an injunction because the strike threatened the nation.

C The government forced workers to return to work during a cooling-off period.

D The government agreed to settle and give the law officials increased wages.

CHAPTER 21

Government's Role in the Economy

CHAPTER BENCHMARKS

SS.7.E.1.3 Review the concepts of supply and demand, choice, scarcity, and opportunity cost as they relate to the development of the mixed market economy in the United States.

SS.7.E.1.5 Assess how profits, incentives, and competition motivate individuals, households, and businesses in a free market economy.

SS.7.E.2.1 Explain how federal, state, and local taxes support the economy as a function of the United States government.

SS.7.E.2.3 Identify and describe United States laws and regulations adopted to promote economic competition.

SS.7.E.2.5 Explain how economic institutions impact the national economy.

LAFS.68.RH.1.1 Cite specific textual evidence to support analysis of primary and secondary sources.

LAFS.68.RH.1.2 Determine the central ideas or information of a primary or secondary source; provide an accurate summary of the source distinct from prior knowledge or opinions.

Chapter Overview

The government of the United States plays a major role in the American economy. The government provides public goods for all citizens. It uses many different measurements to monitor the country's economic health. The government also establishes rules to regulate businesses, protect consumers, prevent discrimination, and promote economic competition. In addition, it tries to combat income inequality and help people who are living in poverty.

WHAT I NEED TO KNOW

TERMS

- ☐ private good
- ☐ public good
- ☐ externality
- ☐ monopoly
- ☐ antitrust law
- ☐ merger
- ☐ natural monopoly
- ☐ real GDP
- ☐ business cycle
- ☐ recession
- ☐ depression
- ☐ unemployment rate
- ☐ fixed income
- ☐ inflation
- ☐ bear market
- ☐ bull market
- ☐ welfare
- ☐ Temporary Assistance for Needy Families (TANF)
- ☐ workfare
- ☐ compensation

CHAPTER 21

Government's Role in the Economy

CHAPTER BENCHMARKS, *continued*

LAFS.68.RH.2.4 Determine the meaning of words and phrases as they are used in a text, including vocabulary specific to domains related to history/social studies.

LAFS.68.WHST.3.7 Conduct short research projects to answer a question (including a self-generated question), drawing on several sources and generating additional related, focused questions that allow for multiple avenues of exploration.

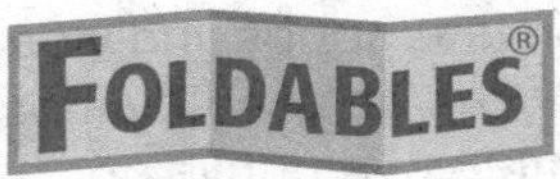

Government's Role in the Economy

Create the Foldable® below and write the chapter title on the cover tab. Label the three tabs below the title with the lesson titles. While studying the chapter, record important terms and main ideas that will help you describe how government is involved in the economy on a national and local level. On the back of the Foldable, describe minimum wage and the effect it has on your life today and predict how it might affect your life in the future.

Step 1
Begin with two sheets of lined paper.

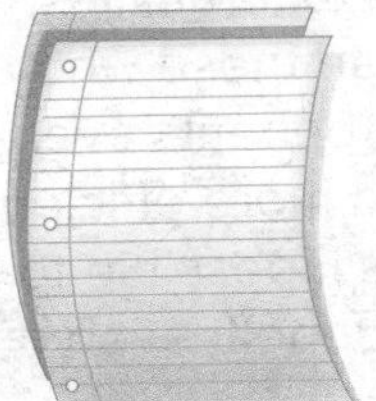

Step 2
Stack the two sheets of paper but align them so one sheet is about an inch below the other sheet.

Step 3
Fold the bottom part of the stack up to create three equal tabs. Flip over. Staple at the fold and label as directed.

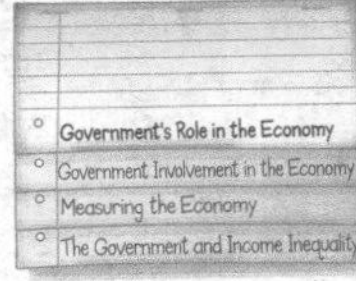

Government Involvement in the Economy

SS.7.E.1.5, SS.7.E.2.1, SS.7.E.2.3, SS.7.E.2.5

Providing Public Goods

Most goods produced by businesses are private goods. **Private goods** have two main features:

1. People must pay to use or own private goods.
2. Only one person can use a private good. For example, if you buy a cell phone, no one else can buy that exact same phone. Clothing, food, and computers are examples of private goods.

Public goods are different from private goods. Individuals do not pay for public goods, and they can be used by more than one person. A highway is an example of a public good. If you drive down a highway, that doesn't stop others from doing so too. The entire community can use public goods. Police protection, public parks, and libraries are examples of public goods. They benefit everyone in the community.

Private businesses do not usually provide public goods, because it would be difficult to charge everyone who uses them. For example, how much should a person be charged for police protection or the use of a sidewalk? It is more efficient for the government to provide public goods like these and pay for them with the taxes and other fees it collects.

Externalities

Economic activities and the use of public goods can cause side effects called externalities. **Externalities** are positive or negative effects of an action that impact somebody else.

Sometimes public goods create *positive* externalities. These are benefits enjoyed by more people than those who use the goods. For example, having good roads benefits everyone—not just drivers. Products can be shipped more efficiently on good roads. Better transportation makes it possible to sell the products for lower prices. Lower prices benefit everyone.

Economic activities can also produce *negative* externalities. These are costs that are suffered by third parties. For example, a car provides transportation, but it also causes air pollution. Even people who do not drive feel the effects of bad air.

1. DIFFERENTIATING

For each public good listed below, identify whether it is provided by the local, state, or federal government.

__________ City parks

__________ Highway patrol officers

__________ Armed forces

__________ Public libraries

__________ Interstate highways

2. DRAWING CONCLUSIONS

Every state government requires students to show proof of vaccination before they are permitted to attend public school. What negative externalities is the government preventing with this requirement? Do you believe this is a good policy? Why or why not?

____

____

____

____

____

____

____

____

Name ______________________ Date ______________ Class ________

Government tries to encourage positive externalities. This is one reason why the government provides free public education to children. Well-educated children grow up to be well-educated workers. Thus, education usually leads to positive externalities. On the other hand, government works to prevent negative externalities. This is why the government has laws regulating auto exhaust, for example.

Maintaining Competition

Goods and services are sold in markets, and markets work best when there are large numbers of buyers and sellers. When there is only one seller in the market, that seller controls the market. This is called a **monopoly.** In a monopoly, the seller can charge any price it wants. Customers have no choice. They must pay what the monopoly demands or go without the product. The government of the United States encourages economic competition and discourages the creation of monopolies.

Antitrust Laws

A *trust* is several businesses that band together to operate as a monopoly. To maintain economic competition, the government has passed several **antitrust laws.** The first was the Sherman Antitrust Act of 1890. It prohibited monopolies and other forms of business that prevent competition. In 1914, Congress passed the Clayton Antitrust Act. It strengthened the Sherman Act and banned specific business practices that limit competition. For example, the act prohibited one person from serving on the board of directors of two competing companies.

Mergers

When two or more companies combine to form a single business, this is called a **merger.** Sometimes a merger threatens competition. When this happens, the Clayton Antitrust Act gives the government power to stop the merger. The Federal Trade Commission (FTC) can stop or make changes to any merger that violates antitrust laws.

3. DETERMINING CENTRAL IDEAS

Competition is a key institution in free market economies. How does competition impact the national economy?

____

____

____

____

____

4. CONSTRUCTING AN ARGUMENT

Do you think antitrust laws have a place in a free market economy. Why or why not?

____

____

____

____

____

____

____

____

____

____

____

5. EXPLAINING

Explain why governments generally choose to regulate natural monopolies rather than break them up.

____

____

____

____

____

____

____

6. EXPRESSING

Some Americans want to abolish regulatory agencies such as the FDA and OSHA, claiming that they stifle the free market and intrude on private property rights. On a separate sheet of paper, explain whether you believe such agencies are needed. Choose one agency and describe how life in the United States might be different if it did not exist.

Natural Monopolies

Sometimes, however, it is more efficient—and cheaper—to have one company produce a good or service. This is called a **natural monopoly.** Many public services, such as natural gas and electricity, are delivered by natural monopolies. Usually natural monopolies have to abide by government regulations. Such regulations monitor the monopoly so it does not raise prices too high or lower the quality of service. Occasionally, a local government takes ownership of a natural monopoly that provides basic services such as water.

In recent years, some local governments have moved to end certain natural monopolies to bring back competition. This process is called deregulation. However, deregulation does not always result in lower prices for consumers. Consequently, these governments are reconsidering the deregulation.

Protecting Consumer Health and Safety

The government also plays an important role in protecting the public's health and safety. The following chart lists several government regulatory agencies and their function.

DEPARTMENT OR AGENCY	PURPOSE
Consumer Product Safety Commission (CPSC)	Protects the public from risks of serious injury or death from consumer products
Environmental Protection Agency (EPA)	Protects human health and the natural environment (air, water, land)
Federal Trade Commission (FTC)	Promotes and protects consumer interests and competition in the marketplace
Food and Drug Administration (FDA)	Makes sure food, drugs, medical equipment, and cosmetics are truthfully labeled and safe for consumers
Occupational Safety and Health Administration (OSHA)	Makes sure workers have safe and healthful workplaces

LESSON 1 SUMMARY, *continued*

REVIEW LESSON 1

1. Use the chart below to describe the government's role in the economy.

PROVIDE PUBLIC GOODS	
MAINTAIN COMPETITION	
PROTECT CONSUMER HEALTH AND SAFETY	

2. **PREDICTING CONSEQUENCES** Using the information in your chart, write an essay that answers this question: How does each role of the U.S. government contribute to the economy of the United States? Use a separate sheet of paper for your essay.

LESSON 2 SUMMARY

Measuring the Economy

SS.7.E.1.3, SS.7.E.1.5, SS.7.E.2.5

1. RECOGNIZING RELATIONSHIPS

In a free market economy, how are prices determined?

2. ANALYZING INFORMATION

Why is real GDP a better indicator of economic performance than GDP?

Economic Performance

Prices are the signals that help people, companies, and the government make economic decisions. Prices are an important component of a market economy, but they can show information about the Gross Domestic Product (GDP) that can be misleading. For example, if a country has a bigger GDP in one year than it had the year before, it might seem that the country's economy has grown. However, if the GDP increased simply because of rising prices—and not because of increased economic output—then the economy has *not* grown.

Real GDP

GDP grows only when the nation produces more, not when products cost more. This is why economists cannot rely on the GDP alone to show economic performance. Instead, they use a measurement called real GDP. **Real GDP** is GDP after the changes caused by price increases have been removed. It is basically the same thing as GDP in an economy where prices do not change. This is why real GDP is a more accurate measure of an economy's performance over time than GDP alone.

Real GDP allows business and government leaders to make more accurate economic plans. It also shows whether these plans are working. In a healthy economy, real GDP will grow. That means good jobs and economic opportunities for all.

Business Cycles

The American economy does not grow steadily. It goes through periods of ups and downs. This series of economic growth and decline is called the **business cycle.** Business cycles have two parts:

1. The cycle starts when real GDP goes down from a peak, or is in a contraction. These are times when businesses may close and people lose their jobs.
2. Eventually, real GDP stops declining and reaches the lowest point of the business cycle, the trough. Real GDP begins to rise again, or expand, as the economy begins to recover.

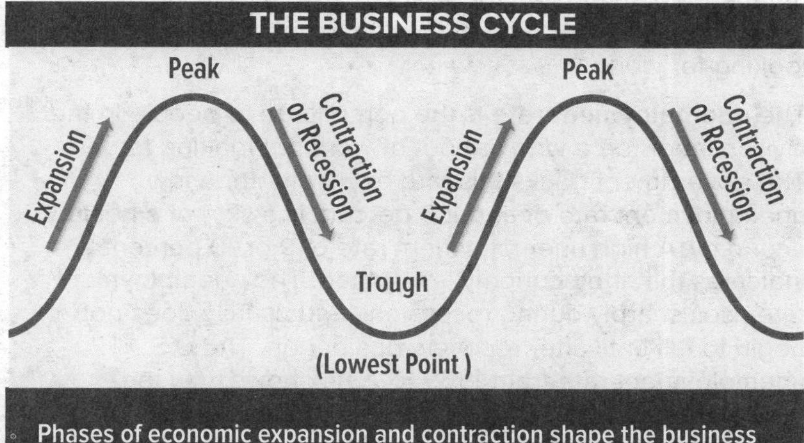

Phases of economic expansion and contraction shape the business cycle. In the real world, the length of time for business cycles varies.

Contractions usually are short. If real GDP stays down for more than six months, the economy is in a **recession.** Recessions usually last less than a year. The recession of December 2007 to June 2009 is an exception to this rule, though. This 18-month recession was the longest since the 1930s. Periods of expansion are usually longer than periods of recession. Recent expansions have lasted from 6 to 10 years. The new peak can be even higher than the previous one.

The Great Depression

A **depression** is a period of severe economic decline. A recession might turn into a depression if real GDP continues to fall rather than beginning to rise. The United States had a major depression—known as the Great Depression—that began in 1929 and reached a trough in 1933. Real GDP fell by half during this period. One in four workers was unemployed. Many banks closed, and many stocks became worthless.

3. HYPOTHESIZING

Based on the law of supply and demand, would you expect prices to rise or fall during a recession? Why?

4. DETERMINING CAUSE AND EFFECT

How is business competition likely to be affected as the economic cycle enters into a recession?

ANALYZING VISUALS

5. INTERPRETING Based on the graph, in 1994, what stage in the business cycle do you think the U.S. economy was in: expansion, peak, or trough? How can you tell?

Because of the Great Depression, the government enacted many new programs to protect people financially. Many economists believe that a depression of this size will never happen again.

Other Measures of Performance

In addition to real GDP, economists use other measures to determine how well the economy is doing. One way is by tracking the number of people who have or do not have jobs. Economists usually look at the civilian labor force. *Civilian* means "people outside the military." The civilian labor force consists of everyone age 16 or older who is either working or looking for work.

The **unemployment rate** is the percentage of people in the civilian labor force who are out of work but looking for jobs. The government tracks this rate every month. A low unemployment rate of about 5 percent is a sign of a healthy economy. A high unemployment rate of 9 or 10 percent indicates that the economy is troubled. The unemployment rate rises sharply during recessions and usually does not begin to fall until after recovery has begun. The U.S. unemployment rate from 1969 to 2014 shows how the measurement rises and falls in line with the business cycle.

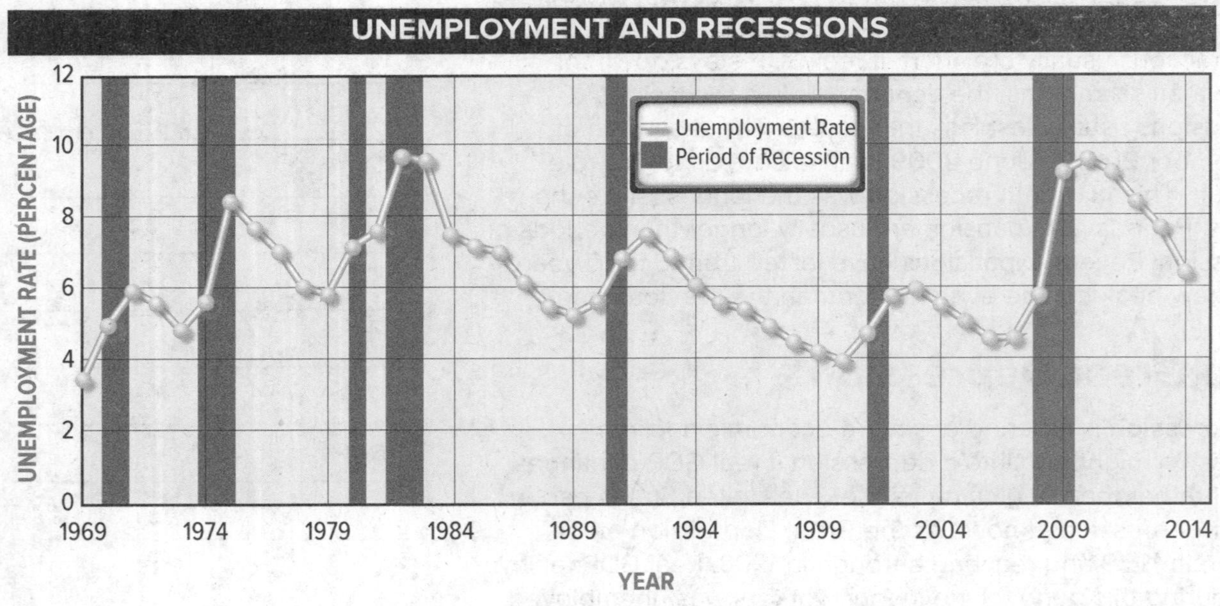

Source: National Bureau of Economic Research; Bureau of Labor Statistics

Economists also measure economic health by looking at prices. When prices do not change much, consumers and businesses benefit. Stable prices are especially important for people who are retired and live on a fixed income. A **fixed income** stays the same each month and does not increase to keep pace with rising prices.

Money keeps its value when prices are stable, but when prices go up, money loses some of its purchasing power. For example, if a hamburger that costs a dollar doubles in price to two dollars, you will need twice as much money to buy the same hamburger. The higher price means that a dollar buys less.

An increase in price for one item generally is not a concern, but an increase of many prices is. A long-term increase in the general level of prices is called **inflation.** Rising inflation is a sign of economic trouble. The government tracks inflation each month by checking the prices of about 400 products commonly used by consumers. The prices of these products make up the consumer price index (CPI). If the overall level of the CPI goes up, inflation is occurring.

6. SPECULATING

Price acts as an incentive to consumers. How might consumers react to changing prices during a period of inflation?

____

____

____

____

____

____

____

____

Economic Indicators

Real GDP, unemployment, and the CPI tell economists how the economy is doing now. Other statistics, such as stock indexes or the Leading Economic Index, tell where the economy is headed.

Stock Indexes

Stock prices are set by supply and demand. Supply is the number of stocks available. Demand is the number of stocks investors want to purchase. Demand for a stock can change when a company has a change in profits or releases a new product. If demand changes, the stock price will change too. Economists do not look at the price of just one company's stock. They examine overall changes in *all* stock prices.

7. EVALUATING

Imagine that you hear a person say, "I don't own any stocks, so it doesn't affect me if the stock market rises or falls." Is this statement correct? Explain your answer.

The Dow Jones Industrial Average (DJIA) and the Standard and Poor's (S&P) 500 are the most common stock indexes. The DJIA tracks prices of 30 representative stocks. The S&P 500 index tracks 500 stocks by their total market values rather than by their prices. Total market value is the price of a company's stock times the number of shares owned by investors.

Stock indexes reveal investors' attitudes about the future performance of the economy. When investors lack confidence in the economy, they stop buying stock and stock prices fall. This is referred to as a **"bear market."** It can signal a slowing of real GDP or a coming recession. A rising stock market is called a **"bull market."** During bull markets, investors expect the economy to grow. Investors have confidence and buy more stocks. Stock prices rise. A bull market is a good sign that real GDP will increase.

The Leading Economic Index®

The Leading Economic Index combines data from 10 sources, such as the S&P, the number of hours worked in manufacturing, the number of building permits issued in the previous month, and other data. No single indicator is always accurate, but this combined average is more precise.

The index is called "leading" because it points to the way real GDP is usually headed. For example, if the leading index goes down, real GDP usually declines a few months later. If the leading index goes up, real GDP usually rises. The Leading Economic Index is a good measure for predicting future economic performance.

REVIEW LESSON 2

1. Use the chart below to fill in the parts of the business cycle. Write the correct term at each arrow, at the lowest point, and at the two highest points.

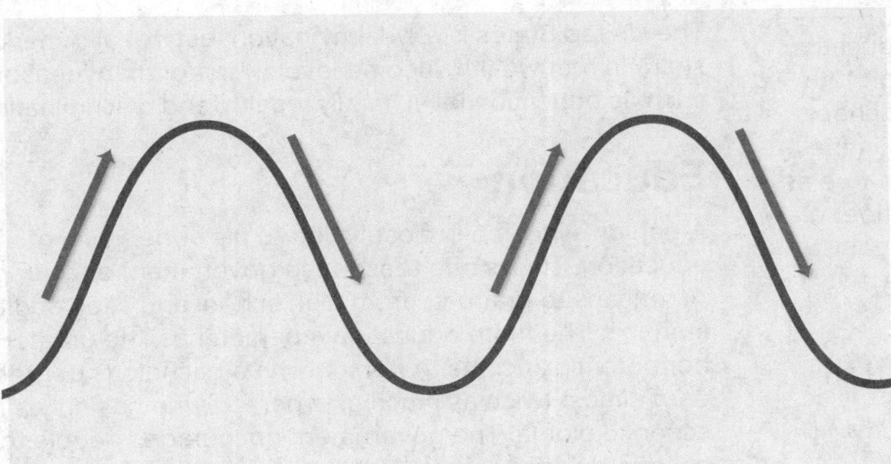

2. **RECOGNIZING RELATIONSHIPS** Using the information in the chart, write an essay that answers the question: What information is analyzed to determine where the economy is at present and where it is going? Explain your answers. Use a separate sheet of paper for your essay.

LESSON 3 SUMMARY

The Government and Income Inequality

1. CONSTRUCTING AN ARGUMENT

In the United States, education for kindergarten through 12th grade is free in public schools. Should public colleges in the United States be tuition-free as well? Use a separate sheet of paper to argue for or against the idea of free college education.

ANALYZING VISUALS

2. SPECULATING

What technology tool are these students using? How might this investment in technology for education affect these students' economic future?

____

____

____

____

____

____

____

____

SS.7.E.1.3, SS.7.E.2.3, SS.7.E.2.5

Income Inequality

The United States is a wealthy nation, but not all Americans share in that wealth. Income levels vary for many reasons, such as education level, family wealth, and discrimination.

Education

A person's income is closely tied to his or her level of education. This is one reason the government encourages Americans to graduate from high school and seek additional learning. The more education a person has, the greater his or her potential income. A person with a bachelor's degree can earn almost twice as much as a person who has only a high school diploma. The government encourages people to go to college by offering low-cost loans and grants to help students pay tuition. Other programs help students from low-income families and those with disabilities prepare for college.

When students drop out of high school, they hurt the nation's economy. They do not learn the skills they need to get good-paying jobs. They usually have lower wages and higher unemployment rates than graduates. To encourage teens to stay in school, the federal government has given money to state and local governments to create dropout prevention programs.

Education is strongly supported by all levels of government.

Family Wealth

Family wealth also affects income. People born into wealthy families often have better educational opportunities. Better education then leads to better opportunities for jobs with higher pay. People also might be able to join an established family business and earn a good income. Their children might then inherit that wealth from their parents.

Discrimination

Discrimination can limit the amount some people can earn. Women, minorities, and disabled people might face discrimination that keeps them from getting jobs for which they are qualified. They might also have trouble getting promotions and earning higher salaries. Discrimination has an impact on the economy as a whole. For example, women generally earn less than men. Congress has passed a number of laws to help protect people from discrimination.

NAME OF LAW	PURPOSE
Equal Pay Act of 1963	Requires that men and women be paid the same for the same work
Civil Rights Act of 1964	Prohibits discrimination based on gender, race, color, religion, and national origin
Equal Employment Opportunity Act of 1972	Gives the government more power to enforce the Civil Rights Act of 1964
Americans With Disabilities Act of 1990	Provides job protection for people with physical and mental disabilities
Lilly Ledbetter Fair Pay Act of 2009	Allows employees to sue companies that have treated them unfairly due to their gender

The government encourages businesses to practice affirmative action. Affirmative action policies are intended to increase the number of minorities and women in the workplace. Affirmative action helps to make up for past discrimination.

Poverty

Millions of Americans live in poverty, unable to earn enough to pay for basic needs such as food, clothing, and shelter. Most welfare programs are funded by the federal government to help families in need. **Welfare** is money or necessities given to the poor. The government uses income guidelines to decide whether a family or an individual qualifies for aid. These annual guidelines are based on the cost of basic necessities.

3. REFLECTING

What are some ways anti-discrimination laws help the economy?

4. DETERMINING CENTRAL IDEAS

How does the welfare system benefit society? Does it have any negative consequences?

____

____

____

____

____

____

Temporary Assistance for Needy Families (TANF) is short-term welfare. The federal government pays for the program, but it is run by the individual states. In 1996, TANF replaced an earlier welfare program from the 1930s. TANF has stricter rules and works to encourage people to find jobs quickly. In many states, this program requires people to work in order to receive help. This is called **workfare.** Many times, workfare involves community service. Program participants might also have to attend job training or education programs.

Another program, called unemployment insurance, pays compensation to workers who lose their jobs through no fault of their own. **Compensation** is payment to make up for lost wages until the worker finds a new job. Usually this payment is given for a limited time. Workers' compensation is a benefit for employees who are injured on the job. This compensation payment covers lost wages and medical care.

REVIEW LESSON 3

1. Use the chart below to identify the effects that some factors might have on an individual's income level.

INCOME INEQUALITY	
Factor	**Effect on Income**
Education level	
Family wealth	
Discrimination	
Job loss	

2. **ASSESSING** Write an essay to answer the question: Which reason listed in the chart do you think has the greatest effect on the economy of the United States? Explain your answer. Use a separate sheet of paper for your essay.

Benchmark Skill Activities

DIRECTIONS: Write your answers on a separate sheet of paper.

LAFS.68.WHST.3.7

1. CONSTRUCTING AN ARGUMENT

Use your FOLDABLES® to write an essay that answers this question: Should the minimum wage be increased? In addition to the information on your Foldable, conduct online research to find other views on this question.

In your essay, present your own position on the question, then summarize opposing viewpoints and explain why you disagree. Generate at least two questions you would pose to those who do not share your opinion.

LAFS.68.RH.1.1

2. ANALYZING DATA

The following chart contains figures from the Consumer Price Index.

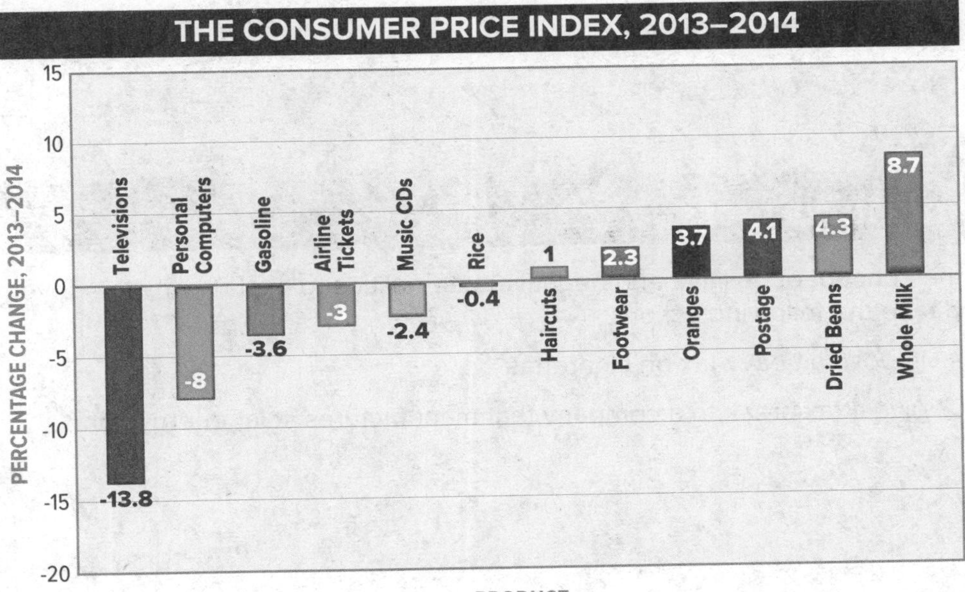

Source: Bureau of Labor Statistics, 2014.

What does the chart show about the prices of various items? Does this pattern indicate that inflation is happening? Explain your answer.

LAFS.68.RH.1.2

3. INTERPRETING

A large corporation accused of having a monopoly in the oil business was once referred to as an "octopus." Imagine that you are a political cartoonist. What other animal or creature would you use to represent a monopoly? Explain your choice. If you want, you can draw a cartoon to support your explanation.

LAFS.68.RH.2.4

4. COMPARING AND CONTRASTING

What are the similarities and differences between a recession and a depression?

LAFS.68.RH.1.2, SS.7.E.2.1

5. MAKING INFERENCES

Use the concept of positive and negative externalities to explain why the government would take the following actions:

1. impose a heavy tax on cigarettes
2. give a tax break to a company that manufactures solar energy panels

Benchmark Note Cards

DIRECTIONS: Use these note cards to help you prepare for the test.

SS.7.E.1.3 Review the concepts of supply and demand, choice, scarcity, and opportunity cost as they relate to the development of the mixed market economy in the United States.

THE BUSINESS CYCLE AND SUPPLY AND DEMAND	• During an expansion, demand for goods and services increases. Consequently, supply increases as well. • During a contraction, demand for goods and services falls, which causes supply to fall as well.

SS.7.E.1.5 Assess how profits, incentives, and competition motivate individuals, households, and businesses in a free market economy.

COMPETITION AND MONOPOLIES	Goods and services are sold in markets, and markets work best when there are large numbers of buyers and sellers. If there is no competition, then only one seller controls the market. This is called a monopoly.

SS.7.E.2.1 Explain how federal, state, and local taxes support the economy as a function of the United States government.

TAXES AND THE ECONOMY	Federal, state, and local governments use taxes to pay for public goods. Many public goods support the economy. • Roads and bridges make the transportation of goods more efficient. This lowers the prices of goods for consumers. • Free education creates a well-educated workforce that benefits the economy.

SS.7.E.2.3 Identify and describe United States laws and regulations adopted to promote economic competition.

ANTITRUST LAWS	The government created antitrust laws to maintain economic competition. These laws make it illegal for businesses to form monopolies. No company can be the only company to sell a product or provide a service. This avoids fixing prices. The Sherman Antitrust Act of 1890 prohibited monopolies and other forms of business that prevent competition. The Clayton Antitrust Act of 1914 strengthened the Sherman Act. It banned specific business practices that limit competition and gave the government power to stop some mergers.

CONSUMER HEALTH AND SAFETY	Government agencies that regulate industries in order to protect consumers from unsafe products include: • Consumer Product Safety Commission (CPSC)—Protects the public from risks of injury or death from consumer products • Environmental Protection Agency (EPA)—Protects human health and the natural environment (air, water, land) • Federal Trade Commission (FTC)—Promotes and protects consumer interests and competition in the marketplace • Food and Drug Administration (FDA)—Makes sure food, drugs, medical items, and cosmetics are truthfully labeled and safe • Occupational Safety and Health Administration (OSHA)—Makes sure workers have safe and healthful workplaces
LAWS PREVENTING DISCRIMINATION	The federal government has passed a number of laws designed to protect people from discrimination and promote fairness in the workplace. These laws help people who are discriminated against to get better wages and access to jobs. They include: • Equal Pay Act of 1963 • Civil Rights Act of 1964 • Equal Employment Opportunity Act of 1972 • Americans with Disabilities Act of 1990 • Lilly Ledbetter Fair Pay Act of 2009

SS.7.E.2.5 Explain how economic institutions impact the national economy.

THE STOCK MARKET	Changes in stock prices can have a huge impact on the national economy. A bear market is a falling market that sometimes signals a coming recession. A bull market is a rising market that often signals economic expansion.
WELFARE	The federal government provides welfare to help struggling families meet their basic needs, such as Temporary Assistance for Needy Families (TANF). Unemployment insurance pays workers who lose their jobs through no fault of their own. It makes up for lost wages until they can find a new job. Workers' compensation helps people injured on the job.

Chapter 21

VISUAL SUMMARY

DIRECTIONS: Complete the graphic organizer below.

GOVERNMENT'S ROLE IN THE ECONOMY

Provides public goods

Promotes competition through antitrust laws
-
-

Protects consumer health and safety

Regulates natural monopolies

Promotes education

Measures economic performance by tracking:
- Real GDP
- Unemployment rate
- Consumer price index
- Stock indexes
- Leading Economic Index®

Helps the needy by providing:
-
-
-
-

Promotes fairness via antidiscrimination laws, including:
-
-
-
-
-

USING PRIMARY SOURCES

REFLECT The following remarks are from President Barack Obama's weekly address on August 30, 2014. Read the remarks, and then answer the questions that follow on a separate sheet of paper.

> *"To build a stronger middle class in today's changing economy, we've got to keep fighting. We've got to fight for the right to affordable health insurance for everybody. The right to fair pay, family leave, and workplace flexibility. The right to a fair living wage.*
>
> *Let me focus on that last one for a minute. In America, no one who works full-time should ever have to raise a family in poverty. A hard day's work deserves a fair day's pay. And raising the minimum wage would be one of the best ways to give a boost to working families. It would help around 28 million Americans from all walks of life pay the bills, provide for their kids, and spend that money at local businesses. And that grows the economy for everyone.*
>
> *The bottom line is, America deserves a raise. But until we've got a Congress that cares about raising working folks' wages, it's up to the rest of us to make it happen. And in the year and a half since I first asked Congress to raise the minimum wage, Americans of all walks of life are doing just that. . . .*
>
> *I've tried to do my part by requiring companies that get contracts with the federal government to pay their workers a fair wage of ten dollars and ten cents an hour. . . .*
>
> *That's how America built the greatest middle class the world has ever known. Not by making sure a fortunate few at the top are doing well, but by making sure that everyone who's willing to work hard and play by the rules can get ahead. That's the bedrock this country is built on. Hard work. Responsibility. Sacrifice. And looking out for one another as one united American family."*
>
> —President Barack Obama

1. Summarize the president's comments. Is he asking Congress to do something? Is he asking other groups to do something?
2. How might an increase in the minimum wage affect the economic incentive of an unemployed person? An employer?
3. Would raising the minimum wage produce any positive externalities? Negative externalities?

Chapter Practice Test

DIRECTIONS: Circle the best answer for each question.

SS.7.E.1.5 (High)

Read the following statement from President Barack Obama.

> *. . . [T]he success of every American will be tied more closely than ever before to the level of education that they achieve. The jobs will go to the people with the knowledge and the skills to do them—it's that simple. In this kind of knowledge economy, giving up on your education and dropping out of school means not only giving up on your future, but it's also giving up on your family's future and giving up on your country's future.*
>
> —President Barack Obama, 2010

Which conclusion is best supported by the statement?

A Local governments should have more control over public education.

B Private schools are more efficient than public schools.

C Teachers deserve to be paid higher salaries.

D Education usually leads to positive externalities.

SS.7.E.2.3 (High)

Which government agency is most related to promoting economic competition?

A Federal Trade Commission

B Food and Drug Administration

C Federal Bureau of Investigation

D Consumer Product Safety Commission

3 **SS.7.E.1.5 (Moderate)**

Examine the following chart.

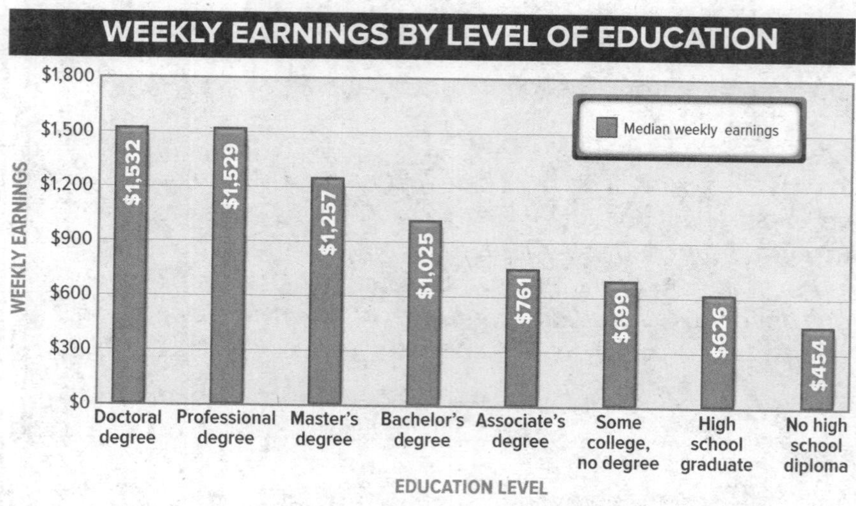

Based on the chart, which of the following statements is correct?

A The supply of doctoral degrees is higher than the supply of bachelor's degrees.

B People with associate's degrees compete with people with master's degrees for the same jobs.

C There is a strong economic incentive for continuing education after completing high school.

D The opportunity cost of attaining a professional degree is the same as that of attaining a master's degree.

---

4 **SS.7.E.1.3 (Moderate)**

At which point in the economic cycle is demand for labor at its lowest?

A expansion

B trough

C contraction

D peak

5 **SS.7.E.1.3 (Moderate)**

Examine the cause-and-effect graphic.

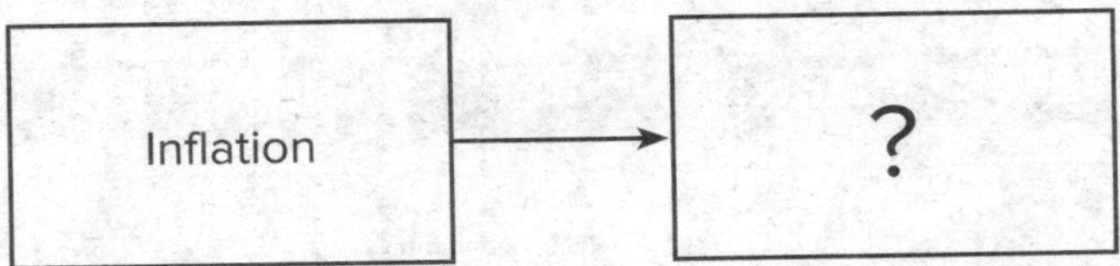

Which of the following would best complete the graphic?

A Increased employment

B A bear market

C Less economic competition

D Decreased consumer demand

SS.7.E.2.5 (High)

You hear a television report about how stock prices have been rising for the past three months. Which is the most reasonable conclusion you should draw?

A The economy is probably in expansion.

B A bear market is underway on Wall Street.

C Real GDP will begin to decline soon.

D Inflation is starting to get out of control.

7 **SS.7.E.1.3 (High)**

The following chart shows periods of unemployment and recession in the United States from 1969 through 2014.

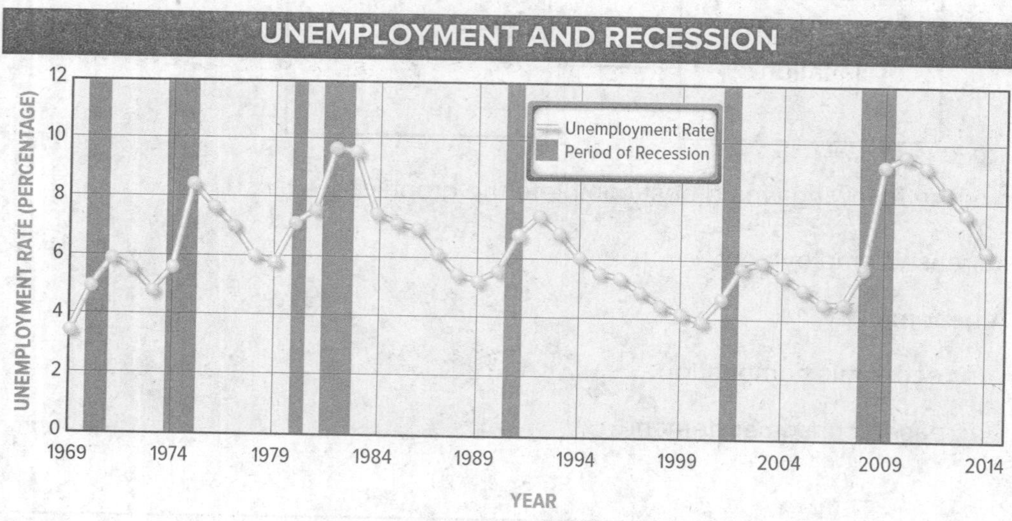

Source: National Bureau of Economic Research; Bureau of Labor Statistics

Based on the chart, in which of the following years was demand for consumer goods probably highest?

A 1990

B 1999

C 2004

D 2009

8 **SS.7.E.2.3 (Moderate)**

Federal laws have been passed to discourage which of the following?

A economic competition

B positive externalities

C monopolies

D workfare programs

9 **SS.7.E.2.5 (High)**

The excerpt below is from a book titled *Three Years Down.*

> *The selling pressure was . . . coming from everywhere. The wires to other cities were jammed with frantic orders to sell. So were the cables, radio and telephones to Europe and the rest of the world. Buyers were few, sometimes wholly absent. . . . Leading stocks had lost as much as 77% of their peak value. The Dow Jones Index was off 40% since September 3. . . .*
>
> —Jonathan Norton Leonard, *Three Years Down*

What does this excerpt describe?

A a positive externality

B a bear market

C a negative externality

D a bull market

10 **SS.7.C.2.1 (Moderate)**

Which of these is a public good provided by the federal government?

A garbage disposal

B fire protection

C city parks

D armed forces

CHAPTER 22

The Government and Banking

CHAPTER BENCHMARKS

SS.7.E.1.2 Discuss the importance of borrowing and lending in the United States, the government's role in controlling financial institutions, and list the advantages and disadvantages of using credit.

SS.7.E.1.4 Discuss the function of financial institutions in the development of a market economy.

SS.7.E.2.2 Describe the banking system in the United States and its impact on the money supply.

SS.7.E.2.5 Explain how economic institutions impact the national economy.

ELD.K12.ELL.SI.1 English language learners communicate for social and instructional purposes within the school setting.

LAFS.68.RH.1.1 Cite specific textual evidence to support analysis of primary and secondary sources.

LAFS.68.RH.1.2 Determine the central ideas or information of a primary or secondary source; provide an accurate summary of the source distinct from prior knowledge or opinions.

LAFS.68.RH.1.3 Identify key steps in a text's description of a process related to history/social studies (e.g., how a bill becomes law, how interest rates are raised or lowered).

Chapter Overview

The health of an economy is based on the flow of money. One job of government is to monitor and manage that flow. The government can adjust the flow of money. Those adjustments help determine whether the economy grows or shrinks.

Financial institutions help people save and manage their own money. However, these institutions must follow government rules. There are rules about interest rates and deposits as well as loans to individuals and businesses. In the United States, the Federal Reserve System, called "the Fed," oversees banks and manages the flow of money. The Fed also acts as a bank for the government. The Fed helps protect the money people deposit in banks.

WHAT I NEED TO KNOW

TERMS

- ☐ coin
- ☐ currency
- ☐ electronic money
- ☐ deposit
- ☐ commercial bank
- ☐ savings and loan association (S&L)
- ☐ credit union
- ☐ deposit insurance
- ☐ central bank
- ☐ Federal Reserve System
- ☐ monetary policy
- ☐ open market operations (OMO)
- ☐ discount rate
- ☐ reserve requirement
- ☐ checking account
- ☐ savings account
- ☐ certificate of deposit (CD)
- ☐ money market account

CHAPTER BENCHMARKS, *continued*

LAFS.7.SL.1.1 Engage effectively in a range of collaborative discussions (one-on-one, in groups, and teacher-led) with diverse partners on grade 7 topics, texts, and issues, building on others' ideas and expressing their own clearly.

LAFS.7.SL.1.3 Delineate a speaker's argument and specific claims, evaluating the soundness of the reasoning and the relevance and sufficiency of the evidence.

LAFS.68.WHST.1.2 Write informative/explanatory texts, including the narration of historical events, scientific procedures/experiments, or technical processes.

The Government and Banking

Make this Foldable® and label the three tabs with the titles of the lessons. Under each tab, briefly outline what you learn by recording main ideas and listing supporting information or terms underneath. Relate what you read to your experience with money, banks, and banking. On the back of the Foldable, draw a time line and sequentially note important events discussed in the chapter. Make sure you include information on the formation and growth of banking and the Federal Reserve System.

Step 1
Fold lined paper horizontally to the margin.

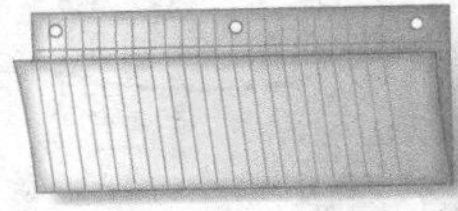

Step 2
Fold the right side and the left side of the paper across the middle to form three equal parts.

Step 3
Cut the two fold lines from the top edge to the bottom fold.

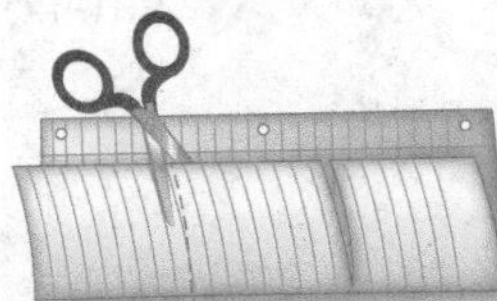

Step 4
Label the tabs as shown.

LESSON 1 SUMMARY

Money

1. GIVING EXAMPLES

What is one example of bartering that shows why it is difficult to do?

____

____

____

____

____

____

____

____

ANALYZING VISUALS

2. EVALUATING

Based on the information in the web diagram, why would pebbles be a poor choice to use as money?

____

____

____

____

____

____

SS.7.E.1.2, SS.7.E.1.4, SS.7.E.2.2

All About Money

Money is anything people agree to use in exchange for goods. Historically, money has included shells, beads, gold, and silver. Using money makes life easier for everyone.

Functions of Money

Money works in three ways:

- as a medium of exchange
- as a store of value
- as a measure of value

Money is a medium, or means, of exchange because people trade money for goods and services. Without money, people would need to barter. This is difficult because people value things differently. Money is a store of value because we can save it until we find something we want to buy with it. Money is a measure of value because it is used to measure the value of a good or service. When we say something costs $20, we are measuring the value of that good or service.

Characteristics of Money

For an item to serve as money, it must have four characteristics. These four qualities give money its value.

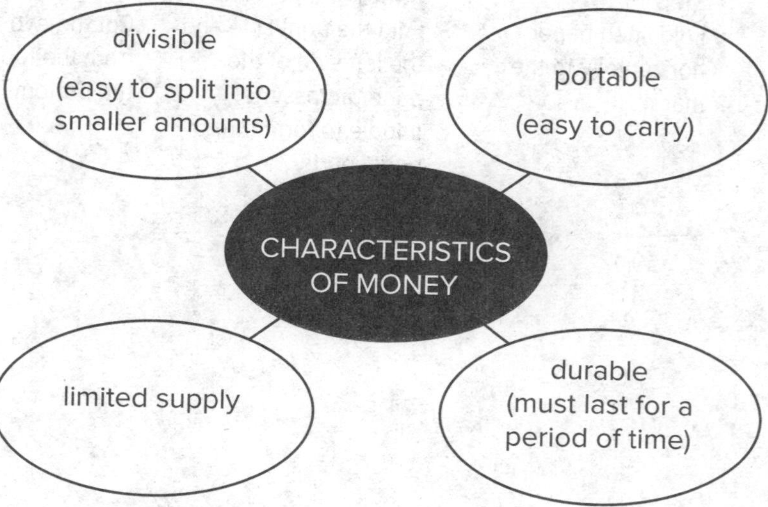

Name ______________________ Date ______________ Class ________

Forms of Money

The United States uses three kinds of money: coins, paper bills, and electronic money. Pennies, nickels, dimes, and quarters are **coins,** or pieces of metal. Paper bills are flat, rectangular pieces of high-quality paper. Together, coins and paper bills are considered **currency.**

Unlike coins and paper bills, you cannot hold **electronic money** in your hand. It exists only as computer entries at a bank or other financial institution. Money in a bank account is electronic money.

Financial Institutions

People and businesses often keep their money in financial institutions, such as banks. When customers put money into a financial institution, they make a **deposit.** Deposits can be made with currency or with electronic money. Employers often pay their employees by depositing pay directly into workers' bank accounts.

Financial institutions use these deposits to make loans to other customers. Banks earn money by charging interest and other fees on these loans. They also pay interest on the deposits they accept. They try to make a profit by charging higher interest rates on their loans and paying lower interest rates on their deposits.

Types of Financial Institutions

There are three main types of financial institutions: **commercial banks, savings and loan associations (S&Ls),** and **credit unions.** Each is described in the chart below.

3. REASONING

What do people and businesses gain by depositing their money in financial institutions?

____

____

____

____

4. MAKING CONNECTIONS

How does the U.S. banking system reflect the idea of a market economy?

____

____

____

____

____

____

____

COMMERCIAL BANKS	SAVINGS AND LOAN ASSOCIATIONS (S&Ls)	CREDIT UNIONS
• largest and most vital part of financial system • offer full financial services: accept deposits, offer checking accounts, make loans	• offer similar services to commercial banks • focus on individuals more than businesses	• nonprofit cooperative owned by depositors • depositors often have something in common, such as working in the same industry • accept deposits, offer checking accounts, and make loans • tend to charge lower interest on loans • give loans only to members

5. CITING TEXT EVIDENCE

Underline the details under the sections Protecting Deposits and Regulating Financial Institutions that show financial institutions are a safe place to keep money. Why do you think this is important?

____

____

____

____

____

____

Protecting Deposits

When you deposit money in a financial institution, it is protected by a **deposit insurance** program. Introduced in the 1930s, deposit insurance protects deposits up to a certain amount if the institution goes out of business. Commercial banks and S&Ls are covered by the Federal Deposit Insurance Corporation (FDIC). The National Credit Union Share Insurance Fund (NCUSIF) covers credit unions.

Deposit insurance is important because financial institutions lend out most of the money they receive as deposits. If the institution goes out of business, depositors would lose their money. Deposit insurance pays depositors up to $250,000 on all accounts in one bank in the event of a bank failure.

Regulating Financial Institutions

Financial institutions are regulated by the government. A financial institution cannot open without a charter, either from a state or the federal government. The government only issues a charter if the institution has enough money to do business. In addition, the people running the business must have the right money-management skills.

After issuing a charter, the state and federal agencies monitor the institution. Officials make sure the institution follows the law and stays in good financial condition.

REVIEW LESSON 1

1. Use the chart below to note key facts about financial institutions.

FINANCIAL INSTITUTIONS		
Purpose(s)	Types	Regulation

2. **SUMMARIZING** Use the information in your chart to write a detailed definition for the term *financial institution*.

LESSON 2 SUMMARY

The Federal Reserve System

SS.7.E.1.4, SS.7.E.2.2, SS.7.E.2.5

The Fed's Structure

During several financial crises in the early 1900s, banks did not have enough money to make loans. People hoped that things would be better with a central bank. A **central bank** is a bankers' bank. Banks can go to it to borrow money when times are difficult. So the government created the **Federal Reserve System,** or "the Fed." All American banks with a national charter were required to give money to this new central bank. In turn, they received some stock in the bank.

Today, the Fed serves a variety of functions. It manages currency, regulates commercial banks, serves as the government's bank, and conducts monetary policies. The structure of the Fed, illustrated in the diagram below, helps it perform these jobs.

ANALYZING VISUALS

1. MAKING INFERENCES
Why do you think the Fed has three federal advisory councils in addition to the Board of Governors?

____

____

____

____

____

____

Structure of the Fed

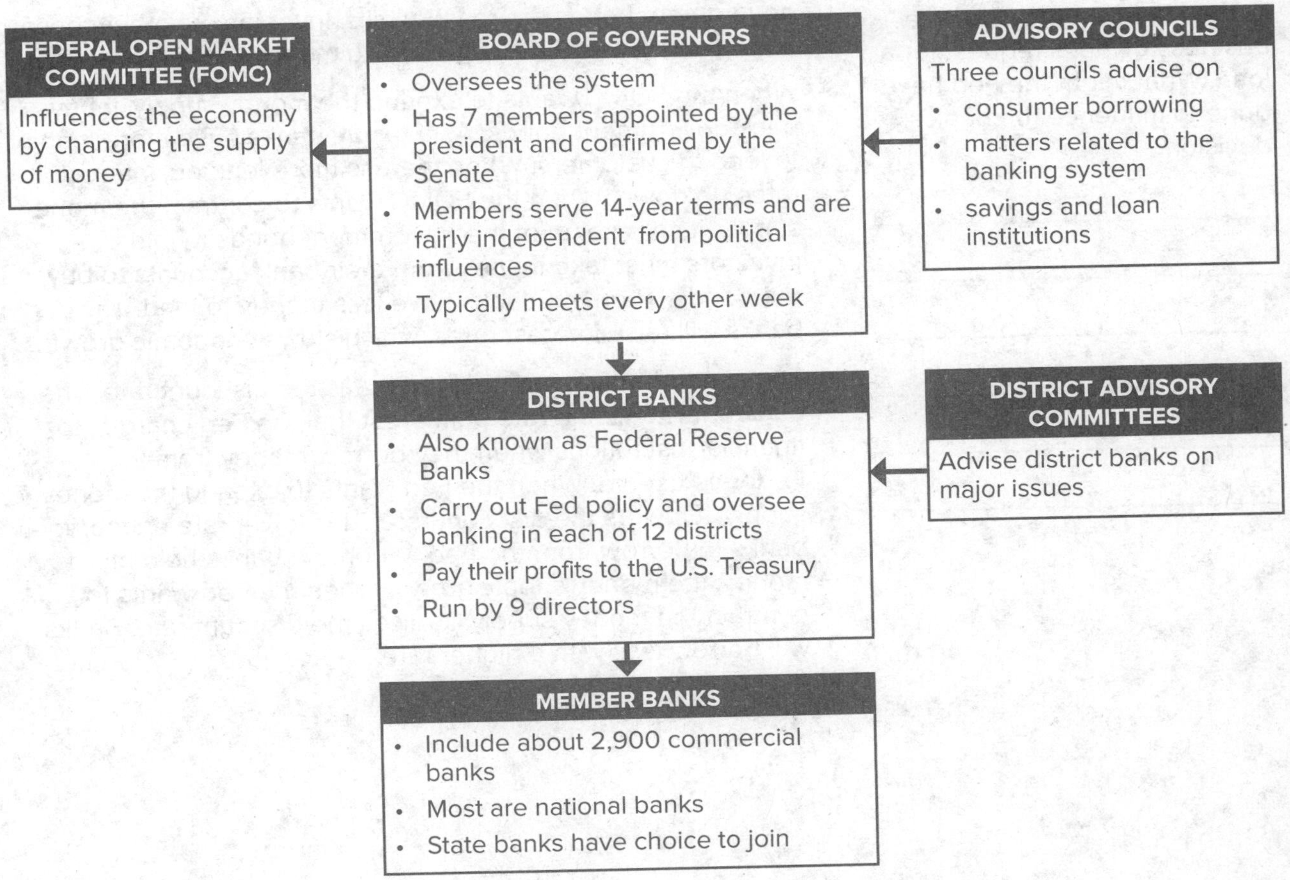

FEDERAL OPEN MARKET COMMITTEE (FOMC)

Influences the economy by changing the supply of money

BOARD OF GOVERNORS

- Oversees the system
- Has 7 members appointed by the president and confirmed by the Senate
- Members serve 14-year terms and are fairly independent from political influences
- Typically meets every other week

ADVISORY COUNCILS

Three councils advise on
- consumer borrowing
- matters related to the banking system
- savings and loan institutions

DISTRICT BANKS

- Also known as Federal Reserve Banks
- Carry out Fed policy and oversee banking in each of 12 districts
- Pay their profits to the U.S. Treasury
- Run by 9 directors

DISTRICT ADVISORY COMMITTEES

Advise district banks on major issues

MEMBER BANKS

- Include about 2,900 commercial banks
- Most are national banks
- State banks have choice to join

2. MAKING CONNECTIONS

How does the Fed's monetary policy make use of the principles of supply and demand?

3. REASONING

The bank has turned down a business owner's request for a loan. What might the Fed have done to influence the bank's decision?

What the Fed Does

Of all the Fed's functions, managing the nation's money supply is the most important. This function helps maintain a strong economy.

Conducting Monetary Policy

The Fed conducts monetary policy. **Monetary policy** means adjusting the money supply to promote economic growth and keep prices stable. Supply and demand determine the interest rate, which is the price of money. If the Fed increases the supply of money, interest rates drop. People borrow more and spend more. The economy grows. If the Fed reduces the money supply, interest rates increase. People borrow less and spend less. The economy slows.

Using the Tools of Monetary Policy

The Fed uses three tools to control the money supply. The most important tool is called open market operations. **Open market operations (OMO)** refers to the actions the FOMC takes that affect the money supply. It can buy or sell government bonds or Treasury bills. Investors who buy these bonds and bills are actually lending money to the government.

When the FOMC wants to expand the money supply, it buys back government bonds. As a result, banks have more money to lend to customers. When there is more lending, interest rates go down. When the FOMC wants to contract the money supply, it sells some of the government bonds it holds. Investors must take money from their bank accounts to buy the bonds. Then the banks have less money to lend. The banks will raise interest rates, which slows economic growth.

The second tool of monetary policy is the discount rate. The **discount rate** is the rate of interest that the Fed charges to financial institutions when they borrow money from the Federal Reserve. When the Fed wants to expand the money supply, it lowers the discount rate. This lower rate encourages banks to borrow from the Fed. When the banks hold more money, the money supply grows. When the Fed wants to contract the money supply, it raises the discount rate. Banks will borrow less with a higher rate.

Name ______________________ Date ______________ Class ________

The third tool of monetary policy is the reserve requirement. The **reserve requirement** is the portion of a new deposit that a financial institution cannot lend out. For example, if the reserve requirement is 30 percent, the bank must keep $30 of a $100 deposit as a reserve. The bank can lend the remaining $70.

If the Fed wants to change the size of the money supply, it can change the size of the reserve requirement. To expand the money supply, the Fed could lower the reserve requirement. The bank has to set aside less money, so it has more money available to lend. To contract the money supply, the Fed could raise the reserve requirement. When the bank has to set aside a larger percentage of each deposit, it has less money to lend.

Effects of Monetary Policy

	Expand Money Supply	Contract Money Supply
Open Market Operations	• FOMC buys bonds. • Banks have more money to lend. • Banks lower interest rates.	• FOMC sells bonds. • Investors withdraw money from banks to buy bonds. • Banks have less money to lend. • Banks raise interest rates.
Discount Rate	• The Fed lowers the discount rate. • Banks can borrow more from the Fed.	• The Fed raises the discount rate. • Banks likely borrow less from the Fed.
Reserve Requirement	• The Fed lowers the reserve requirement. • Banks have more money available to lend.	• The Fed raises the reserve requirement. • Banks have less money available to lend.

Regulating the Financial System

The Fed created most of the forms you fill out when you take out a loan. That is because the Fed writes the rules for lending. These rules require clear explanations of the terms of a loan. They also prohibit lenders from using dishonest tactics.

The Fed writes other rules for member banks. These rules include how banks report their reserve requirements and how they make loans. The Fed also can decide whether member banks are allowed to merge.

4. MAKING CONNECTIONS

What do you think would happen to the interest rate charged by a bank if the Fed increased the reserve requirement? Why?

____

____

____

____

____

____

5. PROBLEM SOLVING

How could the Fed use the discount rate to slow the economy?

____

____

____

____

____

____

Name ______________________ Date ____________ Class ________

6. ANALYZING INFORMATION

Is the Fed a financial institution? Explain.

____
____
____
____
____
____

Maintaining the Currency

The Fed does not actually print paper money. The Bureau of Engraving and Printing does that. The Fed stores and distributes paper money, though. It also pulls old money out of circulation. The Fed exchanges the worn and damaged bills for newer ones. This keeps the nation's money supply in good condition.

Acting as the Government's Bank

The Fed's fourth job is to act as the government's bank. When people pay their federal taxes, that money is deposited with the Fed. The Fed holds that and other government revenue until it is needed. When the government needs to make a purchase or a payment, it can write a check on these deposits. Such payments include monthly social security checks.

REVIEW LESSON 2

1. Use the diagram below to note key facts about the Federal Reserve System.

THE FEDERAL RESERVE

Structure	Functions
• Led by ______________ • Has advisory councils about ______________ ______________ • Controls money supply through ______________ • ______________ carry out Fed policy in each of _____ districts. • Includes about 2,900 commercial ______________	• Adjusts money supply to ______________ ______________ • Writes rules for ______________ • Maintains ______________ • Acts as ______________

2. ✎ **SUGGESTING A SOLUTION** Imagine that the nation's economy is showing signs that it is slowing down. On a separate sheet of paper, write an essay to explain what the Federal Reserve should do. Give reasons for your answer.

LESSON 3 SUMMARY

Banks and Banking

SS.7.E.1.4, SS.7.E.2.2

Banks in the Economy

Banks and other financial institutions accept deposits. They then use part of those monies on deposit to make loans to other customers.

Taking Deposits

Banks offer several deposit account options. Consumers must weigh the different deposit account options and choose the one best suited to their needs.

Money deposited in a **checking account** can be withdrawn at any time by writing a check or using a debit card. People use checking accounts to pay bills or make purchases. Some checking accounts pay interest, but the interest rate is usually lower than for other types of accounts.

Most **savings accounts** pay interest on deposits. They also allow people to make withdrawals. Banks want to encourage people to keep money in the bank, so they pay interest. The banks can use money on deposit to make loans.

A **certificate of deposit (CD)** is an account that pays higher interest than a savings account. However, there is a specific period of time that the money must be left in the bank. It could be six months, a year, or longer. A penalty is paid if a person takes money out of the CD before that time. The penalty is a lower rate of interest.

A **money market account** also pays interest, and it allows people to write checks. There might be some requirements with money market accounts, such as keeping a minimum balance. The number of withdrawals that can be taken also might be limited.

Making Loans

Banks can use part of each deposit to make loans to individuals and businesses. People use loans to buy a car or a home or to pay large expenses such as a home repair or college tuition. Businesses borrow money to pay their employees or to fund new products or locations. Bank loan officers must make sure the borrower understands the loan amount, the interest rate, and the repayment terms.

1. MAKING INFERENCES

Why do banks offer so many different types of deposit accounts?

____

____

____

____

____

____

2. PREDICTING CONSEQUENCES

How can loans both help and hurt the economy?

____

____

____

____

____

____

Name ______________________ Date ______________ Class __________

3. EVALUATING

Has technology made banking easier or more complicated? Explain.

____

____

____

____

____

____

New Ways of Banking

Technology has created new banking options. People can bank by telephone, cell phone, automated teller machine (ATM), and computer. They can use the Internet to monitor their accounts, transfer money, and pay bills. Some services allow people to make payments using their cell phones instead of checks or credit cards.

REVIEW LESSON 3

1. Use the diagram below to note how the banking system in the United States works.

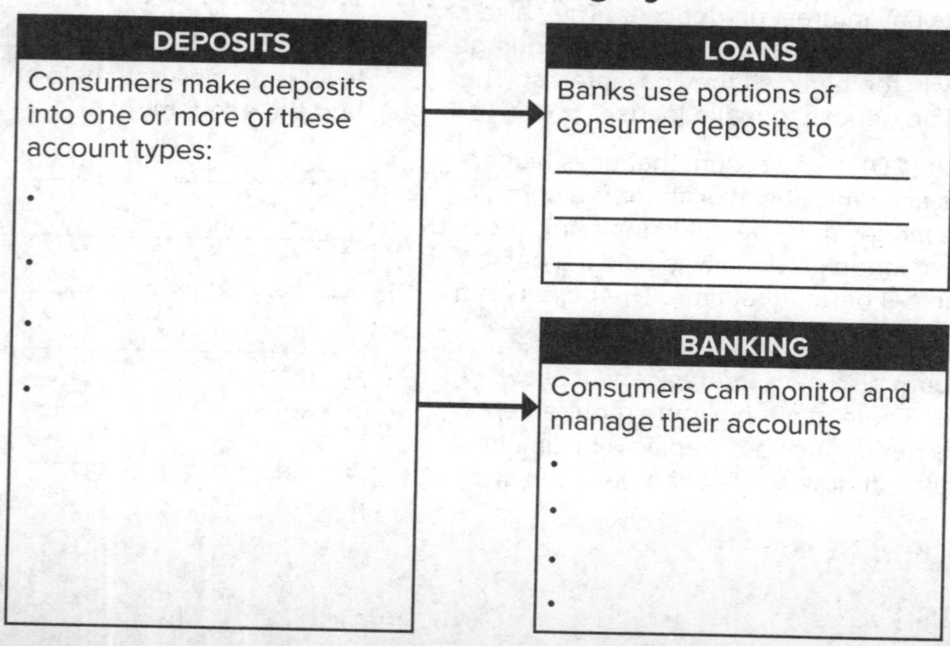

The U.S. Banking System

DEPOSITS

Consumers make deposits into one or more of these account types:

-
-
-
-

LOANS

Banks use portions of consumer deposits to

____

____

____

BANKING

Consumers can monitor and manage their accounts

-
-
-
-

2. **ANALYZING INFORMATION** Use the information in your diagram to write an essay that answers this question: What are two ways consumers benefit from the U.S. banking system? Use a separate sheet of paper to write your essay.

Benchmark Skill Activities

DIRECTIONS: Write your answers on a separate sheet of paper.

LAFS.68.WHST.1.2

1. INFORMATIVE/EXPLANATORY

Use your FOLDABLES to write an essay about the role of money and banking in your day-to-day life.

LAFS.68.RH.1.3

2. VISUALIZING

Create a diagram that illustrates how Federal Reserve monetary policy influences the nation's economy.

LAFS.7.SL.1.3

3. EVALUATING

The president of the Federal Reserve Bank of Philadelphia made the following argument.

> "Think of the impact low interest rates have had on auto sales and housing prices in this most recent expansion. These low interest rates were a consequence of the ripple effect of monetary policy. The FOMC lowered the federal funds rate, effectively lowering the cost of funds to mortgage lenders and automakers, who were then able to offer low rates to consumers. With that evidence, I think it easy to see that monetary policy has a powerful and long lasting impact on our nation's economy."
>
> —Anthony M. Santomero, President, Federal Reserve Bank of Philadelphia, October 17, 2005

Evaluate Santomero's argument. Identify his claims and supporting evidence. Are his reasons sound? Is his evidence relevant and sufficient?

LAFS.68.RH.1.2

4. ANALYZING NEWS MEDIA

Find an article or other news story about the Federal Reserve. Use the main idea and supporting details of the story to write a summary. Then, compare the article with the information about the Fed in this chapter.

LAFS.7.SL.1.1, ELD.K12.ELL.SI.1

5. IDENTIFYING ALTERNATIVES

The federal government has considered replacing the $1 paper bill with a $1 coin. With a partner or a small group, discuss how such a change would need to be made. Talk about how it might affect banking and the economy. Decide together whether such a change is worthwhile.

Benchmark Note Cards

DIRECTIONS: Use these note cards to help you prepare for the test.

SS.7.E.1.2 Discuss the importance of borrowing and lending in the United States, the government's role in controlling financial institutions, and list the advantages and disadvantages of using credit.

BORROWING AND LENDING	Lending helps financial institutions make a profit through the interest rates they charge on loans. Financial institutions lend out most of the money they take in as deposits. Loans give individuals and businesses the money they need to meet financial goals, such as buying a car or house or paying other large expenses.

GOVERNMENT CONTROL OF FINANCIAL INSTITUTIONS	• Deposit insurance protects the money customers put in a financial institution. • The government regulates financial institutions by setting requirements for charters and monitoring the institutions for obedience to the law. • The Federal Reserve makes the rules for loans and determines the paperwork that needs to be completed. • The Fed uses the discount rate and reserve requirement to manage the flow of money into and out of financial institutions.

SS.7.E.1.4 Discuss the function of financial institutions in the development of a market economy.

FINANCIAL INSTITUTIONS IN A MARKET ECONOMY	• Consumers have a choice of different types of financial institutions: commercial banks, savings and loan associations, and credit unions. • Financial institutions give consumers a place to save and manage their money. • Financial institutions give consumers a choice of accounts to meet their needs: checking accounts, savings accounts, certificates of deposit, and money market accounts. • Financial institutions add money into the economy by making loans to individuals and businesses.

SS.7.E.2.2 Describe the banking system in the United States and its impact on the money supply.

THE BANKING SYSTEM IN THE UNITED STATES	The banking system in the United States is overseen by a central bank called the Federal Reserve, or the Fed. The Fed also includes 12 district banks and about 2,900 member banks. It manages the nation's currency, directs economic policies, and acts as the government's bank. It also regulates commercial banks, savings and loan institutions (S&Ls), and credit unions. Banking can be done in person at a financial institution, over the telephone, at an ATM, on a computer, or on a cell phone.

THE U.S. MONEY SUPPLY	• The United States uses paper and coin currency and electronic money. • The Fed controls the nation's money supply by adjusting open market operations, the discount rate, and the reserve requirement. • Open market operations are the buying and selling of government bonds and Treasury bills. • The discount rate is the interest rate charged to financial institutions when they borrow money from the Fed. • The reserve requirement is the part of a new deposit that a financial institution cannot loan out.

SS.7.E.2.5 Explain how economic institutions impact the national economy.

ECONOMIC INSTITUTIONS AND THE ECONOMY	• The Fed expands the money supply to promote economic growth. It reduces the money supply to slow the economy. • Banks accept deposits and use the money to make loans. • Businesses use borrowed money to increase production. • Individuals use borrowed money to make purchases.

Chapter 22

VISUAL SUMMARY

DIRECTIONS: Complete the graphic organizer below.

THE FEDERAL RESERVE

Functions as the nation's central bank

Manages U.S. currency— ______

Regulates commercial banks— ______

Serves as the government's bank— ______

Directs economic policies— ______

↓

FINANCIAL INSTITUTIONS

Accept deposits and make loans to customers

Three types: ______

Offer different types of accounts: ______

Make a profit through ______

Regulated by ______

Must have ______

Borrow money from ______

↓

INDIVIDUALS AND BUSINESSES

Use money as a medium of exchange, a measure of value, and a store of value

Take out loans from financial institutions to ______

Earn interest on ______

Can bank:

- in person
-
-
-

USING PRIMARY SOURCES

CITE EVIDENCE The following excerpt is from a speech given by Janet L. Yellen, chair of the Board of Governors of the Federal Reserve System. Read the excerpt, and then answer the questions that follow on a separate sheet of paper.

Implications for Monetary Policy

My own outlook for the economy and inflation is broadly consistent with the central tendency of the projections [estimates of future events] submitted by FOMC participants at the time of our June meeting. Based on my outlook, I expect that it will be appropriate at some point later this year to take the first step to raise the federal funds rate and thus begin normalizing monetary policy. But I want to emphasize that the course of the economy and inflation remains highly uncertain, and unanticipated developments could delay or accelerate this first step. We will be watching carefully to see if there is continued improvement in labor market conditions, and we will need to be reasonably confident that inflation will move back to 2 percent in the next few years.

Let me also stress that this initial increase in the federal funds rate, whenever it occurs, will by itself have only a very small effect on the overall level of monetary accommodation [adjustment] provided by the Federal Reserve. Because there are some factors, which I mentioned earlier, that continue to restrain the economic expansion, I currently anticipate that the appropriate pace of normalization will be gradual, and that monetary policy will need to be highly supportive of economic activity for quite some time. The projections of most of my FOMC colleagues indicate that they have similar expectations for the likely path of the federal funds rate. But, again, both the course of the economy and inflation are uncertain. If progress toward our employment and inflation goals is more rapid than expected, it may be appropriate to remove monetary policy accommodation more quickly. However, if progress toward our goals is slower than anticipated, then the Committee may move more slowly in normalizing policy.

Long-Run Economic Growth

Before I conclude, let me very briefly place my discussion of the economic outlook into a longer-term context. The Federal Reserve contributes to the nation's economic performance in part by using monetary policy to help achieve our mandated goals of maximum employment and price stability. But success in promoting these objectives does not, by itself, ensure a strong pace of long-run economic growth or substantial improvements in future living standards. The most important factor determining continued advances in living standards is productivity growth, defined as the rate of increase in how much a worker can produce in an hour of work. Over time, sustained increases in productivity are necessary to support rising household incomes.

(continued on the next page)

Here the recent data have been disappointing. The growth rate of output per hour worked in the business sector has averaged about 1-1/4 percent per year since the recession began in late 2007 and has been essentially flat over the past year. In contrast, annual productivity gains averaged 2-3/4 percent over the decade preceding the Great Recession. I mentioned earlier the sluggish pace of wage gains in recent years, and while I do think that this is evidence of some persisting labor market slack, it also may reflect, at least in part, fairly weak productivity growth.

There are many unanswered questions about what has slowed productivity growth in recent years and about the prospects for productivity growth in the longer run. But we do know that productivity ultimately depends on many factors, including our workforce's knowledge and skills along with the quantity and quality of the capital equipment, technology, and infrastructure that they have to work with. As a general principle, the American people would be well served by the active pursuit of effective policies to support longer-run growth in productivity. Policies to strengthen education and training, to encourage entrepreneurship and innovation, and to promote capital investment, both public and private, could all potentially be of great benefit in improving future living standards in our nation.

—Janet L. Yellen, "Recent Developments and the Outlook for the Economy," July 10, 2015

1. What goal does Chairman Yellen identify for the FOMC in the next year?
2. What limitations to the goal does she anticipate?
3. Underline the two sentences that explain how fast or slow the FOMC will act.
4. According to Yellen, why is monetary policy important to the Federal Reserve?
5. How does Yellen define "productivity growth"?
6. In Yellen's words, ". . . the recent data have been disappointing." Why?
7. Of the government policies that Yellen suggests for improving productivity, which do you believe is most important? Why?

Chapter Practice Test

DIRECTIONS: Circle the best answer for each question.

SS.7.E.2.2 (Moderate)

Richard W. Fisher gave the following remarks at the 6th Annual Real Estate Symposium of the North Dallas Chamber of Commerce in Dallas, Texas, on August 30, 2006.

> *"One of the most successful and brilliant aspects of this legislation was the creation of 12 regional banks that would influence monetary policymaking. Having representatives from all parts of the country brings a deeper, more diverse perspective to the policy debate, giving a clearer view of what is really happening in the U.S. economy."*
>
> —Richard W. Fisher, "Primer on Inflation"

Which part of the Federal Reserve is being described in this source?

A district banks

B member banks

C Board of Governors

D federal advisory councils

SS.7.E.2.2 (Moderate)

What is the main difference between a credit union and a commercial bank?

A when money can be withdrawn

B who can use it

C what accounts are offered

D how much can be deposited

3 **SS.7.E.1.4 (High)**

Which type of deposit account makes it easiest for consumers to fulfill their daily needs and wants?

A savings account

B checking account

C certificate of deposit

D money market account

4 **SS.7.E.2.2 (High)**

Look at the chart below.

AVERAGE DAILY CONSUMER SPENDING	
January	$119
February	$100
March	$80
April	$95
May	$72
June	$56

Which action is the Fed most likely to take in response to this information?

A raise the discount rate

B sell U.S. Treasury bills

C sell government bonds

D lower the reserve requirement

5 **SS.7.E.1.2 (Moderate)**

?			
Makes sure the institution has enough money to do business	Makes sure the people running the institution have the right skills	Makes sure the institution obeys the law	Makes sure the institution stays in good financial health

What is an appropriate title for this graphic organizer?

A Government Regulation of Financial Institutions

B Government Deposit Insurance Programs

C Jobs of the Federal Reserve System

D Roles of Financial Institutions

---

6 **SS.7.E.1.4, SS.7.E.2.5 (Moderate)**

Commercial banks offer consumers different types of deposit accounts. Which principle of a free market economy does this illustrate?

A opportunity cost

B scarcity

C choice

D supply and demand

7 **SS.7.E.2.2 (Low)**

When you pay by cell phone, what type of money are you using?

A electronic money

B paper bills

C currency

D coins

---

8 **SS.7.E.1.2, SS.7.E.1.4 (Moderate)**

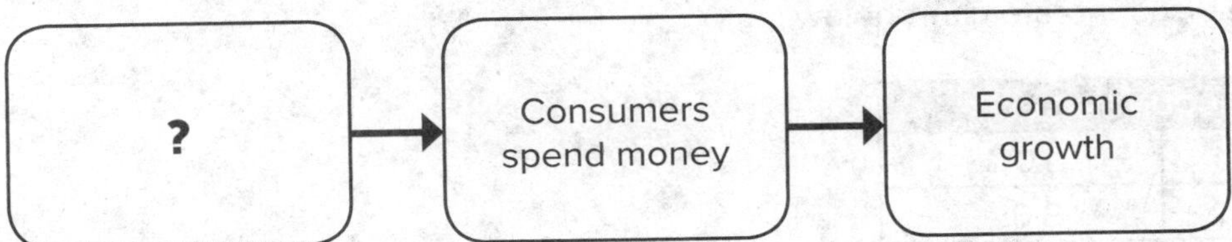

What belongs in the first box of the flow chart?

A Fed reduces the money supply

B FOMC sells government bonds

C Consumers deposit savings at a commercial bank

D Commercial banks make loans to individuals and businesses

9 **SS.7.E.2.2 (Moderate)**

How do banks make a profit?

A by borrowing money from the Fed

B by lending out larger percentages of consumer deposits

C by lending money at higher interest rates than they pay on deposits

D by accepting more in consumer deposits than they give out in loans

---

10 **SS.7.E.2.2 (High)**

Look at the discount rate chart below.

DISCOUNT RATE	
Quarter 1	1.0%
Quarter 2	3.0%
Quarter 3	3.5%
Quarter 4	5.0%

What is the most likely effect of the change in the discount rate?

A Consumers earn lower interest rates.

B Consumers spend less money.

C Commercial banks borrow more money from the Fed.

D Commercial banks lend out greater portions of their deposits.

CHAPTER 23

Financing the Government

Chapter Overview

The federal government, state governments, and local governments all create budgets for a fiscal year. The federal government gets its revenue from income taxes, payroll taxes, and corporate taxes. It uses its revenue to pay for Social Security, Medicare, national defense, and other programs. State governments get their revenue from the federal government, sales tax, and personal income tax. They use that revenue to pay for education, public welfare, state police, prisons, and parks. Local governments get most of their revenue from property taxes. They use the revenue to pay for education, police and fire protection, building and maintaining streets, and other services.

Governments may have budget surpluses or budget deficits. Unexpected events such as natural disasters and international conflicts can sometimes lead to budget deficits. State and local governments must balance their budget. The federal government, however, can borrow money when there is a deficit and incur debt. The federal government uses taxes and spending to reach its economic goals.

CHAPTER BENCHMARKS

SS.7.C.3.14 Differentiate between local, state, and federal governments' obligations and services.

SS.7.E.1.2 Discuss the importance of borrowing and lending in the United States, the government's role in controlling financial institutions, and list the advantages and disadvantages of using credit.

SS.7.E.1.6 Compare the national budget process to the personal budget process.

SS.7.E.2.1 Explain how federal, state, and local taxes support the economy as a function of the United States government.

LAFS.68.RH.1.2 Determine the central ideas or information of a primary or secondary source; provide an accurate summary of the source distinct from prior knowledge or opinions.

LAFS.68.RH.2.4 Determine the meaning of words and phrases as they are used in a text, including vocabulary specific to domains related to history/social studies.

LAFS.68.RH.2.5 Describe how a text presents information (e.g., sequentially, comparatively, causally).

LAFS.68.RH.3.8 Distinguish among fact, opinion, and reasoned judgment in a text.

LAFS.68.WHST.1.1 Write arguments focused on discipline-specific content.

WHAT I NEED TO KNOW

TERMS

- ☐ fiscal year
- ☐ mandatory spending
- ☐ discretionary spending
- ☐ appropriations bill
- ☐ intergovernmental revenue
- ☐ sales tax
- ☐ entitlement program
- ☐ property tax
- ☐ balanced budget
- ☐ budget surplus
- ☐ budget deficit
- ☐ debt
- ☐ fiscal policy
- ☐ automatic stabilizer

Financing the Government

CHAPTER BENCHMARKS, *continued*

LAFS.68.WHST.2.4 Produce clear and coherent writing in which the development, organization, and style are appropriate to task, purpose, and audience.

LAFS.68.WHST.3.7 Conduct short research projects to answer a question (including a self-generated question), drawing on several sources and generating additional related, focused questions that allow for multiple avenues of exploration.

Financing the Government

Create the Foldable® below. Label the tabs with the lesson titles. Under the left tab, compare your revenue and expenditures to that of the federal government and explain the importance of having a budget. Under the right tab, explain how governments and individuals strive to have a balanced budget. On the back of the Foldable, explain when and how the government might use fiscal policy to stimulate the economy.

Step 1
With the paper arranged horizontally, fold the left side over to the right edge and fold paper in half.

Step 2
While the paper is folded in half, fold the top of the paper down to the bottom to fold in half again.

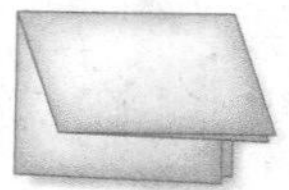

Step 3
Unfold the paper and cut the horizontal fold from the left edge to the center of the paper.

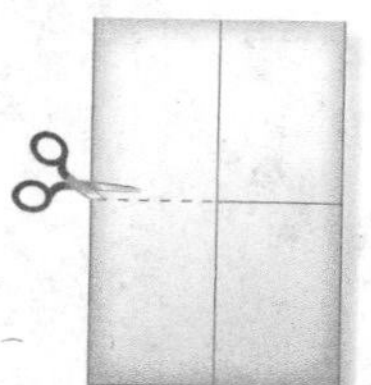

Step 4
Fold shutters down and label as directed.

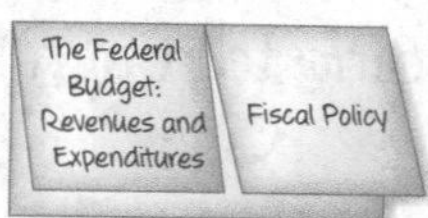

LESSON 1 SUMMARY

The Federal Budget: Revenues and Expenditures

SS.7.C.3.14, SS.7.E.1.6, SS.7.E.2.1

Understanding the Federal Budget

You learned in Chapter 19 how to create a personal budget. You compared your regular income and expenses to check to see if you had a budget deficit or surplus. The federal government creates a budget, too.

The Budget Process

When you created your budget, you did it over a short period. The budget of the federal government covers a fiscal year. A **fiscal year** is any 12-month period for which to keep accounts. The government's fiscal year runs from October 1 of one year to September 30 of the next year.

The budget process begins when the president sends a budget message to Congress by the first Monday in February. This message includes estimates on revenues and expenses, spending priorities, and plans for taxes.

Key members of Congress then agree on a *budget resolution*. This is Congress's plan for revenue and spending. Money can be spent in two broad categories:

- **Mandatory spending** is set by laws outside the budget. Mandatory spending includes Social Security, Medicare, and interest on the national debt.
- **Discretionary spending** involves spending choices that are made and approved each year. This spending includes the budgets of federal agencies and defense.

Next, Congress passes budget resolutions that outline spending and taxes for the next five years. Spending caps are set for areas controlled by committees of Congress. Resolutions are not laws, but they provide frameworks. House committees then write appropriations bills. An **appropriations bill** gives approval for the government to spend the money. This bill must be approved by both houses. It is then sent to the president, who can approve or veto it. Congress can override a veto or rewrite the bill. Sometimes Congress does not approve a budget by the beginning of the next fiscal year. It then approves a *continuing resolution*. With this law, spending continues at the same levels as the previous year.

1. MAKING INFERENCES

The president and Congress follow specific steps each year to create the federal budget. Why do you think this is necessary?

2. MAKING CONNECTIONS

Review the budget process followed by the federal government. On a separate sheet of paper, write down the process you would follow to create your own personal budget. Then, make a list of items that would be part of your mandatory spending. Make a second list to show your discretionary spending.

3. SPECULATING

How might a strong economy affect the government's income?

____

____

____

____

____

Revenues

The money the federal government collects is called revenue. There are three main sources of federal government revenue:

- personal income tax—paid by all people who earn income over a certain amount
- payroll tax—taken from workers' paychecks and used for social insurance programs such as Social Security and Medicare
- corporate tax—paid by corporations on their profits

There are three categories of taxes: progressive, proportional, and regressive. With a progressive tax, the rate for taxes goes up with higher incomes. The federal income tax is progressive. Proportional taxes have a constant tax rate. For example, the tax for Medicare has the same rate for all wage earners. With a regressive tax, people pay a smaller amount in taxes the more money they earn. An example is the sales tax.

ANALYZING VISUALS

4. COMPARING AND CONTRASTING Compare your list of mandatory and discretionary spending to the government's expenditures. How are they different? How is the budget process similar?

____

____

____

____

____

____

____

____

____

____

Expenditures

The amount of money a person, business, or government spends is its expenditures. The government has far greater expenditures and more categories of expenses than individual Americans. Some categories take a large part of the budget. Spending on Social Security and Medicare is likely to increase as more people retire and the population ages. In addition, the government has to pay interest on money it borrows, just like individuals do. Much of the budget goes to these mandatory expenditures. The Congressional Budget Office (CBO) tracks all spending and reports to Congress.

FEDERAL GOVERNMENT EXPENDITURES FOR FISCAL YEAR 2015*

Category	Percentage of Total Expenditures	Description
Social Security	23.2%	includes benefits for retirees
National Defense	16.2%	includes salaries and equipment
Income Security	13.7%	includes unemployment, welfare, and some retirement benefits
Medicare	13.6%	includes health insurance coverage for those 65 and older
Health	13.1%	includes health care and long-term care for low-income people and people with disabilities
Interest on Debt	6.5%	interest on borrowed money
Other	13.7%	includes education, veteran benefits, and highway costs

Source: Economic Report of the President, 2014; *figures given are estimates for 2015

Name ______________________ Date ______________ Class ________

Budgeting for State and Local Governments

State and local governments also prepare budgets. However, by law they cannot have greater expenditures than revenue.

State Governments

State governments get most of the money to run their state from **intergovernmental revenue.** These are funds that one level of government receives from another level. States receive their funds from the federal government.

The second-most important source is **sales taxes.** You pay a sales tax when you buy goods or use some services. Only five states do not have sales tax. Sales taxes are regressive and might make it difficult for poor people to afford some items. That is why many states do not tax essential goods such as food and medicine. Some states also have tax holidays, with no tax on school supplies.

A third source is personal income tax. Florida and four other states do not have a personal income tax. The remaining revenue comes from corporate taxes and various other sources.

5. ANALYZING INFORMATION

Use the Internet to find out more about intergovernmental revenue and how it is used. On a separate sheet of paper, make a chart that shows the information you discover.

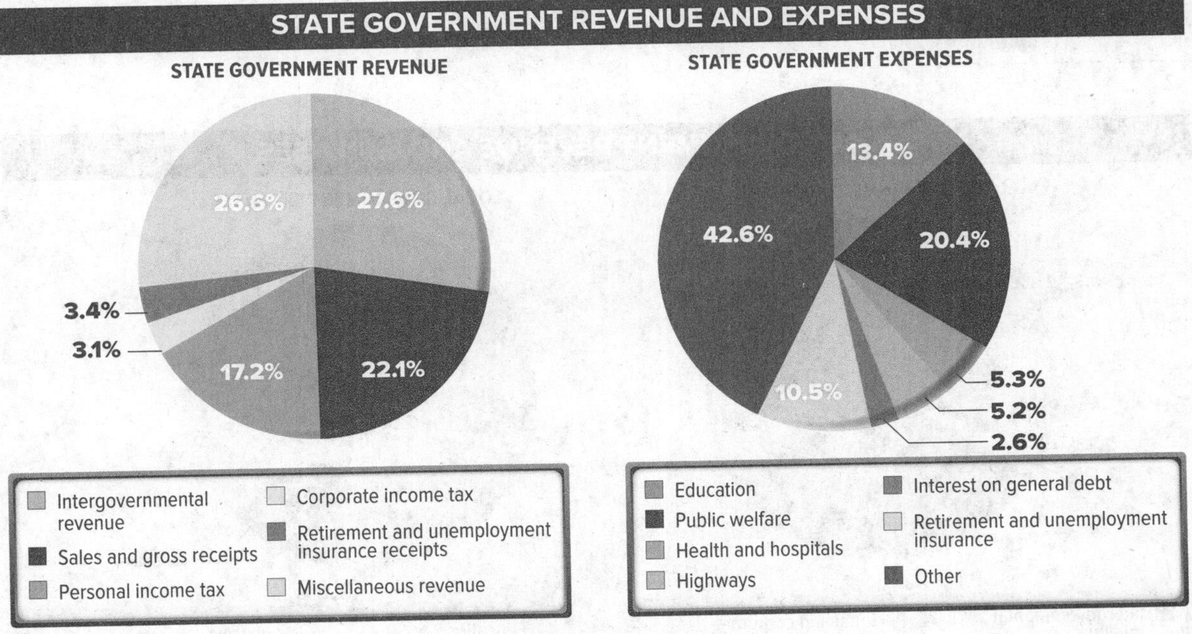

Source: U.S. Bureau of the Census, *Statistical Abstract of the United States*

Name ______________________ Date ______________ Class __________

ANALYZING VISUALS

6. DRAWING CONCLUSIONS Look at the charts on this and the previous page that show expenditures of both state and local governments. Which category is among the largest for both? Why do you think this is so?

States spend their funds on their citizens. The largest share of revenue goes to public welfare. This refers to programs that help people who cannot afford basic needs such as health care, food, and housing. Most of that money is spent on **entitlement programs.** They are called "entitlement" because laws set the requirements for benefits. These include programs such as Medicare. States also spend money on education. A part of that money goes to local governments to help pay for public schools. Some is used to pay part of students' cost to attend state colleges. Police, prisons, and parks are other expenditures that make up a state budget.

Local Governments

The main source of revenue for local governments is the **property tax.** This is a tax based on the value of land and property that people own. Other sources of income include fines and fees. Some local governments also have sales taxes and personal income taxes.

Local governments use their revenue to provide many basic services for their citizens. These services include education, police and fire protection, construction and maintenance of city and county streets, water and sewer service, and trash removal among others.

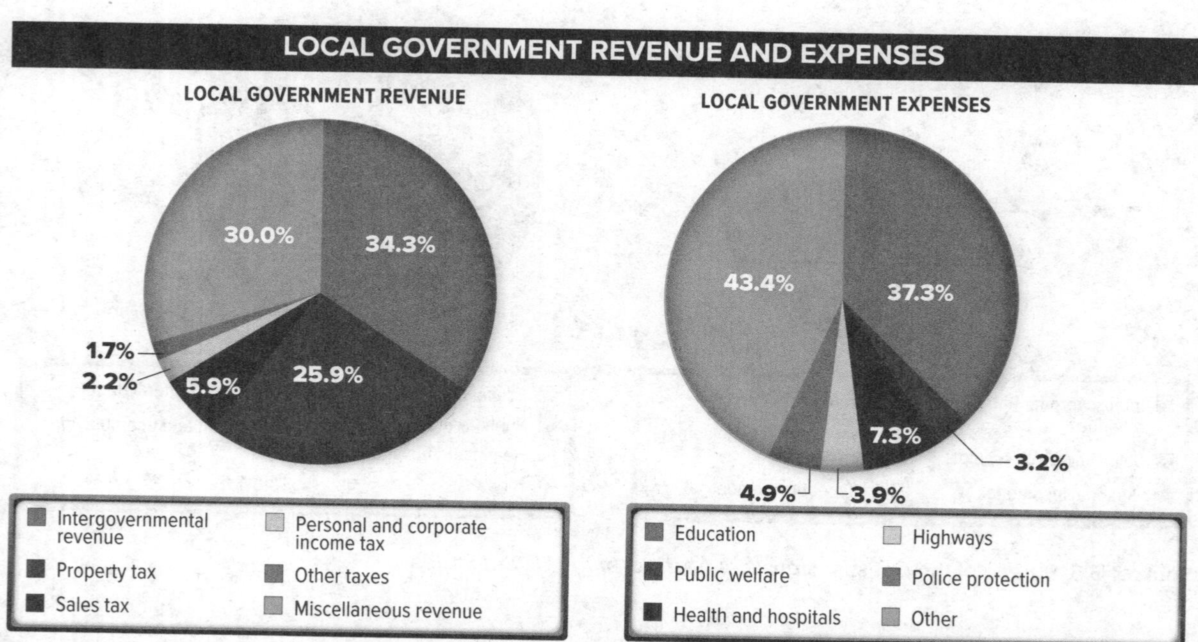

Source: U.S. Bureau of the Census, *Statistical Abstract of the United States*

Name ________________ Date ________________ Class ________

REVIEW LESSON 1

1. Complete the chart below to identify federal, state, and local revenue sources and expenditures.

FEDERAL GOVERNMENT	STATE GOVERNMENT	LOCAL GOVERNMENT
Revenue		
• • •	• • •	• • • • in some states—local sales tax and income taxes
Expenditures		
• • • income security • • health care • • others, such as education, veterans benefits, and highway costs	• • •	• • • construction and maintenance of roads •

2. **PRIORITIZING** For each level of government in the chart, choose the two expenditures you think should be mandatory. Then, for each level of government, choose the type of revenue that you think should be reduced if the economy slows. On a separate sheet of paper, write an essay explaining your reasons for each.

Fiscal Policy

1. DETERMINING CAUSE AND EFFECT

Why is it difficult for the government to follow its budget?

SS.7.E.1.2, SS.7.E.1.6

Surpluses and Deficits

Sometimes it is difficult to stick to a budget. For example, you might have to buy an unexpected birthday present. You might be able to use your savings. However, what will you do if you have more than one unexpected expense?

The government has unexpected expenses, too. If a hurricane hits Florida, the people and businesses will need food and water supplies. They will also need help to repair the damage to utilities and to rebuild roads, homes, and businesses. The government has money set aside in the budget for natural disasters or international conflicts. Too many unexpected events, though, can deplete funds.

Another area of uncertainty is the economy. A strong economy means more revenue. A weak economy means less revenue. When the government makes its budget, it does not know for sure what will happen with the economy.

Balanced—or Unbalanced

Every state except Vermont must have a **balanced budget.** When a budget is balanced, revenue and spending for the year are equal. States are only allowed to borrow money for long-term projects.

To prepare for the unexpected, states save money during years with a **budget surplus.** This happens when a government collects more money than it spends. When the economy is booming, a state's tax revenue can be higher than budgeted. The state saves that money and uses it during years when the economy slows.

Unlike the states, the federal government can spend more than it collects in revenues in a fiscal year. When this happens, the government has a **budget deficit.** The government then borrows money by selling government bonds and Treasury bills. People who buy bonds or T-bills are lending the government money. The government pays back the money with interest when a bond or T-bill matures.

Name ______ Date ______ Class ______

Deficit Becomes Debt

When the government borrows money to cover its budget deficit, it incurs debt. **Debt** is money that has been borrowed and not yet paid back. Each year with a budget deficit means additional debt. Years with a budget surplus allow the government to pay down some of the debt. Overall, the federal debt has increased for many years.

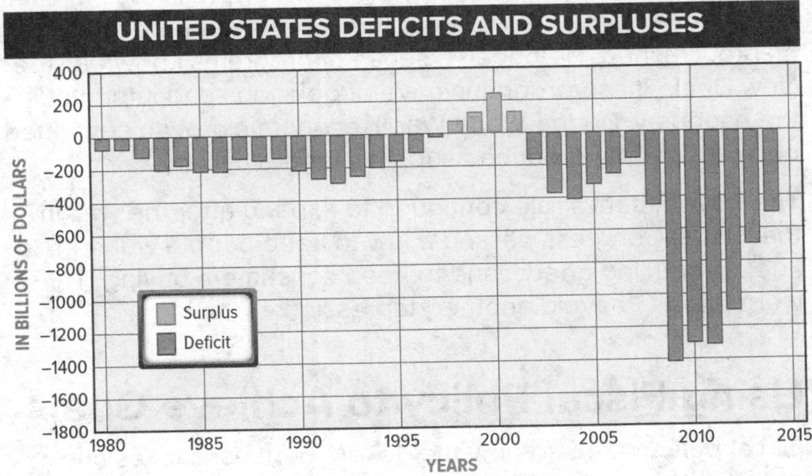

Source: White House Office of Management and Budget; Congressional Budget Office; U.S. Department of the Treasury; U.S. Government Accountability Office

ANALYZING VISUALS

2. MAKING INFERENCES
What can you infer from information in the chart about the government's actions in 2009?

______

______

______

What can you infer from the data for the years 1998 through 2001?

______

______

______

______

______

______

Impact of Deficits and the Federal Debt

Borrowing money has negative effects. Like individuals, the federal government has less money to spend until the debt is paid off. Interest payments make up a large part of the budget. This means less funding is available for new and existing programs.

Another negative effect relates to people's overall investments. People feel safe about investing in government bonds. They then might not have enough money to invest in businesses. As a result, businesses have less money to invest to improve productivity and to grow. This, in turn, slows economic growth.

Government borrowing also can mean a shortage of credit and rising interest rates. This is a result of supply and demand. The more the government borrows, the less money there is available for others. As interest rates on loans and mortgages rise, they will cost more than before.

3. EVALUATING
Do you think individuals or businesses suffer more negative effects from a budget deficit? Explain.

______

______

______

______

______

______

______

______

______

Name _______________ Date _______________ Class _______________

4. SEQUENCING

During the Great Depression, the government worked to manage the economy. Use the flowchart to show the likely steps that led to an improved economy.

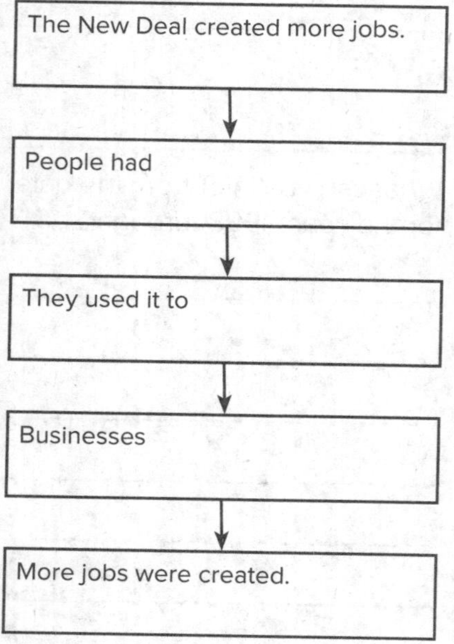
The New Deal created more jobs.
People had
They used it to
Businesses
More jobs were created.

5. DETERMINING CAUSE AND EFFECT

How does fiscal policy stimulate the economy? In the chart below, list the actions that cause economic growth.

Actions:

•

•

Effect: increased demand for goods and services

When a government continually has to borrow money, investors may lose confidence in the government. The government would have to pay a higher interest rate to borrow money. It might decide to cut spending or raise taxes.

Managing the Economy

In the past, the government played a minor role in the economy. This changed during the Great Depression. Franklin D. Roosevelt became president three years after the stock market crashed. He began a series of programs known as the New Deal. These programs gave people jobs and improved the economy. During World War II, economic growth continued because people produced supplies for the military.

The government's role continued to expand after the war. In the 1940s, Congress passed a law to keep people working, to keep producing goods, and to keep consumers buying. These were efforts to avoid another depression.

Using Fiscal Policy to Achieve Goals

Fiscal policy refers to how the government uses taxes and spending to reach its economic goals. When the economy slows down, the government might increase spending, cut taxes, or do both to stimulate the economy. Increased spending leads to a demand for goods and services. Businesses produce more and hire additional workers. Cutting taxes means consumers have more money to spend, which also increases demand.

Problems With Fiscal Policy

However, fiscal policy can cause some problems. Increased spending can increase the federal debt. Leaders also might disagree on how much to spend and what programs to fund. This can result in delays. Programs might take too long to stimulate the economy, or they might not work. Also, fiscal policy is not predictable and could lead to unexpected effects, possibly even negative ones.

Automatic Stabilizers

To help stop problems with fiscal policy, the government uses automatic stabilizers. An **automatic stabilizer** is any economic feature that works to increase income or keep it level without additional government action. Stabilizers include unemployment insurance and the income tax system.

Name ______________________ Date ______________ Class ________

LESSON 2 SUMMARY, *continued*

When an unemployed person is not receiving a paycheck from a job, he or she might receive unemployment payments. This money can be used to pay bills and meet basic needs until the person finds a new job.

Income tax is based on income level, so someone who works less or loses a job pays less in taxes and keeps more of the income. Once a person returns to work, the income increases. In turn, this means that the person will pay more in income tax.

REVIEW LESSON 2

1. Complete the chart below to describe the processes the government uses to manage the economy.

MANAGING THE ECONOMY
A budget surplus is ______________________ A budget deficit is ______________________ A budget deficit can become ______________________
Possible negative effects of a budget deficit: • ______________________ • ______________________ • ______________________ • ______________________
Fiscal policy is ______________________ Possible problems with fiscal policy include ______________________ Problems can be helped with ______________________

2. **HYPOTHESIZING** Imagine a detailed scenario in which the government has had a budget deficit for two years. Describe the scenario with specific examples of at least two effects of the deficit. Then, tell how the government would use fiscal policy to deal with the situation, a problem that might arise, and how an automatic stabilizer might help. Write your essay on a separate sheet of paper.

Benchmark Skill Activities

DIRECTIONS: Write your answers on a separate piece of paper.

LAFS.68.WHST.2.4

1. CONTRASTING

Use your FOLDABLES to write an essay. The government relies on two policies to meet its economic goals. They are monetary policy and fiscal policy. Recall that you learned about monetary policy in the last chapter. In your essay, contrast these two policies.

LAFS.68.RH.1.2, LAFS.68.WHST.1.1, LAFS.68.WHST.3.7

2. DETERMINING POINT OF VIEW

Some people believe that a constitutional amendment is needed to require a balanced federal budget each year. Use the Internet to find viewpoints supporting and opposing such an amendment. Then, state your own opinion about this issue. Support your opinion with evidence from your research and the chapter.

LAFS.68.RH.2.4, LAFS.68.WHST.2.4, SS.7.E.2.1

3. USING DEFINITIONS ACCURATELY

Turn to the chapter Terms list. Choose three terms to include in a paragraph that describes the way the federal government creates a budget.

LAFS.68.RH.2.5

4. IDENTIFYING

Read the paragraph below. Then, answer the questions that follow.

You can create a personal budget by following these steps. First, figure out what your income is for a month. Remember to include what you earn from jobs, your allowance, and any other income such as presents. Then list your expenses for the month. Next, subtract your expenses from your income. Finally, establish your goals and decide how you will spend your money.

How is the paragraph organized: sequentially, comparatively, or causally?

What evidence in the paragraph supports your answer?

LAFS.68.RH.3.8

5. DISTINGUISHING AMONG FACT, OPINION, AND REASONED JUDGMENT

Read the statements below. On the lines, indicate whether each statement is a fact (F), an opinion (O), or a reasoned judgment (J).

1. _______ The federal budget and a personal budget both include mandatory spending items and discretionary spending items.
2. _______ The revenue for local governments will most likely rise as property values increase.
3. _______ It would be best for the country if the federal budget did not have to include entitlement programs.
4. _______ States would have fewer budgetary problems if, like Vermont, they were not required to balance their budgets.
5. _______ The government most likely needs to borrow money after a natural disaster or during wartime.
6. _______ People with greater incomes pay higher levels of income tax.

Benchmark Note Cards

DIRECTIONS: Use these note cards to help you prepare for the test.

SS.7.E.1.2 Discuss the importance of borrowing and lending in the United States, the government's role in controlling financial institutions, and list the advantages and disadvantages of using credit.

GOVERNMENT BORROWING	When the federal government has a budget deficit, it borrows money by selling government bonds and Treasury bills. People who buy bonds or T-bills are lending the government money. The government pays back the money with interest when a bond or a T-bill matures. Borrowing to cover its budget deficit causes the federal government to go into debt. Because the federal government has to pay back its debt with interest, paying for existing and new programs becomes difficult. The federal government's borrowing might affect overall investments. People who invest in bonds might not have enough money to invest in businesses too. This might cause businesses to experience less growth and poor productivity. In turn, this might slow economic growth. When the federal government continually has to borrow money to meet its obligations, investors might lose confidence. The government might have to pay a higher interest rate to borrow money and might then need to cut spending or raise taxes.

BORROWING AND CREDIT	Borrowing by the federal government affects the demand and supply for money. This can result in a shortage of credit and rising interest rates on loans. Loans for consumers and businesses might cost more than they ordinarily would.

SS.7.E.1.6 Compare the national budget process to the personal budget process.

NATIONAL BUDGET PROCESS	The federal government follows a time line to create a budget for a fiscal year. The government's fiscal year runs from October 1 to September 30 of the next year. The president sends a budget message to Congress by the first Monday in February. Members of Congress must have a budget resolution with mandatory and discretionary spending and appropriations bills by April 15. If no budget is passed by September 30, a continuing resolution sets spending for the new year at the levels of the current year.

SS.7.E.2.1 Explain how federal, state, and local taxes support the economy as a function of the United States government.

REVENUES

Federal government gets revenue from

- personal income tax
- payroll tax
- corporate tax

State governments get revenue from

- intergovernmental revenue
- sales tax
- personal income tax

Local governments get revenue from

- property tax
- traffic fines
- permit and special service fees

During a strong economy, more people have jobs and tax revenue is higher. During a weak economy, revenue from taxes is lower because people earn and spend less money. Sometimes during a weak economy, the government raises tax rates so it can pay its bills.

EXPENDITURES

Federal government expenditures include

- Social Security and Medicare
- national defense
- income security
- health care
- borrowed money
- other areas such as education, veteran benefits, and highway costs

State government expenditures include

- entitlement programs
- education
- state police, prisons, parks, and others

Local government expenditures include

- education
- police and fire protection
- road construction and maintenance
- water and sewer treatment and trash removal

Chapter 23

VISUAL SUMMARY

DIRECTIONS: Complete the graphic organizer below.

GOVERNMENT REVENUE AND EXPENDITURES		
	Revenue	Expenditures
Federal Government	• personal income tax • •	Social Security, national defense,
State Government	• intergovernmental revenue • •	education,
Local Government	• property tax • • • •	education,

THE FEDERAL BUDGET AND FISCAL POLICY	
Cause	Effect
Budget Surplus	
	debt
Debt	
	• less money to spend on programs • little economic growth • shortage of credit and rising interest rate on loans • loss of confidence in government
Fiscal Policy	• • •
	• Unemployment insurance provides funds to unemployed people so they can pay bills and meet basic needs. • Progressive income tax allows people who work less or lose a job to pay less in taxes.

USING PRIMARY SOURCES

COMPARE AND CONTRAST Below and on the next page are statements about national debt and fiscal policy. Summarize the point of view in each selection. Then, using examples from each excerpt, compare and contrast the three statements. Write your answers on a separate sheet of paper.

Document A

A national debt, if it is not excessive, will be to us a national blessing. It will be a powerful cement of our union. It will also create a necessity for keeping up taxation . . . which, without being oppressive [harsh], will be a spur [stimulus] to industry. . . .

—Alexander Hamilton, Letter to Robert Morris, April 30, 1781

Document B

We are living with a legacy [tradition] of deficit spending that began almost a decade ago. And in the wake of the financial crisis, some of that was necessary to keep credit flowing, save jobs, and put money in people's pockets. But now that the worst of the recession is over, we have to confront the fact that our government spends more than it takes in. That is not sustainable. Every day, families sacrifice to live within their means. They deserve a government that does the same. So tonight, I am proposing that starting this year, we freeze annual domestic spending for the next five years. . . . The bipartisan [involving two political parties] fiscal commission I created last year . . . conclusion is that the only way to tackle our deficit is to cut excessive spending wherever we find it—in domestic spending, defense spending, health care spending, and spending through tax breaks and loopholes. This means further reducing health care costs, including programs like Medicare and Medicaid, which are the single biggest contributor to our long-term deficit. . . . To put us on solid ground, we should also find a bipartisan solution to strengthen Social Security for future generations.

—President Barack Obama, State of the Union Address, 2011

Document C

Good government policy should spur economic growth, and strengthen the private sector's ability to create new jobs. We must enact policies that promote entrepreneurship and innovation, so America can better compete with the world. What government should not do is pile on more taxation, regulation, and litigation that kill jobs and hurt the middle class. It was Thomas Jefferson who called for "A wise and frugal Government which shall leave men free to regulate their own pursuits of industry . . . and shall not take from the mouth of labor the bread it has earned. . . ." He was right. Today, the federal government is simply trying to do too much. Last year, we were told that massive new federal spending would create more jobs "immediately" and hold unemployment below 8%. In the past year, over three million Americans have lost their jobs, yet the Democratic Congress continues deficit spending, adding to the bureaucracy, and increasing the national debt on our children and grandchildren. The amount of this debt is on pace to double in five years, and triple in ten. The federal debt is already over $100,000 per household. This is simply unsustainable. The President's partial freeze on discretionary spending is a laudable step, but a small one. The circumstances of our time demand that we reconsider and restore the proper, limited role of government at every level.

—Governor Bob McDonnell, Republican Address to the Nation, January 27, 2010

Chapter Practice Test

DIRECTIONS: Circle the best answer for each question.

---

1 **SS.7.E.1.6 (Moderate)**

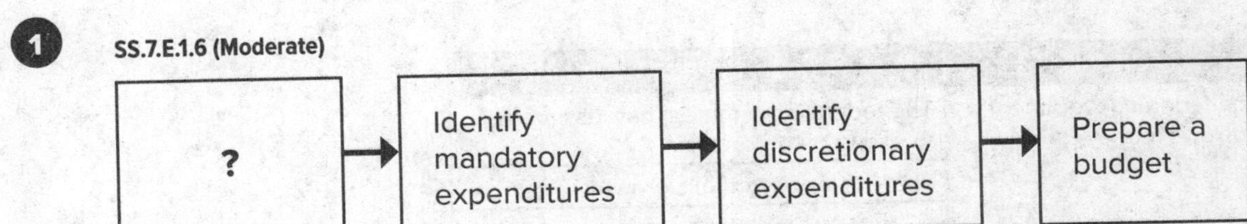

The diagram above shows the process for preparing the national budget and a personal budget. Which step is missing from the diagram?

A Determine the fiscal year

B Identify sources of revenue

C Keep a record of expenses

D Balance the budget

---

2 **SS.7.E.1.6 (Moderate)**

What is an advantage of automatic stabilizers in fiscal policy?

A reduces the national debt

B creates a budget surplus

C requires no new legislation

D equalizes unemployment rate

---

3 **SS.7.E.1.6 (Moderate)**

Which statement accurately describes an item in the federal budget?

A Medicare is a discretionary expense.

B The national debt interest is a discretionary expense.

C Highway spending is a mandatory expense.

D Social Security is a mandatory expense.

4 **SS.7.E.1.2 (Moderate)**

The chart shown here relates to the effects of borrowing by the federal government.

CAUSE	EFFECT
The federal government borrows money.	The federal government has less money to spend on programs.
	There is less economic growth.
	?
	The federal government might have to pay a higher interest rate, cut spending, or raise taxes.

Which effect is missing from the chart?

A There might be a shortage of credit and an increase in interest rates.

B The federal government might have to repay loans sooner than expected.

C The federal government has enough revenue to cover expanding programs.

D Congress needs to pass a balanced budget law.

 **5** **SS.7.E.2.1 (Moderate)**

The diagram shows where state governments get their revenue.

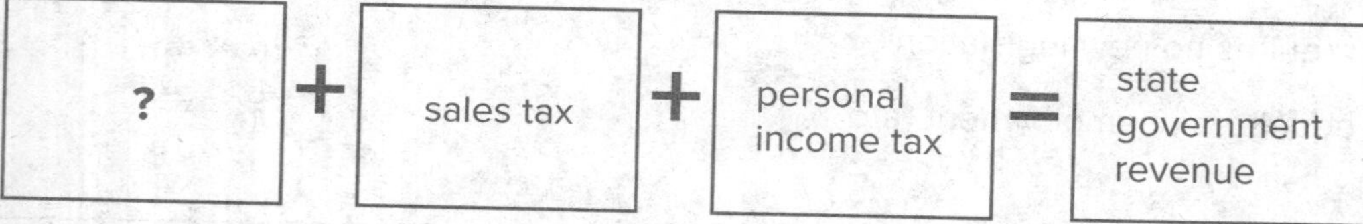

Which revenue source is missing?

A assessment fees

B property tax

C intergovernmental revenue

D bonds

SS.7.E.1.6 (High)

Read the excerpt below from a letter by Jacob Lew, secretary of the Treasury.

> *"Based on this new information, we now estimate that Treasury is likely to exhaust its extraordinary measures on or about Thursday, November 5. At that point, we would be left to fund the government with only the cash we have on hand, which we currently forecast [predict] to be below $30 billion. This amount would be far short of net expenditures on certain days, which can be as high as $60 billion. Moreover, given certain payments that are due in early to mid-November, we anticipate that our remaining cash would be depleted [used up] quickly. Without sufficient cash, it would be impossible for the United States of America to meet all of its obligations for the first time in our history."*
>
> —Jacob Lew, October 1, 2015

Which of the following actions likely led to the situation described in the excerpt?

A Congress agreed on a balanced budget resolution.

B Congress passed appropriations bills, and the president approved them.

C Congress approved a continuing resolution after the fiscal year ended.

D Congress did not pass the annual budget by the end of the fiscal year.

SS.7.E.2.1 (High)

Read the excerpt below.

> *"The income tax is just. It simply intends to put the burdens of government justly upon the backs of the people. I am in favor of an income tax. When I find a man who is not willing to bear his share of the burdens of the government which protects him, I find a man who is unworthy to enjoy the blessings of a government like ours."*
>
> —William Jennings Bryan, speech at the Democratic convention, July 8, 1896

What conclusion can you draw from this excerpt?

A People have a choice about paying taxes.

B Taxes are necessary to raise revenue.

C Selling bonds is the best way to fund government.

D Corporate taxes and payroll taxes should be ended.

8

SS.7.E.2.1 (High)

Which fiscal policy would be appropriate if the government continually has to borrow money?

A decrease government spending and increase taxes

B increase government spending and decrease taxes

C increase government spending with no change in taxes

D decrease taxes with no change in government spending

9

SS.7.E.1.2 (High)

Read the excerpt below from a letter by Jacob Lew, secretary of the Treasury.

> *"Based on this new information, we now estimate that Treasury is likely to exhaust its extraordinary measures on or about Thursday, November 5. At that point, we would be left to fund the government with only the cash we have on hand, which we currently forecast [predict] to be below $30 billion. This amount would be far short of net expenditures on certain days, which can be as high as $60 billion. Moreover, given certain payments that are due in early to mid-November, we anticipate that our remaining cash would be depleted [used up] quickly. Without sufficient cash, it would be impossible for the United States of America to meet all of its obligations for the first time in our history."*
>
> —Jacob Lew, October 1, 2015

What would the government have to do to resolve the situation described in the excerpt?

A It would have to use automatic stabilizers to stop fiscal policy problems.

B It would have to reduce the national debt by paying back more interest.

C It would have to borrow more money.

D It would have to cut taxes to stimulate the economy.

10

SS.7.E.1.6 (High)

Why are all but one state's governments limited in their spending?

A State legislatures will not approve additional spending.

B Limited revenues are collected from property taxes.

C Sales taxes and state income taxes have been increased.

D Their state constitutions require a balanced budget.

CHAPTER 24

International Trade and Economic Systems

Chapter Overview

Because of their limited resources, nations face scarcity. They resolve this problem by trading with other countries. Countries try to make the best use of their resources and manage trade to benefit their own economies. This sometimes means creating trade barriers. More often, it means participating in free trade. International trade also means exchanging currency. In order to trade, nations must know how much their currency is worth when compared to the currency of their trade partners.

Different nations have different economic systems. An economic system is determined by how a nation answers the three basic economic questions: what to produce, how to produce, and for whom to produce. Most nations today have market or mixed-market economies. A few still have command economies, in which the government makes all economic decisions.

A nation's economy helps determine whether it is a developed country or a developing one. The United States is a developed country.

CHAPTER BENCHMARKS

SS.7.C.4.2 Recognize government and citizen participation in international organizations.

SS.7.E.1.3 Review the concepts of supply and demand, choice, scarcity, and opportunity cost as they relate to the development of the mixed market economy in the United States.

SS.7.E.1.5 Assess how profits, incentives, and competition motivate individuals, households, and businesses in a free market economy.

SS.7.E.3.1 Explain how international trade requires a system for exchanging currency between and among nations.

SS.7.E.3.2 Assess how the changing value of currency affects trade of goods and services between nations.

SS.7.E.3.3 Compare and contrast a single resource economy with a diversified economy.

SS.7.E.3.4 Compare and contrast the standard of living in various countries today to that of the United States using gross domestic product (GDP) per capita as an indicator.

ELD.K12.ELL.SI.1 English language learners communicate for social and instructional purposes within the school setting.

WHAT I NEED TO KNOW

TERMS

- ☐ import
- ☐ export
- ☐ comparative advantage
- ☐ single-resource economy
- ☐ diversified economy
- ☐ protectionism
- ☐ tariff
- ☐ quota
- ☐ subsidy
- ☐ free trade
- ☐ balance of trade
- ☐ exchange rate
- ☐ market economy
- ☐ command economy
- ☐ privatization
- ☐ mixed economy
- ☐ developed country
- ☐ developing country

International Trade and Economic Systems

CHAPTER BENCHMARKS, *continued*

LAFS.68.RH.1.2 Determine the central ideas or information of a primary or secondary source; provide an accurate summary of the source distinct from prior knowledge or opinions.

LAFS.68.RH.3.7 Integrate visual information (e.g., in charts, graphs, photographs, videos, or maps) with other information in print and digital texts.

LAFS.7.SL.1.1 Engage effectively in a range of collaborative discussions (one-on-one, in groups, and teacher-led) with diverse partners on grade 7 topics, texts, and issues, building on others' ideas and expressing their own clearly.

LAFS.68.WHST.2.4 Produce clear and coherent writing in which the development, organization, and style are appropriate to task, purpose, and audience.

LAFS.68.WHST.3.8 Gather relevant information from multiple print and digital sources, using search terms effectively; assess the credibility and accuracy of each source.

International Trade and Economic Systems

Create this Foldable® like a small booklet. Label the front *Why and How Nations Trade.* Open the Foldable and label the top of the two inside sections *International Trade* and *Economic Systems and Development.* On the left side, apply what you learn about imports and exports to differentiate between a positive and negative balance of trade. On the right side, apply what you learn to compare and contrast a command economy and a market economy. On the back of the folded booklet, compare a developed country to a developing country. Research the standard of living, industrialization, education, and use of natural resources for each.

Step 1
Arrange a piece of paper horizontally and fold in half from left to right.

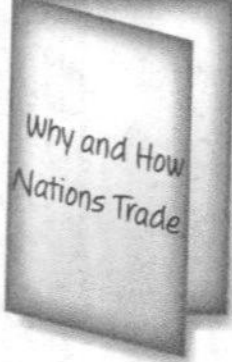

Step 2
Label the inside of your booklet as shown.

International Trade
Economic Systems and Development

LESSON 1 SUMMARY

Why and How Nations Trade

SS.7.C.4.2, SS.7.E.1.3, SS.7.E.3.1, SS.7.E.3.2, SS.7.E.3.3

Trade Between Nations

Nations have limited resources. They cannot provide everything their citizens need and want. Countries resolve the problem of scarcity by trading with other countries. They **import,** or bring into the country, goods they need. They **export,** or sell to other countries, goods they produce.

Comparative advantage makes trade work. **Comparative advantage** is the ability to produce something at a lower opportunity cost than another country can. Take Country A and Country B, for example. Both produce bicycles and bread. In each country, the opportunity cost of making bicycles is the bread it cannot produce while using resources to make bicycles. Country A can produce either one bicycle or 10 units of bread. Country B can produce either one bicycle or 15 units of bread. Therefore, Country A has the comparative advantage in producing bicycles because it has the lower opportunity cost.

OPPORTUNITY COST	
Country A	**Country B**
1 bicycle **or** 10 units of bread	1 bicycle **or** 15 units of bread

A country's comparative advantage is determined by its natural, labor, and capital resources. For example, a nation like China—which has a large population of unskilled workers—has a comparative advantage in manufactured goods. Nations with large areas of fertile land, such as the United States, have a comparative advantage in farm goods.

Some economies rely on a single export and are called **single-resource economies.** They can face problems when demand or prices for the resource in the market change. **Diversified economies** are economies that export a variety of products. They are better able to withstand market changes.

1. ANALYZING DATA

Country C can produce 1 bicycle or 12 units of bread. Country D can produce 1 bicycle or 9 units of bread. Compared with Countries A and B, which country has the best competitive advantage for bicycles? Why?

2. CONTRASTING

Why are diversified economies better able to withstand changes in the international market?

3. CONSTRUCTING AN ARGUMENT

List three possible reasons that you could give to persuade someone to buy products made in the United States, even at a higher price.

____
____
____
____
____
____
____
____

Managing Trade

Most consumers want the lowest possible prices. Therefore, stores supply products from nations with low labor costs, such as China. Consumers benefit from the lower prices of these goods. However, buying these products takes business away from American companies that produce similar goods. The loss of business could force those domestic companies to cut production and possibly their workforce.

Trade Barriers

To protect their businesses, countries sometimes practice protectionism. **Protectionism** is the use of policies to limit imports. Protectionist policies can take three forms: **tariffs,** import **quotas,** or **subsidies.** These methods have an important effect—they raise prices on the imported goods.

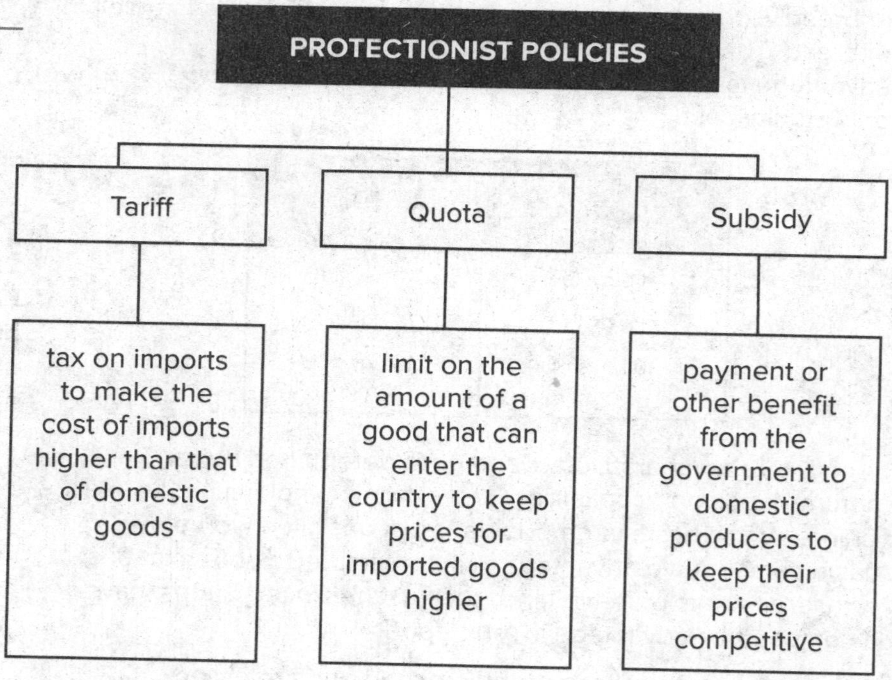

PROTECTIONIST POLICIES

Tariff	Quota	Subsidy
tax on imports to make the cost of imports higher than that of domestic goods	limit on the amount of a good that can enter the country to keep prices for imported goods higher	payment or other benefit from the government to domestic producers to keep their prices competitive

Free Trade Agreements

Most countries today are working to reduce trade barriers. This is called **free trade.** They do this because the total cost of barriers to trade tends to be higher than the benefits. Countries try to increase trade by joining with key trading partners to set up areas of free trade.

For example, the United States, Canada, and Mexico signed the North American Free Trade Agreement (NAFTA) in 1994. This created the largest free trade zone in the world. The three nations agreed to remove most trade barriers. Trade among them has more than tripled, bringing lower prices and a greater variety of goods to consumers. However, these lower-priced imports hurt many domestic companies, which sold less of their products and had to close. Thousands of people lost their jobs.

Europeans also saw the benefits of free trade. The European Union (EU) was formed by 28 European nations to combine their economies. It created the largest economy in the world and a huge free-trade zone. Goods, workers, and services can move freely across national borders. Most EU nations even share a common currency call the euro, making trade easier.

Africa and Asia have similar organizations. The African Union (AU) promotes unity and economic development in Africa. The Asia-Pacific Economic Cooperation (APEC) promotes free trade and economic development among its members.

4. COMPARING AND CONTRASTING

What do NAFTA and the EU have in common? How are they different?

______

The World Trade Organization

In 1995, a group of nations formed the World Trade Organization (WTO). The WTO handles trade agreements and disputes among its 160 member nations. It also tries to help countries that want to build their economies. Some critics, however, believe that the WTO hurts more than it helps. They say the WTO favors big corporations and hurts workers, the environment, and poor countries.

Name ______________________ Date ______________ Class __________

ANALYZING VISUALS

5. READING A GRAPH Based on the information in the graphs, which nations have a positive balance of trade?

____

____

Which have a negative balance of trade?

____

____

What other question could you ask about these graphs?

____

____

____

Balance of Trade

A country's imports might not always be equal in value to its exports. The difference in those values is the nation's **balance of trade.** A nation's balance of trade can result in a surplus or a deficit, just like in a budget.

Positive Balance of Trade

When a nation's exports are worth more money than its imports, the nation has a positive balance of trade, or a trade surplus. In international markets, currencies are bought and sold like goods and services. Also like goods or services, the value of currency can change. When a country has a trade surplus for an extended period of time, the value of its currency increases.

Negative Balance of Trade

When a nation imports more than it exports, it has a negative balance of trade, or a trade deficit. Trade deficits that last for years can hurt a nation. The low demand for domestic goods can lead to job losses. Also, the value of the nation's currency will drop.

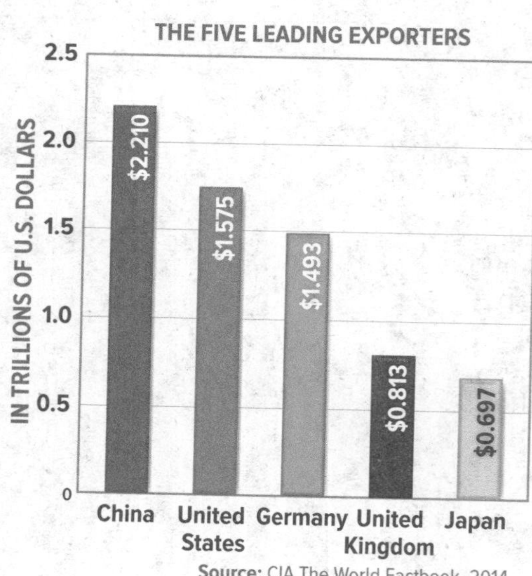

Source: CIA The World Factbook, 2014

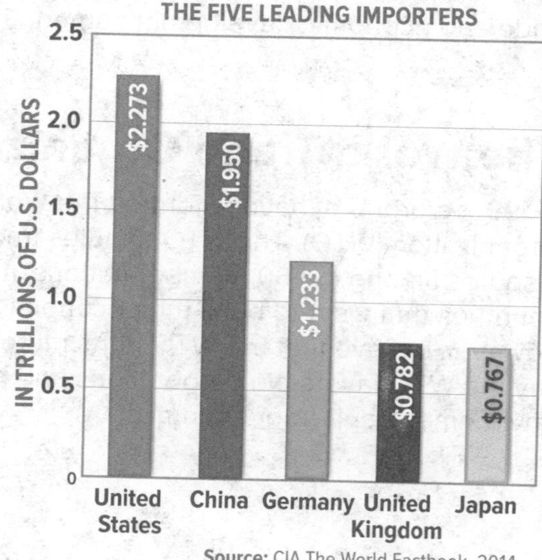

Source: CIA The World Factbook, 2014

Role of Currency and Exchange Rates

Nations prefer to use their own currency when they trade. For that reason, countries need to know the value of different currencies in relation to each other. Those relative values are set by supply and demand. The value of one currency in terms of another is its **exchange rate.**

When the United States imports goods from India, India wants to be paid in its own currency, the rupee. As a result, the United States must sell dollars and buy rupees. This increases the supply of dollars in the international currency market. The higher supply of dollars in the currency market decreases the value of the dollar. That is one reason too many imports can hurt a nation.

A lower currency value is not all bad. The smaller value means the prices of goods drop. Those lower prices could attract interest from other countries. The country could then increase its exports.

6. HYPOTHESIZING

What would likely happen to a country's trade if the value of its currency increased? Why?

____

____

____

____

____

____

____

____

REVIEW LESSON 1

1. Use the chart below to note details about how international trade works.

DECIDING WHAT TO TRADE	MANAGING TRADE	EFFECTS OF TRADE
• What can be exported? • • What comparative advantage does the country have?	• Diversified economies are stronger than _______________ _______________ • Protectionism (trade barriers) _______________ _______________ _______________ • _______________ reduces barriers.	• Balance of _______________ positive = _______________ _______________ • Currency exchange rate _______________ _______________

2. ✏ **SUGGESTING A SOLUTION** Country X is setting new international trade policies. Using a separate sheet of paper, write an essay explaining what Country X should do to get the greatest benefit from these policies.

Economic Systems and Development

1. ANALYZING INFORMATION

What might be the risks to workers in a market economy? What could workers do to lower these risks?

SS.7.E.1.3, SS.7.E.1.5, SS.7.E.3.3, SS.7.E.3.4

Market Economies

How a society answers the three basic economic questions determines its economic system. In a **market economy,** individuals decide what to produce, how to produce, and for whom to produce.

How a Market Economy Works

In a market economy, individuals make decisions in their own best interest. Individuals, not the government, determine the factors of production: natural resources, capital, labor, and entrepreneurship. The decisions made by individuals also determine supply and demand. Together, supply and demand determine the prices of goods and services. This interaction between supply and demand drives the market economy.

Characteristics of a Market Economy

Market economies work best because economies in general are complex. This complexity makes it difficult for a single authority to control an economy. However, market economies have benefits and disadvantages.

Characteristics of a Market Economy

Benefits	Disadvantages
• People have freedom of choice. • People have a high level of satisfaction. • Competition allows consumers to find the best prices.	• The economy goes through periods of growth and decline. People hurt during down times. • The profit motive can lead companies to treat workers and the environment badly.

Market economies are commonly found in countries with high Gross Domestic Products (GDP) per capita. GDP per capita is the total value of goods and services produced in a country divided by the number of people in that country. GDP per capita lets us compare economic output of different countries with different-sized economies.

Name ______________________ Date ______________ Class __________

Command Economies

In a **command economy,** the government owns the factors of production and makes the economic decisions. Individuals have little say about the functioning of the economy.

Most command economies developed from an ideology called socialism. *Socialism* is the belief that the means of production should be owned and controlled by society, either directly or indirectly through the government. Socialists believed this would guarantee greater equality among citizens.

Command economies require central planning. In times of emergency, central planning can be the best course of action. Resources can be directly sent where they are needed most.

Characteristics of a Command Economy

In general, though, command economies are not very efficient. Countries with command economies tend to have low GDPs per capita. Consumers are frequently faced with shortages and poor-quality goods. Command economies also grow more slowly than market economies do. Of the countries in the chart, Cuba is an example of a country with a command economy. The other countries have market-based economies.

COUNTRY	GDP PER CAPITA IN U.S. DOLLARS
Cuba	$6,790
Mexico	$10,173
Turkey	$10,975
Japan	$38,634
United States	$52,980
Denmark	$59,819

Source: The World Bank, 2013 figures

ANALYZING VISUALS

2. INTERPRETING Based on the data in the chart, how does the standard of living in Cuba likely compare with that of the other countries? Explain.

____
____
____
____
____
____
____

3. DIFFERENTIATING

What elements of a command economy does the United States have? What elements of a market economy does it have?

____
____
____
____
____
____
____
____
____
____

4. MAKING INFERENCES

Which type of economy is a developed country most likely to have: a single-resource economy or a diversified economy? Why?

____

____

____

____

____

____

____

____

Switch to a Market Economy

In the 1990s, many command economies in Eastern Europe switched to market economies. The change was not an easy one. First, the economy had to be privatized. **Privatization** is the process of changing state-owned businesses and farms into ones owned by private citizens. Second, citizens had to learn how to be consumers in an economy based on prices. Third, businesses had to learn how to work to earn a profit. Some countries are still struggling with these changes.

China has had more success. Since adopting some market features in the 1970s, China has seen a dramatic rise in GDP and GDP per capita. It now has the world's second-largest economy after the United States.

Mixed Economies

Like many other nations today, the United States has a **mixed economy.** In a mixed economy, both the market and the government guide the economy.

Because the market plays a greater role than the government, the United States is said to have a market-oriented economy. However, the government still performs important roles. It provides goods and services such as education and roads. It also works to make sure that markets are competitive. Finally, it regulates businesses to protect workers and consumers.

Developed and Developing Countries

Countries with strong market-based economies tend to have a high standard of living. The standard of living is measured by such things as having plentiful goods and quality health care. These countries are called **developed countries.** They include the United States, Canada, Japan, Germany, and about 30 other countries around the world. These countries tend to have diversified economies.

Some countries are expanding their export industries in an effort to become developed. These nations are called newly industrialized countries. They include China and India. Their industrial output, however, is not yet equal to that of developed countries.

Many countries do not have the advanced economies of the developed countries or the growth of newly industrialized countries. These nations are called **developing countries.** They produce fewer products for internal use and for export. They also have low GDPs per capita. These countries face a number of obstacles to development.

5. REASONING

What reasons might a developing country have to refuse to join in a free trade agreement?

____

____

____

____

____

____

Obstacles to Development

Population growth can make development difficult. If a country's population grows faster than its GDP, the GDP per capita declines. Furthermore, a larger population requires more jobs. To protect jobs and new industries, many developing countries have trade barriers in place. Economists think these barriers prevent economic growth.

Resources present another obstacle. Developing countries often lack the ability to access or export their resources. They also tend to have single-resource economies and depend on that single export for economic growth. If that one export fails or if prices drop, the country's whole economy suffers.

Developing countries often borrow money to help their economies grow. However, their economies do not always grow enough to pay off the debt. When that happens, much of their income must be used to pay the debt instead of helping the economy grow.

War and corruption also make development difficult. War damages resources and disrupts the economy. Corruption means money for development projects is stolen by self-interested leaders.

Even one of these problems is difficult to solve. However, many developing nations must deal with two or three of these issues. As a result, economic growth is even harder for these countries to achieve.

Name ______________________ Date ______________ Class __________

REVIEW LESSON 2

1. Use the chart below to note details about how countries and economies are classified.

ECONOMIC SYSTEMS AND DEVELOPMENT	
Economies	
Market Economy	• Higher GDPs per capita • • •
Command Economy	• Lower GDPs per capita • • • •
Countries	
Developed Nations	• Strong, diversified economy • • •
Newly Industrialized Nations	• Lower output than developed nations • •
Developing Nations	• Not very productive • •

2. **DETERMINING CAUSE AND EFFECT** Using a separate sheet of paper, write an essay describing the types of countries and economies that have the highest standard of living. In your essay, explain why this is the case.

Benchmark Skill Activities

DIRECTIONS: Write your answers on a separate sheet of paper.

LAFS.68.WHST.2.4

1. COMPARING AND CONTRASTING

Use your FOLDABLES to write an essay that compares and contrasts market economies, command economies, and mixed economies.

LAFS.68.RH.1.2

2. PARAPHRASING

In 2001, President George W. Bush spoke about international trade at the World Bank. Read the excerpt from his speech below and then restate it in your own words.

> "We know that nations that open their economies to the benefits of trade are more successful in climbing out of poverty. . . . We also know that free trade encourages the habits of liberty that sustain freedom."
>
> —President George W. Bush

LAFS.7.SL.1.1, ELD.K12.ELL.SI.1

3. THEORIZING

With a partner or a small group, discuss whether a country can survive without international trade. Use details from this chapter to support your opinion.

LAFS.68.RH.3.7

4. COMPARING

Study the following graphs of the world's leading exporters and importers. Then, explain whether each country has a positive or a negative balance of trade.

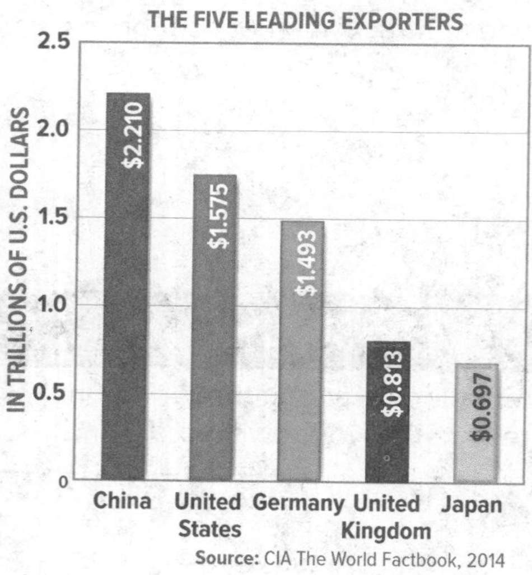

Source: CIA The World Factbook, 2014

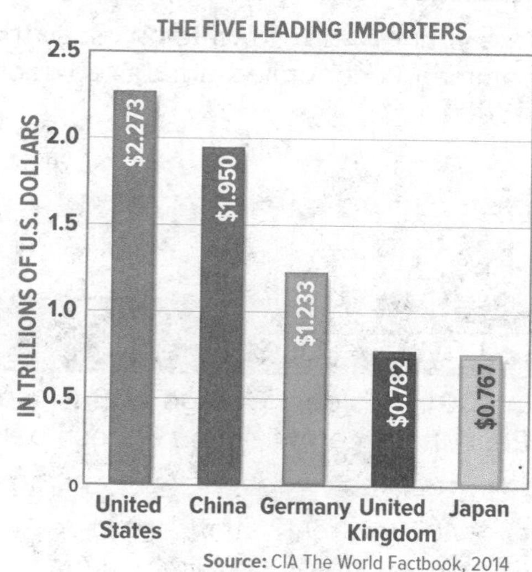

Source: CIA The World Factbook, 2014

LAFS.68.WHST.3.8

5. EVALUATING

Choose one of the following trade groups: NAFTA, the EU, the WTO, the African Union, or APEC. Find three sources about the group. Create an annotated bibliography of the sources. For each source:

- list the source in a standard citation format
- write a paragraph analyzing its reliability and usefulness

Benchmark Note Cards

DIRECTIONS: Use these note cards to help you prepare for the test.

SS.7.C.4.2 Recognize government and citizen participation in international organizations.

INTERNATIONAL ORGANIZATIONS	• **North American Free Trade Agreement (NAFTA)**—agreement among the United States, Canada, and Mexico to reduce trade barriers among the three nations • **European Union (EU)**—organization of 28 European nations that unites their economies, establishes a common currency, and allows free movement across borders • **African Union (AU)**—promotes unity and economic development in Africa • **Asia-Pacific Economic Cooperation (APEC)**—promotes free trade and economic development among its members • **World Trade Organization (WTO)**—organization of 160 nations that oversees trade agreements and tries to settle trade disputes

SS.7.E.1.3 Review the concepts of supply and demand, choice, scarcity, and opportunity cost as they relate to the development of the mixed market economy in the United States.

THE U.S. MIXED MARKET ECONOMY	• The United States has a market-oriented economy. The market—including choice, supply, and demand—plays a greater role in guiding the economy than government. • Government provides some goods and services, such as education and roads. It also ensures competitive markets and regulates businesses to protect workers and consumers.

SS.7.E.1.5 Assess how profits, incentives, and competition motivate individuals, households, and businesses in a free market economy.

THE FREE MARKET ECONOMY	• The interaction of supply and demand drives a market economy. • Private individuals own the factors of production: natural resources, capital, labor, and entrepreneurship. • Sellers compete to attract buyers. Buyers compete for the best price. • Because businesses are driven by profit, working conditions and wages can suffer.

SS.7.E.3.1 Explain how international trade requires a system for exchanging currency between and among nations.

INTERNATIONAL TRADE AND CURRENCY	Countries want to make trades using their own currency. They need to be able to compare currency values to determine trade values. They also need to be able to convert one currency into another to complete the trade.

SS.7.E.3.2 Assess how the changing value of currency affects trade of goods and services between nations.

CURRENCY VALUES AND TRADE	Currency values affect a nation's ability to export goods. • If a country's currency is low in value, its goods will cost less and the country will be able to export more. • If a country's currency is high in value, its goods will cost more and the country will export less.

SS.7.E.3.3 Compare and contrast a single-resource economy with a diversified economy.

RESOURCES AND ECONOMIES	**Single-Resource Economy** • Relies on a single export • Can be damaged by changes in the market • Likely to be the economy of a developing nation **Diversified Economy** • Exports a variety of products • Can withstand changes in the market • More likely to be the economy of a developed nation

SS.7.E.3.4 Compare and contrast the standard of living in various countries today to that of the United States using gross domestic product (GDP) per capita as an indicator.

STANDARD OF LIVING AND GDP PER CAPITA	The standard of living is measured by the availability of goods and health care. A high standard of living is more likely to be found in developed countries with high GDPs per capita. These countries include the United States, Canada, Japan, Germany, and 31 other nations. Countries with a lower standard of living tend to also have lower GDPs per capita.

Chapter 24

VISUAL SUMMARY

INTERNATIONAL TRADE

COMPARATIVE ADVANTAGE	FREE TRADE	BALANCE OF TRADE
Nations trade what they have for what they need. Comparative advantage is	Trade barriers such as tariffs, quotas, and subsidies Free trade	Balance of trade is If exports are worth more, If imports are worth more,

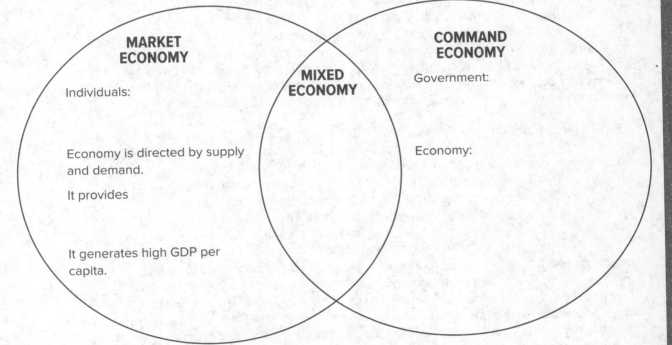

Individuals:

Economy is directed by supply and demand.

It provides

It generates high GDP per capita.

MIXED ECONOMY

COMMAND ECONOMY

Government:

Economy:

DEVELOPED NATIONS

DEVELOPING NATIONS

USING PRIMARY SOURCES

ANALYZE PRIMARY SOURCES Below are two primary sources related to trade. Read the sources. Then, on a separate sheet of paper, answer the questions that follow.

Document A

The excerpt below is from a speech by President Bill Clinton on the signing of the North American Free Trade Agreement (NAFTA).

"I believe we have made a decision now that will permit us to create an economic order in the world that will promote more growth, more equality, better preservation of the environment, and a greater possibility of world peace. We are on the verge of a global economic expansion that is sparked by the fact that the United States at this critical moment decided that we would compete, not retreat.

In a few moments, I will sign the North American free trade act into law. NAFTA will tear down trade barriers between our three nations. It will create the world's largest trade zone and create 200,000 jobs in this country by 1995 alone. The environmental and labor side agreements negotiated by our administration will make this agreement a force for social progress as well as economic growth. Already the confidence we've displayed by ratifying NAFTA has begun to bear fruit. We are now making real progress toward a worldwide trade agreement so significant that it could make the material gains of NAFTA for our country look small by comparison.

Today we have the chance to do what our parents did before us. We have the opportunity to remake the world. For this new era, our national security we now know will be determined as much by our ability to pull down foreign trade barriers as by our ability to breach distant ramparts. Once again, we are leading. And in so doing, we are rediscovering a fundamental truth about ourselves: When we lead, we build security, we build prosperity for our own people. . . .

. . . Make no mistake, the global economy with all of its promise and perils is now the central fact of life for hard-working Americans. It has enriched the lives of millions of Americans. But for too many those same winds of change have worn away at the basis of their security. For two decades, most people have worked harder for less. Seemingly secure jobs have been lost. And while America once again is the most productive nation on Earth, this productivity itself holds the seeds of further insecurity. After all, productivity means the same people can produce more or, very often, that fewer people can produce more. This is the world we face.

We cannot stop global change. We cannot repeal the international economic competition that is everywhere. We can only harness the energy to our benefit. Now we must recognize that the only way for a wealthy nation to grow richer is to export, to simply find new customers for the products and services it makes. That, my fellow Americans, is the decision the Congress made when they voted to ratify NAFTA."

—President Bill Clinton, Remarks on the signing of NAFTA, December 8, 1993

Document B

The text below is from the preamble, or introduction, of the North American Free Trade Agreement.

> *The Government of Canada, the Government of the United Mexican States and the Government of the United States of America, resolved to:*
>
> *STRENGTHEN the special bonds of friendship and cooperation among their nations;*
>
> *CONTRIBUTE to the harmonious [peaceful] development and expansion of world trade and provide a catalyst [stimulant] to broader international cooperation;*
>
> *CREATE an expanded and secure market for the goods and services produced in their territories;*
>
> *REDUCE distortions to trade; . . .*
>
> —North American Free Trade Agreement

Answer the following questions:

1. How are Documents A and B related?
2. What is the purpose of each document?
3. Reread the first paragraph in Document A. Underline the details that explain how NAFTA may benefit the world.
4. Reread the last paragraph in Document A. Underline the reasons why the United States should sign the agreement.
5. In Document B, what does "reduce distortions to trade" mean? What have you read about in this chapter that might be distortions to trade?
6. In Document B, cooperation is mentioned twice. Why is cooperation important for free trade?
7. What benefits do the members of NAFTA expect to gain from this agreement?
8. Based on what you read about NAFTA in this chapter, has the agreement achieved its stated goals?

Chapter Practice Test

DIRECTIONS: Circle the best answer for each question.

---

1 **SS.7.E.3.4 (Moderate)**

COUNTRY	GDP PER CAPITA
Norway	$68,400
Australia	$65,400
United States	$56,300
Turkey	$20,500

Source: CIA World Factbook, 2015 estimates

Based on the chart, which country likely has the highest standard of living?

A Australia

B Norway

C Turkey

D United States

2 **SS.7.C.4.2 (High)**

Read the excerpt from an editorial in the magazine *National Review.*

> *"Agreements like NAFTA and the WTO force nations to respect contracts, which encourages responsible investment and, hence, economic growth. And, you see, economic growth creates a middle class, and a middle class, eventually, demands democracy. That is the story of the 20th century and, God willing, it will be the story of the 21st."*
>
> —Jonah Goldberg, "What protesters don't get," February 14, 2002

With which statement is Jonah Goldberg most likely to agree?

A International trade helps spread democracy.

B International trade requires economic growth in order to work.

C International trade helps spread mixed-market economies.

D International trade requires monitoring by international organizations.

3 **SS.7.E.3.3 (Moderate)**

Which statement about single-resource economies is true?

A They are more likely to be part of a free trade organization.

B They are more likely to be newly industrialized.

C They are more likely to be a developing nation.

D They are more likely to survive price changes in the market.

---

4 **SS.7.E.3.2 (High)**

COUNTRY Y	
Quarter	**Change in Currency Value**
1	↓ 2.00%
2	↑ 0.50%
3	↓ 1.25%
4	↓ 0.75%

Based on the chart, what likely happened to Country Y's trade over the course of the year?

A The price of its exports dropped.

B It developed a trade deficit.

C The price of its imports dropped.

D It developed a diversified economy.

SS.7.E.3.4 (Moderate)

Japan's GDP per capita is similar to that of the United States. What else is most likely true about Japan?

A It has a single-resource economy.

B It belongs to a free trade organization.

C It exports similar products as the United States.

D It has a standard of living similar to that of the United States.

SS.7.E.3.3 (Moderate)

COUNTRY	RESOURCES
A	large population, lots of farmland
B	educated workers, minerals, forests
C	farm laborers, fossil fuels
D	small population, sunshine, beaches

Which country on the chart is most likely to have a diversified economy?

A Country A

B Country B

C Country C

D Country D

7 **SS.7.E.3.1 (Moderate)**

The United States agrees to a trade with the European Union.

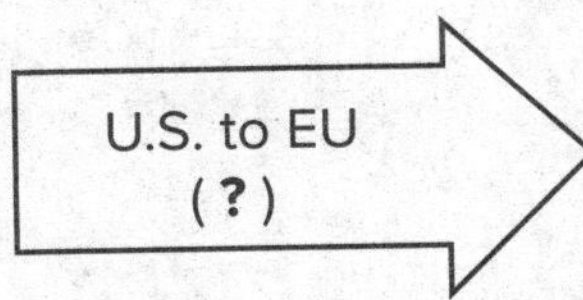

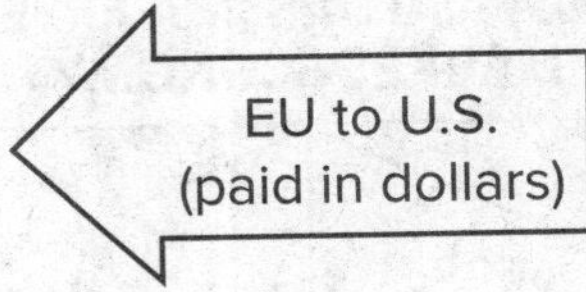

What should replace the question mark in the diagram?

A paid in euros

B paid in goods

C paid in dollars

D paid in services

---

8 **SS.7.C.4.2 (Moderate)**

Why is the World Trade Organization (WTO) controversial?

A Some people believe its standards for trade are too strict.

B It only helps its member nations, not the entire world.

C It only makes trade agreements and does not settle disputes.

D Some people believe it favors developed nations over poor ones.

9 **SS.7.E.1.5 (Moderate)**

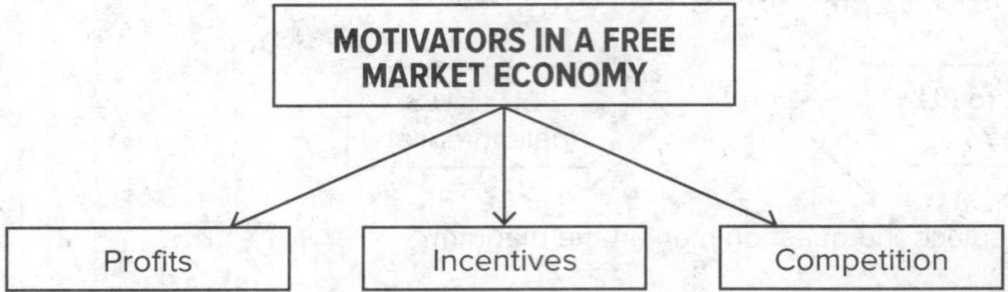

Which example does not represent one of the free market motivators shown in the graphic?

A Two dealerships that sell similar cars charge about the same price.

B An entrepreneur with an original idea starts producing a new product.

C A new federal highway is constructed between two major cities.

D A company automates more tasks to cut costs.

10 **SS.7.E.1.3 (High)**

For the United States to have a pure market economy, what would have to change?

A The government would have to privatize businesses.

B The government would have to stop regulating the economy.

C The government would have to protect workers and consumers.

D The government would have to control the factors of production.

CHAPTER 25

The United States and Foreign Affairs

Chapter Overview

Global interdependence provides people and nations with opportunities to trade so they can meet their needs. It also leads to cooperation among nations across the globe. However, global interdependence can also create challenges, including economic inequality, environmental issues, immigration, and terrorism.

Governmental organizations have been formed to deal with international issues. Member nations fund these organizations, set up rules, and make decisions. Nongovernmental organizations (NGOs) are run through individual volunteer efforts and private donations. NGOs deal with both national and international issues. Government and citizen participation in these organizations affect millions of people worldwide.

The United States and organizations like the United Nations help protect the human rights of people around the globe. American foreign policy is based on protecting and promoting the principles of democracy, including human rights. Still, the nation and the world continue to face challenges.

CHAPTER BENCHMARKS

SS.7.C.2.14 Conduct a service project to further the public good.

SS.7.C.4.1 Differentiate concepts related to United States domestic and foreign policy.

SS.7.C.4.2 Recognize government and citizen participation in international organizations.

SS.7.C.4.3 Describe examples of how the United States has dealt with international conflicts.

SS.7.E.2.5 Explain how economic institutions impact the national economy.

SS.7.E.3.4 Compare and contrast the standard of living in various countries today to that of the United States using gross domestic product (GDP) per capita as an indicator.

LAFS.68.RH.1.1 Cite specific textual evidence to support analysis of primary and secondary sources.

LAFS.68.RH.1.2 Determine the central ideas or information of a primary or secondary source; provide an accurate summary of the source distinct from prior knowledge or opinions.

WHAT I NEED TO KNOW

TERMS

- ☐ global interdependence
- ☐ trade war
- ☐ ethnic group
- ☐ terrorism
- ☐ refugee
- ☐ diplomat
- ☐ nongovernmental organization (NGO)
- ☐ prisoner of war
- ☐ human right
- ☐ genocide
- ☐ weapon of mass destruction (WMD)

PEOPLE, PLACES, EVENTS

- ☐ United Nations (UN)
- ☐ North Atlantic Treaty Organization (NATO)
- ☐ World Health Organization (WHO)
- ☐ International Committee of the Red Cross
- ☐ al-Qaeda
- ☐ Taliban
- ☐ Islamic State in Iraq and the Levant (ISIL)

CHAPTER 25

The United States and Foreign Affairs

CHAPTER BENCHMARKS, *continued*

LAFS.68.RH.2.4 Determine the meaning of words and phrases as they are used in a text, including vocabulary specific to domains related to history/social studies.

LAFS.68.WHST.1.1 Write arguments focused on discipline-specific content.

LAFS.68.WHST.1.2 Write informative/explanatory texts, including the narration of historical events, scientific procedures/ experiments, or technical processes.

LAFS.68.WHST.2.4 Produce clear and coherent writing in which the development, organization, and style are appropriate to task, purpose, and audience.

LAFS.68.WHST.3.7 Conduct short research projects to answer a question (including a self-generated question), drawing on several sources and generating additional related, focused questions that allow for multiple avenues of exploration.

LAFS.68.WHST.3.9 Draw evidence from informational texts to support analysis reflection, and research.

The United States and Foreign Affairs

Make this three-pocket Foldable® and label the pockets with the titles of the three lessons. Use quarter sheets of notebook paper or note cards as information cards. Number note cards to correspond to the lesson pocket in which they are sorted and stored. As you read the chapter, write terms, acronyms, and events relating to the chapter on the front of each note card and information about each on the back. On the back of your Foldable, draw a large circle and label it World Affairs. Inside this circle, draw a smaller circle and label it USA. Apply what you know about current events to explain the position of the United States in world affairs.

Step 1
Take a legal sized piece of paper (8.5" x 14") and place it lengthwise on your desk. Fold the bottom edge of the paper one-third of the way up the page.

Step 2
Fold the left and right sides of the paper to create three equal sections.

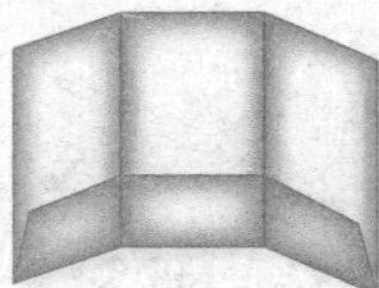

Step 3
Tape or staple the open right and left sides of the pockets.

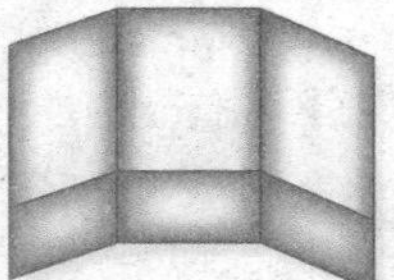

Step 4
Label the pockets and use note cards or cut notebook paper for notes.

LESSON 1 SUMMARY

Global Interdependence and Issues

SS.7.C.4.1, SS.7.C.4.2, SS.7.E.2.5, SS.7.E.3.4

Global Interdependence

As you have learned, countries cannot produce everything they need. For example, if Americans want to eat bananas, they have to import them. Nations thus rely on other nations for goods and services. This relationship is known as **global interdependence.**

Global Trade

If every nation could meet all of its needs, there would be no need for global trade. However, nations have different needs, comparative advantages, and resources. This makes trade among nations necessary.

The United States exports many goods. Developing nations need food, medicine, and defense weapons. Other nations buy American wheat, corn, computer software, aircraft, medical equipment, and machinery. People around the world want American movies, music, and video games.

The United States also imports goods. One major import is oil. Americans use almost 20 million barrels of oil each day. About half of that oil is imported.

Comparative advantage also fuels international trade. China, for example, has low manufacturing costs, which results in cheaper goods. Other nations want to buy these less expensive Chinese products, including electronics, textiles, and toys.

In addition, global trade satisfies global needs for specific natural resources. For example, in South Africa, the Democratic Republic of the Congo, and Botswana, industrial diamonds are a natural resource. The United States does not have this natural resource, so it imports industrial diamonds from these nations to make certain goods.

1. DETERMINING CAUSE AND EFFECT

How do nations benefit when they trade with one another?

____

____

____

____

____

____

____

____

2. ANALYZING INFORMATION

Use the Internet to find information related to American outsourcing to China and job loss in the United States. On a separate sheet of paper, write a summary of your findings and answer the following questions: Should the United States continue its trade relationship with China? Why or why not? Use your research to support your opinion.

ANALYZING VISUALS

3. IDENTIFYING POINTS OF VIEW Look at the chart. What point of view about trade agreements does the chart represent? Explain your answer.

______

______

______

______

______

Global Economic Cooperation

Sometimes nations cooperate to solve trade issues. Trade agreements among European Union (EU) members have removed most trade barriers among them. The North American Free Trade Agreement (NAFTA) among the United States, Canada, and Mexico does the same. Other parts of the world have similar trade agreements.

Global Issues

As nations interact more with each other, people have become aware of problems that affect the whole world. It will take global cooperation to resolve them. Sometimes, though, political and cultural forces are obstacles.

Costs of Competition and Trade

Trade agreements usually lead to lower prices. They also provide consumers with greater choices. However, trade can bring problems. The chart below shows possible effects of trade agreements.

POSSIBLE CONSEQUENCES OF TRADE AGREEMENTS

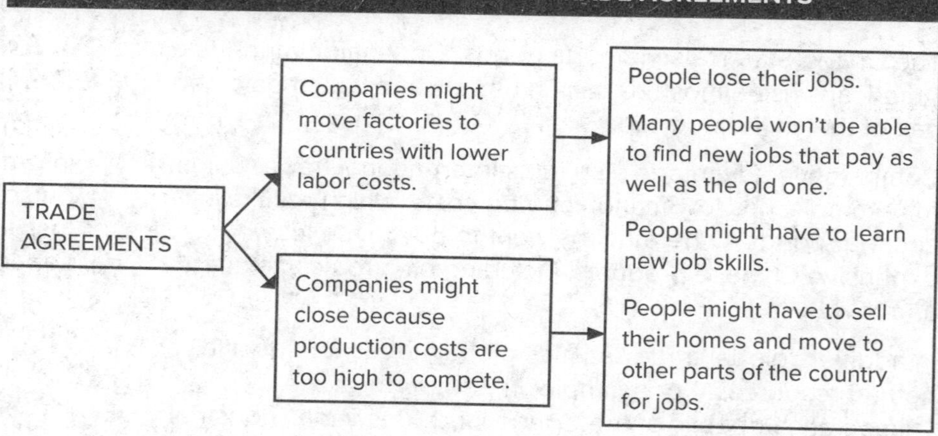

LESSON 1 SUMMARY, *continued*

Nations sometimes want to protect their industries from countries that have cheaper labor. A country might put up a trade barrier, such as a tariff, on these imported products. These trade barriers help domestic industries. However, they have a cost because they make products more expensive.

Countries might retaliate with their own tariffs on imported goods. This could cause a trade war. A **trade war** is an economic conflict that occurs when one or more nations put up trade barriers to punish another nation for its trade barriers against them. During a trade war, prices are higher and buyers have fewer choices. Consumers suffer when this happens.

Rich and Poor Nations

Economic inequality exists among nations. Some nations have experienced strong economic growth. Others are making progress. Still other nations are growing very slowly, if at all.

In developed nations, the economy does well. These countries usually have a high GDP per capita. They also tend to have stable political systems, which means they are not subject to major change. Developed nations include the United States, Germany, and Canada.

Developing countries tend to have low GDP per capita and low rates of growth. There are several reasons for this. Some of these nations have few natural resources and an unskilled or uneducated labor force. Many times the government is unstable. Health issues such as access to clean water and good health care might be additional problems.

Global Politics

Nations have different forms of government. They also differ in their views on what is best for the world. Still, economic interdependence sometimes makes nations cooperate. For example, the United States and Saudi Arabia have had a trade relationship for more than 75 years. The two governments have been at odds over the Israel-Palestine conflict, terrorism, human rights, abuse of women, Iran, and other political issues. Still, Saudi Arabia remains a leading trade partner with the United States.

4. SYNTHESIZING

Underline the definition of *trade war.* Then, use two words from the definition and explain what happens when a trade war occurs. In your answer, explain if either side in the war benefits, and if so, how.

______

5. SPECULATING

How might a country's unstable political system lead to a low GDP?

______

ANALYZING VISUALS

6. IDENTIFYING ALTERNATIVES What alternatives can you suggest to each of the causes listed in the chart?

____
____
____
____
____
____
____
____

7. IDENTIFYING POINTS OF VIEW

Consider the different points of view on protecting the environment. What point of view might someone in the construction business have? Why?

____
____
____
____
____
____
____

Environmental Issues

Concern for the environment is a growing global issue. The chart below lists some of these environmental problems.

ENVIRONMENTAL ISSUES	
Causes	**Effects**
Chemicals released by factories and cars	Pollute the air and water
Chemicals from burning coal for energy	Harm trees and fish when carried back to Earth by rain
Burning coal and oil	Might be the cause of changes in Earth's climate
Deforestation, the mass removal of trees	Leads to flooding and mudslides, and lessens the amount of carbon dioxide that trees absorb

It is not easy to solve these problems. Protecting forests might reduce the amount of land on which farmers can grow crops. Also, using cleaner sources of energy is expensive. Many developing nations are concerned that protecting the environment will slow economic growth.

Some people try to conserve natural resources to limit damage to the environment. For example, using less paper will result in fewer forests being cleared. Views on conservation differ, though. Some believe that limiting how businesses operate leads to rising costs. Others say that failing to conserve resources now will lead to greater costs in the future. They think that taking care of air, ground, and water pollution will be more expensive in the future.

Other Global Challenges

Global interdependence can lead to other problems. As in the past, people immigrate to the United States looking for better jobs and living conditions. This happens in other nations as well. Problems can occur when people already living in the country resent the increased demand on land, jobs, and services. There also might be differences among religious and ethnic groups. An **ethnic group** shares a common national, cultural, or racial background.

LESSON 1 SUMMARY, *continued*

Terrorism is another global challenge. **Terrorism** is the use of violence or the threat of violence to force governments to act in a certain way. War, conflict, famine, or natural disasters are also global problems. In these situations, people often must abandon their homes to escape the danger. These people are called **refugees.** Other people around the world have to deal with lack of food, clean water, and basic health care. Countries need to cooperate to solve these problems.

8. CONTRASTING

How are immigrants different from refugees?

____

____

____

____

____

REVIEW LESSON 1

1. Complete the chart below to describe the roles competition and trade and environmental issues play in global interdependence.

GLOBAL INTERDEPENDENCE	
Competition and Trade	
Positive	
Negative	
Environmental Issues	
Problems	
Solutions and Their Implications	

2. **DETERMINING CENTRAL IDEAS** Use the information in the chart to write an essay about the issues surrounding global interdependence. Write your essay on a separate sheet of paper.

LESSON 2 SUMMARY

The United States and International Organizations

1. MAKING INFERENCES

Why is setting up rules an important step in the formation of governmental organizations?

SS.7.C.4.1, SS.7.C.4.2

The Purpose of International Organizations

Nations often have to deal with difficult problems. Some problems affect one nation or one part of the world, such as an earthquake or a tsunami. In response, countries from around the globe send food, water, and medical supplies. Other problems affect many nations, such as climate change, pollution, and trade. **Diplomats,** officials who represent their country's governments, work together to find solutions for global issues.

Governmental Organizations

Governmental organizations are formed to deal with international issues. Member nations fund these organizations, set up rules to govern them, and make decisions. Some of these organizations, like the World Trade Organization, have a single purpose. Other organizations, such as the European Union or the United Nations, have multiple goals.

Nongovernmental Organizations (NGOs)

Some international organizations operate independently of a government. They are run by private citizens in order to meet a need or to work for a cause. They rely on volunteers and private donations. These types of groups are called **nongovernmental organizations (NGOs).**

Name ______ Date ______ Class ______

LESSON 2 SUMMARY, *continued*

Because NGOs are not part of any government, they can provide assistance to any nation and to both sides in a war. In developing nations, most NGOs focus on public health, feeding the hungry, fighting disease, or promoting economic development. Those focusing on environmental problems work worldwide. Some try to protect human rights and tend to focus on nations with harsh governments.

NONGOVERNMENTAL ORGANIZATIONS		
NGO	**Region**	**Area of Concern**
Amnesty International	Worldwide	Human Rights
CARE International	Worldwide	Poverty, Education, Economic Development, Health
Cousteau Society	North America	Environment
Doctors Without Borders	Worldwide	Health, Disaster Response/ Relief
Heifer International	Worldwide	Hunger, Poverty, Economic Development
Hunger Project	North America	Hunger
International Committee of the Red Cross	Worldwide	Human Rights, Public Health, Disaster Response/ Relief
MacArthur Foundation	Worldwide	Human Rights, Economic Development, Peace, Education, Environment
MAP International	Worldwide	Health, Disaster Response/ Relief
Nature Conservancy	Worldwide	Environment
Oxfam International	Worldwide	Poverty, Hunger, Human Rights, Economic Development
Sweatshop Watch	North America	Human Rights (specifically for workers)

2. MAKING GENERALIZATIONS

Why might an NGO be able to provide help more quickly than a governmental organization when a disaster strikes?

ANALYZING VISUALS

3. CATEGORIZING Look at the information in the chart. On a separate sheet of paper, categorize the NGOs in several ways. For example, one category might be "Worldwide." Another category might be "Disaster Relief/Rescue." Share your information with a partner.

4. DRAWING CONCLUSIONS

Why is the International Court of Justice an important unit of the United Nations?

5. THEORIZING

What international event or conflict happening today could be a focus of the United Nations? Why?

International Organizations

International organizations and the people who participate in them provide a tremendous service to the world. Some of these organizations are governmental, while others are NGOs.

The United Nations

The United Nations (UN) was founded in 1945 at the end of World War II. It began as a peacekeeping body. Today, its role is even greater. The UN deals with many issues such as human rights, health emergencies, and poverty.

MAIN BODIES OF THE UNITED NATIONS	
General Assembly	• main forum for 193 member states • each member nation has a voice
Security Council	• consists of 5 permanent members (United States, Russia, United Kingdom, France, China) and 10 other members elected to two-year terms • deals with immediate threats to world peace • each permanent member can veto or block actions

The UN has many other units that handle different issues. For example, the International Court of Justice, also called the World Court, deals with legal disputes between nations. The UN helps children worldwide with its United Nations Children's Fund (UNICEF). It also encourages science, education, and culture through the United Nations Educational, Scientific and Cultural Organization (UNESCO).

North Atlantic Treaty Organization

The North Atlantic Treaty Organization (NATO), created in 1949, has 28 member nations in North America and Europe. Its purpose is to maintain and defend the freedom and safety of its members. It also works with nonmember nations to keep peace. For example, member nations have sent armed forces to Afghanistan and Iraq.

Name ______________________ Date ______________ Class __________

World Trade Organization

The World Trade Organization (WTO) has a global membership of about 160 nations. It focuses on free trade and resolving trade conflicts among member nations. Some developing nations criticize the WTO for favoring developed nations and their businesses. Other critics believe the WTO ignores environmental issues in favor of trade and profit.

World Health Organization

As part of the United Nations, the World Health Organization (WHO) looks for ways to fight and prevent disease around the world. The WHO has created standards that help developing nations promote their people's health. It also conducts research on public health issues. Successes of the WHO include ending smallpox, educating people around the world about the HIV virus, and decreasing polio around the world by 99 percent.

Peace Corps

The Peace Corps is a volunteer group run by the government of the United States. It was created by President John F. Kennedy in the 1960s to challenge students to work for peace around the world. The hope was for Americans and people of other nations to understand each other better. Since its creation, more than 220,000 volunteers have served. Today volunteers go to more than 60 countries to work in education, public health, and business development.

International Committee of the Red Cross

The International Committee of the Red Cross (ICRC) is an NGO. It is based in Switzerland and unites aid societies around the world. Its aid groups, called the Red Cross or the Red Crescent, help people who are victims of war or natural disasters. The ICRC remains neutral. During wars, it works to protect civilians and makes sure that prisoners of war are treated properly. **Prisoners of war** are soldiers captured by enemy forces. The ICRC also helps find missing persons and provides people in war-torn countries with food, clothing, and shelter.

6. MAKING CONNECTIONS

Why do you think the World Health Organization's efforts to improve people's health are especially helpful to developing nations?

____
____
____
____
____
____
____
____

7. MAKING INFERENCES

Why do you think Peace Corps volunteers work mainly in developing nations?

____
____
____
____
____
____

Name ______________________ Date ____________ Class ________

REVIEW LESSON 2

1. Complete the chart below to describe the work of some governmental and nongovernmental organizations.

GOVERNMENTAL ORGANIZATIONS	NONGOVERNMENTAL ORGANIZATIONS
United Nations • • • • • • •	International Committee of the Red Cross • • • •
NATO • •	Doctors Without Borders • •
WTO •	Amnesty International •
WHO • •	Sweatshop Watch •
Peace Corps • •	CARE International • • • •

2. **COMPARING AND CONTRASTING** Using a separate sheet of paper, write an essay comparing and contrasting governmental organizations and NGOs. Include examples of both types of organizations to show the similarities and differences.

LESSON 3 SUMMARY

The United States and World Affairs

SS.7.C.4.1, SS.7.C.4.2, SS.7.C.4.3

Human Rights

Ethnic groups have different ideas, customs, art, and beliefs. This is their culture. Regardless of these cultural differences, all people have human rights. A **human right** is a basic freedom that all people should have. Human rights include

- the right to food, safety, and shelter
- the right to be protected under the law
- the right to exercise freedom of thought

The Universal Declaration of Human Rights

Soon after the UN was formed, its members developed a list of basic human rights. The document is called the Universal Declaration of Human Rights. It consists of 30 articles, or statements, that list the human rights all people should have. The first two articles form the foundations for all the other articles. Article 1 states that "all human beings are born free and equal." Article 2 says that all people should have human rights regardless of race, color, gender, language, religion, national or social origin, or other status. The other articles focus on other basic rights as well as economic and social rights. Some nations don't always grant their citizens all these rights. Efforts to protect these rights continue.

Violations of Human Rights

Some nations continue to repress people's rights. Repression prevents people from expressing themselves or from freely engaging in a "normal" life. For example, some nations control, or censor, the information their citizens read or hear in the media. Nations that engage in censorship include North Korea, China, Saudi Arabia, and Iran.

Ethnic tensions and cultural differences in some countries have led to **genocide.** This is the attempt to kill everyone of a particular ethnic group. Ethnic fighting has occurred in the African nations of Rwanda and Burundi as well as in the Darfur region of Sudan.

1. EVALUATING

Do you think the UN Universal Declaration of Human Rights is sufficient to protect against abuses of human rights? Explain.

____

____

____

____

____

____

2. ANALYZING INFORMATION

Use reliable sites on the Internet to gather information about one of the following:

- a nation that engages in censorship
- a country in which ethnic tensions have led to genocide

Look for information that indicates what life is like in that place, the reaction or action of the United States, and any governmental organizations or NGOs that have intervened. On a separate sheet of paper, summarize your findings. Share them with the class.

3. RECOGNIZING RELATIONSHIPS

What was the underlying cause of the Cold War?

____

____

____

____

4. DRAWING CONCLUSIONS

In what way was U.S. foreign policy toward the Soviet Union during the Cold War related to democratic principles?

____

____

____

____

____

____

____

____

Protecting Human Rights

The United States promotes human rights and protests countries that take away those rights. Sometimes the United States does not trade with those countries.

The UN Human Rights Council observes and reports on human rights. It hopes that making abuses public will pressure governments to end such abuses. The Council can refer cases to the International Criminal Court if governments violate human rights. NGOs such as Amnesty International and Human Rights Watch also observe and identify nations that violate human rights.

Democracy, Liberty, and Conflict

Democratic governments and human rights are connected. Nations with democratic governments have a better record of respecting these rights than those nations with other forms of government.

The Growth of Democracy

At one time, more people lived in nations where rulers were not elected. Today, about 60 percent of all countries have democracies. As a democratic nation, the United States has had the goal of spreading democracy and freedom beyond its borders. Presidents during World War I and World War II expressed that desire.

After World War II, differences between the political and economic systems of many Western countries and those of the Soviet Union caused conflict. The United States and most of Western Europe had democratic governments and market-based economies. The Soviet Union and Eastern Europe followed communism, with a one-party government system and the state controlling all economic activities.

Name ______ Date ______ Class ______

The Cold War

These differences led to the Cold War. This war between the United States and the Soviet Union did not include actual combat. During this time, the United States worked to contain, or keep, the Soviet Union's control and communism from spreading. To do so, the United States sometimes supported rulers who abused the human rights of their people. The United States also engaged in two conflicts to try to contain communism: the Korean War and the Vietnam War.

Eventually, the people of the Soviet Union and Eastern Europe revolted against their communist governments. The Cold War ended. The Soviet Union broke apart into 15 separate nations, one of them being Russia. These nations worked toward establishing democracies and market economies. However, some countries still have communist governments. Further, in some parts of South America and Africa, people still live with limited or no freedom.

ANALYZING VISUALS

5. ANALYZING GRAPHS
Examine the graph. Which continent has the most free countries? Which continents rank second and third in having the most free countries?

______

______

______

Which region is the least free? Why do you think this is?

______

______

______

______

______

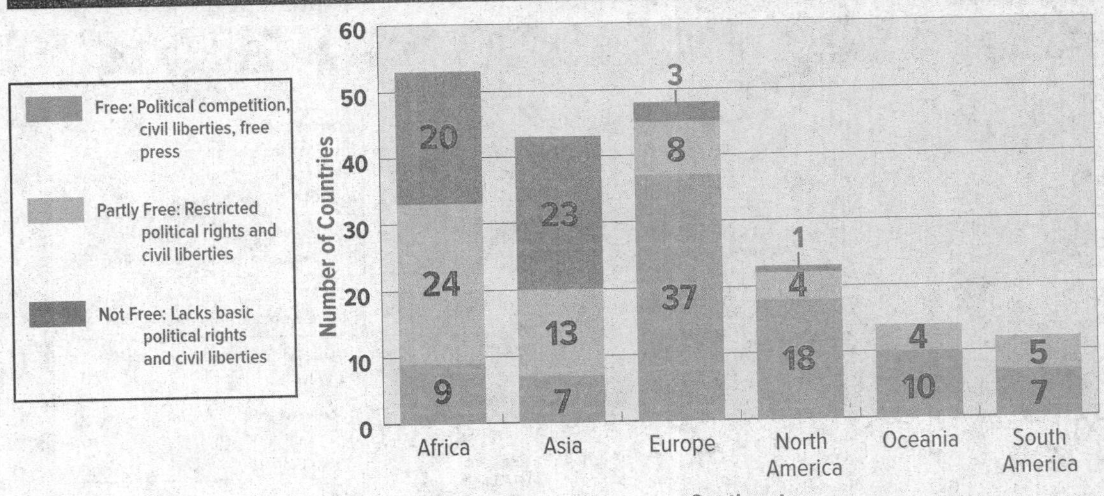

6. DRAWING CONCLUSIONS

Stopping terrorist groups is a major challenge for the U.S. and other nations. Why is it important that they succeed?

____

____

____

____

____

ANALYZING MAPS

7. IDENTIFYING

Based on the map, which locations in the United States were attacked by terrorists?

____

____

____

Recent Conflicts

September 11, 2001, marks the day of the most deadly terrorist attack on the United States. Members of al-Qaeda were responsible for the deaths of more than 3,000 people in the United States on that day.

Homeland Security

In response to the attacks on September 11, 2001, the United States created the Department of Homeland Security. This government body is charged with preventing terrorist attacks, reducing the threat of these attacks, and helping to recover from attacks or natural disasters.

Patriot Act

The Patriot Act of 2001 was also passed in response to the September 11 attacks. It gave the government the power to gather information assumed to be related to terrorism. It also allowed federal agents to search the home of a person believed to be a terrorist. Government agents could monitor the person's phone and computer. These searches could be conducted without obtaining a search warrant. Americans have different perspectives about the Patriot Act. Although changes have been made to the original act, some people still believe it violates people's civil liberties.

Global Terrorism

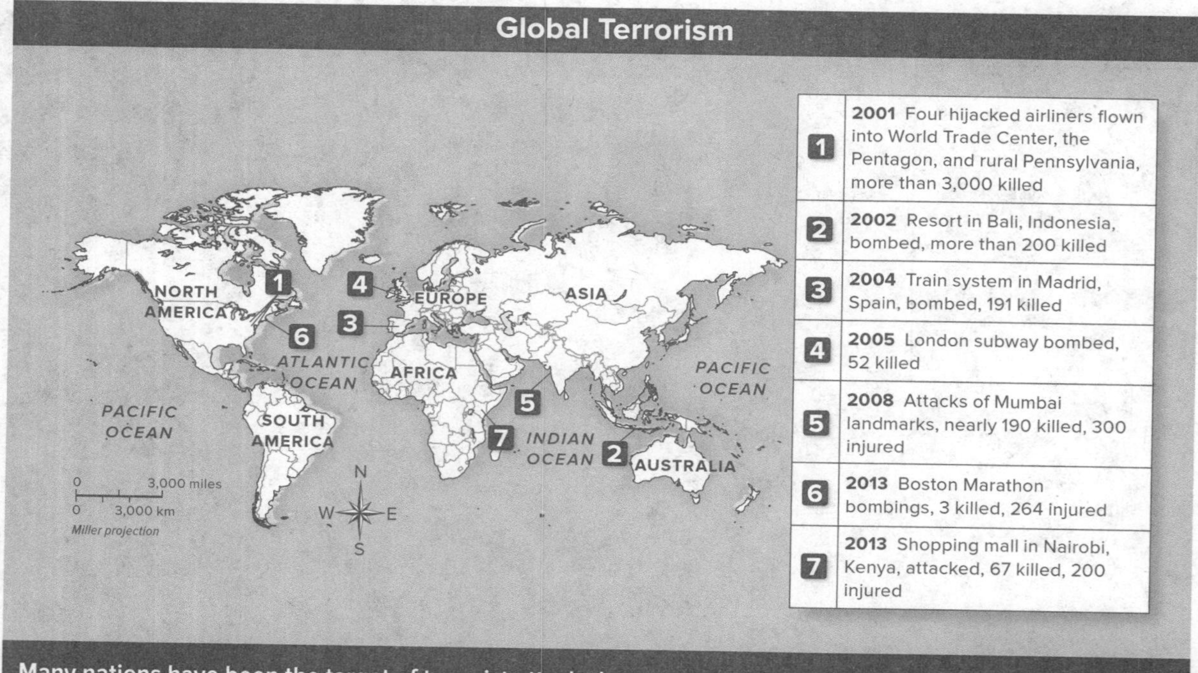
NORTH AMERICA
EUROPE
ASIA
AFRICA
SOUTH AMERICA
AUSTRALIA
ATLANTIC OCEAN
PACIFIC OCEAN
PACIFIC OCEAN
INDIAN OCEAN
1
2
3
4
5
6
7
0 3,000 miles
0 3,000 km
Miller projection
N
S
E
W
1 2001 Four hijacked airliners flown into World Trade Center, the Pentagon, and rural Pennsylvania, more than 3,000 killed
2 2002 Resort in Bali, Indonesia, bombed, more than 200 killed
3 2004 Train system in Madrid, Spain, bombed, 191 killed
4 2005 London subway bombed, 52 killed
5 2008 Attacks of Mumbai landmarks, nearly 190 killed, 300 injured
6 2013 Boston Marathon bombings, 3 killed, 264 injured
7 2013 Shopping mall in Nairobi, Kenya, attacked, 67 killed, 200 injured

Many nations have been the target of terrorist attacks by groups such as al-Qaeda, the Taliban, and ISIL.

Afghanistan

One month after the attacks on September 11, American planes and troops attacked Afghanistan. At that time, the Taliban ruled Afghanistan. They had allowed al-Qaeda to train terrorists in their country. Taliban leaders also knew the location of Osama bin Laden, al-Qaeda's leader, but they refused to cooperate with the United States. The attack by the United States removed the Taliban from power. However, bin Laden was not found.

The war in Afghanistan continued as the Taliban returned and repeatedly attacked. The United States sent more soldiers to try to end the conflict and to help Afghanistan's government. In May 2011, Osama bin Laden was killed during a raid by American troops in Pakistan.

8. HYPOTHESIZING

What international challenges do you think will need to be addressed by the United States in the future?

____

____

____

____

____

____

Iraq

Soon the United States became involved in a conflict with Iraq. President George W. Bush worried that terrorists would use nuclear and other weapons of mass destruction. A **weapon of mass destruction (WMD)** is a weapon that can kill or harm large numbers of people. Leaders feared that Iraqi dictator Saddam Hussein would provide WMDs to terrorist groups. In early 2003, the United States and several other countries attacked Iraq, defeated its army, and overthrew its government. Saddam Hussein was later executed for his crimes against the Iraqi people.

This conflict has remained controversial because no WMDs were found. It was difficult to build a democracy in Iraq, and rebel groups continued to attack American forces even after the Iraqi government was overthrown. Today, some U.S. troops remain to help the new Iraqi government.

Foreign Policy Challenges Continue

The United States still faces global challenges. Concerns over Iran's development of nuclear weapons are ongoing, although relations have improved. Terrorist groups in Pakistan remain a danger. The conflict between Israel and the Palestinians is still unresolved. In 2014, the United States returned to Iraq to fight a militant group called the Islamic State in Iraq and the Levant (ISIL). ISIL, which hoped to create an Islamic state in the region, captured several Iraqi cities. Other nations around the world face internal conflict. The United States continues to work toward ending such conflicts and to promote democracy and human rights.

Name ______________________ Date ______________ Class ______________

REVIEW LESSON 3

1. Complete the chart below to identify issues related to U.S. foreign policy and international conflicts as well as the relationship to human rights, democracy, and freedom.

	UNITED STATES ACTION AND REASONS
How does the United States protect human rights?	
How did the United States fight the Cold War? How did fighting the Cold War protect human rights?	
Why did the United States create the Department of Homeland Security and pass the Patriot Act of 2001?	

2. **IDENTIFYING CENTRAL IDEAS** Write an essay in which you identify ways U.S. policies and dealings in conflicts have safeguarded human rights and promoted democracy and freedom. Write your essay on a separate sheet of paper.

Benchmark Skill Activities

DIRECTIONS: Write your answers on a separate piece of paper.

LAFS.68.WHST.1.1, LAFS.68.WHST.2.4, SS.7.C.4.1, SS.7.C.4.3

1. SPECULATING

Use your FOLDABLES to write an essay.

The United States plays an active role in events that occur in many nations around the world. Write an essay in which you imagine you are the U.S. president. Justify why the United States takes the position it does on world issues such as human rights and terrorism.

LAFS.68.WHST.1.1, LAFS.68.WHST.2.4, SS.7.C.4.1

2. CONSTRUCTING AN ARGUMENT

The United States entered into conflicts in Afghanistan and Iraq during the 2000s. Using information you learned in the chapter, write an argument in support of or against one of these actions. Explain your reasoning.

LAFS.68.RH.2.4

3. USING DEFINITIONS ACCURATELY

Define the following terms as they apply to global issues: *global interdependence, trade war, ethnic group, terrorism,* and *refugee*. Explain their meanings and relationship to global issues.

LAFS.68.WHST.1.2, SS.7.C.4.2

4. SPECIFYING

Identify three to five governmental organizations or nongovernmental organizations that work to protect human rights. Explain the role of government and citizens in these organizations.

LAFS.68.RH.1.1, LAFS.68.RH.1.2, LAFS.68.WHST.1.1, LAFS.68.WHST.3.7, LAFS.68.WHST.3.9, SS.7.C.4.1

5. ANALYZING DATA

The Patriot Act of 2001 was passed after the September 11, 2001, attacks. Do research on the Internet to find arguments for and against this act. Then, write an essay in which you indicate your view toward the Patriot Act. Use evidence from your research to support your viewpoint.

LAFS.68.WHST.2.4, SS.7.C.2.14

6. ORGANIZING

Choose a nongovernmental agency that focuses on a mission such as feeding the hungry, fighting disease, or protecting the environment. Do a public service project for the organization. The project might be distributing flyers to make people aware of the organization or volunteering to help with one of its activities. Write the steps you need to take to get your project going, such as contacting the organization and planning your activity. After you complete the project, write a description of your project and how it supported the organization's goals.

Benchmark Note Cards

DIRECTIONS: Use these note cards to help you prepare for the test.

SS.7.C.4.1 Differentiate concepts related to United States domestic and foreign policy.

GLOBAL INTERDEPENDENCE	Global interdependence refers to people and nations relying on one another for goods and services. Trade occurs because nations have different needs, comparative advantages, and resources. For this reason, the United States exports and imports many goods.
GLOBAL ISSUES	The United States strives to work with other nations regardless of different political views. Sometimes, trade wars come into play when one country puts a trade barrier into effect and another nation responds with its own trade barriers.
THE ENVIRONMENT	Many environmental issues affect the United States and the world. Harmful effects have been caused by factories, energy production, and deforestation. It can be difficult and expensive to solve these problems. However, conservation now might prevent greater costs in the future.
IMMIGRANTS AND REFUGEES	The United States is actively involved in policy decisions related to immigration and refugees. It must consider that some people resent the increased demand on land, jobs, and services that immigrants may cause. In addition, tensions might arise among religious and ethnic groups.
U.S. POLICIES ON HUMAN RIGHTS	The United States promotes human rights and protests countries that take away those rights. It sometimes does not trade with those countries. The United States also promotes democracy to ensure the protection of human rights and liberties.

SS.7.C.4.2 Recognize government and citizen participation in international organizations.

INTERNATIONAL ORGANIZATIONS	International organizations, whether governmental or nongovernmental, provide services to the world. They deal with problems that affect many nations and work with governments to find solutions.
GOVERNMENTAL ORGANIZATIONS	Governmental organizations are formed to deal with international issues. • The United Nations (UN) was formed after World War II as a peacekeeping organization. UN members developed the Universal Declaration of Human Rights. This declaration states that all people are free and equal and should have the same basic rights. • The North Atlantic Treaty Organization (NATO) maintains and defends the freedom and safety of its members. • The World Trade Organization (WTO) focuses on trade and resolving trade conflicts among member nations. • The World Health Organization (WHO) looks for ways to fight and prevent disease. • Peace Corps volunteers work in education, public health, and business development around the world.
NONGOVERN-MENTAL ORGANIZATIONS	Nongovernmental organizations operate independently of a government. They depend on volunteers and private donations. NGOs are free to provide assistance to any nation and to both sides in a conflict or war.

BENCHMARK NOTE CARDS, *continued*

SS.7.C.4.3 Describe examples of how the United States has dealt with international conflicts.

THE COLD WAR	During the Cold War, the United States worked to keep the Soviet Union's control and communism from spreading. The United States also engaged in two conflicts in an attempt to prevent the spread of communism: the Korean War and the Vietnam War.
TERRORIST ATTACKS	After the attacks of September 11, 2001, the United States • created the Department of Homeland Security to help prevent terrorist attacks, reduce the threat of attacks, and help in recovery from attacks, and • passed the Patriot Act of 2001, which gave the government the power to gather information it believes is related to terrorism.
AFGHANISTAN	After the September 11, 2001, attacks, the United States waged a war against Taliban-ruled Afghanistan. The Taliban had refused to cooperate with the United States to bring the head of al-Qaeda, Osama bin Laden, to justice. In 2011, Osama bin Laden was killed during a U.S. raid in Pakistan.
IRAQ	President George W. Bush worried that terrorists would obtain weapons of mass destruction from Iraqi dictator Saddam Hussein. In 2003, the United States and other countries attacked Iraq, defeated its army, and overthrew its government. Saddam Hussein was executed for crimes against the Iraqi people. No weapons of mass destruction were found.
FOREIGN POLICY CHALLENGES	In 2014, the United States returned to Iraq to fight a militant group called the Islamic State in Iraq and the Levant (ISIL). The United States continues to work toward ending such conflicts and to promote democracy and human rights.

BENCHMARK NOTE CARDS, *continued*

SS.7.E.2.5 Explain how economic institutions impact the national economy.

ECONOMIC INSTITUTIONS AND TRADE AGREEMENTS	The World Trade Organization serves as a place for member governments to meet to resolve trade issues. Some argue that the WTO favors developed nations, such as the United States, and their businesses. Others argue that the WTO ignores environmental issues. The United States entered into the North American Free Trade Agreement (NAFTA) with Canada and Mexico. Trade agreements can lead to lower prices for goods and provide consumers with greater choices. Trade agreements can also lead to companies closing or moving to countries with lower costs.

SS.7.E.3.4 Compare and contrast the standard of living in various countries today to that of the United States using gross domestic product (GDP) per capita as an indicator.

RICH AND POOR NATIONS	Economic progress differs among nations. Developed nations tend to have a high GDP per capita and strong economic growth. Developed nations include the United States, Germany, and Canada. Developing countries tend to have a low GDP per capita and slow economic growth.

Chapter 25

VISUAL SUMMARY

DIRECTIONS: Complete the graphic organizer below.

THE GLOBAL COMMUNITY

Nations relying on other nations for goods and services is known as ________________________________.

Global trade occurs because ________________________________.

Global economic cooperation is promoted by ________________ such as NAFTA.

Global issues include:

- ________________
- ________________
- ________________
- ________________
- immigration
- terrorism

INTERNATIONAL ORGANIZATIONS

The purpose of international organizations is to ________________________________.

Member nations fund ________________ and set up rules for how they operate.

________________ are run by private citizens to meet a need or work for a cause.

The United Nations was founded as a ________________.

THE UNITED STATES AND THE WORLD

UN members wrote the ________________, which states that all human beings are born free and equal.

Violations of human rights include: ________________.

The United States responds to countries that take away human rights by ________________.

During the Cold War, the United States tried to prevent the spread of ________________.

During the Cold War, the United States engaged in two conflicts: ________________.

After 9/11, the United States created ________________.

The Patriot Act gave the government the power to ________________.

Concerns about terrorism led the United States to become involved in conflicts in ________________.

USING PRIMARY SOURCES

INTERPRET Below are two primary sources related to foreign policy. President Barack Obama made his statement in 2014. President George Washington gave his address in 1796. Read both sources. Then, answer the questions that follow on a separate sheet of paper.

Document A

Today, the United States of America is changing its relationship with the people of Cuba.

In the most significant changes in our policy in more than fifty years, we will end an outdated approach that, for decades, has failed to advance our interests, and instead we will begin to normalize relations between our two countries. Through these changes, we intend to create more opportunities for the American and Cuban people, and begin a new chapter among the nations of the Americas.

There's a complicated history between the United States and Cuba. . . . We are separated by just over 90 miles. But year after year, an ideological and economic barrier hardened between our two countries.

Meanwhile, the Cuban exile [forced to live in a foreign country] community in the United States made enormous contributions to our country—in politics and business, culture and sports. Like immigrants before, Cubans helped remake America, even as they felt a painful yearning for the land and families they left behind. All of this bound America and Cuba in a unique relationship, at once family and foe [enemy].

Proudly, the United States has supported democracy and human rights in Cuba through these five decades. We have done so primarily through policies that aimed to isolate the island, preventing the most basic travel and commerce that Americans can enjoy anyplace else. And though this policy has been rooted in the best of intentions, no other nation joins us in imposing these sanctions, and it has had little effect beyond providing the Cuban government with a rationale for restrictions on its people. Today, Cuba is still governed by the Castros and the Communist Party that came to power half a century ago.

Neither the American, nor Cuban people are well served by a rigid policy that is rooted in events that took place before most of us were born. Consider that for more than 35 years, we've had relations with China—a far larger country also governed by a Communist Party. Nearly two decades ago, we reestablished relations with Vietnam, where we fought a war that claimed more Americans than any Cold War confrontation. . . .

. . . [W]e are taking steps to increase travel, commerce, and the flow of information to and from Cuba. This is fundamentally about freedom and openness, and also expresses my belief in the power of people-to-people engagement. . . . Nobody represents America's values better than the American people, and I believe this contact will ultimately do more to empower the Cuban people. . . .

—President Barack Obama, 2014

Document B

Against the insidious [harmful] wiles [deception] of foreign influence (I conjure [appeal to] you to believe me, fellow citizens) the jealousy of a free people ought to be constantly awake, since history and experience prove that foreign influence is one of the most baneful [destructive] foes of republican government. But that jealousy, to be useful must be impartial; else it becomes the instrument of the very influence to be avoided; instead of a defense against it. Excessive partiality for one foreign nation and excessive dislike of another cause those whom they actuate [stimulate] to seed anger only on one side, and serve to veil [hide] and even second the arts of influence on the other. . . .

The great rule of conduct for us in regard to foreign nations is in extending our commercial relations, to have with them as little political connection as possible. So far as we have already formed engagements, let them be fulfilled with perfect good faith. Here let us stop. . . . It is our true policy to steer clear of permanent alliances with any portion of the foreign world; so far, I mean, as we are now at liberty to do it; for let me not be understood as capable of patronizing infidelity [disloyalty] to existing engagements. I hold the maxim [saying] no less applicable to public than to private affairs, that honesty is always the best policy. I repeat it, therefore, let those engagements be observed in their genuine sense. But in my opinion, it is unnecessary and would be unwise to extend them.

—President George Washington, 1796

1. How are Documents A and B similar and different?
2. Reread the second paragraph of Document A. Underline the details in that paragraph that tell what President Obama wants to do, and why.
3. What justification does President Obama give for changing the status between the countries?
4. Reread the second paragraph of Document B. Underline the details in that paragraph that tell what President Washington believed about the United States and its foreign policy.
5. What did President Washington believe was the main rule for relations with foreign nations?
6. Do you think President Obama and the American people today would agree with President Washington's policy? Why?

Chapter Practice Test

DIRECTIONS: Circle the best answer for each question.

SS.7.C.4.1 (Moderate)

Read the three headlines below. How are these headlines similar?

China Blocks Citizens' Access to Foreign Web sites

United States Adopts Economic Sanctions Against Sudan for Violence Against Civilians

Former Rwandan Official Convicted of Genocide in UN Court

A They all have to do with problems in developed nations.

B They all have to do with violations of human rights.

C They all have to do with trade barriers and trade wars.

D They all have to do with conflicts involving terrorists.

SS.7.E.2.5 (Moderate)

Which of the following affects trade relationships of the United States?

A Peace Corps

B NAFTA

C United Nations

D North Atlantic Treaty Organization

3 **SS.7.C.4.3 (High)**

Read the excerpt below.

> *"The United States of America is an enemy of those who aid terrorists and of the barbaric criminals who profane [disrespect] a great religion by committing murder in its name."*
>
> —President George W. Bush

Which action of President George W. Bush does the excerpt justify?

A strikes on ISIL training camps in Syria and Iran

B economic sanctions against Sudan for ethnic conflict

C war against the Taliban regime and al-Qaeda terrorists in Afghanistan

D approval of the Universal Declaration of Human Rights

SS.7.C.4.2 (Moderate)

Which action demonstrates government participation in an international organization?

A A Peace Corps volunteer helps train educators in Ecuador.

B An International Committee of the Red Cross worker helps Japanese survivors of a tsunami and an earthquake.

C A U.S. armed services member participates in a project to repair a road in a war-torn country.

D NATO members send a peacekeeping force to aid protestors in Libya.

SS.7.C.4.2 (Moderate)

CHARACTERISTICS
Global membership
Focuses on resolving conflicts among members
Criticized by some for ignoring environmental issues
Criticized by some for favoring business of developed countries

Which organization do these characteristics describe?

A World Health Organization

B World Trade Organization

C International Committee of the Red Cross

D United Nations

SS.7.C.4.2 (Moderate)

Which action is an example of how citizens participate in international organizations?

A A committee of the World Trade Organization issues a report on free trade.

B An American student gathers information about actions taken by the United Nations in developing nations.

C An American Peace Corps volunteer teaches children in Rwanda to read and write.

D A member of the UN Security Council proposes sanctions against countries hiding terrorists.

7 **SS.7.E.3.4 (High)**

NATION X	
Political System	unstable
Economic Growth	slow
Natural Resources	few
Labor Force	unskilled

Which statement is a likely description of Nation X?

A It is a developing nation with a low GDP per capita.

B It is a developed nation with a low GDP per capita.

C It is a developing nation with a high GDP per capita.

D It is a developed nation with a high GDP per capita.

---

8 **SS.7.C.4.3 (Low)**

Which of the following reasons did the United States give to justify an action related to the war on terror?

A Iraq had weapons of mass destruction.

B Afghanistan and Iraq were responsible for the September 11 attacks.

C Saddam Hussein led a communist regime in Iraq.

D Iran was hiding the leader of al-Qaeda.

9 **SS.7.C.4.1 (Moderate)**

Suppose a country with economic ties to the United States is accused of human rights violations. What is one of the first steps the United States might take based on its foreign policy regarding human rights?

A It will use military force.

B It will begin a trade war.

C It will end economic aid.

D It will deliver a protest.

 10 **SS.7.C.4.3 (High)**

Which of these statements is true about how the United States has continued to deal with global challenges?

A The United States has placed economic sanctions on Afghanistan.

B The United States and its allies sent ground troops to end the conflict between Israel and the Palestinians.

C The United States returned to Iraq in 2014 to fight the militant group ISIL.

D The United States and its allies destroyed the weapons of mass destruction in Iraq.

End-of-Course Practice Test

This End-of-Course Practice Test will give you practice on the Florida standards assessments. It will also help you to determine your knowledge of the course content. Circle each correct answer. There will be only one answer per question.

SS.7.C.1.1 (High)

The excerpts below are from the U.S. Constitution.

Excerpt A: *All legislative Powers herein granted shall be vested in a Congress of the United States. . . . The executive Power shall be vested in a President of the United States of America. . . . The judicial Power of the United States, shall be vested in one supreme Court, and in such inferior Courts as the Congress may from time to time ordain and establish.*

Excerpt B: *The Citizens of each State shall be entitled to all Privileges and Immunities of Citizens in the several States.*

Excerpt C: *This Constitution, and the Laws of the United States which shall be made in Pursuance thereof, and all Treaties made, or which shall be made, under the Authority of the United States, shall be the supreme Law of the Land.*

Excerpt D: *A well regulated Militia, being necessary to the security of a free State, the right of the people to keep and bear Arms, shall not be infringed.*

—U.S. Constitution

Which excerpt reflects the Enlightenment ideas of separation of powers as expressed by Montesquieu?

A Excerpt A

B Excerpt B

C Excerpt C

D Excerpt D

2 **SS.7.C.1.2 (Moderate)**

This excerpt is from the English Bill of Rights.

> *. . . [S]uspending the laws or the execution of laws by regal [royal] authority without consent of Parliament is illegal. . . .*
>
> —English Bill of Rights

Which of the following concepts does the excerpt support?

A English citizens had a social contract with their monarch.

B English citizens had rights that no monarch could violate.

C English citizens should not be prohibited from the free exercise of religion.

D English citizens had the right to choose their form of government.

SS.7.C.1.3 (High)

Why did the British Parliament repeal the Stamp Act, which taxed many types of colonial documents?

A Colonists dumped British tea into Boston Harbor.

B Colonists wrote to King George asking him to repeal the act.

C Colonists threatened to declare independence from Britain.

D Colonists began boycotting British goods.

4

SS.7.C.1.4 (Moderate)

Which of the following complaints against the British government was included in the Declaration of Independence?

A executing colonists without benefit of a jury trial

B requiring colonists to lodge British soldiers in their homes

C ordering colonists to move off of lands claimed by Native Americans

D forcing colonists to serve in Parliament

SS.7.C.1.5 (Moderate)

The excerpt below is from Article VI of the U.S. Constitution.

> *This Constitution, and the Laws of the United States which shall be made in Pursuance thereof; and all Treaties made, or which shall be made, under the Authority of the United States, shall be the supreme Law of the Land; and the Judges in every State shall be bound thereby, any Thing in the Constitution or Laws of any State to the Contrary notwithstanding.*
>
> —U.S. Constitution

Which weakness in the Articles of Confederation is addressed in this part of the Constitution?

A There was no executive branch to enforce national laws.

B The states had more power than the national government.

C Laws required the approval of nine states.

D There was no national court system.

SS.7.C.1.6 (Moderate)

This excerpt is the Preamble of the U.S. Constitution.

> *We the People of the United States, in Order to form a more perfect Union, establish Justice, insure domestic Tranquility, provide for the common defence, promote the general Welfare, and secure the Blessings of Liberty to ourselves and our Posterity, do ordain and establish this Constitution for the United States of America.*
>
> —U.S. Constitution

Based on the excerpt, what is the meaning of the phrase "form a more perfect Union"?

A The government would treat all people fairly and equally under the law.

B The government would promote liberty and freedom for all Americans.

C The government would bring the states together to act as a single nation for the good of all.

D The government would protect citizens from conflict in the country and prevent civil war.

7 **SS.7.C.1.6 (High)**

The excerpt below is the Preamble of the U.S. Constitution.

> *We the People of the United States, in Order to form a more perfect Union, establish Justice, insure domestic Tranquility, provide for the common defence, promote the general Welfare, and secure the Blessings of Liberty to ourselves and our Posterity, do ordain and establish this Constitution for the United States of America.*
>
> —U.S. Constitution

Which of the following excerpts from the Constitution supports the intention of the phrase "to form a more perfect Union" in the Preamble?

A From Article I: "The House of Representatives shall choose their Speaker and other Officers; and shall have the sole Power of Impeachment."

B From Article IV: "New States may be admitted by the Congress into this Union."

C From Article VI: "All Debts contracted and Engagements entered into, before the Adoption of this Constitution, shall be as valid against the United States under this Constitution, as under the Confederation."

D From Article VII: "The Ratification of the Conventions of nine States, shall be sufficient for the Establishment of this Constitution between the States so ratifying the Same."

SS.7.C.1.7 (High)

The following excerpt is from *The Federalist*, No. 78.

> *. . . [T]he courts were designed to be an intermediate body between the people and the legislature, in order, among other things, to keep the latter within the limits assigned to their authority.*
>
> —*The Federalist*, No. 78 (1788)

Which of the following principles is being described in this passage?

A judicial review

B checks and balances

C judicial nullification

D popular sovereignty

SS.7.C.1.7 (High)

The following excerpt is from *The Federalist*, No. 47.

> *The accumulation of all powers, legislative, executive and judicia[l] in the same hands, whether of one, few, or many, and whether hereditary, self-appointed, or elective, may justly be pronounced the very definition of tyranny.*
>
> —*The Federalist*, No. 47 (1788)

Which of the following concepts does this passage support?

A separation of powers

B due process of law

C federalism

D judicial precedent

10 **SS.7.C.1.8 (High)**

This passage is from Article VI of the U.S. Constitution.

> *This Constitution, and the Laws of the United States which shall be made in Pursuance thereof; and all Treaties made, or which shall be made, under the Authority of the United States, shall be the supreme Law of the Land; and the Judges in every State shall be bound thereby, any Thing in the Constitution or Laws of any State to the Contrary notwithstanding.*
>
> —U.S. Constitution

Which of the following statements is an Anti-Federalist view of this section of the Constitution?

A It describes a strong national government better able to preserve civil rights.

B It describes unbalanced power between the Senate and the House of Representatives.

C It describes how states and their citizens are at the mercy of a powerful national government.

D It describes the liberties won during the American Revolution.

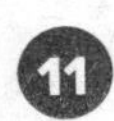

SS.7.C.1.9 (Low)

What is meant by the term *rule of law*?

A Government is based on the consent of the governed.

B Elected leaders must follow the law; no one is above the law.

C Government is limited in power by a constitution or written agreement.

D People are born with certain basic rights; government may not take them away.

12

SS.7.C.3.10 (Moderate)

What type of law deals with the limits of the government's power?

A criminal

B civil

C constitutional

D military

13

SS.7.C.3.10 (Moderate)

Category A robbery driving drunk assault	**Category B** contract disputes divorce personal injury
Category C absence without leave desertion mutiny	**Category D** racial discrimination eminent domain treason

Which category in this table represents civil law?

A Category A

B Category B

C Category C

D Category D

14 **SS.7.C.2.1 (Low)**

Which statement states a requirement for a person to become a naturalized U.S. citizen?

A being at least 18 years of age

B having one parent who is a natural-born U.S. citizen

C living in the United States for at least ten years

D being born in any of the 50 states

---

15 **SS.7.C.2.2 (Moderate)**

Duties of U.S. Citizens	So Citizens Can
• Obey laws	• live together peacefully
• Defend the nation	• protect the country
• Serve in court	• ensure the rights of the accused
• Pay taxes	• **?**
• Attend school	• become good citizens

Which of the following items correctly completes the table?

A prepare for work life

B protect our health

C run the government

D learn to collaborate

SS.7.C.2.4 (Moderate)

In this cartoon, soldiers are blocking members of different religions from gaining access to a woman who represents the "justice" of the nation.

Library of Congress Prints and Photographs Division [LC-USZC4-13015]

Which principle in the Bill of Rights is illustrated by the topic of this cartoon?

A the guarantee of free speech

B the prohibition of government censorship

C the freedom to protest a law

D the prohibition of an official national religion

17 **SS.7.C.2.4 (Low)**

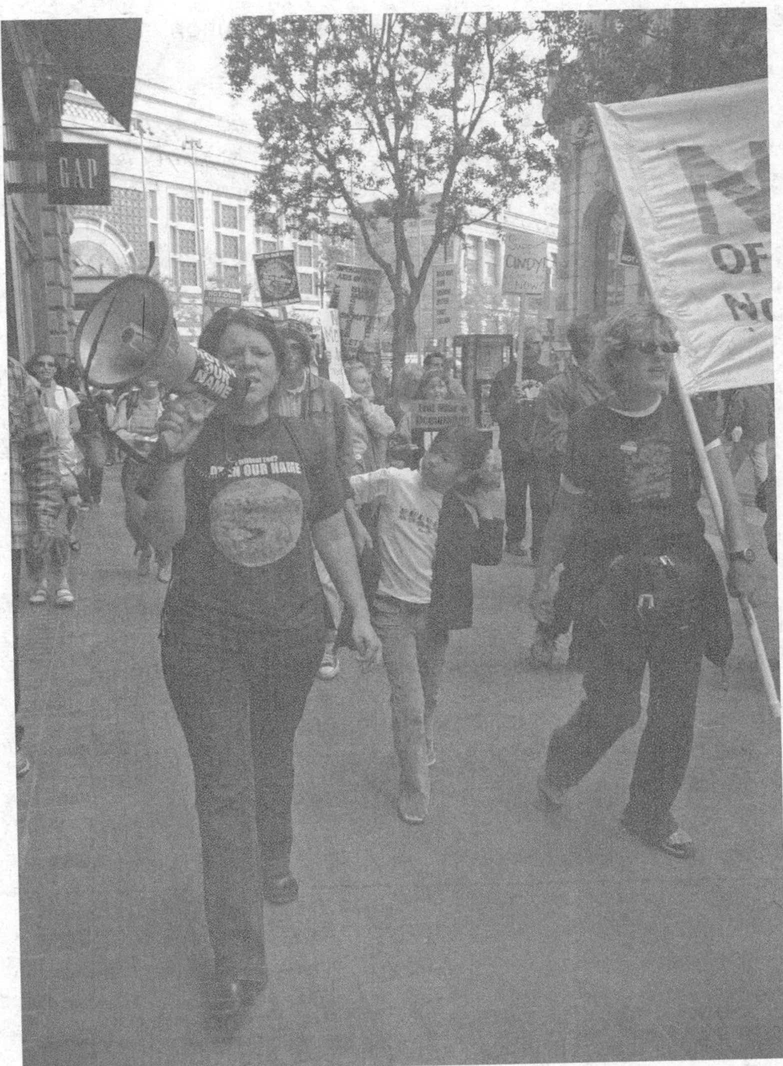

Which civil liberties protected under the Bill of Rights are being exercised in this photograph?

A right to vote, right to health care

B freedom of assembly, freedom of speech

C right to a speedy trial, right to an education

D right to a job, freedom of religion

18 **SS.7.C.2.5 (High)**

The excerpt below is from the First Amendment to the U.S. Constitution.

> *Congress shall make no law respecting an establishment of religion, or prohibiting the free exercise thereof; or abridging the freedom of speech, or of the press; or the right of the people peaceably to assemble, and to petition the Government for a redress of grievances.*
>
> —U.S. Constitution

Which of the following individuals has incorrectly claimed a constitutional right?

A Timothy affixes a bumper sticker to his car that reads "I hate the president." He says that his First Amendment rights allow him to do this.

B Hannah fills her front lawn with campaign signs for the candidate she supports. When her neighbors object, she cites her First Amendment rights.

C As a joke, Jason enters a crowded theater and shouts that the building is on fire. He claims that his action is permissible under the First Amendment.

D Serena and her friends ask city council for a permit to hold a quiet demonstration about the closing of a neighborhood park, saying that she has a First Amendment right to do so.

---

19 **SS.7.C.2.5 (High)**

During his trial for armed robbery, the judge denies Donald the opportunity to present witnesses who say Donald was with them at the time of the robbery. An appeals court overturns Donald's conviction, saying that the trial judge had violated Donald's constitutional rights. Which of the following amendments applies to this case?

A First Amendment (freedom of speech)

B Second Amendment (right to bear arms)

C Fourth Amendment (search and seizure)

D Sixth Amendment (due process of law)

20 **SS.7.C.3.6 (Moderate)**

How did the Nineteenth Amendment impact the rights of Americans?

A It protected the right of women to vote in all national and state elections.

B It allowed voters to elect their senators directly.

C It eliminated the requirement of poll taxes for national elections.

D It set the minimum age for voting at 21.

SS.7.C.3.6 (High)

The excerpt below is from the First Amendment to the U.S. Constitution.

> *Congress shall make no law respecting an establishment of religion, or prohibiting the free exercise thereof; or abridging the freedom of speech, or of the press; or the right of the people peaceably to assemble, and to petition the Government for a redress of grievances.*
>
> —U.S. Constitution

Which responsibility of U.S. citizens is easier to fulfill because of this amendment?

A Respect the rights of others.

B Serve in court.

C Be an informed citizen.

D Pay taxes.

SS.7.C.3.7 (High)

This excerpt is from the Twenty-fourth Amendment to the U.S. Constitution.

> *The right of citizens of the United States to vote in any primary or other election for President or Vice President, for electors for President or Vice President, or for Senator or Representative in Congress, shall not be denied or abridged by the United States or any State by reason of failure to pay any poll tax or other tax.*
>
> —U.S. Constitution

How did the passage of this amendment affect the political process in the United States?

A It resulted in more low-income people being allowed to vote.

B It resulted in more women being allowed to vote.

C It permitted people of all economic backgrounds to contribute to political campaigns.

D It encouraged more college-age Americans to become involved in politics.

 **SS.7.C.3.7 (High)**

The following are excerpts from the Fifth and Fourteenth Amendments to the U.S. Constitution.

> **Fifth Amendment**
> *No person shall be . . . deprived of life, liberty, or property, without due process of law. . . .*
>
> **Fourteenth Amendment**
> *No State shall make or enforce any law which shall abridge the privileges or immunities of citizens of the United States; nor shall any State deprive any person of life, liberty, or property, without due process of law; nor deny to any person within its jurisdiction the equal protection of the laws.*
>
> —U.S. Constitution

Based on the excerpt, which of the following conclusions is accurate?

A The Fourteenth Amendment applies to all Americans; the Fifth Amendment had applied only to white landowners.

B The meaning of *due process* changed over the years; the Fourteenth Amendment defined it more clearly.

C The Fourteenth Amendment prevents states from denying due process; the Fifth Amendment had been applied only to the national government.

D The Supreme Court had ruled that the *due process* clause of the Fifth Amendment was unconstitutional, so the clause needed to be reintroduced into the Constitution.

 **SS.7.C.3.12 (Moderate)**

What was an outcome of the Supreme Court's 1954 decision in *Brown* v. *Board of Education*?

A Segregation was lawful as long as blacks and whites were treated equally.

B The right of public school students to free speech was strengthened.

C States were ordered by the federal government to desegregate public schools.

D Separate facilities for blacks and whites were not unconstitutional.

SS.7.C.3.12 (High)

The passage below is taken from a landmark 1966 Supreme Court ruling.

> *Prior to any questioning, the person must be warned that he has a right to remain silent, that any statement he does make may be used as evidence against him, and that he has a right to the presence of an attorney, either retained or appointed.*
>
> —from Supreme Court ruling

What is the name of the ruling from which this passage was taken?

A *Bush* v. *Gore*

B *Plessy* v. *Ferguson*

C *Miranda* v. *Arizona*

D *Marbury* v. *Madison*

SS.7.C.3.12 (High)

Which important principle was reinforced by the Supreme Court ruling in *United States* v. *Nixon* (1974)?

A habeas corpus

B double jeopardy

C separation of powers

D the rule of law

27 **SS.7.C.2.8 (Moderate)**

Which position is favored by members of the Republican Party?

A less government regulation of the economy

B more federal oversight of educational resources

C the creation of a national health insurance program

D more government spending on jobs for the poor

28 **SS.7.C.2.8 (Moderate)**

Which issue represents a basic agreement between Republicans and Democrats?

A Spending on the military should be increased dramatically to protect Americans from terrorism.

B Economic growth is an effective means of remedying unemployment.

C The U.S. should increase offshore oil drilling to reduce dependence on foreign energy sources.

D Taxes should be cut on corporations and wealthy individuals to promote the economy.

SS.7.C.2.9 (Moderate)

Which of the following individuals is most qualified to be president of the United States?

A Paulina is 34 years old and a U.S. citizen. She earned degrees in civics and law and has held public office since college.

B Luther, a U.S. citizen for 40 years, is a master plumber and volunteers at his kids' elementary school.

C Audra is a naturalized citizen of the United States. She teaches high school social studies and geography.

D Roman is a U.S. citizen and holds degrees in social studies and political science. He is currently the governor of his state.

SS.7.C.2.9 (High)

This poster is for an imaginary candidate in a recent election.

ELECT JAN SMITH!
- Supports new neighborhood park
- Will fight for expansion of police force
- Committed to bringing new businesses to town
- Lives and works in your city
- Brings years of business experience to the office

ELECT JAN SMITH!

What conclusion can you draw about the candidate's qualifications?

A Jan Smith is not qualified because she has lived in the city too long.

B Jan Smith is qualified because she wants to expand the police force.

C Jan Smith is not qualified because she wants to improve the economy.

D Jan Smith is qualified because she knows about and works in the city.

31 **SS.7.C.2.10 (Moderate)**

What is the main purpose of direct lobbying?

A to influence legislation on behalf of interest groups

B to shape public policy by bringing cases to court

C to convince people to join interest groups

D to promote public awareness of important issues

---

32 **SS.7.C.2.10 (Moderate)**

Which role is the media playing when a newspaper prints an article about a federal judge taking bribes from a criminal organization?

A trendsetter

B entertainer

C agenda setter

D watchdog

SS.7.C.2.11 (Moderate)

The following radio advertisement is for a political candidate.

> Hi. I'm Wally Jones, manager of the local baseball team. This November I'm voting for Bob Smith for mayor—and so should you! Bob Smith will hit a "home run" for our city as mayor. That's why I urge you to cast YOUR ballot for a real "team player!"
>
> —Bob Smith

Which technique is being used in this radio advertisement?

A bias

B symbolism

C lobbying

D propaganda

SS.7.C.2.12 (High)

You live near a block of vacant, run down houses and would like to see city leaders replace them with a park that would benefit your community.

Which of the following actions should be your first step in attempting to make this change?

A Call the fire station and police about the run-down houses.

B Contact your state senator to voice your opinion.

C Research what city leaders are planning for your community.

D Write a letter to the governor about the problem.

35 **SS.7.C.2.12 (Low)**

There have been many auto accidents at a busy intersection near your home. Whom should you contact to address the issue?

A the mayor or a city council member

B your state senator or state representative

C a member of the local school board

D the U.S. Department of Transportation

36 **SS.7.C.2.13 (High)**

Examine the information about the minimum wage.

ARGUMENTS FOR RAISING THE MINIMUM WAGE
• Workers would get to a living wage.
• The government could spend less on social programs.
• Workers would be less likely to quit their jobs.
• ?

Which of the following points could correctly be added to the table?

A Overly qualified people would compete for low-level jobs.

B The economy would be stimulated because people would have more money to spend.

C The price of goods and services would increase.

D Inflation would grow out of control.

SS.7.C.4.1 (Moderate)

Which of the following is a foreign policy issue?

A requiring welfare recipients to undergo drug testing

B strengthening laws that prevent companies from polluting

C providing cost of living increases in veterans' disability payments

D imposing an economic embargo on another nation

SS.7.C.4.2 (Moderate)

Which is an example of citizen participation in an international organization?

A taking a tour of NATO headquarters

B giving a donation to the International Red Cross

C writing a senator about U.S. involvement in Middle East peace negotiations

D watching a TV documentary about the United Nations

SS.7.C.4.3 (High)

The excerpt below is from a speech by President George H. W. Bush.

> *This conflict started August 2nd when the dictator of Iraq invaded a small and helpless neighbor. Kuwait—a member of the Arab League and a member of the United Nations—was crushed; its people, brutalized. Five months ago, Saddam Hussein started this cruel war against Kuwait. Tonight, the battle has been joined.*
>
> —President George H. W. Bush, January 16, 1991

Which international action was President Bush justifying with this speech?

A using diplomacy to resolve a dispute

B using military action to halt hostile aggression

C initiating a trade ban against a foreign nation

D cutting off diplomatic relations with a country

SS.7.C.3.1 (Low)

Which of the following forms of government is most like an autocracy?

A representative democracy

B absolute monarchy

C direct democracy

D oligarchy

SS.7.C.3.2. (Moderate)

Which type of government is illustrated in this graphic?

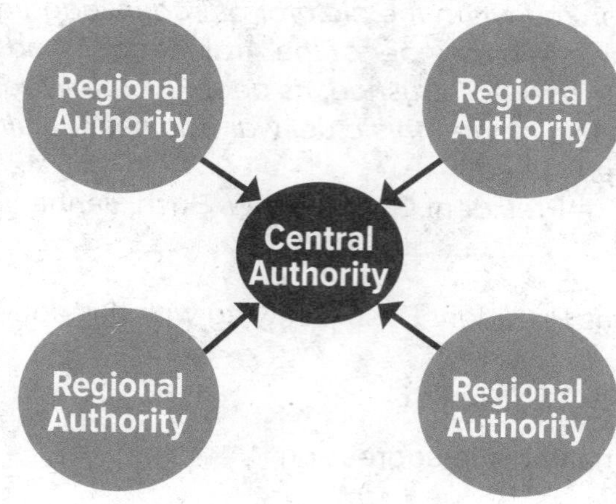

A unitary government

B confederal government

C federal government

D direct democracy